The Futures Directory

the
FUTURES DIRECTORY

An international listing and description
of organizations and individuals active
in future studies and long-range planning

Compiled by
John McHale and Magda Cordell McHale
with
Guy Streatfeild and Laurence Tobias

Center for Integrative Studies
School of Advanced Technology
State University of New York
Binghampton

A **FUTURES** Special Publication from

IPC Science and Technology Press

Westview Press

Published 1977 in England by IPC Science and Technology Press Limited,
IPC House, 32 High Street, Guildford, Surrey, England GU1 3EW.

Published 1977 in the United States of America by Westview Press Inc.,
1898 Flatiron Court, Boulder, Colorado 80301, USA.
Frederick A. Praeger, Publisher and Editorial Director.

Library of Congress Cataloging in Publication Data
Main entry under title: The Futures Directory includes
indexes.
1 Forecasting — Directories.
I McHale, John. II McHale, Magda Cordell.
CB158.F87   001.4'3'025   76-51285
ISBN 0 902852 64 7 (IPC Science and Technology Press)
ISBN 0 89158 224 X (Westview Press)

Printed and bound in England

Contents

Directory Guide

The Directory gives an outline description of organizations and individuals throughout the world concerned with the study of the future in various ways. The listing is not intended to be an exhaustive inventory of the field. But it does provide substantive information on all those who have so identified themselves through participation in a series of survey studies carried out at the Centre for Integrative Studies, State University of New York at Binghamton. The most recent of these studies was undertaken during 1974-1975 in co-sponsorship with the United Nations Institute for Training and Research (UNITAR)[1]

Criteria for inclusion in these surveys were based on:

● production of work in the field as formally defined;
● frequency with which organizations and individuals were referred to in the literature;
● other activities which contribute to the overall development of the field, e.g., conference and work group organizations, co-ordination of projects, documentation work;
● potential contributions to the formation of and influence on future developments, even where these were not identified as futures studies and/ or long-range planning activities per se.

Though these surveys were primarily designed to elicit a profile of futures studies and associated long-range planning, they were not restricted to those primarily engaged in such work. We were also concerned with the identification of activities which affect future developments in the longer term, but are not formally defined as futures studies.

Examples of this latter category would include:

● Science policy, technology assessment, social indicators work, etc.
● Corporate planning of various kinds.
● Work of some governmental and non-governmental organizations that are concerned with the future consequences and implications of human action.
● Research and development activities which might influence and shape the future.

The responses to the surveys have given detailed information, as far as was possible, of the activities of the participants - what they were doing in the area

---

1
  John McHale, Magda Cordell McHale, Futures Studies, An International Survey (New York, UNITAR, 1975).
  Typologicial Survey of Futures Research in the USA, 1969-1970 (NIMH Contract No HSM-42-69-47).
  Continuation of Above Survey (1971-1972) NIMH Contract No HSM-42-71-72.
  International returns through circulation of a survey form via *Futures* journal during 1970, and its extended use by other centres in various world regions.

of futures studies, with what kind of objectives and using which approaches and methods.

The Directory entries have been distilled from these responses according to a uniform pattern, and they have been checked during January-February, 1976, by the respective participants to ensure up-to-date accuracy.

As our policy for this first Directory was to base the entries only on actual responses to surveys rather than to compile these from available materials, we have not attempted to fill certain obvious gaps and omissions where no entry information was received. Nor have we given details of the many academic programmes in futures studies and planning - and future-oriented courses in other disciplines - which have been the natural consequence of the field's development.

Organization Entries

Type of centre
Categories of organization types suggested were:

National govermental: e.g. National Research Council of Canada.
International governmental: e.g. Asian Institute for Economic Development. and Planning, Thailand.
International non-governmental: e.g. World Future Study Federation, Italy.
Industry: e.g. Philips Research Laboratories Future Research Group, The Netherlands.
Business: e.g. Sears, Roebuck and Company Planning and Research, USA.
Academic centre: e.g. Polish Academy of Sciences Institute of Philosophy and Sociology, Division of Social Prognosis, Poland.
Commission/advisory group: e.g. Puget Sound Governmental Conference, USA.
National voluntary association: e.g. Club de Amigos de la Futurologia, Spain.
International voluntary association: e.g. Salzburg Assembly: Impact of the New Technology, Austria.
International professional organization: e.g. Association Internationale Futuribles, France.
Trade Union: e.g. World Federation of Agricultural Workers, Belgium.
Independent research centre: e.g. Japan Techno-Economics Society.
Membership society: e.g. World Future Society, USA.
Ad hoc *study group:* e.g. Stensen Institute Teilhard de Chardin Centre for Studies and Research,Italy.

Entries are either listed as being *Primarily engaged in* futures studies, long-range planning, or both, or they are *Concerned with long-term futures,* in which case a percentage estimate of *Time allocated* to this activity is noted.

Orientation of work being done is divided into categories for: *Direction of work in forecasting, Direction of work in research,* and *Direction of work in planning,* although in actual practice these clearly overlap. Where possible, participants have ranked topic areas in order of importance to their work with 1 as the highest rank. Categories of topic areas were suggested as follows: (Some have specified additional areas)

Forecasting	*Research*	*Planning*
Economic	Alternative futures	Social
Social	Social impacts of technology	Economic
Technological	Resource utilization	Technological
Resources	Policy research	Environmental
Environmental	Environmental	Urban
Educational	Futures methodology	Regional
Population	Social priorities	Educational
Scientific	Value systems	Resources
Manpower	Population	Corporate
Cultural	Manpower	Scientific
Market	The individual in the future	Political
Military	The family in the future	Labour
	Consumer affairs	Military

Methods used

Methodological approaches are listed and where possible ranked, (1, 2, 3......) according to importance in the participant's work. The methodological approaches suggested were as follows: (Some participants supplemented these by methods of their own)

Expert panels	Delphi techniques
Extrapolation techniques	Operational models
Individual expert forecasting	Cross impact analysis
Statistical models	Causal modelling
Brainstorming	Network analysis
Scenario building	Relevance trees
Simulation	Gaming
Historical analogy	Contextual mapping
Probabilistic forecasting	

Time range of work

Entries indicate the time range with which participants are most concerned. Categories for time range of work were suggested as: short range, *5 - 10 years;* medium range, *10 - 25 years;* and long range, *beyond year 2000.*

Source of support for work

Sources from which funding is received are listed by type and the support range is indicated by percentages. Types of funding organization suggested were as follows: (Some participants listed additional types)

Local government
National government
International agencies
Private business
Foundations
Voluntary associations

Work done for

Time spent in futures studies and/or long-range planning is often done specifically for the organization from which funds are received, but not always. Entries indicate the percentage of time spent in these activities for the various types of organization suggested above.

Number of persons working at professional level
Entries denote the total number of persons employed in the organization in
some aspect of futures studies and/or long-range planning on a *full-time* basis
and *part-time.*

Individual entries

Sex

Age
Entries are listed in one of six categories: *less than 25 years old; 25-29, 30-39,
40-49, 50-59, 60 or over.*

Educational qualification
Entries indicate whether the individual concerned has: attended *Some college or
less,* a *Bachelor's degree, Master's degree, Doctoral degree,* or *Other graduate/
professional degree.*

Formal training
Fields of major formal training are listed and, where possible, ranked (1, 2, 3......).
Fields suggested were as follows: (Some participants specified additional fields)

> Social/behavioural sciences
> Engineering
> Humanities
> Physical sciences
> Mathematics
> Life sciences (includes medicine)
> Law
> Design (includes environmental and industrial
>   design, city and regional planning)
> Journalism
> Arts (includes studio and performing)
> Cinema/television

Informal training
Fields of informal training, through work experience and/or interest are listed
and where possible ranked (1, 2, 3......). The same fields denoted above
were suggested.

Engaged in
Entries show whether the individual is primarily engaged in *Futures studies, Long-
range planning,* or *Both futures studies and long-range planning.*

Areas in which work done
Entries show the approximate percentage of time that the individual spends in
any of a number of areas. Areas suggested were as follows: (Some participants
specified additional areas)

In organization primarily concerned with futures studies and/or long-range
planning.

In organization concerned with other studies including long-range planning.
As individual consultant.
In planning unit of a governmental agency.
In planning unit of a business enterprise.
In planning unit of an international organization.
As academic, in teaching futures studies or long-range planning.

Direction of work in forecasting
Direction of work in research
Direction of work in planning
Methods used　　　　　　　　　　　　(All as for organizations)
Time range of work
Source of support for work
Work done for

Occupational function
Entries indicate the individual's present major occupational function. When he
has more than one, they are, where possible, ranked in order of importance
(1, 2, 3......). Functions suggested were as follows: (Some individuals specified
additional categories)

> Research worker
> Educator
> Consultant
> Administrator
> Manager

Worked for government as
Entries show whether the individual has worked for government as an *Elected
official, Administrator* or *Researcher.*

Worked for industry/business in
Entries show whether the individual has worked for industry or business in
Management, Research and Development, Planning, Trade Union or *Consultancy.*

Worked for education
Entries show whether the individual has worked for education in *Teaching,
Research* or *Administration.*

Worked for service sector in
Entries show whether the individual has worked in *Law, Medicine, Social welfare,
Religion, Communications media,* or *Design.*

Additional information
A brief additional description of an individual's or organization's special concern
is added where appropriate.

John McHale and Magda Cordell McHale

Publishers Note

All entries are arranged alphabetically according to the first word, ignoring the definite article in the case of organizations. Individuals are arranged alphabetically according to surname; in the case of more than one surname, the last one determines under which letter of the alphabet the entry will appear, whether or not the surnames are linked by a hyphen.

The numeral preceding the name of the organization or individual is the sequential alphabetic number running through the Directory and this is used in the indexes. The numeral set in sloping type at the end of each entry on the right is the computer retrieval number, which can be ignored by users of the Directory.

All entries have been reproduced from information supplied by the organization or individual. Responsibility for the faithfulness of this reproduction must remain with the publishers, but no attempt has been made independently to verify the accuracy of the original information.

The address of the Centre for Integrative Studies is now:-

College of Social Sciences,
University of Houston,
Houston,
Texas 77004,
U.S.A.
Tel. 713/749-1121.

This change occurred after the Directory had gone to press.

ORGANIZATIONS

A **1. Abt Associates, Inc**
President, Clark C. Abt, 55 Wheeler St, Cambridge, Ma 02138, USA.
Type of centre: National government. *Concerned with long-term futures.*
Time allocated (%): 20.
Direction of work in forecasting: I Economic, 2 Technological.
Direction of work in research: I Policy research, 2 Resource utilization,
3 Social impacts of technology, 4 Manpower, 5 Social priorities, 6 Population,
7 The individual in the future.
Direction of work in planning: I Economic, 2 Educational, 3 Social, 4 Urban,
5 Regional, 6 Corporate, 7 Environmental, 8 Labour, 9 Resources.
Methods used: I Cross impact analysis, 2 Statistical models, 3 Operational models,
4 Expert panels, 5 individual expert forecasting, 6 Historical analogy,
7 Brainstorming, 8 Extrapolation techniques.
Time range of work: 5 - 10 years.
Source of support for work (%): IO International agencies, IO Governments,
8O National government.
Number of persons working at professional level: 3OO Part time, 7OO Full time.   *(195)*

2. Academy for Contemporary Problems
2030 M St, NW, Washington DC 20036, USA.
Type of centre: Knowledge broker.
Concerned with long-term futures.
Direction of work in forecasting: Technological, Resources, Population.
Direction of work in research: Social impacts of technology, Alternative futures,
Resource utilization, Value systems, Population, The individual in the future,
The family in the future, Futures methodology.
Direction of work in planning: Technological, Social, Urban, Regional, Educational.
Economic, Political, Resources.
Methods used: Scenario building, Contextual mapping, Brainstorming, Relevance
trees, Network analysis.
Source of support for work (%): IOO Foundations.
Work done for (%): 20 National government, 30 Local government,
5O International agencies.
Number of persons working at professional level: I Full time, 3 Part time.   *(143)*

3. Advanced Concepts Centre
Director, Dr R.W. Durie, Fontaine Bldg, Environment Canada, Ottawa KIA OH3
Canada.
Type of centre: National government.
Primarily engaged in: Both futures studies and long-range planning.
Direction of work in forecasting: Social, Cultural.
Direction of work in research: Social impacts of technology, Alternative futures,
Environmental, Policy research, Low-impact technology.
Direction of work in planning: Environmental, Policy.

Methods used: Scenario building, Contextual mapping, Brainstorming, Individual expert forecasting.

Time range of work: Long range.

Work done for (%): IOO National government.

Number of persons working at professional level: 3 Full time, 4 Part time.   *(377)*

4. Aéroport de Paris

Director, Corporate Planning, Gerard Franck, 29I Blvd Raspail, 75675 Paris, Cedex I4, France.

Type of centre: National government. *Concerned with long-term futures.*

Time allocated (%): 2O.

Direction of work in forecasting: Technological, Economic, Environmental, Air traffic.

Direction of work in planning: Transport.

Methods used: Probabilistic forecasting, Delphi techniques, Cross impact analysis, Scenario building, Extrapolation techniques, Brainstorming, Statistical models, Network analysis, Operational models, Simulation.

Time range of work: IO - 25 years;

Work done for (%): IOO Own organization.

Number of persons working at professional level: 5 Part time.   *(67)*

5. Akzo NV

Vice President of Long-Range Planning, Arnhem Ijessellaan 82, PO Box I86, The Netherlands.

Type of centre: Industry.

Concerned with long-term futures.

Time allocated (%) Less than IO.

Methods used: Extrapolation techniques, Brainstorming, Individual expert forecasting, Simulation.

Time range of work: 5 - IO years.   *(22)*

6. Aluminium Company of America

Corporate Planning, I5OI Alcoa Bldg, Pittsburgh, Pa I52I9, USA.

Type of centre: Business.

Primarily engaged in: Long-range planning.

Direction of work in forecasting: I Economic, 2 Market, 3 Resources, 4 Environmental, 5 Technological.

Direction of work in research: Alternative futures, Resource utilization.

Direction of work in planning: I Corporate, 2 Economic, 3 Resources, 4 Environmental, 5 Political.

Methods used: I Extrapolation techniques, 2 Individual expert forecasting, 3 Statistical models, 4 Simulation.

Time range of work: 5 - IO years.

Source of support for work (%): IOO Private business.

Work done for (%): IOO Private business.

Number of persons working at professional level: 2O Full time.   *(300)*

7. American Institute of Biological Sciences

Asst Director for Education, Richard A. Dodge, I4OI Wilson Blvd, Arlington Va 222O9, USA.

Type of centre: National professional organization/Membership society.

Concerned with long-term futures.
Direction of work in forecasting: I Scientific, 2 Educational, 3 Environmental,
4 Population, 5 Resources, 6 Manpower, 7 Technological, 8 Economic.
Direction of work in research: I Alternative futures, 2 Social impacts of technology,
3 Environmental.
Direction of work in planning: I Scientific, 2 Educational, 3 Technological.
Methods used: I Expert panels, 2 Operational models, 3 Brainstorming.
Time range of work: 5 - IO years.
Source of support for work (%): 5 Private business, 25 Voluntary associations,
7O National government.
Work done for (%): 2O National government, 2O Voluntary associations.
Number of persons working at professional level: 3 Part time, 8 Full time.　　　*(267)*

8. American Journal of Psychotherapy

Editor-in-Chief, Stanley Lesse, 15 West 81st St, New York, NY 1OO24, USA.
Type of centre: Membership society.
Concerned with long-term futures.
Time allocated (%): Less than IO.
Methods used: I Cross impact analysis, 2 Probabilistic forecasting, 3 Individual
expert forecasting.
Time range of work: IO - 25 years.
Source of support for work (%): IOO Voluntary associations.
Work done for (%): IO Voluntary associations.
Number of persons working at professional level: I Part time.　　　*(455)*

9. The American Lutheran Church

Office of Research and Analysis, Director, Carl F. Reuss, 422 South Fifth St,
Minneapolis, Mn 554I5, USA.
Type of centre: National voluntary association.
Concerned with long-term futures.
Time allocated (%): Less than IO.
Methods used: I Expert panels, 2 Individual expert forecasting, 3 Brainstorming,
4 Historical analogy, 5 Network analysis.
Time range of work: 5 - IO years.
Source of support for work (%): IOO Internal.
Number of persons working at professional level: 6 Part time.　　　*(246)*

1O. American Management Association

PO Box 88, Hamilton, NY I3346, USA.
Type of centre: Membership society.
Primarily engaged in: Long-range planning.
Direction of work in planning: I Corporate, 2 Educational.
Methods used: I Brainstorming, 2 Probabilistic forecasting, 3 Expert panels,
4 Historical analogy.
Time range of work: 5 - IO years.
Source of support for work (%): 2O National government, 5O Private business.
Number of persons working at professional level: 3 Full time, 6 Part time.　　　*(171)*

11. American Psychological Association

Administrative Officer for Scientific Affairs, Miriam Kelty, 1200 17th St, NW,
Washington, DC 20036, USA.
Type of centre: Membership society.
Concerned with long-term futures.
Time allocated (%): 20.
Methods used: 1 Brainstorming, 2 Individual expert forecasting, 3 Expert panels,
4 Extrapolation techniques, 5 Delphi techniques, 6 Historical analogy, 7 Scenario
building.
Time range of work: 5 - 10 years.
Source of support for work (%): 5 National government, 95 Membership dues.
Work done for (%): 5 National government, 5 Foundations.
Number of persons employed at professional level: 4 Full time.   *(149)*

12. The American University

The World Population Society, President, Washington, DC 20016, USA.
Type of centre: Membership society.
Concerned with long-term futures.
Direction of work in forecasting: 1 Population, 2 Social, 3 Scientific, 4 Educational,
5 Environmental, 6 Resources.
Time range of work: 5 - 10 years.
Source of support for work (%): 50 Foundations, 50 Voluntary associations.
Work done for (%): 100 Voluntary associations.
Number of persons working at professional level: 1 Full time.   *(163)*

13. Arthur D. Little, Inc

25 Acorn Park, Cambridge, Ma 02140, USA.
Type of centre: Consultants.
Concerned with long-term futures.
Time allocated (%): 30.
Direction of work in forecasting: Virtually all areas (see Directory guide).
Direction of work in research: Virtually all areas (see Directory guide).
Direction of work in planning: Virtually all areas (see Directory guide).
Methods used: All methods (see Directory guide).
Time range of work: 5 - 25 years.
Source of support for work (%): 5 Local government, 5 International agencies,
10 National government, 80 Private business.
Work done for (%): 2 Local government, 2 International agencies, 3 National
government, 24 Private business.
Number of persons working at professional level: 20 Full time, 600 Part time.   *(6)*

14. Asian Institute for Economic Development and Planning

Director, Vinyu Vichit-Vadakan, PO Box 2-136, Sri Ayudkya Rd, Bangkok,
Thailand.
Type of centre: International government.
Primarily engaged in: Long-range planning.
Direction of work in forecasting: Economic, Social, Environmental, Manpower,
Resources, Population.
Direction of work in research: Social impacts of technology, Manpower,
Environmental, Resource utilization, Social priorities, Policy research, Population.
Direction of work in planning: Social, Urban, Regional, Economic, Environmental.

Methods used: Scenario building, Brainstorming, Expert panels, Network analysis, Historical analogy, Individual expert forecasting.
Time range of work: 5 - IO years.
Source of support for work (%): IO Foundations, 3O National government, 6O International agencies.
Work done for (%): 4O International agencies, 6O National government.
Number of persons employed in professional level: IO Full time.   (224)

15. Asian Productivity Organization
Aoyama, Dai-Ichi Mansions, 4-14, Akasaka 8-Chome, Minato-ku, Tokyo IO7, Japan.
Type of centre: International government.
Concerned with long-term futures.
Time allocated (%): Less than IO.
Methods used: Brainstorming, Expert panels, Network analysis, Historical analogy.
Time range of work: 5 - IO years.
Source of support for work (%): IOO Contributions of member countries.
Work done for (%): 3 Five year plan.
Number of persons working at professional level: 3 Part time.   (13)

16. Association of International Futuribles
1O, Rue Cernuschi, 75OI7 Paris, France.
Type of centre: International professional organization. Academic centre, Membership society.
Primarily engaged in: Futures studies.
Direction of work in forecasting: I Social, 2 Environmental, 3 Economic, 4 Educational, 5 Cultural, 6 Resources, 7 Population.
Direction of work in research: I Alternative futures, 2 Environmental, 3 Resource utilization, 3 Value systems, 4 Social priorities, 5 The individual in the future, 6 Consumer affairs, 7 Social impacts of technology, 8 Manpower.
Direction of work in planning: I Social, 2 Environmental, 3 Urban, 4 Educational, 5 Economic, 6 Resources.
Methods used: I Scenario building, 2 Brainstorming, 3 Contextual mapping, 4 Expert panels.
Time range of work: 5 - Beyond year 2OOO.
Source of support for work (%): IO Voluntary associations, I5 Private business, I5 Foundations, 25 National government, 35 Membership fées.
Work done for (%): 2O Private business, 25 National government, 55 General activities of the association.
Number of persons working at professional level: 3 Full time, 3O Part time.   (318)

17. Associazione per lo Sviluppo dell'Industria nel Mezzogiorno (SVIMEZ)
Director, Gian M. Dell'Angelo, Via di Porta, Pinciana, 6 Rome, Italy.
Type of centre: Independent research. *Concerned with long-term futures.*
Time allocated (%): 3O.
Direction of work in forecasting: Population.
Direction of work in research: Manpower, Resource utilization, Policy research, Population, Planning.
Methods used: Extrapolation techniques, Statistical models, Historical analogy.
Time range of work: 5 - IO years.
Source of support for work (%): 5O National government, 4O Voluntary associations.
Number of persons working at professional level: 2 Part time, 2 Full time.   (54)

18. Australian Post Office

National telecommunications planning (7th Floor), I.A. Newstead, 140 Queen St, Melbourne, Victoria 3000, Australia.
Type of centre: National government.
Concerned with long-term futures.
Time allocated (%): Less than 10.
Methods used: 1 Scenario building, 2 Expert panels, 3 Delphi techniques, 4 Extrapolation techniques, 5 Cross impact analysis, Relevance Trees, Network analysis, Historical analogy, Individual expert forecasting, Simulation.
Time range of work: 5 - Beyond year 2000.
Source of support for work (%): 100 National government.
Work done for (%): 100 National government.
Number of persons working at professional level: 350 Full time.   *(406)*

19. Austrian Academy of Sciences, Institute for Research in Socio-Economic Development

Fleischmarkt 20, A - 1010 Wien, Austria.
Type of centre: Academic
Primarily engaged in: Both futures studies and long-range planning.
Direction of work in forecasting: 1 Economic, 2 Social, 3 Educational, 4 Resources, 5 Population.
Direction of work in research: 1 Alternative futures, 2 Value systems, 3 Policy research, 4 Population.
Direction of work in planning: 1 Political, 2 Economic, 3 Educational, 4 Resources, 5 Social.
Methods used: 1 Simulation, 2 Historical analogy, 2 Causal modelling, 3 Statistical models, 4 Extrapolation techniques, 5 Scenario building, 6 Operational models.
Time range of work: 10 - 25 years.
Source of support for work (%): 100 National government
Work done for (%): 100 National government.
Number of persons working at professional level: 4 Full time.
Additional information: There is an Austrian Society for futures research, founded in 1974. The President is Gerhart Bruchmann; Paul Blau, Vice-President. It is an umbrella organization.   *(109)*

20. Austrian Institute for Economic Research

A-1103 Wien, Postfach 91, Austria.
Type of centre: Independent research.
Concerned with long-term futures.
Time allocated (%): 30,
Direction of work in forecasting: Economic.
Methods used: 1 Extrapolation techniques, 2 Statistical models.
Time range of work: 5 - 10 years.
Source of support for work (%): 10 Local government, 10 Voluntary associations, 80 National government.
Work done for (%): 10 Local government, 10 Voluntary associations, 80 National government.
Number of persons working at professional level: 20 Part time.   *(63)*

B ## 21. Bar-Ilan University
Department of Psychology, Ramat-Gan, Israel.
Type of centre: Academic. *Concerned with long-term futures.*
Time allocated (%): Less than 10.
Methods used: 1 Individual expert forecasting, 2 Statistical models, 3 Expert panels.
Time range of work: 5 - 10 years.
Source of support for work (%): 20 Local government, 80 Foundations.
Work done for (%): 20 Local government, 80 Science.
Number of persons working at professional level: 10 Part time.   (72)

22. Bariloche Foundation
Carlos A. Mallman, President, CC 138 - Bariloche, Rio Negro, Argentina.
Type of centre: Academic and independent research.
Concerned with long-term futures.
Time allocated (%): 10.
Direction of work in research: Social impacts of technology, Alternative futures,
Environmental, Resource utilization, Value systems, Social Priorities, Population,
Futures methodology.
Methods used: Gaming, Scenario building, Simulation, Causal modelling,
Normative modelling.
Time range of work: 5 - 10 years and beyond year 2000.
Source of support for work (%): 20 International agencies, 80 Own foundation.
Work done for (%): 100 Own Foundation.
Number of persons working at professional level: 8 Full time.
Additional information: Concerned with long-range resource analysis, social and
economic projections, global modelling and mathematical methodologies.   (452)

23. Battelle Columbus Laboratories
Associate Manager, William L. Swager, 505 Ring Ave, Columbus, Oh 43201, USA.
Type of centre: Independent research.
Concerned with long-term futures.
Time allocated (%): Less than 10.
Direction of work in forecasting: Technological, Scientific, Environmental, Resources,
Economic, Population, Social.
Direction of work in research: Social impacts of technology, Policy research,
Environmental, Resource utilization.
Direction of work in planning: Technological, Economic.
Methods used: Probabilistic forecasting, Delphi techniques, Gaming, Cross impact
analysis, Scenario building, Extrapolation techniques, Brainstorming, Statistical
models, Expert panels, Relevance trees, Individual expert forecasting, Simulation.
Time range of work: 5 - 10 years.
Source of support for work (%): 10 Local government, 45 National government,
45 Private business.
Work done for (%): 1 Local government, 2 Private business, 3 National government.
Number of persons employed at professional level: 10 Full time, 40 Part time.
Additional information: A considerable amount of futures-related work is
conducted by many BCL's staff of over 2000 professionals. The combination of
many of the terms and concepts mean that this entry should be viewed as descriptive,
rather than definitive.   (131)

24. Battelle, Geneva Research Centre

Directeur General, Dr Helmut Hoegl, 7, Rte de Prize, CH - 1227 Carouge, Geneva, Switzerland.
Type of centre: Independent research.
Concerned with long-term futures.
Time allocated (%): 2O.
Direction of work in forecasting: Economic, Social, Market, Scientific, Resources, Population.
Direction of work in research: Social impacts of technology, Alternative futures, Consumer affairs, Value systems, Futures methodology.
Direction of work in planning: Scientific, Technological, Urban, Regional, Economic, Corporate.
Methods used: I Brainstorming, 2 Statistical models, 3 Extrapolation techniques, 4 Simulation, 5 Scenario building, 6 Cross impact analysis, 7 Probabilistic forecasting, 8 Delphi techniques.
Time range of work: 5 - 1O years.
Source of support for work (%): 1O International government, 2O National government, 2O Foundations, 5O Private business.
Number of persons working at professional level: 2O Full time, 6O Part time.   *(73)*

25. Battelle Institut eV

6 Frankfurt am Main 9O, Postfach 9OO16O, West Germany.
Type of centre: Independent sponsored research.
Concerned with long-term futures.
Time allocated (%): 1O.
Direction of work in forecasting: Technological, Economic, Social, Market, Scientific, Environmental, Defence, Manpower, Resources, Population.
Direction of work in research: Social impacts of technology, Manpower, Environmental, Futures methodology, Resource utilization, Social priorities.
Direction of work in planning: Scientific, Technological, Social, Urban, Regional, Educational, Economic, Corporate, Environmental, Defence, Labour, Resources.
Methods used: Probabilistic forecasting, Delphi techniques, Gaming, Brainstorming, Statistical models, Relevance trees, Simulation.
Time range of work: 5 - 1O years.
Source of support for work (%): 1O Local government, 55 National government, 1O International government, 25 Industry.
Number of persons working at professional level: 4OO Full time.   *(103)*

26. Battelle Institut eV, Economics and Social Sciences Department

6 Frankfurt am Main 9O, Postfach 9OO16O, West Germany.
Type of centre: Independent research.
Primarily engaged in: Both futures studies and long-range planning.
Direction of work in forecasting: Technological, Economic, Social, Market, Environmental, Manpower, Resources, Population.
Direction of work in research: Social impacts of technology, Technological innovation, Alternative futures, Manpower, Environmental, Resource utilization, Value systems, Social priorities, Population Futures methodology.
Direction of work in planning: Technological, Social, Urban, Regional, Educational, Economic, Corporate, Environmental, Labour, Resources.
Methods used: All methods (see Directory guide).
Time range of work: 5 - 25 years.

Source of support for work (%): 5 Local government, 5 International agencies,
40 Private business, 50 National government.
Work done for (%): 5 Local government, 5 International agencies, 40 Private
business, 50 National government.
Number of persons working at professional level: 10 Part time, 75 Full time.   *(343)*

27. B.C. Telephone Company

Corporate Planning, 768 Seymour St, Vancouver, BC V6, 3K9, Canada.
Type of centre: Industry.
Primarily engaged in: Both futures studies and long-range planning.
Direction of work in forecasting: Technological, Population, Social, Economic,
Environmental.
Direction of work in research: Alternative futures, Population, Futures methodology.
Direction of work in planning: Technological, Corporate.
Methods used: Probabilistic forecasting, Delphi techniques, Extrapolation techni-
ques, Brainstorming, Statistical models, Expert panels, Network analysis, Historical
analogy, Operational models, Individual expert forecasting, Simulation, Causal
modelling.
Time range of work: 5 years - beyond year 2000.
Source of support for work (%): 100 Private business.
Work done for (%): 100 Private business.
Number of persons working at professional level: 48 Full time.   *(358)*

28. Bell Canada

Business Planning Group, Room 1105, 620 Belmont, Montreal, Canada.
Type of centre: Business.
Primarily engaged in: Both futures studies and long-range planning.
Direction of work in forecasting: 1 Social, 2 Technological, 3 Economic, 4 Market,
5 Educational, 6 Scientific.
Direction of work in research: 1 Social impacts of technology, 2 Policy research,
3 Alternative futures, 4 Value systems, 5 Social priorities, 6 The individual in the
future, 7 Futures methodology, 8 Resource utilization, 9 Environmental.
Direction of work in planning: 1 Corporate, 2 Social, 3 Technological,
4 Economic, 5 Scientific, 6 Urban, 7 Educational.
Methods used: 1 Expert panels, 2 Delphi techniques, 3 Extrapolation techniques,
4 Scenario building, 5 Cross impact analysis, 6 Historical analogy, 7 Individual
expert forecasting, 8 Probabilistic forecasting, 9 Relevance trees, 10 Survey research,
11 Brainstorming, 12 Statistical models.
Time range of work: 10 - 25 years.
Source of support for work (%): 100 Private business.
Work done for (%): 5 Local government, 15 National government, 80 Private business.
Number of persons working at professional level: 2 Part time, 9 Full time.   *(207)*

29. The Bendix Corporation

Bendix Center, Felix Kaufmann, Southfield, Mi 48076, USA.
Type of centre: Industry.
Concerned with long-term futures.
Time allocated (%): 10.
Direction of work in forecasting: 1 Market, 2 Economic, 3 Environmental,
4 Technological, 5 Political, 6 Social, 7 Resources, 8 Manpower, 9 Military.
Direction of work in research: Social impacts of technology.

Direction of work in planning: I Corporate, 2 Economic, 3 Regional.
Methods used: I Probabilistic forecasting, 2 Extrapolation techniques, 3 Statistical models, 4 Cross impact analysis, 5 Individual expert forecasting, 6 Expert panels.
Time range of work: 5 - IO years.
Source of support for work (%): IOO Private business.
Number of persons working at professional level: 3O Full time.   *(253)*

30. Bonn University

Institute of Industry and Traffic Policy, Adenauer Allee 24-26 D-53OO Bonn, Gesellschaft fuer wirtschafts-und verkehrswissenschaftliche Forschung eV, Zum kleinen Oelberg 44, D-533O Koenigswinter 41 and Institut fuer das Spar-, Giro- und Kreditwesen an der Universitaet Bonn, Coburger Strasse 2, D-53OO Bonn.
Type of centre: Academic. *Concerned with long-term futures.*
Time allocated (%): 5O.
Direction of work in forecasting: Economic, Transportation, Money.
Direction of work in research: Manpower, Consumer affairs, Environmental, Transportation, Money.
Direction of work in planning: Scientific, Urban, Regional, Economic, Political, Environmental, Transportation, Money.
Methods used: Extrapolation techniques, Brainstorming, Historical analogy.
Time range of work: 5 - 25 years.
Source of support for work (%): IO Private business, 3O Local government, 6O National government.
Work done for (%): IO Private business, 2O Local government, 7O National government.
Number of persons working at professional level: 3 Part time, 18 Full time.
Additional information: These are actually three institutes working together.
(Director: Professor F. Voigt is tied to three institutions which work in collaboration.)
                                                                                    (135)

31. Bristol University

School of Education, 35 Berkeley Square, Bristol 8 UK.
Type of centre: Academic. *Concerned with long-term futures.*
Time allocated (%): Less than IO.
Methods used: Extrapolation techniques, Brainstorming, Individual expert forecasting.
Time range of work: IO - 25 years.
Number of persons working at professional level: I Part time.   *(274)*

32. British Tourist Authority

64 St James St, London SW1, UK.
Type of centre: National government. *Concerned with long-term futures.*
Time allocated (%): Less than IO.
Methods used: Delphi techniques, Scenario building, Extrapolation techniques, Statistical models, Historical analogy, Individual expert forecasting, Causal modelling.
Time range of work: 5 - 25 years.
Source of support for work (%): 3O Private business, 6O National government.
Work done for (%): 5O National government.
Number of persons working at professional level: 4 Part time.   *(281)*

33. Bundesforschungsanstalt fuer Landeskunde und Raumordnung
D 5300 Bonn-Bad Godesberg, Michaelstr 8, Postfach 130, West Germany.
Type of centre: Research institution attached to the Federal government.
Primarily engaged in: Long-range planning.
Direction of work in planning: 1 Population, 2 Economic, 3 Environmental.
4 Labour.
Methods used: 1 Statistical models, 2 Network analysis, 3 Simulation.
Time range of work: 5 - 10 years.
Source of support for work (%): 100 Federal government.
Work done for (%): 100 Federal government.
Number of persons working at professional level: 39 Full time.   *(85)*

34. Bureau d'Etudes et de Réalisations Urbaines
157 Rue des Blairs 92220 Bagneux, France.
Type of centre: National government. *Concerned with long-term futures.*
Primarily engaged in: Both futures studies and long-range planning.
Direction of work in forecasting: 1 Population, 2 Social, 3 Economic, 4 Resources,
5 Market, 6 Environmental.
Direction of work in research: 1 Manpower, 1 Population, 2 Resource utilization,
3 Environmental, 4 Futures methodology.
Direction of work in planning: 1 Urban, 2 Regional, 3 Environmental, 4 Economic,
5 Resources, 6 Labour.
Methods used: 1 Individual expert forecasting, 2 Statistical models, 3 Scenario
building, 4 Expert panels.
Time range of work: 5 - 25 years.
Source of support for work (%): 10 International agencies, 10 Private business,
10 Voluntary associations, 30 Local government, 40 National government.
Number of persons working at professional level: 65 Full time.   *(202)*

35. Bureau Fédéral de Statistique
Hallwylstr 15, CH-3003 Berne, Switzerland.
Type of centre: National government.
Concerned with long-term futures.
Time allocated (%): Less than 10.
Direction of work in forecasting: Economic, Social, Educational, Manpower, Popu-
lation.
Methods used: Extrapolation techniques, Statistical models.
Time range of work: 5 - 10 years and beyond year 2000.
Source of support for work (%): 100 National government.
Work done for (%): 100 National government.
Number of persons working at professional level: 4 Part time.   *(234)*

36. Bureau d'Informations et de Prévisions Economiques (BIPE)
122 Ave Charles de Gaulle, 92522 Neuilly, France.
Type of centre: Membership society/non-profit organization.
Primarily engaged in: Both futures studies and long-range planning.
Direction of work in forecasting: Technological, Economic, Social, Educational,
Manpower.
Direction of work in research: Manpower, Resource utilization.
Direction of work in planning: Technological, Social, Educational, Economic.
Methods used: Probabilistic forecasting, Delphi techniques, Scenario building,

Extrapolation techniques, Brainstorming, Statistical models, Expert panels,
Operational models, Individual expert forecasting.
Time range of work: 5 - beyond year 2000.
Source of support for work (%):   45 Private business, 55 National government.   *(106)*

37. Bureau du Plan

Commissaire au Plan, Robert Maldague, Ave des Arts 47-49, 1040 Brussels, Belgium.
Type of centre: National government. *Concerned with long-term futures.*
Time allocated (%):   Less than 10.
Direction of work in forecasting: Economic, Social, Cultural, Educational,
Environmental, Manpower, Resources, Population, Regional.
Direction of work in planning: Social, Regional, Economic, Environmental,
Labour, Resources.
Methods used: Probabilistic forecasting, Causal modelling, Delphi techniques,
Extrapolation techniques, Brainstorming, Statistical models, Expert panels, Simulation.
Time range of work: 5 - 10 years.
Source of support for work (%):   100 National government.
Work done for (%):   50 Local government, 50 National government.
Number of persons working at professional level: 153 Full time.   *(385)*

38. Bureau de Recherches Géologiques et Minières

Mr. Guillemin, Executive Director, BP 6009, 45018 Orléans
Cedex, France.
Type of centre: National government.
Concerned with long-term futures.
Time allocated (%):   Less than 10.
Methods used: 1 Scenario building, 2 Expert panels, 3 Delphi techniques.
Time range of work: 5 - 25 years.
Source of support for work (%):   100 National government.
Work done for (%):   10 International government, 90 National government.
Number of persons working at professional level: 12 Part time.   *(408)*

39. Burmah Oil Company Limited

Financial Development Co-ordinator, Corporate Development Division, Burmah House,
Pipers Way, Swindon SN3 1RE, UK.
Type of centre: Industry.
Primarily engaged in: Long-range planning.
Direction of work in forecasting: Environmental.
Direction of work in planning: Corporate.
Methods used: Probabilistic forecasting, Simulation, Scenario building, Brainstorming,
Expert panels, Historical analogy, Operational models, Individual expert forecasting.
Time range of work: 10 - 25 years.
Source of support for work (%):   100 Private business.
Work done for (%):   100 Private business.   *(75)*

40. Busch Centre, University of Pennsylvania

400 Vance Hall, Philadelphia, Pa 19174, USA.
Type of centre: Academic
Primarily engaged in: Long-range planning.
Direction of work in planning: Corporate.
Methods used: Scenario building.

Time range of work: 5 - 25 years.
Source of support for work (%): 2O National government, 8O Private business.
Work done for (%): 2O National government, 8O Private business.
Number of persons working at professional level: 4O Full time.   *(466)*

C 4I. Cairo University
Institute of African Research and Studies, Department of Natural Resources, Giza,
Egypt.
Type of centre: Academic.
Concerned with long-term futures.
Time allocated (%): Less than IO.
Direction of work in research: I Environmental, 2 Resource utilization, 3 Population,
4 Manpower, 5 Social impacts of technology.
Direction of work in planning: I Environmental, 2 Resources, 3 Labour, 4 Urban,
5 Economic, 6 Political.
Methods used: Individual expert forecasting.
Time range of work: 5 - beyond year 2OOO.
Source of support for work (%): IO International agencies, 3O National government.
Work done for (%): IO International agencies, 9O National government.
Number of persons working at professional level: 3 Part time, 3 Full time.   *(185)*

42. Canada Post Office
F.G. Thompson, Station 26O, Sir Alexander Campbell Bldg, Confederation
Heights, Ottawa K1A OB1, Canada.
Type of centre: National government.
Direction of work in forecasting: Technological, Economic, Social, Population.
Methods used: Delphi techniques, Scenario building, Extrapolation techniques,
Brainstorming, Statistical models, Expert panels, Operational models.
Time range of work: 5 - beyond year 2OOO.
Source of support for work (%): IOO National government.
Work done for (%): IOO National government.
Number of persons working at professional level: 3 Part time.
Additional information: Currently preparing the background papers to act as a
resource for six to eight scenarios of Canada 2OOO.   *(405)*

43. Canadian Industries Ltd
Corporate planning, Hughie Rowlinson, Manager, Montreal, Canada.
Type of centre: Industry.
Concerned with long-term futures.
Time allocated (%): Less than IO.
Methods used: I Extrapolation techniques, 2 Operational models, 3 Scenario
building, 4 Relevance trees, 5 Probabilistic forecasting.
Time range of work: 5 - IO years.
Source of support for work (%): IOO Private business.
Work done for (%): IOO Private business.
Number of persons working at professional level: 4 Full time, 6 Part time.   *(366)*

44. Canadian International Development Agency
I22 Bank St, Ottawa, K1A OG4, Canada.
Type of centre: National government.
Concerned with long-term futures.

Time allocated (%): 10 of policy branch.
Direction of work in forecasting: 1 Social, 2 Economic, 3 International.
Direction of work in research: 1 International co-operation, 2 Policy research.
Direction of work in planning and development: 1 Social, 2 Economic, 3 Political,
4 Corporate.
Methods used: 1 Expert panels, 2 Trend extrapolation and regression analysis, 3 Causal
Modelling, 4 Brainstorming, 5 Factor analysis.
Time range of work: 5 - 20 years.
Source of support for work (%): 100 National government.
Work done for (%): 80 National government, 20 International agencies.
Number of persons working at professional level: 3 Full time.   *(226)*

45. Caribbean Food and Nutrition Institute
Dr. Robert Cook, PO Box 140, Kingston 7, Jamaica.
Type of centre: International government.
Concerned with long-term futures.
Time allocated (%): 30.
Methods used: 1 Expert panels, 2 Extrapolation techniques, 3 Operational
models, 4 Individual expert forecasting, 5 Historical analogy.
Time range of work: 5 - beyond year 2000.
Source of support for work (%): 11 National government, 39 International
government, 50 Foundations.
Work done for (%): 100 National government.
Number of persons working at professional level: 8 Part time.   *(39)*

46. Case Western Reserve University
Dept of Political Science, Kenneth Grundy, Chairman, Cleveland, Oh 44106, USA.
Type of centre: Academic.
Concerned with long-term futures.
Time allocated (%): 10.
Methods used: 1 Operational models, 2 Causal modelling, 3 Brainstorming,
4 Probabilistic forecasting.
Time range of work: Beyond year 2000.
Source of support for work (%): 100 University research centre.
Number of persons working at professional level: 2 Full time.   *(170)*

47. Cedric Price - Architects
38 Alfred Place, London WC1E 7DP UK.
Type of centre: Independent research.
Primarily engaged in: Long-range planning.
Direction of work in forecasting: Environmental.
Direction of work in research: 1 Manpower, 2 Environmental.
Direction of work in planning: 1 Environmental, 2 Educational, 3 Regional, 4 Labour.
Methods used: 1 Probabilistic forecasting, 2 Brainstorming, 3 Scenario building,
4 Operational models.
Time range of work: 10 - 25 years.
Source of support for work (%): 5 National government, 40 Private business,
50 Self-supported.
Work done for (%): 10 Private business, 10 Voluntary associations, 20 National
government.
Number of persons working at professional level: 1 Full time, 4 Part time.   *(120)*

48. Central Bureau of Statistics
Statistisk Sentralbyra, Dronningens Gt I6, Oslo 1, Norway.
Type of centre: National government. *Concerned with long-term futures.*
Time allocated (%): Less than IO.
Methods used: Statistical models, Operational models.
Time range of work: IO - 25 years.
Source of support for work (%): IOO National government.
Work done for (%): 2 National government.
Number of persons working at professional level: 11 Full time.
Additional information: The work in this field is limited to population progress
and long-term economic planning. The aim is to produce and analyse statistics.   *(129)*

49. Central Office for International Railway Transport
Gryphenhubeliweg 30, 3006 Berne, Switzerland.
Type of centre: International government. *Concerned with long-term futures.*
Time allocated (%): 30.
Methods used: I Law studies and comparative studies, 2 Expert panels, 3 Individual
expert forecasting.
Time range of work: IO - 25 years.
Source of support for work (%): IOO Member states of organization.
Work done for (%): IOO Member states of organization.
Number of persons working at professional level: 8 Part time.
Additional information: Concerned with unification and development of
international transport law by railways.   *(56)*

5O. Central Planning Bureau.
Director, Prof C.A. Van Den Beld, Van Stolkweg I4, The Hague, The Netherlands.
Type of centre: National government.
Primarily engaged in: Futures studies.
Direction of work in forecasting: I Economic, 2 Social, 2 Educational, 2 Manpower,
3 Environmental, 3 Project analysis.
Methods used: Delphi techniques, Scenario building, Extrapolation techniques,
Brainstorming, Expert panels, Individual expert forecasting, Simulation, Model
construction.
Time range of work: 5 - 25 years.
Source of support for work (%): IOO National government.
Work done for (%): I Local government, 2 International agencies, 3 Private business,
95 National government.
Number of persons working at professional level: I4O Full time.   *(121)*

51. Central Statistical Office
Great George St, London SW1, UK.
Type of centre: National government. *Concerned with long-term futures.*
Time allocated (%): Less than IO.
Methods used: I Statistical models, 2 Extrapolation techniques.
Time range of work: IO - 25 years.
Source of support for work (%): IOO National government.
Work done for (%): IOO National government.
Additional information: The Central Statistical Office is not directly involved in any
futures studies, but as the co-ordinating branch of the government statistical service
it is concerned with some long-range studies. In particular the Government Actuaries

Dept is responsible for population projections, at present to year 2011; the Dept of Employment produce projections of the working population; the Dept of Education and Science produce projections of the school population and the numbers of teachers; and the Dept of the Environment produce projections of housing demand.   *(98)*

52. Central Water Planning Unit
Reading Bridge House, Reading RG1 8 PS Berks, UK.
Type of centre: National government.
Primarily engaged in: Both futures studies and long-range planning.
Direction of work in forecasting: I Resources, 2 Demand (water), 3 Scientific, 4 Economic, 5 Environmental, 6 Technological.
Direction of work in research: I Resource utilization, 2 Environmental, 3 Futures methodolgy.
Direction of work in planning: I Resources, 2 Scientific, 3 Technological, 4 Environmental.
Methods used: I Simulation, 2 Network analysis, 3 Operational models, 4 Probabilistic forecasting, 5 Extrapolation techniques, 6 Statistical models, 7 Expert panels, 8 Relevance Trees, 9 Individual expert forecasting, IO Scenario building.
Time range of work: IO - 25 years.
Source of support for work (%): 5 International agencies, 95 National government.
Work done for (%): 5 International agencies, 95 National government.
Number of persons working at professional level: 45 Full time.   *(117)*

53. Centre for Advanced Study
912 W Illinois, Urbana, II 61801, USA.
Type of centre: Academic.
Concerned with long-term futures.
Time allocated (%): 30.
Methods used: I Individual expert forecasting, 2 Expert panels, 3 Social invention and evaluation of change efforts.
Time range of work: 5 - 25 years.
Source of support for work (%): 20 National government, 80 University.
Work done for (%): 5 Local government, IO National government, 40 University.
Number of persons working at professional level: 7 Part time.   *(339)*

54. Centre for Environmental Studies
Director, Prof David Donnison, 5 Cambridge Terrace, London , NW1, UK.
Type of centre: Independent research.
Concerned with long-term futures.
Time allocated (%): 30.
Direction of work in forecasting: Population .
Direction of work in research: Social priorities, Policy research, Population, Futures methodology.
Direction of work in planning: Social, Urban, Regional.
Methods used: Probabilistic forecasting, Statistical models, Simulation, Causal modelling.
Time range of work: 5 - 25 years.
Source of support for work: (%): IO Foundations, 16 International government, 74 National government.
Work done for (%): IOO As academic pursuit.   *(27)*

55. Centre d'Etudes des Conséquences Général des Grades Techniques Nouvelles

20 Rue Laffitte, 75009 Paris, France.
Type of centre: Independent research.
Primarily engaged in: Both futures studies and long-range planning.
Direction of work in research: Social impacts of technology, The individual in the future.
Methods used: General reflection and contact with very diverse personalities.
Time range of work: 5 - beyond year 2000.
Source of support for work (%): 20 Private individuals, 80 Private business.
Work done for (%): 100 Association members.
Number of persons working at professional level: 2 Full time, 6 Part time.   *(156)*

56. Centre d'Etudes des Problèmes Sociaux et Professionels de la Technique

Secretary-General, Pierre Feldheim, 44 Ave Jeanne, B-1050 Brussels, Belgium.
Type of centre: Academic.
Primarily engaged in: Both futures studies and long-range planning.
Direction of work in forecasting: Social, Educational, Manpower.
Direction of work in research: Manpower.
Direction of work in planning: Educational.
Methods used: Extrapolation techniques, Brainstorming, Statistical models, Expert panels, Network analysis, Operational models, Individual expert forecasting.
Time range of work: 5 - 10 years.
Source of support for work (%): 100 National government.
Work done for (%): 100 National government.
Number of persons working at professional level: 1 Part time, 9 Full time.   *(279)*

57. Centre d'Etudes sur la Recherche et l'Innovation

Director, Raymond Saint Paul, 116 Blvd Pereire, Paris, 17E France.
Type of centre: Independent research.
Concerned with long-term futures.
Time allocated (%): 10.
Direction of work in forecasting: 1 Technological, 1 Economic, 1 Market, 2 Scientific.
Direction of work in research: 1 Futures methodology, 2 Policy research, 3 Social impacts of technology.
Direction of work in planning: 1 Technological, 1 Economic, 1 Political, 2 Social.
Methods used: Delphi techniques, Cross impact analysis, Scenario building, Extrapolation techniaues, Network analysis, Simulation, Operational models.
Time range of work: 5 - 25 years.
Source of support for work (%): 5 Voluntary associations, 25 Private business, 70 National government.
Work done for (%): 10 International agencies, 30 Private business, 60 National government.
Number of persons working at professional level: 4 Full time, 15 Part time.   *(414)*

58. Centre for Integrative Studies

School of Advanced Technology, State University of New York at Binghamton, Binghamton, NY 13901, USA.
Type of centre: Academic.
Primarily engaged in: Futures studies and long-range planning.
Direction of work in forecasting: Resources, Social, Technological, Scientific,

2

Cultural, Environmental, Population.
Direction of work in research: Social impacts of technology, Alternative futures, Social priorities, The individual in the future, Population.
Direction of work in planning: Technological, Resources, Socio/cultural.
Methods used: Individual expert forecasting, Expert panels, Brainstorming, Contextual Mapping, Probabilistic forecasting, Scenario building, Extrapolation techniques, Historical analogy.
Time range of work: IO - Beyond year 2OOO.
Source of support for work (%): 3O University, 3O International agencies, 3O Foundations, IO National government.
Work done for (%): 3O University, 3O International agencies, 3O Foundations, IO National government.
Number of persons working at professional level: 4 Part time, 4 Full time.   *(467*

59. Centre International de Recherche sur l'Environment et de la Développement
Ecole Practique des Hautes Etudes, Director, Ignacy Sachs, 54, Blvd Raspail, 7527O Paris, Cedex O6, France.
Type of centre: Academic. *Concerned with long-term futures.*
Time allocated (%): 5O.
Direction of work in forecasting: I Economic, I Environmental, 3 Social, 4 Scientific.
Direction of work in research: I Alternative futures, 2 Environmental, 3 Social impacts of technology, 4 Resource utilization.
Direction of work in planning: I Environmental, 2 Scientific, 3 Technological.
Methods used: I Scenario building, 2 Contextual mapping, 3 Expert panels.
Time range of work: IO - 25 years.
Source of support for work (%): 5O National government, 5O International agencies.
Work done for (%): 5O National government, 5O International agencies.
Number of persons working at professional level: 2 Full time, IO Part time.   *(12.*

6O. Centre National d'Etudes Spatiales
129 Rue de L'Université, Paris 7, France.
Type of centre: National government.
Concerned with long-term futures.
Time allocated (%): Less than IO.
Direction of work in forecasting: Technological, Economic.
Direction of work in research: Social impacts of technology.
Direction of work in planning: Resources.
Methods used: I Brainstorming, 2 Extrapolation techniques, 3 Individual expert forecasting, 4 Probabilistic forecasting, 5 Relevance trees, 6 Scenario building.
Time range of work: 5 - beyond year 2OOO.
Source of support for work (%): IOO National government.
Work done for (%): IOO National government.
Number of persons working at professional level: I5 Full time, 3O Part time.   *(18*

61. Centre for Peaceful Change
Kent State University, Kent, Oh 44242, USA.
Type of centre: Academic.
Concerned with long-term futures.

Time allocated (%): 3O.
Methods used: I Operational models, 2 Simulation, 3 Historical analogy, 4 Scenario
building, 5 Brainstorming, 6 Gaming, 7 Probabilistic forecasting, 8 Expert panels.
Source of support for work (%): IOO University.
Work done for (%): IOO University.
Number of persons working at professional level: 3 Part time, 3 Full time.
Additional information: A living memorial to the slain students, May I97O.
Objective is the training of social change agents. *(127)*

62. Centre for the Study of Alternative Futures

Director, May Maury Harding, Southwestern at Memphis, 2OOO North Parkway,
Memphis, Tn 38112, USA.
Type of centre: Academic.
Primarily engaged in: Both futures studies and long-range planning.
Direction of work in planning: I Urban, 2 Regional, 3 Social.
Methods used: I Cross impact analysis, 2 Delphi techniques, 3 Probabilistic
forecasting, 4 Scenario building, 5 Extrapolation techniques, 6 Network analysis,
7 Operational models.
Time range of work: IO - 25 years.
Source of support for work (%): 5 Voluntary associations, IO Local government,
I5 Southwestern college budget, 7O Foundations.
Work done for (%): 3O Voluntary associations, 7O Local government.
Number of persons working at professional level: I Full time, IO Part time. *(335)*

63. Centre for the Study of Developing Societies

29, Rajpur Rd, Delhi 11OO54, India.
Type of centre: Academic. *Concerned with long-term futures.*
Time allocated (%): 5O.
Methods used: I Brainstorming, 2 Designing new paradisms and identifying
strategies/policies for moving towards them, 3 Causal modelling, 4 Historical
analogy, 5 Scenario building, 6 Probabilistic forecasting, 7 Gaming, 8 Contextual
mapping, 9 Individual expert forecasting, IO Network analysis.
Time range of work: 5 - 25 years.
Source of support for work (%): 2O International agencies, 3O National
government, 5O Social science research council, national committee on science and
technology, national committee on environmental planning.
Work done for (%): IO Voluntary associations, 2O National government,
2O International agencies, 5O Own work.
Number of persons working at professional level: 2 Part time, 2 Full time.
Additional information: Specific focus of work: international and global context
of national development; planning of national goals and strategies. *(18O)*

64. Centre for the Study of the Future

Director, Carl Townsend, 411O NE Alameda, Portland, Or 94212, USA.
Type of centre: International voluntary associations.
Primarily engaged in: Futures studies.
Direction of work in forecasting: Religious.
Direction of work in research: Religious.
Direction of work in planning: Religious.
Methods used: Gaming, Scenario building, Brainstorming, Expert panels, Historical
analogy, Simulation.

Time range of work: 5 - 10 years.
Source of support for work (%): 100 Member Fees.
Work done for (%): 100 Other subscribers.
Number of persons working at professional level: 2 Full time.   *(387)*

65. Centre for the Study of Social Policy

Director, Willis Harman, Stanford Research Institute, Menlo Park, Ca 94025, USA.
Type of centre: Independent research.
Concerned with long-term futures.
Time allocated (%): 40.
Direction of work in research: 1 Policy research, 2 Alternative futures, 3 Value systems, 4 Futures methodology.
Methods used: Synthesis of results from all methods (see Directory guide).
Time range of work: 10 - 25 years.
Source of support for work (%): 15 Foundations, 85 National government.
Work done for (%):   5 Foundations, 35 National government.
Number of persons working at professional level: 1 Full time, 8 Part time.   *(433)*

66. Newark College of English, Centre for Technology Assessment

Dr Murray Turoff, 323 High St, Newark, NJ 07102, USA.
Type of centre: Academic.
Primarily engaged in: Both future studies and long-range planning.
Methods used: All methods (see Directory guide).
Time range of work: 5 - 25 years.
Number of persons working at professional level: 8 Part time.   *(286)*

67. Centro Nazionale Italiano

Technologie Educative, 84 Via Marche, 00187 Rome, Italy.
Type of centre: National association of agencies.
Concerned with long-term futures.
Time allocated (%): 20.
Direction of work in forecasting: Educational.
Direction of work in research: Social impacts of technology.
Direction of work in planning: Educational.
Methods used: 1 Scenario building, 2 Expert panels, 3 Operational models.
Time range of work: 10 - 25 years.
Source of support for work (%): 10 Private business, 20 Voluntary associations, 30 Foundations, 40 National government.
Work done for (%): 10 Private business, 40 Foundations, 50 National government.
Number of persons working at professional level: 5 Part time.   *(277)*

68. Centrum Voor Sociaal Beleid

Prinsstraat 13, B-2000 Antwerpen, Belgium.
Type of centre: Academic.
Concerned with long-term futures.
Time allocated (%): 50.
Direction of work in forecasting: 1 Social, 2 Economic.
Direction of work in research: 1 Social priorities, 2 Policy research, 3 Alternative futures, 4 Social impacts of technology.
Direction of work in planning: 1 Social.

Methods used: I Individual expert forecasting, 2 Statistical models, 3 Causal modelling.
Time range of work: 5 - IO years.
Source of support for work (%): IOO Sui generis.
Number of persons working at professional level: 7 Full time.
Additional information: Specific focus of work: social security systems and income redistribution; alternative ways of financing social security systems; and poverty in the welfare state. *(183)*

69. Chamber of Mines Research Organization
Human Resources Laboratory, PO Box 61809, Marshalltown, Johannesburg 2107, South Africa.
Type of centre: Industry.
Concerned with long term futures.
Time allocated (%): 20.
Methods used: I Simulation, 2 Extrapolation techniques, 3 Historical analogy, 4 Individual expert forecasting, 5 Scenario building.
Time range of work: IO - 25 years.
Source of support for work (%): IOO Private business.
Work done for (%): IOO Private business.
Number of persons working at professional level: 3 Full time. *(394)*

70. Champion International Corp
Vice President Corporate planning and development, 777 Third Ave, New York, NY, 10017, USA.
Type of centre: Industry. *Concerned with long-term futures.*
Time allocated (%): 50.
Direction of work in forecasting: Economic.
Direction of work in planning: Corporate, Resources.
Methods used: Scenario building, Individual expert forecasting.
Time range of work: 5 - IO years.
Number of persons working at professional level: 3 Full time, I7 Part time. *(111)*

71. Chemurgic Council for Renewable Resources
Vice President, Merritt L. Kastens, 530 Fifth Ave, New York, NY, USA.
Type of centre: Membership society.
Concerned with long-term futures.
Direction of work in forecasting: Technological, Scientific.
Direction of work in research: Resource utilization.
Direction of work in planning: Scientific, Technological, Educational, Economic, Political, Corporate.
Methods used: I Expert panels, 2 Individual expert forecasting.
Time range of work: IO - 25 years.
Source of support for work (%): 50 Private business, 50 Members.
Work done for (%): IOO Public.
Number of persons working at professional level: I Full time. *(154)*

72. Cities Service Company
Vice President of Planning and Economies, PO Box 300, Tulsa, Ok 74101, USA.
Type of centre: Industry.

Concerned wihh long-term futures.
Time allocated (%): 3O.
Direction of work in forecasting: I Resources, 2 Economic, 3 Technological, 3 Environmental, 4 Market, 6 Social, 7 Cultural.
Direction of work in research: I Alternative futures, 2 Consumer affairs, 2 Resource utilization, 3 Environmental.
Direction of work in planning: I Resources, 2 Technological, 3 Economic.
Methods used: I Scenario building, 2 Individual expert forecasting, 3 Historical analogy, 4 Cross impact analysis.
Time range of work: 5 - IO years.
Source of support for work (%): IOO Private business.
Work done for (%): IO Voluntary associations, 9O Private business.
Number of persons working at professional level: I2 Full time.   *(102)*

73. Club de Amigos de la Futurologia
Gra Via 6O8 8th D, Barcelona 7, Spain.
Type of centre: Membership society/National voluntary association.
Concerned with long-term futures. Time allocated (%): 5O.
Direction of work in forecasting: I Educational, 2 Cultural, 3 Environmental, 4 Resources, 5 Population.
Direction of work in research: I The Individual in the future, 2 The family in the future, 3 Resource utilization, 4 Environmental, 5 Alternative futures.
Direction of work in planning: I Educational, 2 Urban, 3 Environmental, 4 Resources, 5 Political.
Methods used: I Individual expert forecasting, 2 Brainstorming, 3 Network analysis.
Time range of work: 5 - IO years and beyond year 2OOO.
Source of support for work (%): 5 Private business, 5 Foundations, 9O Voluntary associations.
Work done for (%): 5 Private business, 5 Foundations, 9O Voluntary associations.   *(361)*

74. The Coca-Cola Company
Long-Range Planning, PO Box 1734, Atlanta, Ga 3O3O1, USA.
Type of centre: Business.
Primarily engaged in: Both futures studies and long-range planning.
Direction of work in forecasting: I Economic, 2 Environmental, 3 Market.
Direction of work in research: I Environmental, 2 Consumer affairs, 3 Alternative futures.
Direction of work in planning: I Corporate, 2 Economic, 3 Technological.
Methods used: I Extrapolation techniques, 2 Individual expert forecasting, 3 Expert panels, 4 Scenario building, 5 Simulation, 6 Operational models, 7 Causal modelling.
Time range of work: IO - 25 years.
Source of support for work (%): IOO Private business.
Work done for (%): 5 Foundations, I5 Voluntary associations, 8O Private business.
Number of persons working at professional level: 5 Full time.   *(302)*

75. Colgate University
Institutional Planner, Richard Heck, Hamilton NY 13346, USA.
Type of centre: Academic.
Concerned with long-term futures.
Time allocated(%): Less than IO.

Methods used: I Statistical models, 2 Extrapolation techniques, 3 Historical analogy, 4 Operational models, 5 Individual expert forecasting, 6 Simulation, 7 Expert panels.
Time range of work: 5 - IO years.
Source of support for work (%): IOO College funds.
Work done for (%): IOO College.
Number of persons working at professional level: I Full time. *(272)*

76. Commissariat Général du Plan
Bernard Cazes, I8 Rue de Martignal, 75OO7 Paris, France.
Type of centre: National government.
Concerned with long-term futures.
Time allocated (%): Less than IO.
Methods used: I Extrapolation techniques, 2 Probabilistic forecasting, 3 Scenario building, 5 Individual expert forecasting, 4 Expert panels.
Time range of work: IO - 25 years.
Source of support for work (%): IOO National government.
Work done for (%): IOO National government.
Number of persons working at professional level: I Full time, 3 Part time. *(17)*

77. Commissariat Général au Tourisme
Blvd de l'Imperatrice, NR5, IOOO Bruxelles, Belgium.
Type of centre: National government.
Concerned with long term futures.
Time allocated (%): IO.
Methods used: Cross impact analysis, Extrapolation techniques, International conferences and seminars.
Time range of work: 5 - IO years.
Source of support for work (%): IOO National government.
Work done for (%): IOO National government.
Number of persons working at professional level: 2 Part time. *(164)*

78. Commission Interministerielle de l'Eau
Chairman, A.E. Crahay, Cité Administrative de l'Etat, 2O Rue Montagne de l'Oratoire Quartier Vesale, 1O1O Brussels, Belgium.
Type of centre: National government.
Concerned with long-term futures.
Time allocated (%): 2O.
Direction of work in forecasting: Technological, Economic, Social. Environmental, Resources.
Direction of work in research: Environmental.
Direction of work in planning: Scientific, Technological, Social, Urban, Regional, Environmental, Resources.
Methods used: Extrapolation techniques, Statistical models.
Time range of work: 5 - 25 years.
Source of support for work (%): IOO National government.
Work done for (%): IOO National government.
Number of persons working at professional level: I Part time, 2 Full time. *(25)*

79. Commission Fédérale pour une Conception Globale Suisse des Transports

Effingerstr. I4, CH - 3000 Bern, Switzerland.
Type of centre: National government.
Primarily engaged in: Long-range planning.
Direction of work in planning: I Traffic and transportation.
Methods used: I Simulation, 2 Extrapolation techniques, 3 Statistical models.
Time range of work: Beyond year 2000.
Source of support for work (%): I00 National government.
Work done for (%): I00 National government.
Number of persons working at professional level: I9 Full time.   *(10)*

80. The Committee for the Future, Inc

2325 Porter St, NW, Washington, DC 20008 USA.
Type of centre: International non-government.
Primarily engaged in: Both futures studies and long-range planning.
Direction of work in forecasting: I Normative holistic, 2 Social, 3 Technological,
4 Environmental, 5 Resources, 6 Educational.
Direction of work in research: I Social priorities, 2 Futures methodology, 3 Policy
research, 4 Alternative futures, 5 Social impacts of technology.
Direction of work in planning: I Corporate, 2 Educational.
Methods used: I Syncon, 2 Expert panels, 3 Brainstorming, 4 Scenario building.
4 Operational models, 5 Causal modelling, 6 Historical analogy, 7 Cross impact analysis,
8 Extrapolation techniques, 9 Contextual mapping, I0 Individual expert forecasting,
11 Network analysis.
Time range of work: Beyond year 2000.
Source of support for work (%): I0 Private business, I0 Voluntary associations,
20 National government, 20 Foundations, 40 Private donation.
Work done for (%): 30 National government, 70 General public.
Number of persons working at professional level: 3 Full time, I0 Part time.   *(235)*

81. Communications - Electronics (USAMC CE), Directorate for

Chief, H.T. Darracott, 5001 Eisenhower Ave, Alexandria, Va 22333, USA.
Type of centre: National government. *Concerned with long-term futures.*
Time allocated (%): 20.
Direction of work in forecasting: I Technological, 2 Military, 3 Manpower, 4 Resources.
Direction of work in research: Resource utilization.
Direction of work in planning: Military.
Methods used: Extrapolation techniques.
Time range of work: 5 - I0 years.
Source of support for work (%): I00 National government.
Work done for (%): I00 National government.
Number of persons working at professional level: 25 Part time.   *(265)*

82. Confederacion de Organizaciones Turisticas de la America Latina (COTAL)

Secretaria Permanente-Viamonte, 640 Buenos Aires, Argentina.
Type of centre: International professional organization.
Concerned with long-term futures.
Time allocated (%): 50.
Direction of work in forecasting: Economic.
Methods used: Statistical models, Expert panels.

Time range of work: 5 - I0 years.
Source of support for work (%): I00 COTAL
Work done for (%): I00 COTAL (30)

83. Conference on Alternative Economic Futures for Hawaii
c/o George Chaplin, PO Box 311O, Honolulu, Hi, USA.
Type of Centre: Ad Hoc study group.
Primarily engaged in: Both futures studies and long-range planning.
Direction of work in forecasting: Economic.
Direction of work in research: Alternative futures.
Direction of work in planning: Social, Economic, Political.
Methods used: I Probabilistic forecasting, 2 Statistical models, 3 Expert panels,
4 Scenario building.
Time range of work: 5 - I0 years.
Source of support for work (%): 75 Private business, 25 Labour.
Work done for (%): I00 Community.
Number of persons working at professional level: I Part time. (460)

84. Congressional Research Service, Environmental Policy Division
Chief, Wallace D. Bowman, Washington, DC 2054O, USA.
Type of centre: National government.
Concerned with long-term futures.
Time allocated (%): 20.
Methods used: I Expert panels, 2 Brainstorming, 3 Individual expert forecasting,
4 Summarize and compare studies of others.
Time range of work: 5 - I0 years.
Source of support for work (%): I00 National government.
Work done for (%): I00 National government.
Number of persons working at professional level: 38 Full time. (77)

85. Consejo Nacional de Investigaciones Cientificas y Technologicas
President, Dr Rodrigo Beledon, APTO 10318, San Jose, Costa Rica.
Type of centre: National government.
Primarily engaged in: Both futures studies and long-range planning.
Direction of work in forecasting: I Scientific, 2 Technological, 3 Educational,
4 Manpower, 5 Resources, 6 Environmental.
Direction of work in research: I Social impacts of technology, 2 Policy research,
3 Resource utilization, 4 Environmental, 5 Alternative futures.
Direction of work in planning: I Scientific, 2 Technological, 3 Social.
Time range of work: I0 - 25 years.
Source of support for work (%): 5 International agencies, 95 National government.
Work done for (%): I00 National government.
Number of persons working at professional level: 6 Part time, 6 Full time.
Additional information: Focus of work is to establish scientific and technological
policies and to promote research. (20)

86. Conservatoire National des Arts et Métiers
Institut Technique de Prévision Economique et Sociale, P.M. Guerin, Directeur,
Ministère de l'Education, 292 Rue Saint Martin, Paris, France.
Type of centre: National government.
Primarily engaged in: Both futures studies and long-range planning.

Direction of work in forecasting: Technological, Economic, Social, Market, Scientific.
Direction of work in research: Social impacts of technology, Policy research, Futures methodology.
Methods used: Delphi techniques, Cross impact analysis, Scenario building, Extrapolation techniques, Expert panels, Relevance trees, Network analysis, Simulation.
Time range of work: 5 - 25 years.
Source of support for work (%): IO Private business, 9O National government.
Number of persons working at professional level: 5 Full time, I2 Part time.   *(419)*

87. Contracultura
Miguel Grinberg, CC Central 1332, 1OOO Capital, Argentina.
Type of centre: Independent research. **Concerned with long-term futures.**
Time allocated (%): 5O.
Direction of work in forecasting: Cultural.
Direction of work in research: Environmental.
Direction of work in planning: Educational.
Methods used: Meditation and analysis.
Time range of work: 5 - IO years.
Source of support for work (%): IOO Subscriptions.
Work done for (%): IOO Readers.
Number of persons working at professional level: I Part time, I Full time.   *(229)*

88. Council for Science and Society
Sir Michael Swann, Chairman, 3/4 St, Andrew's Hill, Third Floor, London EC4 5 BY, UK.
Type of centre: National Voluntary Association.
Time allocated (%): IO.
Methods used: Expert panels.
Time range of work: 5 - IO years.
Source of support for work (%): IOO Foundations.
Number of persons working at professional level: I Full time, I Part time.   *(66)*

89. CREDOC
45 Blvd de la Gare, 75O13 Paris, France.
Type of centre: National governmental. **Concerned with long-term futures.**
Concerned with long-term futures.
Time allocated (%): Less than IO.
Methods used: I Scenario building, 2 Contextual mapping, 3 Extrapolation techniques, 4 Expert panels, 5 Individual 'expert' analysis.
Time range of work: IO - 25 years.
Source of support for work (%): 66 National government, 33 Private business.
Work done for (%): 66 National government, 33 Private business.
Number of persons working at professional level: 2 Part time, I Full time.   *(463)*

D 9O. DATAR
Director, Jacques Durand, 1 Ave Charles Floquet, Paris 7, France.
Type of centre: National government.
Concerned with long-term futures.
Time allocated (%): 4O.
Methods used: I Scenario building, 2 Contextual mapping, 3 Expert panels, 4 Individual expert forecasting, 5 Brainstorming.
Time range of work: IO - 25 years.

Source of support for work (%): IOO National government.
Work done for (%): 25 Local government, 75 National government.
Number of persons working at professional level: IO Full time.   *(404)*

91. Denmark Towards the Year 1990
Handelshøjskolen I Arhus, Herredsuej 14, 821O Arhus V, Denmark.
Type of centre: Independent research group.
Primarily engaged in: Long-term futures.
Time allocated (%): Less than IO.
Methods used: Extrapolation techniques, Expert panels, Cross impact analysis, Scenario
building, Morphology.
Time range of work: 5 - 25 years.
Source of support for work (%): 75 Danish research councils, 25 School of business
administration.
Number of persons working at professional level: 4 Full time.   *(228)*

92. Delft Technological University
Institute for Town Planning Research (ISO) Berlageweg 1. Delft, The Netherlands.
Type of centre: Academic.
Concerned with long-term futures.
Time allocated (%): 5O.
Direction of work in research: Social impacts of technology, Environmental,
Consumer affairs, Futures methodology, The family in the future.
Direction of work in planning: Urban, Environmental.
Methods used: Statistical models, Operational models, Simulation.
Time range of work: 5 - IO years.
Source of support for work (%): IOO National government.
Number of persons working at professional level: 7 Full time.   *(4)*

93. Department of Agriculture
Office of Planning and Evaluation, Room 115 - A, Administration Building,
Washington DC 2025O, USA.
Type of centre: National government.
Primarily engaged in: Both futures studies and long-range planning.
Direction of work in forecasting: I Economic, 2 Resources, 3 Technology.
Direction of work in planning. I Economic, 2 Resources, 3 Rural development.
Methods used: I Statistical models, 2 Individual expert forecasting, 3 Scenario building.
Time range of work: 5 - 5O years.
Source of support for work (%): IOO National government.
Work done for (%): IOO National government.
Number of persons working at professional level: 3 Full time.   *(12)*

94. Department of Agriculture, International and Special Programs
Graduate School, Dr Joseph Pendera, National Press Building, Suite 366,
Washington, DC 20004, USA.
Type of centre: Academic.
Time allocated (%): Less than IO.
Methods used: I Expert panels, 2 Delphi techniques, 3 Scenario building,
4 Extrapolation techniques, 5 Contextual mapping, 6 Statistical models, 7 Simulation,

8 Causal modelling, 9 Gaming, IO Probabilistic forecasting, 11 Cross impact analysis,
12 Brainstorming, 13 Network analysis, 14 Relevance trees, 15 Historical analogy,
16 Operational models, 17 Individual expert forecasting.
Time range of work: IO - 25 years.
Source of support for work (%): IOO National government.
Work done for (%): IO International agencies, 9O National government.
Number of persons working at professional level: I Part time, 4 Full time.   *(297)*

95. Department of the Environment

Systems Analysis Research Unit, 2 Marsham St, London, UK.
Type of centre: National government.
Primarily engaged in: Both futures studies and long-range planning.
Direction of work in forecasting: I Resources, 2 Technology, 3 Economic, 4 Cultural.
Direction of work in research: I Resource utilization, 2 Futures methodology, 3
Alternative futures.
Direction of work in planning: I Resources, 2 Technological, 3 Environmental,
4 Political.
Methods used: I Causal modelling, 2 Scenario building, 3 Simulation.
Time range of work: IO - 25 years.
Source of support for work (%): IOO National government.
Work done for (%): IOO National government.
Number of persons working at professional level: 4 Part time, 12 Full time.   *(91)*

96. Department of Housing and Community Development

Chief of Program Development, 222 E Saratoga St, Baltimore, Md 212O3 USA.
Type of centre: Local government. *Concerned with long-term futures.*
Time allocated (%): Less than IO.
Methods used: Causal modelling.
Time range of work: IO - 25 years.
Source of support for work (%): 33 Local government, 67 National government.
Work done for (%): 33 Local government, 67 National government.
Number of persons working at professional level: I Full time, 4 Part time.   *(168)*

97. Department of Industry, Trade and Commerce

Office of Science and Technology, Chief, Brian Tucker, 112 Kent St, Ottawa, Ontario
K1A OH5, Canada.
Type of centre: National government. *Concerned with long-term futures.*
Time allocated (%): 2O.
Direction of work in forecasting: I Scientific, 2 Economic, 3 Technological.
Direction of work in research: Policy research.
Direction of work in planning: Technological.
Methods used: Extrapolation techniques.
Time range of work: 5 - IO years.
Source of support for work (%): IOO National government.
Work done for (%): IOO National government.
Number of persons working at professional level: 5 Part time, 5 Full time.
Additional information: Essentially a staff organisation providing scientific and
technological services for the whole department.   *(349)*

98. Department of National Defence

101 Colonel By Drive, Ottawa K1A OK2,Canada.
Type of centre: National government.
Primarily engaged in: Both futures studies and long-range planning.
Direction of work in forecasting: 1 Technological, 1 Economic, 1 Social, 1 Scientific,
1 Military, 2 Cultural, 2 Educational, 2 Manpower, 2 Resources, 2 Population,
3 Market, 3 Environmental.
Direction of work in research: 1 Social impacts of technology, 1 Futures methodology,
2 Alternative futures, 2 Manpower, 2 Policy research, 3 Value systems, 3 Social
priorities, 3 Population, 3 The individual in the future, 3 The family in the future.
Direction of work in planning: 1 Military, 2 Scientific, 2 Technological, 2 Social,
2 Economic.
Methods used: 1 Extrapolation techniques, 2 Probabilistic forecasting, 2 Scenario
building, 2 Statistical models, 2 Causal modelling, 3 Cross impact analysis, 3 Network
analysis.
Time range of work: 10 - 25 years.
Source of support for work (%): 100 National government.
Work done for (%): 100 National government.
Number of persons working at professional level: 7 Full time.   *(337)*

99. Department of State

Bureau of Politico-Military Affairs, Office of Nuclear Policy and Operation,
Washington, DC 20520, USA.
Type of centre: National government. *Concerned with long-term futures.*
Time allocated (%): 30.
Direction of work in forecasting: 1 Political, 2 Military, 3 Technological.
Direction of work in planning: 1 Political, 2 Military, 3 Technological, 4 Scientific.
Methods used: Gaming, Scenario building, Extrapolation techniques, Brainstorming,
Historical analogy, Individual expert forecasting.
Time range of work: 5 - 10 years.
Source of support for work (%): 100 National government.
Work done for (%): 100 National government.
Number of persons working at professional level: 5 Part time.   *(169)*

100. The Diebold Group, Inc

430 Park Ave, New York, NY 10022, USA.
Type of centre: International non-government. *Concerned with long-term futures.*
Time allocated (%): 50.
Direction of work in forecasting: 1 Technological, 2 Economic, 3 Market.
Direction of work in research: 1 Alternative futures, 2 Resource utilization, 3 Policy
research.
Direction of work in planning: 1 Corporate, 2 Technological, 3 Resources.
Methods used: 1 Expert panels, 2 Individual expert forecasting, 3 Scenario building.
Time range of work: 10 - 25 years.
Source of support for work (%): 20 National government, 80 Private business.
Work done for (%): 20 National government, 30 Private business.   *(82)*

101. Dreyfuss College
Division of the Future, Projector, Irving H. Buchen, Fairleigh, Dickinson University, Madison, NJ 07940, USA.
Type of centre: Academic. *Concerned with long term futures.*
Time allocated (%): 30.
Direction of work in forecasting: Social, Educational, Environmental, Manpower, Resources.
Direction of work in research: Social impacts of technology, Alternative futures, Manpower, Consumer affairs, Value systems, Social priorities, The individual in the future, The family in the future, Futures methodology.
Direction of work in planning: Social Urban, Regional, Educational, Economic, Political, Corporate, Environmental, Labour, Resources.
Methods used: All methods (see Directory Guide).
Time range of work: IO - 25 years.
Source of support for work (%): 5 National government, IO Foundations, IO Voluntary associations, 2O Local government, 2O Private business.
Work done for (%): IO Private business, IO Foundations, IO Voluntary associations, 2O Local government. *(288)*

E 102. Earth Resources Research Ltd
Director, Graham Searle, 4O James St, London WI, UK.
Type of centre: Independent research.
Primarily engaged in: Both futures studies and long-range planning.
Direction of work in forecasting: I Resources, 2 Technological, 3 Economic, 4 Environmental, 5 Social, 6 Cultural.
Direction of work in research: I Resource utilization, 2 Policy research, 3 Social impacts of technology, 4 Environmental;
Direction of work in planning: Political, Resources, Environmental, Economic, Social.
Methods used: I Scenario building, 2 Brainstorming, 3 Expert panels, 4 Extrapolation techniques, 5 Historical analogy.
Time range of work: IO - 25 years.
Source of support for work (%): 5 National government, IO International agencies, IO Private business, 6O Foundations, 15 Voluntary associations.
Work done for (%): IO National government, 5 International agencies, 85 Voluntary associations.
Number of persons working at professional level: 3 Part time, I2 Full time. *(447)*

103. Earthrise, Futures Lab
Thomas Carleton, PO Box 12O, Annex Station, Providence, RI 0290I USA.
Type of centre: Academic.
Primarily engaged in: Both futures studies and long-range planning.
Direction of work in research: I Alternative futures, 2 Futures methodology.
Direction of work in planning: I Environmental, 2 Social.
Methods used: I Scenario building, 2 Simulation, 3 Gaming, 4 Brainstorming.
Time range of work: IO - 25 years.
Source of support for work (%): 9O Academic sources.
Work done for (%): 9O In-house studies.
Number of persons working at professional level: 2 Part time, 2 Full time. *(334)*

104. East Africa Institute of Social Research
Makerere Institute of Social Research, PO Box 16022 Kampala, Uganda.
Type of centre: Academic centre. *Concerned with long-term futures.*
Time allocated (%): 50.
Direction of work in forecasting: I Economic, 2 Social, 3 Cultural, 4 Market, 5 Educational.
Direction of work in research: I Social priorities, 2 Manpower, 3 Policy research,
4 Resource utilization.
Direction of work in planning: I Economic, 2 Urban, 3 Regional, 4 Social.
Methods used: I Probabilistic forecasting, 2 Historical analogy.
Time range of work: 5 - IO years.
Source of support for work (%): IOO National government.
Work done for (%): 40 Local government, 60 National government.
Number of persons working at professional level: 20 Part time, IOO Full time.   *(141)*

105. East African Marine Fisheries Research Organization
PO Box 668, Zanzibar, Tanzania, Africa.
Type of centre: International governmental.
Primarily engaged in: Both futures studies and long-range planning.
Direction of work in forecasting: Resources.
Direction of work in research: Resource utilization
Direction of work in planning: Resources.
Methods used: I Statistical models, 2 Individual expert forecasting.
Time range of work: IO - 25 years.
Source of support for work (%): 85 National government, I5 International agencies.
Work done for (%): 50 National government, IO International agencies. 20 Private
Business, 20 General public.
Number of persons working at professional level: 7 Full time.   *(444)*

106. Economic Commission for Europe
FAO Timber Division, Palais des Nations, Geneva, Switzerland.
Type of centre: International government.
Concerned with long-term futures.
Time allocated (%): 30.
Methods used: I Probabilistic forecasting, 2 Historical analogy, 3 Extrapolation techniques.
4 Statistical models, 5 Individual expert forecasting.
Time range of work: 5 - beyond year 2000.
Source of support for work (%): 100 International agencies.
Work done for (%): 100 International agencies.
Number of persons working at professional level: 5 Part time.   *(107)*

107. Economic Development Institute
Raudararstig 31, Reykjavik, Iceland.
Type of centre: National government.
Primarily engaged in: Long-range planning.
Direction of work in forecasting: I Population, 2 Economic, 3 Manpower, 4 Resources,
5 Social.
Direction of work in planning: I Economic, 2 Regional, 3 Social, 4 Military, 5 Labour.
Methods used: I Individual expert forecasting, 2 Expert panels, 3 Statistical models.
4 Operational models, 5 Extrapolation techniques, 6 Contextual mapping, 7 Simulation,
8 Network analysis.
Source of support for work (%): IOO Revenue from own investment funds.

Work done for (%): lOO National government.
Number of persons working at professional level: 2 Part time, 9 Full time.   *(381)*

108. Economic Planning Centre

Erottajankatu 15-17, SF-OO13O Helsinki 13, Finland
Type of centre: National government.
Primarily engaged in: Long-range planning.
Direction of work in forecasting: I Economic, 2 Resources, 3 Manpower.
Direction of work in planning: I Economic, 2 Resources, 3 Regional, 4 Energy.
Methods used: Delphi techniques, Scenario building, Extrapolation techniques,
Brainstorming, Statistical models, Expert panels, Historical analogy, Individual
expert forecasting, Causal modelling, Econometric models.
Time range of work: lO - 25 years.
Source of support for work (%): lOO National government.
Work done for (%): lOO National government.
Number of persons working at professional level: l9 Full time.   *(367)*

109. Economic and Social Commission for Asia and the Pacific

Agriculture Division, Chief S. Kawakatsu, Sala Santitham, Rajdamnern Ave, Bangkok,
Thailand.
Type of centre: International government.
Primarily engaged in: Both futures studies and long-range planning.
Direction of work in forecasting: I Economic, 2 Social, 3 Market, 4 Manpower,
5 Resources, 6 Population.
Direction of work in research: I Policy research, 2 Resource utilization.
Direction of work in planning: I Economic, 2 Political, 3 Social, 4 Resources.
Methods used: I Expert panels, 2 Historical analogy, 3 Operational models.
Time range of work: 5 - 25 years.
Source of support for work (%): lO National government, 9O International agencies.
Work done for (%): lO International agencies, 9O National government.
Number of persons working at professional level: l4 Full time.   *(221)*

110. Economic and Social Commission for Asia and the Pacific

Division of Social Development, K.R. Emnich, Sala Santitham, Bangkok, Thailand.
Type of centre: International government.
Concerned with long-term futures.
Time allocated (%): 2O.
Direction of work in forecasting: Social, Cultural, Manpower.
Direction of work in research: Social impacts of technology, Value systems, Social
priorities, Policy research.
Direction of work in planning: Social.
Methods used: Extrapolation techniques, Expert panels, Historical analogy, Individual
expert forecasting, Causal modelling.
Time range of work: 5 - lO years.
Source of support for work (%): lO National government, l5 Foundations, 75 Inter-
national agencies.
Work done for (%): lO International agencies.
Number of persons working at professional level: 2 Part time.   *(132)*

111. Economic and Social Commission for Asia and the Pacific

Population Division, Chief, N. Carl Firsen, Sala Santitham, Rajdamnern Ave, Bangkok, Thailand.
Type of centre: International government. *Concerned with long-term futures.*
Time allocated (%): 40.
Direction of work in forecasting: I Population, 2 Manpower.
Direction of work in research: I Population, 2 Manpower.
Direction of work in planning: Population.
Methods used: Component projections.
Time range of work: IO - 25 years.
Source of support for work (%): IOO International agencies.
Work done for (%): IO International agencies, 9O National government.
Number of persons working at professional level: 5 Full time.   *(104)*

112. Education Exploration Centre Inc

Co-ordinator and President, Anita Fatland, 3IO4 - 16th Ave, South, Minneapolis.
Mn 554O7, USA.
Type of centre: Non-governmental supporter of educational alternatives.
Concerned with long-term futures.
Time allocated (%): Less than IO.
Direction of work in research: Alternative futures.
Direction of work in planning: Educational.
Methods used: I Brainstorming, 2 Historical analogy.
Time range of work: IO - 25 years.   *(57)*

113. Educational Resources Information Centre (ERIC)

Clearinghouse for Social Studies, Social Science Education, 855 Broadway, Boulder, Co 8O3O2, USA.
Type of centre: National government. *Concerned with long-term futures.*
Time allocated (%): Less than IO.
Direction of work in forecasting: Educational.
Time range of work: 5 - IO years.
Source of support for work (%): IOO National government.
Work done for (%): National government.
Additional information: Scope of organization is very broad and treats futures as one of many areas in the social studies/social sciences. Deals with dissemination in the nation, therefore is always on the lookout for appropriate educational documents dealing with the future.   *(36)*

114. Eindhoven University of Technology

Project Group 'Global Dynamics', Prof Ir. O. Rademaker, PO Box 513, Eindhoven, The Netherlands.
Type of centre: Academic. *Concerned with long-term futures.*
Time allocated (%): 2O.
Direction of work in forecasting: Long-term world modelling and control studies.
Methods used: I Simulation, 2 Extrapolation techniques, 3 Scenario building.
Time range of work: IO - beyond year 2OOO.
Source of support for work (%): IOO National government.
Work done for (%): 2O Professionals, General public.   *(130)*

115. Electrical Research Association
Long-Range Planning Department, Brian Buss, Cleeve Rd, Leatherhead, Surrey, UK.
Type of centre: Independent research.
Primarily engaged in: Both futures studies and long range planning.
Direction of work in forecasting: I Technological, 2 Market, 3 Economic, 4 Social.
.*Direction of work in research:* I Social impacts of technology, 2 Alternative futures, 3 Resource utilization, 4 Social priorities.
Direction of work in planning: I Technological, 2 Corporate, 3 Resources.
Methods used: I Cross impact analysis, 2 Scenario building, 3 Extrapolation techniques.
Time range of work: IO - 25 years.
Source of support for work (%): 5 National government, 95 Private business.
Work done for (%): 5 National government, 95 Private business.
Number of persons working at professional level: 6 Full time.   *(172)*

116. Emergency Committee for World Government
Frederik Hendriklaan 26, The Hague, The Netherlands.
Type of centre: International non-government.
Primarily engaged in: Long-range planning.
Direction of work in forecasting: I Political, 2 Social, 3 Educational.
Direction of work in research: I Social priorities, 2 Policy research, 3 Futures methodology.
Direction of work in planning: Political.
Methods used: I Operational models, 2 Probabilistic forecasting.
Time range of work: 5 - IO years.
Source of support for work (%): IOO Members.
Work done for (%): IOO International agencies.
Number of persons working at professional level: IO Part time.
Additional information: In the process of formation: when completed - will set up potential World Government, then launch appeal for acknowledgement as highest authority on earth.   *(344)*

117. Europe Plus Thirty
c/o European Commission, Brussels, Belgium.
Type of centre: International non-government/international government.
Primarily engaged in: Both futures studies and long-range planning.
Direction of work in forecasting: Technological, Soc⁺ I, Cultural, Educational, Scientific, Environmental, Military, Manpower, Resources, Population, Meteorological, Economic. Financial.
Direction of work in research: Social impacts of technology, Alternative futures.
Methods used: Brainstorming, Expert panels, Historical analogy.
Time range of work: Beyond year 2OOO.
Source of support for work (%): IOO International agencies.
Work done for (%): IOO International agencies.
Number of persons working at professional level: 4 Full time, 45 Part time.   *(259)*

118. European Association of National Productivity Centres
Secretary General, Rue de la Concorde, 6O, 1O5O Brussels, Belgium.
Type of centre: International non-government.
Concerned with long-term futures.
Time allocated (%): IO.

Methods used: I Scenario building, 2 Extrapolation techniques, 3 Expert panels.
Time range of work: 5 - IO years.
Source of support for work (%): IOO National government.
Work done for (%): IO Productivity centres.
Number of persons working at professional level: I Part time, I Full time.　　　　*(285)*

119. European Centre for Leisure and Education
Director, Premysl Maydl, Jilska 1, Prague 1, Czechoslovakia.
Type of centre: National government.
Concerned with long-term futures.
Time allocated (%): Less than IO.
Direction of work in forecasting: Cultural.
Direction of work in research: Social impacts of technology.
Direction of work in planning: Social.
Methods used: I Expert panels, 2 Statistical models.
Time range of work: IO - 25 years.
Source of support for work (%): 5O National government, 5O International agencies.
Work done for (%): 5O National government, 5O International agencies.
Number of persons working at professional level: I Part time.　　　　*(435)*

120. European Centre for Population Studies
Secretary General, Dr G. Beyer, The Hague, Pauwenlaan 17, The Netherlands.
Type of centre: Independent research/membership society/international voluntary association.
Primarily engaged in: Both futures studies and long-range planning.
Direction of work in forecasting: Educational, Population, Agriculture.
Direction of work in research: Manpower, Population, The family in the future.
Direction of work in planning: Urban, Labour.
Methods used: Individual expert forecasting, Statistical models.　　　　*(212)*

121. European Co-ordination Centre for Research and Documentation in Social Sciences
Grunangergasse 2, 1O1O Vienna, Austria.
Type of centre: International non-government.
Concerned with long-term futures.
Time allocated (%): 4O.
Methods used: I Cross impact analysis, 2 Extrapolation techniques, 3 Causal modelling, 4 Statistical models.
Time range of work: IO - 25 years.
Source of support for work (%): IOO National governments
Work done for (%): IOO All interested persons and organizations.
Number of persons working at professional level: 3 Full time.　　　　*(81)*

122. European Cultural Foundation
Jan Van Goyenkade 5, 1OO7 Amsterdam, The Netherlands.
Type of centre: International non-governmental.
Primarily engaged in: Both futures studies and long-range planning.
Direction of work in forecasting: I Educational, 2 Environmental, 3 Manpower, 4 Cultural.
Direction of work in research: I Alternative futures, 2 Environmental, 3 Manpower.
Direction of work in planning: I Educational, 2 Environmental, 3 Urban, 4 Labour.

Methods used: I Cross impact analysis, 2 Brainstorming, 3 Expert panels, 4 Network analysis. 5 Scenario building, 6 Individual 'expert' forecasting, 7 Extrapolation techniques, 8 Contextual mapping.
Time range of work: 5 - 25 years.
Source of support for work (%): 5 Local government, 25 National government, 3O International agencies, 3O Private business, IO Foundations.
Work done for (%): 25 Local government, 35 National government, 4O International agencies.
Number of persons working at professional level: 2O Part time, IO Full time.   *(448)*

123. Exxon Corp

Corporate Planning Dept, 1251 Ave of the Americas, New York, NY 1OO2O, USA.
Type of centre: Business.
Primarily engaged in: Long-range planning.
Direction of work in forecasting: I Energy, 2 Economic.
Direction of work in planning: Corporate.
Methods used: Extrapolation techniques.
Time range of work: 5 - IO years.
Source of support for work(%): IOO Private business.
Work done for (%): IOO Private business.
Number of persons working at professional level: 4O Part time.   *(307)*

F   124. Federal Statistical Office

Sokolovska 142, 186 13 Praha 8, Czechoslovakia.
Type of centre: National government.
Concerned with long-term futures.
Time allocated (%): Less than IO.
Direction of work in forecasting: Economic.
Methods used: I Subjective methods, 2 Extrapolation techniques, 3 Probabilistic forecasting.
Time range of work: 5 - IO years and beyond year 2OOO.
Source of support for work (%): IOO National government.
Work done for (%): IOO National government.
Number of persons working at professional level: 7 Part time.   *(409)*

125. Federated Department Stores

Director, Corporate Planning, 222 West Seventh St, Cincinnati, Oh 452O2, USA.
Type of centre: Business.
Primarily engaged in: Long-range planning.
Direction of work in forecasting: Market.
Direction of work in research: Resource utilization.
Direction of work in planning: Corporate.
Methods used: I Causal modelling, 2 Operational models, 3 Individual expert forecasting.
Time range of work: 5 - IO years.
Source of support for work (%): IOO Private business.
Work done for (%): IOO Private business.
Number of persons working at professional level: 4 Full time, 5 Part time.   *(138)*

126. Firestone Tyre and Rubber Company

Corporate Research and Planning, 1200 Firestone Parkway Akron, Oh, 44317 USA.
Type of centre: Industry.
Concerned with long-term futures.
Time allocated (%): 30.
Direction of work in forecasting: Economic, Market, Resources.
Direction of work in research: Resource utilization.
Direction of work in planning: Technological, Economic, Corporate, Resources.
Methods used: 1 Statistical models, 2 Extrapolation techniques, 3 Operational models, 4 Delphi techniques, 5 Brainstorming.
Time range of work: 5 - 10 years.
Source of support for work (%): 100 Private business.
Work done for (%): 30 Private business.
Number of persons working at professional level: 25 Part time.   *(301)*

127. Fondation C.N. Ledoux pur les Réflexions sur le Futur

President, Serge Antoins, 25610 Arc et Semans, France.
Type of centre: International voluntary association.
Primarily engaged in: Both futures studies and long-range planning.
Time range of work: 5 - Beyond year 2000.
Source of support for work (%): 20 National government, 20 Foundations, 60 Private business.
Work done for (%): 10 Local government, 10 Foundations, 20 National government. 30 International agencies, 30 Private business.
Number of persons working at professional level: 1 Part time.
Additional information: The foundation has an overall role as a meeting centre for all future-oriented studies or future-oriented works in any field.   *(257)*

128. Food and Agriculture Organization of the United Nations FAO

Economic and Social Policy Department, Assistant Director-General, E.M. Ojala, Via Delle Terne di Caracalla, Rome, Italy.
Type of centre: International government.
Concerned with long-term futures.
Time allocated (%): 10.
Direction of work in forecasting: 1 Resources, 2 Market, 3 Economic, 4 Manpower, 5 Population.
Direction of work in research: 1 Futures methodology, 2 Resource utilization.
Direction of work in planning: 1 Resources, 2 Economic, 3 Regional.
Methods used: 1 Statistical models, 2 Extrapolation techniques, 3 Individual expert forecasting, 4 Simulation, 5 Probabilistic forecasting.
Time range of work: 10 - 25 years.
Source of support for work (%): 100 National government.
Work done for (%): 100 National government.
Additional information: (This entry relates only to the work of the Economic and Social Policy Department of FAO in the field of long-term agricultural commodity projections and planning). Assists governments at national and multi-national levels, in agricultural sector analysis, planning and policy formation, through direct technical advice on request, and related methodological research, analytical studies and training.   *(52)*

129. Forecasting International Ltd

President, Marvin Cetron, 1001 N Highland St, Arlington, Va 22201, USA.
Type of centre: Independent research.
Primarily engaged in: Both futures studies and long-range planning.
Direction of work in forecasting: I Technological, 2 Social, 3 Cultural, 4 Economic,
5 Environmental, 6 Military, 7 Resources, 8 Market.
Direction of work in research: I Social impacts of technology, 2 Policy research,
3 Value systems, 4 Social priorities, 5 Consumer affairs, 6 Alternative futures,
7 Futures methodology, 8 Environmental.
Direction of work in planning: I Technological, 2 Scientific, 3 Corporate, 4 Military,
5 Social, 6 Urban, 7 Regional, 8 Economic, 9 Political, IO Environmental.
Methods used: I Brainstorming, 2 Scenario building, 3 Extrapolation techniques,
4 Expert panels, 5 Relevance trees, 6 Delphi techniques.
Time range of work: IO - 25 years.
Source of support for work (%): 9O National government, 2 International agencies,
8 Private business.
Work done for (%): 95 National government, I International agencies, 4 Private
business.
Number of persons working at professional level: IO Part time, I5 Full time.   *(454)*

130. Forschungs - Institut für Internationale Technisch - Wirtschaftliche Zusammenarbeit der RWTH Aachen

D-5100 Aachen Vereinsstrasse 3-5 West Germany.
Type of centre: Academic. *Concerned with long-term futures.*
Time allocated (%): Less than IO.
Time range of work: 5 - IO years.   *(133)*

131. Forum for the Advancement of Students in Science and Technology (FASST)

I785 Massachusetts Ave, NW, Washington, DC 20076, USA.
Type of centre: National educational student association.
Concerned with long-term futures.
Time allocated (%): 3O.
Methods used: Brainstorming.
Time range of work: IO - 25 years.
Source of support for work (%): 2O National government, 8O Private business.
Number of persons working at professional level: 4 Full time.   *(162)*

132. Furman University

Dept of Sociology, Dan J. Cover, Greenville, SC 29613, USA.
Type of centre: Academic. *Concerned with long-term futures.*
Time allocated (%): IO.
Direction of work in forecasting: I Social, 2 Technological.
Direction of work in research: I The individual in the future, 2 Social impacts of
technology.
Direction of work in planning: Urban.
Methods used: I Extrapolation techniques, 2 Gaming, 3 Delphi techniques.
Time range of work: IO - 25 years.
Source of support for work (%): 5 National government, 5 Furman University.
Work done for (%): 5 National government.
Number of persons working at professional level: I Full time.   *(247)*

133. Future Options Room
3701 Connecticut Ave, 404, Washington DC 20008, USA.
Type of centre: International non-governmental.
Primarily engaged in: Both futures studies and long-range planning.
Direction of work in forecasting; I Educational 2 Environmental, 3 Cultural, 4 Social,
5 Economic, 6 Technological, 7 Market, 8 Scientific.
Time range of work: 5 - beyond year 2000.
Source of support for work (%): 60 National government, 30 Private business,
IO Private Sources.
Work done for (%): 40 National government, 30 Internal, 30 Private business.
Number of persons working at professional level: 5 Part time, 3 Full time.   *(464)*

134. Future Research Corp
12 Shattuck St, PO Box 1169, Nashua, NH, 03060, USA.
Type of centre: Business.
Primarily engaged in: Both futures studies and long range planning.
Direction of work in forecasting: I Technological, 2 Market.
Direction of work in research: I Alternative futures, 2 Social impacts of technology.
Methods used: I Individual expert forecasting, 2 Brainstorming.
Time range of work: 5 - beyond year 2000.
Source of support for work (%): 5 Local government, 5 National government,
40 Educational institute, 50 Private business.
Work done for (%): 5 Local government, 5 National government, 40 Educational
institute, 50 Private business.
Number of persons working at professional level: 2 Full time.
Additional information: Publisher of Futureport, a newsletter on the future: for
planners, educators and others.   *(386)*

135. Future Shape of Technology Foundation
Prinsessegracht 23, The Hague, The Netherlands.
Type of centre: National voluntary association.
Primarily engaged in: Futures studies.
Direction of work in forecasting: Technological.
Direction of work in research: I Social impacts of technology, 2 Resource
utilization.
Methods used: I Individual expert forecasting, 2 Expert panels, 3 Scenario building.
Time range of work: 5 - 25 years.
Source of support for work (%): IO Voluntary associations, 40 National government,
50 Private business.
Work done for (%): IOO Dutch public.
Number of persons working at professional level: I Part time, 5 Full time.   *(16)*

136. The Futures Group
President, Theodore J. Gordon, 124 Hebron Ave, Glastonbury, Ct 06033, USA.
Type of centre: Independent research.
Primarily engaged in: Futures studies.
Direction of work in forecasting: Technological, Economic, Social, Scientific,
Environmental, Resources.
Direction of work in research: Social impacts of technology, Alternative futures,
Consumer affairs, Environmental, Value systems, Social priorities, Policy research,

The individual in the future, Futures methodology, The family in the future.
Direction of work in planning: Scientific, Technological, Social, Corporate, Environmental.
Methods used: Probabilistic forecasting, Delphi techniques, Gaming, Cross impact analysis, Scenario building, Extrapolation techniques, Brainstorming, Statistical models, Expert panels, Relevance trees, Network analysis, Historical analogy, Operational models, Simulation, Causal modelling.
Time range of work: 5 - beyond year 2000.
Source of support for work (%): 50 National government, 50 Private business.
Work done for (%): 50 National government, 50 Private business.
Number of persons working at professional level: 5 Part time, 30 Full time.   **(248)**

137. General Electric Company

Business Environment Research and Forecasting. Staff Associate, Ian H. Wilson, Fairfield, Ct 06431, USA.
Type of centre: Industry.
Primarily engaged in: Both futures studies and long-range planning.
Direction of work in forecasting: I Social, 2 Political, 3 Economic, 4 Manpower.
Direction of work in research: I Value systems, 2 Alternative futures, 3 Social priorities, 4 Social impacts of technology.
Direction of work in planning: Corporate.
Methods used: I Expert panels, 2 Individual expert forecasting, 3 Scenario building, 4 Cross impact analysis, 5 Delphi techniques, 6 Historical analogy, 7 Brainstorming.
Time range of work: 5 - 15 years.
Source of support for work (%): 100 Private business.
Work done for (%): 100 Private business.
Number of persons working at professional level: 2 Full time.   **(314)**

138. General Electric Tempo

Walter House, PO Drawer QQ Santa Barbara, Ca, 93102, USA.
Type of centre: Industry.
Primarily engaged in: Both futures studies and long-range planning.
Direction of work in forecasting: I Military, 2 Technological, 3 Environmental.
Direction of work in research: I Alternative futures, 2 Defence technology, 4 Population, 3 World politics.
Direction of work in planning: I Military, 2 Corporate, 3 Political, 4 Economic.
Methods used: I Individual expert forecasting, 2 Causal modelling, 3 Statistical models, 4 Extrapolation techniques, 5 Probabilistic forecasting.
Time range of work: 10 - 25 years.
Source of support for work (%): 10 Local government, 10 International agencies, 20 Private business, 60 National government.
Work done for (%): 10 Local government, 10 International agencies, 20 Private business, 60 National government.
Number of persons working at professional level: 15 Part time, 120 Full time.   **(294)**

139. Geological and Mines Department

PO Box 9, Mbadane, Swaziland.
Type of centre: National government.
Concerned with long-term futures.
Time allocated (%): 50.

Methods used: Evaluation of resources in relation to social, economic and political environment.
Time range of work: 5 - IO years.
Source of support for work (%): 2O International agencies, 8O National government.
Work done for (%): IOO National government.
Number of persons working at professional level: 6 Part time. *(420)*

14O. Georgetown University
Centre for Strategic and International Studies, 18OO K Street, NW, Washington, DC 2OOO6, USA.
Type of centre: International government.
Concerned with long-term futures.
Direction of work in forecasting: I Economic, I Resources, 2 Military.
Direction of work in research: I Alternative futures, I Policy research, 2 Resource utilization.
Direction of work in planning: I Economic, 2 Political, 3 Resources, 4 Military.
Methods used: 2 Probabilistic forecasting, 2 Expert panels, 3 Individual expert forecasting, 4 Historical analogy, 5 Scenario building.
Time range of work: 5 - IO years.
Source of support for work (%): 5O Private business, 5O Foundations.
Work done for (%): 5O Private business, 5O Foundations.
Number of persons working at professional level: 9 Full time. *(342)*

141. Gesellschaft für Hochschule und Forschung
Talstr 83, CH-8OO1, Zurich, Switzerland.
Type of centre: National voluntary association/membership society.
Concerned with long-term futures.
Time allocated (%): 5O.
Direction of work in forecasting: Educational, Scientific, Technological, Social, Cultural, Resosuces.
Direction of work in research: Manpower, Social priorities, Social impacts of technology, Resource utilization, Population, The individual in the future, The family in the future.
Direction of work in planning: Scientific, Educational, Technological, Social, Political.
Methods used: I Expert panels, 2 Operational models.
Time range of work: 5 - 25 years.
Source of support for work (%): 3O Individual (members), 7O Private business.
Work done for: (%): IOO The public.
Number of persons working at professional level: I Full time. *(15)*

142. Gesellschaft für Marktforschung, Marktplanung und Marketingfinberalung Mbh
Divo Inmar, 6 Frankfurt-Niederrad, Hahnstr 4O, West Germany.
Type of centre: International professional organization.
Concerned with long-term futures.
Time allocated (%): IO.
Direction of work in forecasting: I Market, 2 Technological, 3 Environmental.
Methods used: I Extrapolation techniques, 2 Probabilistic forecasting, 3 Statistical models, 4 Brainstorming, 5 Scenario building, 6 Historical analogy, 7 Individual expert forecasting, 8 Delphi techniques, 9 Relevance trees.
Time range of work: 5 - IO years.

Source of support for work (%):   2O National government, 8O Private business.
Work done for (%):   5 National government, 2O Private business.
Number of persons working at professional level: 8 Full time.   *(5O)*

143. Gesellschaft für Zunkunftsfragen eV

c/o Deutsche BP AG, 2OOO Hamburg 6O, Postfach 6OO34O, West Germany.
Type of centre: National voluntary association.
Primarily engaged in: Futures studies.
Methods used: I Delphi techniques, 2 Individual expert forecasting, 3 Scenario building.
Time range of work: IO - 25 years.
Source of support for work (%):   IO Foundations, 9O Private membership.
Work done for (%):   IOO The aims of the association itself.   *(44)*

144. Government Actuaries Department

Steel House, Tothill Street, London, SW1H 9LS, UK.
Type of centre: National government.
Primarily engaged in: Futures studies.
Direction of work in forecasting: Economic, Population.
Direction of work in research: Population.
Methods used: I Probabilistic forecasting, 2 Extrapolation techniques, 3 Statistical models.
Time range of work: 5 - beyond year 2OOO.
Source of support for work (%):   IOO National government.
Work done for (%):   IOO National government.
Number of persons working at professional level: 6 Part time, 35 Full time.   *(417)*

145. Government of Canada

Ministry of State for Science and Technology, Secretariat for Future Studies Technology Assessment Division, Ottawa, Canada.
Type of centre: National government.
Primarily engaged in: Futures studies.
Direction of work in forecasting: I Social, 2 Technological, 3 Economic, 4 Resources, 5 Population, 6 Market, 7 Cultural.
Direction of work in research: I Alternative futures, 2 Policy research, 3 Futures methodology, 4 Resource utilization, 5 Social priorities, 6 Population, 7 Social impacts of technology, 8 Value systems.
Direction of work in planning: I Technological, 2 Social, 3 Resources, 4 Economic. 5 Scientific.
Time range of work: IO - 25 years.
Source of support for work (%):   IOO National government.
Work done for (%):   IOO National government.
Number of persons working at professional level: 2 Part time, 5 Full time.   *(140)*

146. Government of The Netherlands

Ministry of General Affairs, Scientific Council for Government Policy, Plein 1813 No. 2, The Hague, The Netherlands.
Type of centre: National government.
Primarily engaged in: Both futures studies and long-range planning.
Time range of work: IO - beyond year 2OOO.
Source of support for work (%):   IOO National government.

Work done for (%): IOO National government.
Number of persons working at professional level: 5 Part time, 18 Full time.
Additional information: The council informs government of possible long-term developments of society - it should stimulate integration of long-term planning in and out of government and it may make proposals to cope with deficiencies in research and long term planning. *(331)*

147. The Greater London Council
Eivind Gilje, Room 519A,County Hall, London SE1 7 PB, UK.
Type of centre: Local government.
Concerned with long-term futures.
Time allocated (%): Less than IO.
Methods used: I Operational models, 2 Statistical models, 3 Scenario building, 4 Contextual mapping, 5 Causal modelling, 6 Expert panels.
Time range of work: IO - 25 years.
Source of support for work (%): IOO Local government.
Work done for (%): IOO Local government. *(327)*

148. Group of Science Organization
President, T. Erdey-Cruz, Minnich FU 18, 1051 Budapest, Hungary.
Type of centre: Academic. *Concerned with long-term futures.*
Time allocated (%): Less than IO.
Direction of work in forecasting: Technological, Scientific, Manpower, Resources,
Direction of work in research: Social impacts of technology, Futures methodology.
Methods used: Delphi techniques, Extrapolation techniques, Brainstorming, Historical analogy.
Time range of work: IO - 25 years.
Source of support for work (%): IOO National government.
Work done for (%): IOO National government.
Number of persons working at professional level: 3 Full time, 5 Part time. *(353)*

149. Group for Techno-Economic Studies
Information and Research Services, Council for Scientific and Industrial Research, PO Box 395, Pretoria 0001, South Africa.
Type of centre: Statutory body.
Concerned with long-term futures.
Time allocated (%): Less than IO.
Direction of work in forecasting: I Technological, 2 Scientific.
Direction of work in research: I Alternative futures, 2 Futures methodology.
Direction of work in planning: I Technological, 2 Scientific, 3 Regional.
Methods used: I Monitoring, 2 Delphi techniques, 3 Relevance trees.
Time range of work: 5 - 25 years.
Source of support for work (%): IOO National government.
Work done for (%): IOO National government.
Number of persons working at professional level: I Part time. *(407)*

15O. Gulf and Western Industries Inc
Market Planning Department, 1 Gulf and Western Plaza, New York, NY 10023, USA.
Type of centre: Industry.
Primarily engaged in: Both futures studies and long-range planning.
Direction of work in forecasting: I Market, 2 Economic.

Direction of work in planning: Corporate.
Methods used: Gathering and analysis of available data, discussion with specialists.
Time range of work: 5 - IO years.
Source of support for work (%): IOO Private business.
Work done for (%): IOO Private business.
Number of persons working at professional level: 8 Full time.   *(310)*

H 151. Harris Associates

John K. Harris, Social Scientist, 248O 16th St, NW, Washington, DC 2OOO9, USA.
Type of centre: Consultancy firm. **Concerned with long-term futures.**
Time allocated (%): 5O.
Direction of work in forecasting: I Manpower, 2 Social, 3 Technological, 4 Educational, 5 Environmental.
Direction of work in research: I Value systems, 2 Social priorities, 3 Alternative futures, 4 Manpower.
Direction of work in planning: I Social, 2 Political, 3 Urban.
Methods used: I Network analysis, 2 Delphi techniques, 3 Individual expert forecasting, 4 Cross impact analysis.
Time range of work: IO - 25 years.
Source of support for work (%): 5O National government, 5O Voluntary associations.
Work done for (%): 5O National government, 5O Voluntary associations.
Number of persons working at professional level: I Full time.   *(328)*

152. Hawaii Commission on The Year 2OOO

c/o Carl Smith, Carl Smith, Wichman and Case, PO Box 656, Honolulu, Hawaii 968O9, USA.
Type of centre: Publicly established and supported commission.
Primarily engaged in: Both futures studies and long-range planning and community-wide education.
Direction of work in forecasting: Holistic approach required by statutory mandate for the Commission on the year 2OOO.
Direction of work in research: I Alternative futures, 2 Value systems, 3 Policy research, 4 Futures methodology.
Direction of work in planning: I Social, 2 Economic, 3 Urban.
Methods used: I Brainstorming, 2 Expert panels, 3 Scenario building.
Time range of work: Beyond year 2OOO.
Source of support for work (%): 9O Local government, IO Private business.
Work done for (%): IOO State and people of Hawaii.
Number of persons working at professional level: I Part time.   *(459)*

153. Hawaii State Research Centre for Futures Study

Social Science Research Institute, 1914 University Ave, University of Hawaii, Honolulu, Hawaii 96822, USA.
Type of centre: Academic.
Primarily engaged in: Futures studies.
Direction of work in forecasting: Social.
Direction of work in research: I Alternative futures, 2 The individual in the future, 3 Futures methodology, 4 Social impacts of technology, 5 Value systems, 6 Resource utilization, 7 The family in the future.
Direction of work in planning: Social.

Methods used: Causal modelling.
Time range of work: IO - beyond year 2OOO.
Source of support for work (%): 25 Private business, 75 Local government.
Number of persons working at professional level: I Full time, 5 Part time. *(430)*

154. Hazan International

38 Rue de Moscow, 75OO8 Paris, France.
Type of centre: Industry.
Concerned with long-term futures.
Time allocated (%): 5O.
Direction of work in forecasting: I Economic, 2 Technological, 3 Market.
Direction of work in research: Environmental, Resource utilization.
Direction of work in planning: Scientific, Technological, Social, Economic.
Methods used: Delphi techniques, Extrapolation techniques, Brainstorming, Expert panels, Historical analogy, Individual expert forecasting.
Time range of work: 5 - IO years.
Source of support for work (%): IOO Private business.
Work done for (%): IOO Private business.
Number of persons working at professional level: 4 Full time. *(I98)*

155. Henkel KGaA

Director, Planning and Control, D-4OOO Dusseldorf 1, Postfach 11OO, West Germany.
Type of centre: Industry.
Concerned with long-term futures.
Time allocated (%): 3O.
Methods used: I Extrapolation techniques, 2 Delphi techniques, 3 Brainstorming.
Time range of work: 5 - IO years.
Source of support for work (%): IOO Private business.
Work done for (%): IOO Private business.
Number of persons working at professional level: IO Full time. *(203)*

156. Hitachi Limited

Corporate Planning Office, Vice President of Long-Range Planning, No 5 - 1, 1 Chome, Marunouchi, Chiyoda-ku, Tokyo 1OO, Japan.
Type of centre: Business.
Primarily engaged in: Both futures studies and long-range planning.
Direction of work in forecasting: I Market, 2 Economic.
Direction of work in research: I Alternative futures, 2 Manpower, 3 Resource utilization, 4 Environmental.
Direction of work in planning: Corporate.
Methods used: I Statistical models, 2 Extrapolation techniques, 3 Scenario building.
Time range of work: 5 - IO years.
Source of support for work (%): IOO Private business.
Work done for (%): IOO Private business.
Number of persons working at professional level: 8 Full time. *(209)*

157 Howard League for Penal Reform

125 Kennington Park Road, London, SE 11, UK.
Type of centre: International non-government.
Concerned with long-term futures.

Time allocated (%): IO.
Time range of work: 5 - IO years.
Source of support for work (%): 3O Foundations, 7O Private individuals (members).
Number of persons working at professional level: I Full time.   *(3)*

158. Hudson Institute
Quaker Ridge Road, Croton-on-Hudson, NY 1O52O, USA.
Type of centre: Independent research.
Primarily engaged in: Both futures studies and long-range planning.
Direction of work in forecasting: I Economic, 2 Military, 3 Resources, 4 Social.
Direction of work in research: I Policy research, 2 Resource utilization, 3 Alternative futures, 4 Social impacts of technology, 5 Social priorities, 6 Value systems.
Direction of work in planning: I Military, 2 Economic, 3 Social.
Methods used: I Scenario building, 2 Historical analogy, 3 Individual expert forecasting, 4 Brainstorming, 5 Extrapolation techniques.
Time range of work: 5 - beyond year 2OOO.
Source of support for work (%): IO Grants, 3O Private business, 6O National government.
Work done for (%): IO Institute projects, 3O Private business, 6O National government.
Number of persons working at professional level: 45 Full time.   *(190)*

159. Human Sciences Research Council
Institute for Research Development, Private Bag X 41, Pretoria OOO1, South Africa.
Type of centre: National government. *Concerned with long-term futures.*
Time allocated (%): Less than IO.
Number of persons working at professional level: 2 Part time.   *(422)*

16O. Hungarian Academy of Sciences
Institute of Sociology, Budapest 1, URI-U 49, Hungary.
Type of centre: Academic.
Primarily engaged in: Both futures studies and long-range planning.
Direction of work in research: I Value systems, 2 Social impacts of technology, 3 Science in the future, 4 Population, 5 Environmental.
Methods used: I Statistical models, 2 Historical analogy, 3 Expert panels, 4 Individual expert forecasting, 5 Delphi techniques, 6 Cross impact analysis.
Time range of work: 5 - IO years.
Source of support for work (%): 2O National government, 8O Academy of science.
Work done for (%): 2O National government, 8O Academy of science.
Number of persons working at professional level: 3O Full time.   *(28)*

161. ICAITI
Avenida la Reforme, 4-47, Zona 1O, Guatemala.
Type of centre: International research. *Concerned with long-term futures.*
Time allocated (%): Less than IO.
Methods used: Extrapolation techniques, Brainstorming, Expert panels, Historical analogy.
Time range of work: 5 - IO years.
Source of support for work (%): 6O International agencies, 2O Private business, 2O Government.
Number of persons working at professional level: IO Part time.   *(249)*

162. ICPS

1415 Budapest, Hungary.
Type of centre: International non-government. *Concerned with long-term futures.*
Time allocated (%): 20.
Time range of work: 5 - 10 years.
Source of support for work (%): 100 Voluntary associations.
Work done for (%): 10 International agencies, 20 Voluntary associations.
Number of persons working at professional level: 2 Full time.   *(222)*

163. IFES

Fleismarkt 3 - 5, Wien 1010, Austria.
Type of centre: Independent research.
Concerned with long-term futures.
Time allocated (%): Less than 10.
Methods used: Probabilistic forecasting, Scenario building, Delphi techniques.
Brainstorming, Extrapolation techniques, Expert panels, Statistical models,
Simulation, Relevance trees.
Time range of work: 5 - 25 years.
Source of support for work (%): 20 Private business, 30 National government,
50 Local government.
Work done for (%): 20 Private business, 30 National government, 50 Local
government.
Number of persons working at professional level: 5 Part time.   *(150)*

164. IIT Research Institute

10 West 35th St, Chicago, Il 60616, USA.
Type of centre: Independent research.
Concerned with long-term futures.
Time *allocated (%):* 20.
Direction of work in forecasting: Technological, Economic.
Direction of work in research: Social impacts of technology, Environmental,
Resource utilization.
Direction of work in planning: Scientific, Technological.
Methods used: Cross impact analysis, Individual expert forecasting.
Time range of work: 5 - 10 years.
Source of support for work (%): 25 Local government, 75 National government.
Work done for (%): 5 Local government, 1 National government, 5 State government.
Number of persons working at professional level: 5 Part time.   *(42)*

165. Incentive SpA

President, Antonio de Martini, Viale Liege 33 - B4, 00198 Rome, Italy.
Type of centre: Business. *Concerned with long-term futures.*
Time allocated (%): Less than 10.
Methods used: Brainstorming, Individual expert forecasting.
Time range of work: 5 - 10 years.
Number of persons working at professional level: I Full time.   *(293)*

166. Indian Lead, Zinc Information Centre

7 Shopping Centre, Block B6, Safdarjung Enclave, New Delhi, 11016,
India.
Type of centre: International non-government.
Concerned with long-term futures.

Direction of work in forecasting: I Market, 2 Technological, 3 Economic.
Direction of work in research: I Resource utilization, 2 Alternative futures,
3 Environmental.
Methods used: I Brainstorming, 2 Individual forecasting.
Time range of work: 5 - IO years.
Source of support for work (%): IOO Private business.
Number of persons working at professional level: 4 Part time.   *(176)*

167. Indiana University of Pennsylvania

Dept of Political Science, Institute for the Study of the Future, 1O1 Keith Hall Annex,
Indiana, Pa 157O1, USA.
Type of centre: Ad Hoc study group/academic.
Primarily engaged in: Both futures studies and long-range planning.
Direction of work in forecasting: I Environmental, 2 Technological, 3 Social.
Direction of work in research: I Policy research, 2 Social impacts of technology.
Direction of work in planning: I Political, 2 Environmental, 3 Technological,
4 Regional.
Methods used: I Simulation, 2 Expert panels, 3 Probabilistic forecasting.
Time range of work: IO - 25 years.
Source of support for work (%): 25 Institution, 75 Foundations.
Work done for (%): 25 National government, 25 International institution, 5O Local
government.
Number of persons working at professional level: I Full time, 3 Part time.   *(273)*

168. Industrial Management Centre Inc

President, James R. Bright, 1411 West Ave, Austin, Tx 787O1, USA.
Type of centre: Independent research.
Primarily engaged in: Both futures studies and long-range planning.
Direction of work in forecasting: I Technological, 2 Social.
Direction of work in research: I Futures methodology, 2 Alternative futures.
Direction of work in planning: I Technological, 2 Scientific, 3 Corporate.
Methods used: I Extrapolation techniques, 2 Scenario building, 3 Relevance trees,
4 Operational models.
Time range of work: 5 - 25 years.
Source of support for work (%): IO National government, 9O Private business.
Work done for (%): 2O National government, 8O Private business.
Number of persons working at professional level: 3 Part time.
Additional information: Specific focus is training others in technological forecasting
work.   *(255)*

169. Institut für Angewandte Systemanalyse und Prognose

3 Hannover, Alte Herrenhauser Str, IO, West Germany.
Type of centre: Independent research.
Primarily engaged in: Both futures studies and long-range planning.
Direction of work in forecasting: Technological, Economic, Market, Environmental,
Manpower, Resources, Population.
Direction of work in research: Alternative futures, Environmental, Resource
utilization, Population, Futures methodology.
Direction of work in planning: Technological, Economic, Political, Environmental,
Labour, Resources.

Methods used: Scenario building, Hierarchical complex systems approach, Expert panels.
Time range of work: IO - beyond year 2OOO.
Source of support for work (%): 7O National government, 2O Local government, IO Private business.
Work done for (%): IOO National government;
Number of persons working at professional level: I5 Part time, 5 Full time.   *(470)*

17O. Institut für Europaïsche Politik
53OO Bonn, Stockenstr, 1 - 5, West Germany.
Type of centre: Independent research.
Concerned with long-term futures.
Time allocated (%): 2O.
Methods used: I Brainstorming, 2 Extrapolation techniques, 3 Expert panels.
Time range of work: 5 - IO years.   *(357)*

171. Institut de Recherche d'Informatique (IRIA)
Domaine de Voluceau, Rocquencourt 78IO5, Le Chesnay, France.
Type of centre: National government. *Concerned with long-term futures.*
Time allocated (%): 2O.
Direction of work in forecasting: I Scientific, 2 Technological, 3 Educational.
Direction of work in research: I Policy research, 2 Value systems.
Direction of work in planning: I Scientific, 2 Technological, 3 Educational.
Methods used: I Brainstorming, 2 Probabilistic forecasting, Delphi techniques, Gaming, Cross impact analysis, Statistical models, Expert panels, Relevance trees, Network analysis, Simulation, Causal modelling.
Time range of work: 5 - IO years.
Source of support for work (%): IOO National government.
Work done for (%): IO Private business, 9O National government.
Number of persons working at professional level: 8O Full time.   *(80)*

172. Institut für Regional und Landerplanung
Ecole Polytechnique Fédérale, P. Atteslander, Zurich, Switzerland.
Type of centre: Academic. *Concerned with long-term futures.*
Time allocated (%): IO.
Direction of work in forecasting: I Social, 2 Population.
Direction of work in research: I Environmental, 2 Social priorities.
Direction of work in planning: I Urban, 2 Regional.
Methods used: I Simulation, 2 Expert panels, 3 Cross impact analysis, 4 Brainstorming.
Time range of work: IO - beyond year 2OOO.
Source of support for work (%): IOO National government.
Work done for (%): IO Local government, IO Other, 8O National government.
Number of persons working at professional level: I2 Full time, 25 Part time.   *(230)*

173. Institut für Sozio-Ökonomische Entwicklungsforschung
A-1O1O Vienna, Fleischmarkt 2O, Austria.
Type of centre: Academic.
Primarily engaged in: Both futures studies and long-range planning.
Direction of work in forecasting: I Economic, 2 Educational, 3 Resources, 4 Population, 5 Social, 6 Manpower.

3

Direction of work in research: Alternative futures, Consumer affairs, Environmental, Resource utilization, Social priorities, Policy research, The family in the future, Futures methodology.

Direction of work in planning: Social, Educational, Economic, Political, Environmental, Labour, Resources.

Methods used: I Simulation, 2 Causal modelling, 3 Statistical models, 4 Extrapolation techniques, 5 Scenario building, 6 Historical analogy.

Time range of work: IO - 25 years.

Source of support for work (%): IOO National government.

Number of persons working at professional level: 4 Full time.   *(440)*

174. Institut für Systemtechnik und Innovationsforschung der Fraunhofergesellschaft

75 Karlsruhe Waldstadt, Breslauerstr 48, West Germany.

Type of centre: National government.

Primarily engaged in: Both futures studies and long-range planning.

Direction of work in forecasting: I Technological, 2 Environmental, 3 Resources.

Direction of work in research: I Environmental, 2 Resource utilization, 3 Value systems.

Direction of work in planning: I Technological, 2 Political, 3 Scientific.

Methods used: I Extrapolation techniques, I Simulation, 2 Scenario building, 2 Network analysis, 3 Brainstorming, 4 Delphi techniques.

Time range of work: IO - beyond year 2OOO.

Source of support for work (%): IO Private business, 9O National government.

Work done for (%): IO Private business, 9O National government.

Number of persons working at professional level: 5 Part time, 25 Full time.   *(401)*

175. Institut du Transport Aérian (ITA)

4 Rue de Solferino, Paris 75OO7, France.

Type of centre: International non-government. *Concerned with long-term futures.*

Time allocated (%): 2O.

Methods used: Probabilistic forecasting, Scenario building, Brainstorming, Statistical models, Relevance trees, Network analysis, Historical analogy, Operational models.

Time range of work: 5 - IO years.

Number of persons working at professional level: 3 Part time, 3 Full time.   *(96)*

176. Institute of Cybernetics

Section 7O2, Science Policy Studies, USSR, Kiev 127, Bul-4O-Ley Oktyabya 142/144, USSR.

Type of centre: National governmental.

Primarily engaged in: Both futures studies and long-range planning.

Direction of work in forecasting: I Technological, 2 Scientific, 3 Manpower, 4 Economic.

Direction of work in research: I Policy research, 2 Alternative futures, 3 Social impacts of technology, Manpower, 5 Social Priorities.

Direction of work in planning: I Technological, 2 Scientific, 3 Economic, 4 Social.

Methods used: I Expert panels, 2 Relevance trees, 3 Delphi techniques, 4 Network analysis, 5 Simulation, 6 Extrapolation techniques, 7 Contextual mapping, 8 Statistical models.

Time range of work: 5 - 25 years.

Source of support for work (%): 2O Local government, 6O National government,

20 Foundations.
Work done for (%): IO Local government, 3O Foundations, 6O National government.
Number of persons working at professional level: 5O Part time, 7O Full time.   *(439)*

177. Institute for Defence Analysis
4OO Army-Navy Drive, Arlington, Va 222O2, USA.
Type of centre: Federal contract research.
Primarily engaged in: Long-range planning.
Direction of work in forecasting: I Military, 2 Scientific.
Direction of work in research: I Policy research, 2 Resource utilization.
Direction of work in planning: I Technological, I Military, 3 Economic.
Methods used: Extrapolation techniques, Statistical models, Expert panels, Network analysis, Operational models, Individual expert forecasting, Simulation, All techniques of analysis in science, technology, operations research, econometrics, human performance, history.
Time range of work: 5 - IO years.
Source of support for work (%): IOO National government.
Work done for (%): IOO National government.
Number of persons working at professional level: Few Part time, 2OO Full time.   *(51)*

178. Institute for Economic and Social Research
Project Director, Prof. Hans Linneman, Free University, PO Box 7161, Amsterdam, The Netherlands.
Type of centre: Academic.
Concerned with long-term futures.
Time allocated (%): 4O.
Methods used: Statistical models, Simulation, Causal modelling.
Time range of work: Beyond year 2OOO.
Source of support for work (%): IO Private business, IO Foundations, 8O National government.
Work done for (%): 25 National government, 25 Foundations, 5O Academic.
Number of persons working at professional level: 4 Full time, 8 Part time.   *(74)*

179. Institute of Employment Research
D-85OO Nurnberg 1, Regensburger Str, 1O4, Postfach, West Germany.
Type of centre: National government. *Concerned with long-term futures.*
Time allocated (%): 3O.
Direction of work in forecasting: I Manpower, 2 Educational.
Direction of work in research: I Manpower, 2 Social impacts of technology.
Direction of work in planning: I Labour, 2 Educational.
Methods used: I Extrapolation techniques, 2 Statistical models, 3 Causal modelling, 4 Brainstorming.
Time range of work: IO - 25 years.
Source of support for work (%): 5 International agencies, 95 National government.
Work done for (%): 5 International agencies, 95 National government.
Number of persons working at professional level: I5 Full time.   *(115)*

180. Institute for Future Technology
c/o Science Museum, 2-1 Kitanomaru Koen, Chiyoda-ku, Tokyo, Japan.
Type of centre: Independent research. *Concerned with long-term futures.*
Time allocated (%): 4O.

Direction of work in forecasting: I Technological, 2 Environmental.
Direction of work in research: I Social impacts of technology, 2 Environmental,
3 Futures methodology.
Direction of work in planning: I Technological, 2 Environmental, 3 Social,
4 Educational.
Methods used: I Brainstorming, 2 Causal modelling, 3 Expert panels, 4 Cross impact
analysis, 5 Statistical models, 6 Scenario building, 7 Delphi techniques, 8 Operational
models, 9 Relevance trees, IO Historical analogy, 11 Extrapolation techniques,
I2 Contextual mapping, I3 Simulation, I4 Individual expert forecasting, I5 Network
analysis.
Time range of work: 5 - IO years.
Source of support for work (%): 4O National government, 6O Public co-operation.
Work done for (%): 16 National government.
Number of persons working at professional level: IO Full time.   *(179)*

181. Institute of Geological Sciences
Dr A.W. Woodland, CBE, Director; London SW7 2DE.
Type of centre: National government.
Primarily engaged in: Futures studies.
Direction of work in forecasting: I Resources, 2 Environmental.
Direction of work in research: I Resource utilization, 2 Environmental.
Direction of work in planning: Resources.
Methods used: I Contextual mapping, 2 Statistical models, 3 Historical analogy.
Time range of work: IO - 25 years.
Source of support for work (%): IOO National government.
Work done for (%): IOO National government.
Number of persons working at professional level: I5O Part time, 45O Full time.   *(256)*

182. Institute for Juvenile Research
114O South Paulina, Chicago II, 6OO12, USA.
Type of centre: State Government. *Concerned with long-term futures.*
Time allocated (%): Less than IO.
Direction of work in forecasting: Scientific.
Direction of work in research: Policy research, The individual in the future,
The family in the future.
Direction of work in planning: Scientific.
Methods used: Probabilistic forecasting, Scenario building, Extrapolation techniques,
Brainstorming, Simulation.
Time range of work: IO - 25 years.
Source of support for work (%): 3 Foundations, I2 National government, 85 Local
government.
Work done for (%): 2O National government, 8O Local government.
Number of persons working at professional level: I5 Full time.   *(423)*

I83. Institute of Legal Medicine and Criminology
Lyon, France.
Type of centre: Academic.
Concerned with long-term futures.
Time allocated (%): Less than IO.
Time range of work: 5 - IO years.
Work done for (%): IOO National government.
Number of persons working at professional level: 4 Part time.   *(113)*

184. Institute for Philosophy and Sociology
110 OO Praha 1, Jilska 1, Czechoslovakia.
Type of centre: Academic.
Concerned with long-term futures.
Time allocated (%): 30.
Methods used: Expert panels, Individual expert forecasting.
Time range of work: IO - 25 years.
Source of support for-work (%): IOO National government.
Work done for (%): 3O National government.
Number of persons working at professional level: I5 Full time.   *(427)*

Institute for Public Policy Alternatives
See: State University of New York at Albany.

185. Institute for Research on Public Policy
Director, A.W.R. Carrothers, No 514, 3535 Chemin Queen Mary, Montreal, Quebec, H5V 1H8, Canada.
Type of centre: Independent research.
Primarily engaged in: Both futures studies and long-range planning.
Direction of work in forecasting: I Population, 2 Social, 3 Resources.
Direction of work in research: I Policy research, 2 Population, 3 Resource utilization.
Direction of work in planning: I Social, 2 Economic, 2 Political, 3 Resources.
Time range of work: IO - beyond year 2000.
Source of support for work (%): 33 Local government, 33 Private business. 33 National government.
Work done ,for (%): IOO Canadians in general/policy makers at all levels.
Number of persons working at professional level: 4 Full time.
Additional information: This is a new institutem dedicated to independent research for the improvement of public policy making in Canada at all levels   *(323)*
of government.

186. Institute for Scientific Information
325 Chestnut St, Philadelphia, Pa 191O6, USA.
Type of centre: Business. *Concerned with long-term futures.*
Time allocated (%): IO.
Source of support for work (%): IO National government.
Work done for (%): IO National government.
Number of persons working at professional level: 3 Part time.   *(32)*

187. Institute of Social Psychology
Professor, Abraham Moles, 12, Rue Goethe, 67OO Strasbourg, France.
Type of centre: Academic.
Concerned with long-term futures.
Time allocated (%): 2O.
Direction of work in research: The individual in the future, Futures methodology.
Direction of work in planning: Social, Urban, Environmental.
Methods used: Probabilistic forecasting, Delphi techniques.
Time range of work: IO - 25 years.
Work done for (%): 5 - IO Private business.
Number of persons working at professional level: I Full time.   *(4O2)*

188. Institute of Strategic Studies

Deputy Dean, Dr Serafin Talisayon, Philippine Centre for Advanced Studies
University of The Philippines System, Diliman, Quezon City, Philippines.
Type of centre: National government. *Concerned with long-term futures.*
Time allocated (%): 20.
Methods used: I Causal modelling, 2 Expert panels, 3 Simulation, 4 Delphi techniques,
5 Statistical models, 6 Individual expert forecasting, 7 Historical analogy.
Source of support for work (%): IOO National government.
Work done for (%): IOO National government.   *(380)*

189. Institute for the Study of International Organization

Prof Asa Briggs, Stanmer House, Stanmer Park, Brighton BN1 9 QA, UK.
Type of centre: International government/international non-government/international
voluntary association.
Concerned with long-term futures. Time allocated (%): 20.
Direction of work in forecasting: Economic, Social, Cultural, Environmental, Population,
International organization response to problems.
Methods used: Delphi techniques, Cross impact analysis, Scenario building, Individual
expert forecasting.
Time range of work: 5 - beyond year 2000.
Source of support for work (%): IOO Foundations.
Work done for (%): 20 International agencies, 80 Foundations.
Number of persons working at professional level: I Part time, 2 Full time.   *(325)*

190. Institute for Technology and Economics (ITE)

Director, Dr Wolfgang Michalski, Neuer Junfernstieg 21, 2 Hamburg 36, West Germany.
Type of centre: Independent research. *Concerned with long-term futures.*
Primarily engaged in: Both futures studies and long-range planning.
Direction of work in forecasting: I Resources, 2 Economic, 3 Technological.
Direction of work in research: I Resource utilization, 2 Environmental, 3 Alternative
futures, 4 Futures methodology.
Direction of work in planning: I Resources, 2 Economic, 3 Technological.
Methods used: I Simulation, 2 Probabilistic forecasting, 3 Extrapolation techniques.
Time range of work: 5 - IO years.
Source of support for work (%): 40 Private business, 60 National government.
Work done for (%): 40 Private business, 60 National government.
Number of persons working at professional level: 2 Part time, 14 Full time.   *(262)*

191. Institute of Terrestrial Ecology

Merlewood Research Station, Grange-over-Sands, Cumbria, LA11 6JU, UK.
Type of centre: National government.
Concerned with long-term futures.
Time allocated (%): 30.
Methods used: I Statistical models, 2 Simulation, 3 Network analysis, 4 Causal modelling,
3 Relevance trees, 6 Gaming, 7 Delphi techniques.
Time range of work: IO - 25 years.
Source of support for work (%): IOO National government.
Work done for (%): 30 National government.
Number of persons working at professional level: I5 Full time.   *(142)*

192. Institute for World Order Inc
1140 Ave of the Americas, New York, NY 10036, USA.
Type of centre: 1 National voluntary association (with some international academic affiliations), 2 Independent research.
Primarily engaged in: Futures studies.
Direction of work in forecasting: 1 Social, 2 Military, 3 Environmental, 4 Educational.
Direction of work in research: 1 Alternative futures, 2 Value systems.
Time range of work: 10 - 25 years.
Source of support for work: Foundations, Voluntary Associations, Individual donors, Private business.
Work done for (%): 100 International agencies.
Number of persons working at professional level: 2 Part time (plus 100 associates in the USA and abroad), 8 Full time.   *(458)*

193. Instituto de la Juventud
Marques Del Riscal, 16, Madrid 4, Spain.
Type of centre: Academic.
Concerned with long-term futures.
Time allocated (%): 30.
Direction of work in forecasting: 1 Youth in the future, 2 Social priorities, 3 Value systems, 4 The Individual in the future, 5 The family in the future, 6 Social impacts of technology.
Direction of work in planning: 1 Youth policy, 2 Social, 3 Scientific, 4 Political.
Methods used: Cross impact analysis, Brainstorming, Expert panels, Operational models.
Time range of work: 5 - beyond year 2000.
Source of support for work (%): 5 Foundations, 5 Voluntary associations, 10 International agencies, 80 National government.
Work done for (%): 30 International agencies, 70 National government.
Number of persons working at professional level: 18 Full time, 27 Part time.   *(97)*

194. Instituto Nuevas Alternativas, SA
Cordoba 23-A, Mexico 7, DF.
Type of centre: International professional organisation. *Concerned with long-term futures.*
Time allocated (%): 40.
Direction of work in research: Social impacts of technology, Environmental, Alternative futures.
Direction of work in planning: Social, Urban, Regional, Educational, Environmental.
Methods used: Contextual mapping, Brainstorming, Expert panels, Historical analogy, Individual expert forecasting, Common sense.
Time range of work: 5 - 10 years.
Source of support for work (%): 10 National government, 20 Private business, 20 Foundations, 50 International agencies.
Work done for (%): 10 National government, 20 Private business, 20 Foundations, 50 International agencies.
Number of persons working at professional level: 5 Part time.   *(436)*

195. Instituttet for Fremtidsporskning
Vester Parimagsgade 3, 1606 Copenhagen V, Denmark.
Type of centre: Independent research centre/membership society.
Primarily engaged in: Futures studies.
Direction of work in forecasting: Technological, Economic, Social, Cultural, Market,

Educational, Scientific, Environmental, Manpower, Resources, Food, Population.
Direction of work in research: All areas (see Directory guide).
Methods used: Probabilistic forecasting, Delphi techniques, Gaming, Cross impact analysis, Scenario building, Extrapolation techniques, Contextual mapping, Brainstorming, Statistical models, Expert panels, Relevance trees, Network analysis, Simulation.
Time range of work: IO - beyond year 2OOO.
Source of support for work (%): 2O Private business, IO Foundations, 7O Members of the institute.
Work done for (%): 2O Private business, IO Foundations, 7O Members of the institute.
Number of persons working at professional level: 6 Part time, 5 Full time.   *(376)*

196. Inter-American Committee on the Alliance for Progress
Executive Secretary, Walter J. Sedwitz, Room 11O3, 1725 Eye St, NW, Washington, DC 20OO6, USA.
Type of centre: International government.
Concerned with long-term futures.
Time allocated (%): 3O.
Methods used: I Statistical models, 2 Individual expert forecasting, 3 Expert panels, 4 Extrapolation techniques, 5 Simulation.
Time range of work: 5 - 25 years.
Source of support for work (%): 5 International agencies, 5 Foundations, 9O National government.
Work done for (%): IOO National government.
Number of persons working at professional level: 4O Part time.   *(49)*

197. Interfuture
President Dr Paul W. Conner, 535 Fifth Ave, Suite 31O3, New York, NY 1OO17, USA.
Type of centre: Academic.
Primarily engaged in: Futures studies.
Direction of work in research: I International co-operation, 2 Environmental, 3 The individual in the future.
Methods used: Intercultural case studies.
Time range of work: 5 - IO years.
Work done for (%): 5O Individuals, 5O Universities and colleges.
Number of persons working at professional level: 5 Part time, IO-I5 Full time.   *(78)*

198. Intergovernmental Committee for European Migration
53 Bonn-Bad Godesberg, Friedrichstr, 1O, West Germany.
Type of centre: International government.
Concerned with long-term futures.
Additional information: This is the German Branch Office and its research is carried out at Headquarters Section for Research and Planning, Rue du Valais, 9, Geneva, Switzerland   *(79)*

199. International Agency for Research on Cancer
Director, Dr John Higginson, 15O Cours Albert Thomas, 69OO8 Lyon, France.
Type of centre: International government.
Concerned with long-term futures.
Direction of work in research: Environmental.

Methods used: I Brainstorming, 2 Expert panels, 3 Scientific analogy, 4 Statistical models.
Time range of work: IO - 25 years.
Source of support for work (%): IOO National governments.
Work done for (%): IOO National government.
Number of persons working at professional level: 26 Full time.   *(177)*

200. International Amateur Radio Union

Region 1 Division, 51 Pettits Lane, Romford, RM1 4HJ, Essex, UK.
Type of centre: International non-government.
Primarily engaged in: Long-range planning.
Direction of work in forecasting: Scientific.
Direction of work in research: Resource utilization.
Methods used: I Expert panels, 2 Probabilistic forecasting, 3 Individual expert forecasting.
Time range of work: 5 - IO years.
Source of support for work (%): 5O Voluntary associations.
Work done for (%): 25 Voluntary associations.
Number of persons working at professional level: 3 Part time.   *(68)*

201. International Association of Educators for World Peace

Executive Office of the Secretary-General, PO Box 3282, Blue Springs Station, Huntsville, Al 3581O, USA.
Type of centre: International non-government.
Primarily engaged in: Both futures studies and long-range planning.
Direction of work in forecasting: I Cultural, Educational, 2 Social, Resources, Population, 3 Technological, Scientific, Environmental.
Direction of work in research: I Social priorities, Individual in the future, 2 Social impacts of technology, Futures methodology, 3 Alternative futures.
Direction of work in planning: I Educational, 2 Social.
Methods used: I Expert panels, 2 Brainstorming, 3 Historical analogy.
Time range of work: 5 - beyond year 2OOO.
Source of support for work (%): 5 Local government, 5 International agencies. IO Foundations, IO Voluntary associations, I5 Private business, 5O Personal donations.
Work done for (%): 5 Local government, 5 International agencies, 5 Private business, IO Voluntary associations, 75 Personal and individual.
Number of persons working at professional level: 3 Full time, 47 Part time.   *(369)*

202. International Association for The Physical Sciences of the Ocean

c/o Secretary, Dr E.C. La Fond, Naval Undersea Centre, San Diego, Ca 92132, USA.
Type of centre: International non-government.
Primarily engaged in: Futures studies.
Direction of work in forecasting: Scientific.
Direction of work in research: Environmental.
Direction of work in planning: I Scientific, 2 Environmental.
Methods used: I Individual expert forecasting, 2 Expert panels, 3 Statistical models.
Time range of work: 5 - 25 years.
Source of support for work (%): IOO International agencies.
Work done for (%): IOO National government agencies.   *(225)*

203. The International Association of Ports and Harbours (IAPH)
Deputy Secretary General, Katsuya Yokoyama, Kotohira-kaikan Building, No. I,
Kotohire-Cho, Minato-Ku, Tokyo 105, Japan.
Type of centre: International voluntary association.
Concerned with long-term futures.
Time allocated (%): IO.
Direction of work in forecasting: Economic, Environmental.
Direction of work in research: Environmental.
Direction of work in planning: Economic, Environmental.
Methods used: Expert panels.
Time range of work: 5 - IO years.
Source of support for work (%): 50 International government, 50 Voluntary
associations.
Work done for (%): 20 Voluntary associations, 80 International government.
Number of persons working at professional level: 2 Full time.   *(83)*

204. International Association for Water Law
President, Guillermo J. Cano, Arenales 2040 7 - B, Buenos Aires, Argentina.
Type of centre: International non-government.
Concerned with long-term futures.
Time allocated (%): *30.*
Methods used: I Expert panels, 2 Brainstorming.
Time range of work: IO - 25 years.
Source of support for work (%): IOO Membership fees.
Work done for (%): 20 Local government, 80 National government.   *(182)*

205. International Association for Water Law
Via Montevideo, Rome, Italy.
Type of centre: International non-government.
Concerned with long-term futures.
Time allocated (%): Less than IO.
Direction of work in forecasting: Law on water resources.
Direction of work in research: Water resources, Law trends.
Direction of work in planning: Legal reforms.
Methods used: I Expert panels, 2 Historical analogy.
Time range of work: 5 - IO years.
Source of support for work (%): IO National government, 90 Voluntary associations.
Work done for (%): 50 National government, 50 International agencies.
Number of persons working at professional level: 4 Part time.   *(136)*

206. International Bank for Reconstruction and Development (World Bank)
1818 H Street, NW, Washington DC, 20433, USA.
Type of centre: International government.
Concerned with long-term futures.
Time allocated (%): 20.
Methods used: All methods (see Directory guide).
Time range of work: IO - 25 years.
Source of support for work (%): IOO International agencies.
Work done for (%): IOO International agencies.
Number of persons working at professiosnal level: 300 Full time.   *(194)*

207. International Bank for Reconstruction and Development

Transportation and Urban Projects Dept, Director, Edward Jaycox, 1818 H Str, NW Washington, DC. 20433, USA.

Type of centre: International government.
Concerned with long-term futures.
Time allocated (%): 20.
Direction of work in research: Resource utilization.
Methods used: I Scenario building, 2 Extrapolation techniques, 3 Operational models, 4 Brainstorming.
Time range of work: IO - 25 years.
Source of support for work (%): IOO International agencies.
Work done for (%): IOO International agencies.
Number of persons working at professional level: 5O Part time.   *(275)*

208. International Centre of Methodology for Future and Development Studies

Str Mihail Moxa 3 - 5, Bucharest 8, Romania.

Type of centre: International professional organisation.
Primarily engaged in: Futures studies.
Direction of work in forecasting: I Social, 2 Resources, 3 Environmental, 4 Educational, 5 Technological.
Direction of work in research: I Futures methodology, 2 Alternative futures, 3 Environmental, 4 Resource utilization.
Direction of work in planning: I Environmental, 2 Educational, 3 Social.
Methods used: I Brainstorming, 2 Delphi techniques, 3 Operational models, 4 Probabilistic forecasting, 5 Simulation, 6 Cross impact analysis.
Time range of work: 5 - beyond year 2OOO.
Source of support for work (%): IOO University of Bucharest.
Work done for (%): 45 International agencies, 55 University of Bucharest.
Number of persons working at professional level: 5 Part time, 7 Full time.   *(144)*

209. International Confederation of Free Trade Unions (ICFTU)

Tokyo Office, Eiichi Ochiai, Kawate Building 1 - 5 - 8, Nishi-Shimbashi, Minato-ku, Tokyo, 1O5 Japan.

Type of centre: Trade union/international non-governmental.
Concerned with long-term futures.
Time allocated (%): Less than IO.
Direction of work in forecasting: I Economic, 2 Educational, 3 Manpower, 4 Resources, 5 Population, 6 Technological, 7 Environmental.
Direction of work in research: I Social impacts of technology, 2 Manpower, 3 Environmental, 4 Resource utilization, 5 Social priorities, 6 Population.
Direction of work in planning: I Labour, 2 Regional, 3 Educational, 4 Social, 5 Environmental.
Methods used: I Statistical models, 2 Expert panels, 3 Individual expert forecasting.
Time range of work: 5 - IO years.
Work done for (%): IOO Own organization.
Number of persons working at professional level: 2 Full time.   *(363)*

210. International Co-operation Council
World Headquarters, 17819 Roscoe Blvd, Northridge, Ca 91324, USA.
Type of centre: Non-profit council of new age organization and individuals.
Concerned with long-term futures.
Time allocated(%):   20.
Direction of work in forecasting: Social, Cultural, Educational, Scientific, Religious.
Direction of work in research: Social impacts of technology, Alternative futures,
Value systems, Social priorities, The individual in the future, The family in the future,
Futures methodology.
Direction of work in planning: Scientific, Social Educational.
Methods used: I Operational models, 2 Historical analogy.
Time range of work: Beyond year 2000.
Source of support for work (%):   5 Foundations, 30 Voluntary associations.
60 Meetings and memberships.
Work done for (%):   5 Foundations, 75 Voluntary associations.
Number of persons working at professional level: 3 Part time.   *(23)*

211. International Council for the Exploration of the Sea
Charlottenlund Slot, DX 2920, Charlottenlund, Denmark.
Type of centre: International government.
Primarily engaged in: Futures studies.
Direction of work in forecasting: I Scientific, Environmental, Resources, 2 Technological.
Direction of work in research: Environmental, Resource utilization.
Direction of work in planning: Scientific.
Methods used: Expert panels.
Time range of work: I - 5 years.
Source of support for work (%):   I00 National government.
Number of persons working at professional level: 4 Full time.   *(211)*

212. International Council of Monuments and Sites (ICOMOS)
75 Rue du Temple, Paris 3, France.
Type of centre: International non-government.
Concerned with long-term futures.
Methods used: I Expert panels, 2 Historical analogy, 3 Operational models.
Time range of work: 5 - beyond year 2000.
Work done for (%):   I0 Local government, 45 National government, 45 International
government.
Number of persons working at professional level: 2 Part time, 2 Full time.   *(34)*

213. International Council of Scientific Unions
51 Blvd de Montmorency, 75016 Paris, France.
Type of centre: International professional organization.
Concerned with long-term futures.
Time allocated (%):   I0.
Direction of work in forecasting: I Scientific, 2 Educational, 2 Environmental, 2 Resources.
Direction of work in research: I Environmental, I Resource utilization, 2 Social impacts
of technology.
Direction of work in planning: I Scientific, 2 Educational, 2 Environmental.
Methods used: Brainstorming, Expert panels, Simulation.
Time range of work: 5 - I0 years.

Source of support for work (%): 3 Foundations, 20 International agencies.
Work done for (%): 5 Voluntary associations, 20 International agencies. *(393)*

214. International Development Association
International Bank for Reconstruction and Development, Regional Projects Department
Europe, Middle East and North Africa, Director, Willi Wapenhans, 1818 H Street,
NW Washington DC 20433, USA.
Type of centre: International government.
Concerned with long-term futures.
Time allocated (%): 50.
Direction of work in forecasting: Economic, Social, Resources, Population.
Direction of work in research: Social impacts of technology, Social priorities, Resource
utilization.
Direction of work in planning: Social, Economic, Resources.
Methods used: Probabilistic forecasting, Simulation, Statistical models, Expert panels,
Historical analogy, Operational models, Individual expert forecasting, Causal modelling.
Time range of work: 5 - 25 years.
Source of support for work (%): 100 International agencies.
Work done for (%): 100 International agencies. *(210)*

215. International Fiscal Association
c/o Erasmus University, Woudestein, PO Box 1738 Rotterdam, The Netherlands.
Type of centre: International non-government. *Concerned with long-term futures.*
Time allocated (%): 20.
Direction of work in forecasting: Scientific.
Direction of work in planning: Scientific.
Methods used: Expert panels.
Time range of work: 5 - 10 years.
Additional information: Aim of the association is the study and advancement of
international and comparative law in regard to public finance, and especially
international and comparative fiscal law and the financial and economic aspects
of taxations. *(373)*

216. International Hydrographic Organization
Ave, President J.F. Kennedy, Monte Carlo, Monaco.
Type of centre: International government.
Concerned with long-term futures.
Methods used: Expert panels.
Time range of work: 5 - 10 years.
Source of support for work (%): 100 National government.
Work done for (%): 100 National government.
Number of persons working at professional level: 7 Full time. *(2)*

217. International Institute for Educational Planning (in UNESCO)
Director, Hans Weiler, 7 Rue Eugene Delacroix, Paris 16E, France.
Type of centre: International government.
Primarily engaged in: Long-range planning.
Direction of work in forecasting: Educational.
Direction of work in research: Policy research.
Direction of work in planning: Educational.
Methods used: 1 Statistical models, 2 Brainstorming, 3 Probabilistic forecasting,

4 Expert panels, 5 Simulation, 6 Individual expert forecasting.
Time range of work: 5 - IO years.
Source of support for work (%):   5O National governments, 5O International agencies.
Work done for (%):   25 International agencies, 75 National governments.
Number of persons working at professional level: IO Part time, 14 Full time.   *(396)*

218. International Institute for Labour Studies

154 Route de Lausanne, Geneve, Switzerland.
Type of centre: International government.
Concerned with long-term futures.
Time allocated (%):   Less than IO.
Direction of work in forecasting: Social.
Direction of work in research: I Social priorities, 2 Social impacts of technology.
Methods used: I Individual expert forecasting, 2 Scenario building, 3 Expert panels,
4 Delphi techniques, 5 Extrapolation techniques.
Time range of work: 5 - 25 years.
Additional information: Methods of futurology research have been applied and developed
with respect to certain projects which appear to require such an approach. Futurology
methods were used for the 1972 project on the Future of Industrial Relations. For
this project one person was employed full time and approximately IO part time
(including external collaborators). Have also published on future social policy trends. *(21)*

219. International Institute of Management

Griegstr 5, D-1OOO, Berlin 33, West Germany.
Type of centre: Academic.
Concerned with long-term futures.
Time allocated (%):   4O.
Direction of work in forecasting: Technological, Scientific, Manpower.
Direction of work in research: Social impacts of technology, Policy research, Manpower.
Direction of work in planning: Technological, Regional, Political, Labour.
Methods used: Probabilistic forecasting, Simulation, Extrapolation techniques, Statistical
models, Historical analogy, Operational models.
Time range of work: IO - 25 years.
Source of support for work (%):   IO Local government, IO Foundations, 8O National
government.
Number of persons working at professional level: 3 Full time.   *(84)*

22O. International Institute Tropical Agriculture

W.K. Gamble, PHB 532O Ibadan, Nigeria.
Type of centre: International agricultural research centre.
Concerned with long-term futures.
Methods used: I Expert panels, 2 Brainstorming, 3 Individual expert forecasting,
4 Causal modelling.
Time range of work: 5 - IO years.
Source of support for work (%):   IO Foundations, 15 National government,
75 International agencies.
Work done for (%):   15 National government.
Number of persons working at professional level: 12 Part time, 5O Full time.   *(271)*

221. International Labour Office
154 Rue de Lausanne, 1211 Geneva 22, Switzerland.
Type of centre: International government.
Concerned with long-term futures.
Time allocated (%): lO.
Methods used: Extrapolation techniques, Brainstorming, Statistical models, Expert panels, Operational models, Individual expert forecasting.
Time range of work: 5 - 25 years.
Source of support for work (%): lOO National government.
Work done for (%): lOO National governments', employers' and workers' organizations.
Number of persons working at professional level: 5O Part time.   *(384)*

222. International Police Association
Police Headquarters, Sutton Road, Maidstone, ME 15, Kent, UK.
Type of centre: International non-government.
Concerned with long-term futures.
Time allocated (%): lO.
Methods used: Historical analogy.
Time range of work: 5 - lO years.
Source of support for work (%): lOO Voluntary associations.
Work done for (%): lOO Voluntary associations.
Number of persons working at professional level: 2O Part time.   *(322)*

223. International Society for Research on Civilization, Diseases and Environment
Headquarters, Luxembourg Ville, Weimershot, B-1O4O Brussels, 1O Rue d'Italie, Belgium.
Type of centre: International voluntary association.
Methods used: Annual conference.
Time range of work: 5 - 25 years.
Source of support for work (%): 5 Local government.   *(424)*

224. Iowa 2OOO
c/o Institute of Public Affairs, University of Iowa, Iowa City, Iowa 52242, USA.
Type of centre: Commission/advisory group.
Primarily engaged in: Futures studies.
Direction of work in forecasting: l Economic, 2 Energy, 3 Environmental, 4 Social.
Direction of work in research: l Alternative futures, 2 Social priorities.
Methods used: l Probabilistic forecasting, 2 Scenario building, 3 Cross impact analysis, 4 Brainstorming, 5 Individual expert forecasting, 6 Expert panels.
Time range of work: Beyond year 2OOO.
Source of support for work (%): lOO - State appropriation, Title I grant, Private donations, and extension, division support from the three State Universities.
Number of persons working at professional level: l Part time.   *(456)*

225. The Irish Conservation Society
Treasurer, W.M. Griffin, 34 Brookwood Heights, Artane, Dublin 5, Eire.
Type of centre: Membership society.
Concerned with long-term futures.

Time allocated (%): 20.
Method used: I Expert panels, 2 Statistical models, 3 Historical analogy.
Time range of work: 5 - IO years.   *(368)*

226. The Israeli Institute of International Affairs

Chairman of the Executive Board, Prof, Marion Mushkat, PO Box 17027 Tel Aviv 61170, Israel.
Type of centre: Independent research/National voluntary association/membership society.
Concerned with long-term futures.
Time allocated (%): IO.
Direction of work in forecasting. Economic, Social, Population.
Direction of work in research: Population, Migration problems.
Direction of work in planning: Social, Economic.
Methods used: Cross impact analysis, Statistical models, Expert panels, Causal modelling.
Time range of work: 5 - IO years.
Source of support for work (%): IO Local government, IO Voluntary associations, 20 National government, 30 Foundations.
Work done for (%): 5 Voluntary associations, 20 Local government, 25 Foundations, 50 National government.
Number of persons working at professional level: 4 Part time.   *(213)*

227. Instituto per la Ricerca e la Formzione al Futuro (IRADES)

Via Paisiello, 6-Rome, OO198, Italy.
Type of centre: Independent research.
Primarily engaged in: Futures studies.
Direction of work in forecasting: I Educational, 2 Social, 3 Environmental.
Direction of work in research: I The individual in the future, 2 Value systems, 3 Alternative futures, 4 Futures methodology, 5 The family in the future.
Direction of work in planning: I Educational.
Methods used: I Brainstorming, 2 Scenario building, 3 Delphi techniques, 4 Extrapolation techniques.
Time range of work: Beyond year 2000.
Source of support for work (%): IO National government, IO Private business, IO Foundations, 40 Voluntary associations.
Work done for (%): IO National government, IO International agencies, 80 Voluntary associations.
Number of persons working at professional level: 3 Part time, 8 Full time.   *(341)*

228. Italian Institute for Foreign Trade

Via Liszt, 21, Rome, Italy.
Type of centre: National government. *Concerned with long-term futures.*
Time allocated (%): 20.
Direction of work in forecasting: Market.
Direction of work in research: Consumer affairs.
Direction of work in planning: Economic.
Methods used: I Expert panels, 2 Individual expert forecasting, 3 Brainstorming.
Time range of work: 5 - IO years.
Source of support for work (%): IOO National government.
Work done for (%): IOO National government.
Number of persons working at professional level: I2 Full time.   *(241)*

J 229. Japan Computer Usage Development Institute

Director, Dr Yoheji Masuda, Kasumigaseki Bldg, 3 Chome Kasumigaseki, Tokyo, Japan.
Type of centre: Membership society.
Primarily engaged in: Futures studies.
Direction of work in forecasting: I Technological, 2 Environmental, 3 Economic.
Direction of work in research: I Social impacts of technology, 2 Futures methodology.
Direction of work in planning: Social.
Methods used: I Scenario building, 2 Delphi techniques, 3 Cross impact analysis, 4 Historical analogy.
Time range of work: 5 - IO years.
Source of support for work (%): 40 National government, 60 Foundations.
Work done for (%): 40 Private business, 60 National government.
Number of persons working at professional level: 5 Part time, 12 Full time.   *(410)*

230. Japan Techno-Economics Society

2-4-5 Iidabashi, Chiyoda-kn, Tokyo, Japan.
Type of centre: Independent research.
Concerned with long-term futures.
Time allocated (%): 20.
Direction of work in forecasting: I Technological, 2 Social, 3 Environmental, 4 Economic.
Direction of work in research: I Social impacts of technology, 2 Environmental, 3 Alternative futures, 4 Manpower, 5 Value systems, 6 Futures methodology, 7 Resource utilization.
Direction of work in planning: I Technological, 2 Corporate, 3 Environmental.
Methods used: Simulation, Statistical models, Relevance trees, Brainstorming, Causal modelling, Delphi techniques, Cross impact analysis, Extrapolation techniques.
Time range of work: 5 - beyond year 2000.
Source of support for work (%): IO National government, 5 International agencies, 50 Private business, 5 Foundations, 30 Public Corporation.
Work done for (%): 30 National government, 30 International agencies, 15 Private business, 5 Foundations, 20 Public corporations.
Number of persons working at professional level: 17 Full time.
Additional information: Concerned with motivation for R & D staff, technology transfer and quality of working environment.   *(453)*

231. Joint Unit for Planning Research

Director, Peter Cowan, 172 Tottenham Court Rd, London W1, UK.
Type of centre: Academic.
Concerned with long-term futures.
Time allocated (%): 20.
Direction of work in forecasting: Environmental.
Direction of work in research: Environmental.
Direction of work in planning: I Urban, 2 Regional.
Methods used: I Scenario building, 2 Delphi techniques, 3 Statistical models.
Time range of work: IO - 25 years.
Source of support for work (%): IOO Centre for Environmental Studies, London.
Work done for (%): IOO Centre for Environmental Studies, London.
Number of persons working at professional level: 23 Full time.   *(292)*

K ### 232. Kapur Solar Farms
Bijwasan-Naja-Garth Road, PO Kapas Hera, New Delhi 110037, India.
Type of centre: Independent research. ***Concerned with long-term futures.***
Time allocated (%): 20.
Direction of work in research: Social impacts of technology, Environmental, Energy,
Solar energy.
Time range of work: 5 - 25 years.
Work done for (%): 20 Voluntary associations.
Number of persons working at professional level: I Full time, 2 Part time.   *(395)*

L ### 233. Laboratoire de Prospective Appliquée
BP 734-07, 75326 Paris, Cedex 07, France.
Type of centre: National voluntary association.
Primarily engaged in: Both futures studies and long-range planning.
Direction of work in forecasting: I Social, 2 Economic, 3 Geo-politics, 4 Cultural,
5 Environmental.
Direction of work in research: 1 Social priorities, 2 Alternative futures, 3 Futures
methodology, 4 Geo-politics, 5 Environmental, 6 Value systems.
Direction of work in planning: I Social, 2 Economic, 3 Environmental, 4 Regional,
5 Urban, 6 Geo-politics.
Methods used: I Individual expert forecasting, 2 Expert panels, 3 Brainstorming,
4 Contextual mapping, 5 Operational models, 6 Scenario building, 7 Historical analogy,
8 Simulation.
Time range of work: IO - 25 years.
Source of support for work (%): IO Private business, IO Voluntary associations,
8O National government.
Work done for (%): IO Private business, IO Voluntary associations, 8O National
government.
Number of persons working at professional level: 2 Full time, I2 Part time.   *(317)*

234. Library of Congress
Congressional Research Service, Science Policy Research Division, Washington, DC
20540, USA.
Type of centre: National government.
Concerned with long-term futures.
Time allocated (%): 20.
Methods used: Probabilistic forecasting, Individual expert forecasting, Delphi techniques,
Gaming, Cross impact analysis, Scenario building, Extrapolation techniques, Brainstorming,
Expert panels, Historical analogy.
Time range of work: 5 - beyond year 2000.
Source of support for work (%): 100 National government, legislative branch.
Work done for (%): 100 National government, legislative branch.
Number of persons working at professional level: 75 Full time, I5 Part time.
Additional information: Science Policy Research Division is spearheading an effort
to enable all of the Congressional Research Service to participate in formal futures
work. This is partly a response to pending legislation requiring that every committee
of the House of Representatives be concerned with futures work.   *(199)*

235. Local Government Operational Research Unit
Director, Brian Whitworth, 201 Kings Road, Reading RG1. 42H, UK.
Type of centre: Independent research.
Primarily engaged in: Both futures studies and long-range planning.

Direction of work in forecasting: Social, Environmental, Resources, Population.
Direction of work in research: Environmental, Resource utilization, Policy research.
Direction of work in planning: Social, Urban, Regional, Environmental.
Methods used: Scenario building, Operational models, Simulation, Causal modelling.
Time range of work: 5 - 25 years.
Source of support for work (%): 25 National government, 75 Local government.
Work done for (%): 25 National government, 75 Local government.
Number of persons working at professional level: 2 Part time, 40 Full time.
Additional information: It is open to question as to whether the work of the Unit can properly be described as futures studies or long-range planning. Undertakes research and development of methodologies for planning, relevant to the needs of local government. *(125)*

236. Local Government Relations Division
Executive Department, 240 Cottage SE Salem, Or 97310, USA.
Type of centre: State government.
Concerned with long-term futures.
Time allocated (%): 50.
Methods used: I Scenario building, Futures conferences.
Time range of work: 10 - 25 years.
Source of support for work (%): 33 Government state, 67 National government.
Work done for (%): 50 Government state.
Number of persons working at professional level: 11 Full time. *(187)*

237. The London School of Economics and Political Science (LSE)
CREDOC, Edmond Lisle, Houghton Street, Aldwych, London WC2A 2AE, UK.
Type of centre: Academic.
Concerned with long-term futures.
Time allocated (%): 10.
Direction of work in forecasting: Economic, Social, Cultural, Educational, Manpower, Resources, Population.
Direction of work in research: Manpower, Social priorities, Policy research, Population, The family in the future, Futures methodology.
Direction of work in planning: Social, Urban, Educational, Economic, Resources.
Methods used: Probabilistic forecasting, Extrapolation techniques, Statistical models Historical analogy, Individual expert forecasting, Simulation, Causal modelling.
Time range of work: 10 - 25 years. *(227)*

238. Louisiana State University
School of Environmental Design, Gerald J. McLindon, Dean, Room 304 Field House, Batch Rouge, La, 70803, USA.
Type of centre: Academic.
Concerned with long-term futures.
Time allocated (%): 50.
Direction of work in forecasting: Social, Environmental.
Direction of work in research: Environmental, Futures methodology.
Direction of work in planning: Urban, Regional, Environmental.
Methods used: Gaming, Cross impact analysis, Extrapolation techniques, Contextual mapping, Brainstorming, Expert panels, Historical analogy, Individual expert forecasting, Simulation.
Time range of work: 10 - beyond year 2000.

Source of support for work (%): 2 Foundations, 98 State.
Work done for (%): 100 Educational program.
Number of persons working at professional level: 5 Part time, 35 Full time.   *(167)*

239. Lutheran Resource Commission
Executive Director, Henry Endress, 1348 Connecticut Ave, NW, Suite 828,
Washington, DC 20036, USA.
Type of centre: Church agency. *Concerned with long-term futures.*
Time allocated (%): 20.
Direction of work in forecasting: 1 Resources, 2 Social, 3 Educational.
Direction of work in research: 1 Resources utilization, 2 Social priorities.
Direction of work in planning: Resources.
Source of support for work (%): 100 Church bodies.
Work done for (%): 100 Church.
Number of persons working at professional level: 4 Full time.   *(282)*

M 240. Macmillan Bloedel Limited
Strategic Planning and Development, Vice President, R.L. Gillen, 1075 W Georgia St,
Vancouver, BC Canada.
Type of centre: Industry.
Concerned with long-term futures.
Time allocated (%): 20.
Methods used: 1 Probabilistic forecasting, 1 Simulation, 1 Delphi techniques,
Scenario building, 1 Extrapolation techniques, Brainstorming, 1 Statistical models,
Expert panels, 1 Historical analogy, Operational models, 1 Individual expert forecasting.
Time range of work: 5 - 10 years.
Work done for (%): 100 Private business.
Number of persons working at professional level: 1 Full time, 10 Part time.   *(306)*

241. Management and Organization Development, Inc
Chairman of the Board, Philip R. Harris, 2702 Costebelle Drive, La Jolla, Ca 92037, USA.
Type of centre: Independent research. *Concerned with long-term futures.*
Time allocated (%): 20.
Direction of work in forecasting: Manpower.
Direction of work in research: Future of Corporation.
Methods used: 1 Extrapolation techniques, 2 Brainstorming, 3 Simulation.
Time range of work: 5 - 10 years.
Source of support for work (%): 10 Local government, 20 National government,
70 Private business.
Work done for (%): 10 Local government, 10 National government, 10 Voluntary
associations, 70 Private business.
Number of persons working at professional level: 70 Part time.   *(383)*

242. Mankind 2000 (Humanité 2000)
1, Rue Aux Laines, 1000 Brussels, Belgium.
Type of centre: International voluntary association.
Primarily engaged in: Futures studies.
Direction of work in forecasting: Contextual clarification and integration.
Direction of work in research: 1 Social innovation, 2 The individual in the future.
Methods used: Extrapolation techniques, Contextual mapping, Brainstorming, Expert
panels, Individual expert forecasting.

Time range of work: lO - 25 years.
Source of support for work (%): lOO Voluntary associations.
Work done for (%): lOO Voluntary associations.
Number of persons working at professional level: 2 Part time.
Additional information: Individual members of the association are involved in a
range of futures studies and long-range planning. *(146)*

243. Marga Institute of Development Studies
75 Ward Place, Columbo 7, Sri Lanka.
Type of centre: Independent research.
Concerned with long-term futures.
Direction of work in forecasting: Educational, Manpower, Resources, Population.
Direction of work in research: Social impacts of technology, Alternative futures,
Manpower, Resource utilization, Population, Futures methodology, Futures of society
in general.
Direction of work in planning: Urban, Educational, Labour.
Methods used: Statistical models, Expert panels, Historical analogy.
Time range of work: lO - 25 years.
Source of support for work: Mainly international agencies.
Work done for: Mainly for own society.
Number of persons working at professional level: 59 Full time, 3O Part time,
4 Consultants. *(200)*

244. Massachusetts Institute of Technology
Centre for Policy Alternatives, Director, Herbert J. Hollomon, 77 Massachusetts Ave,
Cambridge, Ma ∪2139, USA.
Type of centre: Academic.
Primarily engaged in: Both futures studies and long-range planning.
Direction of work in forecasting: I Manpower, 2 Technological, 3 Economic, 4 Educational.
Direction of work in research: I Policy research.
Time range of work: 5 - 25 years.
Source of support for work (%): 2O Foundations, 8O National government.
Work done for (%): 2O International agencies, 7O National government.
Number of persons working at professional level: lO Full time, 2O Part time. *(242)*

245. Massachusetts Institute of Technology
Dept of Urban Studies and Planning, Special Program for Urban and Regional Studies
of Developing Areas, Cambridge, Ma O2139, USA.
Type of centre: Academic.
Concerned with long-term futures.
Direction of work in research: Social impacts of technology, Environmental, Manpower,
Social priorities, Resource utilization, Population, Policy research.
Direction of work in planning: I Urban, 2 Regional, 3 Social, 3 Economic, 3 Environ-
mental,.
Methods used: Statistical models, Historical analogy, Operational models, Simulation,
Causal modelling.
Time range of work: 5 - 25 years.
Number of persons working at professional level: 4O Part time. *(276)*

246. Massachusetts Institute of Technology

Research Program of Communication Policy, 53 - 401 MIT, Cambridge, Ma 02139, USA.
Type of centre: Academic.
Concerned with long-term futures.
Time allocated (%): 50.
Direction of work in research: I Social impacts of technology, 2 Policy research.
Methods used: I Individual expert forecasting, 2 Expert panels.
Time range of work: 5 - 25 years.
Ssouce of support for work (%): 25 Foundations, 75 National government.
Work done for (%): 33 National government, 67 Publications.
Number of persons working at professional level: I5 Part time.   *(157)*

247. Massachusetts Institute of Technology

System Dynamics Group, Jay W. Forrester, Room F40 - 253, 77 Massachusetts Ave,
Cambridge, Ma 02139, USA.
Type of centre: Academic.
Primarily engaged in: Both futures studies and long-range planning.
Direction of work in forecasting: I Economic, 2 Social, 3 Environmental, 4 Resources,
5 Population.
Direction of work in research: I Alternative futures, 2 Value systems, 3 Futures
methodology, 4 Population, 5 Environmental.
Methods used: I System dynamics, 2 Causal modelling, 3 Simulation, 4 Historical
analogy.
Time range of work: 5 - beyond year 2000.
Source of support for work (%): IO Local government, IO Private business, IO Individuals,
20 National government, 50 Foundations.
Number of persons working at professional level: 20 Full time.   *(214)*

248. Mens en Ruimte

Directeur General, H.M. Baeyens, Froissartstraat, 118, Brussels, Belgium.
Type of centre: Independent study group/non-profit organization.
Primarily engaged in: Both futures studies and long-range planning.
Direction of work in research: Environmental, Social priorities, Population.
Direction of work in planning: Social, Urban, Regional, Environmental.
Methods used: Extrapolation techniques, Contextual mapping, Expert panels, Historical
analogy, Individual expert forecasting.
Time range of work: 5 - 25 years.
Source of support for work (%): IO International agencies, IO Foundations, 20 Local
government, 20 Foreign governments, 40 National government.
Work done for (%): IO International agencies, IO Foundations, 20 Local government.
20 Foreign governments, 40 National government.
Number of persons working at professional level: I2 Full time.   *(173)*

249. Metal Box

37 Baker St, London, W1A 1AN, UK.
Type of centre: Industry. *Concerned with long-term futures.*
Time allocated (%): Less than IO.
Additional information: Long-range planning is done as part of the corporate planning
unit, or as part of R & D. The corporate planning unit is concerned with the future
of the markets. Corporate research and development forecasts future trends, is concerned
with finding new technologies, and only to the extent that it must know what technology
the company requires for the future.   *(206)*

250. Michigan State University
College of Agriculture and Natural Resources, Department of Agricultural Economics,
Faculty Member, John N. Ferris, East Lansing, Mi, 48823, USA.
Type of centre: Academic. **Concerned with long-term futures.**
Time allocated (%): 20.
Methods used: I Statistical models, 2 Simulation, 3 Extrapolation techniques,
4 Individual expert forecasting, 5 Delphin Techniques.
Time range of work: IO - 25 years.
Source of support for work (%): 60 Local government, 20 National government,
IO International agencies, IO Private business.
Work done for (%): 5 Local government, 2 National government, 2 International
agencies.
Number of persons working at professional level: IO Part time.   *(437)*

251. Michigan State University
Office of Medical Education, Research and Development, Professor of Medical Education,
Robert C. Brictson, A206 East Fee Hall, East Lansing, Mi, 48824, USA.
Type of centre: Academic. **Concerned with long-term futures.**
Time allocated (%): 40.
Direction of work in forecasting: I Social, 2 Educational, 3 Resources, 4 Population,
5 Market.
Direction of work in research: I Social priorities, 2 Policy research, 3 Social impacts
of technology, 4 Alternative futures.
Direction of work in planning: I Educational, 2 Technological, 3 Social, 4 Urban.
Methods used: I Simulation. 2 Individual expert forecasting, 3 Expert panels,
4 Brainstorming, 5 Statistical models, 6 Scenario building, 7 Delphi techniques.
Time range of work: 5 - 25 years.
Source of support for work (%): 50 Local government, 50 National government.
Work done for (%): 40 Medicine and Education.   *(438)*
Number of persons working at professional level: 20 Full time.

252. Microfutures Group, Inc
President, Brian Quickstad, 200 Park Ave, Suite 300 East, New York, NY 10017, USA.
Type of centre: Commission/advisory group. **Concerned with long-term futures.**
Time allocated (%): 50.
Direction of work in forecasting: I Educational, 2 Market, 3 Resources.
Direction of work in research: I Policy research, 2 Alternative futures, 3 Value systems,
4 Resource utilization, 5 Social impacts of technology, 6 The individual in the future.
Direction of work in planning: I Urban, 2 Educational, 3 Organizational/institutional,
4 Corporate.
Methods used: I Contextual mapping, 2 Individual expert forecasting, 3 Probabilistic
forecasting.
Time range of work: IO - 25 years.
Source of support for work (%): 45 Private business, 55 National government.
Work done for (%): IO Private business, 30 National government, 60 Own projects.
Number of persons working at professional level: I Full time, 20 Part time.   *(375)*

253. Mineral Economics Research Division, Energy, Mines and Resources
Chief, Dr Peter Andrews, 588 Booth St, Ottowa H1A DE4, Canada.
Type of centre: National government.
Concerned with long-term futures.

Time allocated (%): 3O.
Methods used: 2 Statistical models, 3 Delphi techniques, 4 Probabilistic forecasting, 5 Expert panels, 6 Historical analogy.
Time range of work: IO - 25 years.
Source of support for work:(%): IOO National government.
Work done for (%): IOO National government.
Number of persons working at professional level: 2 Part time, 2 Full time.   *(362)*

254. Ministero del Bilancio e della Programmazione Economica
Via XX Settembre 97, Rome, Italy.
Type of centre: National government.
Concerned with long-term futures.
Time allocated (%): 2O.
Direction of work in forecasting: Economic, Social, Cultural, Educational, Scientific, Environmental, Manpower, Resources, Population.
Direction of work in planning: Social Urban, Regional, Educational, Economic, Environmental, Labour, Resources.
Methods used: Probabilistic forecasting, Causal modelling, Delphi techniques, Extrapolation techniques.
Time range of work: 5 - 25 years.   *(403)*

255. Ministry of Church and Education
Dept of Research and Planning, Oslo DEP, Norway.
Type of centre: National government. *Concerned with long-term futures.*
Concerned with long-term futures.
Time allocated (%): 3O.
Direction of work in forecasting: Social, Cultural, Educational.
Direction of work in research: Alternative futures, Resource utilization, Policy research.
Direction of work in planning: Social, Educational.
Methods used: Gaming, Scenario building, Extrapolation techniques, Contextual mapping, Statistical models, Operational models, Simulation, Causal modelling.
Time range of work: 5 - 25 years.
Source of support for work (%): IOO National government.
Work done for (%): IOO National government.
Number of persons working at professional level: 6 Full time.   *(291)*

256. Ministry of Communications
Kaisaniemenkatu IO, OO1OO Helsinki 1O, Finland.
Type of centre: National government. *Concerned with long-term futures.*
Time allocated (%): 5O.
Direction of work in forecasting: Technological.
Direction of work in research: Social impacts of technology.
Direction of work in planning: Technological.
Methods used: Statistical models.
Time range of work: 5 - 25 years.
Source of support for work (%): IOO National government.
Work done for (%): 15 International agencies, 85 National government.
Number of persons working at professional level: 9 Full time.   *(371)*

257. Ministry of Finance

Planning Division, Oslo-DEP, Oslo 1, Norway.
Type of centre: National government.
Primarily engaged in: Long-range planning.
Direction of work in forecasting: I Economic, 2 Manpower, 3 Resources, 4 Population,
5 Environmental, 6 Educational.
Direction of work in research: Alternative.futures, Environmental, Social priorities,
Population.
Direction of work in planning: Regional, Economic, Environmental, Manpower, Social systems.
Methods used: I Statistical models, I Operational techniques.
Time range of work: 5 - 25 years.
Source of support for work (%): IOO National government.
Number of persons working at professional level: 13 Full time.   *(94)*

258. Ministry of Housing and Physical Planning

Bostadsdepartementet, Fack, S-1O3 2O Stockholm 16, Sweden.
Type of centre: National government.
Primarily engaged in: Long-range planning.
Direction of work in planning: I Environmental, 2 Regional, 3 Resources.
Methods used: Probabilistic forecasting, Individual expert forecasting, Cross impact
analysis, Extrapolation techniques, Contextual mapping, Expert panels.
Time range of work: IO - beyond year 2OOO.
Source of support for work (%): IOO National government.
Work done for (%): IOO National government.
Number of persons working at professional level: I2 Part time.   *(118)*

259. Ministry of Industry, Mines, and Tourism

PO Box 451, Mbabane, Swaziland.
Type of centre: National government.
Concerned with long-term futures.
Time allocated (%): 4O.
Direction of work in forecasting: I Economic, 2 Social.
Methods used: I Individual expert forecasting.
Time range of work: 5 - IO years.
Source of support for work (%): IOO National government.
Work done for (%): 3O National government, 7O Private business.
Number of persons working at professional level: 9 Full time.   *(40)*

26O. Ministry of Justice Prison Administration

International Penal and Penitentiary Foundation, Koninginnegracht 19, The Hague,
The Netherlands.
Type of centre: Industry.
Concerned with long-term futures.
Direction of work in forecasting: Social, Cultural.
Direction of work in research: Value systems.
Methods used: Expert panels, Individual expert forecasting.
Time range of work: 5 - IO years.   *(43)*

261. Ministry of Transport and Public Works

Study Dept, Plemanweg 1, The Hague, The Netherlands.
Type of centre: National government.
Concerned with long-term futures.
Methods used: Delphi techniques, Scenario building, Extrapolation techniques, Brainstorming, Statistical models, Relevance trees, Historical analogy, Operational models, Simulation, Causal modelling.
Time range of work: 5 - 25 years.
Source of support for work (%): IOO National government.
Work done for (%): 98 National government, 2 Foundations,.
Number of persons working at professional level: 7 Full time.
Additional information: The work is broad in scope, working in interministerial groups and groups of own Ministry on a high level, in preparing advice and reports for the Ministry, the Ministerial Board, or general groups, concerning general socio-economic or scientific problems.   *(443)*

262. Ministry of Treasury Economics and Intergovernmental Affairs

Office of Economic Policy, Laszlo Bodnar, Province of Ontario, Toronto, Canada.
Type of centre: Provincial government policy planning branch.
Concerned with long-term futures.
Time allocated (%): 5O.
Direction of work in forecasting: Economic, Social, Market, Manpower, Resources, Population.
Direction of work in research: Manpower, Resource utilization, Policy research, Population.
Direction of work in planning: Social, Urban, Regional, Economic, Political, Resources.
Methods used: I Statistical models, 2 Probabilistic forecasting, 3 Scenario building, 4 Simulation, 5 Individual expert forecasting.
Time range of work: IO - 25 years.
Source of support for work (%): IOO Provincial government.
Work done for (%): IOO Provincial government.
Number of persons working at professional level: I4 Full time.   *(32O)*

263. The Mitre Corporation

Senior Vice President, Charles Zraket, 182O Dolley Madison Blvd, McLean, Va 221O1, USA.
Type of centre: Independent research.
Concerned with long-term futures.
Time allocated (%): 4O.
Direction of work in research: I Environmental, 2 Resource utilization.
Direction of work in planning: I Technological, 2 Environmental, 3 Resources.
Methods used: I Cross impact analysis, 2 Brainstorming, 3 Individual expert forecasting.
Time range of work: IO - 25 years.
Source of support for work (%): IOO National government.
Work done for (%): 4O National government.
Number of persons working at professional level: 2OO Full time.   *(193)*

264. Monsanto Company

J. Kenneth Craver, 8OO N. Lindbergh Blvd, St Louis, Mo 63166, USA.
Type of centre: Industry.
Primarily engaged in: Both futures studies and long-range planning.
Direction of work in forecasting: I Technological, I Economic, I Social, 2 Scientific,

2 Environmental , 2 Legislative, 2 Regulatory, 3 Cultural.
Direction of work in research: I Social impacts of technology, I Futures methodology,
2 Alternative futures, 2 Social priorities, 3 Resource utilization.
Direction of work in planning: I Corporate, 2 Technological.
Methods used: I Cross impact analysis, I Statistical models, I Individual expert
forecasting, 2 Probabilistic forecasting, 2 Extrapolation techniques, 2 Expert panels,
2 Simulation.
Time range of work: 5 - IO years.
Source of support for work (%): IOO Private business.
Work done for (%): IOO Private business.
Number of persons working at professional level: 5 Full time.   *(268)*

265. Motivation Programmers, Inc
Research Director, Betty Demby, 77O Lexington Ave, New York, NY 1OO21, USA.
Type of centre: Independent research.
Concerned with long-term futures.
Time allocated (%): IO.
Methods used: I Expert panels, 2 Probabilistic forecasting, 2 Delphi techniques,
4 Scenario building, 5 Individual expert forecasting, 6 Simulation, 7 Brainstorming,
8 Statistical models.
Time range of work: 5 - IO years.
Source of support for work (%): IOO Private business.
Work done for (%): IOO Private business.
Number of persons working at professional level: 3 Full time, 5 Part time.
Additional information: The organization is concerned with new product developments,
communications and entertainment.   *(365)*

266. Nagoya Group for Future Science
School of Economics, Nagoya University, Furo-cho, Chikusa-ku, Nagoya, Japan.
Type of centre: Membership society.
Primarily engaged in: Both futures studies and long-range planning.
Time range of work: 5 - beyond year 2OOO.   *(462)*

267. Nathaniel Lichfield and Associates
Economic, Planning, Development and Transportation Consultants, I3 Chalcot Gardens,
Englands Lane, London NW3 4YB, UK.
Type of centre: International professional organization.
Primarily engaged in: Both futures studies and long-range planning.
Direction of work in forecasting: Economic, Social, Market, Environmental, Resources,
Population.
Direction of work in research: Social impacts of technology, Alternative futures,
Environmental, Resource utilization, Value systems, Social priorities, Policy research,
Population, The individual in the future, The family in the future, Futures methodology.
Direction of work in planning: Technological, Social, Urban, Regional, Economic,
Corporate, Environmental, Labour, Resources.
Methods used: Probabilistic forecasting, Social cost benefit analysis, Delphi techniques,
Cross impact analysis, Scenario building, Extrapolation techniques, Brainstorming,
Statistical models, Expert panels, Network analysis, Historical analogy, Operational
models, Individual expert forecasting, Simulation, Causal modelling.
Time range of work: 5 - 25 years.
Source of support for work (%): 5 Foundations, 5 Voluntary associations, I5 Inter-

national agencies, 25 Local government, 25 National government, 25 Private business.
Work done for (%):   5 Foundations, 5 Voluntary associations, I5 International agencies,
25 Local government, 25 National government, 25 Private business.
Number of persons working at professional level: IO Part time, IO Full time.   *(87)*

268. National Defence Research Institute

Försvarets Forskningsanstalt, S-IO4 5O Stockholm, Sweden.
Type of centre: National government.
Concerned with long-term futures.
Time allocated (%):   Less than IO.
Direction of work in forecasting: Technological, Economic, Social, Cultural, Scientific,
Environmental, Military, Manpower, Resources, Population.
Direction of work in research: Social impacts of technology, Alternative futures,
Policy research, Futures methodology.
Direction of work in planning: Scientific, Military.
Methods used: Delphi techniques, Causal modelling, Scenario building, Gaming,
Contextual mapping, Extrapolation techniques, Relevance trees, Brainstorming, Historical
analogy, Individual expert forecasting.
Time range of work: IO - 25 years.
Source of support for work (%):   IOO National government.
Work done for (%):   IOO National government.
Number of persons working at professional level: 4 Part time, 6 Full time.
Additional information: The organization focuses on changes in international power
balance and methods of coping with threats to national security. One entire department
of the Institute (9O Professionals including those above) is concerned with defence
planning in the short to medium range (5 - 25 years).   *(134)*

269. National Planning Association

Mark C. Kendally, 1666 Connecticut Ave, Washington DC 2OOO9, USA.
Type of centre: Independent research.
Concerned with long-term futures,
Direction of work in forecasting: I Economic, 2 Population, 3 Manpower.
Direction of work in research: I Consumer affairs, 2 Manpower.
Methods used: I Econometric modelling, 2 Statistical models, 2 Causal modelling,
3 Individual expert forecasting.
Time range of work: I - 25 years.
Source of support for work (%):   5 Local government, 5 Private business, 6O National
government, 3O Foundations.
Work done for (%):   5 National government, 5 Private business, 6O Local government,
3O Foundations.
Number of persons working at professional level: 5O Full time.   *(324)*

270. National Research Council

Laugavegur 13, Reykjavik, Iceland.
Type of centre: National Government.
Concerned with long-term futures.
Time allocated (%):   IO.
Methods used: I Expert panels, 2 Brainstorming, 3 Historical analogy.
Time range of work: 5 - IO years.
Source of support for work (%):   IOO National government.
Work done for (%):   IOO National government.
Number of persons working at professional level: I Full time, 26 Part time.   *(41)*

271. National Research Council of Canada
Environmental Secretariat, Ottawa, KIA OR6, Canada.
Type of centre: National government.
Concerned with long-term futures.
Time allocated (%): 30.
Methods used: I Expert panels, 2 Brainstorming, 3 Delphi techniques.
Time range of work: 5 - IO years.
Source of support for work (%): IOO National government.
Work done for (%): IOO All sectors.
Number of persons working at professional level: 25 Full time, 25O Part time. *(7)*

272. National Research Council of Canada.
Marine Dynamics and Ship Laboratory, Head, S.T. Mathews, Building M-22, Montreal
Road Labs, Ottawa, K1A OR6, Canada.
Type of centre: National government.
Concerned with long-term futures.
Time allocated (%): IO.
Methods used: I Individual expert forecasting, 2 Probabilistic forecasting.
Time range of work: 5 - IO years.
Source of support for work (%): IOO National government.
Number of persons working at professional level: 8 Part time. *(390)*

273. Netherlands Central Bureau of Statistics
Prinses Beatrixlaan 428, Voorburg, The Netherlands.
Type of centre: National government.
Concerned with long-term futures.
Time allocated (%): Less than IO.
Methods used: I Statistical models, 2 Econometric models, 3 Extrapolation
techniques, 4 Simulation, 5 Brainstorming, 5 Expert panels.
Time range of work: 5 - beyond year 2OOO.
Source of support for work (%): IOO National government.
Number of persons working at professional level: I6 Part time. *(55)*

274. Nederlands Interuniversitair Demografisch Institut
(NIDI), Prinses Beatrixiaan, 428, Voorburg, The Netherlands.
Type of centre: Academic/national government.
Concerned with long-term futures.
Time allocated (%): 4O.
Direction of work in forecasting: Economic, Educational, Population.
Direction of work in research: Policy research, Population.
Direction of work in planning: Labour.
Methods used: I Extrapolation techniques, 2 Statistical models, 3 Brainstorming.
Time range of work: 5 - IO years.
Source of support for work (%): 5O National government, 5O Foundations.
Work done for (%): I5 International agencies, I5 Private business, 3O National
government, 4O Foundations.
Number of persons working at professional level: 5 Full time. *(415)*

275. Neue Helvetische Gesellschaft

Sekretariat, Alpenstr 26, CH - 3006 Bern Switzerland.
Type of centre: National government.
Primarily engaged in: Futures studies.
Direction of work in forecasting: Technological, Economic, Social, Cultural, Educational, Scientific, Environmental, Resources, Population.
Methods used: Probabilistic forecasting, Historical analogy, Statistical models, Expert panels.
Time range of work: 10 - 25 years.
Source of support for work (%): 50 Private business, 50 Voluntary associations.   *(374)*

Newark College of English
See: Centre for Technology Assessment.

276. Newcastle Upon Tyne University

Department of Town and Country Planning, Head, Paul Brenikov, The University, Newcastle Upon Tyne NE1 7RO, UK.
Type of centre: Academic/independent research.
Primarily engaged in: Long-range planning.
Direction of work in forecasting: 1 Environmental, 2 Resources, 3 Population, 4 Economic, 5 Social.
Direction of work in research: 1 Environmental, 2 Alternative futures, 3 Population, 4 Futures methodology.
Direction of work in planning: 1 Urban, 1 Regional, 2 Environmental.
Methods used: Can make use of virtually all methods (see Directory guide) as and when teaching and research projects warrant their use.
Time range of work: 5 - 25 years.
Source of support for work (%): 10 Foundations, 20 Local government, 70 National government.
Work done for (%): 50 Local government, 50 National government.
Number of persons working at professional level: 17 Full time   *(137)*

277. New York Centre of World Game Studies

345 East 69th St, Apt 119, New York, NY 10021, USA.
Type of centre: Independent research.
Primarily engaged in: Futures studies.
Direction of work in forecasting: 1 Social, 1 Cultural, 1 Educational, 2 Technological, 2 Scientific, 3 Resources.
Direction of work in research: 1 Alternative futures, 1 Resource utilization, 2 Social impacts of technology, 3 Social priorities, 2 Futures methodology, 3 Value systems.
Direction of work in planning: Scientific, Technological, Social, Educational, Resources.
Methods used: 1 Scenario building, 1 Brainstorming, 2 Gaming, 3 Simulation.
Time range of work: 5 - 25 years.
Source of support for work (%): 100 Voluntary associations.
Work done for (%): 100 Voluntary associations.
Number of persons working at professional level: 1 Full time, 10 Part time.   *(428)*

278. Norwegian Productivity Institute

PO Box 8401, Hammersborg, Oslo 1, Norway.
Type of centre: National semi-governmental. *Concerned with long-term futures.*
Time allocated (%): 20.

Methods used: I Extrapolation techniques, 2 Expert panels, 3 Statistical models, 4 Brainstorming.
Time range of work: 5 - 25 years.
Source of support for work (%): IO Foundations, IO Voluntary associations, 3O National government, 5O Private business.
Work done for (%): IO Foundations, IO Voluntary associations, 3O National government, 5O Private business.
Number of persons working at professional level: 5 Part time.   *(299)*

279. Norwegian Society for Future Studies (SEFREM)

Director, O.T. Grande, PO Box 84O1, Hammersborg, Oslo 1, Norway.
Type of centre: Membership society. *Concerned with long-term futures.*
Primarily engaged in: Both futures studies and long-range planning.
Direction of work in research: I Alternative futures, 2 Futures methodology, 3 Resource utilization, 4 Social priorities, 5 Policy research, 6 Population, 7 Environmental, 8 The family in the future, 9 The individual in the future, 1O Value systems, 11, Manpower, 12 Social impacts of technology.
Direction of work in planning: I Regional, 2 Resources, 3 Environmental, 4 Social, 5 Scientific, 6 Urban, 7 Technological, 8 Economic, 9 Educational, 1O Political, 11 Corporate, 12 Labour.
Methods used: I Cross impact analysis, 2 Scenario building, 3 Statistical models, 4 Network analysis, 5 Expert panels, 6 Delphi techniques, 7 Probabilistic forecasting.
Time range of work: 5 - beyond year 2OOO.
Source of support for work (%): IO International agencies, IO Foundations, I5 Local government, 2O Private business, 2O Voluntary associations, 25 National government.
Work done for (%): IO International agencies, IO Foundations, I2 Local government, 2O Private business, 2O Voluntary associations, 25 National government.
Number of persons working at professional level: I Full time, IO Part time.   *(266)*

28O. Nottingham University

School of Agriculture, Director, Dr J.E. Bessel, Sutton Bonnington, Loughborough, Leics LE12 5RD, UK.
Type of centre: Academic. *Concerned with long-term futures.*
Time allocated (%): 5O.
Direction of work in forecasting: I Economic, 2 Population.
Direction of work in planning: I Economic.
Methods used: I Statistical models, 2 Causal modelling, 3 Extrapolation techniques, 4 Probabilistic forecasting.
Time range of work: 5 - IO years.
Source of support for work (%): IOO National government.
Work done for (%): IOO National government.
Number of persons working at professional level: 2 Part time, 2 Full time.   *(295)*

281. NTL Institute for Applied Behavioural Science

Professional Development Division, PO Box 9155, Rosslyn Station, Va 222O9, USA.
Type of centre: Adult education.
Concerned with long-term futures.
Time allocated (%): Less than IO.
Direction of work in forecasting: I Social, 2 Educational.
Direction of work in research: I Value systems, 2 The individual in the future,

3 The family in the future.
Direction of work in planning: I Social, 2 Educational.
Methods used: I Brainstorming, 2 Scenario building, 3 Individual expert forecasting.
Time range of work: 5 - IO years.
Number of persons working at professional level: I Full time.   *(243)*

O 282. Occidental Petroleum Corp
Director of Planning, 10889 Wilshire Blvd, Los Angeles, Ca 80024, USA.
Type of centre: Business.
Concerned with long-term futures.
Direction of work in forecasting: I Market, I Resources, 3 Technological, 4 Economic.
Direction of work in research: Manpower.
Direction of work in planning: I Corporate, 2 Resources, 3 Economic.
Methods used: I Scenario building, 2 Expert panels, 3 Extrapolation techniques.
Time range of work: 5 - IO years.
Source of support for work (%): IOO Private business.
Work done for (%): IOO Private business.
Number of persons working at professional level: 50 Full time, IOO Part time.   *(309)*

283. OECD Development Centre
Mr Paul Marc Henry, President, 94 Rue Chardon Lagache, 75016 Paris, France.
Type of centre: International government.
Concerned with long-term futures.
Direction of work in forecasting: I Technological, I Economic, I Resources, 2 Market,
2 Educational, 2 Scientific, 2 Environmental, 2 Manpower.
Direction of work in research: I Policy research, 2 Social impacts of technology,
2 Manpower, 2 Consumer affairs, 2 Environmental, 2 Resource utilization, 2 Social
priorities, 3 Alternative futures, 3 Futures methodology.
Direction of work in planning: I Educational, I Economic, I Environmental,
2 Scientific, 2 Technological, 2 Urban, 2 Regional.
Methods used: All methods (see Directory guide).
Time range of work: 5 - 25 years.
Source of support for work (%): IOO National government.
Work done for (%): IOO National government.   *(418)*

284. Office of Health Economics
162 Regent St, London W1R DD, UK.
Type of centre: Independent research.
Concerned with long-term futures.
Time allocated (%): 40.
Direction of work in forecasting: I Social, 2 Economic, 3 Scientific, 4 Resources.
Direction of work in research: I Social priorities, 2 Resource utilization, 3 Policy
research, 4 Social impacts of technology.
Direction of work in planning: I Social, 2 Economic, 3 Political, 4 Resources.
Methods used: I Individual expert forecasting, 2 Expert panels, 3 Scenario building,
3 Extrapolation techniques, 3 Contextual mapping, 3 Brainstorming, 3 Statistical
models.
Time range of work: 5 - IO years.
Source of support for work (%): IOO Private business.
Work done for (%): 40 Private business.
Number of persons working at professional level: 3 Full time.   *(76)*

285. Office of Population Censuses and Surveys
St Catherines House, 1O Kingsway, London WC2B 6JP, UK.
Type of centre: National government. *Concerned with long-term futures.*
Time allocated (%): 5O.
Direction of work in forecasting: Population.
Direction of work in research: Population.
Methods used: Statistical models.
Time range of work: 5 - beyond year 2OOO.
Source of support for work (%): IOO National government.
Work done for (%): IOO National government.
Number of persons working at professional level: I Part time, 3 Full time.   *(261)*

286. Office of the Prime Minister
Economic Division, Auberge de Castille, Valletta, Malta.
Type of centre: National government.
Direction of work in forecasting: Economic, including manpower.
Direction of work in research: Economic.
Direction of work in planning: Economic.
Methods used: Probabilistic forecasting, Statistical models, Extrapolation techniques.
Time range of work: 5 - IO years.
Source of support for work (%): IOO National government.
Work done for (%): IOO National government.
Number of persons working at professional level: 11 Full time.   *(359)*

287. The Ontario Educational Communications Authorities
Chairman, T. Ranald Ide, 213O Yonge St, Toronto, Ontario M4S 2C1, Canada.
Type of centre: Provincial government.
Concerned with long-term futures.
Time allocated (%): Less than IO.
Direction of work in research: I The individual in the future, 2 The family in the
future, 3 Value systems, 4 Social priorities.
Direction of work in planning: I Educational, 2 Social.
Methods used: I Expert panels, 2 Individual expert forecasting, 3 Brainstorming,
4 ·Delphi techniques.
Time range of work: 5 - 25 years.
Source of support for work (%): IOO Local government.
Number of persons working at professional level: 2 Full time, 4 Part time.   *(201)*

288. The Open University
Design Group, Faculty of Technology, The Open University, Milton Keynes, UK.
Type of centre: Academic.
Concerned with long-term futures.
Time allocated (%): Less than IO.
Methods used: Gaming, Scenario building, Simulation.
Time range of work: 5 - 25 years.
Source of support for work (%): IOO National government.
Number of persons working at professional level: 5 Full time.   *(355)*

289. The Open University
Oxford Research Unit, 11-12 Bevington Rd, Oxford, UK.
Type of centre: Academic. *Concerned with long-term futures.*
Time allocated (%): 5O.

4

Direction of work in forecasting: Social, Cultural, Educational, Environmental.
Direction of work in research: I Social priorities, I The individual in the future,
2 Environmental, 2 Futures methodology, 3 Alternative futures, 3 The family in the future.
Direction of work in planning: I Social, I Environmental, 2 Educational, 3 Urban, 3 Regional.
Methods used: Community participation.
Time range of work: 5 - beyond year 2000.
Source of support for work (%): IOO National government.   *(191)*

290. Operational Research and Analysis Establishment
Chief, George Lindsey, 101 Colonel By Drive, Ottawa, K1A OK2, Canada.
Type of centre: National government.
Concerned with long-term futures.
Time allocated (%): 30.
Direction of work in forecasting: I Military, 2 Social, 3 Manpower, 4 Resources.
Direction of work in research: I Policy research, 2 Manpower, 3 Alternative futures.
Direction of work in planning: I Military, 2 Scientific, 3 Economic, 4 Environmental.
Methods used: I Statistical models, 2 Causal modelling, 3 Operational models,
4 Probabilistic forecasting, 5 Simulation, 6 Gaming, 7 Scenario building.
Time range of work: IO - 25 years.
Source of support for work (%): IOO National government.
Work done for (%): IOO National government.
Number of persons working at professional level: IO Part time, 25 Full time.   *(348)*

291. Operations Research, Inc
W. Thomas Callahan, Silver Spring Md 20910, USA.
Type of centre: Independent research.
Concerned with long-term futures.
Time allocated (%): 30.
Methods used: Probabilistic forecasting, Simulation, Delphi techniques, Gaming,
Scenario building, Extrapolation techniques, Brainstorming, Statistical models, Expert
panels, Relevance trees, Historical analogy, Operational models, Individual expert
forecasting.
Time range of work: 5 - 25 years.
Source of support for work (%): 5 Private business, IO Local government,
85 National government.
Work done for (%): 2 Private business, 3 Local government, 25 National government.
Number of persons working at professional level: I5O Full time.   *(290)*

292. Organization for Economic Co-operation and Development (OECD)
2 Rue Andre Pascal, 75016 Paris, France.
Type of centre: International government.
Concerned with long-term futures.
Time allocated (%): IO.
Methods used: I Collective long-term studies (multidisiplinary), 2 Brainstorming,
3 Statistical models, 4 Individual expert forecasting, 5 Delphi techniques, Extrapolation
techniques.
Time range of work: 5 - 25 years.
Source of support for work (%): IOO National government.
Work done for (%): IOO Common interest or member countries.   *(270)*

293. Osterreischische Gesellschaft für Zukunftspolitik
Wipplingerstr 36 - 38, A - 1010, Vienna, Austria.
Type of centre: Membership society.
Primarily engaged in: Futures studies.
Direction of work in forecasting: (Practically all areas see Directory guide).
Time range of work: 5 - 10 years.
Source of support for work (%): 5 National government, 15 Membership fees,
80 Foundations.
Work done for (%): 5 National government, 95 Public interest.
Number of persons working at professional level: 1 Part time.
Additional information: This organization will be running the symposium 'Austria 1985'.

(388)

294. Osterreischische Studiengesellschaft für Atomenergie GMbH
A-1082 Wien, Lenaugasse 10, Austria.
Type of centre: Independent research.
Concerned with long-term futures.
Time allocated (%): Less than 10.
Methods used: Brainstorming, Expert panels.
Time range of work: 5 - 10 years.
Source of support for work (%): 25 Private business, 75 National government.
Work done for (%): 100 National government.
Number of persons working at professional level: 3 Part time.

(400)

Overseas Development Group
See: University of East Anglia.

295. Pacific Asian Affairs Council
Director, Pacific House, 2004 University Ave, Honolulu, Hi 96822, USA.
Type of centre: Academic.
Concerned with long-term futures.
Time allocated (%): 10.
Time range of work: 5 - 10 years.
Source of support for work (%): 34 Foundations, 66 Local government.
Number of persons working at professional level: 1 Part time.

(237)

296. Parliamentary Group for World Government (PGWG)
House of Commons, London SW1, UK.
Type of centre: All party group of MPs and associate members.
Concerned with long-term futures.
Direction of work in planning: 1 Political, 2 Educational, 3 Functional.
Time range of work: 10 - 25 years.
Source of support for work (%): 80 Foundations.
Work done for (%): 100 Common Heritage of mankind.
Number of persons working at professional level: 3 Full time.

(338)

297. Participation Publishers
Robert Theobold, PO Box 1531 Wickenburg, Az 85358, USA.
Type of centre: Business.
Primarily engaged in: Futures studies.
Methods used: Individual expert forecasting.
Time range of work: 5 - 25 years.
Number of persons working at professional level: 3 Full time.

(278)

298. Patterns and Systems International, Inc
703 Knoll Drive, San Carlos, Ca 94070, USA.
Type of centre: Non-profit research corporation.
Primarily engaged in: Both futures studies and long-range planning.
Direction of work in forecasting: Technological, Economic, Social, Cultural, Market,
Educational, Scientific, Environmental, Military, Manpower, Resources, Population,
Composite.
Direction of work in research: l Policy research, 2 Alternative futures, 2 Futures
methodology.
Direction of work in planning: l Educational, l Corporate, l Military.
Methods used: l Scenario building, 2 Morphological, iterative study of field coherence.
3 Brainstorming.
Time range of work: 10 - 25 years.
Source of support for work (%): 20 Local government, 20 Private business,
60 National government.
Work done for (%): 20 Local government, 20 Private business, 60 National
government.
Number of persons working at professional level: l Full time, 3 Part time.   *(53)*

299. Philips Research Laboratories
Future Research Group, Eindhoven, The Netherlands.
Type of centre: Industry.
Primarily engaged in: Futures studies.
Direction of work in forecasting: Technological, Economic, Social.
Direction of work in research: Social impacts of technology, Consumer affairs,
Resource utilization, Value systems.
Direction of work in planning: l Regional, 2 Technological.
Methods used: Delphi techniques, Cross impact analysis, Scenario building, Brainstorming,
Expert panels.
Time range of work: 10 - 25 years.
Source of support for work (%): 100 Private business.
Work done for (%): 30 Foundations, 70 Private business.
Number of persons working at professional level: 7 Full time.   *(218)*

300. N.V. Philips' Gloeilampenfabrieken
Department CV and P, Eindhoven, The Netherlands.
Type of centre: Industry.
Methods used: Probabilistic forecasting, Extrapolation techniques, Brainstorming,
Statistical models, Expert panels, Historical analogy, Operational models, Individual
expert forecasting, Causal modelling, Simulation.
Time range of work: 10 - 25 years.   *(304)*

301. Plan Europe 2000
European Cultural Foundation, Amsterdam 1007, Jan Van 5, Goyenkadf, The Netherlands.
Type of centre: Independent research.
Primarily engaged in: Futures studies.
Direction of work in forecasting: Social, Cultural, Educational, Scientific,
Environmental.
Direction of work in research: Alternative futures, Environmental, Value Systems,
Policy research, The individual in the future, Futures methodology, The family in the
future.

Direction of work in planning: Scientific, Urban, Regional, Educational, Environmental, Resources.
Methods used: Brainstorming, Expert panels, Historical analogy, Operational models, Individual expert forecasting.
Time range of work: IO - beyond year 2000.
Source of support for work (%): 5 Local government, 5 National government, 5 International agencies, 5 Voluntary associations, 30 Foundations, 60 Private business.
Work done for (%): 5 Local government, 5 National government, 5 International agencies, 5 Voluntary associations, 30 Foundations, 60 Private business.
Number of persons working at professional level: 3 - 5 Full time, 5 - IO Part time. *(197)*

302. Planning Commission of the Ministers' Council
Deputy Chairman, Prof Pajestka, OO 507 Warsaw, Plac Irzech Krzyzy 3/5, Poland.
Type of centre: National government.
Concerned with long-term futures.
Time allocated (%): IO.
Direction of work in forecasting: All areas except military (see Directory Guide).
Direction of work in research: All areas (see Directory guide).
Direction of work in planning: All areas except corporate and military (see Directory Guide).
Methods used: I Scenario building, 2 Network analysis, 3 Probabilistic forecasting, 4 Cross impact analysis, 5 Statistical models, 6 Operational models.
Time range of work: 5 - beyond year 2000.
Source of support for work (%): IOO National government.
Work done for (%): IO International agencies, 45 Local government, 45 National government.
Number of persons working at professional level: 80 Full time. *(326)*

303. Planning Dynamics, Inc
Chairman, Edward J. Green, Babb Bldg, 850 Ridge Ave, Pittsburgh Pa 15212, USA.
Type of centre: Planning consultant.
Primarily engaged in: Long-range planning.
Direction of work in forecasting: Economic, Educational.
Direction of work in research: Resource utilization, Policy research.
Direction of work in planning: Scientific, Educational, Economic, Corporate.
Methods used: Probabilistic forecasting, Operational models, Scenario building.
Time range of work: 5 - IO years.
Source of support for work (%): IO National government, 20 Foundations, 30 Voluntary associations, 50 Private business.
Work done for (%): IO National government, 30 Voluntary associations, 50 Private business.
Number of persons working at professional level: 5 Full time. *(283)*

304. Planning and Forecasting Consultants
President, Dale W. Steffes, 863 Frostwood, Houston, Tx 77024, USA.
Type of centre: Business.
Primarily engaged in: Both futures studies and long-range planning.
Direction of work in forecasting: Technological, Economic, Social, Resources, Political.
Direction of work in planning: Corporate.

Methods used: I Scenario building, 2 Cross impact analysis, 2 Individual expert forecasting, 2 Monitoring.
Time range of work: IO - 25 years.
Source of support for work (%): IOO Private business.
Work done for (%): IOO Private business.
Number of persons working at professional level: I Part time.   *(421)*

305. Plurilog
37, Ave Adrien, Ledoux F - 77220 Gretzarmainwilliers, France.
Type of centre: Independent research/international voluntary association membership society.
Methods used: I Probabilistic forecasting, 2 Extrapolation techniques, 3 Delphi techniques, 4 Expert panels, 5 Historical analogy.
Time range of work: IO - 25 years.
Number of persons working at professional level: 8 Part time.   *(350)*

306. Polish Academy of Sciences
Institute of Philosophy and Sociology, Division of Social Prognosis, Nowy Swiat 72, OO - 330 Warsaw, Poland.
Type of centre: Academic.
Primarily engaged in: Futures studies.
Direction of work in forecasting: I Cultural, 2 Social.
Direction of work in research: I Life styles in the future, 2 Futures methodology, 3 Value systems, 4 The individual in the future, 5 The family in the future, 6 Social priorities, 7 Consumer affairs, 8 Social impacts of technology.
Direction of work in planning: I Educational, 2 Social.
Methods used: I Individual expert forecasting, 2 Extrapolation techniques, 3 Simulation, 4 Scenario building.
Time range of work: IO - 25 years.
Source of support for work (%): IOO National government.
Work done for (%): 3O Self, 7O National government.
Number of persons working at professional level: 3 Part time, I2 Full time.   *(434)*

307. Polish Academy of Science
Research and Prognostics Committee, Poland of 2OOO, Palac Kultury i Nauki, Warsaw. Poland.
Type of centre: Academic.
Primarily engaged in: Both futures studies and long-range planning.
Direction of work in forecasting: I Social, 2 Cultural, 3 Population, 4 Educational, 5 Resources, 6 Economic, 7 Manpower.
Direction of work in research: All areas (see Directory guide).
Direction of work in planning: Social.
Methods used: Probabilistic forecasting, Simulation, Scenario building, Extrapolation techniques, Expert panels, Individual expert forecasting.
Time range of work: IO - 25 years.   *(374)*

308. Political and Economic Planning (PEP)
Director, John Pinder, 12 Upper Belgrave St, London, SW1, UK.
Type of centre: Independent research.
Concerned with long-term futures.
Time allocated (%): Less than IO.

Methods used: Thinking about findings from empirical research that show new trends in society.
Time range of work: 5 - IO years.
Source of support for work (%): 20 Private business, 3O National government, 5O Foundations.
Number of persons working at professional level: I2 Full time.   *(9)*

3O9. Portland State University
Futures Research Institute, Systems Science PH-O Program, Harold A. Linstone, PO Box 751, Portland, Or 972O7, USA.
Type of centre: Academic.
Primarily engaged in: Both futures studies and long-range planning.
Direction of work in forecasting: I Technological, 2 Economic, 3 Social.
Direction of work in research: I Futures methodology, 2 Alternative futures, 3 Social impacts of technology.
Direction of work in planning: I Regional, 2 Environmental.
Methods used: All methods (see Directory guide).
Time range of work: 5 - 25 years.
Source of support for work (%): IO Private business, IO Foundations, 8O Government.
Work done for (%): IO Private business, IO Foundations, 8O Government.
Number of persons working at professional level: 5 Part time.   *(215)*

31O. Post Office Telecommunications
Long-Range Studies Division (TSS 6.1), 2O7 Old St, London, EC1, UK.
Type of centre: Business.
Primarily engaged in: Both futures studies and long-range planning.
Direction of work in forecasting: I Economic, 2 Market, 3 Social, 4 Resources, 5 Technological.
Direction of work in research: I Policy research, 2 Social impacts of technology, 3 Alternative futures, 4 Resource utilization, 5 Environmental.
Direction of work in planning: I Corporate, 2 Economic, 3 Environmental, 4 Urban, 5 Technological.
Methods used: I Causal modelling, 2 Scenario building, 3 Relevance trees, 4 Expert panels, 5 Statistical models, 6 Delphi techniques.
Time range of work: IO - 25 years.
Source of support for work (%): IOO Internal Funding.
Work done for (%): IOO Own Organization.
Number of persons working at professional level: 25 Full time.
Additional information: Work focus: Telecommunications planning including demand studies, technology assessment and analysis of economic, social, and environmental impact of innovations --- e.g. impact of telecommunications on energy saving, office location, urban and regional planning. An 'Intelligence Information Service' is provided on a subscription basis, and is available for United Kingdom business and government organizations.   *(289)*

311. Prognos AG
CH - 4O11 Basel, Viaduktstr 65, Switzerland.
Type of centre: Independent research.
Primarily engaged in: Both futures studies and long-range planning.
Direction of work in forecasting: I Economic, 2 Market, 3 Social, 4 Educational, 5 Environmental, 6 Technological.

Direction of work in research: I Consumer affairs, 2 Social impacts of technology, 3 Environmental, 4 Population, 5 Futures methodology.
Direction of work in planning: I Corporate, 2 Urban, 3 Regional, 4 Economic, 5 Educational,.
Methods used: I Individual expert forecasting, 2 Extrapolation techniques, 3 Scenario building, 4 Causal modelling, 5 Simulation, 6 Probabilistic forecasting, 7 Delphi techniques, 8 Brainstorming, 9 Statistical models.
Time range of work: IO - beyond year 2OOO.
Source of support for work (%): I5 Local government, I5 National government, 7O Private business.
Work done for (%): I5 Local government, I5 National government, 7O Private business.
Number of persons working at professional level: 75 Full time.   *(296)*

312. Programmes Analysis Unit (PAU)

Dr P.M.S. Jones, Director, Chilton, Didcot, Oxon, OX11 ORF, UK.
Type of centre: National government.
Primarily engaged in: Both futures studies and long-range planning.
Direction of work in forecasting: I Technological, Economic, Market, 2 Social, Environmental, Resources, 3 Manpower.
Direction of work in research: I Social impacts of technology, Environmental, Resources utilization, Policy research, 2 Value systems, Futures methodology.
Direction of work in planning: Technological.
Methods used: Probabilistic forecasting, Delphi techniques, Cross impact analysis, Scenario building, Extrapolation techniques, Brainstorming, Statistical models, Expert panels, Relevance trees, Network analysis, Historical analogy, Operational models, Individual expert forecasting, Simulation Causal modelling, Techno-economic assessment.
Time range of work: IO - 25 years.
Source of support for work (%): IOO National government.
Work done for (%): IOO National government.
Number of persons working at professional level: 3O Full time.   *(192)*

313. Puget Sound Governmental Conference

Director of Research, Robert L. Shindler, 216 First Ave South, Seattle, Wa 98IO4, USA.
Type of centre: Commission/advisory group.
Primarily engaged in: Long-range planning.
Direction of work in forecasting: I Economic, 2 Population, 3 Urban growth (land use).
Direction of work in research: I Alternative futures, 2 Population, 3 Policy research.
Direction of work in planning: I Urban, 2 Regional, 3 Environmental.
Methods used: I Statistical models, 2 Individual expert forecasting, 3 Scenario building.
Time range of work: IO - 25 years.
Source of support for work (%): 25 Local government, 75 National government.
Work done for (%): 4O Local government, 6O National government.
Number of persons working at professional level: 21 Full time.   *(59)*

314. Pugwash Conference on Science and World Affairs

Secretary General, B.T. Feld, 9 Great Russell Mansions, 6O Great Russell St, London WC1, UK.
Type of centre: International non-government.
Concerned with long-term futures.
Time allocated (%): 4O.
Methods used: Expert panels.

Time range of work: 5 - IO years.
Source of support for work (%): 5O Foundations, 5O Voluntary associations.
Work done for (%): 7O International agencies.
Number of persons working at professional level: I Full time, 2 Part time.   *(321)*

315. Pulp and Paper Research Institute of Canada
Economics and Planning Section, Head, Dr K.M. Thompson, 57O St, John's Blvd,
Pointe Claire, PQ, H9R 3T9 Canada.
Type of centre: Co-operative industrial research.
Concerned with long-term futures.
Time allocated (%): Less than IO.
Methods used: I Delphi techniques, 2 Extrapolation techniques, 3 Relevance trees.
Time range of work: 5 - 25 years.
Source of support for work (%): 3O National government, 7O Private business.
Work done for (%): IOO Private business.
Number of persons working at professional level: 3 Part time.   *(313)*

316. Radio Corporation of America (RCA)
Corporate Strategy Development, Dave Wetherill, Room 5O6O, 3O Rockefeller Plaza,
New York, NY 1OO2O, USA.
Type of centre: Business.
Primarily engaged in: Long-range planning.
Direction of work in forecasting: Economic.
Direction of work in planning: Corporate.
Methods used: I Extrapolation techniques, 2 Scenario building, 3 Statistical models,
4 Expert panels.
Time range of work: 5 - IO years.
Source of support for work (%): IOO Private business.
Work done for (%): IOO Private business.
Number of persons working at professional level: 7 Full time.   *(100)*

317. Reading University
Department of Geography, Urban System Research Unit, Peter Hall, Whiteknights
Reading RG6 2AF, UK.
Type of centre: Academic. *Concerned with long-term futures.*
Time allocated (%): Less than IO.
Methods used: Operational models.
Time range of work: 5 - IO years.
Source of support for work (%): IOO Foundations.
Work done for (%): IOO Pure research.
Number of persons working at professional level: 3 Part time.   *(251)*

318. Research for Better Schools
Executive Director, Jo Ann Weinberger, 17OO Market St, Philadelphia, Pa 191O3, USA.
Type of centre: Independent research centre. *Concerned with long-term futures.*
Time allocated (%): Less than IO.
Methods used: I Brainstorming, 2 Expert panels.
Time range of work: 5 - IO years.
Source of support for work (%): 75 National government.
Number of persons working at professional level: I Part time, 2 Full time.   *(391)*

319. Resources for the Future, Inc
1755 Massachusetts Ave, NW, Washington DC 20036, USA.
Type of centre: Independent research.
Concerned with long-term futures.
Time allocated (%): 50.
Methods used: Individual expert forecasting, Statistical models, Scenario building, Expert panels.
Time range of work: 5 - 25 years.
Source of support for work (%): 8 National government, 89 Foundations, 3 Other (Misc).
Work done for (%): 100 Organizational goals.
Number of persons working at professional level: 3 Part time, 49 Full time.
Additional information: Concerned with long-range resource analysis, technology assessment, economic projections and environmental analysis.   *(449)*

320. Royal Norwegian Council for Scientific and Industrial Research
PO Box 279 Blindern, Gaustadaaleen 30, Oslo 3, Norway.
Type of centre: National government.
Concerned with long-term futures.
Time allocated (%): 20.
Methods used: 1 Brainstorming, 2 Extrapolation techniques, 3 Scenario building.
Time range of work: 10 - 25 years.
Source of support for work (%): 40 National government.
Work done for (%): 50 National government, 50 Private business.
Number of persons working at professional level: 1 Full time, 20 Part time.   *(69)*

321. Royal Swedish Academy of Engineering Sciences
(Ingenjörsvetenskapsakademien), PO Box 5073, S- 102 42 Stockholm 5, Sweden.
Type of centre: Academic.
Concerned with long-term futures.
Time allocated (%): 20.
Methods used: Cross impact analysis, Contextual mapping, Historical analogy, Individual expert forecasting, Causal modelling.
Time range of work: 10 - 25 years.
Source of support for work (%): 20 Foundations, 40 National government, 40 Private business.
Work done for (%): 20 Foundations, 40 National government, 40 Private business.
Number of persons working at professional level: 5 Part time, 5 Full time.   *(90)*

S 322. St Gallen Zentrum für Zukunftsforschung
General Guisan Str 92, 9010 St Gallen, Switzerland.
Type of centre: Academic.
Primarily engaged in: Futures studies.
Direction of work in forecasting: 1 Economic, 2 Population, 3 Manpower, 4 Educational;
Direction of work in research: 1 Social impacts of technology, 2 Futures methodology, 3 Population, 4 Manpower, 5 Policy research.
Methods used: 1 Causal modelling, 2 Statistical models, 3 Extrapolation techniques, 4 Delphi techniques, 5 Cross impact analysis.
Time range of work: 10 - 25 years.
Source of support for work (%): 100 National government.
Work done for (%): 100 National government.
Number of persons working at professional level: 5 Part time, 10 Full time.

Additional information: The Organization's aim is the presentation of alternative long-range future developments against a background of Government national economic policies. *(99)*

323. Saint Louis University
Dept of Sociology, Clement S. Mihanovich, Professor of Sociology, 211 North Grand Blvd, St Louis, Mo 63103, USA.
Type of centre: Academic.
Concerned with long-term futures.
Time allocated (%): Less than IO.
Direction of work in forecasting: Social.
Direction of work in research: Social priorities.
Direction of work in planning: Technological.
Methods used: I Delphi techniques, 2 Simulation, 3 Causal modelling, 4 Extrapolation techniques, 5 Statistical models.
Time range of work: IO - 25 years.
Number of persons working at professional level: 50 Part time. *(238)*

324. Salzburg Assembly: Impact of New Technology (Saint)
Schloss Leopoldskron, PO Box 129, A-5010 Salzburg, Austria.
Type of centre: International voluntary association.
Primarily engaged in: Futures studies.
Direction of work in forecasting: I Scientific, 2 Technological, 3 Economic, 4 Social.
Methods used: I Expert panels.
Time range of work: IO - 25 years.
Source of support for work (%): IOO Subscriptions or members.
Work done for (%): IOO Conferences for members.
Number of persons working at professional level: I Part time. *(64)*

325. San Jose State University
School of Education, Instructional Technology Dept, Prof Ronald L. Hunt, San Jose, Ca. 95192, USA.
Type of centre: Academic.
Concerned with long-term futures.
Time allocated (%): Less than IO.
Methods used: I Expert panels, 2 Operational models, 3 Brainstorming.
Time range of work: 5 - IO years.
Source of support for work (%): 30 National government, 70 Local government.
Work done for (%): 2 National government, 8 Local government.
Number of persons working at professional level: I Part time. *(269)*

326. Scandinavian Institutes for Administrative Research
Stenkullavagen 43, S-112 65 Stockholm, Sweden.
Type of centre: Independent research.
Concerned with long-term futures.
Direction of work in forecasting: I Social, 2 Environmental.
Direction of work in research: Social impacts of technology.
Direction of work in planning: Corporate.
Methods used: I Historical analogy, 2 Brainstorming, 3 Contextual mapping.
Time range of work: 5 - IO years.
Source of support for work (%): 5 Local government, IO National government,

IO International agencies, I5 Foundations, 6O Private business.
Work done for (%): 5 Local government, IO National government, IO International
agencies, 6O Private business.
Number of persons working at professional level: IO Part time, 3O Full time.   *(351)*

327. Science Council of Canada

15O Kent St, Ottawa, K1P 5P4, Canada.
Type of centre: National government.
Concerned with long-term futures.
Direction of work in forecasting: I Technological, 2 Social, 3 Resources, 4 Environmental,
5 Economic.
Direction of work in research: I Policy research, 2 Alternative futures, 3 Social impacts
of technology.
Direction of work in planning: I Technological, 2 Scientific, 3 Political.
Methods used: I Expert panels, 2 Individual expert forecasting, 3 Contextual mapping,
4 Scenario building, 5 Probabilistic forecasting.
Time range of work: IO - 25 years.
Source of support for work (%): IOO National government.
Work done for (%): IOO National within 75% federal focus.
Number of persons working at professional level: I5 Part time, I5 Full time.   *(284)*

328. Science Policy Foundation

Director, Maurice Goldsmith, Benjamin Franklin House, 36 Craven Street, London WC2N 5NC
UK.
Type of centre: Educational trust.
Concerned with long-term futures.
Time allocated (%): 2O.
Methods used: I Brainstorming, 2 Extrapolation techniques, 3 Expert panels,
4 Probabilistic forecasting, 5 Delphi techniques.
Time range of work: 5 - IO years.
Number of persons working at professional level: 2 Part time.   *(457)*

329. Science Policy Research Unit (SPRU)

Prof, Christopher Freeman, University of Sussex, Falmer, Brighton BN1 9RF, UK.
Type of centre: Academic.
Concerned with long-term futures.
Time allocated (%): 5O.
Direction of work in forecasting: I Technological, I Social, I Environmental, 2 Resources,
Direction of work in research: I Social impacts of technology, I Alternative futures,
I Futures methodology, 2 Resource utilization, 2 Value systems, 2 Social priorities,
3 Environmental, 3 Policy research.
Direction of work in planning: I Technological, I Social, 2 Environmental, 2 Resources,
3 Scientific.
Methods used: I Scenario building, I Extrapolation techniques, I Statistical models,
I Individual expert forecasting, I Simulation.
Time range of work: 5 - beyond year 2OOO.
Source of support for work (%): 5 Private business, IO International agencies,
I5 Foundations, 7O National government.
Work done for (%): 5 Private business, IO International agencies, I5 Foundations,
7O National government.
Number of persons working at professional level: 4 Part time, I5 Full time.   *(128)*

330. SCIENCE SPRL
Manfred Siebker, Ave Louise 177, 1050 Brussels, Belgium.
Type of centre: Independent research.
Concerned with long-term futures.
Time allocated (%): 30.
Methods used: I Delphi techniques, I Cross impact analysis, I Scenario building,
I Brainstorming, I Relevance trees, 2 Statistical models, 2 Expert panels, 2 Network
analysis, 2 Historical analogy, 2 Operational models.
Time range of work: IO - beyond year 2000.
Source of support for work (%): IO National government, 20 Other, 30 Private
business, 40 International agencies.
Work done for (%): IO National government, 20 Other, 30 Private business,
40 International agencies.
Number of persons working at professional level: 4 Full time, 6 Part time.   *(364)*

331. Scottish Home and Health Department
St Andrews House, Edinburgh EH1 3DE, Scotland, UK.
Type of centre: National government.
Concerned with long-term futures.
Time allocated (%): Less than IO.
Direction of work in forecasting: Social, Manpower, Population.
Direction of work in research: Manpower, Policy research.
Direction of work in planning: Health services.
Methods used: I Expert panels, 2 Extrapolation techniques, 3 Probabilistic forecasting,
4 Individual expert forecasting.
Time range of work: 5 - IO years.
Source of support for work (%): IOO Local government.
Number of persons working at professional level: IO Part time, I Full time.   *(432)*

332. Sears, Roebuck and Co
Director, Planning and Research, R.E. Barmeier, Sears Tower, Dept 702P, Chicago,
II 60684, USA.
Type of centre: Business.
Primarily engaged in: Both futures studies and long-range planning.
Direction of work in forecasting: I Economic, 2 Social, 3 Cultural, 4 Market,
5 Environmental, 6 Manpower, 7 Population, 8 Resources, 9 Technological.
Direction of work in research: I Alternative futures, 2 Value systems, 3 Social priorities,
4 The individual in the future, 5 The family in the future, 6 Futures methodology,
7 Consumer affairs, 8 Social impacts of technology, 9 Environmental, IO Policy research,
11 Population, I2 Manpower, I3 Resource utilization.
Methods used: I Probabilistic forecasting, 2 Scenario building, 3 Cross impact analysis,
4 Statistical models, 5 Expert panels, 6 Individual expert forecasting, 7 Simulation,
8 Delphi techniques.
Time range of work: IO - 25 years.
Source of support for work (%): IOO Private business.
Work done for (%): IOO Private business.   *(62)*

333. Secretariat for Future Studies
Fack, S-103 20 Stockholm 16, Sweden.
Type of centre: National government.
Primarily engaged in: Both futures studies and long-range planning.

Direction of work in forecasting: Technological, Economic, Social, Cultural, Market, Educational, Scientific, Environmental, Manpower, Resources, Population.
Direction of work in research: Social impacts of technology, Alternative futures, Manpower, Consumer affairs, Environmental, Resource utilization, Value systems, Social priorities, Policy research, Population, The individual in the future, The family in the future, Futures methodology.
Direction of work in planning: Scientific, Technological, Social, Urban, Regional, Educational, Economic, Political, Corporate, Environmental, Labour, Resources.
Time range of work: lO - beyond year 2OOO.
Source of support for work (%): lOO National government.
Work done for (%): lOO National government.
Number of persons working at professional level: 4 Full time.   *(126)*

334. Seneca College
Centre for International Programs, Director, Ranjit Kumar, 175O Finch Ave East, Willowdale 428, Ontario, Canada.
Type of centre: Academic.
Concerned with long-term futures.
Time allocated (%): 2O.
Direction of work in planning: Technological, Educational.
Time range of work: 5 - lO years.
Source of support for work (%): 25 National government, 25 Donations.
Work done for (%): lO International agencies, lO Voluntary associations.
Number of persons working at professional level: l Full time, 2 Part time.   *(336)*

335. The Simulation and Gaming Association
4833 Greentree Rd, Lebanon, Oh 45O36, USA.
Type of centre: International professional organization.
Concerned with long-term futures. Time allocated (%): lO.
Methods used: l Simulation, 2 Gaming.
Time range of work: lO - 25 years.
Source of support for work (%): lOO Membership.
Number of persons working at professional level: l Part time.   *(389)*

336. Social and Cultural Planning Office
J.C. Van Markenlann, Rijswijk (2-H), The Netherlands.
Type of centre: National government. *Concerned with long-term futures.*
Time allocated (%): 5O.
Direction of work in forecasting: l Social, 2 Cultural.
Direction of work in research: Interrelation of policy sectors.
Direction of work in planning: Social.
Methods used: l Statistical models, 2 Causal modelling.
Time range of work: lO - 25 years.
Source of support for work (%): lOO National government.
Work done for (%): lOO National government.
Number of persons working at professional level: 23 Full time.   *(37)*

337. Société d'Etude Economiques et Sociales and Société d'Etude de la Planification et de la Prévision
President, Pierre Goetschin, 5 Place de la Cathedrale, 1OO5 Lausanne, Switzerland.
Type of centre: Academic.

Primarily engaged in: Both futures studies and long-range planning.
Direction of work in forecasting: Technological, Economic, Social, Scientific, Manpower.
Direction of work in research: Alternative futures, Social priorities, Policy research, Futures methodology.
Direction of work in planning: Scientific, Technological, Social, Economic, Political, Corporate.
Methods used: Probabilistic forecasting, Historical analogy, Delphi techniques, Cross impact analysis, Scenario building, Extrapolation techniques, Brainstorming, Expert panels, Relevance trees, Network analysis.
Time range of work: 5 - beyond year 2000.
Source of support for work (%): 100 Voluntary associations.
Work done for (%): 100 Own members.
Number of persons working at professional level: 40 Part time, 1 Full time.   *(196)*

338. Société d'Etudes et de Documentation Economiques Industrielles et Sociales
90 Rue du Bac, 75007 Paris, France.
Type of centre: Independent research. *Concerned with long-term futures.*
Time allocated (%): Less than 10.
Direction of work in forecasting: 1 Social, 2 Environmental, 3 Economic, 4 Educational 5 Resources, 6 Cultural, 7 Population, 8 Scientific.
Direction of work in research: 1 Social priorities, 2 Alternative futures, 3 Environmental, 4 Value systems, 5 The individual in the future, 6 Social impacts of technology, 7 Manpower.
Direction of work in planning: 1 Social, 2 Environmental, 3 Urban, 4 Labour, 5 Economic.
Methods used: 1 Individual expert forecasting.
Time range of work: 5 - 25 years.
Source of support for work (%): 98 Sale of publications, 2 Studies under contract.
Number of persons working at professional level: 2 Full time, 150 Part time.   *(319)*

339. Société d'Etudes et de Recherches en Sciences Sociales
Director, Raymond Fichelet, 10-12 Rue Richer, Paris 75000, France.
Type of centre: Independent research.
Concerned with long-term futures.
Time allocated (%): 50.
Direction of work in research: 1 Alternative futures, 2 Futures methodology, 3 Change in social structures, 4 Social priorities.
Direction of work in planning: 1 Urban, 2 Social, 3 Health systems.
Methods used: 1 Futurization groups, 2 Scenario building, 3 Network analysis, 4 Historical analogy.
Time range of work: 10 - 25 years.
Source of support for work (%): 20 Private business, 80 National government.
Work done for (%): 10 Private business, 30 National government.
Number of persons working at professional level: 2 Part time, 4 Full time.   *(26)*

340. Society for Long-Range Planning
8th Floor, Terminal House, Grosvenor Gardens, London SW1W 0AR, UK.
Type of centre: Membership society.
Primarily engaged in: Long-range planning.
Direction of work in planning: Corporate.
Number of persons working at professional level: 1 Part time, 1 Full time.   *(451)*

341. Southam Press Limited

Tele-Information, Vice President, Michael A. Harrison, Suite 908, 321 Floor St East, Toronto 285, Ontario, Canada.
Type of centre: Industry. *Concerned with long-term futures.*
Time allocated (%): Less than 10.
Methods used: 1 Individual expert forecasting, 2 Historical analogy, 3 Brainstorming.
Time range of work: 5 - 10 years.
Source of support for work (%): 100 Private business.
Work done for (%): 100 Private business.
Number of persons working at professional level: 2 Part time.   *(252)*

342. Southern Growth Policies Board

Executive Director, Dr William L. Bowden, PO Box 12293, 100 Par Drive, Research Triangle Park, NC 27709, USA.
Type of centre: Regional agency.
Primarily engaged in: Both futures studies and long-range planning.
Direction of work in forecasting: Environmental, Resources, Population, Economic, Technological, Manpower.
Direction of work in research: Social impacts of technology, Environmental, Resource utilization, Social priorities, Population, Manpower.
Direction of work in planning: Regional, Social, Urban, Economic, Political, Environmental, Resources.
Methods used: Synthesis of information from all methods - (see Directory guide).
Time range of work: 5 - 10 years.
Source of support for work (%): 30 National government, 30 Foundations, 10 Voluntary associations, 30 State governments.
Work done for (%): 100 For 15 State Region.
Number of persons working at professional level: 3 Part time, 3 Full time.   *(446)*

343. Sperry Rand Corp

Vice President of Long-Range Planning, Marcus Ave, Great Neck, NY 11020, USA.
Type of centre: Industry.
Concerned with long-term futures.
Time allocated (%): 20.
Direction of work in forecasting: 1 Military, 2 Technological.
Direction of work in planning: 1 Corporate, 2 Technological.
Methods used: 1 Extrapolation techniques, 2 Probabilistic forecasting.
Time range of work: 5 - 10 years.
Source of support for work (%): 90 National government.
Work done for (%): 90 National government.   *(105)*

344. Sperry Univac

Staff Scientist, Earl C. Joseph, PO Box 3525, St, Paul, Mn 55165, USA.
Type of centre: Industry.
Concerned with long-term futures.
Time allocated (%): 20.
Direction of work in forecasting: 1 Technological, 1 Economic, 1 Market, 1 Scientific, 1 Military, 1 Resources, 2 Social, 2 Cultural, 2 Educational, 2 Population.
Direction of work in research: 1 Social impacts of technology, 1 Alternative futures, 1 Manpower, 1 Consumer affairs, 1 Environmental, 1 Resource utilization, 1 Policy research, 2 Value systems, 2 Social priorities, 2 Population, 2 The individual in the

future, 2 The family in the future, 3 Futures methodology.
Direction of work in planning: I Technological, I Economic, I Corporate, I Military,
I Resources, 2 Scientific, 2 Educational, 2 Labour, 3 Environmental, 4 Social, 4 Urban,
4 Regional, 5 Political.
Methods used: All methods (see Directory guide).
Time range of work: 5 - beyond year 2000.
Source of support for work (%): 50 National government, 50 Private business.
Work done for (%): 50 National government, 50 Private business.   *(239)*

345. Standard Oil Company

Corporate Planning and Development Dept, (Indiana), 200 E. Randolph Dr, Chicago,
II 60601, USA.
Type of centre: Industry.
Primarily engaged in: Long-range planning.
Direction of work in forecasting: I Economic, 2 Resources, 3 Market.
Direction of work in research: Resource utilization.
Direction of work in planning: Corporate.
Methods used: Delphi techniques, Simulation, Brainstorming, Scenario building,
Individual expert forecasting, Operational models.
Time range of work: 5 - 10 years.
Source of support for work (%): 100 Private business.
Work done for (%): 100 Private business.
Number of persons working at professional level: 29 Full time.   *(101)*

346. Stanford Research Institute

President and Executive Director, C. Anderson, Menlo Park, Ca 94025, USA.
Type of centre: Independent research.
Concerned with long-term futures.
Time allocated (%): 50.
Time range of work: 5 - 25 years.
Source of support for work (%): 66 Government clients, 34 Commercial clients.
Work done for (%): 66 Government clients, 34 Commercial clients.
Number of persons working at professional level: 100 Part time, 1500 Full time.   *(124)*

347. Stanford Research Institute

Centre for the Study of Social Policy, Educational Policy Research Centre, Menlo Park,
Ca 94025, USA.
Type of centre: National government. *Concerned with long-term futures.*
Time allocated (%): 50.
Direction of work in forecasting: I Cultural, 2 Educational, 3 Scientific.
Direction of work in research: I Policy research, 2 Alternative futures, 3 Cultural
transformation, 4 Futures methodology.
Direction of work in planning: I Educational, 2 Social.
Methods used: I Contextual mapping, 2 Scenario building, 3 Network analysis,
4 Historical analogy.
Time range of work: 5 - beyond year 2000.
Source of support for work (%): 2 Private business, 2 Voluntary associations,
15 Foundations, 80 National government.
Work done for (%): 2 International agencies, 2 Voluntary associations, 3 Local government,
3 Private business, 10 Foundations, 80 National government.
Number of persons working at professional level: 5 Part time, 15 Full time.   *(231)*

348. Stanford University

Bechtel International Centre, World Analysis Centre, PO Box 5816, Stanford, Ca 94305, USA.
Type of centre: Academic.
Primarily engaged in: Long-range planning.
Direction of work in forecasting: I Social, 2 Economic, 3 Cultural, 4 Political, 5 Environmental.
Direction of work in research: I Value systems, 2 Alternative futures, 3 Social impacts of technology, 4 Environmental, 5 Resource utilization, 6 Population.
Direction of work in planning: I Social, 2 Economic, 3 Political, 4 Environmental, 5 Technological, 6 Regional, 7 Educational, 8 Resources.
Methods used: I Cross impact analysis, 2 Expert panels, 3 Brainstorming, 4 Causal modelling.
Time range of work: 5 - beyond year 2000.
Source of support for work (%): I00 University.
Work done for (%): 50 National governments, 50 International agencies.
Number of persons working at professional level: I0 Part time.   *(445)*

349. State University of New York at Albany

Institute for Public Policy Alternatives, 99 Washington Ave, Albany, NY 12210, USA.
Type of centre: Academic.
Primarily engaged in: Both futures studies and long-range planning.
Direction of work in research: Policy research.
Time range of work: 5 - I0 years.
Source of support for work (%): I00 State government.
Work done for (%): I00 State government.
Number of persons working at professional level: 4 Part time, 4 Full time.   *(5)*

350. Stensen Institute

Teilhard de Chardin Centre for Studies and Research, Viale Don Minzoni, 25 A 50129, Florence, Italy.
Type of centre: Ad hoc study group.
Primarily engaged in: Futures studies.
Direction of work in forecasting: Economic, Social, Cultural, Educational, Scientific, Environmental, Population, Religion.
Direction of work in research: Alternative futures, Social priorities, Population, The individual in the future, The family in the future, Futures methodology.
Methods used: I Extrapolation techniques, 2 Expert panels, 3 Individual expert forecasting, 4 Historical analogy.
Time range of work: I0 - 25 years.
Source of support for work (%): 50 Private business, 50 Foundations.
Number of persons working at professional level: 5 Part time.   *(35)*

351. Stockholm International Peace Research Institute (SIPRI)

Sveavagen 166, 11346 Stockholm, Sweden.
Type of centre: Independent research. *Concerned with long-term futures.*
Time allocated (%): I0.
Methods used: Probabilistic forecasting, Expert panels, Extrapolation techniques, Individual expert forecasting, Historical analogy.
Time range of work: 5 - I0 years.
Source of support for work (%): I00 National government.

Work done for (%): 16 Local government, 16 National government, 16 International government, 16 Private business, 16 Foundations, 16 Voluntary associations.
Number of persons working at professional level: 16 Full time. *(88)*

352. Study Group for Science Organization
Hungarian Academy of Sciences, Munnich, Ferenc-Utca 18, H-1051 Budapest, Hungary.
Type of centre: Academic research.
Concerned with long-term futures.
Time allocated (%): 20.
Direction of work in forecasting: Technological, Social, Educational, Scientific.
Direction of work in research: Social impacts of technology, Scientific and technical development, Futures methodology.
Direction of work in planning: Scientific, Technological, Social.
Methods ysed: Probabilistic forecasting, Individual expert forecasting, Cross impact analysis, Scenario building, Brainstorming, Statistical models.
Time range of work: 5 - 25 years.
Source of support for work (%): 100 Hungarian Academy of Science.
Work done for (%): 10 International agencies, 20 National government,
70 Hungarian Academy of Science.
Number of persons working at professional level: 2 Part time, 2 Full time. *(159)*

353. Sun Fun
Director, Perry E. Smart, 52 Forest Rd, Wallingford, Ct 06492, USA.
Type of centre: Business.
Concerned with long-term futures.
Time allocated (%): Less than 10.
Direction of work in forecasting: Market.
Direction of work in research: Value systems, The family in the future.
Direction of work in planning: Corporate.
Methods used: Scenario building, Brainstorming, Individual expert forecasting.
Time range of work: 5 - 10 years.
Source of support for work (%): 100 Private business.
Work done for (%): 100 Private business.
Number of persons working at professional level: 1 Part time.
Additional information: Focus of work: aims to shift individuals into leisure activities such as bicycling, miniature golf, and other outdoor recreation activities. *(426)*

354. Swiss Council of Sciences
9 Wildhainweg, PO Box 2732, CH 3001 Berne, Switzerland.
Direction of work in planning: Scientific, Educational.
Methods used: 1 Expert panels, 2 Individual expert forecasting, 3 Extrapolation techniques, 4 Simulation.
Source of support for work (%): 100 National government.
Work done for (%): 100 National government.
Number of persons working at professional level: 4 Part time. *(46)*

355. Swiss Federal Institute of Technology
Institute for National, Regional and Local Planning, Weinfergest 35, 8006 Zurich, Switzerland.
Type of centre: Academic. *Concerned with long-term futures.*
Time allocated (%): 50.

Direction of work in forecasting: I Environmental, 2 Economic, 3 Social, 4 Resources, 5 Population.
Direction of work in research: I Alternative futures, 2 Environmental, 3 Policy research, 4 Social priorities, 5 Resource utilization, 5 Population, 5 Futures methodology.
Direction of work in planning: I Regional, 2 Urban.
Methods used: I Statistical models, 2 Extrapolation techniques, 3 Scenario building, 4 Individual expert forecasting.
Time range of work: 5 - beyond year 2000.
Source of support for work (%): IOO National government.
Work done for (%): 3O Local government, 7O National government.
Number of persons working at professional level: I2 Part time, 2O Full time.   *(340)*

356. Swiss Society for Futures Research

Ecole Polytechnique Fédérale, President, Bruno Fritsch, Schenchferstr 68, Zurich, Switzerland.
Type of centre: Membership society. **Concerned with long-term futures.**
Time allocated (%): 5O.
Direction of work in forecasting: Technological, Economic, Environmental, Resources, Population.
Direction of work in research: Social impacts of technology, Environmental, Alternative futures, Social priorities, Value systems.
Direction of work in planning: Economic, Political, Environmental.
Methods used: Delphi techniques, Scenario building, Statistical models, Expert panels, Simulation.
Time range of work: IO - 25 years.
Work done for (%): 2O Local government, 4O National government.
Number of persons working at professional level: 6 Part time.   *(352)*

System Dynamics Group

See: Massachusetts Institute of Technology.

357. Systemplan eV

Institut für Umweltforschung und Entwichlungsplanung, D 69 Heidelberg, Tiergartenstr 15, West Germany.
Type of centre: Independent research.
Primarily engaged in: Both futures studies and long-range planning.
Direction of work in forecasting: I Social, I Integrative, 2 Scientific, 3 Technological.
Direction of work in research: I Policy research, I Integrative, 2 Social priorities, 3 Value systems, 4 Social impacts of technology, 5 Alternative futures, 6 Futures methodology.
Direction of work in planning: I Regional, I Integrative, 2 Urban, 3 Technological, 4 Political, 5 Social, 6 Scientific.
Methods used: I Brainstorming, I Systems analysis, 2 Expert panels, 3 Scenario building, 4 Relevance trees, 5 Cross impact analysis, 6 Delphi techniques.
Time range of work: 5 - 25 years.
Source of support for work (%): IO Local government, IO International agencies, 3O Foundations, 5O National government.
Work done for (%): IO Local government, IO International agencies, 3O Foundations, 5O National government.
Number of persons working at professional level: IO Part time, 35 Full time.   *(233)*

T 358. Ted McIlvenna

1523 Franklin St, San Francisco, Ca 94109, USA.
Type of centre: National voluntary association..
Concerned with long-term futures.
Time allocated (%): 20.
Direction of work in forecasting: Social, Cultural, Market, Resources, Population.
Direction of work in research: Alternative futures, Value systems, Population,
The individual in the future.
Direction of work in planning: Social, Economic.
Methods used: Scenario building, Causal modelling, Brainstorming, Contextual
mapping, Individual expert forecasting, Operational models.
Time range of work: 5 - 25 years.
Source of support for work (%): 20 Voluntary associations, 80 Foundations.
Number of persons working at professional level: 15 Part time.   *(158)*

359. Tehran University

Institute of Psychology, 19, 24th of Esfand Square, Tehran 14, Iran.
Type of centre: Research institute attached to University of Tehran.
Concerned with long-term futures.
Number of persons working at professional level: 4 Full time, 20 Part time.   *(223)*

360. The Teilhard Centre for The Future of Man

The Secretary, St Marks Chambers, Kennington Park Rd, London, SE11 4PW, UK.
Type of centre: Membership society.
Primarily engaged in: Futures studies.
Direction of work in forecasting: States of mind and morals.
Direction of work in research: Psycho-genesis.
Direction of work in planning: Evolutionary structures of consciousness.
Methods used: Rhetorical presentation and democratic analysis.
Time range of work: 5 - 10 years.
Source of support for work (%): 100 Own membership.
Work done for (%): 100 Own membership.
Number of persons working at professional level: 10 Part time.   *(61)*

Teilhard de Chardin Centre for Studies and Research

See: Stensen Institute.

361. Tenneco Inc

Vice President of Long-Range Planning, Tenneco Bldg, Houston, Tx 77002, USA.
Type of centre: Business.
Primarily engaged in: Both futures studies and long-range planning.
Direction of work in forecasting: 1 Market, 2 Economic, 3 Technological.
Direction of work in planning: 1 Corporate, 2 Economic, 3 Resources.
Methods used: 1 Brainstorming, 2 Statistical models, 3 Scenario building,
4 Simulation, 5 Individual expert forecasting.
Time range of work: 5 - 10 years.
Source of support for work (%): 100 Private business.
Work done for (%): 100 Private business.
Number of persons working at professional level: 7 Full time   *(205)*

362. Thomson/CSF
Research Director, L. Gerardin, 87 Rue La Boëtie, 75008 Paris, France.
Type of centre: Industry.
Primarily engaged in: Futures studies.
Direction of work in research: I Alternative futures, 2 Social impacts of technology, 3 Futures methodology.
Direction of work in planning: Corporate.
Methods used: I Cross impact analysis, I Structural modelling, 2 Scenario building, 3 Extrapolation techniques.
Time range of work: IO - 25 years.
Source of support for work (%): IOO Private business.
Work done for (%): 5O National government, 5O Private business.
Number of persons working at professional level: 3 Full time.   *(356)*

363. Twenty First Century Media Inc
606 Fifth Ave, E Northport, NY 11731, USA.
Type of centre: Business.
Primarily engaged in: Futures studies.
Direction of work in forecasting: Technological.
Methods used: Brainstorming, Individual expert forecasting.
Time range of work: 5 - IO years.
Work done for (%): IOO Readers.
Number of persons working at professional level: I Full time.   *(431)*

U   364. UN Centre for Housing, Building and Planning (ESA/CHBP)
New York, NY 10017, USA.
Type of centre: International government.
Concerned with long-term futures.
Direction of work in forecasting: I Social, 2 Environmental, 3 Technological, 4 Economic.
Direction of work in research: I Social priorities, 2 Policy research, 3 Environmental, 4 Resource utilization, 5 Social impacts of technology.
Direction of work in planning: I Urban, I Regional, 2 Social, 3 Technological, 4 Environmental.
Methods used: I Network analysis, 2 Expert panels, 3 Operational models, 4 Statistical models, 5 Individual expert forecasting, 6 Probabilistic forecasting.
Time range of work: 5 - IO years.
Source of support for work (%): IOO Contributions from member states.
Work done for (%): 33 National government, 33 International agencies, 33 Private business.
Number of persons working at professional level: 6 Part time, 3O Full time.   *(108)*

365. UN Conference on Trade and Development (UNCTAD)
(Trade and Economic Integration), Palais des Nations, Geneva, Switzerland.
Type of centre: International government.
Concerned with long-term futures.
Time allocated (%): IO.
Direction of work in forecasting: Economic.
Direction of work in research: Policy research.
Direction of work in planning: Economic.
Methods used: I Expert panels, 2 Individual expert forecasting.

Time range of work: 5 - 25 years.
Source of support for work (%): IO National government, 9O International agencies.
Work done for (%): 3O National government, 7O International agencies.
Number of persons working at professional level: 5 Part time, IO Full time.   *(188)*

366. UN Energy Section
G.V. Rao, United Nations Plaza, New York, NY 10017, USA.
Type of centre: International government. **Concerned with long-term futures.**
Time allocated (%): Less than IO.
Direction of work in forecasting: Technological, Economic, Resources.
Direction of work in research: Resource utilization, Policy research, Futures methodology.
Direction of work in planning: Technological, Regional, Economic, Environmental, Resources.
Methods used: I Expert panels, 2 Extrapolation techniques, 3 Statistical models, 4 Historical analogy, 5 Individual expert forecasting.
Time range of work: 5 - 25 years.
Source of support for work (%): IOO International government.
Number of persons working at professional level: 2 Part time.   *(24)*

367. UN Economic Commission for Europe
Palais des Nations, CH-1121, Geneva 1O, Switzerland.
Type of centre: International government.
Concerned with long-term futures.
Time allocated (%): IO.
Methods used: I Expert panels, 2 Probabilistic forecasting, 3 Extrapolation techniques, 4 Statistical models, 5 Individual expert forecasting.
Time range of work: IO - 25 years.
Source of support for work (%): IOO International agencies.
Work done for (%): IOO International agencies.
Number of persons working at professional level: I5 Part time.   *(45)*

368. UN Economic Commission for Europe
Projections and Programming Division, Director, Mr J. Royer, Palais des Nations, Geneva, Switzerland.
Type of centre: International government. **Concerned with long-term futures.**
Time allocated (%): 5O.
Direction of work in forecasting: I Economic, 2 Social, 3 Technological.
Direction of work in planning: Technological, Social, Economic.
Methods used: Statistical models, Expert panels, Simulation.
Time range of work: 5 - 25 years.
Source of support for work (%): IOO International agencies.
Work done for (%): IOO International agencies.   *(110)*

369. UN Economic Commission for Europe
Trade and Technology Division, Director, Norman Scott, Palais des Nations, Geneva, Switzerland.
Type of centre: International government.
Concerned with long-term futures.
Time allocated (%): 2O.
Methods used: I Probabilistic forecasting, 2 Extrapolation techniques, 3 Statistical models, 4 Expert panels, 5 Individual expert forecasting.

Time range of work: 5 - 25 years.
Source of support for work (%): IOO International agencies.
Work done for (%): IOO International agencies.
Number of persons working at professional level: IO Part time.   *(303)*

370. UN - Food and Agriculture Organization
Regional Office, Phraatit Rd, Bankok 2, Thailand.
Type of centre: International professional organization.
Primarily engaged in: Both futures studies and long-range planning.
Direction of work in forecasting: I Technological, 2 Educational, 3 Resources,
4 Scientific, 5 Environmental.
Direction of work in research: I Resource utilization, 2 Policy research,
3 Environmental, 4 Social impacts of technology.
Direction of work in planning: I Regional, 2 Technological, 3 Scientific, 4 Educational,
5 Environmental, 6 Resources.
Methods used: Extrapolation techniques, Network analysis, Historical analogy.
Time range of work: 5-beyond year 2OOO.
Source of support for work (%): IOO International agencies.
Work done for (%): 5 Foundations, 5 Voluntary associations, IO International agencies,
80 National government.
Number of persons working at professional level: I Part time, I Full time.   *(178)*

371. UN Office of Science and Technology
New York, NY 1OO17, USA.
Type of centre: International government. *Concerned with long-term futures.*
Time allocated (%): 2O.
Direction of work in forecasting: Technological, Scientific.
Direction of work in research: Policy research, Futures methodology.
Direction of work in planning: Scientific, Technological.
Methods used: Expert panels, Operational models.
Time range of work: 5 - IO years.
Source of support for work (%): IOO International agencies.
Work done for (%): IOO International agencies.
Number of persons working at professional level: 3 Part time.   *(89)*

372. UN Population Division
Director, Leon Tabah, New York, NY 1OO17, USA.
Type of centre: International government.
Concerned with long-term futures.
Time allocated (%): 5O.
Direction of work in forecasting: Technological; Economic, Social, Cultural, Educational,
Scientific, Environmental, Manpower, Resources, Population.
Direction of work in research: All areas (see Directory guide).
Direction of work in planning: Scientific, Technological, Social, Urban, Regional,
Educational, Economic, Political, Corporate, Environmental, Labour, Resources.
Methods used: Probabilistic forecasting, Extrapolation techniques, Cross impact analysis,
Expert panels, Statistical models, Simulation, Operational models.   *(312)*

373. UNESCO
Dept of Environmental Sciences and Natural Resources Research, Michel Batisse,
7 Place de Fontenoy, 75700 Paris, France.
Type of centre: International government.
Concerned with long-term futures.
Time allocated (%): 30.
Methods used: Probabilistic forecasting, Brainstorming, Statistical models, Expert
panels, Operational models.
Time range of work: 5 - 10 years.
Source of support for work (%): 100 International agencies.
Work done for (%): 10 National government, 20 International agencies.
Number of persons working at professional level: 50 Part time.   *(311)*

374. UNESCO
Dept of Free Flow of Information and Development of Communication,
7 Place de Fontenoy, 75700 Paris, France.
Type of centre: International government.
Concerned with long-term futures.
Time allocated (%): 30.
Direction of work in forecasting: 1 Communication, 2 Social, 3 Economic, 4 Technol-
ogical, 5 Educational.
Direction of work in research: 1 Communication, 2 Policy research, 3 Social impacts
of technology, 4 Social priorities, 5 Value systems.
Direction of work in planning: 1 Communication, 2 Social, 3 Technological, 4 Economic.
Methods used: 1 Expert panels, 2 Operational techniques, 3 Individual expert forecasting,
4 Statistical models.
Time range of work: 5 - 10 years.
Number of persons working at professional level: 6 Full time, 6 Part time.   *(14)*

375. UNESCO
Science Sector, 7, Place de Fontenoy, 75700 Paris, France.
Type of centre: International government.
Concerned with long-term futures.
Time allocated (%): 40.
Methods ysed: 1 Expert panels, 2 Brainstorming, 3 Delphi techniques.
Time range of work: 100 International agencies.
Work done for (%): 100 International agencies.
Number of persons working at professional level: 100 Part time.   *(166)*

376. Union of Soviet Socialist Republics Academy of Sciences
Institute for Social Research, Section of Social Forecasting, Dr Igor V. Bestuzhev-Lada,
46, Novo-Chezemushki, 117418 Moscow, USSR.
Type of centre: Academic.
Primarily engaged in: Futures studies.
Direction of work in forecasting: 1 Social, 2 Cultural, 3 Environmental.
Direction of work in research: 1 Futures methodology, 2 Value systems, 3 Consumer
affairs, 4 Alternative futures, 5 Social priorities, 6 Social impacts of technology.
Methods used: 1 Individual expert forecasting, 2 Expert panels, 3 Delphi techniques,
4 Extrapolation techniques, 5 Scenario building, 6 Brainstorming, 7 Relevance trees,
8 Historical analogy.
Time range of work: 10 - 25 years.

Source of support for work (%): 1OO National government.
Work done for (%): 1OO National government.
Number of persons working at professional level: 5 Part time, 15 Full time.   *(186)*

377. United Kingdom Atomic Energy Authority

Economics and Programmes Branch, 11 Charles II St, London, SW1, UK.
Type of centre: National government.
Concerned with long-term futures.
Time allocated (%): 3O.
Direction of work in forecasting: 1 Technological, 2 Scientific, 3 Economic,
4 Environmental, 5 Resources.
Direction of work in research: 1 Environmental, 1 Resources utilization.
Direction of work in planning: 1 Scientific.
Methods used: 1 Probabilistic forecasting, 2 Expert panels, 3 Scenario building,
4 Extrapolation techniques, 5 Operational models, 6 Brainstorming, 7 Statistical
models, 8 Contextual mapping, 8 Relevance trees.
Time range of work: 5 - beyond year 2OOO.
Source of support for work (%): 1OO National government.
Work done for (%): 3O National government.
Number of persons working at professional level: 1 Full time, 7 Part time.   *(346)*

378. United States Army War College

Strategic Studies Institute, Dr Anthony Wermuth, PO Box 329, Carlisle Barracks, Pa
171O3, USA.
Type of centre: National government.
Concerned with long-term futures.
Time allocated (%): 3O.
Methods used: 1 Brainstorming, 2 Delphi techniques, 3 Expert panels, 4 Gaming,
5 Historical analogy, 6 Simulation.
Time range of work: 5 - 25 years.
Source of support for work (%): 1OO US Army.
Work done for (%): 1OO US Army.
Number of persons working at professional level: 15 Full time, 2O Part time.   *(236)*

379. United States Chamber of Commerce

Council on Trends and Perspective, 1615 H St NW, Washington, DC 2OO62, USA.
Type of centre: National voluntary association.
Primarily engaged in: Futures studies.
Methods used: 1 Individual expert forecasting, 2 Expert panels, 3 Scenario building.
4 Brainstorming, 5 Statistical models.
Time range of work: 5 - 1O years.
Ssource of support for work (%): 1OO Private business.
Work done for (%): 1OO Private business.
Number of persons working at professional level: 4 Full time.
Additional information: The Council studies a variety of major long-term national
issues that are of interest to the business community: consumerism, corporate
responsibility, and economic growth.   *(33)*

380. United States Department of the Army
Ellsworth E. Sietz, 3205 Plantation Parkway, Fairfax, Va 22030, USA.
Type of centre: National government.
Primarily engaged in: Long-range planning.
Direction of work in forecasting: Technological.
Direction of work in research: Resource utilization.
Direction of work in planning: Technological, Military.
Methods used: Probabilistic forecasting, Individual expert forecasting, Extrapolation techniques, Brainstorming, Expert panels, Operational models, Simulation, Causal modelling.
Time range of work: 5 - 25 years.
Source of support for work (%): 100 National government.
Work done for (%): 100 National government.
Number of persons working at professional level: 3 Full time.   *(245)*

381. United States Department of Labour
Bureau of Labour Statistics, Commissioner, Julius Shiskin, Washington, DC 20212, USA.
Type of centre: National government.
Concerned with long-term futures.
Time allocated (%): Less than 10.
Methods used: 1 Statistical models, 2 Individual expert forecasting, 3 Extrapolation techniques.
Time range of work: 10 - 25 years.
Source of support for work (%): 100 National government.
Work done for (%): 100 National government.
Number of persons working at professional level: 73 Full time.   *(38)*

382. United States Steel Corporation
Long Range Planning, 600 Grant St, Pittsburgh, Pa 15230, USA.
Type of centre: Industry.
Primarily engaged in: Both futures studies and long-range planning.
Direction of work in forecasting: 1 Market, 2 Economic, 3 Technological, 4 Social.
Direction of work in planning: 1 Corporate, 2 Economic, 3 Resources, 4 Technological.
Methods used: Can be any of the methods (see Directory guide).
Time range of work: Medium range.
Source of support for work (%): 100 Private business.
Work done for (%): 100 Private business.
Number of persons working at professional level: 6 Part time.   *(305)*

383. Universal Postal Union (UPU)
Case Postale, Weltpoststr 4, 3000 Berne 15, Switzerland.
Type of centre: International government.
Concerned with long-term futures.
Time allocated (%): 30.
Methods used: 1 Expert panels, 2 Statistical models, 3 Individual expert forecasting, 4 Historical analogy.
Time range of work: 5 - 25 years.
Source of support for work (%): 100 Postal administrations.
Work done for (%): 30 Postal administrations.
Number of persons working at professional level: 4 Part time, 25 Full time.   *(411)*

384. Universidad Central del Ecuador
Facultad de Dere Cho, Instituto Superior de Investigaciones Sociales, Ciudad Universitaria, Quito, Ecuador.
Type of centre: Research centre of University.
Concerned with long-term futures.
Direction of work in forecasting: I Social, 2 Economic.
Direction of work in research: I Social priorities, 2 Futures methodology, 3 Social impacts of technology, 4 Alternative futures.
Methods used: I Statistical models, 2 Historical analogy, 3 Probabilistic forecasting, 4 Gaming, 5 Expert panels, 6 Operational models, 7 Network analysis.
Time range of work: 5 - IO years.
Source of support for work (%):   IOO University.
Work done for (%):   IOO University.
Number of persons working at professional level: 5 Part time, I2 Full time.   *(232)*

385. Universita Internazionale Degli Studi Sociali
Mr Giorgio Nebbia, Viale Pola 12, 1 - OO198 Rome, Italy.
Type of centre: Academic.
Concerned with long-term futures.
Time allocated (%):   IO.
Source of support for work (%):   IOO University.
Work done for (%):   5 Other University.
Number of persons working at professional level: I Full time, 2 Part time.   *(413)*

386. Universität Mannheim (see also University of Mannheim)
Sonderforschungsbereich 24, 68 Mannheim, West Germany.
Type of centre: National government.
Concerned with long-term futures.
Time allocated (%):   Less than IO.
Direction of work in research: The individual in the future.
Methods used: Statistical models, Individual expert forecasting.
Time range of work: 5 - IO years.
Source of support for work (%):   IOO National government.
Work done for (%):   IOO National government.
Number of persons working at professional level: I Part time, 3 Full time.   *(151)*

387. Université Nationale du Zaire
Campus de Lubumdashi,PO Box 1825, Lubumbashi, Republic du Zaire.
Type of centre: Academic.
Primarily engaged in: Futures studies.
Source of support for work (%):   5O Local government, 5O National government.
Work done for (%):   5O Local government, 5O National government.   *(161)*

388. University of Aston
Design and Innovation Group, Secretary, C.H. Buck, Gosta Green, Birmingham 4, UK.
Type of centre: Academic.
Concerned with long-term futures.
Time allocated (%):   3O.
Direction of work in forecasting: I Technological, 2 Resources, 3 Environmental.
Direction of work in research: I Futures methodology, 2 Resource utilization, 3 3 Alternative futures.

Direction of work in planning: I Technological, 2 Resources, 3 Corporate.
Methods used: I Extrapolation techniques, 2 Morphological, 3 Brainstorming, 4 Delphi techniques, 5 Scenario building, 6 Gaming, 7 Simulation.
Time range of work: IO - 25 years.
Work done for (%): 2O Local government, 2O National government, 6O Private business.
Additional information: Formally recognised university body to which any member of the university may belong. *(145)*

389. University of Birmingham
Centre for Urban and Regional Studies, Selly Wiek House, Selly Wiek Road, Birmingham B29, 76F, UK.
Type of centre: Academic.
Concerned with long-term futures.
Time allocated (%): 2O.
Direction of work in research: I Policy research, 2 Social priorities, 3 Environmental.
Direction of work in planning: I Urban, 2 Regional, 3 Social, 4 Economic, 5 Political, 6 Environmental.
Methods used: I Historical analogy, 2 Causal modelling, 3 Statistical models, 4 Extrapolation techniques.
Time range of work: 5 - beyond year 2OOO.
Source of support for work (%): IO Local government, 2O Foundations, 2O University, 5O National government.
Work done for (%): 5O Local government, 5O National government.
Number of persons working at professional level: I2 Part time. *(379)*

390. University of Bradford Management Centre
Emm Lane, Bradford, West Yorkshire, BD9 4JL, UK.
Type of centre: Academic. *Concerned with long-term futures.*
Time allocated (%): 2O.
Methods used: I Statistical models, 2 Network analysis, 3 Simulation, 4 Probabilistic forecasting, 5 Gaming.
Time range of work: IO - 25 years.
Source of support for work (%): IO Local government, 9O National government.
Work done for (%): 3 Local government, I2 Other.
Number of persons working at professional level: 3 Full time *(70)*

391. University of California
Dept of City and Regional Planning, Richard L. Meier, Berkeley, California 94720, USA.
Type of centre: Academic.
Primarily engaged in: Both futures studies and long-range planning.
Direction of work in forecasting: Technological, Economic, Social, Cultural, Educational, Scientific, Environmental, Manpower, Resources, Population.
Direction of work in research: All areas (see Directory guide).
Direction of work in planning: Scientific, Technological, Social, Urban, Regional, Educational, Economic, Political, Environmental, Resources.
Methods used: Probabilistic forecasting, Gaming, Cross impact analysis, Scenario building, Extrapolation techniques, Contextual mapping, Brainstorming, Statistical models, Relevance trees, Network analysis, Historical analogy, Simulation, Causal modelling.

Time range of work: 5 - beyond year 2000.
Source of support for work (%): IO International agencies, IO Private business,
IO Foundations, IO Voluntary associations, 2O National government, 40 Local government.
Number of persons working at professional level: IO Full time, 7O Part time.   *(416)*

392. University of California
Department of Psychiatry, Program on Psychosocial Adaptation and the Future,
Director, Roderick Gorney, 76O Westwood Plaza, Los Angeles, Ca 90024, USA.
Type of centre: Academic.
Primarily engaged in: Both futures studies and long-range planning.
Direction of work in forecasting: Psychosocial.
Direction of work in research: I Social priorities, 2 Value systems, 3 Alternative
futures, 4 Policy research, 5 The individual in the future.
Direction of work in planning: I Social, 2 Political.
Methods used: I Survey research, 2 Expert panels, 3 Individual expert forecasting,
3 Field experiment, 3 Literature-based experiment.
Time range of work: IO - 25 years.
Source of support for work (%): 5 Private business, IO UCLA Department of
Psychiatry, 85 Foundations.
Work done for (%): 9O Foundations, IO UCLA Department of Psychiatry.
Number of persons working at professional level: 4 Part time, 5 Full time.
Additional information: Concerned with analysis of mass entertainment and cultural
patterns as vehicle for charting and creating psychosocial adaptations to the future.   *(441)*

393. University of California
Institute of Urban and Regional Development, Berkeley, Ca. 94720, USA.
Type of centre: Academic.
Concerned with long-term futures.
Time allocated (%): Less than IO.
Direction of work in forecasting: I Economic, 2 Technological, 3 Population,
4 Environment.
Direction of work in research: I Population, 2 Resource utilization, 3 Alternative futures,
4 Social impacts of technology.
Direction of work in planning: I Urban, 2 Social, 3 Regional.
Methods used: Probabilistic forecasting, Gaming, Scenario building, Statistical models,
Simulation.
Time range of work: 5 - beyond year 2000.
Source of support for work (%): 8O National government, 2O University.
Number of persons working at professional level: 2O Part time.   *(461)*

394. University of California
Urban Resources Study Centre, Fred E. Case, Graduate School of Management,
Los Angeles, Ca 90024, USA.
Type of centre: Academic.
Primarily engaged in: Both futures studies and long-range planning.
Direction of work in forecasting: I Economic, 2 Social, 3 Market, 4 Environmental.
Direction of work in research: I Alternative futures, 2 Value systems, 3 Alternative
governmental futures, developments.
Direction of work in planning: I Urban, 2 Economic, 3 Political, 4 Social.
Methods used: I Statistical models, 2 Delphi techniques, 3 Extrapolation techniques,
4 Individual expert forecasting, 5 Simulation, 6 Scenario building.

Time range of work: 5 - 25 years.
Source of support for work (%): 5 Private business, 5 Foundations, 2O Local government, 7O State government.
Work done for (%): IO National government, IO Private business, 4O Local government, 4O State government.
Number of persons working at professional level: 3 Part time, 8-15 Full time.   *(329)*

395. University College Dublin
Dept of Social Science, Belfield, Dublin 4, Eire.
Type of centre: Academic. *Concerned with long-term futures.*
Time allocated (%): Less than IO.
Direction of work in research: Social priorities, Policy research.
Direction of work in planning: Social, Educational.
Methods used: Surveys.
Time range of work: 5 - IO years.
Source of support for work (%): IO Private business, IO Foundations, IO Voluntary associations, IO University, 6O National government.
Work done for (%): I Local government, 2 National government, 2 Foundations, 2 Voluntary associations, 3 University.
Number of persons working at professional level: 5 Part time.   *(95)*

396. University of Dayton
Research Institute, Ralph C. Lenz, Jr, Joseph P. Martino, Dayton, Ohio 45469, USA.
Type of centre: Academic.
Primarily engaged in: Both futures studies and long-range planning.
Direction of work in forecasting: I Technological, 2 Resources, 3 Military, 4 Economic, 5 Market, 6 Social.
Direction of work in research: I Futures methodology, 2 Resource utilization, 3 Social impacts of technology, 4 Alternative futures, 5 Social priorities.
Direction of work in planning: I Technological, 2 Military, 3 Resources, 4 Urban, 5 Corporate, 6 Regional.
Methods used: I Extrapolation techniques, 2 Cross impact analysis, 3 Delphi techniques, 4 Scenario building, 5 Relevance trees, 6 Causal modelling.
Time range of work: 5 - 25 years.
Source of support for work (%): 2O Local government, 4O National government, 25 Private business, I5 University.
Work done for (%): 25 Local government, 45 National government, 25 Private business, 5 University.
Number of persons working at professional level: 4 Part time, 2 Full time.   *(450)*

397. University of East Anglia
Overseas Development Group, Norwich, NR4 7TJ, UK.
Type of centre: Academic.
Concerned with long-term futures.
Time allocated (%): 2O.
Direction of work in forecasting: I Economic, 2 Social, 3 Resources, 4 Population, 5 Environmental.
Direction of work in research: I Resource utilization, 2 Policy research, 3 Social impacts of technology, 4 Environmental.
Direction of work in planning: I Economic, 2 Regional, 3 Social, 4 Resources.
Time range of work: 5 - IO years.

Source of support for work (%):   25 National government, 30 International agencies, 20 Private business, 20 Foundations, 5 Voluntary associations.
Work done for (%):   25 National government, 30 International agencies, 20 Private business, 20 Foundations, 5 Voluntary associations.
Number of persons working at professional level: 24 Full time.   *(465)*

398. University of Edinburgh
Centre for Human Ecology, Director, Dr. J.L. Hale, St George Square, Edinburgh EH8 9JU, UK.
Type of centre: Academic.
Primarily engaged in: Both futures studies and long-range planning.
Direction of work in forecasting: I Environmental, 2 Resources.
Direction of work in research: I Social impacts of technology, 2 Environmental, 3 Resource utilization.
Direction of work in planning: I Environmental, 2 Regional.
Methods used: I Expert panels, 2 Base-line of case-studies.
Time range of work: 5 - 25 years.
Source of support for work (%):   100 University.
Number of persons working at professional level: I Full time.   *(378)*

399. University of Edinburgh
Planning Research Unit, 57 George Square, Edinburgh EH8 9JU, UK.
Type of centre: Academic.
Primarily engaged in: Both futures studies and long-range planning.
Direction of work in forecasting: I Environmental, 2 Resources, 3 Population.
Direction of work in research: I Environmental, 2 Alternative futures, 3 Resource utilization, 4 Policy research.
Direction of work in planning: I Regional, 2 Environmental, 3 Urban, 4 Educational, 5 Technological.
Methods used: I Scenario building, 2 Probabilistic forecasting, 3 Brainstorming.
Time range of work: 10 - 25 years.
Source of support for work (%):   25 Local government, 25 National government, 50 Foundations.
Work done for (%):   20 Local government, 20 National government, 20 Foundations.
Number of persons working at professional level: 10 Full time.   *(258)*

400. University of Georgia
The Executive Forum, Dept of Management, College of Business Administration, Athens, Ga 30602, USA.
Type of centre: Academic.
Concerned with long-term futures.
Time allocated (%):   10.
Direction of work in forecasting: Social, Educational.
Direction of work in research: The family in the future.
Direction of work in planning: Urban, Regional.
Methods used: Statistical models, Expert panels.
Time range of work: 5 - 25 years.
Source of support for work (%):   5 Local government, 5 National government, 5 Private business, 5 Foundations.
Work done for (%):   5 Private business, 90 Local government.
Number of persons working at professional level: 10 Full time, 30 Part time.   *(165)*

401. University of Houston at Clear Lake City

Program in Studies of the Future, Christopher Dede, 2700 Bay Area Blvd, Houston, Tx 77058, USA.

Type of centre: Academic.
Primarily engaged in: Both futures studies and long-range planning.
Direction of work in forecasting: I Social, 2 Cultural, 3 Educational, 4 Economic, 5 Technological, 6 Scientific, 7 Environmental, 8 Resources, 9 Manpower, IO Market.
Direction of work in research: I Alternative futures, 2 Social priorities, 3 Social impacts of technology, 4 Value systems, 5 Resource utilization, 6 Policy research, 7 The family in the future, 8 The individual in the future.
Direction of work in planning: I Social, 2 Educational, 3 Economic, 4 Scientific, 5 Technological, 6 Urban, 7 Corporate, 8 Resources.
Methods used: I Scenario building, 2 Individual expert forecasting, 3 Delphi techniques, 4 Cross impact analysis, 5 Gaming, 6 Simulation, 7 Historical analogy, 8 Brainstorming, 9 Expert panels.
Time range of work: IO - 25 years.
Source of support for work (%): IOO University.
Work done for (%): IOO University.
Number of persons working at professional level: 4 Full time, IO Part time. **(264)**

402. University of Illinois at Chicago Circle

Vice Chancellor for Academic Affairs, Dr Joseph Lipson, PO Box 4348, Chicago, Il 60880, USA.

Type of Centre: Academic. *Concerned with long-term futures.*
Time allocated (%): IO.
Methods used: I Expert panels, 2 Individual expert forecasting, 4 Simulation, 5 Scenario building, 5 Operational models, 6 Extrapolation techniques, 7 Causal modelling, 8 Historical analogy.
Time range of work: 5 - 25 years.
Source of support for work (%): 2 Foundations, 8 National government, 90 Local government.
Work done for (%): 2 Foundations, 4 Local government, 4 National government, 90 University.
Number of persons working at professional level: IOO Part time. **(260)**

403. University of Iowa College of Law

Centre for World Order Studies, Burns Wesson, Iowa City, Ia 52242, USA.

Type of centre: Academic.
Concerned with long-term futures.
Time allocated (%): Less than IO.
Methods used: Brainstorming, Simulation.
Time range of work: IO - 25 years.
Source of support for work (%): IOO Foundations.
Number of persons working at professional level: 3 Full time. **(48)**

404. University of Lancaster

Institute for Research and Development in Post-compulsory Education, Bailrigg, Lancaster, UK.

Type of centre: Academic.
Concerned with long-term futures.
Time allocated (%): 30.
Direction of work in forecasting: Educational, Manpower.

5

Direction of work in research: Manpower, Policy research.
Direction of work in planning: Educational.
Methods used: I Causal modelling, 2 Statistical models, 3 Simulation, 4 Probabilistic forecasting.
Time range of work: 5 - IO years.
Source of support for work (%): 3O National government, 3O International agencies, 4O Other.
Number of persons working at professional level: I Part time, I Full time.   *(244)*

405. University of Leeds
Dept of Fuel and Combustion Science, Prof A. Williams, Leeds LS2 9JT, UK.
Type of centre: Academic.
Concerned with long-term futures.
Time allocated (%): IO.
Methods used: Simulation.
Time range of work: IO - 25 years.
Source of support for work (%): IOO National government.
Number of persons working at professional level: 2 Full time.   *(29)*

406. University of Linköping
Prof Eve Malmquist, 581 83 Linkoping, Sweden.
Type of centre: Academic. *Concerned with long-term futures.*
Time allocated (%): 2O.
Direction of work in forecasting: Educational, Scientific.
Direction of work in research: Alternative futures.
Direction of work in planning: Scientific, Educational.
Methods used: Scenario building, Individual expert forecasting.
Time range of work: IO - 25 years.
Source of support for work (%): IOO Foundations.
Work done for (%): 2O Foundations.
Number of persons working at professional level: 2I Part time.   *(116)*

407. The University of Manchester
Dept of Liberal Studies in Science, Harry Rothman, Manchester, UK.
Type of centre: Academic.
Concerned with long-term futures:
Time allocated (%): 3O.
Direction of work in forecasting: Technological, Environmental, Resources, Scientific.
Direction of work in research: Social impacts of technology, Environmental, Resource utilization, Value systems, Policy research, Futures methodology.
Direction of work in planning: Scientific, Technological.
Source of support for work (%): 9O National government.
Number of persons working at professional level: 3 Part time, 6 Full time.   *(442.*

408. University of Mannheim (see also Universität Mannheim)
Industry Seminar, Gert V. Kortzfleisch, 68 Mannheim 1, Schloss, West Germany.
Type of centre: Independent research.
Primarily engaged in: Long-range planning.
Direction of work in forecasting: 2 Technological, 3 Social, 4 Environmental, 5 Resources 6 Population, 7 Economic.

Direction of work in research: l Value systems, 2 The individual in the future,
3 Simulation technology, 4 Social impacts of technology.
Direction of work in planning: l Technological, 2 Regional, 3 Corporate.
Methods used: l Simulation, 2 Operational models, 3 Causal modelling,
4 Extrapolation techniques.
Time range of work: lO - beyond year 2OOO.
Source of support for work (%): lOO Foundations.
Work done for (%): lOO Foundations.
Number of persons working at professional level: 3 Part time, 11 Full time.   *(181)*

4O9. University of Maryland, Dept of Economics

Interindustry Forecasting Project, College Park, Md 2O742, USA.
Type of centre: Academic.
Primarily engaged in: Futures studies.
Direction of work in forecasting: l Economic, 2 Technological, 3 Environmental.
4 Manpower.
Methods used: Statistical models, Simulation, Causal modelling.
Time range of work: 5 - lO years.
Source of support for work (%): 5 Foundations, lO National government, 85 Private
business.
Work done for (%): lO National government, 9O Private business.
Number of persons working at professional level: 3 Part time, 6 Full time.   *(240)*

41O. University of Minnesota

Quigley Centre of International Studies, Minneapolis, Mn 55455, USA.
Type of centre: Academic.
Concerned with long-term futures.
Time allocated (%): Less than lO.
Source of support for work (%): lOO Foundations.
Work done for (%): 4O Foundations.
Number of persons working at professional level: 3 Part time.   *(148)*

411. University of Oregon

Dept of Political Science, Institute of Policy Studies, H.J. Strauss, Eugene, Or 974O3, USA.
Type of centre: Academic.
Concerned with long-term futures.
Time allocated (%): 2O.
Methods used: l Expert panels, 2 Delphi techniques.
Time range of work: 5 - lO years.
Source of support for work (%): 5 Foundations, 95 Local government.
Work done for (%): lO Local government.
Number of persons working at professional level: 2 Part time, 2 Full time.   *(316)*

412. University of Oslo

Chair in Conflict and Peace Research, Johan Galtung, PO Box 1O7O, Oslo 3, Norway.
Type of centre: Academic.
Concerned with long-term futures.
Time allocated (%): 3O.
Direction of work in research: Alternative futures, Futures methodology, Social
priorities, Value systems, The individual in the future, Policy research.
Direction of work in planning: Educational, Economic, Political.

Time range of work: IO - beyond year 2OOO.
Source of support for work (%): 3O International agencies, 7O Foundations.
Work done for (%): 3O International agencies.
Number of persons working at professional level: 3 Part time, 4 Full time.   *(184)*

413. University of South Africa
School Business Leadership, A.T. Morkel. Pretoria OOO1, South Africa.
Type of centre: Academic. *Concerned with long-term futures.*
Time allocated (%): Less than IO.
Methods used: I Extrapolation techniques, 2 Individual expert forecasting, 3 Scenario building, 4 Cross impact analysis.
Time range of work: 5 - IO years.
Number of persons working at professional level: 2 Part time.   *(37O)*

414. University of South Florida
Leisure Studies Program, Tampa, Fl 33629 USA.
Type of centre: International non-government.
Concerned with long-term futures.
Time allocated (%): 2O.
Methods used: I Secondary analysis, 2 Historical analogy, 3 Cross impact analysis.
Time range of work: IO - 25 years.
Source of support for work (%): 5 Voluntary associations, IO National government, IO International agencies, 75 Local government.
Work done for (%): 5 Foundations, IO National government, IO International agencies, 75 Local government.
Number of persons working at professional level: 2 Part time, 2 Full time.   *(155)*

415. University of Southern California
Graduate School of Business Administration, Centre for Futures Research, University Park, Los Angeles, Ca 9OOO7, USA.
Type of centre: Academic.
Primarily engaged in: Both futures studies and long-range planning.
Direction of work in forecasting: I Economic, 2 Technological, 3 Social, 4 Cultural, 4 Educational, 4 Scientific, 4 Manpower, 4 Resources, 4 Population.
Direction of work in research: I Futures methodology, 2 Policy research, 3 Alternative futures, 4 Social impacts of technology, 4 Manpower, 4 Value systems, 4 Social priorities, 4 Population, 4 The individual in the future.
Direction of work in planning: I Regional, 2 Corporate, 3 Technological, 4 Scientific, 4 Social, 4 Urban, 4 Educational, 4 Economic, 4 Political.
Methods used: I Delphi techniques, 2 Simulation, 3 Extrapolation techniques, 4 Probabilistic forecasting, 4 Gaming, 4 Cross impact analysis, 4 Scenario building, 4 Contextual mapping, 4 Brainstorming, 4 Statistical models, 4 Expert panels, 4 Historical analogy, 4 Operational models, 4 Individual expert forecasting, 4 Causal modelling.
Time range of work: IO - 25 years.
Source of support for work (%): IO Foundations, I5 Local government, 25 Private business, 5O National government.
Work done for (%): IO Foundations, I5 Local government, 25 Private business, 5O National government.
Number of persons working at professional level: I2 Part time.   *(332)*

416. University of Stellenbosch
Bureau for Economic Research, Unit for Futures Research, Stellenbosch 7600, South Africa.
Type of centre: Academic.
Primarily engaged in: Futures studies.
Direction of work in forecasting: Technological, Social, Cultural, Environmental, Educational, Resources, Manpower, Economic, Population.
Methods used: I Extrapolation techniques, 2 Expert panels, 3 Scenario building, 4 Probabilistic forecasting.
Time range of work: IO - 25 years.
Source of support for work (%): 3 Foundations, I7 Other public corporations and utilities, 80 Private business.
Work done for (%): 3 Foundations, 80 Private business.
Number of persons working at professional level: 2 Part time, 4 Part time.　　　*(372)*

417. University of Strathclyde
Abacus, Dept of Architecture and Building Science, Glasgow G4 ONG, UK.
Type of centre: Academic.
Concerned with long-term futures.
Time allocated (%): 50.
Direction of work in research: I Environmental, 2 Value systems, 3 Futures methodology.
Direction of work in planning: I Corporate, 2 Urban, 3 Regional.
Methods used: I Simulation, 2 Operational models, 3 Gaming.
Time range of work: 5 - beyond year 2000.
Source of support for work (%): IOO National government.
Work done for (%): IO Private business, 40 National government, 50 Local government.
Number of persons working at professional level: IO Full time.　　　*(153)*

418. University of Tokyo
Prof Shinkichi Eto, 3 - 8 - 1 Komara, Meguro-ku, Tokyo, Japan.
Type of centre: Academic. *Concerned with long-term futures.*
Time allocated (%): IO.
Direction of work in forecasting: International relations.
Direction of work in research: Policy research.
Direction of work in planning: Political.
Methods used: I Simulation, 2 Gaming, 3 Scenario building, 4 Historical analogy, 5 Operational models, 6 Individual expert forecasting.
Time range of work: IO - 25 years.
Source of support for work (%): 40 Foundations, 60 National government.
Work done for (%): IOO Academic purposes.
Number of persons working at professional level: 5 Part time.　　　*(287)*

419. University of Washington
Program in Social Management of Technology, Seattle, Wa 98195, USA.
Type of centre: Academic.
Concerned with long-term futures.
Time allocated (%): 30.
Methods used: I Brainstorming, 2 Causal modelling, 3 Historical analogy.
Time range of work: 5 - IO years.
Source of support for work (%): 50 Government state, 50 Foundations.
Number of persons working at professional level: 3 Full time.　　　*(160)*

420. University of Washington

Urban Systems Research Centre, Director, Prof, J.B. Schneiden, 125 More Hall (FX-1O)
Seattle, Wa 98195, USA.
Type of centre: Academic.
Concerned with long-term futures.
Time allocated (%):   2O.
Direction of work in forecasting: I Technological, 2 Economic, 3 Social, 4 Population,
5 Environmental.
Direction of work in research: I Social impacts of technology, 2 Resource utilization,
3 Environmental, 4 Value systems, 5 Social priorities.
Direction of work in planning: I Urban, 2 Regional, 3 Technological, 4 Social,
5 Educational, 6 Economic, 7 Environmental.
Methods used: All methods (see Directory guide) and Morphological analysis.
Time range of work: 5 - 25 years.
Source of support for work (%):   IOO National government.
Work done for (%):   5O Local government, 5O National government.
Number of persons working at professional level: 2 Part time, 2 Full time.   *(152)*

421. The University of Wisconsin

Project Destiny, University Extension, Prof of Engineering, Paul J. Grogan, Madison,
Wi 537O6, USA.
Type of centre: Academic.
Concerned with long-term futures.
Time allocated (%):   IO.
Direction of work in forecasting: I Technological, 2 Environmental, 3 Resources,
4 Scientific.
Direction of work in research: I Resource utilization, 2 Environmental, 3 Alternative
futures, 4 Futures methodology.
Direction of work in planning: I Technological, 2 Scientific, 3 Environmental,
4 Resources.
Methods used: I Delphi techniques, 2 Scenario building, 3 Cross impact analysis,
4 Extrapolation techniques, 5 Expert panels, 6 Relevance trees.
Time range of work: 5 - beyond year 2OOO.
Source of support for work (%):   IOO Institutional revenues.
Work done for (%):   5O National government, 5O Private business.
Number of persons working at professional level: I Part time.   *(31)*

V 422. Videa 1OOO.

Robert de Havilland, 2O Rockledge Rd, Hartsdale, NY 1O53O, USA.
Type of centre: Business.
Concerned with long-term futures.
Time allocated (%):   3O.
Methods used: I Individual expert forecasting, 2 Expert panels.
Time range of work: 5 - IO years.
Source of support for work (%):   IOO Private business.
Work done for (%):   IOO Private business.
Number of persons working at professional level: I Part time, I Full time.   *(250)*

423. WACY 2000

Secretary, John Goodman, 7A Elmcroft Ave, London NW11, ORS, UK.
Type of centre: International non-government.
Primarily engaged in: Long-range planning.
Direction of work in forecasting: Environmental, Celebration.
Methods used: Brainstorming.
Time range of work: IO - beyond year 2000.
Source of support for work (%): 2 Universities, 98 Local government.
Number of persons working at professional level: I2 Part time.
Additional information: Exists to celebrate year 2000.   *(345)*

424. Weyerhaeuser Company

Tacoma, Wa 98401, USA.
Type of centre: Business. **Concerned with long-term futures.**
Time allocated (%): Less than IO.
Direction of work in forecasting: I Technological, I Economic, I Market, I Resources,
2 Social, 2 Environmental, 2 Manpower.
Direction of work in research: I Resource utilization, 2 Environmental, 3 Alternative
futures.
Direction of work in planning: Corporate, Resources.
Methods used: All methods (see Directory guide).
Time range of work: 5 - year 2000.
Source of support for work (%): IOO Private business.
Work done for (%): IOO Private business.
Number of persons working at professional level: IOO Full time.   *(208)*

425. The Whirlpool Corp

Technology Forecasting and Technology Assessement Manager, Richard G. Davis,
Benton Harbor, Mi 49022, USA.
Type of centre: Industry. **Concerned with long-term futures.**
Time allocated (%): 30.
Direction of work in forecasting: I Technological, 2 Social, 3 Resources, 4 Environmental.
Direction of work in research: I Social impacts of technology, 2 Value systems,
3 Social priorities, 4 Resource utilization, 5 Environmental, 6 Consumer affairs, 7 The
family in the future.
Direction of work in planning: I Technological, 2 Social, 3 Resources, 4 Environmental,
5 Corporate.
Methods used: I Historical analogy, 2 Simulation, 3 Cross impact analysis, 4 Extrapolation
techniques, 5 Relevance trees, 6 Delphi techniques.
Time range of work: 5 - IO years.
Source of support for work (%): IOO Private business.
Work done for (%): IO Local government, 9O Private business.
Number of persons working at professional level: 8 Full time, 2O Part time.   *(398)*

426. Wirtschafts und Sozialwissenschaftliches Institut des Deutschen Gewerk-schaftbundes

4 Dusseldorf, Hans Bockler-Str 39, West Germany.
Type of centre: Trade union.
Concerned with long-term futures.
Time allocated (%): 2O.
Methods used: I Statistical models, 2 Extrapolation techniques, 3 Scenario building.

Time range of work: 5 - IO years.
Source of support for work (%): 5O National government, 5O German trade union-confederation (DGB)
Work done for (%): 4O National government, 6O Trade unions.
Number of persons working at professional level: 5 Full time, IO Part time.   *(18)*

World Bank
See: International Bank for Reconstruction and Development.

427. World Confederation of Teachers
C. Damen, 5O, Rue Joseph II, Brussels 1O4O, Belgium.
Type of centre: International professional organization/international non-government/trade union.
Concerned with long-term futures.
Time allocated (%): 3O.
Direction of work in planning: Social, Educational.
Methods used: Expert panels.
Time range of work: IO - 25 years.
Source of support for work (%): 3O International agencies.
Number of persons working at professional level: I Full time, 3 Part time.   *(47)*

428. World Federation of Agricultural Workers
5O, Rue Joseph II, 1O4O Brussels, Belgium.
Type of centre: Trade Union.
Concerned with long-term futures.
Direction of work in forecasting: Social.
Direction of work in research: Social priorities.
Direction of work in planning: Labour.
Number of persons working at professional level: I Part time, I Full time.
Additional information: Concerned with defence of agricultural workers, social professional and human interests, especially labour conditions and social progress.   *(58)*

429. World Future Society
President, Edward Cornish, PO Box 3O369 Bethesda Branch, Washington DC 2OO14, USA.
Type of centre: International non-governmental.
Primarily engaged in: Futures studies.
Direction of work in forecasting: I Educational, 2 Scientific, 3 Social.
Direction of work in research: I Alternative futures, 2 Social impacts of technology, 3 The individual in the future.
Direction of work in planning: I Social, 2 Educational.
Methods used: Expert panels, Individual expert forecasting.
Time range of work: 5 - 5O years.
Source of support for work (%): 5 National government., 9O Voluntary associations, 5 Sales of publications.
Work done for (%): IO National government.
Number of persons working at professional level: 9 Part time, 9 Full time.   *(468)*

43O. World Future Studies Federation
Secretary General, Eleonora Masini, Casella Postale 62O3, Roma Prati, Italy.
Type of centre: Membership society.
Erimarily engaged in: Both futures studies and long-range planning.

Direction of work in forecasting: I Social, 2 Cultural, 3 Educational, 4 Scientific.
Direction of work in research: I Alternative futures, 2 Value systems, 3 Social priorities,
4 The individual in the future, 5 Social impacts of technology, 6 Futures methodology.
Direction of work in planning: I Social, 2 Educational, 3 Scientific, 4 Political.
Methods used: I Expert panels, 2 Individual expert forecasting, 3 Scenario building,
4 Brainstorming, 5 Historical analogy, 6 Delphi techniques, 7 Extrapolation techniques,
8 Simulation.
Time range of work: Beyond year 2000.
Source of support for work (%): 50 National government, 30 Voluntary associations,
20 International agencies.
Work done for (%): 30 Voluntary associations, 70 International agencies.
Additional information: The Federation has two people who work on a professional
basis, and has about 200 individual and 30 organization members. *(469)*

431. World Institute
PO Box 7458, Jerusalem, Israel.
Type of centre: Independent research.
Concerned with long-term futures.
Time allocated (%): 20.
Methods used: Probabilistic forecasting, Extrapolation techniques, Scenario building,
Historical analogy, Individual expert forecasting.
Time range of work: 5 - 10 years.
Number of persons working at professional level: 4 Part time, 8 Full time. *(392)*

432. World Institute Council
President, Julius Stulman, 777 United Nations Plaza, New York, NY 10017, USA.
Type of centre: International research and education institution.
Concerned with long-term futures.
Time allocated (%): 50.
Direction of work in forecasting: I Educational, 2 Cultural, 3 Economic.
Direction of work in research: I Futures methodology, 2 Value systems, 3 Alternative
futures.
Direction of work in planning: I Educational, 2 Scientific, 3 Technological.
Methods used: I Probabilistic forecasting, I Delphi techniques, 2 Expert panels,
3 Individual expert forecasting.
Time range of work: 10 - beyond year 2000.
Source of support for work (%): 50 International agencies.
Work done for (%): 25 Fields within Fields (a journal).
Additional information: As a non-profit research and educational institution the
Council serves government bodies and educational institutions, supports research
in human ecology, and publishes and disseminates such works and ideas as it believes
will lead to solutions to the urgent problem facing mankind. *(60)*

433. World Meteorological Organization
Director for Programme Planning, O.M. Ashford, Case Postale No 5, CH - 1211 Geneva,
Switzerland.
Type of centre: International government.
Concerned with long-term futures.
Time allocated (%): Less than 10.
Methods used: Statistical models, Simulation, Causal modelling.
Time range of work: 5 - 10 years.

Source of support for work (%):   100 International agencies.
Number of persons working at professional level: 4 Part time.   (65)

434. World Organization of National Colleges, Academies, and Academic Associations of General Practitioners and Family Physicians (WONCA)

Honorary Secretary, Dr David A. Game, 50 Lambert Road, Royston Park, South Australia, Australia.
Type of centre: International professional organization.
Direction of work in forecasting: Educational, Scientific.
Direction of work in research: The family in the future.
Time range of work: 5 - 10 years.
Source of support for work (%):   100 Voluntary associations.
Work done for (%):   100 Voluntary associations.
Number of persons working at professional level: 80 Part time.   (354)

435. World Problems Project

1 Rue aux Laines, 1000 Brussels, Belgium.
Type of centre: International non-government.
Concerned with long-term futures.
Direction of work in forecasting: All world problems existing and potential perceived as a network.
Direction of work in research: Value systems.
Methods used: Delphi techniques, Contextual mapping, Brainstorming, Network analysis.
Source of support for work (%):   25 Voluntary associations, 75 Private individuals.
Work done for (%):   50 International agencies, 50 Voluntary associations.
Additional information: Objective is the creation of a data base to assess in above methods.   (147)

436. World Resources Inventory

2500 Market St, Philadelphia, Pa 19104, USA.
Type of centre: Independent research centre.
Primarily engaged in: Long-range planning.
Direction of work in research: Alternative futures, Environmental, Resource utilization, Futures methodology.
Direction of work in planning: Technological, Social, Regional, Environmental, Resources.
Methods used: Probabilistic forecasting, Simulation, Delphi techniques, Gaming, Cross impact analysis, Scenario building, Extrapolation techniques, Brainstorming, Statistical models, Expert panels, Relevance trees, Network analysis, Historical analogy, Operational models, Individual expert forecasting.
Time range of work: 5 - beyond year 2000.
Work done for (%):   100 Earth.   (280)

437. World Without War Council Inc

175 5th Ave, No 2101 Flatiron Bldg, New York, NY 10010, USA.
Type of centre: National voluntary association.
Concerned with long-term futures.
Time allocated (%):   50.
Direction of work in forecasting: 1 Political, 2 Educational, 3 Social.
Direction of work in reseaarh: 1 Value systems, 2 Policy research, 3 Alternative futures.

Direction of work in planning: I Political, 2 Educational.
Methods used: Expert panels, Network analysis, Historical analogy, Individual expert forecasting.
Time range of work: 5 - beyond year 2000.
Source of support for work (%): 20 Voluntary associations, 80 Foundations.
Work done for (%): 3 Private business, 3 Foundations, I0 National government, 20 Voluntary associations.
Number of persons working at professional level: 5 Part time.   *(425)*

438. Zentrum Berlin für Zukunftsforschung eV (ZBZ)

D-1000 Berlin 12, Giesebrechtsr, I5, West Germany.
Type of centre: Independent research.
Primarily engaged in: Both futures studies and long-range planning.
Direction of work in forecasting: I Social, 2 Economic, 3 Technological.
Direction of work in research: I Alternative futures, 2 Social impacts of technology, 3 Social priorities.
Direction of work in planning: I Urban, 2 Environmental, 3 Social.
Methods used: I Scenario building, 2 Relevance trees, 3 Individual expert forecasting, 4 Expert panels, 5 Delphi techniques, 6 Extrapolation techniques, 7 Brainstorming.
Time range of work: I0 - beyond year 2000.
Source of support for work (%): I0 Private business, I0 Voluntary associations, 80 National government.
Work done for (%): 20 Local government, 80 National government.
Number of persons working at professional level: I2 Part time, I4 Full time.
Additional information: Publishes Journal: 'Analysen und Prognosen'.   *(119)*

439. Zero Population Growth

1346 Connecticut Ave, NW Washington, DC 20036, USA.
Type of centre: Membership society.
Concerned with long-term futures.
Time allocated (%): Less than I0.
Source of support for work (%): I00 Members.
Work done for (%): I Own use.   *(122)*

INDIVIDUALS

A
1. Ronald Abler
Associate Professor, Pennsylvania State University, 403 Deike Bldg, University Park, Pa 16802, USA.
Sex: Male.　　*Age:* 30-39.
Educational qualification: Doctoral degree.
Formal training: Social/behavioural sciences.
Direction of work in forecasting: I Cultural, 2 Social, 3 Technological.
Direction of work in research: Social impacts of technology.
Methods used: I Historical analogy, 2 Extrapolation techniques.
Time range of work: IO - 25 years.
Source of support for work (%): 20 National government, 80 Local government.
Work done for (%): 20 National government, 80 Local or regional government.
Occupational function: Educator.
Worked in education: I In research, 2 Teaching.
Additional information: Concerned with future communications, technology and settlement patterns.　　　　　　　　　　　　　　　　　　　　　*(43)*

2. K.V. Abraham
Manager Corporate Planning and Analysis, Weyerhaeuser Company, Tacoma, Wa 98401, USA.
Sex: Male.　　*Age:* 30-39.
Educational qualification: Master's degree.
Formal training: Engineering.
Informal training: Social/behaviourial sciences.
Primarily engaged in: Long-range planning.
Areas in which work done (%): 50 In planning unit of a business enterprise, 50 In planning unit of an international organization.
Direction of work in forecasting: Economic, Market, Resources.
Direction of work in research: Futures methodology.
Direction of work in planning: Technological, Economic, Corporate, Resources.
Methods used: Probabilistic forecasting, Extrapolation techniques, Brainstorming, Statistical models, Historical analogy, Operational models, Simulation.
Time range of work: 5 - beyond year 2000.
Source of support for work (%): IOO Private business.
Work done for (%): IOO Private business.
Occupational function: Manager.
Worked in industry/business in: Management, Planning.
Additional information: Concerned with long-range resource analysis of timber; finance analysis; and growth.　　　　　　　　　　　　　　　　　　　　*(265)*

3. Mark Abrams
Social Science Research Council, State House, High Holborn, London, WC1, UK.
Sex: Male.　　*Age:* 60 or over.
Educational qualification: Doctoral degree.

Formal training: Social/behavioural sciences.
Informal training: I Social/behavioural sciences, 2 Education, 3 Journalism.
Direction of work in forecasting: I Social, 2 Cultural, 3 Educational, 4 Market, 5 Economic.
Direction of work in research: I Value systems, 2 Social priorities.
Direction of work in planning: Educational.
Methods used: I Mass sample surveys, 2 Extrapolation techniques, 3 Statistical models.
Time range of work: 5 - IO years.
Source of support for work (%): 3O Local government, 7O National government.
Work done for (%): 5 Local or regional government, 2O National government.
Occupational function: I Manager, 2 Research worker, 3 Administrator.
Worked in government as: Researcher.
Worked in industry/business in: I Management, 2 Research and development.
Worked in education: I In research, 2 Teaching.
Additional information: Not primarily engaged but concerned with long-term future in the areas of social indicators, and change in social values.. *(148)*

4. Benson D. Adams
51O6 Viking Road, Bethesda, Md 2OO14, USA.
Sex: Male.   *Age:* 30-39.
Educational qualification: Doctoral degree.
Formal training: Social/behavioural sciences.
Informal training: Physical sciences, mathematics, engineering.
Primarily engaged in: Both futures studies and long-range planning.
Areas in whcih work done (%): IOO in planning unit of a governmental agency.
Direction of work in forecasting: I Political, 2 Military, 3 Technological.
Direction of work in planning: I Military, 2 Political, 3 Technological, 4 Scientific.
Methods used: Gaming, Extrapolation techniques, Expert panels, Operational models, Simulation, Scenario building, Brainstorming, Historical analogy, Individual expert forecasting.
Time range of work: 5 - IO years.
Source of support for work (%): IOO National government.
Work done for (%): IOO National government.
Occupational function: Research worker.
Worked in government as : Researcher.
Worked in industry/business in: Management.
Worked in education: In research.
Additional information: Concerned with national security policy. *(222)*

5. John D. Adams
Consultant to Organizations, 32O2 23rd St, North, Arlington, Va 22201, USA.
Sex: Male.   *Age:* 30-39.
Educational qualification: Doctoral degree.
Formal training: Social/behavioural sciences, Mathematics.
Informal training: Social/behavioural sciences.
Areas in whcih work done (%): IO As individual consultant, IO As academic, in teaching futures studies or long-range planning, 8O In organization concerned with other studies including long-range planning.
Direction of work in forecasting: I Social, 2 Educational.
Direction of work in research: I Value systems, 2 The individual in the future, 3 The family in the future.

Direction of work in planning: I Social, 2 Educational.
Methods used: I Training, 2 Scenario building, 3 Individual expert forecasting.
Time range of work: IO - 25 years.
Source of support for work (%): IOO Self employed, on contractual bases with clients.
Occupational function: I Consultant, 2 Educator.
Worked in education: Teaching, Administration.
Additional information: Concerned with development of theory and data about
transitional dynamics. Engaged in private consultation to organizations in areas of
stress reduction and personal development.   *(305)*

6. Marvin Adelson

Prof, School of Architecture and Urban Planning, University of California, Los Angeles,
Ca 90024, USA.
Sex: Male.   *Age:* 40-49.
Educational qualification: Doctoral degree.
Formal training: I Social behavioural sciences, 2 Engineering.
Informal training: I Mathematics, 2 Education, 3 Design, 4 Humanities, 5 Arts.
Primarily engaged in: Futures studies.
Areas in which work done (%): 5 As individual consultant, 5O As academic, in teaching
futures studies or long-range planning.
Direction of work in forecasting: I Educational, 2 Social.
Direction of work in research: I Alternative futures, 2 Value systems, 3 Social priorities,
4 Policy research, 5 The individual in the future, 5 The family in the future, 7 Futures
methodology.
Direction of work in planning: I Educational, 2 Urban.
Methods used: I Scenario building, 2 Delphi techniques, 3 Probabilistic forecasting,
4 Individual expert forecasting, 5 Historical analogy.
Time range of work: 5 - beyond year 2OOO.
Source of support for work (%): IO Voluntary associations, IO University, 2O Private
business, 6O National government.
Work done for (%): IO Voluntary associations, IO University, 2O Private business,
6O National government.
Occupational function: I Educator, 2 Administrator, 3 Consultant, 4 Research worker.
Worked in industry/business in: I Research and development, 2 Planning, 3 Manage-
ment, 4 Consultancy.
Worked in education: I Teaching, in administration, 2 In research.
Worked in service sector: Social welfare.
Additional information: Concerned with social futures.   *(524)*

7. John Adler

Director, Programming and Budgeting Dept, International Bank for Reconstruction and
Development, International Development Assoc, 1818 H St NW, Washington DC
20433, USA.
Sex: Male   *Age:* 6O or over.
Educational qualification: Doctoral degree.
Formal training: I Social/behavioural sciences, 2 Law.
Informal training: Management.
Primarily engaged in: Both futures studies and long-range planning.
Areas in which work done (%): IOO In planning unit of an international organization.
Direction of work in research: Social priorities.
Direction of work in planning: Corporate.

Methods used: Operational models.
Time range of work: 5 - IO years.
Source of support for work (%): IOO International agencies.
Work done for (%): IOO International agencies.
Occupational function: I Administrator, 2 Manager, 3 Research worker.
Worked in government as: Researcher.
Worked in education: Teaching.   *(261)*

8. R.O. Aines

Manager, Operational and Strategic, International Harvester Company, 4O1 N Michigan
Ave, Chicago, II 6O611, USA.
Sex: Male.   *Age:* 4O-49 years.
Educational qualification: Doctoral degree.
Formal training: Economics.
Informal training: Managerial/behavioural sciences, Education.
Primarily engaged in: Planning systems.
Areas in which work done (%): IOO In planning unit of a business enterprise.
Direction of work in forecasting: Economic.
Direction of work in research: Resource utilization.
Direction of work in planning: Corporate/divisional.
Methods used: Probabilistic forecasting, Brainstorming, Statistical models,
Operational models, Simulation.
Time range of work: I - IO years.
Source of support for work (%): IOO Private business.
Work done for (%): IOO Private business.
Occupational function: I Manager, 2 Consultant, 3 Educator.
Worked in government as: Researcher/planner.
Worked in industry/business in: Planning.
Worked in education: Teaching.   *(143)*

9. H.R. Albrecht

International Institute, Tropical Agriculture, PO Box 532O, Ibadan, Nigeria.
Sex: Male.   *Age:* 6O or over.
Educational qualification: Doctoral degree.
Formal training: Life sciences.
Informal training: I Education, 2 Extension methods.
Areas in which work done (%): 5 In planning unit of an international organization,
IO In planning unit of a government agency, IO As individual consultant, 7O In
organization concerned with other studies including long-range planning.
Direction of work in forecasting: I Scientific, 2 Economic, 3 Environmental,
4 Educational.
Direction of work in research: I Farm production, 2 Environmental, 3 Consumer
affairs, 4 Social impacts of technology.
Direction of work in planning: I Farm production, 2 Scientific, 3 Technological,
4 Educational, 5 Economic.
Methods used: I Expert panels, 2 Brainstorming, 3 Individual expert forecasting,
4 Causal modelling.
Time range of work: 5 - IO years.
Source of support for work (%): I5 National government, 2O Foundations,
75 International agencies.
Work done for: I5 National government.

Occupational function: Administrator.
Worked in government as: I Administrator, 2 Researcher.
Worked in industry/business in: I Research and development, 2 Consultancy.
Worked in education: I In administration, 2 In research, 3 Teaching.
Additional information: Involved in the improvement of food crop production
capabilities, and the development of tropical countries   *(336)*

10. S. Takdir Alisjahbana

290 Jalan Drive, Saharjo, Jakarta-Selatan, Indonesia.
Sex: Male   *Age:* 60 or over.
Educational qualification: Master's degree.
Formal training: Education, Law, Philosophy, Anthropology, Linguistics.
Informal training: Social/behavioural sciences, Humanities, Arts-literature.
Primarily engaged in: Both futures studies and long-range planning.
Areas in which work done (%): 30 In organization concerned with other studies
including long range planning, 10 as academic, in teaching futures studies or long range
planning, 15 Reading and writing.
Direction of work in forecasting: Cultural, Educational, Social.
Direction of work in research: Value systems.
Direction of work in planning: Language, Art.
Methods used: I Analysis of value systems, 2 Brainstorming, 3 Scenario building,
4 Historical analogy.
Time range of work: 5 - 10 years for development in Indonesia, Beyond year 2000
for world societal and cultural development.
Source of support for work (%): 100 Own personal resources.
Work done for (%): 60 Own institution and interest.
Occupational function: Creative thinker, scholar and artist, Educator.
Worked in education as: Teaching, In research.
Additional information: Concerned with the future of a world society and world
culture through the increasing density of communication and transportation, and
the unity of mankind in the world.   *(550)*

11. Clopper Almon

7303 Dartmouth Ave, College Park, Md 20740, USA.
Sex: Male.   *Age:* 40-49.
Formal training: Social/behavioural sciences.
Informal training: Social/behavioural sciences, Humanities, Mathematics.
Primarily engaged in: Futures studies.
Areas in which work done (%): 30 In organization primarily concerned with futures
studies and/or long-range planning, 30 As academic in teaching futures studies or
long-range planning, 40 Other teaching.
Direction of work in forecasting: I Economic, 2 Manpower, 3 Market.
Methods used: Econometric models.
Time range of work: 5 - 10 years.
Source of support for work (%): 5 Foundation, 10 Local government, 85 Private
business.
Occupational function: I Teaching, 2 In research.
Worked in education: I Teaching, 2 In research.   *(302)*

12. Roy Amara

President, Institute for the Future, 2740 Sand Hill Rd, Menlo Par, Ca 94025, USA.
Sex: Male.   *Age:* 40-49.
Educational qualification: Doctoral degree.
Formal training: 1 Engineering, 2 Mathematics, 3 Education.
Informal training: 1 Physical sciences, 2 Social/behavioural sciences.
Primarily engaged in: Both futures studies and long-range planning.
Areas in which work done (%): 100 in organization primarily concerned with futures
studies and/or long-range planning.
Direction of work in forecasting: 1 Social, 2 Economic, 3 Technological, 4 Market,
5 Environmental, 8 Manpower, 7 Population.
Direction of work in research: Social impacts of technology, Alternative futures, Manpower,
Consumer affairs, Environmental, Resource utilization, Value systems, Social priorities,
Policy research, Population, The individual in the future, The family in the future,
Futures methodology.
Direction of work in planning: 1 Corporate, 2 Technological, 3 Social, 4 Economic.
Methods used: 1 Probabilistic forecasting, Scenario building, 3 Expert panels,
4 Individual expert forecasting, 5 Delphi techniques.
Time range of work: 5 - 10 years.
Source of support for work (%): 10 Foundations, 40 Private business, 50 National
government.
Work done for (%): 10 Foundations, 40 Private business, 50 National government.
Occupational function: 1 Administrator, 2 Manager, 3 Research worker   *(53)*

13. C. Eugene Anderson

Director of Corporate Development , Tenneco, PO Box 2511, Houston, Tx
77001, USA.
Sex: Male.   *Age:* 30-39.
Educational qualification: Doctoral degree.
Formal training: Business.
Informal training: Mathematics.
Primarily engaged in: Both futures studies and long-range planning.
Areas in which work done (%): 100 In planning unit of business enterprise.
Direction of work in forecasting: 1 Market, 2 Economic, 3 Technological.
Direction of work in planning: 1 Corporate, 2 Economic, 3 Resources.
Methods used: 1 Brainstorming, 2 Statistical models, 3 Scenario building,
4 Simulation, 5 Individual expert forecasting.
Time range of work: 5 - 10 years.
Source of support for work (%): 100 Private business.
Work done for (%): 100 Private business.
Occupational function: Manager.
Worked in industry/business in: Management, Planning.
Worked in education: Teaching.   *(262)*

14. Hans Skifter Anderson

Fyensved 15,2800 Lyngby, Denmark.
Sex: Male.   *Age:* 30-39.
Educational qualification: Master's degree.
Formal training: Mathematics.
Informal training: 1 Design, 2 Social/behavioural sciences.
Primarily engaged in: Both futures studies and long-range planning.

Areas in which work done (%): IOO In organization concerned with other studies including long-range planning.
Direction of work in forecasting: I Technological, 2 Social, 3 Economic, 4 Scientific.
Direction of work in research: I Policy research, 2 Social impacts of technology, 3 Resource utilization.
Direction of work in planning: I Scientific, 2 Technological, 3 Social.
Methods used: Extrapolation techniques, Brainstorming, Expert panels, Relevance trees.
Time range of work: IO - 25 years.
Source of support for work (%): IOO National government.
Work done for (%): IOO Research centre.
Occupational function: Research worker.
Worked in government as: Researcher.
Worked in industry/business in: Research and development.
Additional information: Concerned with the future of the building industry, construction technology, and the building environment.   *(288)*

15. Peter Andrews

Chief, Mineral Economics Research Division, Energy, Mines and Resources, 588 Booth St, Ottawa K1A OB4, Canada.
Sex: Male.   *Age:* 4O-49.
Educational qualification: Doctoral degree.
Formal training. I Physical sciences, 2 Social/behavioural sciences.
Informal training: I Social/behavioural sciences, 2 Physical sciences.
Direction of work in forecasting: Economic.
Direction of work in research: I Policy research, 2 Resource utilization.
Direction of work in planning: Economic.
Time range of work: IO - 25 years.
Source of support for work (%): IOO National government.
Work done for (%): IOO National government.
Occupational function: Manager.
Worked in government as: Administrator.
Worked in industry/business in: Administrator.
Additional information: Concerned with long-range mineral resource analysis (as a manager, not a researcher).   *(447)*

16. Serge Antoine

12 Rue de la Fontaine, 91 Bifures, France.
Sex: Male.   *Age:* 4O-49.
Educational qualification: Master's degree.
Formal training: Civil service.
Informal training: Design.
Primarily engaged in: Both futures studies and long-range planning.
Areas in which work done (%): IO Organization primarily concerned with futures studies and/or long-range planning, 2O In planning unit of a governmental agency.
Direction of work in forecasting: Environmental.
Direction of work in research: Alternative futures, Environmental.
Direction of work in planning: Regional, Environmental.
Methods used: Scenario building, Brainstorming, Relevance trees.
Time range of work: 5 - beyond year 2OOO.
Source of support for work (%): 2O Foundations, 8O National government.
Work done for (%): IO Foundations, IO Voluntary associations, 8O National government.

Occupational function: Administrator.
Worked in government as: Administrator.
Additional information: Concerned with long-range resource analysis. **(321)**

17. Pavel Apostol
Bu-7 Bucharest I, Calea Dorobantilor 102 - 110, Bloc 2, SC. B, EF.II, Apt, 38 Romania.
Sex: Male. *Age:* 50-59.
Educational qualification: Doctoral degree.
Formal training: I Philosophy, 2 Social/behavioural sciences.
Informal training: Mathematics.
Areas in which work done (%): 20 In organization primarily concerned with futures studies and/or long-range planning, 30 As academic, in teaching futures studies or long-range planning.
Direction of work in forecasting: I Educational, 2 Social progress.
Direction of work in research: I The individual in the future, 2 Social priorities, 3 Value systems.
Direction of work in planning: Educational.
Methods used: I Scenario building, 2 Operational models, 3 Extrapolation techniques, 4 Network analysis.
Time range of work: IO - 25 years.
Source of support for work (%): IO National government, 30 Voluntary associations, 60 Personal.
Work done for (%): IO National government, 20 Voluntary associations, 20 Personal.
Occupational function: I Educator, 2 Research worker.
Worked in government as: Researcher.
Worked in education: Teaching, In research. **(528)**

18. Francisco Aquirre B
Icaiti, Apartado Postal 1552, Guatemala.
Sex: Male. *Age:* 50-59.
Educational qualification: Master's degree.
Formal training: Life sciences.
Informal training: Management.
Direction of work in forecasting: Technological.
Direction of work in research: Environmental, Resource utilization, Policy research.
Direction of work in planning: Technological.
Methods used: Brainstorming, Expert panels, Historical analogy.
Time range of work: IO - 25 years.
Source of support for work (%): IO International agencies, 20 Local government, 20 Private business.
Work done for (%): IOO Institute of technology.
Occupational function: Manager.
Additional information: Worked in education as: Professor of industrial microbiology.
(311)
19. Patrick Armstrong
Parliamentary Group for World Government, House of Commons, London SW1, UK.
Sex: Male. *Age:* 60 or over.
Educational qualification: Master's degree.
Formal training: Humanities.
Informal training: Journalism, Education, Music.
Primarily engaged in: Both futures studies and long-range planning.

Areas in which work done (%): IOO In organization primarily concerned with futures studies and/or long-range planning.
Methods used: Probabilistic forecasting, Instinct.
Time range of work: IO - 25 years.
Source of support for work (%): 5O Voluntary associations.
Work done for (%): IOO Voluntary associations.
Occupational function: Administrator, Research worker, Educator, Consultant, Factotum.
Additional information: Concerned with generating a greater sense of world community. through education, and generating political will through parliamentary means to make global institutions in certain fields. *(4O5)*

2O. Mary F. Arnold

3O61 S. Josephine St, Denver, Co 8O21O, USA.
Sex: Female. *Age:* 5O-59.
Educational qualification: Doctoral degree.
Formal training: I Social/behavioural sciences, 2 Life sciences.
Informal training: I Humanities, 2 Education, 3 Engineering.
Primarily engaged in: Long-range planning.
Areas in which work done (%): 5O As individual consultant, 5O In organization concerned with other studies including long-range planning.
Direction of work in forecasting: Health needs.
Direction of work in research: I Social impacts of technology, 2 Futures methodology.
Direction of work in planning: Health serivces.
Methodsz used: I Expert panels, 2 Network analysis, 3 Operational models, 4 Causal modelling, 5 Probabilistic forecasting, 6 Brainstorming, 7 Delphi techniques, 8 Cross impact analysis.
Time range of work: IO - 25 years.
Occupational function: I Consultant, 2 Educator, 3 Research worker.
Worked in government as: I Administrator, 2 Researcher.
Worked in education: I Teaching, 2 In research.
Worked in service sector: I Medicine, 2 Social welfare.
Additional information: Concerned with human services, Health delivery systems and social indicators. *(425)*

21. R.A. Arnold

Director of Corporate Planning, The B.F. Goodrich Co, 5OO S Main St, Akron, Oh 44318, USA.
Sex: Male. *Age:* 4O-49.
Educational qualification: Master's degree.
Formal training: I Engineering, 2 Business administration.
Primarily engaged in: Long-range planning.
Areas in which work done (%): IOO In planning unit of a business enterprise.
Direction of work in forecasting: I Market, 2 Economic, 3 Technological.
Direction of work in planning: I Corporate, 2 Economic, 3 Technological.
Methods used: I Statistical models, 2 Historical analogy, 3 Probabilistic forecasting, 4 Cross impact analysis.
Time range of work: 5 - IO years.
Source of support for work (%): IOO Private business.
Work done for (%): IOO Private business.
Occupational function: Administrator.
Worked in industry/business in: Management. *(135)*

22. Samuel Aroni
School of Architecture and Urban Planning, University of California, Los Angeles, Ca 90024, USA.
Sex: Male. *Age:* 40-49.
Educational qualification: Doctoral degree.
Formal training: Engineering, Design.
Areas in which work done (%): 20 Research on futures studies.
Direction of work in research: Futures methodology, Images of the future.
Methods used: Images of the future.
Time range of work: 5 - beyond year 2000.
Source of support for work (%): 100 University.
Work done for (%): 100 University.
Occupational function: 1 Educator, 2 Research worker.
Worked in education as: 1 Teaching, 2 In research, 3 In administration. *(571)*

23. P. Atteslander
Bellevuestrasse 25, CH-3271 Bellmund, Switzerland.
Sex: Male. *Age:* 40-49.
Educational qualification: Doctoral degree.
Formal training: 1 Social/behavioural sciences, 2 Design.
Informal training: 1 Journalism, 2 Education.
Primarily engaged in: Both futures studies and long-range planning.
Areas in which work done (%): 10 In planning unit of a government agency, 10 Writing books, 20 In organization primarily concerned with futures studies and/or long-range planning, 10 As individual consultant, 40 As academic, in teaching futures studies or long-range planning.
Direction of work in forecasting: Social, Cultural, Scientific, Environmental.
Direction of work in research: 1 Social impacts of technology, 2 Futures methodology, 3 Social priorities, 4 Policy research.
Direction of work in planning: Scientific, Urban, Regional.
Methods used: 1 Cross impact analysis, 2 Brainstorming, 3 Delphi techniques, 4 Expert panels.
Time range of work: 10 - 25 years.
Source of support for work (%): 20 Foundations, 80 Local government.
Work done for (%): 20 National government, 80 Local or regional government.
Occupational function: 1 Educator, 2 Research worker, 3 Consultant.
Worked in government as: 1 Researcher, 2 Administrator.
Worked in industry/business in: 1 Research and development, 2 Planning, 3 Consultancy, 4 Management.
Worked in education: 1 Teaching, 2 In research, 3 In administration.
Worked in service sector: 1 Medicine, 2 Social welfare. *(291)*

24. R. Aubrac
Director, Office of General Affairs and Information, Food and Agricultural Organization, of the UN, Via Delle Terme di Caracalla, Rome, Italy.
Sex: Male. *Age:* 60 or over.
Educational qualification: Doctoral degree.
Formal training: 1 Engineering, 2 Law.
Informal training: Social/behavioural sciences, Mathematics.
Areas in whichn work done (%): 10 In planning unit of an international organization. 15 In organization concerned with other studies including long-range planning.

Direction of work in research: Resource utilization.
Direction of work in planning: Technological.
Methods used: Expert panels.
Time range of work: IO 25 years.
Source of support for work (%): IOO International agencies.
Work done for (%): IOO International agencies.
Occupational function: I Administrator, 2 Manager.
Worked in government as: I Administrator, 2 Elected official.
Worked in industry/business in: I Management, 2 Planning.
Additional information: Concerned with transfer of scientific and technological knowledge.

(298)

25. Harvey Averch

Chairman, Federal Council Committee on Forecasting models, c/o Social Systems and Human Resource Division, The National Science Foundation, 18OO G Street, NW Washington, DC 2O55O, USA.
Sex: Male.   *Age:* 30-39.
Educational qualification: Doctoral degree.
Formal training: Social/behavioural sciences.
Informal training: Social/behavioural sciences, Education, Mathematics.
Areas in which work done (%): 6O In planning unit of a governmental agency.
Methods used: Cross impact analysis, Expert panels.
Time range of work: 5 - IO years.
Occupational function: Administrator.
Worked in government as: Researcher.

(116)

B 26. Munzadi Babole

PO Box 213O, Lubumbashi, Republic of Zaire.
Sex: Male.   *Age:* 4O-49.
Educational qualification: Doctoral degree.
Formal training: Social/behavioural sciences.
Informal training: Social/behavioural sciences.
Areas in which work done (%): 5O As academic, in teaching futures studies or long-range planning.
Direction of work in forecasting: Social.
Direction of work in research: Social impacts of technology.
Direction of work in planning: Social.
Methods used: Probabilistic forecasting.
Time range of work: IO - 25 years.
Occupational function: I Research worker, 2 Teacher.
Worked in government as: Researcher.
Worked in industry/business in: Research and development.
Worked in education: Teaching, In research.
Worked in service sector: Social welfare.
Additional information: Concerned with sociological and anthropological research, particularly on the question of integration of tribal society with modern worldwide society.

(210)

27. M. Baboulene
President Directeur General, Bureau d'Etudes et de Réalisations Urbaines, 157 Rue des Blaines, 92220 Bagneux, France.
Sex: Male.   *Age:* 50-59.
Educational qualification: Other graduate/professional degree.
Formal training: I Mathematics, 2 Physical sciences, 3 Social/behavioural sciences.
Informal training: I Journalism, 2 Engineering, 3 Education.
Primarily engaged in: Long-range planning.
Areas in which work done (%): 20 In planning unit of a governmental agency, concerned with other studies including long-range planning.
Direction of work in forecasting: I Economic, 2 Resources, 3 Population, 4 Market.
Direction of work in research: Manpower, Population.
Direction of work in planning: I Economic, 2 Regional, 3 Urban.
Methods used: I Statistical models, 2 Operational models, 3 Simulation, 4 Probabilistic forecasting.
Time range of work: 5 - 25 years.
Source of support for work (%): IO Private business, 2O Local government, 2O International agencies, 5O National government.
Work done for (%): IO Private business, 2O Local or regional government, 2O International agencies, 5O National government.
Occupational function: I Consultant, 2 Administrator.
Worked in government as: Administrator.
Worked in industry/business in: I Planning, 2 Management.
Worked in service sector: I Social welfare, 2 Religion.   *(259)*

28. Herman Baeyens
Tuinbouwlaan, 23 PO Box 1710 Dilbeek, Belgium.
Sex: Male.   *Age:* 40-49.
Educational qualification: Doctoral degree.
Formal training: I Law, 2 Social/behavioural sciences.
Informal training: I Design, 2 Social/behavioural sciences.
Primarily engaged in: Both futures studies and long-range planning.
Areas in which work done (%): IO As academic, in teaching futures studies or long-range planning, 2O In organization concerned with other studies including long-range planning, 7O In organization primarily concerned with futures studies and/or long-range planning.
Direction of work in research: Environmental.
Direction of work in planning: Urban, Regional.
Methods used: Extrapolation techniques, Expert panels, Historical analogy, Individual expert forecasting.
Time range of work: 5 - IO years.
Source of support for work (%): IO Foundations, IO International agencies, 3O Local government, 5O National government.
Work done for (%): IO International agencies, IO Foundations, 3O Local or regional government, 5O National government.
Occupational function: I Research worker, 2 Consultant, 3 Manager, 4 Educator.
Worked in industry/business in: Research and development, Planning, Consultancy.
Worked in education: Teaching.   *(227)*

29. Archie J. Bahm

Professor of Philosophy Emeritus, University of New Mexico, 1915 Las Lomas Road, NE, Albuquerque, New Mexico 87106, USA.
Sex: Male.   *Age:* Over 60.
Educational qualification: Doctoral degree.
Formal training: I Philosophy, 2 Humanity, 3 Social/behavioural sciences.
Informal training: Asian philosophies.
Primarily engaged in: Futures studies.
Areas in which work done (%): 100 Personal projects, retired.
Direction of work in forecasting: Future of philosophy.
Methods used: Extrapolation techniques, Study of obsolescence in philosophies.
Time range of work: Beyond year 2000.
Source of support for work (%): 100 Personal income.
Work done for (%): 5 Voluntary associations, 95 Personal.
Occupational function: Research worker.
Worked in education: I Teaching, 2 In research.   *(575)*

30. Richard Bailey

72 Ashley Gardens, Westminster, London SW1, UK.
Sex: Male.   *Age:* 60 or over.
Educational qualification: Bachelor's degree.
Formal training: Social/behavioural sciences, Journalism.
Informal training: Journalism.
Direction of work in forecasting: I Economic, 2 Resources, 3 Manpower.
Direction of work in research: I Resource utilization, 2 Alternative futures.
Direction of work in planning: I Economic, 2 Technological.
Methods used: I Historical analogy, 2 Brainstorming.
Time range of work: 5 - 10 years.
Source of support for work (%): 10 Voluntary associations, 80 Private business.
Work done for (%): 20 International agencies, 20 Voluntary associations, 60 Private business.
Occupational function: Research worker, Consultant.
Worked in government as: Administrator.
Additional information: Concerned with economic development and resource allocation.
                                                                               (133)

31. F.W.G. Baker

97 Rue de Sèvres, 92100 Boulogne, France.
Sex: Male.   *Age:* 40-49.
Educational qualification: Bachelor's degree.
Formal training: Life sciences.
Informal training: Physical sciences, Journalism, Arts.
Direction of work in forecasting: I Scientific, 2 Resources.
Direction of work in planning: I Scientific, 2 Environmental, Resources, 3 Educational.
Methods used: I Expert panels, 2 Simulation.
Time range of work: 5 - 10 years.
Source of support for work (%): 20 International agencies.
Work done for (%): 5 Voluntary associations, 20 International agencies.
Occupational function: Administrator.
Additional information: Concerned with future of science, long-range resource analysis. *(473)*

32. Barbara Baruchello

IRADES, Istituto per la Ricerca e la Formazione al Futuro, Via Paisiello 6, Rome.
OO198, Italy.
Sex: Female. *Age:* 25-29.
Educational qualification: Bachelor's degree.
Formal training: Humanities.
Informal training: I Management, 2 Education, 3 Design, 4 Arts, 5 Cinema/television.
Primarily engaged in: Futures studies.
Areas in which work done (%): IOO In organization primarily concerned with futures studies and/or long-range planning.
Direction of work in research: I The individual in the future, 2 Alternative futures.
Time range of work: Beyond 2000 AD.
Source of support for work (%): IOO Private association.
Work done for (%): IOO Private association.
Occupational function: Educator.
Worked in industry/vusiness in: I Management, 2 Research and development.
Worked in service sector: Communication media.
Additional information: Concerned with education towards the future.   *(419)*

33. Michel Batisse

Director, Dept. of Environmental Sciences and Natural Resource Research, UNESCO,
7 Place de Fontenoy, 75700 Paris, France.
Sex: Male. *Age:* 50-59.
Educational qualification: Doctoral degree.
Formal training: I Physical sciences, 2 Engineering.
Informal training: I Social/behavioural sciences.
Primarily engaged in: Both futures studies and long-range planning.
Areas in which work done (%):   20 In planning unit of an international organization,
80 In organization concerned with other studies including long-range planning.
Direction of work in forecasting: I Resource, 2 Environmental, 3 Scientific,
4 Educational.
Direction of work in research: I Environmental, 2 Resource utilization.
Direction of work in planning: I Scientific, 2 Educational.
Methods used: Expert panels, Operational models.
Time range of work: 5 - IO years.
Source of support for work (%): IOO International agencies.
Work done for (%): IOO International agencies.
Occupational function: I Administrator, 2 Manager.
Worked in government as: I Administrator, 2 Researcher.
Additional information: Concerned with natural resources and environment.   *(376)*

34. R.E. Beamish

The Great-West Life Assurance Company, 60 Osborne St, North Winnipeg, Manitoba,
R3C 3A5, Canada.
Sex: Male. *Age:* 50-59.
Educational qualification: Doctoral degree.
Formal training: Life sciences.
Informal training: I Business, 2 Humanities, 3 Education.
Areas in which work done (%): 2 As academic, in teaching futures studies or long-range planning, 8 In planning unit of a business enterprise.
Direction of work in forecasting: I Medical, 2 Social, 3 Technological.

Direction of work in research: I The individual in the future, 2 The family in the future.
Direction of work in planning: I Medical, 2 Scientific, 3 Social.
Methods used: I Expert panels, 2 Scenario building.
Time range of work: IO - 25 years.
Source of support for work (%): IOO Private business.
Work done for (%): IO Private business.
Occupational function: I Administrator, 2 Educator.
Worked in industry/business in: Management.
Worked in education: Teaching, In research.
Worked in service sector: Medicine.
Additional information: Concerned with the future of medicine: implications of
social, economic and medical changes for the insurance industry.   *(454)*

35. Harold S. Becker

Vice President and Treasurer, The Futures Group, 124 Hebron Ave, Glastonbury,
Ct O6O33, USA.
Sex: Male.   *Age:* 4O-49.
Educational qualification: Master's degree.
Formal training: Management, Engineering, Operations research.
Informal training: Social/behavioural sciences, Education.
Primarily engaged in: Futures studies, short-range and long-range planning.
Areas in which work done (%): IOO In organization primarily concerned with futures
studies and/or long-range planning.
Direction of work in forecasting: Technological, Economic, Social, Scientific,
Environmental, Resources.
Direction of work in research: Social impacts of technology, Futures methodology,
Alternative futures, Environmental, Resource utilization, Value systems, Social
priorities, Policy research, The individual in the future.
Direction of work in planning: Scientific, Technological, Social, Corporate.
Methods used: Probabilistic forecasting, Simulation, Delphi techniques, Gaming, Cross
impact analysis, Scenario building, Extrapolation techniques, Brainstorming, Statistical
models, Expert panels, Relevance trees, Historical analogy, Operational models,
Individual expert forecasting.
Time range of work: 2 - 25 years.
Source of support for work (%): 6O Private business, 4O National government.
Work done for (%): 4O National government, 6O Private business.
Occupational function: Administrator, Manager, Research worker.
Worked in government as: Manager.
Worked in industry/business in: Management, Research and development, Planning.
Worked in education: Teaching.   *(186)*

36. Stafford Beer

Firkins, Old Avenue, West Byfleet, Surrey KT14 6AD, UK.
Sex: Male.   *Age:* 4O-49.
Educational qualification: Master's degree.
Formal training: Humanities.
Informal training: I Humanities, 2 Mathematics, 3 Engineering, 3 Arts, 4 Social/
behavioural sciences, 5 Life sciences, 6 Physical sciences, 7 Design, 9 Education.
Primarily engaged in: Both futures studies and long-range planning.
Areas in which work done (%): IO As academic in teaching futures studies or long-
range planning, 2O Private work and writing, 7O As individual consultant.

Direction of work in forecasting: Technological, Economic, Social, Cultural, Market, Educational, Scientific, Environmental, Resources.
Direction of work in research: Social impacts of technology, The family in the future, Alternative futures, Environmental, Resource utilization, Value systems, Social priorities, Policy research, The individual in the future, Futures methodology.
Direction of work in planning: Scientific, Technological, Social, Urban, Regional, Educational, Economic, Political, Corporate, Environmental, Resources.
Methods used: I Cybernetic analysis, 2 Probabilistic forecasting, 2 Gaming, 2 Scenario building, 2 Extrapolation techniques, 2 Contextual mapping, 2 Brainstorming, 2 Statistical models, 2 Network analysis, 2 Operational models, 2 Simulation.
Time range of work: 5 - beyond year 2000.
Source of support for work (%): 5 Local government, 25 Private business, 70 National government.
Work done for (%): 5 Local government, 25 Private business, 70 National government.
Occupational function: I Consultant, 2 Research worker, 3 Educator.
Worked in government as: Researcher.
Worked in education: Teaching. *(130)*

37. Wendell Bell

Yale University, Department of Sociology, New Haven, Ct 06520, USA.
Sex: Male. *Age:* 40-49.
Educational qualification: Doctoral degree.
Formal training: Social/behavioural sciences.
Primarily engaged in: Futures studies.
Areas in which work done (%): 30 Research on images of the future, 30 As academic, in teaching futures studies or long-range planning.
Direction of work in research: I Value systems, 2 Social priorities, 3 Alternative futures.
Methods used: Interviewing national leaders.
Time range of work: I0 - 25 years.
Source of support for work (%): 30 Foundations, 70 University.
Occupational function: I Educator, 2 Research worker.
Worked in education: I In research, 2 Teaching, 3 In administration. *(109)*

38. A. Douglas Bender

Vice President, Planning and Operations, R and D, Smith Kline and French Laboratories, 1500 Spring Garden St, Philadelphia, Pa 19101, USA.
Sex: Male. *Age:* 30-39.
Educational qualification: Doctoral degree.
Formal training: Life sciences.
Informal training: I Mathematics, 2 Social/behavioural sciences.
Areas in which work done (%): I5 In Planning unit of a business enterprise.
Direction of work in forecasting: I Technological, 2 Economic, 3 Market.
Direction of work in research: I Alternative futures, 2 Resource utilization, 3 Futures methodology.
Direction of work in planning: I Technological, 2 Scientific, 3 Economic.
Methods used: I Statistical models, 2 Scenario building, 3 Delphi techniques.
Time range of work: I0 - 25 years.
Source of support for work (%): I00 Private business.
Work done for (%): I00 Private business.
Worked in industry/business in: I Research and development, 2 Planning, 3 Management.
Additional information: Concerned with future of medicine. *(1)*

39. L. Berger

5 Dizengoff St, Tel Aviv, Israel.
Sex: Male.   *Age:* 60 or over.
Formal training: Social/behavioural sciences.
Informal training: Social/behavioural sciences, Humanities.
Primarily engaged in: Both futures studies and long-range planning.
Areas in which work done (%): 25 In organization primarily concerned with futures studies and/or long-range planning, 75 As academic, in teaching futures studies or long-range planning.
Direction of work in forecasting: Economic, Social, Cultural, Scientific, Population.
Direction of work in research: Social priorities, Population, The individual in the future, The family of the future.
Direction of work in planning: Social, Economic;
Methods used: Probabilistic forecasting, Historical analogy, Delphi techniques, Extrapolation techniques.
Time range of work: 5 - 10 years.
Source of support for work (%): 25 Foundations, 75 National government.
Occupational function: Research worker.
Worked in government as: Researcher.
Worked in industry/business in: Research and development.
Worked in education: Teaching, In research.   *(172)*

40. Jeff Berner

Director, Innerspace Project, PO Box 503, Mill Valley, Ca 94941, USA.
Sex: Male.   *Age:* 30-39.
Educational qualification: Bachelor's degree.
Formal training: Humanities.
Informal training: 1 Humanities, 2 Journalism, 3 Education.
Direction of work in forecasting: 1 Cultural, 2 Social.
Direction of work in research: 1 The individual in the future, 2 Value systems, 3 Alternative futures.
Methods used: Probabilistic forecasting, Brainstorming, Individual expert forecasting.
Time range of work: 10 - 25 years.
Source of support for work (%): 100 Private business.
Occupational function: Educator,
Worked in industry/business in: Consultancy.
Worked in education: Teaching.
Additional information: Concerned with future 'usefulness' of the aesthetic/spiritual interface.   *(478)*

41. J.E. Bessell

Director of Ungazmi, Nottingham University, Dept of Agriculture, Sutton Bonington, Loughborough, Leicestershire LE12 5RD, UK.
Sex: Male.   *Age:* 50-59.
Educational qualification: Doctoral degree.
Formal training: Mathematics.
Informal training: Social/behavioural sciences, Mathematics, Management.
Areas in which work done (%): 20 As individual consultant, 30 In organization primarily concerned with futures studies and/or long-range planning, 50 As academic teaching and conducting research.
Direction of work in forecasting: 1 Economic, 2 Population.

Direction of work in planning: Economic.
Methods used: 1 Statistical models, 2 Causal modelling, 3 Extrapolation techniques, 4 Probabilistic forecasting.
Time range of work: 5 - 10 years.
Source of support for work (%): 100 National government.
Work done for (%): 50 National government.
Occupational function: Administrator, Manager, Research worker.
Worked in government as: Researcher.
Worked in industry/business in: Research and development.
Worked in education: Teaching, In research.   *(361)*

42. G. Beyer

Secretary General, European Centre for Population Studies,
The Hague, Pauwenlaan 17, The Netherlands.
Sex: Male.   *Age:* 60 or over.
Educational qualification: Doctoral degree.
Formal training: Humanities, Demography.
Informal training: 1 Demography, 2 Humanities.
Primarily engaged in: Futures studies.
Areas in which work done (%): 50 In organization concerned with other studies including long-range planning, 50 In organization primarily concerned with futures studies and/or long-range planning.
Direction of work in forecasting: Social, Manpower, Population.
Direction of work in research: Manpower, Population, The family in the future.
Direction of work in planning: Urban, Military, Resources.
Methods used: Individual expert forecasting.
Time range of work: 5 - 10 years.
Source of support for work (%): 100 Self.
Work done for (%): 100 Private business.
Occupational function: 1 Manager, 2 Research worker.
Worked in government as: Researcher.
Worked in industry/business in: Research and development.
Worked in education: In research.   *(270)*

43. Alexander B. Bigler

2941 Wilson Ave, Oakton, Va 22124, USA.
Sex: Male.   *Age:* 30-39.
Educational qualification: 'Other' graduate/Professional degree.
Formal training: Social behavioural sciences, Design.
Informal training: 1 Engineering, 2 Physical sciences.
Primarily engaged in: Both futures studies and long-range planning.
Areas in which work done (%): 10 As individual consultant, 40 In planning unit of a governmental agency, 50 In organization concerned with other studies including long-range planning.
Direction of work in forecasting: 1 Technological, 2 Environmental, 3 Market.
Direction of work in research: 1 Social impacts of technology, 2 Alternative futures, 3 Environmental, 2 Policy research.
Direction of work in planning: 1 Recreation, 2 Technological, 3 Urban, 4 Regional, 5 Environmental.
Methods used: 1 Brainstorming, 2 Cross impact analysis, 3 Network analysis.
Time range of work: 5 - 10 years.

Source of support for work (%): 5 Voluntary associations, l5 Local government, National government, International agencies, 8O Private business.
Work done for (%): 5 Private business, l5 Local or regional government, 8O National government.
Occupational function: l Consultant, 2 Research worker, 3 Manager.
Worked in government as: l Researcher, 2 Administrator.
Worked in education: In research.   *(76)*

44. Craig Bigler

Associate State Planning Co-ordinator, Office of the Governor, 118 State Capitol, Salt Lake City, Ut 84114, USA.
Sex: Male.   *Age:* 3O-39.
Educational qualification: Bachelor's degree.
Formal training: Social/behavioural sciences.
Informal training: Physical sciences.
Areas in which work done (%): 25 In organization primarily engaged with futures studies and/or long-range planning, 25 In organization concerned with other studies including long-range planning, 5O In planning unit of a governmental agency.
Direction of work in forecasting: l Economic, 2 Population, 3 Social, 4 Environmental, 5 Resources, 6 Cultural, 7 Market.
Direction of work in research: l Alternative futures, 2 Population, 3 Social priorities, 4 Environmental, 5 Policy research.
Direction of work in planning: l Economic, 2 Political, 3 Environmental, 4 Resources, 5 Social.
Methods used: l Expert panels, 2 Historical analogy, 3 Operational models, 4 Extrapolation techniques, 4 Simulation, 5 Brainstorming, 6 Statistical models, 7 Delphi techniques.
Time range of work: 5 - 25 years.
Source of support for work (%): 25 State government, 75 National government.
Work done for (%): lO Local or regional government, 4O State government.
Occupational function: l Administrator.
Worked in government as: l Administrator, 2 Researcher.
Worked in education: In research.
Additional information: Concerned with economic and social development/change, and related environmental impacts.   *(1O2)*

45. Richard T. Bigwood

Director, Planning Research Unit, University of Edinburgh, 57 George Square, Edinburgh, EH8 9JU, UK.
Sex: Male.   *Age:* 5O-59.
Educational qualification: Other graduate/professional degree.
Formal training: Design.
Informal training: l Education, 2 Humanities, 3 Social/behavioural sciences, 4 Engineering.
Primarily engaged in: Both futures studies and long-range planning;
Areas in which work done (%): lO As individual consultant, 2O As academic, in teaching futures studies or long-range planning, 7O In organization primarily concerned with futures studies and/or long-range planning.
Direction of work in forecasting: l Environmental, 2 Resources, 3 Educational.
Direction of work in research: l Environmental, 2 Value systems, 3 Resource utilization, 4 Alternative futures, 5 Futures methodology.
Direction of work in planning: l Regional, 2 Urban, 3 Educational, 4 Environmental,

5 Corporate, 6 Resources.
Methods used: I Probabilistic forecasting, 2 Historical analogy, 3 Scenario building,
3 Operational models, 4 Brainstorming, 5 Expert panels.
Time range of work: IO - 25 years.
Source of support for work (%): 3O Local government, 3O Foundations, 4O National government.
Work done for (%): I5 Foundations, 2O National government, 25 Local or regional government.
Occupational function: Directing research.
Worked in government as: I Researcher, 2 Administrator.
Worked in industry/business in: I Planning, 2 Management, 3 Research and development,
4 Consultancy.
Worked in education: I In research, 2 Teaching, 3 In administration.
Worked in service sector: Design.   *(322)*

46. Roger Bilstein

University of Houston at Clear Lake City, 27OO Bay Area Blvd, Houston, Tx 77O58, USA.
Sex: Male.   *Age:* 30-39.
Educational qualification: Doctoral degree.
Formal training: I Humanities, 2 Social/behavioural sciences.
Informal training: Engineering.
Areas in which work done (%): IO As academic, in teaching futures studies or long-range planning.
Direction of work in forecasting: I Social, 2 Technological, 3 Environmental.
Direction of work in research: I Social impacts of technology, 2 Social priorities.
Direction of work in planning: I Social, 2 Environmental, 3 Technological.
Methods used: I Historical analogy, 2 Extrapolation techniques.
Time range of work: 5 - IO years.
Source of support for work (%): IO University.
Work done for (%): IO Informal classes.
Occupational function: Educator.
Worked in government as: Researcher.
Worked in education: I Teaching, 2 In research.
Additional information: Concerned with social and cultural implications of technology,
technology assessment. Specific interest: aerospace transportation.   *(5O6)*

47. Dag Bjornland

Transportokonomisk Institutt, Oslo 4, Stasjonsveljen 4, Norway.
Sex: Male.   *Age:* 30-39.
Educational qualification: Master's degree.
Formal training: Social/behavioural sciences.
Informal training: Social/behavioural sciences.
Areas in which work done (%): IOO In organization concerned with other studies
including long-range planning.
Direction of work in forecasting: I Economic, 2 Social, 3 Environmental.
Direction of work in research: I Social priorities, 2 Alternative futures.
Direction of work in planning: I Urban, 2 Economic, 3 Regional.
Methods used: I Historical analogy, 3 Scenario building, 5 Causal modelling,
IO Extrapolation techniques.
Time range of work: 5 - 25 years.
Source of support for work (%): IOO National government.

Work done for (%): 2O National government.
Occupational function: I Research worker, 2 Administrator.
Worked in government as: I Researcher.
Additional information: Concerned with long-range resource analysis, technology assessment, social indicators.   *(474)*

48. R.E. Blackith
Zoology Dept, Trinity College, Dublin 2, Eire.
Sex: Male.   *Age:* 5O-59.
Educational qualification: Doctoral degree.
Formal training: I Life sciences, 2 Physical sciences, 3 Mathematics.
Informal training: Humanities.
Areas in which work done (%): IO As academic, in teaching futures studies or long-range planning.
Direction of work in forecasting: I Population, 2 Resources.
Methods used: I Statistical models, 2 Historical analogy.
Time range of work: 5 - IO years.
Occupational function: Research worker.
Worked in education: In research.
Additional information: Concerned with population projections related to food and other sources.   *(455)*

49. A. Wade Blackman
Science and Technology Policy Office, National Science Foundation, 18OO G Street, NW, Washington, DC 2O55O, USA.
Sex: Male.   *Age:* 4O-49.
Educational qualification: Doctoral degree.
Formal training: I Engineering, 2 Business Management.
Informal training: I Engineering, 2 Management, 3 Physical sciences, 4 Mathematics, 5 Social/behavioural sciences.
Primarily engaged in: Both futures studies and long-range planning.
Areas in which work done (%): IO In planning unit of a governmental agency, 9O In organization concerned with futures studies or long-range planning.
Direction of work in planning: I Technological, 2 Scientific, 3 Social, 4 Resources.
Methods used: Probabilistic forecasting, Gaming, Delphi techniques, Scenario building, Cross impact analysis, Contextual mapping, Extrapolation techniques, Statistical models, Brainstorming, Relevance trees, Expert panels, Historical analogy, Network analysis, Individual expert forecasting, Operational models, Causal modelling, Simulation.
Time range of work: IO - 25 years.
Source of support for work (%): IOO National government.
Work done for (%): IOO National government.
Occupational function: I Consultant, 2 Manager.
Worked in government as: Administrator.
Worked in industry/business in: I Management, 2 Research and development, 3 Planning.
(174)

5O. Eskil Block
Pyrolavagen 23, 1816O Lidingo, Sweden.
Sex: Male.   *Age:* 4O-49.
Educational qualification: Doctoral degree.
Formal training: Physical sciences, Social/behavioural sciences, Mathematics, Engineering.
Informal training: Life sciences, Humanities, Journalism, Education, Cinema/television.

Primarily engaged in: Futures studies.
Areas in which work done (%): IOO In planning unit of a governmental agency.
Direction of work in forecasting: Technological, Economic, Social, Cultural, Scientific,
Environmental, Military, Resources, Population.
Direction of work in research: I Futures methodology, 2 Alternative futures.
Methods used: Scenario building, Extrapolation techniques, Contextual mapping,
Relevance trees, Historical analogy, Individual expert forecasting.
Time range of work: IO - beyond year 2OOO.
Source of support for work (%): IOO National government.
Occupational function: Research worker, Consultant.
Worked in government as: Administrator, Researcher.
Worked in education: Teaching, In research.
Worked in service sector: Communication media. *(181)*

51. Laszlo Bodnar
Office of Economic Policy, Ministry of Treasury, Economics and Intergovernmental
Affairs, Province of Ontario, Toronto, Canada.
Sex: Male.　*Age:* 5O-59 years.
Educational qualification: Master's degree.
Formal training: Social/behavioural sciences.
Informal training: Humanities.
Primarily engaged in: Long-range planning.
Areas in which work done (%): IOO In planning unit of a governmental agency.
Direction of work in forecasting: Resources.
Direction of work in research: Resource utilization.
Direction of work in planning: Resources.
Methods used: I Scenario building, 2 Cross impact analysis, 3 Brainstorming.
Time range of work: IO - 25 years.
Source of support for work (%): IOO Provincial government.
Work done for (%): IOO Provincial government.
Occupational function: Research worker.
Worked in government as: Researcher.
Additional information: Concerned with agriculture; food production in general. *(387)*

52. Carl Boehret
67O Speyer, Freiherr-Vom-Stein-Str 2, Hochschule für Verwaltungs-Wissenschaften,
West Germany.
Sex: Male.　*Age:* 4O-49.
Educational qualification: Doctoral degree.
Formal training: Social/behavioural sciences, Design.
Informal training: Engineering, Education.
Areas in which work done (%): 2 In organization primarily concerned with futures
studies and/or long-range planning, 2 In planning unit of a business enterprise,
5 In planning unit of a governmental agency, I5 As academic, in teaching futures
studies or long-range planning.
Direction of work in forecasting: Social, Political systems.
Direction of work in research: I Value systems, 2 Social priorities, 3 Alternative futures,
4 Futures methodology.
Direction of work in planning: I Political, 2 Urban, 3 Environmental.
Methods used: I Gaming, 2 Scenario building, 3 Delphi techniques, 4 Historical
analogy, 5 Simulation, 6 Causal modelling, 7 Cross impact analysis, 8 Extrapolation
techniques.

6

Time range of work: IO - 25 years.
Source of support for work (%): IO Voluntary associations, 2O Local government, 2O National government, 5O University.
Work done for (%): 5 Foundations, 2O National government, 35 University, 2O Local or regional government.
Occupational function: I Educator, 2 Research worker.
Worked in government as: Administrator.
Worked in industry/business in: I Trade union, 2 Planning.
Worked in education: I Teaching, 2 In research.
Worked in service sector: Social welfare.   *(424)*

53. Volker Bornschier
Soziologisches Institut der Universität Zurich, Zeltweg 63, 8032 Zurich, Switzerland.
Sex: Male.   *Age:* 30-39.
Educational qualification: Doctoral degree.
Formal training: Social/behavioural sciences.
Primarily engaged in: Futures studies.
Areas in which work done (%): IO In organization primarily concerned with futures studies and/or long-range planning, 7O Personal research, 2O As academic, in teaching futures studies or long-range planning.
Direction of work in forecasting: Economic.
Direction of work in research: I Social impacts of technology, 2 Value systems, 3 Alternative futures.
Methods used: I Simulation, 2 Causal modelling, 3 Statistical models, 4 Operational models, 5 Historical analogy.
Time range of work: 5 - IO years.
Source of support for work (%): 5O Local government, 5O National government,
Occupational function: I Research worker, 2 Educator.
Worked in education: I In research, 2 Teaching.
Additional information: Concerned with futures of the social and economic order in the world.   *(37)*

54. Phillip Bosserman
Deputy Director, University of South Florida, Institute for Studies of Leisure, Tampa, Fl 33620, USA.
Sex: Male.   *Age:* 4O-49.
Educational qualification: Doctoral degree.
Formal training: I Social/behavioural sciences, 2 Humanities.
Informal training: I Education, 2 Arts, 3 Cinema/television.
Primarily engaged in: Long-range planning.
Areas in which work done (%): 5 As individual consultant, 7O As academic, in teaching futures studies or long-range planning, 25 In planning unit of an international organization.
Direction of work in research: I Policy research, 2 Value systems, 3 Social priorities, 4 The individual in the future.
Methods used: I Secondary analysis, 2 Historical analogy, 3 Cross impact analysis.
Time range of work: IO - 25 years.
Source of support for work (%): 5 Foundations, IO International agencies, IO National government, 75 Local government.
Work done for (%): 5 Foundations, IO National government, IO International agencies. 75 Local or regional government.

Occupational function: I Research worker, 2 Administrator, 3 Educator, 4 Consultant.
Worked in government as: Administrator.
Worked in education: I Teaching, 2 In research, 3 In administration.
Worked in service sector: Religion.
Additional information: Concerned with social indicators on leisure, quality of life; secondary analysis of data to determine long-range trends.   *(204)*

55. M.C. Botez
Director, International Centre of Methodology for Future and Development Studies, Str Mihail Moxa 3 - 5, Bucharest 8, Romania.
Sex: Male.   *Age:* 30-39.
Educational qualification: Doctoral degree.
Formal training: Mathematics.
Informal training: I Humanities, 2 Social/behavioural sciences.
Primarily engaged in: Futures studies.
Areas in which work done (%): 40 In planning unit of an international organization, 35 Individual research programs, 25 As academic, in teaching futures studies or long-range planning.
Direction of work in forecasting: I Social, 2 Resources, 3 Environmental.
Direction of work in research: I Futures methodology, 2 Alternative futures, 3 Value systems, 4 Environmental.
Direction of work in planning: I Scientific, 2 Environmental, 3 Educational.
Methods used: I Probabilistic forecasting, 2 Statistical models, 3 Gaming, 4 Brainstorming, 5 Extrapolation techniques, 6 Operational models, 7 Simulation.
Source of support for work (%): IOO University funds.
Work done for (%): 35 International agencies, 65 University.
Occupational function: I Research worker, 2 Educator.
Worked in education: I In research, 2 Teaching.
Worked in service sector: 3 Design.
Additional information: Concerned with general methodology of future studies; social design in a systems approach.   *(191)*

56. Wayne I. Boucher
Vice President and Secretary, Futures Group, 124 Hebron Ave, Glastonbury, Ct 06033, USA.
Sex: Male.   *Age:* 40-49.
Educational qualification: Master's degree.
Formal training: Humanities.
Informal training: I Social/behavioural sciences, 2 Education, 3 Business and public administration, (Planning etc).
Primarily engaged in: Both futures studies and planning.
Areas in which work done (%): 95 In organization primarily concerned with futures studies and/or planning, 5 As academic, in teaching futures studies or planning.
Direction of work in forecasting: I Market, 2 Technological, 3 Social.
Direction of work in research: I Futures methodology, 2 Planning systems, futures literature, 3 Policy research.
Direction of work in planning: I Corporate, 2 Political, Governmental, 3 Technological.
Methods used: Probabilistic forecasting.
Time range of work: IO years.
Source of support for work (%): 30 Private business, 70 National government.
Work done for (%): 30 Private business, 70 National government.

Occupational function: I Research worker, 2 Consultant, 3 Administrator.
Worked in industry/business in: I Management, 2 Research and development, 3 Planning.
Worked in education: I Teaching, 2 In research.
Additional information: As of March 1, 1976 Director of Research and Deputy Executive Director of the staff, the National Commission on Electronic Fund Transfers, 1000 Connecticut Avenue NW, Suite 900, Washington DC 20036, USA. *(61)*

57. Elise Boulding

Professor of Sociology, Institute of Behavioural Science, University of Colorado, Boulder, Co 80302, USA.
Sex: Female.   *Age:* 50-59.
Educational qualification: Doctoral degree.
Formal training: Social/behavioural sciences.
Informal training: Humanities, Education, Arts.
Areas in which work done (%): IO As academic, in teaching futures studies or long-range planning.
Direction of work in research: Alternative futures, The family in the future.
Methods used: Scenario building, Contextual mapping, Network analysis, Historical analogy.
Time range of work: Beyond 2000 AD.
Source of support for work (%): IOO Self-supported.
Work done for (%): IOO General public interest.
Occupational function: I Educator, 2 Research worker.
Worked in education: I Teaching, 2 In research, 3 In administration.
Additional information: Concerned with translational networks: the family, women's roles. *(28)*

58. Kenneth Boulding

Professor of Economics, Institute of Behavioural Science, University of Colorado, Boulder, Co 80302, USA.
Sex: Male.   *Age:* Over 60.
Educational qualification: Master's degree.
Formal training: Social/behavioural sciences.
Informal training: Physical sciences, Education, Life sciences, Arts, Humanities.
Methods used: Thinking.
Worked in education: I Teaching, 2 In research *(538)*

59. William L. Bowden

Executive Director, Southern Growth Policies Board, PO Box 12293, 100 Park Drive, Research Triangle Park, NC 27709, USA.
Sex: Male.   *Age:* 50-59.
Educational qualification: Doctoral degree.
Formal training: Education.
Informal training: Education, Television, Design, Social/behavioural sciences.
Primarily engaged in: Both futures studies and long-range planning.
Areas in which work done (%): IOO Organization primarily concerned with futures studies and/or long-range planning.
Direction of work in planning: I Regional, 2 Social, 2 Urban, 2 Economic, 2 Political, 2 Environmental, 2 Resources, 3 Educational.
Occupational function: Administrator.
Worked in education as: In administration, Teaching, In research.

Worked in service sector: Communications media.
Additional information: Concerned with interstate planning of public policies for 15
states in the southern United States. **(557)**

60. Jim Bowman
University of Houston at Clear Lake City, 2700 Bay Area Blvd, Houston, Tx
77058, USA.
Sex: Male. *Age:* 25-29.
Educational qualification: Doctoral degree.
Formal training: 1 Education, 2 Social/behavioural sciences.
Areas in which work done (%): 25 As academic, in teaching futures studies or long-
range planning.
Direction of work in forecasting: 1 Educational, 2 Social, 3 Environmental, 4 Economic.
Direction of work in research: 1 Alternative futures, 2 Social priorities, 3 Value
systems, 4 Futures methodology.
Direction of work in planning: 1 Educational, 2 Social.
Methods used: 1 Scenario building, 1 Relevance trees, 2 Extrapolation techniques,
2 Simulation, 3 Historical analogy, 4 Cross impact analysis, 5 Delphi techniques,
5 Gaming.
Time range of work: 5 - 25 years.
Occupational function: Educator, Consultant.
Worked in education: Teaching.
Additional information: Concerned with educational, societal futures. **(446)**

61. B. Bowonder
Dept of Industrial Management, Indian Institute of Science, Bangalore-12, India 560012.
Sex: Male. *Age:* 25-29.
Educational qualification: Doctoral degree.
Formal training: 1 Engineering, 2 Physical sciences, 3 Industrial management.
Informal training: 1 Futurology, 2 Design.
Primarily engaged in: Both futures studies and long-range planning.
Areas in which work done (%): 25 In organization concerned with other studies
including long-range planning, 75 In organization primarily concerned with futures
studies and/or long-range planning.
Direction of work in forecasting: 1 Technological, 2 Scientific, 3 Resources, 4 Population,
5 Environmental.
Direction of work in research: 1 Science policy and industrial growth, 2 Alternative
futures, 3 Social impacts of technology, 4 Environmental.
Direction of work in planning: 1 Technological, 2 Scientific, 3 Corporate, 4 Environmental.
Methods used: 1 Extrapolation techniques, 2 Delphi techniques, 3 Scenario building,
4 Relevance trees, 5 Operational models.
Time range of work: 10 - 25 years.
Source of support for work (%): 100 A university-like institute.
Occupational function: Post-doctoral fellow.
Worked in education: In research.
Additional information: Concerned with technology/assessment and technology
forecasting as techniques for research and development management and long-range
planning. **(160)**

62. Theodore Brameld
151 Ward Ave, Honolulu, Hi 96822, USA.
Sex: Male.   *Age:* 60 or over.
Educational qualification: Doctoral degree.
Formal training: l Philosophy, 2 Social/behavioural sciences, 3 Education.
Informal training: l Humanities, 2 Education.
Areas in which work done (%): 25 As academic, in teaching futures studies or long-range planning, 25 In organization concerned with other studies including long-range planning.
Direction of work in research: l Alternative futures, 2 Futures methodology.
Direction of work in planning: l Educational, 2 Social, 3 Environmental.
Methods used: l Operational models, 2 Expert panels.
Time range of work: l0 - 25 years.
Source of support for work (%): 50 Voluntary associations, 50 Foundations.
Work done for (%): 50 Foundations, 50 Voluntary associations.
Occupational function: l Educator, 2 Research worker.
Worked in education: Teaching.   *(215)*

63. Paul Brenikov
Head, Newcastle Upon Tyne University, Dept of Town and Country Planning, The University, Newcastle Upon Tyne NE1 7RO, UK.
Sex: Male.   *Age:* 50-59.
Educational qualification: Other graduate/professional degree.
Formal training: Physical sciences, Design, Economic geography.
Informal training: Social/behavioural sciences, Law, Mathematics, Education.
Primarily engaged in. Both futures studies and long-range planning.
Areas in which work done (%): l0 Individual consultant, 40 Academic administration, 50 As academic, in teaching futures studies or long-range planning.
Direction of work in forecasting: Environmental.
Direction of work in research: l Environmental, 2 Resource utilization, 3 Population, 4 Policy research.
Direction of work in planning: l Environmental, 2 Urban, 2 Regional, 3 Resources, 4 Economic.
Methods used: l Operational models, 2 Simulation, 3 Contextual mapping, 4 Scenario building, 5 Gaming, 6 Statistical models, 7 Extrapolation techniques.
Time range of work: 5 - l0 years.
Source of support for work (%): l00 National government.
Work done for (%): l5 Local or regional government, l5 National government, 70 Academic.
Occupational function: l Educator, 2 Administrator, 3 Research worker, 4 Consultant.
Worked in government as: Administrator, Researcher.
Worked in education: Teaching, In research, In administration.
Worked in service sector: Design.   *(184)*

64. Siegfried M. Breuning
129 School St, Wayland, Ma 01778, USA.
Sex: Male.   *Age:* 50-59.
Educational qualification: Doctoral degree.
Formal training: Engineering.
Informal training: l Social/behavioural sciences, 2 Education.
Primarily engaged in: Long-range planning.

Areas in which work done (%): IO In planning unit of a business enterprise, 2O As individual consultant, 7O As academic, in teaching futures studies or long-range planning.
Direction of work in forecasting: I Technological, 2 Social.
Direction of work in research: I Social impacts of technology, 2 Social priorities, 3 Value systems.
Direction of work in planning: I Technological, 2 Social, 3 Corporate.
Methods used: I Gaming, 2 Brainstorming, 3 Simulation.
Time range of work: IO - 25 years.
Source of support for work (%): 2O Private business, 8O Local government.
Work done for (%): IO Voluntary associations, 2O Private business, 3O National government. 4O Local or regional government.
Occupational function: I Educator, 2 Consultant.
Worked in industry/business in: Consultancy.
Worked in education: I Teaching, 2 In research.   *(87)*

65. Robert C. Brictson
Professor of Medical Education, Office of Medical Education, Research and Development, A 2O6 East Fee Hall, Michigan State University, East Lansing, Mi 48824, USA.
Sex: Male.   *Age:* 40-49.
Educational qualification: Doctoral degree.
Formal training: Social/behavioural sciences, Journalism, Humanities, Mathematics.
Informal training: Life sciences, Arts, Education, Law.
Primarily engaged in: Both futures studies and long-range planning.
Areas in which work done (%): 25 In organization primarily concerned with futures studies and/or long-range planning, 25 In organization concerned with other studies including long-range planning, 25 In planning unit of a business enterprise, IO As individual consultant, I5 As academic, in teaching futures studies or long-range planning.
Direction of work in forecasting: I Social, 2 Market, 3 Educational, 4 Resources, 5 Population.
Direction of work in research: I Social priorities, 2 Policy research, 3 Social impacts of technology, 4 Alternative futures.
Direction of work in planning: I Educational, 2 Urban, 3 Social, 4 Technological.
Methods used: I Simulation, 2 Expert panels, 3 Brainstorming, 4 Scenario building, 5 Gaming.
Time range of work: 5 - 25 years.
Source of support for work (%): IOO University.
Work done for (%): IOO University medical education, Michigan State University.
Occupational function: I Research worker, 2 Educator, 3 Consultant.
Worked in industry/business in: I Research and development, 2 Management, 3 Planning.
Worked in education: I In administration, 2 In research, 3 Teaching.
Additional information: Concerned with future of medicine, technology impact, modernization, social indicators and quality of life, social change.   *(540)*

66. James R. Bright
President, Industrial Management Centre, Inc, 1411 West Ave, Austin, Tx 787O1, USA.
Sex: Male.   *Age:* 50-59.
Educational qualification: Master's degree.
Formal training: Engineering.
Informal training: I Education, 2 Engineering, 3 Journalism.

Primarily engaged in: Both futures studies and long-range planning.

Areas in which work done (%): IO In organization primarily concerned with futures studies and/or long-range planning, 2O As individual consultant, 7O As academic, in teaching futures studies or long-range planning.

Direction of work in forecasting: I Technological, 2 Social, 3 Market.

Direction of work in research: I Technological innovation, 2 Social impacts of technology.

Direction of work in planning: I Technological, 2 Scientific, 3 Educational.

Methods used: I Extrapolation techniques, 2 Scenario building, 3 Relevance trees.

Time range of work: 5 - 25 years.

Source of support for work (%): 2O National government, 8O Private business.

Work done for (%): 2O National government, 8O Private business.

Occupational function: I Educator, 2 Consultant.

Worked in industry/business in: Management.

Worked in education: I Teaching, 2 In research.

Additional information: Concerned with technological forecasting.   *(319)*

67. K.J. Brimley

5 Dognell Green, Welwyn Garden City, AL8 7BL, UK.

Sex: Male.   *Age:* 5O-59.

Educational qualification: Bachelor's degree.

Formal training: Physical sciences.

Informal training: I Physical sciences, 2 Engineering, 3 Design.

Direction of work in forecasting: I Technological, 2 Market.

Direction of work in research: Resource utilization.

Direction of work in planning: Technological.

Time range of work: 5 - IO years.

Occupational function: I Manager, 2 Administrator.

Worked in industry/business in: Management, Research and development.

Additional information: Concerned with technological assessment and its relation to the built environment and its control.   *(142)*

68. William L. Brockhaus

Graduate School of Business Administration, Dept of Management, University of Southern California, University Park, Los Angeles, Ca 9OOO7, USA.

Sex: Male.   *Age:* 3O-39.

Educational qualification: Doctoral degree.

Formal training: I Business administration.

Informal training: I Social/behavioural sciences, 2 Education.

Areas in which work done (%): 25 As academic, in teaching futures studies or long-range planning, 75 As individual consultant.

Direction of work in forecasting: I Population, 2 Educational, 3 Environmental, 4 Technological, 5 Social, 6 Economic, 7 Resources, 8 Cultural, 9 Market, IO Scientific.

Direction of work in research: I The family in the future, 2 Population, 3 Policy research, 4 Social impacts of technology, 5 Value systems, 6 Environmental, 7 The individual in the future.

Direction of work in planning: I Educational, 2 Social, 3 Environmental, 4 Corporate. 5 Political, 6 Economic, 7 Regional.

Methods used: I Scenario building, 2 Delphi techniques, 3 Statistical models.

Time range of work: IO - 25 years. ·

Source of support for work (%): IOO Private business.

Work done for (%): 4O Private business.

Occupational function: I Educator, 2 Consultant.
Worked in government as: I Researcher, 2 Administrator.
Worked in industry/business in: I Management, 2 Research and development.
Worked in education: I Teaching, 2 In research, 3 In administration.
Additional information: Concerned with methodological developments relevant to all areas of substantial applications. *(426)*

69. L.G. Brookes

United Kingdom Atomic Energy Authority, 11 Charles II St, London SW1, UK.
Sex: Male.　　*Age:* 50-59.
Educational qualification: Bachelor's degree.
Formal training: I Social/behavioural sciences, 2 Mathematics.
Informal training: Physical sciences, Engineering.
Primarily engaged in: Both futures studies and long-range planning.
Areas in which work done (%): IO As academic, in teaching futures studies or long-range planning, 90 In planning unit of a governmental agency.
Direction of work in forecasting: I Resources, 2 Economic, 3 Technological, 4 Environmental, 5 Social.
Direction of work in research: I Resource utilization, 2 Alternative futures.
Direction of work in planning: I Resources, 2 Technological, 3 Scientific, 4 Environmental.
Methods used: I Probabilistic forecasting, 2 Causal modelling, 3 Extrapolation techniques, 4 Expert panels, 5 Statistical models.
Time range of work: IO - beyond year 2000.
Source of support for work (%): IOO National government.
Work done for (%): IOO National government.
Occupational function: I Consultant, 2 Research worker, 3 Administrator, 4 Manager, 5 Educator.
Worked in government as: I Administrator, 2 Researcher. *(112)*

70. Corrin Brownlee

Field Politics Centre, Goucher College, Towson, Baltimore, Md 21204, USA.
Sex: Male.　　*Age:* 50-59.
Educational qualification: Doctoral degree.
Formal training: Social/behavioural sciences.
Informal training: Physical sciences, Life sciences, Humanities, Education, Arts, Cinema/television, Law.
Direction of work in forecasting: Global.
Direction of work in research: I Alternative futures, 2 Value systems, 3 The Individual in the future, 4 Metalaw.
Direction of work in planning: Global.
Methods used: Probabilistic forecasting, Individual expert forecasting, Delphi techniques, Cross impact analysis, Scenario building, Extrapolation techniques, Brainstorming, Expert panels, Relevance trees, Network analysis, Historical analogy, Operational models.
Time range of work: 5 years to beyond year 2000.
Source of support for work (%): IOO Academic institution and self.
Work done for (%): IOO Teaching.
Occupational function: I Educator, 2 Consultant.
Worked in education: Teaching.
Worked in service sector: Communication media. *(69)*

71. Gerhart Bruckmann
Austrian Futures Research Society, Universitatsstr 7, A-1010 Wien, Austria.
Sex: Male.   *Age:* 40-49.
Educational qualification: Doctoral degree.
Formal training: I Economic statistics, 2 Mathematics, 3 Social/behavioural sciences, 4 Engineering.
Informal training: Humanities.
Primarily engaged in: Both futures studies and long-range planning.
Areas in which work done (%): 20 As individual consultant, 20 In organization concerned with other studies including long-range planning, 60 As academic, in teaching futures studies or long-range planning.
Direction of work in forecasting: I Economic, 2 Social.
Direction of work in research: I Alternative futures, 2 Futures methodology, 3 Social priorities, 4 Value systems.
Methods used: Scenario building, Extrapolation techniques, Individual expert forecasting, Causal modelling.
Time range of work: 10 - beyond year 2000.
Source of support for work (%): 30 Voluntary associations, 30 International agencies, 40 National government.
Work done for (%): 30 International agencies, 70 National government.
Occupational function: I Educator, 2 Consultant, 3 Administrator.
Worked in education: Teaching, In research, In administration.   *(140)*

72. H.G. Brudner
Fairleigh Dickinson University, Rutherford, NJ 07070, USA.
Sex: Female.   *Age:* 30-39.
Educational qualification: Doctoral degree.
Formal training: I Social/behavioural sciences, 2 Education.
Informal training: I Law, 2 Humanities.
Areas in which work done (%): 10 As individual consultant, 40 In organization primarily concerned with futures studies and/or long-range planning, 50 As academic, in teaching futures studies of long-range planning.
Direction of work in forecasting: I Social, 2 Technological, 3 Cultural.
Direction of work in research: I Social impacts of technology, 2 Alternative futures, 3 Policy research.
Direction of work in planning: Educational.
Methods used: I Network analysis, 2 Delphi techniques, 3 Gaming.
Time range of work: 5 - 25 years.
Source of support for work (%): 95 University.
Occupational function: Educator.
Worked in industry in: Consultancy.
Worked in education: Teaching.
Additional information: Concerned with impact of technology on social, political and economic institutions. Forecasting alternative techniques in education.   *(439)*

73. Bruno Fritsch
President, Swiss Society for Futures Research, Ecole Polytechnique Fédèrale, Scheuchzerstr 68, Zurich, Switzerland.
Sex: Male.   *Age:* 40-49.
Educational qualification: Doctoral degree.
Formal training: Economics.

Informal training: Mathematics.
Primarily engaged in: Both futures studies and long-range planning.
Areas in which work done (%): IO In organization primarily concerned with futures studies and/or long-range planning, IO As individual consultant, 5O Teaching, 3O As academic, in teaching futures studies or long-range planning.
Direction of work in forecasting: Economic, Environmental.
Direction of work in research: Social impacts of technology, Value systems.
Direction of work in planning: Economic, Environmental.
Methods used: Delphi techniques, Scenario building, Statistical models, Operational models.
Time range of work: IO - 25 years.
Source of support for work (%): 6O National government.
Occupational function: Professor.
Worked in government as: Researcher.
Worked in education: Teaching, In research.
Additional information: Concerned with the future structure of the international system in view of the long-range prospective in population, energy, technology, and resources. *(437)*

74. V.V. Bryan

Vice President of Corporate Development, Bendix Corporation, Bendix Centre, Southfield, Mi 48076, USA.
Sex: Male.   *Age:* 40-49.
Educational qualification: Master's degree.
Formal training: I Management, 2 Engineering.
Informal training: I Physical sciences, 2 Law.
Primarily engaged in: Both futures studies and long-range planning.
Areas in which work done (%): IOO In planning unit of a business enterprise.
Direction of work in forecasting: I Market, 2 Economic, 3 Technological, 3 Environmental, 4 Military, 6 Resources.
Direction of work in research: Environmental.
Direction of work in planning: Corporate.
Methods used: I Operational models, 2 Simulation, 3 Causal modelling, 4 Delphi techniques, 4 Scenario building, 4 Extrapolation techniques, 4 Statistical models.
Time range of work: 5 - IO years.
Source of support for work (%): IOO Private business.
Work done for (%): IOO Private business.
Occupational function: I Administrator, 2 Manager, 3 Consultant.
Worked in industry/business in: I Planning, 2 Management. *(373)*

75. Irving H. Buchen

Projector, Division of the Future, Dreyfuss College, Fairleigh Dickinson University, Madison, NJ 07940, USA.
Sex: Male.   *Age:* 40-49.
Educational qualification: Doctoral degree.
Formal training: Humanities.
Informal training: Journalism, Education, Cinema/television.
Primarily engaged in: Both futures studies and long-range planning.
Areas in which work done (%): IO In organization primarily concerned with futures studies and/or long-range planning, 3O As individual consultant, IO In organization concerned with other studies including long-range planning, 3O As academic, in

teaching futures studies or long-range planning.

Direction of work in forecasting: Social, Cultural, Educational, Manpower.

Direction of work in research: Social impacts of technology, Alternative futures, Manpower, Value systems, Social priorities, The individual in the future, The family in the future, Futures methodology, Organizational theory and structure.

Direction of work in planning: Social, Urban, Regional, Educational, Corporate.

Methods used: 1 Delphi techniques, 2 Cross impact analysis, 3 Probabilistic forecasting, 4 Scenario building, 4 Statistical models, 5 Gaming, 6 Brainstorming, 8 Contextual mapping, 9 Extrapolation techniques, 10 Relevance trees, 11 Historical analogy, 12 Simulation, 13 Causal modelling.

Time range of work: 10 - 25 years.

Source of support for work (%): 5 Local government, 10 Voluntary associations, 10 Private business, 30 Educational institutions.

Work done for (%): 10 Private business, 10 Voluntary associations, 20 Local or regional government.

Occupational function: 1 Educator, 2 Administrator, 3 Research worker, 4 Consultant.

Worked in industry/business in: Planning, Consultancy.

Worked in education: Teaching, In research, In administration.

Worked in service sector: Communication media..   *(353)*

76. C.M. Buckley

Science Policy Research Unit, University of Sussex, Falmer, Brighton, UK.

Sex: Male.   *Age:* 25-29.

Educational qualification: Master's degree.

Formal training: Social/behavioural sciences.

Primarily engaged in: Both futures studies and long-range planning.

Areas in which work done (%): 100 In organization primarily concerned with futures studies and/or long-range planning.

Direction of work in forecasting: 1 Economic, 2 Resources, 3 Technological, 4 Environmental.

Direction of work in research: 1 Policy research, 2 Resource utilization, 3 Environmental.

Direction of work in planning: Technological, Economic, Environmental, Resources.

Methods used: 1 Scenario building, 1 Expert panels, 2 Individual expert forecasting, 3 Statistical models.

Time range of work: 10 - 25 years.

Source of support for work (%): 25 National government, 25 Private business, 50 National industries.

Work done for (%): 25 National government, 25 Private business, 50 National industries.

Occupational function: 1 Research worker, 2 Administrator, 3 Educator.

Worked in government as: Researcher.

Worked in education: In research.

Worked in service sector: Communication media.

Additional information: Working on economic and technological assessment of UK energy policy choices.   *(496)*

77. Brian Buss

Long-Range Planning Dept, Electrical Research Association, Cleeve Road, Leatherhead, Surrey, UK.

Sex: Male.   *Age:* 40-49.

Educational qualification: Some college or less.

Formal training: Engineering.
Informal training: I Physical sciences, 2 Social/behavioural sciences, 3 Education.
Primarily engaged in: Both futures studies and long-range planning.
Areas in which work done (%): IO In planning unit of a business enterprise, 75 In
organization primarily concerned with futures studies and/or long-range planning,
I5 In organization concerned with other studies including long-range planning.
Direction of work in forecasting: I Technological, 2 Market, 3 Economic, 4 Social.
Direction of work in research: I Social impacts of technology, 2 Alternative futures,
3 Resource utilization, 4 Social priorities.
Direction of work in planning: I Technological, 2 Corporate, 3 Resources.
Methods used: I Cross impact analysis, 2 Scenario building, 3 Extrapolation techniques.
Time range of work: IO - 25 years.
Source of support for work (%): 5 National government, 95 Private business.
Work done for (%): 5 National government 95 Private business.
Occupational function: I Manager, 2 Research worker.
Worked in industry/business in: I Research and development, 2 Planning.   *(226)*

78. Salvino Busuttil

Chairman, Dept of Economics, Royal University of Malta, Malta.
Sex: Male.   *Age:* 30-39.
Educational qualification: Doctoral degree.
Formal training: Social/behavioural sciences.
Informal training: I Humanities, 2 Journalism, 3 Education, 4 Cinema/television.
Areas in which work done (%): 2O As academic, in teaching futures studies or long-
range planning.
Direction of work in forecasting: I Social, 2 Environmental, 3 Cultural, 4 Economic.
Direction of work in research: I Social impacts of technology, 2 Alternative futures,
3 Environmental, 4 Value systems, 5 Social priorities, 6 Policy research, 7 The
individual in the future, 8 The family in the future.
Direction of work in planning: I Social, 2 Economic, 3 Educational, 4 Environmental.
Methods used: I Network analysis, 2 Historical analogy, 3 Operational models, 4 Expert
panels, 5 Individual expert forecasting, 6 Brainstorming, 8 Cross impact analysis,
9 Scenario building.
Time range of work: IO - 25 years.
Work done for (%): IO National government, IO Voluntary associations.
Occupational function: Educator.
Worked in government as: Administrator,. Researcher.
Worked in education: Teaching, In research, In administration.
Worked in service sector: Social welfare, Communication media.   *(481)*

79. Robert E. Button

7 Sylvan Lane, Old Greenwich, Ct O687O, USA.
Sex: Male.   *Age:* 5O-59.
Educational qualification: Other graduate/professional degree.
Formal training: Humanities, Law.
Informal training: Education, Arts.
Primarily engaged in: Both futures studies and long-range planning.
Areas in which work done (%): IO In organization primarily concerned with futures
studies and/or long-range planning, 9O In planning unit of a business enterprise.
Direction of work in forecasting: Economic, Social, Cultural.

Direction of work in research: Social impacts of technology, Alternative futures, Social priorities.
Direction of work in planning: Economic, Corporate.
Methods used: Statistical models.
Time range of work: 5 - 10 years.
Source of support for work (%): 5 Colleges, 95 Private business.
Work done for (%): 99 Private business.
Occupational function: Manager.
Worked in government as: Administrator.
Worked in industry/business in: Management, Research and development, Planning.
Worked in education: Teaching.
Worked in service sector: Religion, Communication media.
Additional information: Concerned with future of communications, both as an industry and an influence on society.
(63)

C 80. W. Thomas Callahan

Operations Research, Inc, Silver Spring, Md 20910, USA.
Sex: Male.   *Age:* 30-39.
Educational qualification: Bachelor's degree.
Formal training: 1 Social/behavioural sciences, 2 Humanities, 3 Education.
Informal training: 1 Social/behavioural sciences, 2 Humanities, 3 Mathematics, 4 Education, 5 Life sciences.
Direction of work in research: 1 Manpower, 2 Resource utilization.
Direction of work in planning: 1 Educational, 2 Military, 3 Economic, 4 Social, 5 Political.
Methods used: 1 Delphi techniques, 2 Scenario building, 3 Relevance trees, 4 Extrapolation techniques, 4 Brainstorming, 4 Statistical models, 4 Historical analogy, 4 Individual expert forecasting.
Time range of work: 5 - 25 years.
Source of support for work (%): 100 National government.
Work done for (%): 100 National government.
Occupational function: 1 Consultant, 2 Research worker, 3 Educator.
Worked in industry/business in: Research and development, Consultancy.
Additional information: Concerned with the future of education, international politics, military affairs, and national politics.
(355)

81. Guillermo J. Cano

President, International Association for Water Law, Arenales 2040, 7-B Buenos Aires, Argentina.
Sex: Male.   *Age:* 60 or over.
Educational qualification: Master's degree.
Formal training: Law.
Informal training: 1 Education, 2 Social/behavioural sciences.
Primarily engaged in: Long-range planning.
Areas in which work done (%): 80 As individual consultant, 20 In organization with other studies including long-range planning.
Direction of work in research: 1 Resource utilization, 2 Environmental.
Direction of work in planning: 1 Environmental, 2 Resources.
Methods used: 1 Brainstorming.
Time range of work: 10 - 25 years.
Source of support for work (%): 50 International agencies, 50 Private business.

Work done for (%): 5O International agencies, 5O Voluntary associations.
Occupational function: I Consultant, 2 Research worker.
Worked in government as: I Elected official, 2 Administrator.
Worked in industry/business in: Consultancy.
Worked in education: Teaching.
Worked in service sector: Law.
Additional information: Concerned with the future of natural resources law and
administration.   *(237)*

82. M.F. Cantley

Dept of Operational Research, University of Lancaster, Lancaster, UK.
Sex: Male.   *Age:* 30-39.
Educational qualification: Other graduate/professional degree.
Formal training: Mathematics.
Informal training: Education, Operational research.
Areas in which work done (%): 3O Individual consultant, 7O As academic, in teaching
futures studies or long-range planning.
Direction of work in research: Futures methodology.
Direction of work in planning: Corporate.
Methods used: I Operational models, 2 Causal modelling.
Time range of work: 5 - lO years.
Source of support for work (%): 3O Private business, 7O University.
Occupational function: I Educator, 2 Consultant.
Worked in education: I Teaching, 2 In research.
Additional information: Concerned with teaching long-range planning methods.   *(131)*

83. Charles M. Cargille

President, The World Population Society, The American University, Washington,
DC, 2OO16, USA.
Sex: Male.   *Age:* 4O-49.
Educational qualification: Doctoral degree.
Formal training: I Medicine, 2 Social/behavioural sciences.
Informal training: I Mathematics, 2 Education.
Areas in which work done (%): I5 In organization concerned with other studies
including long-range planning.
Direction of work in research: I Population, 2 Environmental.
Direction of work in planning: I Scientific.
Methods used: I Brainstorming, 2 Expert panels.
Time range of work: 5 - lO years.
Source of support for work (%): 5O Foundations, 5O Membership and loans.
Work done for (%): lOO Voluntary associations.
Occupational function: Research worker.
Worked in government/business in: I Researcher, 2 Administrator.
Worked in service sector: Medicine.
Additional information: Concerned with developing a new society.   *(212)*

84. Thomas Carleton

Futures Lab Director, Earthrise, PO Box 12O, Annex Station, Providence, RI O29O1, USA.
Sex: Male.   *Age:* 25-29.
Educational qualification: Bachelor's degree.
Formal training: I Design, 2 Arts.

Informal training: I Education, 2 Social/behavioural sciences, 3 Physical sciences.
Primarily engaged in: Both futures studies and long-range planning.
Areas in which work done (%): 5O In organization primarily concerned with futures studies and/or long-range planning, 5O As academic, in teaching futures studies or long-range planning.
Direction of work in research: I Futures methodology, 2 Alternative futures.
Direction of work in planning: I Environmental, 2 Social.
Methods used: I Scenario building, 2 Gaming, 3 Simulation, 4 Brainstorming.
Time range of work: IO - 25 years.
Source of support for work (%): 9O Academic sources.
Work done for (%): 9O In-house studies.
Occupational function: I Educator, 2 Manager, 3 Administrator, 4 Consultant.
Worked in education: Teaching.
Worked in service sector: Design.   *(400)*

85, Fred F. Case

Urban Resources Study Centre, Graduate School of Management, University of California, Los Angeles, Ca 9OO24, USA.
Sex: Male.   *Age:* 5O - 59.
Educational qualification: Doctoral degree.
Formal training: Social/behavioural sciences.
Informal training: I Mathematics, 2 Humanities, 3 Arts, 4 Design, 5 Education, 6 Law.
Primarily engaged in: Both futures studies and long-range planning.
Areas in which work done (%): 5 In planning unit of business enterprise, I5 In planning unit of governmental agencies, 8O As academic, in teaching futures studies or long-range planning.
Direction of work in forecasting: I Economic, 2 Social, 3 Resources, 4 Environmental, 5 Population.
Direction of work in research: I Alternative futures, 2 Social priorities, 3 Policy research, 4 Value systems, 5 Environmental.
Direction of work in planning: I Urban, 2 Regional, 3 Social, 4 Environmental.
Methods used: I Delphi techniques, 2 Expert panels, 3 Operational models, 4 Probabilistic forecasting, 5 Extrapolation techniques, 6 Gaming, 7 Statistical models.
Time range of work: IO - 25 years.
Source of support for work (%): IO Private business, IO National government, I5 Foundations, 65 State government.
Work done for (%): 2O National government, 2O Private business, 6O Local or regional government.
Occupational function: I Educator, 2 Research worker, 3 Consultant.
Worked in industry/business in: Consultancy.
Worked in education: I Teaching, 2 In research, 3 In administration.
Additional information: Concerned with urban growth; structuring; socio-economic forecasting; and social indicators.   *(396)*

86. Vincenzo Cazzaniga

Industrial Manager, Via di Porta Latina 8, OO179, Rome, Italy.
Sex: Male.   *Age:* 6O or over.
Educational qualification: Doctoral degree.
Formal training: I Economics, 2 Engineering, 2 Law.
Informal training: I Economics, 2 Law, 3 Engineering.

Primarily engaged in: Both futures studies and long-range planning.
Areas in which work done (%): IO As individual consultant, 2O In planning unit of a governmental agency, 7O In planning unit of an international organization.
Direction of work in forecasting: Economic.
Direction of work in research: Consumer affairs.
Direction of work in planning: Economic.
Methods used: Scenario building, Historical analogy, Individual expert forecasting.
Time range of work: IO - 25 years.
Source of support for work (%): 5O Private business.
Work done for (%): 7O Private business.
Occupational function: Consultant.
Additional information: Concerned with energy studies. *(2)*

87. Silvio Ceccato

Prof, Centro di Cibernetica e Attivitia Linguistiche del CNR, Via Festa del Perdono 3, Milano, Italy.
Sex: Male.   *Age:* 6O or over.
Educational qualification: Other graduate/professional degree.
Formal training: Humanities, Arts.
Informal training: Education.
Areas in which work done (%): IO Travelling, I5 In planning unit of a governmental agency, I5 As academic in teaching futures studies or long-range planning.
Direction of work in forecasting: I Cultural, 2 Educational.
Direction of work in research: I The individual in the future, 2 Value systems. 3 Alternative futures.
Methods used: Analysis of mental life.
Time range of work: IO - 25 years.
Occupational function: Research worker, Educator.
Worked in government as: Researcher.
Worked in education: Teaching, In research. *(433)*

88. Marvin J. Cetron

President, Forecasting International Ltd, 1001 N Highland St, Arlington, Va 22201, USA.
Sex: Male.   *Age:* 4O-49.
Educational qualification: Doctoral degree.
Formal training: Research and development management, Engineering, Physical sciences, Social/behavioural sciences.
Informal training: Engineering, Physical sciences, Social/behavioural sciences.
Areas in which work done (%): 5 Academic, In teaching futures studies or long-range planning, 3O Organization primarily concerned with futures studies and/or long-range planning, 5O Organization concerned with other studies including long-range planning, 5 Planning unit of a business enterprise, 5 Planning unit of a governmental agency, 5 Planning unit of an international organization.
Direction of work in forecasting: I Technological, 2 Social, 3 Cultural, 4 Economic, 5 Environmental, 6 Military, 7 Resources, 8 Market, 9 Manpower.
Direction of work in research: I Social impacts of technology, 2 Policy research, 3 Value systems, 4 Social priorities, 5 Consumer affairs, 6 Alternative futures, 7 Futures methodology, 8 Environmental.
Direction of work in planning: I Technological, 2 Scientific, 3 Corporate, 4 Military, 5 Social, 6 Urban, 7 Regional, 8 Economic, 9 Political, IO Environmental.
Methods used: I Brainstorming, 2 Scenario building, 3 Extrapolation techniques,

4 Expert panels, 5 Relevance trees, 6 Delphi techniques.
Time range of work: lO - 25 years.
Source of support for work (%): 9O National government, 2 International agencies, 8 Private business.
Work done for (%): 95 National government, l International agencies, 4 Private business.
Occupational function: l Administrator, 2 Consultant, 3 Manager, 4 Educator.
Worked in government as: Researcher.
Worked in industry/business in: l Planning, 2 Management.
Worked in education: Teaching.   *(572)*

89. George Chaplin

Editor-in-Chief, The Honolulu Advertiser, PO Box 311O, Honolulu, Hi 968O2, USA.
Sex: Male.   *Age:* Over 6O.
Educational qualification: Bachelor's degree.
Formal training: Journalism.
Informal training: l Humanities, 2 Education, 3 Design, 4 Law.
Areas in which work done (%): 5 - lO In organization primarily concerned with futures studies and/or long-range planning.
Direction of work in forecasting: Economic.
Direction of work in research: Alternative futures.
Direction of work in planning: Social, Economic, Political.
Methods used: l Probabilistic forecasting, 2 Statistical models, 3 Expert panels, 4 Scenario building.
Time range of work: 5 - lO years.
Source of support for work (%): 75 Private business, 25 Labour.
Work done for (%): lOO Community.
Occupational function: Newspaper editor.
Worked in service sector: Communications media.   *(58O)*

9O. Bertrand H. Chatel

Room 3146-E, Office for Science and Technology, United Nations, New York, NY 1OO17, USA.
Sex: Male.   *Age:* 5O-59.
Educational qualification: Other graduate/professional degree.
Formal training: Physical sciences, Social/behavioural sciences, Mathematics, Engineering.
Informal training: Life sciences, Engineering, Journalism.
Areas in which work done (%): lOO In planning unit of an international organization.
Direction of work in forecasting: Technological, Scientific.
Direction of work in research: Social impacts of technology, Policy research, Futures methodology.
Direction of work in planning: Scientific, Technological, Regional.
Methods used: Expert panels, Operational models, Causal modelling.
Time range of work: 5 - lO years.
Source of support for work (%): lOO International agencies.
Occupational function: Administration.
Additional information: Concerned with world and regional plans of action for application of science and technology to development.   *(137)*

91. Hollis Chenery
Vice President, Development Policy, International Bank for Reconstruction and Development, International Development Association, 1818 H Str, NW, Washington, DC 20433, USA.
Sex: Male.   *Age:* 50-59.
Educational qualification: Doctoral degree.
Formal training: Social/behavioural sciences.
Informal training: I Engineering, 2 Mathematics.
Primarily engaged in: Long-range planning.
Areas in which work done (%): IOO In planning unit of a governmental agency.
Direction of work in forecasting: Economic.
Direction of work in research: Policy research.
Direction of work in planning: Economic.
Methods used: I Statistical models, 2 Simulation, 3 Mathematical programming.
Time range of work: 5 - 25 years.
Source of support for work (%): IOO International agencies.
Work done for (%): IOO International agencies.
Occupational function: Administrator.
Worked in government as: I Researcher, 2 Administrator.
Worked in education: I In research, 2 Teaching.
Additional information: Not primarily engaged but concerned with long-term future in teaching economics.   *(126)*

92. G.E. Cherry
Centre for Urban and Regional Studies, University of Birmingham, Birmingham UK.
Sex: Male.   *Age:* 40-49.
Educational qualification: Other graduate/professional degree.
Formal training: I Design, 2 Social/behavioural sciences.
Informal training: I Design, 2 Social/behavioural sciences.
Primarily engaged in: Long-range planning.
Areas in which work done (%): IOO As academic, in teaching futures studies or long-range planning.
Direction of work in research: I Policy research, 2 Environmental.
Direction of work in planning: I Urban, 2 Regional, 3 Social.
Time range of work (%): 5 - IO years.
Source of support for work (%): IOO National government.
Work done for (%): 33 Local or regional government, 33 National government, 33 Foundations.
Occupational function: I Educator, 2 Administrator, 3 Research worker, 4 Consultant.
Worked in government as: Researcher.
Worked in industry/business in: Planning.
Worked in education: I Teaching, 2 In research, 3 In administration.
Additional information: Concerned with social factors.   *(318)*

93. J.H. Chesshire
Science Policy Research Unit, University of Sussex, Falmer, Brighton, UK.
Sex: Male.   *Age:* 25-29.
Educational qualification: Master's degree.
Formal training: Social/behavioural sciences.
Informal training: Politics.
Primarily engaged in: Both futures studies and long-range planning.

Areas in which work done (%): IOO In organization primarily concerned with futures studies and/or long-range planning.
Direction of work in forecasting: Technological, Economic, Environmental, Resources.
Direction of work in research: Environmental, Resource utilization, Policy research.
Direction of work in planning: Technological, Economic, Environmental, Resources.
Methods used: I Expert panels, 2 Individual expert forecasting, 3 Extrapolation techniques, 4 Scenario building.
Time range of work: IO - 25 years.
Source of support for work (%): 25 National government, 25 Private business, 5O Nationalised industries.
Work done for (%): 25 National government, 25 Private business, 5O Joint project for Nationalised industries.
Occupational function: I Research worker, 2 Educator.
Worked in industry/business in: Trade union.
Worked in education: In research.
Additional information: Working on economic and technological assessment of UK energy policy choices.   *(493)*

94. Alexander N. Christakis
Academy for Contemporary Problems, 2O3O N Street, NW, Washington, DC 2OO36, USA.
Sex: Male.   *Age:* 3O-39.
Educational qualification: Doctoral degree.
Formal training: Physical sciences.
Informal training: I Social/behavioural sciences, 2 Humanities, 3 Design.
Primarily engaged in: Both futures studies and long-range planning.
Areas in which work done (%): IO In planning unit of an international organization, IO As academic, in teaching futures studies or long-range planning, 8O In organization primarily concerned with futures studies and/or long-range planning.
Direction of work in forecasting: Technological, Resources, Population.
Direction of work in research: Social impacts of technology, Alternative futures, Resource utilization, Value systems, Population, The individual in the future, The family in the future, Futures methodology.
Direction of work in planning: Technological, Social, Urban, Regional, Educational, Economics, Political, Resources.
Methods used: I Scenario building, 2 Contextual mapping, 3 Brainstorming, 4 Relevance trees, 5 Network analysis.
Time range of work: Beyond year 2OOO.
Source of support for work (%): IOO Foundations.
Work done for (%): 2O National government, 3O Local or regional government, 5O International agencies.
Occupational function: I Research worker, 2 Educator.
Worked in government as: Researcher.
Worked in industry/business in: Research and development, Planning.
Worked in education: Teaching.   *(190)*

95. Cheryl Christensen
Dept of Political Science, University of Pittsburgh, Pittsburgh, Pa 15213, USA.
Sex: Female.   *Age:* 25-29.
Educational qualification: Doctoral degree.
Formal training: Social/behavioural sciences.
Informal training: Education.

Areas in which work done (%): IO As academic, in teaching futures studies or long-range planning.
Direction of work in forecasting: Resources, Population.
Direction of work in research: I Social priorities, 2 Policy research, 3 Resource utilization, 4 Population.
Direction of work in planning: Political.
Methods used: Statistical models.
Time range of work: 5 - IO years.
Source of support for work (%): 5O University.
Work done for (%): IOO Research at international level.
Occupational function: I Educator, 2 Research worker,
Worked in education: I Teaching, 2 In research. *(3)*

96. Betsy Christian
In Care Of: Civil Engrg, UTT, 254O Dole St, Honolulu, Hi 96822, USA.
Sex: Female. *Age:* 4O-49.
Formal training: I Humanities, 2 Social/behavioural sciences, 2 Design, 2 Futuristics.
Informal training: Journalism, Education, Design.
Primarily engaged in: Both futures studies and long-range planning.
Areas in which work done (%): 5O Teaching psychology, 5O Various groups and commissions.
Direction of work in research: Social impacts of technology, Alternative futures, The individual in the future, The family in the future, Education.
Direction of work in planning: Health, Education.
Time range of work: 5 - beyond year 2OOO.
Work done for (%): 2O Local or regional government, 2O Voluntary associations.
Occupational function: Educator.
Worked in industry/business in: Management.
Additional information: Concerned with future of medicine and technology assessment; founded school for gifted and talented. *(217)*

97. William F. Christopher
Director of Marketing, Hooker Chemical Corp, 1515 Summer St, Stamford, Ct O69O5, USA.
Sex: Male. *Age:* 5O-59.
Educational qualification: Master's degree.
Formal training: I Social/behavioural degree, 2 Humanities.
Informal training: I Engineering, 2 Physical sciences, 3 Journalism, 4 Life sciences.
Areas in which work done (%): 3O As individual consultant.
Direction of work in forecasting: I Economic, 2 Market, 3 Technological, 4 Environmental, 5 Social, 6 Scientific.
Direction of work in research: I Futures methodology, 2 Environmental, 3 Social impacts of technology, 4 Alternative futures, 5 Manpower.
Direction of work in planning: I Corporate, 2 Economic, 3 Technological.
Methods used: I Extrapolation techniques, 2 Individual expert forecasting, 3 Expert panels, 4 Scenario building, 5 Brainstorming, 6 Statistical models.
Time range of work: 5 - IO years.
Source of support for work (%): IOO Private business.
Work done for (%): 3O Private business.
Occupational function: Manager.

Worked in industry/business in: Management.
Additional information: Concerned with long-range planning, strategy development for
my company.   *(91)*

98. Anthony Chullikal
18 Via Nicolo Tomasseo, Monteverde, Rome, Italy.
Sex: Male.   *Age:* 50-59.
Educational qualification: Doctoral degree.
Formal training: I Social/behavioural sciences, 2 Humanities, 3 Education.
Informal training: Social/behavioural sciences, Humanities, Education.
Primarily engaged in: Both futures studies and long-range planning.
Areas in which work done (%): 4O In organization concerned with other studies
including long-range planning, IO As academic, in teaching futures studies or long-
range planning, 5O In planning unit of an international organization.
Direction of work in forecasting: I Economic, 2 Social, 3 Cultural, 4 Educational,
5 Environmental, 6 Resources, 7 Population.
Direction of work in research: I Alternative futures, 2 Value systems, 3 Population,
4 The individual in the future, 5 The family in the future.
Direction of work in planning: I Economic, 2 Social, 3 Technological, 4 Educational,
5 Political, 6 Corporate, 7 Environmental.
Methods used: I Expert panels, 2 Brainstorming, 3 Cross impacts analysis, 4 Causal
modelling.
Time range of work: IO - 25 years.
Source of support for work (%): 5 Local government, 5 National government, 2O
International agencies, 5O Voluntary associations.
Work done for (%): 5 Local government, 5 National government, 2O International
agencies, 5O Voluntary associations.
Occupational function: Research worker, Educator, Consultant.
Worked in education: Teaching, In research.
Worked in service sector: Religion, Communication media.   *(100)*

99. Colin W. Clark
Professor of Mathematics, University of British Columbia, Vancouver 8, Canada.
Sex: Male.   *Age:* 40-49.
Educational qualification: Doctoral degree.
Formal training: Mathematics.
Informal training: I Social/behavioural sciences, 2 Physical, 3 Life sciences.
Direction of work in forecasting: Resources.
Direction of work in research: Resource utilization.
Direction of work in planning: Resources.
Methods used: Control theoretical analysis.
Time range of work: Beyond year 2OOO.
Source of support for work (%): 2O Foundations, 8O National government.
Occupational function: Educator.
Worked in education: I Teaching, 2 In research.
Additional information: Concerned with renewable resources.   *(4)*

100. John A. Clark
Science Policy Research Unit, University of Sussex, Falmer, Brighton, BN1 9RF, UK.
Sex: Male.   *Age:* 25-29.
Educational function: Doctoral degree.

Formal training: Physical sciences.
Informal training: I Mathematics, 2 Social/behavioural sciences.
Primarily engaged in: Futures studies.
Areas in which work done (%): IOO In organization primarily concerned with futures studies and/or long-range planning.
Direction of work in forecasting: Agriculture.
Direction of work in research: I Alternative futures, 2 Futures methodology.
Methods used: I Simulation, 2 Causal modelling, 3 Individual expert forecasting, 4 Extrapolation techniques.
Time range of work: Beyond year 2OOO.
Source of support for work (%): 5O National government, 5O International agencies.
Work done for (%): 5O National government, 5O International agencies.
Occupational function: Research worker.   *(491)*

1OI. R.H. Clayton

Ministry of State for Science and Technology, Technological Forecasting and Technology Assessment Division, Technological Forecasting Group, Government of Canada, Ottawa, Canada.
Sex: Male.   *Age:* 25-29.
Educational qualification: Master's degree.
Formal training: Social/behavioural sciences.
Informal training: I Social/behavioural sciences, 2 Physical sciences, 3 Journalism, 4 Arts.
Primarily engaged in: Futures studies.
Areas in which work done (%): 8O In organization primarily concerned with futures studies and/or long-range planning, 2O As academic, in teaching futures studies or long-range planning.
Direction of work in forecasting: I Social, 2 Technological, 3 Economic, 4 Resources, 5 Population, 6 Market, 7 Cultural.
Direction of work in research: I Alternative futures, 2 Policy research, 3 Futures methodology, 4 Resource utilization, 5 Social priorities, 6 Population, 7 Social impacts of technology, 8 Value systems.
Direction of work in planning: I Technological, 2 Social, 3 Resources, 4 Economic, 5 Scientific.
Methods used: I Scenario building, 2 Delphi techniques, 3 Extrapolation techniques, 4 Cross impact analysis, 5 Network analysis, 6 Relevance trees, 7 Simulation.
Time range of work: IO - 25 years.
Source of support for work (%): IOO National government.
Work done for (%): IOO National government.
Occupational function: I Research worker, 2 Manager, 3 Educator, 4 Consultant.
Worked in government as: I Researcher, 2 Administrator.
Worked in education: Teaching.   *(187)*

1O2. Joseph Coates

Congress of the United States, Office of Technology Assessment, Washington DC 2O51O, USA.
Sex: Male.   *Age:* 4O-49.
Educational qualification: Master's degree.
Formal training: I Physical sciences, 2 Humanities.
Informal training: I Social/behavioural sciences, 2 Life sciences, 3 Engineering, 4 Journalism.
Primarily engaged in: Both futures studies and long-range planning.
Areas in which work done (%): 9O In organization concerned with other studies including

long-range planning, 5 As individual consultant, 5 As academic, in teaching futures studies or long-range planning.
Direction of work in forecasting: I Technological, 2 Social, 3 Economic, 4 Cultural, 5 Environmental, 6 Resources.
Direction of work in research: I Social impacts of technology, 2 Alternative futures, 3 Environmental, 4 Value systems, 5 Policy research, 6 Futures methodology.
Direction of work in planning: I Technological.
Methods used: All methods (see Directory guide).
Time range of work: 5 - beyond year 2000.
Source of support for work (%): IOO National government.
Work done for (%): IOO National government.
Occupational function: Administrator.
Worked in government as: Administrator, Researcher.
Worked in industry/business in: Research and development.
Worked in education: Teaching.
Additional information: Concerned with technology assessment and general futures. *(268)*

103. S.D. Cole
Science Policy Research Unit, University of Sussex, Falmer, Brighton, BN1 9RF, UK.
Sex: Male.   *Age:* 30-39.
Educational qualification: Doctoral degree.
Formal training: Physical sciences.
Informal training: I Social/behavioural sciences, 2 Mathematics.
Primarily engaged in: Futures studies.
Areas in which work done (%): IO As individual consultant, 9O In organization primarily engaged with futures studies and/or long-range planning.
Direction of work in forecasting: Technological, Economic, Social, Resources.
Direction of work in research: I Alternative futures, 2 Social impacts of technology.
Methods used: Cross impact analysis, Scenario building, Extrapolation techniques, Statistical models, Historical analogy, Individual expert forecasting, Simulation.
Time range of work: Beyond year 2000.
Source of support for work (%): 5O National government, 5O International agencies.
Work done for (%): 5O National government, 5O International agencies.
Occupational function: Research worker.
Worked in government as: Researcher.
Worked in education: In research.
Additional information: Concerned with social and technological alternatives for the future methods of forecasting. *(489)*

104. Suleiman Cohen
Centre for Development Planning, Erasmus University, Burg. Oudlaan 5O, Rotterdam, The Netherlands.
Sex: Male.   *Age:* 30-39.
Educational qualification: Doctoral degree.
Formal training: Social/behavioural sciences, Mathematics,.
Informal training: History, Methodology of science.
Direction of work in forecasting: I Economic, 2 Manpower, 3 Resources, 4 Educational.
Direction of work in research: I Resource utilization, 2 Manpower, 3 Futures methodology, 4 Social priorities.
Direction of work in planning: I Economic, 2 Labour, 3 Resources, 4 Educational, 5 Political, 6 Regional.

Methods used: I Operational models, 2 Simulation, 3 Causal modelling, 4 Statistical models, 5 Extrapolation techniques, 6 Cross impact analysis.
Time range of work: 5 - 25 years.
Source of support for work (%): 2O National government, 2O International agencies.
Work done for (%): 4O International agencies.
Occupational function: I Research worker, 2 Consultant, 3 Educator.
Worked in industry/business in: Consultant.
Worked in education: I In research, 2 Teaching.
Additional information: Concerned with manpower planning, social indicators, agrarian reform, international division of labour and future resource allocation, and income distribution policies, national and international.   *(569)*

105. Umberto Columbo
Director General, Research and Development Division, Montedison Corp, Largo Donegani, 2, 2O121 Milan, Italy.
Sex: Male.   *Age:* 4O-49.
Formal training: Physical sciences.
Informal training: Social/behavioural sciences, Engineering.
Areas in which work done (%): 9 In planning unit of a business enterprise.
Direction of work in forecasting: I Technological, 2 Resources, 3 Scientific.
Direction of work in planning: I Corporate, 2 Scientific, 2 Technological, 3 Resources.
Methods used: I Expert panels, 2 Brainstorming.
Time range of work: IO - 25 years.
Source of support for work (%): IO Foundations, 9O Private business.
Work done for (%): IO Foundations, 9O Private business.
Occupational function: Manager.
Worked in industry/business in: I Management, 2 Research and development, 3 Planning.
Additional information: Concerned with long-range resource analysis-related technology assessment, long-range business analysis.   *(105)*

106. Blanche Wiesen Cook
Dept of History, John Jay College, City University of New York, 445 West 59th St, New York, NY 1OO19, USA.
Sex: Female.   *Age:* 3O-39.
Educational qualification: Doctoral degree.
Formal training: Humanities.
Informal training: Journalism.
Primarily engaged in: Futures studies.
Areas in which work done (%): 2O As individual consultant, 8O As academic, in teaching futures studies or long-range planning.
Direction of work in forecasting: Economic, Social, Cultural, Scientific. Environmental, Military, Manpower, Resources.
Direction of work in research: I Alternative futures, I Environmental, I Social priorities, I The individual in the future, 2 Social impacts of technology, 2 Value systems, 2 The family in the future, 3 Policy research.
Methods used: Historical analogy.
Time range of work: IO - 25 years.
Occupational function: I Educator, 2 Research worker, 3 Journalist and writer.
Worked in education: Teaching, In research.
Additional information: Concerned with impact of technology on society, impact of military on society, and policy work force in cybernetic future.   *(26)*

107. James Coomer
University of Houston at Clear Lake City, 2700 Bay Area Blvd, Houston, Tx 77058, USA.
Sex: Male.   *Age:* 30-39.
Educational qualification: Doctoral degree.
Formal training: Social/behavioural sciences.
Informal training: Law.
Areas in which work done (%): 10 In planning unit of a governmental agency, 20 As academic, in teaching futures studies or long-range planning.
Direction of work in research: Policy research.
Direction of work in planning: Political.
Methods used: Probabilistic forecasting, Brainstorming.
Time range of work: 10 - 25 years.
Work done for (%): 10 Local government.
Occupational function: Educator.
Worked in government as: 1 Researcher, 2 Administrator.
Worked in education: 1 Teaching, 2 In research.   *(441)*

108. Kenneth J. Cooper
World Analysis Centre, Bechtel International Centre, Stanford University, PO Box 5816, Stanford, Ca 94305, USA.
Sex: Male.   *Age:* 50-59.
Educational qualification: Doctoral degree.
Formal training: Social/behavioural sciences.
Informal training: Humanities, Engineering, Education, Development.
Primarily engaged in: Long-range planning.
Areas in which work done (%): 25 Organization primarily concerned with futures studies and/or long-range planning, 50 Academic, in teaching futures studies or long-range planning. 25 Research - long-range global planning.
Direction of work in forecasting: 1 Social, 2 Economic, 3 Cultural, 4 Political, 5 Environmental.
Direction of work in research: 1 Value systems, 2 Alternative futures.
Direction of work in planning: 1 Social, 2 Economic, 3 Political, 4 Environmental, 5 Technological.
Methods used: 1 Cross impact analysis, 2 Expert panels, 3 Brainstorming, 4 Causal modelling.
Time range of work: 5 Years - beyond year 2000.
Source of support for work (%): 100 University.
Work done for (%): 50 National governments, 50 International agencies.
Occupational function: Educator, Administrator.
Worked in government as: Researcher, Administrator.
Worked in education as: In administration, Teaching, In research.   *(556)*

109. Edward Cornish
President, World Future Society, PO Box 30369, Bethesda Branch, Washington, DC, 20014, USA.
Sex: Male.   *Age:* 40-49.
Educational qualification: Bachelor's degree.
Formal training: Social/behavioural sciences.
Informal training: Journalism.
Primarily engaged in: Futures studies.
Areas in which work done (%): 100 In organization primarily concerned with futures studies and/or long-range planning.

Time range of work: IO - 25 years.
Source of support for work (%): IOO Membership.
Occupational function: I Administrator, 2 Editor.
Worked in service sector: Communication media. *(273)*

11O. Dan J. Cover
Dept of Sociology, Furman University, Greenville, SC 29613, USA.
Sex: Male. *Age:* 3O-39.
Educational qualification: Doctoral degree.
Formal training: Social/behavioural sciences.
Informal training: Social/behavioural sciences.
Areas in which work done (%): IO As academic, in teaching futures studies or long-range planning, 9O Teaching sociology.
Direction of work in forecasting: I Social, 2 Technological.
Direction of work in research: I The individual in the future, 2 Social impacts of technology.
Direction of work in planning: Urban.
Methods used: I Extrapolation techniques, 2 Gaming, 3 Delphi techniques.
Time range of work: IO - 25 years.
Source of support for work (%): 5 University, 5 National government.
Work done for (%): IO University.
Occupational function: Educator. *(309)*
Worked in education: Teaching.

111. Peter Cowan
Director, Joint Unit for Planning Research, 172 Tottenham Court Rd, London W1, UK.
Sex: Male. *Age:* 4O-49.
Educational qualification: Doctoral degree.
Formal training: Design.
Informal training: Social/behavioural sciences, Education.
Direction of work in forecasting: Environmental.
Direction of work in research: Environmental.
Direction of work in planning: I Urban, 2 Regional.
Methods used: I Scenario building, 2 Delphi techniques, 3 Statistical models.
Source of support for work (%): 5O Foundations, 5O Research councils.
Work done for (%): 5O Foundations, 5O Research councils.
Occupational function: I Research worker, 2 Educator.
Worked in government as: Researcher.
Worked in industry/business in: Consultancy.
Worked in education: Teaching, In research, In administration.
Additional information: Concerned with environmental studies. *(357)*

112. J. Kenneth Craver
Monsanto Company, 8OO N Lindbergh Blvd, St Louis, Mo 63166, USA.
Sex: Male. *Age:* 5O-59.
Educational qualification: Master's degree.
Formal training: I Physical sciences, 2 Education.
Informal training: I Physical sciences, 2 Social/behavioural sciences, 3 Education, 4 Journalism.
Primarily engaged in: Both futures studies and long-range planning.

Areas in which work done (%): IOO In organization primarily concerned with futures studies and/or long-range planning.
Direction of work in forecasting: I Technological, I Economic, I Social, 2 Cultural, 2 Scientific, 2 Environmental, 2 Regulatory.
Direction of work in research: I Futures methodology, 2 Social impacts of technology,
Direction of work in planning: I Corporate, 3 Technological.
Methods used: I Cross impact analysis, I Statistical models, I Individual expert forecasting, 2 Probabilistic forecasting, 2 Extrapolation techniques, 2 Expert panels, 2 Simulation.
Time range of work: 5 - IO years.
Source of support for work (%): IOO Private business.
Work done for (%): IOO Private business.
Occupational function: I Manager, 2 Consultant.
Worked in industry/business in: Management, Research and development, Planning.
Additional information: Concerned with long-range corporate planning.   *(333)*

113. Nigel Cross
Faculty of Technology, Open University, Milton Keynes, UK.
Sex: Male.   *Age:* 3O-39.
Educational qualification: Doctoral degree.
Formal training: Design.
Informal training: Social/behavioural sciences.
Areas in which work done (%): 5O As academic, in teaching futures studies or long-range planning.
Direction of work in forecasting: I Social, 2 Technological, 3 Educational.
Direction of work in research: I Alternative futures, 2 Social impacts of technology, 3 Environmental.
Direction of work in planning: Technological.
Methods used: Simulation.
Time range of work: 5 - 25 years.
Source of support for work (%): IOO National government.
Work done for (%): 2O Personal research interest.
Occupational function: Educator.
Worked in education: I In research, 2 Teaching.
Worked in service sector: Design.
Additional information: Concerned with future of design professions -- technological change.   *(438)*

114. Joseph D. Crumlish
Information Officer, National Bureau of Standards, Washington DC 2O234, USA.
Sex: Male.   *Age:* 5O-59.
Educational qualification: Doctoral degree.
Formal training: I Law, 2 Social/behavioural sciences, 3 Education.
Informal training: Journalism.
Direction of work in forecasting: Economic.
Direction of work in research: Alternative futures.
Direction of work in planning: Social.
Methods used: I Scenario building, 2 Extrapolation techniques, 3 Delphi techniques.
Time range of work: IO - 25 years.
Occupational function: Research worker.

Worked in government as: Researcher.
Worked in industry/business in: Research and development.
Worked in education: Teaching.
Worked in service sector: Law. *(154)*

115. R.C. Curnow
Science Policy Research Unit, University of Sussex, Falmer, Brighton BN1 9RF, UK.
Sex: Male. *Age:* 40-49.
Educational qualification: Bachelor's degree.
Formal training: Mathematics.
Informal training: I Engineering, 2 Physical sciences, 3 Social/behavioural sciences.
Primarily engaged in: Both futures studies and long-range planning.
Areas in which work done (%): 5 As individual consultant, IO As academic, in teaching future studies or long-range planning, 5 In planning unit of an international agency.
Direction of work in forecasting: Technological, Social.
Direction of work in research: Policy research.
Direction of work in planning: Technological.
Methods used: All methods (see Directory guide).
Time range of work: Beyond 2000 AD.
Source of support for work (%): IO Private business, 20 International agencies. 70 National government.
Work done for (%): IO National government, IO International agencies, IO Private business.
Occupational function: Research worker.
Worked in industry/business in: Research and development.
Worked in education: In research. *(488)*

116. Paola Dadaglio
IRADES, Istituto per la Ricerca e la Formazione al Futuro, Via Paisiello 6, Rome 00198, Italy.
Sex: Female. *Age:* 25-29.
Educational qualification: Master's degree.
Formal training: Humanities.
Informal training: Education.
Primarily engaged in: Futures studies.
Areas in which work done (%): IOO In organization primarily concerned with futures studies and/or long-range planning.
Direction of work in research: The individual in the future.
Time range of work: Beyond 2000 AD.
Source of support for work (%): IOO Private association.
Work done for (%): IOO Private association.
Occupttional function: Research worker.
Worked in service sector: Communication media.
Additional information: Concerned with education toward the future and future methodologies. *(413)*

117. Svein Dalen
PO Box 8401, Hammersborg, Oslo 1, Norway.
Sex: Male. *Age:* 50-59.
Educational qualification: Other graduate/professional degree.

Formal training: I Social/behavioural sciences, 2 Economics.
Informal training: Humanities.
Primarily engaged in: Both futures studies and long-range planning.
Areas in which work done (%): 20 Unspecified, 50 In organization concerned with other studies including long-range planning, 30 In organization primary concerned with futures studies and/or long-range planning.
Direction of work in forecasting: I Economic, 2 Social, 3 Market.
Direction of work in research: I Alternative futures, 2 Consumer affairs, 3 Value systems.
Direction of work in planning: I Economic, 2 Corporate, 3 Social.
Methods used: I Extrapolation techniques, 2 Brainstorming, 3 Expert panels.
Time range of work: IO - 25 years.
Source of support for work (%): 20 Voluntary associations, 30 National government, 50 Private business.
Work done for (%): IO International agencies, I5 Voluntary associations, 25 National government, 50 Private business.
Occupational function: Administrator.
Worked in industry/business in: I Management, 2 Planning.
Additional information: Concerned with organizing work in the field on a national level; introducing long-range planning in companies and public bodies.   *(365)*

118. Norman C. Dalkey

Room 7619 Boelter Hall, Dept of Systems Engineering, University of California,
Los Angeles, Ca 90024, USA.
Sex: Male.   *Age:* 50-59.
Educational qualification: Doctoral degree.
Formal training: I Humanities, 2 Mathematics, 3 Social/behavioural sciences.
Informal training: I Physical sciences, 2 Engineering.
Primarily engaged in: Both futures studies and long-range planning.
Areas in which work done (%): I5 As individual consultant, 20 As academic, in teaching futures studies or long-range planning, 65 Methodology research.
Direction of work in forecasting: I Technological, 2 Educational, 3 Environmental.
Direction of work in research: I Futures methodology, 2 Value systems, 3 Policy research.
Direction of work in planning: I Urban, 2 Corporate, 3 Technological.
Methods used: I Delphi techniques, 2 Probabilistic forecasting, 3 Relevance trees, 4 Cross impacts analysis.
Time range of work: IO - 25 years.
Source of support for work (%): IO Local government, IO Private business, 80 National government.
Work done for (%): IO Local or regional government, IO National government, IO Private business, 70 General applicable techniques.
Occupational function: I Research worker, 2 Consultant, 3 Educator.
Worked in government as: Researcher.
Worked in industry/business in: Consultancy.
Worked in education: I In research, 2 Teaching.   *(525)*

119. André van Dam

Corn Products, Latin America, Cerrito 866, Buenos Aires, Argentina.
Sex: Male.   *Age:* 50-59.
Educational qualification: Other graduate/professional degree.
Formal training: Social/behavioural sciences.
Informal training: Social/behavioural sciences, Humanities, Journalism.

Primarily engaged in: Both futures studies and long-range planning.
Areas in which work done (%): 3O As academic, in teaching futures studies or long-range planning, 7O In planning unit of a business enterprise.
Direction of work in forecasting: Economic, Social.
Direction of work in research: Third world - development process.
Direction of work in planning: Economic, Corporate.
Methods used: I Network analysis, 2 Expert panels, 3 Scenario building, 4 Delphi techniques.
Time range of work: 5 - IO years.
Source of support for work (%): 3O Self, 7O Private business.
Work done for (%): 3O Voluntary associations, 7O Private business.
Occupational function: Consultant.
Worked in industry/business in: Research and development, Planning.   *(124)*

12O. Caponera Dante
Via Montevideo, Rome, Italy.
Sex: Male.   *Age:* 5O-59.
Educational qualification: Doctoral degree.
Formal training: Law.
Informal training: I Political sciences, 2 Physical sciences.
Primarily engaged in: Both futures studies and long-range planning.
Areas in which work done (%): IO In non-governmental organization, 9O In planning unit of an international organization.
Direction of work in forecasting: Resources.
Direction of work in research: I Resource utilization, 2 Futures methodology, 3 Environmental.
Direction of work in planning: I Resources, 2 Environmental.
Methods used: I Individual expert forecasting, 2 Historical analogy, 3 Network analysis.
Time range of work: 5 - beyond year 2OOO.
Source of support for work (%): 2 Voluntary associations, 98 International agencies.
Work done for (%): IOO International agencies.
Occupational function: I Manager, 2 Research worker.
Worked in government as: Administrator.
Additional information: Concerned with legislative and legal institutional reforms.   *(183)*

121. Martha Darling
BSRC, 4OOO NE 41 St, Seattle, Wa 981O5, USA.
Sex: Female.   *Age:* 3O-39.
Educational qualification: Other graduate/professional degree.
Formal training: International affairs.
Informal training: I Public policy, 2 Social/behavioural sciences, 3 Education.
Direction of work in research: I Policy research, I The individual in the future, 3 Child care policy, The family in the future, 4 Social priorities, 5 Value systems,
Direction of work in planning: I Social, 2 Political, 3 Economic, 4 Educational.
Methods used: Grounded theory.
Time range of work: 5 - IO years.
Source of support for work (%): 3O Foundations, 3O National government, 3O International agencies.
Work done for (%): 5O Foundations, 5O National and local government.
Occupational function: I Policy researcher, 2 Consultant.

Additional information: Concerned with future political and economic relationships between Europe, North America, and Japan; the changing roles of women and men in an industrial society; and comparative child care policy in industrial societies.   *(382)*

122. H.T. Darracott
Chief, Communications-Electronics Div, Directorate for Comm-elct (USAMC CE)
5001 Eisenhower Ave, Alexandria, Va 22333, USA.
Sex: Male.   *Age:* 60 or over.
Educational qualification: Master's degree.
Formal training: Physical sciences.
Informal training: l Engineering, 2 Journalism, 3 Education, 4 Arts, 5 Cinema/
television.
Areas in which work done (%): l5 In planning unit of a governmental agency, l0 In
organization concerned with other studies including long-range planning.
Direction of work in forecasting: l Technological, 2 Scientific, 3 Military.
Direction of work in research: l Alternative futures, 2 Environmental, 3 Resource
utilization.
Direction of work in planning: l Military, 2 Scientific, 3 Technological.
Methods used: Extrapolation techniques.
Time range of work: 5 - l0 years.
Source of support for work (%): l00 National government.
Work done for (%): l00 National government.
Occupational function: Manager.
Worked in government as: l Researcher, 2 Administrator.
Worked in industry/business in: l Research and development, 2 Management.
Worked in education: Teaching.
Additional information: Concerned with analysis of requirements for communication for
updating and for improvement.   *(330)*

123. R. Morton Darrow
Vice President, Planning and Analysis, Prudential Insurance Company of America,
Prudential Plaza, Newark, NJ 07101 USA.
Sex: Male.   *Age:* 40-49.
Educational qualification: Doctoral degree.
Formal training: Social/behavioural sciences.
Informal training: Education.
Primarily engaged in: Futures studies.
Areas in which work done (%): l0 As individual consultant, l0 In planning unit of a
business enterprise, l0 In organization concerned with other studies, including long-
range planning, 70 In organization primarily concerned with futures studies and/or long-
range planning.
Direction of work in forecasting: l Political, 2 Social, 3 Market.
Direction of work in research: l Alternative futures, 2 The family in the future,
3 The individual in the future.
Direction of work in planning: Corporate.
Methods used: l Individual expert forecasting, 2 Historical analogy, 3 Scenario building,
4 Delphi techniques.
Time range of work: l0 - 25 years.
Source of support for work (%): l00 Private business.
Work done for (%): l00 Private business.
Occupational function: l Research worker, 2 Administrator, 3 Consultant, 4 Educator.

Worked in government as: Administrator.
Worked in industry/business in: I Research and development, 2 Planning.
Worked in education: Teaching. *(81)*

124. Jim Dator

The Ontario Educational Communications Authority, Canada Square, 2180 Yonge St,
Toronto, Ontario, M4S 2C1, Canada.
Sex: Male.   *Age:* 40-49.
Educational qualification: Doctoral degree.
Formal training: Social/behavioural sciences.
Informal training: I Humanities, 2 Cinema/television.
Primarily engaged in: Futures studies.
Areas in which work done (%): 85 As academic, in teaching futures studies or long-
range planning, and research.
Direction of work in forecasting: Social.
Direction of work in research: I Alternative futures, 2 The individual in the future,
3 Futures methodology, 4 Social impacts of technology, 5 Value systems, 6 The family
in the future.
Direction of work in planning: Social.
Methods used: I Causal modelling, 2 Individual expert forecasting, 3 Brainstorming,
4 Scenario building, 5 Extrapolation techniques.
Time range of work: Beyond 2000 AD.
Source of support for work (%): 25 Private business, 75 State government.
Work done for (%): 25 Private business, 75 Local or regional government.
Occupational function: Educator.
Worked in education: I Teaching, 2 In research. *(526)*

125. Henry David

Professor of Public Affairs, Lyndon B. Johnson School of Public Affairs, University of
Texas at Austin, Austin, Tx 78712, USA.
Sex: Male.   *Age:* 60 or over.
Educational qualification: Doctoral degree.
Formal training: Social/behavioural sciences.
Informal training: Mathematics, Education.
Direction of work in forecasting: Social, Manpower.
Direction of work in research: Alternative futures, Social priorities, Policy research,
Futures methodology.
Methods used: Probabilistic forecasting, Delphi techniques, Cross impact analysis, Expert
panels.
Time range of work: 10 - 25 years.
Occupational function: I Educator, 2 Research worker. 3 Consultant.
Worked in government as: I Administrator, 2 Researcher.
Worked in industry/business in: Consultancy.
Worked in education: I In administration, 2 In research, 3 Teaching.
Additional information: Chairman, Board of Trustees of Futures Research Organization,
and as consultant on futures research; US editor of Futures journal. *(178)*

126. Paul T. David

Woodrow Wilson Dept of Government of Foreign Affairs, 232 Cabell Hall, University of
Virginia, Charlottesville, Va 22903, USA.
Sex: Male.   *Age:* 60 or over.

7

Educational qualification: Doctoral degree.
Formal training: Social/behavioural sciences.
Informal training: Education.
Time range of work: IO - 25 years.
Source of support for work (%): IOO University.
Occupational function: Educator.
Worked in government as: Administrator.
Worked in education: I Teaching, 2 In research.
Additional information: Concerned with teaching a university course on 'Processes of Change'. *(155)*

127. Kenneth W. Davis

1116 McIntyre, Ann Arbor, Mi 48105, USA.
Sex: Male.   *Age:* 25-29.
Educational qualification: Doctoral degree.
Formal training: I Humanities, 2 Education.
Informal training: I Education, 2 Journalism, 3 Arts, 4 Life sciences.
Areas in which work done (%): 25 As individual consultant, 25 As academic, in teaching futures studies or long-range planning.
Direction of work in forecasting: I Cultural, 2 Educational.
Direction of work in research: I Alternative futures, 2 Value systems, 3 The individual in the future, 4 Futures methodology.
Direction of work in planning: Educational.
Methods used: I Scenario building, 2 Gaming, 3 Brainstorming, 4 Delphi techniques.
Time range of work: IO - 25 years.
Source of support for work (%): IOO Local government.
Work done for (%): IOO Local or regional government.
Occupational function: I Educator, 2 Consultant.
Worked in education: Teaching. *(72)*

128. Richard C. Davis

Technology Forecasting and Technology Assessment, The Whirlpool Corp, Benton Harbour, Mi 49022, USA.
Sex: Male.   *Age:* 50-59.
Educational qualification: Master's degree.
Formal training: I Physical, 2 Humanities.
Informal training: Social/behavioural sciences.
Primarily engaged in: Both futures studies and long-range planning.
Areas in which work done (%): 2 As academic, in teaching futures studies or long-range planning, 3 As individual consultant, 3O In planning unit of a business enterprise, 65 In organization primarily concerned with futures studies and/or long-range planning.
Direction of work in forecasting: I Technological, 2 Social, 3 Resources, 4 Environmental.
Direction of work in research: I Social impacts of technology, 2 Value systems, 3 Social priorities, 4 Resource utilization, 5 Environmental, 6 Consumer affairs, 7 Alternative futures
Direction of work in planning: I Technological, 2 Social, 3 Resources, 4 Environmental.
Methods used: I Literature monitoring, 2 Delphi techniques, 3 Relevance trees, 4 Historical 5 Cross impact analysis, 6 Extrapolation techniques, 7 Expert panels, 8 Scenario building.
Time range of work: 5 - 25 years.
Source of support for work (%): IOO Private business.
Work done for (%): IO Voluntary associations, 9O Private business.

Occupational function: I Research worker, 2 Consultant, 3 Manager, 4 Educator.
Worked in industry/business in: I Planning, 2 Research and development, 3 Consultancy.
Worked in education: Teaching. **(477)**

129. Lawrence H. Day
Bell Canada, Room 1105, 620 Belmont, Montreal, Quebec, Canada.
Sex: Male. *Age:* 30-39.
Educational qualification: Master's degree.
Formal training: Business administration.
Informal training: I Social/behavioural sciences, 2 Education.
Primarily engaged in: Both futures studies and long-range planning.
Areas in which work done (%): 50 In organization primarily concerned with futures studies and/or long-range planning, 50 In planning unit of a business organization.
Direction of work in forecasting: I Social, 2 Technological, 3 Economic, 4 Market, 5 Educational, 6 Environmental.
Direction of work in research: I Social impacts of technology, 2 Policy research, 3 Alternative futures, 4 Value systems, 5 Social priorities, 6 The individual in the future, 7 Futures methodology, 8 Resource utilization, 9 Environmental.
Direction of work in planning: I Corporate, 2 Social, 3 Technological, 4 Economic, 5 Scientific, 6 Urban, 7 Educational.
Methods used: I Expert panels, 3 Delphi techniques, 3 Extrapolation techniques, 4 Scenario building, 5 Cross impact analysis, 6 Historical analogy, 7 Individual expert forecasting, 8 Probabilistic forecasting, 9 Relevance trees, IO Survey research, 11 Brainstorming, 12 Statistical models.
Time range of work: IO - 25 years.
Source of support for work (%): IOO Private business.
Work done for (%): 5 Local or regional government, 5 International agencies, I5 National government, 8O Private business.
Occupational function: I Manager, 2 Research worker.
Worked in industry/business in: I Management, 2 Research and development. **(264)**

130. André-Clement Découfle
Director, Laboratoire de Prospective Appliquee, 6 Rue Dante, 75017 Paris, France.
Sex: Male. *Age:* 30-39.
Educational qualification: Doctoral degree.
Formal training: I Social/behavioural sciences, 2 Law, 3 Humanities.
Informal training: I Education, I Design.
Primarily engaged in: Both futures studies and long-range planning.
Areas in which work done (%): IO As academic, in teaching futures studies or long-range planning, 90 In organization primarily concerned with futures studies and/or long-range planning.
Direction of work in forecasting: I Social, 2 Cultural, 3 Geo-political, 4 Environmental.
Direction of work in research: I Manpower, 2 Consumer affairs, 3 Futures methodology, 4 Social priorities.
Direction of work in planning: I Social, 2 Urban, 3 Resources, 4 Political.
Methods used: Probabilistic forecasting, Scenario building, Contextual mapping, Brainstorming, Expert panels, Network analysis, Historical analogy, Individual expert forecasting.
Time range of work: Beyond 2000 AD.
Source of support for work (%): IO Private business, 90 National government.
Work done for (%): IO Private business, 90 National government.

Occupational function: I Research worker, 2 Consultant, 3 Administrator.
Worked in government as: Administrator, Researcher.
Worked in industry/business in: Consultancy.
Worked in education: Teaching, In administration.
Worked in service sector: Law, Social welfare, Communication media, Design.　　*(384)*

131. Christopher Dede

University of Houston at Clear Lake City, 2700 Bay Area Blvd, Houston, Tx 77058, USA.
Sex: Male.　　*Age:* 25-29.
Educational qualification: Doctoral degree.
Formal training: I Education, 2 Physical sciences, 3 Humanities.
Informal training: I Futures research, 2 Social/behavioural sciences, 3 Life sciences.
Primarily engaged in: Both futures studies or long-range planning.
Areas in which work done (%): IO As individual consultant, 90 As academic, in teaching futures studies or long-range planning.
Direction of work in forecasting: I Educational, 2 Scientific, 3 Technological, 3 Cultural, 4 Social, 6 Economic.
Direction of work in research: I Social impacts of technology, 2 Value systems, 3 Social priorities, 4 Policy research, 5 Alternative futures.
Direction of work in planning: I Scientific, 2 Technological, 3 Educational, 4 Social, 5 Economic, 6 Political.
Methods used: I Scenario building, 2 Individual expert forecasting, 3 Delphi techniques, 4 Cross impact analysis, 5 Gaming, 6 Brainstorming, 6 Simulation, 7 Historical analogy, 8 Expert panels, 9 Extrapolation techniques.
Time range of work: IO - 25 years.
Source of support for work (%): IO Private business, 90 University.
Work done for (%): IO Private business, 90 University.
Occupational function: I Educator, 2 Consultant, 3 Administrator.
Worked in education: I Teaching, 2 In administration.　　*(329)*

132. Betty Demby

Research Director, Motivation Programmers Inc, 770 Lexington Ave, New York 10021, USA.
Sex: Female.　　*Age:* 40-49.
Educational qualification: Master's degree.
Formal training: Social/behavioural sciences.
Informal training: I Journalism, 2 Cinema/television, 3 Arts.
Primarily engaged in: Both futures studies and long-range planning.
Areas in which work done (%): IOO In organization concerned with other studies including long-range planning.
Direction of work in research: I The individual in the future, 2 The family in the future, 3 Alternative futures, 4 Social impacts of technology, 5 Environmental, 6 Social priorities, 7 Value systems.
Direction of work in planning: I Corporate, 2 Economic, 3 Social.
Methods used: I Expert panels, 2 Delphi techniques, 3 Probabilistic forecasting, 4 Scenario building, 5 Individual expert forecasting, 6 Simulation, 7 Brainstorming, 8 Statistical models.
Time range of work: 5 - IO years.
Source of support for work (%): IOO Private business.
Work done for (%): IOO Private business.

Occupational function: I Administrator, 2 Manager, 3 Research worker.
Worked in industry/business in: I Planning, 2 Research and development, 3 Management.

(452)

133. Robert A. Dennis

Acting Director, National Economic Projections, 1666 Connecticut Ave, NW, Washington, DC 20009, USA.
Sex: Male.   *Age:* 25-29 years.
Educational qualification: Master's degree.
Formal training: Social/behavioural sciences.
Informal training: I Mathematics, 2 Physical sciences.
Primarily engaged in: Futures studies.
Areas in which work done (%): 3 As individual consultant, 97 In organization primarily concerned with futures studies and/or long-range planning.
Direction of work in forecasting: I Economic, 2 Manpower, 3 Resources, 4 Population.
Direction of work in research: Consumer affairs.
Methods used: I Econometric modelling, 2 Causal modelling.
Time range of work: 5 - IO years.
Source of support for work (%): IOO Private business.
Work done for (%): 5O National government, 5O Private business.
Occupational function: Research worker.

(390)

134. Louis A. Dernoi

5O9 - 424 Queen St, Ottawa, Ontario, Canada K1R 5 AB.
Sex: Male.   *Age:* 50-59.
Educational qualification: Doctoral degree (candidate), Master's degree.
Formal training: I Design, 2 Humanities, 3 Social/behavioural sciences.
Informal training: I Social/behavioural sciences, 2 Forecasting.
Primarily engaged in: Long-range planning.
Areas in which work done (%): 5O In planning unit of a government agency, 5O As individual consultant.
Direction of work in forecasting: I Work and leisure, 2 Way of life, 3 Social.
Direction of work in research: I Urban life management, 2 Policy research, 3 Social priorities.
Direction of work in planning: I Urban, 2 Regional.
Methods used: I Individual expert forecasting, 2 Scenario building, 3 Brainstorming, 4 Expert panels.
Time range of work: IO - 25 years.
Source of support for work (%): IOO National government.
Work done for (%): IOO National government.
Occupational function: I Research worker, 2 Consultant.
Worked in government as: I Researcher, 2 Consultant.
Worked in education: I Teaching (university).
Worked in industry/business in: Consultancy.
Worked in service sector: Design.
Additional information: Concerned with urban futures, policy planning, future life styles.

(80)

135. W. Diamond

World Bank, 1818 H St, NW, Washington DC, 2O433, USA.
Sex: Male.   *Age:* 5O-59.
Educational qualification: Doctoral degree.

Formal training: History.
Informal training: Banking.
Primarily engaged in: Both futures studies and long-range planning.
Direction of work in forecasting: Economic.
Direction of work in planning: Economic.
Source of support for work (%): lOO International agencies.
Work done for (%): lOO International agencies.
Occupational function: Manager.
Additional information: Concerned with economic developments.   *(251)*

136. G. Diemer

Philips Research Laboratories, Eindhoven, The Netherlands
Sex: Male.   *Age:* 5O-59.
Educational qualification: Doctoral degree.
Formal training: Physical sciences.
Informal training: Social/behavioural sciences, Mathematics, Engineering, Journalism,
Education.   *(277)*

137. Paul Dimitriu

Laboratory for Prospective Research, University of Bucharest, Str Mihail Moxa, 3 - 5,
Bucharest 8, Romania.
Sex: Male.   *Age:* 5O-59.
Educational qualification: Doctoral degree.
Formal training: l Law, 2 Social/behavioural sciences, 3 Humanities.
Informal training: l Humanities, 2 Social/behavioural sciences, 3 Law, 4 Education.
Primarily engaged in: Futures studies.
Areas in which work done (%): 5 As individual consultant, lO In planning unit of an
international organization, 2O In organization primarily concerned with futures studies
and/or long-range planning, 65 As academic, in teaching futures studies or long-range
planning.
Direction of work in forecasting: l Social, 2 Methodology, 3 Cultural.
Direction of work in research: l Social impacts of technology, 2 Policy research,
3 Futures methodology, 4 Social priorities.
Methods used: l Scenario building, 2 Historical analogy, 3 Expert panels, 4 Delphi
techniques, 5 Causal modelling, 6 Simulation, 7 Relevance trees, 8 Morphological method.
Time range of work: lO - beyond year 2OOO.
Source of support for work (%): lOO National government.
Work done for (%): 25 International agencies, 75 National government.
Occupational function: l Research worker, 2 Educator, 3 Consultant.
Worked in education: l In research, 2 Teaching.
Worked in service sector: Law.
Additional information: Concerned with technology assessment, social indicators,
forecasting in international relations, and forecasting in the field of culture.   *(328)*

138. Gennadi Mikhailovich Dobrov

Kiev 127, Bul 4O - Let Oktyabya, 142/144, Institute of Cybernetics of the Academy
of Sciences, The UKROSSR, USSR.
Sex: Male.   *Age:* 4O-49.
Educational qualification: Doctoral degree.
Formal training: Social/behavioural sciences, Engineering.
Informal training: Humanities, Mathematics.

Primarily engaged in: Both futures studies and long-range planning.
Areas in which work done (%): IOO In organization primarily concerned with futures studies and/or long-range planning.
Direction of work in forecasting: I Technological, 2 Scientific, 3 Economics, 4 Manpower, 5 Social.
Direction of work in research: I Policy research, 2 Futures methodology, 3 Manpower, 4 Alternative futures.
Direction of work in planning: I Scientific, 2 Technological, 3 Social, 4 Economic, 5 Resources.
Methods used: I Expert panels, 2 Relevance trees, 3 Delphi techniques, 4 Network analysis, 5 Simulation, 6 Extrapolation techniques, 7 Contextual mapping, 8 Statistical models, 9 Cross impact analysis.
Time range of work: 5 - 25 years.
Source of support for work (%): 2O Local government, 2O Foundations, 6O National government.
Work done for (%): IO Local or regional government, 30 Foundations, 6O National government.
Occupational function: I Research worker, 2 Consultant, 3 Administrator, 4 Educator.
Worked in government as: Researcher.
Worked in education: Teaching.   *(541)*

139. Richard A. Dodge

Assistant Director for Education, American Institute of Biological Sciences, 14O1 Wilson Blvd, Arlington, Va 222O9, USA.
Sex: Male.   *Age:* 4O-49.
Educational qualification: Doctoral degree.
Formal training: I Life sciences, 2 Education.
Informal training: I Journalism, 2 Design, 3 Cinema/television.
Direction of work in forecasting: I Educational, 2 Scientific, 3 Technological.
Direction of work in research: I Futures methodology, 2 Social impacts of technology, 3 Manpower.
Direction of work in planning: I Scientific, 2 Educational, 3 Technological.
Methods used: I Expert panels, 2 Brainstorming, 3 Historical analogy.
Time range of work: 5 - IO years.
Source of support for work (%): 3O Voluntary associations, 7O National government.
Work done for (%): 9O Education.
Occupational function: I Educator, 2 Administrator, 3 Consultant, 4 Manager.
Worked in industry/business in: I Consultancy.
Worked in education: I Teaching, 2 In administration, 3 In research.
Worked in service sector: Communication media.   *(332)*

14O. Charles Doran

Dept of Political Science, Rice University, Houston, Tx 77OO1, USA.
Sex: Male.   *Age:* 3O-39.
Educational qualification: Doctoral degree.
Formal training: Social/behavioural sciences.
Informal training: I Humanities, 2 Mathematics.
Primarily engaged in: Both futures studies and long-range planning.
Areas in which work done (%): IO In organization primarily concerned with futures studies and/or long-range planning, 2O As individual consultant, 7O As academic, in teaching futures studies or long-range planning.

Direction of work in forecasting: I Political, 2 Resources, 3 Military, 4 Environmental, 5 Economic, 6 Social.

Direction of work in research: I Conflict analysis, 2 Policy research, 3 Alternative futures, 4 Environmental.

Methods used: I Statistical models, 2 Individual expert forecasting, 3 Probabilistic forecasting, 4 Historical analogy, 5 Simulation, 6 Causal modelling, 7 Scenario building, 8 Extrapolation techniques.

Time range of work: IO - 25 years.

Source of support for work (%): 2O National government, 8O Private business.

Work done for (%): IO Local or regional government, 3O National government, 6O Private business.

Occupational function: I Educator, 2 Consultant, 3 Research worker.

Worked in education: I Teaching, 2 In research.

Additional information: Concerned with; relationship between resource scarcity and political conflict at the international level. Currently working on probable producer response to U.S. energy alternatives.   *(466)*

141. Claire Dover

Science Correspondent, The Daily Telegraph, 135 Fleet St, London, EC4, UK.

Sex: Female.   *Age:* 3O-39.

Educational qualification: Bachelor's degree.

Formal training: Physical sciences.

Informal training: Life sciences, Social/behavioural sciences, Journalism, Education.

Areas in which work done (%): Organization concerned with other studies including long-range planning.

Direction of work in forecasting: Technological, Scientific, Environmental, Population.

Occupational function: Entertainer.   *(86)*

142. Frank J. Doyle

Chief, Technological Strategy Division, Dept of Industry, Trade, and Commerce, Government of Canada, 112 Kent St, Ottawa M1A OH5, Canada.

Sex: Male.   *Age:* 4O-49.

Educational qualification: Master's degree.

Formal training: I Social/behavioural sciences, 2 MBA.

Primarily engaged in: Both futures studies and long-range planning.

Areas in which work done (%): 5O In organization primarily concerned with futures studies and/or long-range planning, 5O In planning unit of a governmental enterprise.

Direction of work in forecasting: Technological, Economic, Social, Cultural, Population.

Direction of work in research: I Alternative futures, 2 Environmental, 3 Resource utilization, 4 Value systems, 5 Population.

Direction of work in planning: Technological.

Methods used: Delphi techniques, Scenario building, Statistical models, Historical analogy, Operational models.

Time range of work: IO - 25 years.

Source of support for work (%): IOO National government.

Work done for (%): 5O National government.

Occupational function: I Manager, 2 Research worker.

Worked in goverment as: I Researcher, 2 Administrator.

Worked in industry/business in: I Management, 2 Research and development, 3 Planning.

Additional information: Concerned with long-term analysis of economic, social, demographic and technological trends on a global scale.   *(380)*

143. Rachel Elboim Dror

Head, Division of Educational Planning and Administration, School of Education,
The Hebrew University of Jerusalem, Jerusalem, Israel.
Sex: Female. *Age:* 40-49.
Educational qualification: Doctoral degree.
Formal training: I Social/behavioural sciences, 2 Education.
Areas in which work done (%): 50 As academic, in teaching futures studies or long-range
planning, 50 As academic, in teaching educational policy and administration.
Direction of work in research: Alternative futures in education.
Direction of work in planning: Educational.
Methods used: Use of methods varies according to need.
Time range of work: 10 - 25 years.
Source of support for work (%): 100 University.
Work done for (%): 100 University.
Occupational function: I Education, 2 Research worker, 3 Consultant.
Worked in education as: I Teaching, 2 In research, 3 In administration.
Additional information: Concerned with alternative educational futures for Israel. *(583)*

144. Yehezkel Dror

Professor, Policy Scientist, The Eliezer Kaplan School for Economics and Social Sciences,
The Hebrew University of Jerusalem, Jerusalem, Israel.
Sex: Male. *Age:* 40-49.
Educational *qualification:* Doctoral degree.
Formal training: I Social/behavioural sciences, 2 Law.
Informal training: Policy studies, Strategic planning.
Areas in which work done (%): 20 As individual consultant.
60 Planning unit of a governmental agency, 20 Academic, In teaching futures studies
or long-range planning.
Direction of work in forecasting: Military.
Direction of work in research: I Policy research, 2 Futures methodology.
Direction of work in planning: I Military, 2 Political, 3 Social.
Methods used: Mixed and combined policy analysis.
Time range of work: 5 - 25 years.
Source of support for work (%): 60 National government, 10 International agencies,
20 University, 10 Other governments.
Work done for (%): 60 National government, 10 International agencies, 10 Other
governments, 20 Methodology research.
Occupational function: I Policy analyst/advisor, 3 Educator, 3 Research worker.
Worked in government as: I Policy analyst, 2 Consultant.
Worked in education: I In research, 2 Teaching. *(578)*

145. Paul Dubach

Weinberg Str 17, CH-8623 Wetziton, Switzerland.
Sex: Male. *Age:* 40-49.
Educational qualification: Master's degree.
Formal training: Engineering, Education, Design, Methodology.
Informal training: Social/behavioural sciences, Mathematics, Technical assistant to
developing committees.
Primarily engaged in: Both futures studies and long-range planning.
Areas in which work done (%): 25 In organization primarily concerned with futures

studies and/or long-range planning, 7O As individual consultant, 5 As academic, in teaching futures studies or long-range planning.

Direction of work in forecasting: Technological, Economic, Scientific, Environmental, Methodology.

Direction of work in research: Social impacts of technology, Alternative futures, Environmental, Value systems, Futures methodology.

Direction of work in planning: Scientific, Technological, Social, Educational, Environmental.

Methods used: Delphi techniques, Gaming, Scenario building, Extrapolation techniques, Brainstorming, Relevance trees, Simulation, Morphology.

Time range of work: 5 - 25 years.

Source of support for work (%): 25 National government, 75 Private business.

Work done for (%): 25 National government, 75 Private business.

Occupational function: Consultant.

Worked in government as: Researcher.

Worked in industry/business in: I Consultancy, 2 Planning, 3 Management.

Worked in education: Teaching.

Worked in service sector: Design.

Additional information: Concerned with technological development, research planning, technology assessment, methodology, organization of future research groups.   *(275)*

146. J. Dull

Co-ordination and Planning Dept, Exxon International, 1251 Ave of the Americas. New York, NY 1OO2O, USA.

Sex: Male.   *Age:* 30-39.

Educational qualification: Master's degree.

Formal training: I Engineering, 2 Social/behavioural sciences, 3 Mathematics.

Informal training: Engineering.

Areas in which work done (%): IOO In planning unit of a business enterprise.

Direction of work in forecasting: I Market, 2 Economic.

Direction of work in planning: I Corporate, 2 Economic.

Methods used: I Operational models, 2 Probabilistic forecasting, 3 Individual expert forecasting, 4 Extrapolation techniques.

Time range of work: 5 - IO years.

Source of support for work (%): IOO Private business.

Work done for (%): IOO Private business.

Occupational function: Manager.

Worked in industry/business in: Management.   *(92)*

147. Sir Kingsley Dunham

Institute of Geological Sciences, London, SW7 2DE, UK.

Sex: Male.   *Age:* 6O or over.

Educational qualification: Doctoral degree.

Formal training: Physical sciences, Engineering.

Informal training: Humanities, Education, Arts.

Primarily engaged in: Futures studies.

Areas in which work done (%): IO In planning unit of an international organization, 35 In organization concerned with other studies including long-range planning, 45 In organization primarily concerned with futures studies and/or long-range planning.

Direction of work in forecasting: I Resources, 2 Environmental, 3 Scientific.

Direction of work in research: I Resource utilization, 2 Environmental.

Direction of work in planning: I Resources, 2 Environmental.

Source of support for work (%): 5 Voluntary associations, 95 National government.
Work done for (%): 5 Voluntary associations, 95 National government.
Occupational function: I Administrator, 2 Research worker.
Worked in government as: Researcher.
Worked in education: Teaching, In research. *(320)*

148. R.W. Durie

Director, Advanced Concepts Centre, Environment Dept, Ottawa K1A ON3, Canada.
Sex: Male. *Age:* 40-49.
Educational qualification: Doctoral degree.
Formal training: Engineering.
Informal training: I Engineering, 2 Humanities, 3 Social/behavioural sciences, 4 Design.
Primarily engaged in: Both futures studies and long-range planning.
Areas in which work done (%): 50 In organization concerned with other studies
including long-range planning, 50 In planning unit of a governmental agency.
Direction of work in forecasting: Technological, Social, Environmental, Resources.
Direction of work in research: Social impacts of technology, Alternative futures,
Environmental, Value systems, Policy research, The individual in the future, Futures
methodology, Low impact technology.
Direction of work in planning: Scientific, Technological, Social, Regional, Political,
Environmental, Resources.
Methods used: Scenario building, Contextual mapping, Brainstorming.
Time range of work: IO - 25 years.
Source of support for work (%): IOO National government.
Work done for (%): IOO National government.
Occupational function: Facilitator.
Worked in government as: Administrator, Researcher.
Worked in industry/business in: Research and development, Planning.
Worked in education: In research. *(461)*

149. Michael W. Dwyer

Director of Marketing Research, Sperry Division, General Mills Inc, 9200 Wayzata Blvd,
Minneapolis, Mn 55440, USA.
Sex: Male. *Age:* 30-39.
Educational qualification: Master's degree.
Formal training: Social/behavioural sciences, Business.
Informal training: I Business-marketing, 2 Social/behavioural sciences, 3 Education.
Areas in which work done (%): IO As individual consultant, IO In organization
concerned with other studies including long-range planning, 20 In organization primarily
concerned with futures studies and/or long-range planning, 60 In planning unit of a
business enterprise.
Direction of work in forecasting: I Market, 2 Population, 3 Resources, 4 Technological,
Direction of work in research: I Value systems, 2 Population, 3 The individual in the
future, 4 Social impacts of technology, 4 Consumer affairs, 4 Environmental.
Direction of work in planning: Corporate.
Methods used: Probabilistic forecasting, Delphi techniques, Scenario building,
Brainstorming, Statistical models, Expert panels, Simulation.
Time range of work: 5 - IO years.
Source of support for work (%): IOO Private business.
Work done for (%): IO Local or regional government, 90 Private business.
Occupational function: Manager.
Worked in industry/business in: Management. *(70)*

E

150. Stephen C. Ehrmann

Office of Education Research and Assistance, The Evergreen State College, Olympia, Washington 98505, USA.

Sex: Male.   *Age:* 25-29.

Educational qualification: Bachelor's degree, Doctoral candidate.

Formal training: 1 Social/behavioural sciences, 2 Design, 3 Engineering.

Informal training: Education.

Primarily engaged in: Educational research, Futures studies, Organizational research.

Areas in which work done (%): 25 As student, 75 In organization primarily concerned with futures studies and/or long-range planning.

Direction of work in research: 1 Historical analogy, 2 Futures methodology.

Methods used: 1 Causal modelling, 2 Historical analogy, 2 Futures methodology.

Time range of work: 5 - 25 years.

Source of support for work (%): 100 University.

Work done for (%): 100 Educational institution.

Occupational function: 1 Evaluator, 2 Research worker.

Worked in education: In research.   *(304)*

151. Kjell Eide

Dept of Research and Planning, Ministry of Education, Oslo Dep, Norway.

Sex: Male.   *Age:* 40-49.

Educational qualification: Other graduate/professional degree.

Formal training: Social/behavioural sciences.

Direction of work in forecasting: Social, Cultural, Educational.

Direction of work in research: Alternative futures, Resource utilization, Policy research.

Direction of work in planning: Social, Educational.

Methods used: Gaming, Scenario building, Extrapolation techniques, Contextual mapping, Statistical models, Operational models, Simulation, Causal modelling.

Time range of work: 10 - 25 years.

Source of support for work (%): 100 National government.

Work done for (%): 30 National government.

Occupational function: Planner.   *(356)*

152. Silje Eivind

R 519 A, County Hall, GLC, London, SE1 7PB, UK.

Sex: Male.   *Age:* 30-39.

Educational qualification: Other graduate/professional degree.

Formal training: 1 Mathematics, 2 Life sciences, 3 Social/behavioural sciences.

Informal training: 1 Physical sciences, 2 Engineering.

Primarily engaged in: Long-range planning.

Areas in which work done (%): 100 In planning unit of a governmental agency.

Direction of work in forecasting: 1 Population, 2 Social.

Direction of work in research: 1 Population, 2 Alternative futures, 3 Manpower, 4 Policy research.

Direction of work in planning: 1 Urban, 2 Regional, 3 Corporate, 4 Labour, 5 Social.

Methods used: 1 Operational models, 2 Statistical models.

Time range of work: 10 - 25 years.

Source of support for work (%): 100 Local government.

Work done for (%): 100 Local or regional government.

Occupational function: 1 Manager, 2 Administrator, 3 Consultant.

Worked in government as: Researcher.   *(394)*

153. Jacques Ellul
University of Bordeaux, Campus, Pessac 33600, France.
Sex: Male. *Age:* 60 or over.
Educational qualification: Doctoral degree.
Formal training: Social/behavioural sciences, History.
Informal training: Social/behavioural sciences.
Primarily engaged in: Both futures studies and long-range planning.
Areas in which work done (%): 25 In organization primarily concerned with futures studies and/or long-range planning, 25 As academic, in teaching futures studies or long-range planning, 50 Social and ecclesiastical activities.
Direction of work in forecasting: Social, Environmental.
Direction of work in research: Social impacts of technology, The individual in the future, Futures methodology.
Direction of work in planning: Social.
Methods used: Probabilistic forecasting, scenario building, Historical analogy, Individual expert forecasting, Causal modelling.
Time range of work: 10 - 25 years.
Occupational function: Educator.
Worked in education: Teaching, In research.
Worked in service sector: Social welfare, Religion.   *(539)*

154. Isabel Emmett
Afallon, Tan-y-Grisiau, Blaenau Ffestiniog, Merionethshire, Wales, UK.
Sex: Female. *Age:* 40-49.
Educational qualification: Bachelor's degree.
Formal training: Social/behavioural sciences.
Informal training: I Journalism, 2 Humanities, 3 Education.
Areas in which work done (%): 10 As individual consultant, 10 Leisure studies.
Direction of work in research: I Value systems, 2 Policy research, 3 Social priorities.
Direction of work in planning: Leisure.
Time range of work: 10 - 25 years.
Source of support for work (%): 100 Self supported.
Work done for (%): 10 Local or regional government, 10 National government.
Occupational function: Research worker.
Worked in education: I In research, 2 Teaching.
Additional information: Concerned with planning for leisure.   *(30)*

155. K.R. Emrich
Social Research and Planning Office, Social Development Division, Ecafe, Sala Santitham, Bangkok, Thailand.
Sex: Male. *Age:* 40-49.
Educational qualification: Doctoral degree.
Formal training: I Social/behavioural sciences, 2 Engineering.
Informal training: Physical sciences, Social/behavioural sciences, Education.
Areas in which work done (%): 100 In planning unit of an international organization.
Direction of work in forecasting: Social, Cultural.
Direction of work in research: Social impacts of technology, Value systems, Social priorities, Policy research.
Direction of work in planning: Social.
Methods used: Extrapolation techniques, Expert panels, Historical analogy, Individual expert forecasting, Causal modelling.

Time range of work: 5 - lO years.
Source of support for work (%): lOO International agencies.
Work done for (%): lOO International agencies.
Occupational function: l Research worker, 2 Educator.
Worked in government as: l Administrator, 2 Researcher.
Worked in industry/business in: l Research and development, 2 Trade union.
Worked in education: Teaching, In research.
Additional information: Concerned with social indicators; economic, social, psychological, etc, interrelationships; and trend analysis.   *(179)*

156. Henry Endress

Executive Director, Lutheran Resources Commission, 1346 Connecticut Ave, NW, Suite 823, Washington DC 20036, USA.
Sex: Male.   *Age:* 6O or over.
Educational qualification: Bachelor's degree.
Formal training: l Humanities, 2 Journalism.
Informal training: l Business administration, 2 Journalism, 3 Education, 4 Cinema/television.
Areas in which work done (%): lO In planning unit of an international organization, 2O In organization primarily concerned with futures studies and/or long-range planning, 7O As individual consultant.
Direction of work in forecasting: l Resources, 2 Social, 3 Educational.
Direction of work in research: l Resource utilization, 2 Social priorities, 2 Social services.
Direction of work in planning: l Resources, 2 Social, 3 Educational.
Source of support for work (%): lOO Church.
Work done for (%): lOO Church.
Occupational function: l Consultant, 2 Educator, 3 Administrator.
Worked in industry/business in: Consultancy.
Worked in education: In administration.
Worked in service sector: l Religion, 2 Social welfare, 3 Communication media.
Additional information: Concerned with social services, education, and the arts.   *(347)*

157. Hugo O. Engelman

Dept of Sociology, Northern Illinois University, Dekalb, Il 60115, USA.
Sex: Male.   *Age:* 50-59.
Educational qualification: Doctoral degree.
Formal training: Social/behavioural sciences.
Informal training: Law, Education, Humanities.
Direction of work in forecasting: l Social, 2 Cultural, 3 Scientific, 4 Technological, 5 Economic, 6 Educational.
Direction of work in research: l Alternative futures, 2 The individual in the future, 3 The family in the future, 4 Value systems, 5 Futures methods.
Direction of work in planning: Social.
Methods used: Causal modelling.
Time range of work: Beyond year 2OOO.
Occupational function: Educator, Research worker.
Worked in education as: Teaching in research.
Additional information: Concerned with transformation of total societal organization. *(562)*

158. Gordon A. Enk
The Institute on Man and Science, Rensselaerville, NY 12147. USA.
Sex: Male. *Age:* 30-39.
Educational qualification: Doctoral degree.
Formal training: Life sciences, Social/behavioural sciences.
Informal training: I Social/behavioural sciences, 2 Life sciences.
Primarily engaged in: Long-range planning.
Areas in which work done (%): IO In planning unit of a governmental agency, 9O In organization primarily concerned with futures studies and/or long-range planning.
Direction of work in forecasting: Economic.
Direction of work in research: I Environmental, I Resource utilization, I Social priorities, 2 Value systems.
Methods used: Delphi techniques, Scenario building, Brainstorming.
Time range of work: IO - 25 years.
Source of support for work (%): 2O Local government, 4O National government, IO Foundations.
Work done for (%): 5O Local or regional government, 5O National government.
Occupational function: I Consultant, 2 Educator, 3 Research worker, 4 Administrator.
Worked in education: Teaching, In research, In administration.
Additional information: Concerned with land use and natural resources. *(103)*

159. Shinkichi Eto
University of Tokyo, 3 - 8 - 1 Komaba, Meguro-ku, Tokyo, Japan.
Sex: Male. *Age:* 50-59.
Educational qualification: B.L. degree.
Formal training: Law.
Informal training: Life sciences, Social/behavioural sciences, Humanities.
Primarily engaged in: Futures studies.
Areas in which work done (%): IOO As academic, in teaching futures studies or long-range planning.
Direction of work in forecasting: International relations.
Direction of work in research: Social priorities.
Direction of work in planning: Political.
Methods used: I Simulation, 2 Gaming, 3 Historical analogy, 4 Causal modelling.
Time range of work: 5 years.
Occupational function: Professor.
Worked in government as: University professor in a national university. *(352)*

F ## 16O. B.T. Feld
Secretary General, Pugwash Conferences on Science and World Affairs, 9 Great Russell Mansions, 6O Great Russell St, London W.C.1 UK.
Sex: Male. *Age:* 50-59.
Educational qualification: Doctoral degree.
Formal training: Physical sciences.
Informal training: I Education, 2 Social/behavioural sciences, 3 Engineering.
Areas in which work done (%): IO In organization primarily concerned with futures studies and/or long-range planning, 4O In planning unit of an international organization, 5O Research in physics.
Direction of work in forecasting: I Military, 2 Resources, 3 Technological, 4 Population.
Direction of work in research: I Social impacts of technology, 2 Population, 3 Resource utilization.

Direction of work in planning: I Scientific, 2 Technological, 3 Environmental, 4 Military.
Methods used: Expert panels.
Time range of work: 5 - IO years.
Source of support for work (%): 5O University, 5O Foundation.
Occupational function: I Research worker, 2 Administrator, 3 Educator.
Worked in education: I In research, 2 Teaching.
Additional information: Concerned with arms control and disarmament; technology assessment.   *(388)*

161. Pierre Feldheim

Secretary-General, Centre d'Etudes des Problemes Sociaux et Professionels de la Technique, 44 Avenue Jeanne, B-1O5O Brussels, Belgium.
Sex: Male.   *Age:* 5O-59.
Educational qualification: Some college or less.
Formal training: Social/behavioural sciences.
Informal training: Social/behavioural sciences.
Primarily engaged in: Both futures studies and long-range planning.
Areas in which work done (%): 5 In planning unit of a governmental agency, IO As individual consultant, 25 Teaching and administration, 6O In organization concerned with other studies including long-range planning.
Direction of work in forecasting: Social, Educational, Manpower.
Direction of work in research: Manpower.
Direction of work in planning: Educational.
Methods used: Extrapolation techniques, Brainstorming, Statistical models, Expert panels, Network analysis, Operational models, Individual expert forecasting.
Time range of work: 5 - IO years.
Source of support for work (%): IOO National government.
Work done for (%): IOO University.
Occupational function: I Manager, 2 Administrator,3 Research worker, 4 Educator, 4 Consultant.
Worked in government as: Elected official.
Worked in industry/business in: I Management, 2 Trade union.
Worked in education: Teaching.
Additional information: Concerned with manpower studies under all aspects (qualitative, quantative, sociological, reaction, etc).   *(344)*

162. John N. Ferris

Dept of Agricultural Economics, College of Agriculture and Natural Resources, Michigan State University, East Lansing, Mi 48823, USA.
Sex: Male.   *Age:* 4O-49.
Educational qualification: Doctoral degree.
Formal training: Social/behavioural sciences.
Informal training: Social/behavioural sciences.
Primarily engaged in: Both futures studies and long-range planning.
Areas in which work done (%): 5O In organization primarily concerned with futures studies and/or long-range planning. I5 Academic, in teaching futures studies or long-range planning.
Direction of work in forecasting: Economic.
Direction of work in research: Futures methodology.
Direction of work in planning: Economic.

Methods used: I Statistical models, 2 Probabilistic forecasting 3 Simulation,
4 Extrapolation techniques, 5 Expert panels, 6 Delphi techniques.
Time range of work: IO - 25 years.
Source of support for work (%): 6O State government, 3O National government,
IO International agencies.
Work done for (%): 6O State government, 25 National government, IO International
agencies, 5 Church.
Occupational function: I Research worker, 2 Educator, 3 Consultant.
Worked in education: Teaching, In research. *(536)*

163. Abbot L. Ferriss
Dept of Sociology, Emory University, Atlanta, Ga 30322, USA.
Sex: Male. *Age:* 5O-59.
Educational qualification: Doctoral degree.
Formal training: I Social/behavioural sciences, 2 Statistics.
Informal training: I Social/behavioural sciences, 2 Education, 3 Statistics.
Areas in which work done (%): IO As individual consultant, 9O Teaching, administration,
research.
Direction of work in forecasting: I Social, 2 Educational, 3 Manpower, 4 Population.
Direction of work in research: I Population, 2 Manpower.
Methods used: I Statistical models, I Causal modelling, 2 Extrapolation techniques,
3 Contextual mapping.
Time range of work: 5 - IO years.
Occupational function: I Administrator, 2 Educator, 3 Research worker, 4 Consultant.
Worked in government as: I Researcher.
Worked in education: I Teaching, 2 In research, 3 Administration.
Additional information: Concerned with social indicators; model development; analysis
of time series; and monitoring change. *(402)*

164. Bruno de Finetti
Istituto di Matematica, Universita di Roma, Vicenza 23, OO185, Rome, Italy.
Sex: Male. *Age:* 6O or over.
Educational qualification: Doctoral degree.
Formal training: Mathematics.
Informal training: I Education, 2 Insurance, economics, organization.
Direction of work in research: I Social priorities, 2 Policy research, 3 Value systems.
Direction of work in planning: I Educational, 2 Social, 3 Political.
Methods used: I Scenario building, 2 Probabilistic forecasting.
Time range of work: Beyond 2OOO AD.
Occupational function: I Educator, 2 Research worker.
Worked in industry in: I Research and development.
Worked in education: I In research, 2 Teaching.
Additional information: Concerned with need for better social, economic, political systems.
(6)

165. Michael Finley
Staff Consultant, House Foreign Affairs Committee, 217O Rayburn, Washington, DC 2O515, USA.
Sex: Male. *Age:* 3O-39.
Educational qualification: Bachelor's degree.
Formal training: Social/behavioural sciences.
Informal training: I Law, 2 Journalism.
Direction of work in planning: I Regional, I Environmental, I Resources.

Methods used: I Expert panels, 2 Brainstorming, 3 Historical analogy.
Time range of work: IO - 25 years.
Source of support for work (%): IOO National government.
Work done for (%): IOO National government.
Worked in government as: Elected official (staff of).
Additional information: Concerned with the future of United States relations with
Latin America, the Carribean, and Canada.   *(84)*

166. Franco E. Fiorio

Scientific Attache, Italian Embassy, 16O1 Fuller St, NW, Washington, DC 2OOO9, USA.
Sex: Male.   *Age:* 6O or over.
Educational qualification: Doctoral degree.
Formal training: Engineering, Aerospace sciences.
Informal training: Journalism, Law.
Primarily engaged in: Both futures studies and long-range planning.
Areas in which work done (%): 5 In planning unit of an international organization, 85 In
planning unit of a governmental agency, IO As individual consultant.
Direction of work in forecasting: I Technological, 2 Scientific, 3 Resources, 4 Environmental.
Direction of work in research: I Alternative futures, 2 Environmental, 3 Resource
utilization, 4 Social impacts of technology.
Direction of work in planning: I Technological, 2 Scientific, 3 Environmental, 3 Resources.
Methods used: I Extrapolation techniques, 2 Brainstorming, 3 Expert panels, 4 Individual
expert forecasting, 5 Scenario building.
Time range of work: 5 - 25 years.
Source of support for work (%): IOO National government (Italy).
Work done for (%): IO Private business, 9O National government.
Occupational function: Consultant.
Worked in government as: I Administrator, 2 Researcher.
Worked in education: Teaching.
Worked in service sector: Communication media.
Additional information: Not primarily engaged but concerned with long-term future
in areas: Long-range resource analysis; technological assessment; aerospace-practical
application; limits to growth.   *(138)*

167. S.J. Fitzsimmons

Vice President, Abt Associates, Inc, 55 Wheeler St, Cambridge, Ma O2138, USA.
Sex: Male.   *Age:* 3O-39.
Educational qualification: Doctoral degree.
Formal training: Social/behavioural sciences.
Areas in which work done (%): IOO In organization concerned with other studies
including long-range planning.
Direction of work in research: Social impacts of technology, Environmental, Resource
utilization, Social priorities, Policy research.
Direction of work in planning: I Social, 2 Economic, 3 Environmental, 4 Educational.
Methods used: I Statistical models, 2 Operational models, 3 Causal modelling,
4 Brainstorming.
Time range of work: 5 - 25 years.
Source of support for work (%): IO Grants, 9O National government.
Work done for (%): IO Unspecified, 9O National government.
Occupational function: Research worker.
Worked in industry/business in: Research and development.
Additional information: Concerned with social and economic aspects.   *(252)*

168. Steven N. Flajser
Research Assistant Prof, Faculty Search Committee, Program in Social Management of Technology, University of Washington, Seattle, Wa 98195, USA.
Sex: Male.   *Age:* 30-39.
Educational qualification: Doctoral degree.
Formal training: Physical sciences.
Informal training: I Policy sciences, 2 Social/behavioural sciences, 3 Engineering, 4 Education.
Primarily engaged in: Future studies.
Areas in which work done (%): 67 In organization concerned with other studies including long-range planning, 33 As academic, in teaching futures studies or long-range planning.
Direction of work in forecasting: I Environmental, 2 Social, 3 Technological.
Direction of work in research: I Social impacts of technology, I Policy research, 2 Alternative futures, 3 Environmental.
Direction of work in planning: I Environmental, 2 Technological.
Methods used: I Brainstorming, 2 Historical analogy, 3 Cross impact analysis, 4 Delphi techniques, 5 Extrapolation techniques, 6 Causal modelling.
Time range of work: 5 - IO years.
Source of support for work (%): 5O Local government, 5O Foundations.
Occupational function: Educator.
Worked in education: I In research, 2 Teaching, 3 In administration.
Additional information: Concerned with energy policy, environmental policy, and technology assessment.   *(209)*

169. Ossip K. Flechtheim
1 Berlin 33, Rohifsstrasse 18, West Germany.
Sex: Male.   *Age:* 6O or over.
Educational qualification: Doctoral degree.
Formal training: I Social/behavioural sciences, 2 Law.
Informal training: Humanities.
Primarily engaged in: Futures studies.
Areas in which work done (%): IO In organization primarily concerned with futures studies and/or long-range planning, 25 As academic, in teaching futures studies or long-range planning, 65 Research, publishing, lecturing.
Direction of work in research: I Alternative futures, 2 Futures methodology, 3 Social priorities, 4 Policy research, 5 The individual in the future.
Methods used: I Historical analogy, 2 Simulation, 3 Scenario building, 4 Brainstorming.
Time range of work: IO - 25 years.
Work done for (%): IO Voluntary associations.
Occupational function: I Author, 2 Educator.
Worked in government as: Administrator.
Worked in education: I Teaching, 2 In research.   *(32)*

17O. Peter Fleissner
Institut für Sozio-Ökonomische, Entwicklungsforschung, A-1O1O Vienna, Austria.
Sex: Male.   *Age:* 30-39.
Educational qualification: Doctoral degree.
Formal training: Social/behavioural sciences, Mathematics, Physical sciences, Engineering.
Informal training: Life sciences, Humanities, Education.
Primarily engaged in: Both futures studies and long-range planning.

Areas in which work done (%): 9O In organization primarily concerned with futures studies and/or long-range planning, IO As individual consultant.
Direction of work in forecasting: Economic, Social, Population, Manpower.
Direction of work in research: Manpower, Consumer affairs, Value systems, Social priorities, Policy research, The family in the future.
Direction of work in planning: Social, Economic, Political, Labour.
Methods used: Extrapolation techniques, Statistical models, Historical analogy, Simulation, Causal modelling.
Time range of work: IO - 25 years.
Source of support for work (%): IOO National government.
Work done for (%): 2O National government. 8O Academic.
Occupational function: I Research worker, 2 Consultant.
Worked in education: I In research, 2 Teaching.   (546)

171. H. Floyd, Jr
DGA International Inc, 1225 Nineteenth St, NW, Washington DC 2OO36, USA.
Sex: Male.   *Age:* 4O-49.
Educational qualification: Master's degree.
Formal training: Social/behavioural sciences.
Informal training: Engineering, Design, Arts.
Areas in which work done (%): 2O Local government planning commission, 8O In organization concerned with other studies including long-range planning.
Direction of work in forecasting: Technological, Market.
Direction of work in planning: Urban, Corporate, Environmental.
Methods used: I Individual expert forecasting, 2 Scenario building, 3 Probabilistic forecasting.
Time range of work: 5 - IO years.
Source of support for work (%): 2O Local government, 8O Private business.
Work done for (%): 2O Local or regional government, 8O Private business.
Occupational function: Consultant.
Worked in government as: I Researcher, 2 Administrator.
Worked in service sector: Design.
Additional information: Concerned with technological assessment and market planning for business decisions and actions.   (94)

172. Emilio Fontela
University of Geneva, Rue de Candolle, Geneva, Switzerland.
Sex: Male.   *Age:* 3O-39.
Educational qualification: Doctoral degree.
Formal training: Social/behavioural sciences.
Informal training: Mathematics.
Primarily engaged in: Both futures studies and long-range planning.
Areas in which work done (%): 25 As academic, in teaching futures studies or long-range planning, 75 As individual consultant.
Direction of work in forecasting: I Economic, 2 Social.
Direction of work in research: I Futures methodology, 2 Global systems.
Direction of work in planning: I Corporate, 2 Economic.
Methods used: I Cross impact analysis, 3 Gaming, 4 Causal modelling.
Time range of work: 5 - 25 years.
Source of support for work (%): 2O Private business, 8O Foundations.
Work done for (%): I5 Private business, 25 University, 6O Foundations.

Occupational function: I Consultant, 2 Educator.
Worked in industry/business in: I Management.
Worked in education: 2 In research, 3 Teaching.

(97)

173. Pal Forgacs
1415 Budapest, Hungary.
Sex: Male. *Age:* 50-59.
Educational qualification: Other graduate/professional degree.
Formal training: Social/behavioural sciences.
Informal training: Social/behavioural sciences.
Areas in which work done (%): 20 In organization concerned with other studies including long-range planning.
Direction of work in forecasting: I Economic, 2 Social, 3 Environmental.
Direction of work in research: I Social impacts of technology, 2 Manpower, 3 Environmental.
Direction of work in planning: I Social, 2 Economic, 3 Environmental.
Methods used: I Probabilistic forecasting, 2 Statistical models, 3 Expert panels.
Time range of work: 5 - IO years.
Source of support for work (%): IOO Voluntary associations.
Work done for (%): 5O International agencies, 5O Voluntary associations.
Occupational function: Research worker.
Worked in industry/business in: Trade union.
Worked in education: Teaching.
Worked in service sector: Social welfare.
Additional information: Concerned with economic and social aspects of chemical, oil, and allied industries.

(281)

174. Jay W. Forrester
System Dynamics Group, Room E4O - 253, Massachusetts Institute of Technology, 77 Massachusetts Ave, Cambridge Ma O2139, USA.
Sex: Male. *Age:* 50-59.
Educational qualification: Master's degree.
Formal training: Engineering.
Informal training: I Social/behavioural sciences, 2 Physical sciences, 3 Design.
Primarily engaged in: Both futures studies and long-range planning.
Areas in which work done (%): 20 As academic, in teaching futures studies or long-range planning, 20 As individual consultant, 4O In organization primarily concerned with futures studies and/or long-range planning.
Direction of work in forecasting: I Economic, 2 Social, 3 Environmental, 4 Resources, 5 Population.
Direction of work in research: I Value systems, 2 Futures methodology,
Direction of work in planning: Urban.
Methods used: I System dynamics, 2 Causal modelling, 3 Simulation, 4 Historical analogy.
Time range of work: 5 - beyond year 2OOO.
Source of support for work (%): IO Local government, IO Private business, IO Individuals, 2O National government, 5O Foundations.
Work done for (%): IO Private business, 3O Local or regional government, 6O Public.
Occupational function: I Research worker, 2 Educator, 3 Administrator.
Worked in education: I In research, 2 In administration, 3 Teaching.

(272)

175. F.R. Fosberg
Smithsonian Institution, Washington DC 20560, USA.
Sex: Male.   *Age:* 60 or over.
Educational qualification: Doctoral degree.
Formal training: Life sciences.
Informal training: Physical sciences.
Occupational function: Research worker.
Worked in government as: Researcher.
Worked in education: Teaching.
Additional information: Concerned with basic biological and ecological research,
international and local conservation, and counselling on these matters.   *(238)*

176. Jib Fowles
University of Houston at Clear Lake City, 2700 Bay Area Blvd, Houston, Tx 77058, USA.
Sex: Male.   *Age:* 30-39.
Educational qualification: Doctoral degree.
Formal training: Social/behavioural sciences.
Informal training: Humanities.
Primarily engaged in: Futures studies.
Areas in which work done (%): 100 As academic, in teaching futures studies or long-range planning.
Direction of work in forecasting: Social, Cultural.
Direction of work in research: Social impacts of technology, Value systems, Futures
methodology.
Methods used: Individual expert forecasting.
Time range of work: Beyond 2000 AD.
Occupational function: Educator.
Worked in education: Teaching.   *(42)*

177. David Fradin
1030 Minnesota Bldg, St Paul, Minnesota 55110, USA.
Sex: Male.   *Age:* Less than 25.
Educational qualification: Bachelor's degree.
Formal training: 1 Engineering, 2 Business, 3 Journalism.
Informal training: 1 Journalism, 2 Business.
Primarily engaged in: Both futures studies and long-range planning.
Areas in which work done (%): 10 In organization primarily concerned with futures
studies and/or long-range planning, 10 As individual consultant.
Direction of work in forecasting: 1 Technological, 2 Resources, 3 Environmental.
Direction of work in research: 1 Resource utilization, 2 Social impacts of technology,
3 Environmental regulation and impact.
Direction of work in planning: 1 Resources, 2 Technological, 3 Scientific, 4 Environmental
regulation.
Methods used: 1 Brainstorming, 2 Causal modelling, 3 Scenario building, 4 Delphi
techniques.
Time range of work: 10 - 25 years.
Source of support for work (%): 100 Own organization.
Work done for (%): 100 Voluntary associations.
Occupational function: 1 Manager, 2 Administrator, 3 Educator, 4 Research worker,
5 Consultant.   *(211)*

178. Christopher Freeman

Science Policy Research Unit, University of Sussex, Falmer, Brighton BN1 9RF, UK.
Sex: Male. *Age:* 50-59.
Educational qualification: Bachelor's degree.
Formal training: Social/behavioural sciences.
Informal training: Social/behavioural sciences.
Primarily engaged in: Futures studies.
Areas in which work done (%): IO As academic, in teaching futures studies or long-range planning, 90 In organization primarily concerned with futures studies and/or long-range planning.
Direction of work in forecasting: I Economic, 2 Social.
Direction of work in research: Alternative futures.
Methods used: I Common sense, 2 Scenario building, 3 Extrapolation techniques.
Time range of work: IO - beyond year 2000.
Source of support for work (%): IO International agencies, I5 Foundations, 25 Private business, 5O National government.
Work done for (%): IO International agencies, I5 Foundations, 25 Private business, 5O National government.
Occupational function: I Manager, 2 Research worker, 3 Educator.
Worked in industry/business in: I Research and development, 2 Planning.
Worked in education: I In research, 2 In administration, 3 Teaching. *(482)*

179. Maurice Fried

Director, Joint FAO/IAEA Division of Atomic Energy in Food and Agriculture.
International Atomic Energy Agency, Karntnerring 11, A-1O1O Vienna I, Austria.
Sex: Male. *Age:* 50-59.
Educational qualification: Doctoral degree.
Formal training: I Physical sciences, 2 Life sciences.
Areas in which work done (%): 4O In planning unit of an international organization.
Direction of work in research: Agricultural.
Direction of work in planning: I Scientific, 2 Environmental.
Methods used: Expert panels.
Time range of work: 5 - IO years.
Source of support for work (%): 2O National government, 8O International agencies.
Work done for (%): 4O International agencies.
Occupational function: Research administrator.
Worked in government as: Administrator, Researcher.
Additional information: Concerned with long-range planning in agriculture research. *(5)*

180. Yona Friedman

42 Blvd Pasteur, Paris 15E, France.
Sex: Male. *Age:* 50-59.
Educational qualification: Master's degree.
Formal training: Design.
Informal training: Social/behavioural sciences, Mathematics, Education, Arts, Cinema/television.
Primarily engaged in: Futures studies.
Direction of work in forecasting: Technological, Social, Scientific.
Direction of work in research: Social impacts of technology, Alternative futures, Environmental, Resource utilization, Value systems, Social priorities, The individual in the future, The family in the future, Futures methodology.

Direction of work in planning: Technological, Social, Urban, Regional.
Methods used: Cross impact analysis, Network analysis, Simulation.
Time range of work: IO - 25 years.
Occupational function: Research worker, Educator.
Worked in government as: Researcher.
Worked in education: Teaching, In research.
Worked in service sector: Communication media, Design.   *(120)*

Bruno Fritsch: See entry number 73.

181. Jackson T. Frost

The Committee for the Future, Inc, New Worlds Training and Education Centre,
2325 Porter St, NW, Washington, DC 20008, USA.
Sex: Male.   *Age:* 25 - 29.
Educational qualification: Bachelor's degree.
Formal training: I Life sciences, 2 Physical sciences.
Informal training: I Social/behavioural sciences, I Education, 2 Cinema/television,
3 Journalism.
Primarily engaged in: Long-range planning.
Areas in which work done (%): IOO In organization primarily concerned with
futures studies and/or long-range planning.
Direction of work in forecasting: I Cultural, 2 Economic, 3 Social, 2 Environmental,
3 Resources, 3 Population.
Direction of work in research: Social impacts of technology, Alternative futures,
Social priorities, The individual in the future, The family in the future.
Direction of work in planning: Scientific, Technological, Social, Environmental, Resources.
Methods used: Cross impacts analysis, Scenario building, Brainstorming, Expert panels,
Network analysis, Historical analogy.
Time range of work: 5 - beyond year 2000.
Work done for (%): IOO Committee for the future.
Occupational function: Administrator, Research worker.
Worked in industry/business in: Planning.
Worked in education: Teaching.
Worked in service sector: Social welfare, Communication media.   *(510)*

182. Takashi Fujii

School of Economics, Nagoya University, Furo-cho Chikusa-ku, Nagoya, Japan.
Sex: Male.   *Age:* 40-49.
Educational qualification: Doctoral degree.
Formal training: I Social/behavioural sciences, 2 Education, 3 Design, 4 Life sciences.
Informal training: I Social/behavioural sciences, 2 Life sciences, 3 Education, 4 Design.
Primarily engaged in: Both futures studies and long-range planning.
Areas in which work done (%): 20 In organization concerned with other studies
including long-range planning, 30 In planning unit of a governmental agency, 50 As
academic, in teaching futures studies or long-range planning.
Direction of work in forecasting: Economic, Social, Cultural, Market, Educational,
Scientific, Environmental, Manpower, Resources, Population.
Direction of work in research: Environmental, Resource utilization, Value systems,
Social priorities, Policy research, Population, The family in the future, Futures methodology.
Direction of work in planning: Social, Urban, Regional, Economic, Environmental,
Resources.

Methods used: Extrapolation techniques, Contextual mapping, Brainstorming, Statistical models, Network analysis, Historical analogy, Operational models, Simulation, Own methods.
Time range of work: 5 - beyond year 2000.
Source of support for work (%): 30 Local government, 50 National government, 20 Foundations.
Work done for (%): 30 Local government, 50 National government, 20 Foundations.
Occupational function: 1 Professor, 2 Administrator, 3 Consultant.
Worked in government as: Elected official, Administrator.
Worked in education: Teaching, In research, In administration.   *(584)*

G ### 183. Madard Gabel
World Resources Inventory, 3500 Market St, Philadelphia, Pa 19104, USA.
Sex: Male.   *Age:* 25 - 29.
Educational qualification: Bachelor's degree.
Formal training: Design.
Informal training: Physical sciences, Humanities, Education, Arts, Cinema/television.
Primarily engaged in: Long-range planning.
Areas in which work done (%): 25 In organization concerned with other studies including long-range planning, 25 As individual consultant, 25 In organization primarily concerned with futures studies and/or long-range planning, 25 As academic, in teaching futures studies or long-range planning.
Direction of work in research: Alternative futures, Environmental, Resource utilization, Futures methodology.
Direction of work in planning: Technological, Social, Regional, Economic, Environmental, Resources.
Methods used: Probabilistic forecasting, Delphi techniques, Gaming, Cross impact analysis, Scenario building, Extrapolation techniques, Brainstorming, Statistical models, Expert panels, Relevance trees, Network analysis, Historical analogy, Individual expert forecasting, Simulation.
Time range of work: 5 - beyond year 2000.
Source of support for work (%): 50 Voluntary associations, 50 Other (unspecified).
Work done for (%): 100 Earth.
Occupational function: Research worker.
Worked in education: Teaching, In research, In administration.   *(345)*

184. André Gagnaux
c/o Sauter Ltd, Basle Switzerland Research and Development-Environmental Technics, Lorracherstreet 102, 4125 Riehen-CH, Switzerland.
Sex: Male.   *Age:* 50-59.
Educational qualification: Master's degree.
Formal training: 1 Engineering, 2 Law.
Informal training: Engineering.
Direction of work in research: Environmental.
Methods used: 1 Extrapolation techniques, 2 Operational models.
Time range of work: 5 - 10 years.
Source of support for work (%): 100 Private business.
Work done for (%): 100 Private business.
Occupational function: 1 Manager, 2 Engineering, 3 Research worker.
Worked in industry/business in: 1 Management, 2 Research and development.
Additional information: Concerned with technology assessment.   *(117)*

185. J.H. Gagnon

Dept of Sociology, University of New York, Stony Brook, NY, USA.
Sex: Male.   *Age:* 40-49.
Educational qualification: Doctoral degree.
Formal training: Social/behavioural sciences.
Informal training: l Life sciences, 2 Cinema/television.
Areas in which work done (%): 25 As individual consultant, 75 As academic, in
teaching futures studies or long-range planning.
Direction of work in forecasting: l Social, 2 Cultural, 3 Scientific.
Direction of work in research: l Value systems, 2 Social impacts of technology,
3 The individual in the future, 4 Social priorities.
Direction of work in planning: l Social, 2 Scientific, 3 Educational.
Methods used: l Scenario building, 2 Gaming, 3 Contextual mapping.
Time range of work: 5 - lO years.
Source of support for work (%): l5 Foundations, l5 International agencies, 7O University.
Occupational function: Research worker.
Worked in education: l In research, 2 Teaching.
Additional information: Concerned with theory of social change, gaming and simulation,
sociology of sciences.   *(7)*

186. Maria Cristina Gaja

IRADES, Istituto per la Ricerca e la Formazione al Futuro, Via Paisiello 6, Rome OO198,
Italy.
Sex: Female.   *Age:* 25-29.
Educational qualification: Master's degree.
Formal training: Political sciences.
Informal training: Documentation.
Primarily engaged in: Futures studies.
Areas in which work done (%): lOO In organization primarily concerned with futures
studies and/or long-range planning.
Direction of work in forecasting: Social.
Direction of work in research: l The individual in the future, 2 Alternative futures,
3 Futures methodology, 5 Social impacts of technology, 6 Value systems, 6 The family
in the future.
Time range of work: Beyond 2OOO A.D.
Source of support for work (%): lOO Private association.
Work done for (%): lOO Private association.
Occupational function: Research worker.
Worked in service sector: l Communication media, 2 Social welfare.
Additional information: Concerned with documentation and information in future studies.
                                                                               (416)

187. Johan Galtung

Chairman, Conflict and Peace Research, PO Box 1O7O, University of Oslo, Oslo 3, Norway.
Sex: Male.   *Age:* 40-49.
Educational qualification: Doctoral degree.
Formal training: Social/behavioural sciences, Mathematics.
Informal training: Physical sciences, Humanities.
Primarily engaged in: Futures studies.
Areas in which work done (%): 5 In planning unit of an international organization,
5O In organization primarily concerned with futures studies and/or long-range planning.

Direction of work in research: Alternative futures, Value systems, Social priorities, Policy research, The individual in the future, Futures methodology, International.
Direction of work in planning: Educational, Economic, Political, International.
Methods used: Thinking,dialogue.
Time range of work: IO - beyond year 2000.
Source of support for work (%): 30 International agencies, 70 National government.
Work done for (%): 30 International agencies.
Occupational function: I Research worker, 2 Educator, 3 Administrator.
Worked in education: I In research, 2 Teaching, 3 In administration.
Additional information: Concerned with alternative futures, world order models project, images of the world in the year 2000 --- World Indicators Program.   *(240)*

188. Peter C. Gardner

Abt Associates, 55 Wheeler St, Cambridge, Ma O2138, USA.
Sex: Male.   *Age:* 40-49.
Educational qualification: Master's degree.
Formal training: I Social/behavioural sciences, 2 Humanities, 3 Arts.
Informal training: I Education, 2 Design, 3 Cinema/television.
Areas in which work done (%): IO In planning unit of a business enterprise, 90 In organization concerned with other studies including long-range planning.
Direction of work in forecasting: Cultural.
Direction of work in research: I Social priorities, 2 Policy research, 3 Resource utilization, 4 Alternative futures.
Direction of work in planning: I Social, 2 Urban.
Methods used: I Operational models, 2 Expert panels, 3 Scenario building, 4 Brainstorming, 5 Gaming.
Time range of work: 5 - IO years.
Source of support for work (%): 5 Private business, 95 National government.
Work done for (%): 5 Private business, 95 National government.
Occupational function: I Administrator, 2 Manager, 3 Research worker.
Worked in industry/business in: I Management, 2 Research and development.
Worked in service sector: Social welfare.
Additional information: Concerned with design of social systems and related research (day care, elderly services, and others).   *(8)*

189. James E. Gates

Dept of Management, The University of Georgia, Athens, Ga 30601, USA.
Sex: Male.   *Age:* 60 or over.
Educational qualification: Doctoral degree.
Formal training: Social/behavioural sciences.
Informal training: Humanities.
Areas in which work done (%): 3 In planning unit of a government agency, 2 As individual consultant, 3 As academic, in teaching futures studies or long-range planning.
Direction of work in forecasting: Technological.
Direction of work in research: Social impacts of technology.
Direction of work in planning: Social.
Methods used: Probabilistic forecasting, Brainstorming, Expert panels, Individual expert forecasting.
Time range of work: 5 - 25 years.
Occupational function: Educator.

Worked in government as: Administrator.
Worked in industry/business in: Research and development.
Worked in education: 1 In administration, 2 Teaching, 3 In research.   *(214)*

190. Ernst Gehmacher

IFES, Fleischmarkt 3 - 6, Wien 1010, Austria.
Sex: Male.   *Age:* 40-49.
Educational qualification: Other graduate/professional degree.
Formal training: Social/behavioural sciences, Engineering.
Informal training: Life sciences, Mathematics, Journalism, Education.
Direction of work in forecasting: Social, Cultural, Market, Manpower.
Direction of work in research: Manpower, Value systems, Social priorities.
Direction of work in planning: Social, Regional, Political, Labour.
Methods used: Probabilistic forecasting, Delphi techniques, Scenario building,
Extrapolation techniques, Brainstorming, Statistical models, Expert panels, Simulation.
Time range of work: 5 - 25 years.
Source of support for work (%): 20 Private business, 30 National government,
50 Local government.
Work done for (%): 20 Private business, 30 National governments, 50 Local or regional
government,
Occupational function: 1 Manager, 2 Research worker, 3 Educator, Consultant.
Worked in industry/business in: Research and development, Consultancy.
Worked in education: In research.
Worked in service sector: Communication media.
Additional information: Not primarily engaged but concerned with long-term future
in social development and social indicators.   *(198)*

191. H.N. Van Gelder

Algemewe Bank Nederland NV, Vijzelstraat 32, Amsterdam, The Netherlands.
Sex: Male.   *Age:* 40-49.
Educational qualification: Other graduate/professional degree.
Formal training: Mathematics, Management, Economics.
Informal training: 1 Managerial service, Economics, 2 Mathematics, 3 Social/behavioural
sciences.
Areas in which work done (%): 100 In organization concerned with other studies
including long-range planning.
Direction of work in forecasting: 1 Economic, 2 Market, 3 Environmental, 4 Monetary.
Direction of work in research: 1 Resource utilization, 2 Alternative futures, 3 Consumer
affairs, 4 Environmental.
Direction of work in planning: Corporate.
Methods used: 1 Simulation, 2 Optimization, 3 Causal modelling, 4 Statistical models,
5 Extrapolation techniques.
Time range of work: 5 - 10 years.
Source of support for work (%): 100 Private business.
Work done for (%): 100 Private business.
Occupational function: 1 Manager, 2 Consultant, 3 Research worker.
Worked in industry/business in: 1 Planning, 2 Consultancy, 3 Management.
Additional information: Concerned with commercial and business forecasting and
planning; corporate planning.   *(279)*

192. Raymond Georis
Secretary General, European Cultural Foundation, Jan Van Goyenkade 5, 1007 Amsterdam, The Netherlands.
Sex: Male. *Age:* 40-49.
Educational qualification: Doctoral degree.
Formal training: Law, Education.
Informal training: Humanities, Social/behavioural sciences.
Primarily engaged in: Both futures studies and long-range planning.
Areas in which work done (%): 55 Organization primarily concerned with futures studies and/or long-range planning, 45 Organization concerned with other studies including long-range planning.
Direction of work in forecasting: 1 Educational, 2 Environmental, 3 Manpower, 4 Cultural.
Direction of work in research: 1 Alternative futures, 2 Environmental, 3 Manpower.
Direction of work in planning: 1 Educational, 2 Environmental, 3 Urban.
Methods used: 1 Cross impact analysis, 2 Brainstorming, 3 Expert panels, 4 Network analysis, 5 Scenario building, 6 Individual expert forecasting, 7 Extrapolation techniques, 8 Contextual mapping.
Time range of work: 5 - 25 years.
Source of support for work (%): 5 Local government, 25 National government, 30 Private business, 30 International agencies, 10 Foundations.
Work done for (%): 25 Local or Regional government, 35 National government, 40 International agencies.
Occupational function: 1 Manager, 2 Administrator.
Worked in education: 1 In research, 2 In administration. *(559)*

193. L. Gerardin
Research Director, Thomson/CSF, Blvd Haussmann 173, 75009 Paris, France.
Sex: Male. *Age:* 50-59.
Educational qualification: Master's degree.
Formal training: 1 Physical sciences, 2 Humanities.
Informal training: 1 Social/behavioural sciences, 2 History of sciences, 3 Education.
Primarily engaged in: Futures studies.
Areas in which work done (%): 100 In organization primarily concerned with futures studies and/or long-range planning.
Direction of work in research: 1 Alternative futures, 2 Social impacts of technology, 3 Futures methodology.
Methods used: 1 Structural modelling, 1 Cross impact analysis, 2 Scenario building, 3 Extrapolation techniques.
Time range of work: 10 - 25 years.
Source of support for work (%): 100 Private business.
Work done for (%): 50 National government, 50 Private business.
Occupational function: 1 Research worker, 2 Manager.
Worked in industry/business in: Research and development. *(440)*

194. J.I. Gershuny
Science Policy Research Unit, University of Sussex, Falmer, Brighton BN1 9RF, UK.
Sex: Male. *Age:* 25-29.
Educational qualification: Master's degree.
Formal training: Social/behavioural sciences.
Informal training: Mathematics.

Primarily engaged in: Futures studies.
Areas in which work done (%): 2O In organization primarily concerned with futures studies and/or long-range planning, 8O As individual.
Direction of work in forecasting: Transport.
Direction of work in research: I Futures methodology, 2 Policy research.
Methods used: I Scenario building, 2 Brainstorming, 3 Logical calculus, 4 Relevance Trees.
Time range of work: Beyond 2OOO AD.
Source of support for work (%): IOO National government.
Work done for (%): 75 National government, 25 University.
Occupational function: I Research worker, 2 Teaching, 3 Consultant.
Worked in education: I In research, 2 Teaching.   *(498)*

195. Norman Geschwind
Director, Pacific Asian Affairs Council, Pacific House, 2OO4 University Ave, Honolulu, Hi 96822, USA.
Sex: Male.   *Age:* 4O-49.
Educational qualification: Master's degree.
Formal training: Social/behavioural sciences.
Informal training: Social/behavioural sciences, Humanities, Education.
Areas in which work done (%): IOO In organization concerned with other studies including long-range planning.
Occupational function: I Administrator, 2 Educator.
Worked in education: I Teaching, 2 In administration.   *(299)*

196. Samir I. Ghabbour
Dept of Natural Resources, Institute of African Research and Studies, Cairo University, Giza, Egypt.
Sex: Male.   *Age:* 4O-49.
Educational qualification: Doctoral degree.
Formal training: I Life sciences, 2 Education.
Informal training: Social/behavioural sciences.
Direction of work in forecasting: Environmental, Resources.
Direction of work in research: Environmental, Resource utilization.
Direction of work in planning: Urban, Environmental, Resources.
Methods used: I Simulation, 2 Systems analysis.
Time range of work: 5 - beyond year 2OOO.
Source of support for work (%): IO National government, 5O International agencies.
Work done for (%): 5O National government, 5O International agencies.
Occupational function: I Research worker, 2 Educator.
Worked in education: I Teaching, 2 In research.
Additional information: Concerned with future of resource utilizations, alternative patterns of development.   *(242)*

197. Samir Ghosh
Director, Indian Institute of Human Sciences, 114 Sri Aurobindo Rd, PO Konnagar, WB, Near Calcutta, India.
Sex: Male.   *Age:* 4O-49.
Educational qualification: Doctoral degree.
Formal training: 2 Humanities, 3 Life sciences.
Informal training: I Life sciences, 2 Education.

Primarily engaged in: Both futures studies and long-range planning.
Areas in which work done (%): lO As individual consultant, 4O In organization primarily concerned with futures studies and/or long-range planning, lO In organization concerned with other studies including long-range planning, 2O As academic, in teaching futures studies or long-range planning.
Direction of work in forecasting: I Scientific, 2 Cultural, 3 Environmental.
Direction of work in research: I Social priorities, 2 Alternative futures, 3 Value systems.
Direction of work in planning: I Social, 2 Environmental, 3 Scientific.
Methods used: I Biological, 2 Scenario building, 3 Historical analogy, 4 Causal modelling.
Time range of work: Beyond 2OOO AD.
Source of support for work (%): lO Foundations.
Work done for (%): lO Foundations.
Occupational function: I Research worker, 2 Educator, 3 Consultant.
Worked in education: I Teaching, 2 In research.
Worked in service sector: Social welfare.
Additional information: Concerned with biological model of future, future and sex differences. *(9)*

198. R.L. Gillen
Vice President of Strategic Planning and Development, Macmillan Bloedel Ltd, 1O75 W Georgia St, Vancouver, BC, Canada.
Sex: Male.　　*Age:* 4O-48.
Educational qualification: Master's degree.
Formal training: I Social/behavioural sciences, 2 Humanities.
Informal training: I Social/behavioural sciences, 2 Humanities.
Primarily engaged in: Both futures studies and long-range planning.
Areas in which work done (%): lOO In planning unit of a business enterprise.
Direction of work in research: Resource utilization.
Direction of work in planning: I Corporate, 2 Economic.
Methods used: Probabilistic forecasting, Delphi techniques, Extrapolation techniques, Brainstorming, Historical analogy, Individual expert forecasting.
Time range of work: 5 - 25 years.
Work done for (%): lOO Private business.
Occupational function: Administrator.
Worked in industry/business in: I Consultancy, 2 Management, 3 Planning. *(372)*

199. N. Gillett
35 Berkeley Sq, Bristol 8, UK.
Sex: Male.　　*Age:* 5O-59.
Educational qualification: Other graduate/professional degree.
Formal training: Education.
Informal training: I Education, 2 Humanities.
Areas in which work done (%): lO Seminar on school and community.
Direction of work in forecasting: I Social, 2 Educational.
Direction of work in research: I Social priorities, 2 The family in the future, 3 Environmental.
Direction of work in planning: Educational.
Methods used: Extrapolation techniques, Brainstorming, Individual expert forecasting.
Time range of work: lO - 25 years.
Occupational function: Educator.

Worked in education: I Teaching, 2 In administration.
Additional information: Concerned with hopes and expectations of pupils and parents regarding the future of life in the school catchment area.   *(339)*

200. Gail P. Gilroy

American Management Associates, PO Box 88, Hamilton, NY 13346, USA.
Sex: Female.   *Age:* 40-49.
Educational qualification: Some college or less.
Formal training: Retailing.
Informal training: Journalism.
Primarily engaged in: Long-range planning.
Areas in which work done (%): 90 Library research.
Direction of work in planning: I Corporate, 2 Educational, 3 Social.
Time range of work: 5 - IO years.
Occupational function: I Administrator, 2 Research worker.
Worked in industry/business in: I Management, 2 Research and development.
Worked in education: Teaching.   *(225)*

201. Jerome C. Glenn

Executive Director, Future Options Room, 3701 Connecticut Ave, NW, Washington DC, 20008, USA.
Sex: Male.   *Age:* 30-39.
Educational qualification: Master's degree.
Formal training: I Futuristics, 2 Education, 3 Social/behavioural sciences, 5 Life sciences.
Informal training: I Futuristics, 2 Social/behavioural sciences, 3 Education, 4 Cinema/television, 5 Physical sciences, 6 Humanities.
Primarily engaged in: Both futures studies and long-range planning.
Areas in which work done (%): 5 As individual consultant, 5 As academic, in teaching futures studies or long-range planning, IO Futures consultancy, 80 In organization primarily eoncerned with futures studies and/or long-range planning.
Direction of work in forecasting: I Holistic, 2 Social, 3 Technological, 4 Environmental, 5 Resources, 6 Educational.
Direction of work in research: I Social priorities, 2 Futures methodology, 3 Policy research, 4 Alternative futures, 5 Social impacts of technology.
Direction of work in planning: I Corporate, 2 Educational.
Methods used: I System analysis, 2 Causal modelling, 3 Operational models, 4 Brainstorming, 5 Extrapolation techniques, 6 Scenario building, 7 Cross impact analysis, 8 Probabilistic forecasting, 9 Expert panels, IO Individual expert forecasting, 11 Delphi techniques, 12 Contextual mapping, 13 Historical analogy, 14 Network analysis.
Time range of work 5 - beyond year 2000.
Source of support for work (%): IO Private business, 20 National government, 70 Foreign governments.
Work done for (%): 20 National government, 70 Foreign governments, IO Private business.
Occupational function: I Director/co-ordinator, 2 Manager, 3 Administrator, 4 Educator, 5 Research worker, 6 Consultant.
Worked in government as: Administrator.
Worked in industry/business in: Consultancy.
Worked in education: I Teaching, 2 In research, 3 In administration.
Worked in service sector: I Design, 2 Medicine, 3 Communication media.   *(296)*

2

202. Pierre Goftschin

5 Place de la Cathédrale, 1005 Lausanne, Switzerland.
Sex: Male.   *Age:* 50-59.
Educational qualification: Doctoral degree.
Formal training: Social/behavioural sciences, Education, Business.
Informal training: Social/behavioural sciences, Humanities.
Primarily engaged in: Both futures studies and long-range planning.
Areas in which work done (%): 10 As individual consultant, 30 Other business and educational fields, 60 As academic, in teaching futures studies or long-range planning.
Direction of work in forecasting: Technological, Economic, Social, Market, Educational, Manpower.
Direction of work in research: Manpower, Social priorities, Futures methodology.
Direction of work in planning: Educational, Economic, Corporate.
Methods used: Delphi techniques, Cross impacts analysis, Scenario building, Extrapolation techniques, Brainstorming, Statistical models, Expert panels, Relevance trees, Network analysis, Historical analogy, Individual expert forecasting.
Time range of work: 5 - beyond year 2000.
Source of support for work (%): 20 Private business, 80 University and business school.
Work done for (%): 20 Private business, 80 University and business school.
Occupational function: Administrator, Educator, Consultant.
Worked in industry/business in: Consultancy.
Worked in education: Teaching, In research, In administration.   *(253)*

203. Irwin Goldman

Director of Corporate Planning, Merck and Company, Inc, Bldg 32, 5th Floor, Rahway, NJ 07065, USA.
Sex: Male.   *Age:* 50-59.
Educational qualification: Master's degree.
Formal training: Engineering.
Informal training: 1 Social/behavioural sciences, 2 Education, 3 Physical sciences.
Primarily engaged in: Long-range planning.
Areas in which work done (%): 100 In planning unit of a business enterprise.
Direction of work in forecasting: 1 Market, 2 Economic, 3 Social.
Direction of work in research: 2 Value systems, 3 Social priorities.
Direction of work in planning: Corporate.
Methods used: 1 Individual expert forecasting; 2 Scenario building, 3 Expert panels, 4 Delphi techniques, 5 Reading, meetings, thinking etc.
Time range of work: 5 - 10 years.
Source of support for work (%): 100 Private business.
Work done for (%): 100 Private business.
Occupational function: 1 Corporate planner.
Worked in industry/business in: Management, Research and development, Planning.
Worked in education: Teaching.   *(62)*

204. Maurice Goldsmith

Director, Science Policy Foundation, Benjamin Franklin House, 36 Craven Street, London, WC2N 5NG, UK.
Sex: Male.   *Age:* Over 60.
Educational qualification: Bachelor's degree.
Formal training: 1 Social/behavioural sciences, 2 Physical sciences, 3 Journalism, 4 Cinema/television.

8

Informal training: I Life sciences, 2 Humanities, 3 Education, 4 Arts, 5 Mathematics.
Areas in which work done (%): 20 Organization concerned with other studies including long-range planning, 5 Academic in teaching futures studies or long-range planning.
Direction of work in forecasting: All types (see Directory guide), plus science policy.
Methods used: I Brainstorming, 2 Extrapolation techniques, 3 Expert panels, 4 Probabilistic forecasting, 5 Delphi techniques.
Time range of work: 5 - 10 years.
Source of support for work (%): 5 Voluntary associations.
Work done for (%): 20 Voluntary associations.
Occupational function: I Consultant, 2 Administrator, 3 Educator.   *(577)*

205. Lincoln Gordon

Resources for the Future, 1775 Massachusetts Ave, NW, Washington DC 20036, USA.
Sex: Male.   *Age:* Over 60.
Educational qualification: Doctoral degree.
Formal training: Social/behavioural sciences.
Informal training: Social/behavioural sciences, Physical sciences.
Primarily engaged in: Futures studies.
Areas in which work done (%): 100 Organization primarily concerned with futures studies and/or long-range planning.
Direction of work in research: I Resource utilization, 2 Policy research, 3 Population, 4 Alternative futures.
Methods used: I Expert panels, 2 Statistical modelling, 3 Historical analogy.
Time range of work: 10 - 25 years.
Source of support for work (%): 100 Foundations.
Work done for (%): 10 National government, 10 International agencies, 80 Foundations.
Occupational function: Research worker.
Worked in government as: I Administrator, 2 Researcher.
Worked in education: I Teaching, 2 In administration, 3 In research.
Additional information: Concerned with international implications of structural changes in growth patterns, as influences by resource contraints and shifting preferences.   *(560)*

206. Theodore J. Gordon

President, The Futures Group, 124 Hebron Ave, Glastonbury, Ct 06033, USA.
Sex: Male.   *Age:* 40-49.
Educational qualification: Master's degree.
Formal training: Engineering.
Informal training: Physical sciences, Social/behavioural sciences, Mathematics.
Primarily engaged in: Both futures studies and long-range planning.
Areas in which work done (%): 100 In organization primarily concerned with futures studies and/or long-range planning.
Direction of work in forecasting: Technological, Economic, Social, Scientific, Environmental.
Direction of work in research: Social impacts of technology, Alternative futures, Consumer affairs, Value systems, Social priorities, Policy research, The individual in the future, The family in the future, Futures methodology.
Direction of work in planning: Scientific, Technological, Social, Corporate.
Methods used: Probabilistic forecasting, Delphi techniques, Cross impacts analysis, Scenario building, Extrapolation techniques, Brainstorming, Statistical models, Expert panels, Relevance trees, Network analysis, Historical analogy, Operational models, Simulation, Causal modelling.

Time range of work: Beyond 2000 AD.
Source of support for work (%): 50 Private business, 50 National government.
Work done for (%): 50 National government, 50 Private business.
Occupational function: I Administrator, 2 Research worker.
Worked in industry/business in: I Management, 2 Planning, 3 Research and development.
Additional information: Concerned with futures research, policy analysis, and
technological assessment.   *(310)*

207. Umberto Gori

International Relations, Universita Degli Studi di Firense, Facolta di Scienze Politiche,
C. Alfieri, Via Laura 48, 50121 Florence, Italy.
Sex: Male.   *Age:* 40-49.
Educational qualification: Doctoral degree.
Formal training: I Social/behavioural sciences, 2 Law.
Informal training: I Social/behavioural sciences, 2 Humanities, 3 Education, 4 Law.
Primarily engaged in: Both futures studies and long-range planning.
Areas in which work done (%): 20 As individual consultant, 40 In planning unit of a
governmental agency, 40 As academic, in teaching futures studies or long-range planning.
Direction of work in forecasting: International relations.
Direction of work in research: I Policy research, 2 Futures methodology, 3 Alternative
futures.
Direction of work in planning: Political.
Methods used: I Simulation, 2 Scenario building, 3 Probabilistic forecasting, 3 Delphi
techniques, 3 Statistical models, 3 Historical analogy, 3 Operational models, 3 Individual
expert forecasting.
Time range of work: 5 - 10 years.
Source of support for work (%): 50 National government.
Work done for (%): 40 National government.
Occupational function: I Research worker, 2 Educator, 3 Consultant.
Worked in government as: Researcher.
Worked in education: I Teaching, 2 In research, 3 In administration.   *(532)*

208. Roderic Gorney

Director, Program on Psychosocial Adaptation and the Future, Dept of Psychiatry,
University of California, 760 Westwood Plaza, Los Angeles, Ca 90024, USA.
Sex: Male.   *Age:* 50-59.
Educational qualification: Doctoral degree.
Formal training: Life sciences.
Informal training: Cinema/television, Life sciences, Social/behavioural sciences,
Humanities, Arts.
Primarily engaged in: Futures studies.
Areas in which work done (%): 20 In organization primarily concerned with futures
studies and/or long-range planning, 5 As individual consultant, 10 As academic, in
teaching futures studies or long-range planning, 65 Professor of Psychiatry.
Direction of work in forecasting: Psychosocial.
Direction of work in research: I Social priorities, 2 Value systems, 3 Alternative
futures.
Direction of work in planning: I Social, 2 Political.
Methods used: I Survey Research, 2 Expert panels, 3 Individual expert forecasting,
Field experiment, Literature-based experiment.
Time range of work (%): 10 - 25 years.

Source of support for work (%): 5 Private business, 85 Foundations, IO UCLA Dept of Psychiatry.
Work done for (%): 5 Private business, 5 Foundations, 3O UCLA Dept of Psychiatry.
Occupational function: I Educator, 2 Consultant, 3 Administrator.
Worked in education as: I Teaching, 2 In research, 3 In administration.
Worked in service area as: I Medicine, 2 Communications media.
Additional information: Concerned with mass entertainment (television/movies), both as social indicators and as a vehicle for action research.   *(551)*

2O9. George Gowans

Chief, Planning and Program Policy, National Park Service, 19th and C St, NW, Washington, DC 2O24O, USA.
Sex: Male.   *Age:* 4O-49.
Educational qualification: Bachelor's degree.
Formal training: Engineering.
Informal training: Mathematics, Design.
Primarily engaged in: Long-range planning.
Areas in which work done (%): IOO In planning unit of a governmental agency.
Direction of work in forecasting: Environmental.
Direction of work in research: I Environmental, 2 Policy research.
Direction of work in planning: I Environmental, 2 Regional, 3 Social, 4 Economic.
Methods used: I Individual expert forecasting, 2 Statistical models, 3 Brainstorming, 4 Expert panels.
Time range of work: IO - 25 years.
Source of support for work (%): IOO National government.
Work done for (%): IOO National government.
Occupational function: I Manager, 2 Administrator.
Worked in government as: Administrator.
Additional information: Concerned with natural and historical resources, planning and management policy.   *(27)*

21O. Giovanni Gozzer

4O Via Appiano, Rome, Italy.
Sex: Male.   *Age:* 5O-59.
Educational qualification: Doctoral degree.
Formal training: Humanities.
Informal training: Education.
Areas in which work done (%): 8O As individual consultant.
Direction of work in planning: Educational.
Methods used: Eclectic approach.
Time range of work: IO - 25 years.
Occupational function: Consultant.
Worked in government as: Administrator.
Worked in education: Teaching.
Additional information: Concerned with future of education.   *(115)*

211. O.T. Grande

Norwegian Society for Future Studies, PO Box 84O1 Hammersborg, Oslo 1, Norway.
Sex: Male.   *Age:* 4O-49.
Educational qualification: Doctoral degree.

Formal training: I Social/behavioural sciences, 2 Life sciences, 3 Design, 4 Education,
5 Humanities.
Informal training: I Journalism, 2 Law, 3 Mathematics.
Primarily engaged in: Both futures studies and long-range planning.
Areas in which work done (%): IOO In organization primarily concerned with futures
studies and/or long-range planning.
Direction of work in forecasting: I Social, 2 Economic, 3 Cultural.
Direction of work in research: I Alternative futures, 2 Resource utilization, 3 Social
priorities, 4 Value systems, 5 The family in the future, 6 The individual in the future,
7 Population, 8 Futures methodology, 9 Policy research, IO Manpower.
Direction of work in planning: I Regional, 2 Social, 3 Economic.
Methods used: I Cross impact analysis, 2 Scenario building, 3 Statistical models,
4 Expert panels, 5 Operational models, 6 Network analysis.
Time range of work: 5 - beyond year 2OOO.
Source of support for work (%): IOO Voluntary associations.
Work done for (%): 5 Foundations, I5 International agencies, I5 Private business,
I5 Voluntary associations, 25 Local or regional government, 25 National government.
Occupational function: I Manager, 2 Administrator, 3 Consultant, 4 Educator,
5 Research worker.
Worked in government as: I Researcher, 2 Administrator, 3 Elected official.
Worked in industry/business in: I Management, 2 Research and development, 3 Planning,
4 Consultancy.
Worked in education: I Teaching, 2 In research, 3 In administration.   *(331)*

212. Edward J. Green

Chairman, Planning Dynamics, Inc, Babb Bldg, 85O Ridge Ave, Pittsburgh, Pa 15212, USA.
Sex: Male.   *Age:* 6O or over.
Educational qualification: Other graduate/professional degree.
Formal training: I Public administration, 2 Humanities.
Informal training: Social/behavioural sciences.
Primarily engaged in: Both futures studies and long-range planning.
Areas in which work done (%): IO In planning unit of a business enterprise, IO In
planning unit of a governmental agency, 2O As individual consultant, 2O As academic,
in teaching futures studies or long-range planning, 4O In organization primarily
concerned with futures studies and/or long-range planning.
Direction of work in forecasting: I Technological, 2 Economic, 3 Environmental,
4 Educational, 5 Health care.
Direction of work in research: I Futures methodology, 2 Policy research, 3 Resource
utilization.
Direction of work in planning: I Corporate, 2 Health care, 3 Educational, 4 Scientific,
5 Military.
Methods used: I Probabilistic forecasting, 2 Scenario building.
Time range of work: 5 - IO years.
Source of support for work (%): IO Hospitals, IO National government, IO Voluntary
associations, 2O Foundations, 5O Private business.
Work done for (%): IO National government, 2O Voluntary association, 2O Hospitals,
5O Private business.
Occupational function: I Consultant, 2 Educator.
Worked in government as: I Administrator, 2 Elected official, 3 Researcher.
Worked in industry/business in: I Planning, 2 Consultancy, 3 Management.
Worked in education: Teaching.
Worked in service sector: I Religion, 2 Communication media.   *(348)*

213. James Green

Dept of Economics and Statistics, College of Business Administration, University of Georgia, Athens, Ga 3O6O1, USA.
Sex: Male.   *Age:* 5O-59.
Educational qualification: Doctoral degree.
Formal training: Social/behavioural sciences.
Areas in which work done (%): 2O As individual consultant, 8O As academic, in teaching futures studies or long-range planning.
Direction of work in forecasting: I Economic, 2 Market, 3 Resources, 4 Technological.
Direction of work in research: I Social impacts of technology, 2 Resource utilization 3 Value systems, 4 Policy research.
Direction of work in planning: I Economic, 2 Corporate, 3 Environmental, 4 Technological, 5 Social, 6 Urban.
Methods used: I Scenario building, 2 Extrapolation techniques.
Time range of work: 5 - IO years.
Source of support for work (%): IO Local government, IO Private business, 8O University.
Work done for (%): IO Local or regional government, IO Private business, 8O University.
Occupational function: I Educator, 2 Consultant.
Worked in education: I Teaching, 2 In research.
Additional information: Concerned with economic structure and functioning.   *(56)*

214. Thomas Green

PO Box 24 Pompey, NY 13138, USA.
Sex: Male.   *Age:* 4O-49.
Educational qualification: Other graduate/professional degree.
Formal training: Philosophy.
Informal training: I Education, 2 Theology, 3 Social/behavioural sciences, 4 Humanities.
Areas in which work done (%): 5 In planning unit of a business enterprise, IO As individual consultant, IO In organization concerned with other studies including long-range planning, 7O Academics.
Direction of work in forecasting: I Educational, 2 Social, 3 Values.
Direction of work in research: I Policy research, 2 Value systems, 3 The individual in the future.
Direction of work in planning: I Educational, 2 Political, 3 Social, 5 Urban.
Methods used: I Scenario building, 2 Brainstorming, 3 Cross impact analysis, 4 Extrapolation techniques, 5 Probabilistic forecasting, 6 Network analysis, 7 Historical analogy, 8 Individual expert forecasting.
Time range of work: IO - 25 years.
Source of support for work (%): IOO University.
Work done for (%): 2 Voluntary associations, 5 Private business, 5 Foundations.
Occupational function: I Educator, 2 Consultant.
Worked in government as: I Researcher.
Worked in education: I Teaching, 2 In research, 3 In administration.
Worked in service sector: Religion.
Additional information: Concerned with education, government policy and problems of value change.   *(196)*

215. A. Gregory

Dept of Chemical Engineering, The University of Aston in Birmingham, B4 7ET, UK.
Sex: Male.   *Age:* 6O or over.
Educational qualification: Other graduate/professional degree.

Formal training: Physical sciences.
Informal training: I Engineering, 2 Social/behavioural sciences, 3 Design, 4 Education.
Direction of work in forecasting: I Technological, 2 Economic, 3 Resources, 4 Market.
Direction of work in research: I Futures methodology, 2 Resource utilization,
3 Alternative futures, 4 Social impacts of technology.
Direction of work in planning: I Technological, 2 Resources, 3 Corporate.
Methods used: I Morphological methods, 2 Extrapolation techniques, 3 Brainstorming,
4 Delphi techniques, 5 Scenario building, 6 Gaming.
Time range of work: IO - 25 years.
Work done for (%): I5 Local or regional government, I5 National government,
7O Private business.
Occupational function: I Educator, 2 Consultant, 3 Research worker.
Worked in industry/business in: I Management, 2 Research and development.
Worked in education: I Teaching, 2 In research.
Additional information: Concerned with industrial development, particularly associated
with new technology.   *(192)*

216. Miguel Grinberg
C.C. Central 1332, Capital-Argentina.
Sex: Male.   *Age:* 30-39.
Educational qualification: Bachelor's degree.
Formal training: I Journalism, 2 Cinema/television, 3 Education.
Informal training: Social/behavioural sciences.
Primarily engaged in: Both futures studies and long-range planning.
Areas in which work done (%): IOO As individual consultant.
Direction of work in forecasting: I Cultural, 2 Environmental, 3 Educational.
Direction of work in research: I Alternative futures, 2 Environmental, 3 The individual
in the future.
Direction of work in planning: I Educational, 2 Environmental.
Methods used: I Brainstorming, 2 Intuition.
Time range of work: 5 - IO years.
Source of support for work (%): IOO Personal.
Work done for (%): 5O Voluntary associations, 5O Personal.
Occupational function: Research worker.
Worked in education: In research.
Worked in service sector: Communication Media.   *(289)*

217. R.M.E.M. van der Grinten
Werkgroep Globale Dynamica, PO Box 513 Technische Hogeschool HG 8, 12,
Eindhoven, The Netherlands.
Sex: Male.   *Age:* 40-49.
Educational qualification: Doctoral degree.
Formal training: Engineering.
Informal training: Physical sciences, Mathematics, Economics.
Primarily engaged in: Long-range planning.
Areas in which work done (%): IO As academic, in teaching futures studies or long-range
planning, 3O Teaching control engineering, 6O In planning unit of a business enterprise.
Direction of work in forecasting: I Economic, 2 Market, 3 Technological.
Direction of work in research: I Consumer affairs, 2 Resource utilization, 3 Environmental.
Direction of work in planning: I Corporate, 2 Economic, 3 Resources, 4 Scientific.
Methods used: I Extrapolation techniques, 2 Operational models, 3 Simulation,

4 Scenario building.
Time range of work: 5 - l0 years.
Source of support for work (%):   l00 Private business.
Work done for (%):   l0 National government, 30 Voluntary associations, 60 Private business.
Occupational function: l Manager, 2 Consultant.
Worked in industry/business in: l Research and development, 2 Planning.
Worked in education: l Teaching, 2 In research.   *(147)*

218. Robert E. Grochau

The Lutheran Theological Seminary, Gettysburg, Pa, USA.
Sex: Male.   *Age:* 40-49.
Educational qualification: Master's degree.
Formal training: l Religious, 2 Humanities, 3 Social/behavioural sciences.
Informal training: l Social/behavioural sciences, 2 Design.
Direction of work in forecasting: Cultural, Environmental.
Direction of work in research: l Value systems, 2 The family in the future, 3 Alternative .futures.
Direction of work in planning: Religious.
Methods used: l Historical analogy, 2 Causal modelling, 3 Contextual mapping, 4 Probabilistic forecasting.
Time range of work: 5 - l0 years.
Source of support for work (%): l00 The church.
Work done for (%): l00 Voluntary associations.
Occupational function: Administrator, Educator.
Worked in service sector: Religion.   *(82)*

219. Paul J. Grogan

Professor of Engineering, University Extension, Project Destiny, University of Wisconsin, Madison, Wi 53706, USA.
Sex: Male.   *Age:* 50-59.
Educational qualification: Master's degree.
Formal training: Engineering.
Informal training: l Mathematics, 2 Design, 3 Physical sciences.
Areas in which work done (%): l0 As individual consultant, l5 In organization primarily concerned with futures studies and/or long-range planning, l0 As academic, in teaching futures studies or long-range planning.
Direction of work in forecasting: l Technological, 2 Environmental, 3 Economic, 3 Resources, 4 Educational.
Direction of work in research: l Alternative futures, 2 Environmental, 3 Resource utilization, 4 Futures methodology, 5 Social impacts of technology.
Direction of work in planning: l Economic, 2 Urban, 2 Environmental, 3 Scientific, 3 Regional, 4 Technological.
Methods used: l Delphi techniques, 2 Probabilistic forecasting, 3 Cross impact analysis, 4 Scenario building, 5 Extrapolation techniques, 6 Individual expert forecasting, 7 Simulation, 8 Relevance trees.
Time range of work: l0 - 25 years.
Source of support for work (%): 25 Private business, 75 State university.
Work done for (%): 25 Local or regional government, 25 National government, 25 Private business, 25 Voluntary associations.
Occupational function: l Educator, 2 Consultant.

Worked in government as: Administrator.
Worked in education: Teaching.
Additional information: Concerned with application of science and technology, for
public need and environmental protection. *(129)*

220. Martin Grotjahn
410 North Bedford Drive, Beverly Hills,Ca 90210, USA.
Sex: Male. *Age:* 60 or over.
Educational qualification: Doctoral degree.
Formal training: Medical doctor.
Informal training: Psychiatry, Psychoanalysis.
Direction of work in forecasting: Psychoanalysis.
Direction of work in research: Psychoanalysis.
Methods used: Individual expert forecasting.
Time range of work: 10 - 25 years.
Occupational function: Psychiatric therapist.
Worked in service sector: Medicine. *(10)*

221. Kenneth Grundy
Dept of Political Science, Case Western Reserve University, Cleveland, Oh 44106, USA.
Sex: Male. *Age:* 30-39.
Formal training: Social/behavioural sciences.
Informal training: Social/behavioural sciences.
Direction of work in research: 1 Value systems, 2 Alternative futures, 3 Social
impacts of technology.
Methods used: 1 Scenario building, 2 Individual expert forecasting, 3 Causal modelling.
Time range of work: 10 - 25 years.
Source of support for work (%): 100 University.
Occupational function: Educator.
Worked in education: 1 Teaching, 2 In research, 3 In administration. *(224)*

222. Georges Gueron
21 Rue Rollin, 75005 Paris, France.
Sex: Male. *Age:* 60 or over.
Educational qualification: Master's degree.
Formal training: Law.
Informal training: Management.
Primarily engaged in: Both futures studies and long-range planning.
Areas in which work done (%): 50 As individual consultant, 50 Encouraging
organizations concerned with the future.
Direction of work in research: Social impacts of technology, Alternative futures, Social
priorities.
Methods used: General reflection.
Time range of work: 5 - beyond year 2000.
Source of support for work (%): 25 Voluntary associations, 75 Private business.
Work done for (%): 50 Private business, 50 Voluntary associations.
Occupational function: Consultant.
Worked in industry/business in: Management, Consultancy.
Additional information: Concerned with conditions in our era which require decision
and action. *(205)*

223. Claude Guillemin

Directeur, Service Geologique National (BRGM) BP 6009, 45018 Orleans Cedex, France.
Sex: Male.   *Age:* 50-59.
Educational qualification: Doctoral degree.
Formal training: Physical sciences.
Informal training: Social/behavioural sciences.
Direction of work in forecasting: 1 Technological, 1 Resources, 2 Environmental, 3 Economic.
Direction of work in research: 1 Resource utilization.
Direction of work in planning: 1 Resources, 2 Environmental.
Methods used: 1 Scenario building, 2 Brainstorming, 3 Expert panels.
Time range of work: 5 - beyond year 2000.
Source of support for work (%): 100 National government.
Work done for (%): 90 National government.
Occupational function: Manager.
Worked in government as: 1 Researcher, 2 Administrator.
Additional information: Concerned with long-range resource analysis.   *(507)*

224. L. Gunawardena

41 2 - 2 Gregory's Rd, Columbo, Sri Lanka.
Sex: Female.   *Age:* 40-49.
Educational qualification: Master's degree.
Formal training: Social/behavioural sciences.
Informal training: Education, Cook.
Primarily engaged in: Long-range planning and futures studies.
Areas in which work done (%): 100 for a development studies organization.
Direction of work in research: Social impacts of technology, Alternative futures, Resource utilization, Social priorities, Population, The family in the future.
Direction of work in planning: Technological, Educational, Economic, Environmental, Labour, Resources.
Methods used: 1 Historical analogy, 2 Operational models, 3 Expert panels.
Time range of work: 5 - 10 years.
Source of support for work (%): 50 Foundations, 50 International agencies.
Occupational function: Research worker, Consultant.
Worked in government as: Researcher.
Worked in industry/business in: Research and development.
Worked in service sector: Social welfare.
Additional information: Concerned with education, population, the role and problems of women in contemporary Sri Lanka society, health and administration, plantation agriculture, domestic agrcculture, institutions, industry and technology.   *(257)*

H 225. Ernst B. Haas

Dept of Political Science, University of California, Berkeley, Ca 94720, USA.
Sex: Male.   *Age:* 50-59.
Educational qualification: Doctoral degree.
Formal training: Social/behavioural sciences.
Informal training: Humanities.
Areas in which work done (%): 100 As academic.
Direction of work in research: Social impacts of technology, Value systems, Social priorities.

Methods used: All methods (see Directory guide).
Time range of work: 5 - 10 years.
Source of support for work (%): 100 Foundations.
Work done for (%): 100 General audiences.
Occupational function: Educator.
Worked in education: Teaching, In research, In administration.
Additional information: Concerned with international aspects of technology assessment and science policy. *(71)*

226. E. Halal

School of Business, American University, Washington, DC 20016, USA.
Sex: Male.   *Age:* 40-49.
Educational qualification: Doctoral degree.
Formal training: 1 Social/behavioural sciences, 2 Engineering.
Informal training: 1 Social/behavioural sciences, 2 Engineering, 3 Humanities, 4 Education.
Primarily engaged in: Both futures studies and long-range planning.
Areas in which work done (%): 20 As individual consultant, 30 In planning unit of an international organization, 30 Academic work in complex organizations and R & D management, 20 In organization concerned with other studies including long-range planning.
Direction of work in forecasting: 1 Social organization, 2 Technological, 3 Economic, 4 Social.
Direction of work in research: 1 Organization, 3 Social impacts of technology, 3 Manpower, 4 Value systems, 5 Social priorities.
Direction of work in planning: 1 Organization, 2 Corporate, 3 Technological, 4 Economic.
Methods used: 1 Causal modelling, 2 Individual expert forecasting, 3 Scenario building, 4 Delphi techniques.
Time range of work: 10 - 25 years.
Source of support for work (%): 20 Private business, 20 National government, 60 University, (Salary).
Work done for (%): 10 Local or regional government, 30 National government, 30 Private business, 30 University.
Occupational function: 1 Educator, 2 Consultant, 3 Research worker.
Worked in government as: Administrator.
Worked in industry/business in: 1 Management, 2 Consultancy, 3 Research and development.
Worked in education: 1 Teaching, 2 In research. *(170)*

227. L.J. Hale

Director, Centre for Human Ecology, 57 George Square, Edinburgh EH8 9JU, UK.
Sex: Male.   *Age:* 50-59.
Educational qualification: Doctoral degree.
Formal training: Life sciences.
Informal training: 1 Education, 2 Social/behavioural sciences.
Time range of work: 5 - 25 years.
Source of support for work (%): 100 University.
Occupational function: 1 Manager, 2 Educator.
Worked in education: Teaching, In research, In administration. *(462)*

228. Peter Hall

Director, Reading University, Dept of Geography, Urban System Research Unit, Whiteknights, Reading RG6 2AF, UK.
Sex: Male.   *Age:* 40-49.

Educational qualification: Doctoral degree.
Formal training: Social/behavioural sciences.
Informal training: Journalism, Design.
Primarily engaged in: Both futures studies and long-range planning.
Areas in which work done (%): 40 In organization concerned with other studies including long-range planning, 60 As academic, in teaching futures studies or long-range planning.
Direction of work in forecasting: I Environmental, 2 Social, 3 Cultural.
Direction of work in research: I Alternative futures, 2 Environmental, 3 Policy research, 4 Value systems, 5 Futures methodology.
Direction of work in planning: I Urban, 2 Regional, 3 Corporate.
Methods used: I Scenario building, 2 Brainstorming, 3 Statistical models, 4 Simulation.
Time range of work: IO - 25 years.
Source of support for work (%): IOO Foundations.
Work done for (%): IOO Foundations.
Occupational function: I Research worker, 2 Educator, 3 Administrator.
Worked in education: I In research, 2 Teaching, 3 In administration.
Additional information: Concerned with the Europe 2000 Project; and analysis of major planning decisions from a long-term planning viewpoint.   *(315)*

229. V.D. Hallett

International Secretary General Police Headquarters, Sutton Rd, Maidstone, KE 15 Kent, UK.
Sex: Male.   *Age:* 50-59.
Educational qualification: Other graduate/professional degree.
Formal training: I Police, 2 Law, 3 Social/behavioural sciences.
Informal training: I Police, 2 Law, 3 Social/behavioural sciences.
Areas in which work done (%): 50 In planning unit of an international organization, 50 In organization concerned with other studies including long-range planning.
Direction of work in forecasting: I Police, 2 Educational, 3 Social.
Direction of work in research: I Police, 2 Social priorities.
Direction of work in planning: I Police, 2 Resources, 3 Educational.
Methods used: Historical analogy.
Time range of work: 5 - IO years.
Source of support for work (%): IOO Voluntary associations.
Work done for (%): IOO Voluntary associations.
Occupational function: Administrator.
Worked in service sector: Law.   *(389)*

230. Carl Halvorson

Contractor and Developer, Halvorson-Mason Corp, PO Box 1449, Portland, Oregon, USA.
Sex: Male.   *Age:* 50-59.
Educational qualification: Some college or less.
Formal training: Engineering.
Informal training: Journalism.
Direction of work in forecasting: Resources.
Direction of work in research: Resource utilization.
Methods used: Brainstorming.
Time range of work: Beyond 2000 AD.
Occupational function: Entrepreneur,
Worked in industry/business in: Management.   *(90)*

231. May Maury Harding
Director, Centre for the Study of Alternate Futures, Southwestern at Memphis,
2000 North Parkway, Memphis, Tn 38112, USA.
Sex: Female.　*Age:* 40-49.
Educational qualification: Bachelor's degree.
Formal training: I Humanities, 2 Mathematics.
Informal training: I Social/behavioural sciences, 2 Design, 3 Humanities, 4 Education.
Primarily engaged in: Both futures studies and long-range planning.
Areas in which work done (%): IO As academic, in teaching futures studies or long-range planning, I5 In organization continuing education programs, 75 In organization primarily concerned with futures studies and/or long-range planning.
Direction of work in planning: I Urban, 2 Regional, 3 Social.
Methods used: I Cross impact analysis, 2 Delphi techniques, 3 Probabilistic forecasting, 4 Scenario building, 5 Extrapolation techniques, 6 Network analysis, 7 Operational models.
Time range of work: IO - 25 years.
Source of support for work (%): 5 Voluntary associations, IO Local government, I5 University, 7O Foundations.
Work done for (%): 3O Voluntary associations, 7O Local or regional government.
Occupational function: I Administrator, 2 Educator. 3 Manager.
Worked in education: I In administration, 2 Teaching.　　　　*(401)*

232. John K. Harris
Harris Associates, 2480 I6th St, NW, Washington, DC 20009, USA.
Sex: Male.　*Age:* 50-59.
Educational qualification: Other graduate/professional degree.
Formal training: I Social/behavioural sciences, 2 Adult education, 3 Humanities, 4 Systems science.
Informal training: Education, Social psychology.
Primarily engaged in: Both futures studies and long-range planning.
Areas in which work done (%): IO In planning unit of a governmental agency, 2O In organization primarily concerned with futures studies and/or long-range planning, 2O As individual consultant, 5O Training unit of a national organization.
Direction of work in forecasting: I Manpower, 2 Social, 3 Technological, 4 Educational.
Direction of work in research: I Value systems, 2 Social priorities, 3 Alternative futures, 4 Manpower.
Direction of work in planning: I Social, 2 Political, 3 Urban.
Methods used: I Network analysis, 2 Delphi techniques, 3 Individual expert forecasting, 4 Cross impact analysis.
Time range of work: IO - 25 years.
Source of support for work (%): 5O National government, 5O Voluntary associations.
Work done for (%): 5O National government, 5O Voluntary associations.
Occupational function: Consultant.
Worked in government as: Administrator.
Worked in industry/business in: I Management, 2 Trade union, 3 Consultancy.
Worked in education: Teaching.
Worked in service sector: I Social welfare, 2 Religion.　　　　*(395)*

233. John R. Harris
9 - 334 MIT, Cambridge, Ma 02139, USA.
Sex: Male.　*Age:* 40-49.
Educational qualification: Doctoral degree.

Formal training: Social/behavioural sciences.
Informal training: Social/behavioural sciences.
Direction of work in research: Social impacts of technology, Resource utilization, Policy research, Population.
Direction of work in planning: Urban, Regional, Economic.
Methods used: I Causal modelling, 2 Statistical models, 2 Operational models, 3 Historical analogy, 3 Simulation.
Time range of work: 5 - IO years.
Source of support for work (%): 2O University, 2O Foundation, 6O International agencies.
Work done for (%): 2O International agencies, 6O National government.
Occupational function: I Educator, 2 Consultant.
Worked in education: I Teaching, 2 In research.
Additional information: Concerned with economic development.   *(341)*

234. James Harrison

Assistant Director-General Science, UNESCO, 7 Place de Fontenoy, F 757OO Paris, France.
Sex: Male.   *Age:* 5O-59.
Educational qualification: Doctoral degree.
Formal training: Physical sciences.
Informal training: I Social/behavioural sciences, 2 Physical sciences, 3 Engineering.
Direction of work in forecasting: I Scientific, 2 Environmental, 3 Resources.
Direction of work in research: I Environmental, 2 Policy research.
Direction of work in planning: I Scientific, 2 Technological, 3 Educational, 4 Environmental, 5 Resources..
Methods used: I Expert panels, 2 Brainstorming, 3 Delphi techniques.
Time range of work: 5 - IO years.
Source of support for work (%): IOO International agencies.
Work done for (%): IOO International agencies.
Occupational function: I Manager, 2 Administrator.
Worked in government as: I Researcher, 2 Administrator.
Worked in education: Teaching.
Additional information: Concerned with development of science and technology in itself and for the poor countries.   *(216)*

235. Michael A. Harrison

Tele-Information, Southam Press Limited, Suite 9O8, 321 Bloor St East, Toronto 285, Ontario, Canada.
Sex: Male.   *Age:* 4O-49.
Educational qualification: Other graduate/professional degree.
Formal training: I Engineering, 2 Business administration.
Informal training: I Cinema/television, 2 Mathematics, 3 Arts.
Direction of work in forecasting: I Technological, 2 Market, 3 Economic.
Direction of work in research: I The individual in the future.
Direction of work in planning: I Corporate, 2 Technological, 3 Economic.
Methods used: I Scenario building, 2 Individual expert forecasting, 3 Expert panels, 4 Brainstorming, 5 Cross impact analysis, 6 Historical analogy.
Time range of work: 5 - IO years.
Source of support for work (%): IOO Private business.
Work done for (%): IOO Private business.
Occupational function: I Administrator, 2 Consultant.
Worked in government as: I Administrator.

Worked in industry/business in: I Management, 2 Planning, 3 Research and development, 4 Trade union.
Worked in education: Teaching.
Worked in service sector: Communication media.
Additional information: Concerned with communications in the future. *(316)*

236. R.I. Hart

Business Planning Dept, Plessey Telecommunications Ltd, Taplow Court, Taplow, Maidenhead, Berks, SL6 OER, UK.
Sex: Male. *Age:* 40-49.
Educational qualification: Other graduate/professional degree.
Formal training: Engineering.
Informal training: I Economics, 2 Mathematics, 3 Humanities, 4 Social/behavioural sciences.
Primarily engaged in: Both futures studies and long-range planning.
Areas in which work done (%): IOO In planning unit of a business enterprise.
Direction of work in forecasting: I Market, 2 Technological, 3 Economic, 4 Social, 5 Environmental, 6 Manpower.
Direction of work in research: I Alternative futures, 2 Social impacts of technology, 3 Futures methodology.
Direction of work in planning: I Corporate, 2 Technological.
Methods used: Scenario building, Extrapolation techniques, Brainstorming, Statistical models, Expert panels, Relevance trees, Individual expert forecasting, Systems analysis.
Time range of work: 5 - 25 years.
Source of support for work (%): IOO Private business.
Work done for (%): IOO Private business.
Occupational function: Corporate planner.
Worked in industry/business in: I Management, 2 Research and development, 3 Planning.
(93)

237. Audrey D. Hassanein

Giza Farms, Waldorf, Md 20601, USA.
Sex: Female. *Age:* 50-59.
Educational qualification: Some college or less.
Formal training: Education.
Informal training: I Mathematics, 2 Journalism, 3 Arts, 4 Design, 5 Social/behavioural sciences, 6 Humanities.
Primarily engaged in: Both futures studies and long-range planning.
Areas in which work done (%): 25 In organization concerned with other studies including long-range planning, 25 In organization primarily concerned with futures studies and/or long-range planning, 50 As individual consultant.
Direction of work in forecasting: Environmental.
Direction of work in research: Value systems, Social priorities, Policy research, The individual in the future, Futures methodology.
Direction of work in planning: Educational, Environmental.
Methods used: Literature and data searches, Expert panels, Individual expert forecasting.
Time range of work: IO - 25 years.
Source of support for work (%): IO Foundations, 40 National government, 50 International agencies.
Work done for (%): 50 International agencies, 50 University.
Occupational function: Consultant.

Worked in education: Teaching, In research, In administration.
Additional information: Concerned with technology assessment; social indicators; new methodologies for world systems studies; and ethical consideration in exploring space.

(420)

238. Arthur Haulot

95 Avenue des Certolans, Brussels, Belgium.
Sex: Male.   *Age:* 60 or over.
Educational qualification: Doctoral degree.
Formal training: Social/behavioural sciences.
Informal training: I Humanities, 2 Journalism, 3 Arts, 4 Education, 5 Cinema/television.
Direction of work in forecasting: I Economic, 2 Social, 3 Resources, 4 Environmental, 5 Cultural.
Direction of work in research: I Social impacts of technology, I Leisure time, 2 Social priorities, 3 Environmental, 4 The individual in the future, 5 The family in the future.
Direction of work in planning: Scientific, Technological, Social, Urban, Regional, Educational, Economic, Political, Environmental, Labour, Resources.
Methods used: Cross impact analysis, Extrapolation techniques.
Time range of work: 5 - 10 years.
Source of support for work (%): 100 National government.
Work done for (%): 100 National government.
Occupational function: Administrator.
Worked in government as: Administrator.
Worked in education: Teaching.
Additional information: Concerned with future of economy, sociology, and education.

(213)

239. Walter Hause

General Electric, PO Drawer QQ, Santa Barbara, Ca 93102, USA.
Sex: Male.   *Age:* 50-59;
Educational qualification: Master's degree.
Formal training: Engineering.
Informal training: I Engineering, 2 Physical sciences, 3 Mathematics, 4 Social/behavioural sciences.
Primarily engaged in: Both futures studies and long-range planning.
Areas in which work done (%): 80 In organization primarily concerned with futures studies and/or long-range planning, 20 In organization concerned with other studies including long-range planning.
Direction of work in forecasting: I Technological, 2 Economic, 3 Environmental, 4 Social, 5 Resources.
Direction of work in research: I Futures methodology, 2 Alternative futures, 3 Social impacts of technology, 4 Environmental.
Direction of work in planning: I Technological, 2 Corporate, 3 Economic.
Methods used: I Individual expert forecasting, 2 Brainstorming, 3 Probabilistic forecasting, 4 Extrapolation techniques, 5 Scenario building, 6 Historical analogy, 7 Delphi techniques.
Time range of work: 10 - 25 years.
Source of support for work (%): 30 Private business, 70 National government.
Work done for (%): 30 Private business, 70 National government.
Occupational function: I Research worker, 2 Consultant.
Worked in industry/business in: I Management, 2 Research and development.   *(359)*

240. Hans A. Havemann
Forschungsinstitut für Internationale Technisch Wirtschaftliche Zusammenarbeit der Rhein, Westfal. Techn. Hochschule, D - 51 Aachen, Vereinsstr, 3 - 5, West Germany.
Sex: Male.   *Age:* 60 or over.
Educational qualification: Doctoral degree.
Formal training: Engineering.
Informal training: 1 Project management in industry, 2 International development economics.
Areas in which work done (%): 10 In planning unit of a governmental agency, 20 As academic, in teaching futures studies or long-range planning, 20 Planning aspects of developing countries.
Direction of work in forecasting: Technological, Economic, Educational, Scientific.
Direction of work in research: Social impacts of technology, Manpower, Resource utilization.
Direction of work in planning: Technological, Economic, Resources.
Methods used: Extrapolation techniques, Expert panels.
Time range of work: 5 - 10 years.
Source of support for work (%): 10 National government, 90 Local government.
Work done for (%): 5 Local or regional government, 10 National government.
Occupational function: Research worker, Educator.
Worked in industry/business in: Management, Research and development.
Worked in education: Teaching, In research, In administration.
Additional information: Concerned with assessment of technology for international development, international division of labour, production.   *(180)*

241. Robert de Havilland
20 Rockledge Rd, Hartsdale, NY 10530, USA.
Sex: Male.   *Age:* 40-49.
Educational qualification: Bachelor's degree.
Formal training: Journalism.
Informal training: Cinema/television.
Direction of work in forecasting: 1 Technological, 2 Market, 3 Economic, 4 Social, 5 Cultural, 6 Educational.
Methods used: 1 Individual expert forecasting, 2 Expert panels.
Time range of work: 5 - 10 years.
Source of support for work: 100 Private business.
Work done for (%): 100 Foundations.
Occupational function: 1 Manager, 2 Consultant.
Worked in industry in: 1 Consultancy, 2 Management.
Worked in service sector: Communication media.
Additional information: Concerned with the future of television.   *(314)*

242. Yujiro Hayashi
President, Institute for Future Technology, 2 - 1 Kitanomaru Koen, Chiyoda-ku, Tokyo, Japan.
Sex: Male.   *Age:* 50-59.
Educational qualification: Bachelor's degree.
Formal training: Other.
Informal training: 1 Humanities, 2 Social/behavioural sciences, 3 Journalism.
Primarily engaged in: Both futures studies and long-range planning.
Areas in which work done (%): 5 As individual consultant, 5 In planning unit of a government agency, 5 In planning unit of a business enterprise, 5 In planning unit of an

international organization, 5 In organization concerned with other studies including long-range planning, 5 Unspecified, 2O As academic, in teaching futures studies or long-range planning, 5O In organization primarily concerned with futures studies and/or long-range planning.

Direction of work in forecasting: I Social, 2 Cultural.

Direction of work in research: I Alternative futures, 2 Social impacts of technology, 3 Social priorities, 4 Value systems, 5 Environmental.

Direction of work in planning: I Social, 2 Scientific.

Methods used: I Individual expert forecasting, 2 Historical analogy, 3 Scenario building, 4 Expert panels.

Time range of work: IO - 25 years.

Source of support for work (%): IO Private business, 3O National government, 6O Other, unspecified.

Work done for (%): IO National government, IO Private business, 2O International agencies, 6O Other unspecified.

Occupational function: I Consultant, 2 Educator, 3 Organizer.

Worked in government as: Researcher.

Worked in industry/business in: Consultancy.

Worked in education: Teaching.

Worked in service sector: I Social welfare, 2 Communication media.   *(234)*

243. Richard C. Heck
71 Madison St, Hamilton, NY 13336, USA.

Sex: Male.   *Age:* 25-29.

Educational qualification: Master's degree.

Formal training: I Education, 2 Social/behavioural sciences, 3 Mathematics.

Informal training: I Education, 2 Mathematics, 3 Social/behavioural sciences, 4 Life sciences.

Primarily engaged in: Long-range planning.

Areas in which work done (%): IOO In long-range planning unit of an educational enterprise.

Direction of work in forecasting: I Educational, 2 Resources, 3 Population, 4 Environmental, 5 Market, 6 Economic, 7 Social, 8 Manpower, 9 Cultural.

Direction of work in research: I Alternative futures, 2 Resource utilization, 3 Policy research, 4 Population.

Direction of work in planning: I Educational, 2 Economic, 3 Resources, 4 Environmental.

Methods used: I Statistical models, 2 Extrapolation techniques, 3 Historical analogy, 4 Operational models, 5 Individual expert forecasting, 6 Simulation, 7 Expert panels.

Time range of work: 5 - IO years.

Source of support for work (%): IOO University.

Work done for (%): IOO University planning.

Occupational function: I Administrator, 2 Research worker, 3 Manager, 4 Consultant, 5 Educator.

Worked in education: In administration.   *(337)*

244. Carl Heden
Dept of Microbiological Engineering, Kardlinsha Institute Solnavägen I, Stockholm 6O, Sweden.

Sex: Male.   *Age:* 5O-59.

Educational qualification: Doctoral degree.

Formal training: Life sciences.

Informal training: Engineering.
Primarily engaged in: Long-range planning.
Areas in which work done (%): 50 In organization concerned with other studies including long-range planning, 15 In planning unit of a governmental agency, 10 in planning unit of a business enterprise, 25 In planning unit of an international agency.
Direction of work in forecasting: 1 Scientific, 2 Environmental.
Direction of work in research: 1 Social impacts of technology, 2 Resource utilization, 3 Policy research, 4 Value systems, 5 Alternative futures.
Direction of work in planning: 1 Scientific, 2 Technological, 3 Environmental, 4 Resources, 5 Corporate.
Methods used: 1 Scenario building, Individual expert forecasting, Expert panels, 2 Brainstorming, 3 Delphi techniques.
Time range of work: Beyond year 2000.
Source of support for work (%): 25 National government, 50 International agencies, 25 Foundations.
Work done for (%): 50 National government, 25 International agencies, 10 Private business, 15 Foundations.
Occupational function: Research worker.
Worked in government as: Researcher.
Worked in industry/business in: Consultancy.
Worked in education: In research.   *(592)*

245. François Hetman
22 Bis, Rue de Lubeck Paris 16E, France.
Sex: Male.   *Age:* 50-59.
Educational qualification: Doctoral degree.
Formal training: 1 Social/behavioural sciences, 2 Engineering.
Informal training: Humanities, Education.
Primarily engaged in: Both futures studies and long-range planning.
Areas in which work done (%): 10 As individual consultant, 40 In planning unit of an international organization.
Direction of work in forecasting: 1 Economic, 2 Technological, 3 Scientific.
Direction of work in research: 1 Social impacts of technology, 2 Futures methodology, 3 Alternative futures.
Direction of work in planning: 1 Technological, 2 Social, 3 Scientific.
Methods used: 1 Probabilistic forecasting, 2 Scenario building, 3 Relevance trees.
Time range of work: 10 - 25 years.
Source of support for work (%): 40 International agencies, 60 Personal work (publications).
Work done for (%): 40 International agencies, 60 Personal.
Occupational function: 1 Consultant, 2 Research worker, 3 Manager.
Worked in government as: Researcher.
Worked in industry/business in: Research and development.
Additional information: Concerned with futures research methodology, technology assessment, systems analysis.   *(127)*

246. Bruce Hicks
College of Education, University of Illinois, Urbana, Il, USA.
Sex: Male.   *Age:* 50-59.
Educational qualification: Doctoral degree.
Formal training: 1 Physical sciences, 2 Mathematics.

Informal training: 1 Education, 2 Mathematics, 3 Engineering.
Direction of work in research: Environmental, Social priorities, The individual in the future.
Direction of work in planning: Technological, Educational.
Methods used: 1 Individual expert forecasting, 2 Simulation, 3 Brainstorming.
Time range of work: 5 - 10 years.
Source of support for work (%): 20 Voluntary associations, 80 University.
Work done for (%): 20 Voluntary associations, 80 University.
Occupational function: 1 Educator, 2 Research worker, 3 Manager.
Worked in government as: 1 Researcher, 2 Administrator.
Worked in education: 1 Teaching, 2 In research, 3 In administration.
Additional information: Concerned with the future of educational applications of computers.
(59)

247. John Higginson

Director, International Agency for Research on Cancer, 150 Cours Albert Thomas, 69008 Lyon, France.
Sex: Male. *Age:* 50-59.
Educational qualification: Doctoral degree.
Formal training: Life sciences.
Informal training: 1 Physical sciences, 2 Social/behavioural sciences.
Direction of work in research: Environmental.
Methods used: 1 Brainstorming, 2 Expert panels.
Time range of work: 10 - 25 years.
Source of support for work (%): 100 National government.
Work done for (%): 100 National government.
Occupational function: Research worker.
Worked in government as: Researcher.
Worked in service sector: Medicine.
Additional information: Concerned with medicine and environmental carcinogenesis. *(231)*

248. Kim Hill

University of Houston at Clear Lake City, 2700 Bay Area Blvd, Houston, Tx 77058, USA.
Sex: Male. *Age:* 25-29.
Educational qualification: Doctoral degree.
Formal training: Social/behavioural sciences.
Informal training: Social/behavioural sciences.
Areas in which work done (%): 10 As academic, in teaching futures studies or long-range planning.
Direction of work in research: Policy research, Futures methodology.
Time range of work: 5 - 25 years.
Source of support for work (%): 100 University.
Work done for (%): 100 Personal research.
Occupational function: 1 Educator, 2 Research worker.
Worked in education: Teaching, In research.
Additional information: Concerned with the future of politics, international political relationships, and policy choices.
(450)

249. Reuben Hill

University of Minnesota, 1014 Social Science Bldg, Minneapolis, Mn 55455, USA.
Sex: Male.   *Age:* 60 or over.
Educational qualification: Doctoral degree.
Formal training: Social/behavioural sciences.
Areas in which work done (%): 10 As academic, in teaching futures studies or long-range planning.
Direction of work in research: The family in the future.
Methods used: Survey of family imageries and intensions.
Time range of work: 10 - 25 years.
Source of support for work (%): 100 University.
Work done for (%): 10 University.
Occupational function: Educator.
Worked in education: 1 Teaching, 2 In research, 3 In administration.
Additional information: Concerned with future of marriage and family, forms and function, future of population composition.   *(121)*

250. Joseph Hodara

United Nations, Economic Commission for Latin America, 29 Mazarik St, Polanco, Mexico 5 DF, Mexico.
Sex: Male.   *Age:* 30-39.
Educational qualification: Doctoral degree.
Formal training: Social/behavioural sciences.
Informal training: 1 Humanities, 2 Educational.
Primarily engaged in: Both futures studies and long-range planning.
Areas in which work done (%): 70 In planning unit of an international agency, 30 As individual consultant.
Direction of work in forecasting: 1 Social, 2 Resources, 3 Military, 4 Scientific.
Direction of work in research: 1 Alternative futures, 2 Social priorities, 3 Value systems.
Direction of work in planning: 1 Social, 2 Resources, 3 Scientific.
Methods used: 1 Scenario building, 2 Historical analogy, 3 Individual expert forecasting.
Time range of work: 10 - 25 years.
Source of support for work (%): 20 International agencies.
Work done for (%): 20 International agencies.
Occupational function: Research worker.
Worked in government as: Researcher.
Worked in industry/business in: Planning.
Worked in education: Teaching.   *(144)*

251. Ben Hoffman

Planning Officer, Universities Grants Commission, 11 - 395 Berry St, Winnipeg, Manitoba, Canada.
Sex: Male.   *Age:* 40-49.
Educational qualification: Doctoral degree.
Formal training: Social/behavioural sciences.
Informal training: Mathematics, Education, Law.
Primarily engaged in: Both futures studies and long-range planning.
Areas in which work done (%): 5 In planning unit of an international organization, 15 In organization primarily concerned with futures studies and/or long-range planning, 30 In planning unit of a governmental agency, 50 In organization concerned with other studies including long-range planning.

Direction of work in forecasting: I Educational, 2 Population, 4 Economic, 5 Social, 6 Cultural, 7 Resources, 8 Manpower, 9 Technological.

Direction of work in research: I Policy research, 2 Population, 3 Social impacts of technology, 4 Futures methodology, 5 Resource utilization, 6 Value systems, 7 Manpower, 8 Alternative futures.

Direction of work in planning: I Educational, 2 Resources, 3 Technological, 4 Economic, 5 Social, 6 Political.

Methods used: I Cross impact analysis, I Network analysis, I Operational models, I Causal modelling, 2 Probabilistic forecasting, 3 Gaming, 4 Scenario building, 5 Brainstorming, 6 Delphi techniques, 7 Statistical models, 7 Simulation, 8 Extrapolation techniques.

Time range of work: 5 - 25 years.

Source of support for work (%): IOO Local government, provincial level.

Work done for (%): IOO Local or regional government and institutional agencies.

Occupational function: I Administrator, I Chairman special operational search committee, 2 Manager, 3 Consultant, 4 Educator.

Worked in government as: I Administrator, 2 Researcher.

Worked in industry/business in: I Planning, 2 Research and development, 3 Consultancy.

Worked in education: I In administration, 2 In research.

Worked in service sector: I Communication media, 2 Design, 3 Law.   *(422)*

252. H.J. Hoffman

Prognos AG, Viaduktstr 65, 4011 Basle, Switzerland.

Sex: Male.   *Age:* 30-39.

Educational qualification: Master's degree.

Formal training: I Engineering, 2 Physical sciences.

Informal training: I Mathematics, 2 Education, 3 Social/behavioural sciences.

Primarily engaged in: Futures studies.

Areas in which work done (%): IOO In organization primarily concerned with futures studies and/or long-range planning.

Direction of work in forecasting: I Market, 2 Economic, 3 Technological.

Direction of work in research: I Consumer affairs, 2 Social priorities, 3 Social impacts of technology.

Direction of work in planning: I Technological.

Methods used: I Extrapolation techniques, 2 Scenario building, 3 Individual expert forecasting, 4 Historical analogy.

Time range of work: IO - 25 years.

Source of support for work (%): IOO National government.

Work done for (%): IOO National government.

Occupational function: I Research worker, 2 Consultant.

Worked in industry/business in: Consultancy.

Worked in education: I Teaching, 2 In administration, 3 In research.   *(362)*

253. H.P. Hofmeyr

Techno-Economic (Research) Division, Information and Research Services, Council for Scientific and Industrial Research, PO Box 395, Pretoria OOO1, South Africa.

Sex: Male.   *Age:* 30-39.

Educational qualification: Master's degree.

Formal training: Life sciences, Business administration.
Informal training: I Life sciences, 2 Techno-Economics.
Direction of work in forecasting: I Technological, 2 Scientific.
Direction of work in research: I Alternative futures, 2 Futures methodology.
Direction of work in planning: I Technological, 2 Scientific, 3 Regional.
Methods used: Monitoring.
Time range of work: 5 - 25 years.
Source of support for work (%): IOO National government.
Work done for (%): IOO National government.
Occupational function: I Consultant, 2 Research worker.
Worked in government as: Researcher.
Additional information: Concerned with technological development and growth in assessment of R & D and development of aids to planning, e.g. budget allocation for technical R & D. *(504)*

254. Gordon A. Hoke

Centre for Instructional Research and Curriculum Evaluation, College of Education, 270 Education Bldg, University of Illinois, Urbana II 61801, USA.
Sex: Male.   *Age:* 50-59.
Educational qualification: Doctoral degree.
Formal training: I Education, 2 Social/behavioural sciences, 3 Humanities.
Informal training: I Education, 2 Social/behavioural sciences, 3 Humanities, 4 Journalism.
Primarily engaged in: Futures studies.
Areas in which work done (%): 4O In organization concerned with other studies including long-range planning, 4O As individual consultant, IO In organization primarily concerned with futures studies and/or long-range planning, IO As academic, in teaching futures studies or long-range planning.
Direction of work in forecasting: I Educational, 2 Social, 3 Technological.
Direction of work in research: I Social priorities, 2 Social impacts of technology, 3 Value systems, 4 Resource utilization.
Direction of work in planning: I Educational, 2 Social, 3 Regional, 4 Resources.
Methods used: I Contextual mapping, 2 Scenario building, 3 Historical analogy.
Time range of work: 5 - beyond year 2OOO.
Source of support for work (%): 2O Local government, 3O Other institutions, 5O National government.
Work done for (%): 2O Local or regional government, 3O Other institutions, 5O National government.
Occupational function: I Educator, 2 Consultant.
Worked in education: I Teaching, 2 In research, 3 In administration.
Additional information: Concerned with technology assessment, social indicators. *(156)*

255. Paul S. Hoover

Unit One, 7O Allen Hall, University of Illinois, II, 61803, USA.
Sex: Male.   *Age:* 30-39.
Educational qualification: Doctoral degree.
Formal training: Physical sciences.
Informal training: Education.
Areas in which work done (%): 3O In organization primarily concerned with futures studies and/or long-range planning, 7O Administrator of an experimental educational program.

Direction of work in research: I The individual in the future, 2 Alternative futures, 3 Value systems, 4 Policy research.
Direction of work in planning: Educational.
Methods used: I Scenario building, 2 Simulation.
Time range of work: IO - 25 years.
Source of support for work (%): IOO Institution.
Work done for (%): 3O Institution.
Occupational function: I Educator, 2 Administration.
Worked in education: I Teaching, 2 In administration, 3 In research.
Additional information: Concerned with developing educational strategies which take cognizance of one fact that current students will live out their lives in the last decade of the twentieth century.   *(407)*

256. Terry Hopmann

Quigley Centre of International Studies, University of Minnesota, Minneapolis, Mn 55455, USA.
Sex: Male.   *Age:* 3O-39.
Educational qualification: Doctoral degree.
Formal training: Social/behavioural sciences.
Informal training: Humanities.
Areas in which work done (%): 25 As academic, in teaching futures studies or long-range planning.
Direction of work in research: Policy research, Futures methodology, International systems.
Methods used: I Gaming, 2 Statistical models, 3 Simulation, 4 Causal modelling.
Time range of work: IO - 25 years.
Source of support for work (%): 5O University, 5O Foundations.
Occupational function: Educator.
Worked in education: I Teaching, 2 In research, 3 In administration.
Additional information: Concerned with international political and strategic system, disarmament.   *(195)*

257. Irving Louis Horowitz

Professor of Sociology and Political Science, Rutgers University, Studies in Comparative International Development, Livingston College, New Brunswick, NJ O89O3, USA.
Sex: Male.   *Age:* 4O-49.
Educational qualification: Doctoral degree.
Formal training: Social sciences.
Informal training: Journalism, Education.
Direction of work in forecasting: Social,
Direction of work in research: Policy research.
Direction of work in planning: Social, Political.
Source of support for work (%): IO Voluntary associations, 2O National government.
Work done for (%): 3O International agencies.
Additional information: Concerned with social indicators and political sociology.
(Also at Princeton University and Woodrow Wilson centre of international affairs).   *(286)*

258. Earl Hubbard

Wells Hill Rd, Lakeville, Ct O6O39, USA.
Sex: Male.   *Age:* 5O-59.
Educational qualification: Bachelor's degree.
Formal training: Humanities.

Informal training: Arts.
Primarily engaged in: Futures studies.
Areas in which work done (%): 99 Writing, Painting, studying and lecturing on 'His Philosophy'.
Direction of work in forecasting: I Cultural.
Direction of work in research: 2 Value systems, 3 The individual in the future, 4 The family in the future.
Time range of work: Beyond 2000 AD.
Work done for (%): 99 Mankind.
Occupational function: Revelation and inspiration.   *(165)*

259. Benedikt Huber

ETN ORL, Weinberstr 35, Zurich, Switzerland.
Sex: Male.   *Age:* 40-49.
Educational qualification: Master's degree.
Formal training: I Design, 2 Education.
Informal training: Engineering, Journalism.
Primarily engaged in: Both futures studies and long-range planning.
Areas in which work done (%): I5 In planning unit of a business enterprise, 25 In organization primarily concerned with futures studies and/or long-range planning, 60 As academic, in teaching futures studies or long-range planning.
Direction of work in forecasting: Educational, Scientific.
Direction of work in research: Environmental.
Direction of work in planning: I Urban, 2 Regional, 3 Environmental.
Methods used: I Network analysis, 2 Operational models, 3 Historical analogy.
Time range of work: 5 - I0 years.
Source of support for work (%): 40 Local government, 60 National government.
Work done for (%): 50 Local or regional government, 50 Education.
Occupational function: I Educator, 2 Research worker.
Worked in education: Teaching.
Worked in service sector: Design.
Additional information: Concerned with future of the city and city planning.   *(410)*

260. Bettina J. Huber

University of California, Dept of Sociology, Santa Barbara, Ca 93106, USA.
Sex: Female.   *Age:* 30-39.
Educational qualification: Doctoral degree.
Formal training: Social/behavioural sciences.
Informal training: Social/behavioural sciences.
Direction of work in research: Individual images of the future.
Direction of work in planning: Social.
Methods used: Scenario building, Extrapolation techniques.
Time range of work: I0 - 25 years.
Source of support for work (%): I00 University.
Occupational function: Educator.
Worked in education: I Teaching, 2 In research.   *(150)*

261. M. Hubert

Secretary General, European Association of National Productivity Centres, Rue de la Concorde, 60, 1050 Brussels, Belgium.
Sex: Male.   *Age:* 30-39.

Educational qualification: Master's degree.
Formal training: Social/behavioural sciences.
Informal training: Journalism.
Direction of work in planning: I Social, 2 Economic, 3 Labour.
Methods used: I Scenario building, 2 Extrapolation techniques.
Time range of work: 5 - IO years.
Source of support for work (%): IOO Member organization.
Work done for (%): IOO Member organization.
Occupational function: Administrator.
Worked in service sector: Communication media.
Additional information: Concerned with need for and means of raising production.   *(350)*

262. Alois Huning

D - 5603 Wuelfrath, Weissdornweg 12, West Germany.
Sex: Male.   *Age:* 40-49.
Educational qualification: Doctoral degree.
Formal training: I Humanities, 2 Philosophy, 3 Psychology.
Informal training: I Education, 2 Engineering, 3 Journalism.
Direction of work in research: I Social impacts of technology, 2 Value systems,
3 Social priorities, 4 Alternative futures, 5 Policy research, 6 Environmental, 6 The
individual in the future, 6 The family in the future.
Work done for (%): 30 Voluntary associations.
Occupational function: I Educator, 2 Consultant, 3 Manager.
Worked in industry/business in: Management.
Worked in education: I In research, 2 Teaching.
Additional information: Concerned with technology assessment. Social and ethical
consequences of development.   *(11)*

263. Ronald L. Hunt

Professor of Education, San Jose State University, San Jose, Ca 95192, USA.
Sex: Male.   *Age:* 40-49.
Educational qualification: Doctoral degree.
Formal training: Education.
Informal training: Education.
Areas in which work done (%): 25 In planning unit of an international agency.
Direction of work in forecasting: Educational.
Direction of work in research: Futures methodology.
Direction of work in planning: Educational.
Time range of work: IO - 25 years.
Source of support for work (%): IO National government, 40 Local government,
50 Private business.
Work done for (%): 3 National government, IO Local or regional government, I2 Private
business.
Occupational function: Educator.
Worked in government as: I Researcher, 2 Administrator.
Worked in industry/business in: I Consultancy, 2 Research and development, 3 Management.
Worked in education: I Teaching, 2 In research, 3 In administration.
Worked in service sector: Communication media.
Additional information: Concerned with futures education programming.   *(334)*

264. Neil Hurley

944 N1 5th St, New Hyde Park, NY 11040, USA.
Sex: Male. *Age:* 40-49.
Educational qualification: Other graduate/professional degree.
Formal training: Social/behavioural sciences, Humanities.
Informal training: Journalism, Education, Cinema/television.
Primarily engaged in: Both futures studies and long-range planning.
Areas in which work done (%): 10 As individual consultant, 15 As academic, in teaching futures studies including long-range planning, 35 In planning unit of an international organization, 40 In organization concerned with other studies including long-range planning.
Direction of work in forecasting: Social, Cultural, Manpower.
Direction of work in research: Social impacts of technology, Alternative futures, Value systems.
Direction of work in planning: Technological, Educational, Political.
Methods used: Brainstorming, Historical analogy, Operational models, Individual expert forecasting.
Time range of work: 5 - 10 years.
Source of support for work (%): 50 Voluntary associations, 50 Writing and university.
Work done for (%): 25 International agencies, 75 Voluntary associations.
Occupational function: Educator, Consultant.
Worked in education: Teaching, In research.
Worked in service sector: Religion, Communication media.　　　　　*(303)*

265. T. Ranald Ide

Chairman, Communications Authorities, 2180 Yonge St, Toronto, Ontario, M4S 2C1, Canada.
Sex: Male. *Age:* 50-59.
Educational qualification: Other graduate/professional degree.
Formal training: 1 Education, 2 Cinema/television.
Informal training: Arts.
Areas in which work done (%): 30 In planning unit of a governmental agency.
Direction of work in forecasting: 1 Social, 2 Educational, 3 Cultural.
Direction of work in research: 1 Social impacts of technology, 2 The individual in the future, 3 Futures methodology.
Direction of work in planning: 1 Corporate, 2 Educational, 3 Technological.
Methods used: 1 Brainstorming, 2 Expert panels, 3 Operational models.
Time range of work: 10 - 25 years.
Source of support for work (%): 100 Provincial government.
Work done for (%): 30 Provincial government.
Occupational function: 1 Administrator, 2 Educator.
Worked in government as: Administrator.
Worked in education: 1 In administration, 2 Teaching.
Additional information: Concerned with technology assessment and social indicators. *(258)*

266. Lars E. Ingelstam

Secretariat for Future Studies, Fack, 10310 Stockholm 2, Sweden.
Sex: Male. *Age:* 30-39.
Educational qualification: Doctoral degree.
Formal training: Mathematics.
Informal training: Social/behavioural sciences.

Primarily engaged in: Both futures studies and long-range planning.
Areas in which work done (%): 100 In planning unit of a governmental agency.
Direction of work in forecasting: Educational, Resources, Population.
Direction of work in research: Alternative futures, Value systems, Social priorities, Policy research, The individual in the future.
Direction of work in forecasting: Educational, Resources, Population.
Direction of work in research: Alternative futures, Value systems, Social priorities, Policy research, The individual in the future.
Direction of work in planning: Political, Resources.
Methods used: Scenario building.
Time range of work: Beyond 2000 AD.
Source of support for work (%): 100 National government.
Work done for (%): 100 National government.
Occupational function: Manager.
Worked in government as: 1 Researcher, 2 Administrator.
Worked in education: In research.   *(33)*

267. D.C. Ion

49 Southwood Lane, Highgate Village, London, N6 5ED UK.
Sex: Male.   *Age:* 60 or over.
Educational qualification: Master's degree.
Formal training: Physical sciences.
Informal training: Petroleum Exploration, management and planning.
Areas in which work done (%): 100 As individual consultant.
Direction of work in forecasting: Resources.
Direction of work in research: Resource utilization.
Direction of work in planning: Resources.
Methods used: 1 Individual expert forecasting, 2 Historical analogy, 3 Extrapolation techniques.
Time range of work: 10 - 25 years.
Source of support for work (%): 90 Personal.
Work done for (%): 100 Private business.
Occupational function: Consultant.
Worked in industry/business in: 1 Management, 2 Planning.
Additional information: Concerned with long-range resource analysis.   *(159)*

268. Ali Irtem

PK 685, Istanbul (Merkez) Turkey.
Sex: Male.   *Age:* 60 or over.
Educational qualification: Bachelor's degree.
Formal training: Physical sciences.
Informal training: Physical sciences, Life sciences, Social/behavioural sciences, Mathematics, Engineering, Arts, Law, Cybernetics.
Direction of work in forecasting: Technological, Economic, Social, Cultural, Scientific, Military, Cybernetics.
Direction of work in research: Social impacts of technology, Policy research, Cybernetics.
Direction of work in planning: Scientific, Technological, Social, Political, Military, Cybernetics.
Methods used: Simulation, Causal modelling.
Time range of work: 10 - beyond year 2000.
Occupational function: Manager, Research worker, Educator, Consultant.

Worked in government as: Elected official, Researcher.
Worked in education: Teaching, In research.
Additional information: Concerned with cybernetics.   *(161)*

269. Madhur Srinivas Iyengar
Managing Director, M.S. Iyengar and Associates Pvt Ltd, PO Box 2817, New Delhi - 11060, India.
Sex: Male.   *Age:* 50-59.
Educational qualification: Doctoral degree.
Formal training: I Physical sciences, 2 Engineering.
Informal training: I Life sciences, 2 Social/behavioural sciences, 3 Design.
Primarily engaged in: Both futures studies and long-range planning.
Areas in which work done (%): 20 In organization primarily concerned with futures studies and/or long-range planning, 30 As individual consultant, 50 Industrial consultancy.
Direction of work in forecasting: I Technological, 2 Scientific, 3 Economic, 4 Social.
Direction of work in research: Social impacts of technology, Alternative futures.
Direction of work in planning: Scientific, Technological.
Methods used: I Scenario building, 2 Delphi techniques, 3 Individual expert forecasting.
Time range of work: IO - 25 years.
Source of support for work (%): IO National government, 9O Self.
Work done for (%): 2O Local or regional government, 2O National government.
Occupational function: Consultant.
Worked in government as: I Researcher.
Worked in industry/business in: 2 Consultancy.   *(173)*

270. R.W. Jackson
Science Council of Canada, 150 Kent St, Ottawa, KIP 5P4 Canada.
Sex: Male.   *Age:* 50-59.
Educational qualification: Doctoral degree.
Formal training: I Physical sciences, 2 Engineering, 3 Humanities.
Informal training: I Humanities, 2 Physical sciences.
Primarily engaged in: Futures studies.
Areas in which work done (%): 7O In organization primarily concerned with futures studies including long-range planning.
Direction of work in forecasting: I Technological, 2 Social.
Direction of work in research: I Policy research, 2 Alternative futures, 3 Value systems, 4 Social impacts of technology.
Direction of work in planning: I Political, 2 Scientific, 3 Social.
Methods used: I Individual expert forecasting, 2 Expert panels, 3 Scenario building, 4 Contextual mapping.
Time range of work: IO - 25 years.
Source of support for work (%): IOO National government.
Work done for (%): IOO National government.
Occupational function: Researcher.
Worked in industry/business in: Research and development.   *(349)*
Worked in education: In research.

271. Eliezer D. Jaffe
Paul Baerwald School of Social Work, Jerusalem, Israel.
Sex: Male.   *Age:* 40-49.
Educational qualification: Doctoral degree.

Formal training: Social/behavioural sciences.
Informal training: Education.
Areas in which work done (%): IO As individual consultant, 5 In planning unit of a governmental agency, I5 In organization primarily concerned with futures studies and/or long-range planning.
Direction of work in forecasting: Social.
Direction of work in research: Policy research.
Direction of work in planning: Social.
Methods used: I Probabilistic forecasting, 2 Historical analogy, 3 Network analysis.
Time range of work: 5 - IO years.
Source of support for work (%): 25 University, 25 International agencies, 5O Foundations.
Work done for (%): IO National government, IO Private business.
Occupational function: I Research worker, 2 Educator, 3 Consultant.
Worked in government as: Administrator.
Worked in industry/business in: Consultancy.
Worked in education: I Teaching, 2 In research.
Worked in service sector: Social welfare.   *(1O7)*

272. Marie Jahoda

Science Policy Research Unit, University of Sussex, Falmer, Brighton, BN1 9RF, UK.
Sex: Female.   *Age:* 6O or over.
Educational qualification: Doctoral degree.
Formal training: Social/behavioural sciences.
Informal training: Education.
Primarily engaged in: Futures studies.
Areas in which work done (%): IOO In organization primarily concerned with futures studies and/or long-range planning.
Direction of work in forecasting: Social.
Direction of work in research: I Alternative futures, 2 Value systems.
Methods used: Thinking.
Time range of work: IO - 25 years.
Source of support for work (%): IOO National government.
Work done for (%): IOO World.
Occupational function: Research consultant.
Worked in government as: Researcher.
Worked in education: I In research, 2 Teaching.   *(483)*

273. Henri Janne

Institut de Sociologie, Université Libre de Bruxelles, Bruxelles, Belgium.
Sex: Male.   *Age:* 6O or over.
Educational qualification: Doctoral degree.
Formal training: Social/behavioural sciences, Humanities, Education.
Informal training: Journalism, Education.
Areas in which work done (%): IO In organization primarily concerned with futures studies and/or long-range planning, IO In planning unit of an international organization, I5 As individual consultant.
Direction of work in forecasting: Educational.
Direction of work in research: Social impacts of technology, Alternative futures, Value systems.
Direction of work in planning: Educational.

Methods used: Probabilistic forecasting, Expert panels, Individual expert forecasting, Causal modelling.
Time range of work: Beyond 2000 AD.
Source of support for work (%): 5 Local government, 5 International agencies, IO National government, 80 Foundations.
Work done for (%): 35 Foundations.
Occupational function: Consultant.
Worked in government as: I Administrator, 2 Elected official.
Worked in industry/business in: Research and development.
Worked in education: I Teaching, 2 In research.
Additional information: Concerned with research on future systems of education linked with the global social systems. *(24)*

274. Edward Jaycox

Director, Transportation and Urban Projects Dept, International Bank for Reconstruction and Development, International Development Assoc, 1818 H Street, NW, Washington DC 20433, USA.
Sex: Male.　　*Age:* 30-39.
Educational qualification: Doctoral degree.
Formal training: Economics.
Areas in which work done (%): 20 In planning unit of an international organization, 80 Supervisor of lending operations of an international organization.
Direction of work in forecasting: I Resources, 2 Environmental, 3 Population, 4 Market.
Direction of work in research: I Resource utilization, 2 Environmental, 3 Alternative futures.
Direction of work in planning: I Urban, 2 Regional, 3 Resources.
Methods used: I Operational models, 2 Statistical models.
Time range of work: 5 - IO years.
Source of support for work (%): 5 National government, 95 International agencies.
Work done for (%): IOO International agencies.
Occupational function: I Manager, 2 Administrator. *(340)*

275. N.R. Jeffers

Merlewood Research Station, Grange-Over-Sands, Cumbria, LA11 6JU, UK.
Sex: Male.　　*Age:* 40-49.
Educational qualification: Other graduate/professional degree.
Formal training: Mathematics.
Informal training: I Life sciences, 2 Physical sciences.
Primarily engaged in: Long-range planning.
Areas in which work done (%): 20 In organization concerned with other studies including long-range planning, IO In planning unit of an international organization, 30 In organization primarily concerned with futures studies and/or long-range planning, 40 In planning unit of a governmental agency.
Direction of work in forecasting: I Environmental, 2 Scientific.
Direction of work in research: I Environmental, 2 Resource utilization.
Direction of work in planning: I Scientific, 2 Environmental.
Methods used: I Statistical models, 2 Simulation, 3 Operational models.
Time range of work: IO - 25 years.
Source of support for work (%): IOO National government.
Work done for (%): 40 National government.
Occupational function: Administrator.
Worked in government as: Researcher. *(189)*

276. Brian Johnson

Institute for the Study of International Organization, Stanmer House, Stanmer Park, Brighton, BN1 9QA, UK.

Sex: Male.   *Age:* 30-39.

Educational qualification: Other graduate/professional degree.

Formal training: Humanities.

Informal training: Social/behavioural sciences, Humanities, Journalism.

Areas in which work done (%): IO In planning unit of an international organization, I5 Administration, 25 As individual consultant, 5O In organization concerned with other studies including long-range planning.

Direction of work in forecasting: I Social, 2 Environmental, 3 Cultural.

Direction of work in research: I Alternative futures, 2 Social priorities, 3 The individual in the fuutre.

Methods used: Probabilistic forecasting, Scenario building, Relevance trees, Historical analogy, Individual expert forecasting,

Time range of work: Beyond 2OOOAD.

Source of support for work (%): IOO Foundations.

Work done for (%): 33 International agencies, 67 Foundations.

Occupational function: Educator, Consultant.

Worked in government as: Administrator.

Worked in education: In research.

Worked in service sector: Communication media.

Additional information: Concerned with technology assessment, social indicators and institutional change.   *(391)*

277. Denis F. Johnston

1434 - 36 St, NW, Washington, DC 2OOO7, USA.

Sex: Male.   *Age:* 5O-59.

Educational qualification: Doctoral degree.

Formal training: Social/behavioural sciences.

Informal training: I Social/behavioural sciences, 2 Demography.

Direction of work in forecasting: I Social, 2 Economic, 3 Cultural, 3 Population, 4 Technological, 6 Manpower, 7 Educational, 8 Environmental.

Direction of work in research: I Social indicators development, 2 Social priorities, 3 Population, 4 Manpower, 5 Value systems, 6 Alternative futures, 7 Social impacts of technology, 8 Resource utilization.

Methods used: I Extrapolation techniques, 2 Statistical models, 3 Individual expert forecasting, 4 Scenario building.

Time range of work: 5 - 25 years.

Source of support for work (%): IOO National government.

Work done for (%): 2O National government.

Occupational function: I Research worker, 2 Educator.

Worked in government as: I Researcher.

Worked in education: 2 Teaching.

Additional information: Concerned with currently directing the planning and preparing of the second 'Social Indicators', 1975 volume, Office of Management and Budget, Executive Office of the President.   *(164)*

278. M.S. Jones

Director, Programmes Analysis Unit, Chilton, Didcot, Oxfordshire OX11 ORF, UK.

Sex: Male.   *Age:* 4O-49.

Educational qualification: Doctoral degree.

Informal training: I Social/behavioural sciences, 2 Journalism.
Primarily engaged in: Both futures studies and long-range planning.
Areas in which work done (%): 5 As individual consultant, 5 In planning unit of an international organization, 40 In organization with other studies including long-range planning, 50 In organization primarily concerned with futures studies and/or long-range planning.
Direction of work in forecasting: I Social, 2 Environmental, 3 Cultural, 4 Educational.
Direction of work in research: I Value systems, 2 Social priorities, 3 Alternative futures, 4 Environmental, 5 Consumer affairs, 5 The individual in the future.
Direction of work in planning: I Social, 2 Environmental, 3 Educational, 4 Urban.
Time range of work: 5 - 25 years.
Source of support for work (%): 20 Private business, 20 Foundations, 20 Voluntary associations, 20 Unspecified, 20 National government.
Work done for (%): I0 International agencies, I5 Private business, 20 National government. 65 Unspecified.
Occupational function: I Manager, 2 Research worker, 3 Consultant.
Worked in government as: Researcher.
Worked in industry/business in: Consultancy.
Worked in service sector: I Law, 2 Social welfare, 3 Communication media.
Additional information: Concerned with physical and social environment; social indicators; values.

(386)

283. Anthony Judge

Union des Association Internationales, Rue Aux Laines 1, 1000 Bruxelles, Belgium.
Sex: Male.   *Age:* 30-39.
Educational qualification: Master's degree.
Formal training: I Physical sciences, 2 Social/behavioural sciences.
Informal training: I Social/behavioural sciences, 2 Journalism.   *(194)*

284. Robert Jungk

Technische Universität, West Berlin, West Germany.
Sex: Male.   *Age:* 60 or over.
Educational qualification: Doctoral degree.
Formal training: Humanities, Mathematics, Journalism.
Informal training: Education, Design, Cinema/television.
Primarily engaged in: Futures studies.
Areas in which work done (%): I0 In organization concerned with other studies including long-range planning, 30 As academic, in teaching futures studies or long-range planning, 60 Writing on futures studies, for magazines, TV public lectures etc.
Direction of work in research: Social impacts of technology, Alternative futures, Consumer affairs, Value systems, Social priorities, Policy research, Population, The individual in the future, Futures methodology.
Methods used: I Brainstorming, 2 Gaming, 3 Scenario building, 4 Individual expert forecasting, 5 Simulation,
Source of support for work (%): 20 Local government.
Work done for (%): I0 Local or regional government.
Occupational function: Educator, Writer, Columnist.
Worked in education: Teaching, In research.
Additional information: Concerned with looking for future indications in all areas. *(176)*

K 285. Dirk van de Kaa

Ruychrocklaan 125, The Hague, The Netherlands.
Sex: Male.   *Age:* 40-49.
Educational qualification: Doctoral degree.
Formal training: Social/behavioural sciences.
Informal training: Mathematics, Education.
Primarily engaged in: Long-range planning.
Areas in which work done (%): 5 In organization concerned with other studies including long-range planning, 10 As individual consultant, 60 In planning unit of a government agency, 20 In planning unit of an international organization, 5 In organization primarily concerned with futures studies and/or long-range planning.
Direction of work in forecasting: 1 Population, 2 Social, 3 Economic.
Direction of work in research: 1 Population, 2 Policy research, 3 Manpower.
Direction of work in planning: 1 Educational, 2 Political, 3 Labour.
Methods used: 1 Extrapolation techniques, 2 Brainstorming, 3 Statistical models.
Time range of work: 5 - 10 years.
Source of support for work (%): 50 National government, 50 Foundations.
Work done for (%): 20 International agencies, 40 National government, 40 Private business.
Occupational function: 1 Manager, 2 Educator, 3 Consultant, 4 Research worker, 5 Administrator.
Worked in government as: Researcher.
Worked in education: 1 Teaching, 2 In research.   *(513)*

286. Herman Kahn

Quaker Ridge Rd, Croton-on-Hudson, NY 10520, USA.
Sex: Male.   *Age:* 50-59.
Educational qualification: Master's degree.
Formal training: 1 Mathematics, 2 Physical sciences.
Informal training: 1 Social/behavioural sciences, 2 Humanities, 3 Education.
Primarily engaged in: Both futures studies and long-range planning.
Areas in which work done (%): 20 As individual consultant, 10 As academic, in teaching futures studies or long-range planning, 70 In organization concerned with other studies including long-range planning.
Direction of work in forecasting: 1 Economic, 2 Social, 3 Technological, 4 Cultural, 5 Resources, 6 Population.
Direction of work in research: 1 Futures methodology, 2 Alternative futures, 3 Social impacts of technology.
Direction of work in planning: Corporate.
Methods used: 1 Brainstorming, 2 Scenario building, 3 Probabilistic forecasting, 4 Individual expert forecasting.
Time range of work: Beyond 2000 AD.
Source of support for work (%): 10 Grants, 30 Private business, 60 National government.
Work done for (%): 10 Private speaking, 30 Private business, 60 National government.
Occupational function: 1 Research worker, 2 Administrator, 3 Manager, 4 Educator, 5 Consultant.
Worked in industry/business in: 1 Management, 2 Research and development, 3 Consultancy 4 Planning.
Worked in education: Teaching.   *(247)*

287. Max Kaplan

Leisure Studies Program, University of South Florida, Tampa, Fl 33620, USA.
Sex: Male.　*Age:* 60 or over.
Educational qualification: Doctoral degree.
Formal training: I Social/behavioural sciences, 2 Arts.
Areas in which work done (%): I00 In organization concerned with other studies including long-range planning.
Direction of work in forecasting: Cultural.
Direction of work in research: Social impacts of technology.
Direction of work in planning: Social.
Methods used: I Operational models, 2 Brainstorming, 3 Extrapolation techniques.
Time range of work: I0 - 25 years.
Work done for (%): I0 International agencies.
Occupational function: Consultant.
Worked in education: I Teaching, 2 In research, 3 In administration.　*(519)*

288. J.C. Kapur

Kapur Solar Farms, Bijwasan-Naja-Garth Rd, PO Kapas Hera, New Delhi 110037, India.
Sex: Male.　*Age:* 50-59.
Educational qualification: Other graduate/professional degree.
Formal training: I Engineering, 2 Physical sciences, 3 Humanities.
Informal training: I Design, 2 Arts, 3 Social/behavioural sciences.
Primarily engaged in: Both futures studies and long-range planning.
Areas in which work done (%): I0 As academic, in teaching futures studies or long-range planning, 20 In planning unit of a business enterprise, 30 As individual consultant, 40 Industrial management.
Direction of work in forecasting: I Technological, 2 Economic, 3 Social, 4 Cultural,
Direction of work in research: I Social impacts of technology, 2 Alternative futures, 3 Resource utilization.
Direction of work in planning: I Technological, 2 Social, 3 Scientific, 4 Economic, 5 Corporate.
Methods used: I Scenario building, 2 Probabilistic forecasting.
Time range of work: 5 - 25 years.
Source of support for work (%): I00 Personal.
Work done for (%): 20 Private business, 20 Voluntary associations.
Occupational function: I Administration, 2 Consultant, 3 Research worker.
Worked in industry/business in: I Management, 2 Consultancy, 3 Research and development, 4 Planning.
Additional information: Concerned with focus on intermediate and appropriate technologies, for developing societies. Technology and social change. Employment. *(476)*

289. Timo Karttunen

Neste OY, Kaivoratu 10 A, 00101 Helsinki 10, Finland.
Sex: Male.　*Age:* 30-39.
Educational qualification: Doctoral degree.
Formal training: Engineering.
Informal training: Engineering.
Primarily engaged in: Long-range planning.
Areas in which work done (%): I0 In organization concerned with other studies including long-range planning, 20 As individual consultant, 60 In planning unit of a business enterprise, I0 In organization primarily concerned with futures studies and/or long-range planning.

Direction of work in forecasting: I Technological, 2 Economic, 3 Market, 4 Scientific.
Direction of work in research: I Social impacts of technology, 2 Consumer affairs,
3 Alternative futures.
Direction of work in planning: I Corporate, 2 Economic, 3 Technological.
Methods used: I Scenario building, 2 Delphi techniques, 3 Brainstorming, 4 Expert
panels, 5 Simulation.
Time range of work: IO - 25 years.
Source of support for work (%): 5 Local government, 5 National government, 9O Private
business.
Work done for (%): 5 Local or regional government, 5 National government, 9O Private
business.
Worked in industry/business in: Research and development.   *(430)*

29O. Merritt L. Kastens

Editor, Food Industry Futures Magazine, East Lake Rd, Hamilton, NY 13346, USA.
Sex: Male.   *Age:* 5O-59.
Educational qualification: Bachelor's degree.
Formal training: Physical sciences.
Informal training: I Journalism, 2 Engineering.
Primarily engaged in: Both futures studies and long-range planning.
Areas in which work done (%): IOO As individual consultant.
Direction of work in forecasting: I Economic, 2 Social, 3 Cultural, 4 Technological,
5 Market, 6 Scientific, 7 Resources, 8 Environmental, 9 Manpower.
Direction of work in research: Alternative futures, Resource utilization, The family in
the future, Organization.
Direction of work in planning: Corporate.
Methods used: I Individual expert forecasting, 2 Brainstorming, 3 Extrapolation
techniques, 4 Expert panels, 5 Probabilistic forecasting, 6 Scenario building, 7 Delphi
techniques.
Time range of work: 5 - IO years.
Source of support for work: IO National government, 9O Private business.
Work done for (%): IO National government, 9O Private business.
Occupational function: Consultant.
Worked in industry/business in: Management, Research and development, Planning,
Consultancy.
Worked in education: Teaching.
Worked in service sector: Communication media.   *(2O3)*

291. Hideitoshi Kato

Faculty of Law, Gakushuin University, Mejiro, Toshima-ku, Tokyo, Japan.
Sex: Male.   *Age:* 4O-49.
Educational qualification: Master's degree.
Formal training: I Social/behavioural sciences, 2 Humanities, 3 Journalism, 4 Education.
Informal training: I Design, 2 Cinema/television, 3 Humanities, 3 Journalism.
Areas in which work done (%): 5O In organization concerned with other studies including
long-range planning, 5O As academic, in teaching futures studies or long-range planning.
Direction of work in forecasting: I Cultural, 2 Educational.
Direction of work in research: I Alternative futures, 2 Value systems.
Direction of work in planning: I Social, 2 Educational, 3 Urban.
Methods used: I Causal modelling, 2 Brainstorming, 3 Historical analogy, 4 Simulation.
Time range of work: IO - 25 years.

Source of support for work (%): 25 Local government, 50 National government, 25 Foundations.
Work done for (%): 5 Local or regional government, 20 National government, 5 Foundations.
Occupational function: 1 Research worker, 2 Educator, 3 Consultant.
Worked in education: 1 In research, 2 Teaching.
Worked in service sector: Communications media.   *(537)*

292. Felix Kaufman

901 Avon, Ann Arbor, Mi 48104, USA.
Sex: Male.   *Age:* 50-59.
Educational qualification: Doctoral degree.
Formal training: 1 Life sciences, 2 Physical sciences, 3 Social/behavioural sciences, 4 Humanities.
Informal training: 1 Humanities, 2 Social/behavioural sciences, 3 Life sciences, 4 Economics.
Primarily engaged in: Both futures studies and long-range planning.
Areas in which work done (%): 5 As academic, in teaching futures studies or long-range planning, 10 As individual consultant, 5 Associate of Newmark College of Engineering, Centre for Technology Assessment, 80 In planning unit of a business enterprise.
Direction of work in forecasting: 1 Economic, 2 Social, 3 Market, 4 Technological, 5 Resources.
Direction of work in research: 1 Environmental, 2 Alternative futures, 3 Policy research, 4 Social impacts of technology, 5 Futures methodology, 6 Manpower.
Direction of work in planning: 1 Corporate, 2 Economic, 3 Political, 4 Environmental, 5 Technological.
Methods used: 1 Individual expert forecasting, 2 Probabilistic forecasting, 3 Cross impact analysis, 4 Extrapolation techniques, 5 Contextual mapping, 6 Expert panels, 7 Historical analogy, 8 Statistical models, 9 Scenario building.
Time range of work: 5 - beyond year 2000.
Source of support for work (%): 100 Private business.
Work done for (%): 10 National government, 10 International agencies, 80 Private business.
Occupational function: Administrator.
Worked in industry/business in: 1 Management, 2 Planning, 3 Research and development.
Additional information: Concerned with future of medicine; long-range resource analysis; technology assessment; social indicators; economic, social and technological forecasting; international strategic planning.   *(317)*

293. Showei Kawakatsu

c/o Agriculture Division Economic and Social Commission for Asia and the Pacific (ESCAP), Sala Santitham, Rajdamnern Ave, Bangkok, Thailand.
Sex: Male.   *Age:* 40-49.
Educational qualification: Doctoral degree.
Formal training: 1 Social/behavioural sciences, 2 Mathematics.
Informal training: International relations.
Primarily engaged in: Both futures studies and long-range planning.
Areas in which work done (%): 20 In organization primarily concerned with futures studies and/or long-range planning, 80 In planning unit of an international organization.
Direction of work in forecasting: Economic.
Direction of work in research: 1 Policy research, 2 Resource utilization, 3 Alternative futures, 4 Social impacts of technology, 5 The individual in the future.

Direction of work in planning: I Economic, 2 Political.
Methods used: I Statistical models, 2 Expert panels, 3 Historical analogy, 4 Operational models.
Time range of work: 5 - I0 years.
Source of support for work (%): I0 National government, 90 International agencies.
Work done for (%): I0 International agencies, 90 National government.
Occupational function: I Administrator, 2 Research worker.
Worked in government as: Researcher.
Worked in industry/business in: Consultancy.
Worked in education: Teaching.   *(280)*

294. Yoichi Kaya

Engineering Research Institute, University of Tokyo, Bunkyo-ku, Tokyo 113, Japan.
Sex: Male.   *Age:* 40-49.
Educational qualification: Doctoral degree.
Formal training: Engineering, Mathematics.
Informal training: Design, Humanities.
Primarily engaged in: Long-range planning.
Areas in which work done (%): 30 Organization concerned with other studies including long-range planning, 70 As academic, in teaching futures studies or long-range planning.
Direction of work in research: I Resource utilization, 2 Environmental.
Direction of work in planning: I Regional, 2 Environmental.
Methods used: I Operational models, 2 Optimization models, 3 Statistical models.
Time range of work: I0 - 25 years.
Source of support for work (%): 50 National government, 25 Foundations, 25 Voluntary associations.
Work done for (%): 50 National government, 25 Foundations, 25 Voluntary associations.
Occupational function: I Educator, 2 Research worker, 3 Manager.
Worked in education as: I In research, 2 In teaching.   *(561)*

295. Daniel L. Kegan

Office of Institutional Research, Hampshire College, Amherst, Ma O1OO2, USA.
Sex: Male.   *Age:* 30-39.
Educational qualification: Doctoral degree.
Formal training: I Social/behavioural sciences, 2 Engineering.
Areas in which work done for (%): 50 In organization concerned with other studies including long-range planning.
Direction of work in forecasting: I Educational, 2 Social.
Direction of work in research: I Value systems, 2 Social priorities, 3 Social impacts of technology.
Direction of work in planning: I Educational, 2 Social.
Methods used: I Statistical models, 2 Simulation, 3 Expert panels.
Time range of work: 5 - I0 years.
Source of support for work (%): 5 National government, 95 University.
Work done for (%): I00 Own organization - college.
Occupational function: 1 Administrator, 2 Educator, 3 Research worker.
Worked in education: I In research, 2 Teaching, 3 In administration.   *(13)*

296. Suzanne Keller

Dept of Sociology, Princeton University, Princeton NJ O854O, USA.
Sex: Female.   *Age:* 40-49.
Educational qualification: Doctoral degree.

Formal training: I Social/behavioural sciences, 2 Design, 3 Life sciences.
Informal training: I Humanities, 2 Arts.
Primarily engaged in: Both futures studies and long-range planning.
Areas in which work done (%): 5O As academic, in teaching futures studies or long-range planning, 5O Research.
Direction of work in forecasting: I Social, 2 Cultural, 3 Environmental, 4 Technological, 5 Population.
Direction of work in research: I Policy research, 2 The family in the future, 3 Alternative futures.
Direction of work in planning: I Urban, 2 Environmental.
Methods used: I Scenario building, 2 Extrapolation techniques, 3 Historical analogy, 4 Operational models.
Time range of work: IO - 25 years.
Source of support for work (%): IOO National government.
Work done for (%): IOO National government.
Occupational function: I Educator, 2 Research worker, 3 Consultant.
Worked in government as: I Researcher.
Worked in industry/business in: 3 Research and development.
Worked in education: I Teaching.
Worked in service sector: 4 Design.
Additional information: Concerned with long-term future in social institutions, values and community planning. *(44)*

297. Mirian Kelty

American Psychological Assoc, Administrative Officer for Scientific Affairs, 1200 17th Street, NW, Washington, DC20036, USA.
Sex: Female. *Age:* 30-39.
Educational qualification: Doctoral degree.
Formal training: Social/behavioural sciences.
Informal training: I Education, 2 Life sciences, 3 Arts, 4 Humanities, 5 Design.
Areas in which work done (%): IOO Program planning unit of a private non-profit science editors association.
Direction of work in forecasting: I Scientific, 2 Educational, 3 Social, 4 Population, 5 Manpower.
Direction of work in research: I Policy research, 2 Alternative futures, 3 Value systems, 4 Social priorities, 5 Population, 6 Social impacts of technology, 7 Resource utilization, 8 Consumer affairs, 9 Manpower, IO Environmental, 11 The individual in the future, I2 The family in the future.
Direction of work in planning: I Scientific, 2 Educational, 3 Social, 4 Environmental.
Methods used: I Expert panels, 2 Individual expert forecasting, 3 Brainstorming, 4 Historical analogy, 5 Delphi techniques.
Time range of work: 5 - 25 years.
Source of support for work (%): IO Foundations, IO National government, 8O Voluntary associations.
Work done for (%): 5 National government, IO Foundations, 85 Voluntary associations.
Occupational function: I Administrator, 2 Educator, 3 Consultant.
Worked in government as: I Administrator, 2 Researcher.
Worked in education: I In research, 2 Teaching.
Worked in service sector: Social welfare.
Additional information: Concerned with future of psychology/behavioural sciences, with respect to policy formulation, implications of basic and applied research, social/behavioural sciences. *(197)*

298. Lord Kennet

Europe Plus Thirty, c/o The European Commission, Brussels, Belgium.

Sex: Male.   *Age:* 50-59.
Educational qualIfication: Bachelor's degree.
Formal training: I Humanities, 2 Arts.
Informal training: I Politics, 2 Journalism, 3 Humanities, 4 Design, 5 Arts, 6 Social/
behavioural sciences, 7 Physical sciences, 8 Life sciences.
Primarily engaged in: Both futures studies and long-range planning.
Areas in which work done (%): IOO In planning unit of an international organization.
Direction of work in forecasting: Technological, Economic, Social, Cultural, Educational,
Scientific, Environmental, Military, Manpower, Resources, Population.
Direction of work in research: Social impacts of technology, Alternative futures.
Methods used: Brainstorming, Expert panels, Historical analogy.
Time range of work: Beyond 2OOO AD.
Source of support for work (%): IOO International agencies.
Work done for (%): IOO International agencies.
Occupational function: I Director, writer, 2 Administrator.
Worked in government as: I Elected official, 2 Administrator, 3 Researcher.
Worked in industry/business in: I Consultancy, 2 Planning.
Worked in education: Teaching.
Worked in service sector: Communication media.   *(323)*

299. John Kettle

12 Selwood Ave, Toronto, M4E 1B2, Ontario, Canada.

Sex: Male.   *Age:* 4O-49.
Educational qualification: Some college or less.
Formal training: Journalism.
Informal training: I Social/behavioural sciences, 2 Mathematics.
Primarily engaged in: Futures studies.
Areas in which work done (%): 2O As academic, in teaching futures studies or long-range
planning, 2O Journalism, 4O As individual consultant.
Direction of work in forecasting: 2 Economic, 3 Population, 4 Social.
Direction of work in research: Most areas (see Directory guide).
Methods used: I Extrapolation techniques, 2 Statistical models, 3 Individual expert
forecasting, 4 Historical analogy, 5 Scenario building.
Time range of work: IO - 25 years.
Source of support for work (%): IO Voluntary associations, 45 Private business,
45 National government.
Work done for (%): IO Voluntary associations, 45 National government, 45 Private business.
Occupational function: I Consultant.
Worked in industry/business in: 2 Consultancy.
Worked in service sector: Communication media.   *(166)*

3OO. S.N. Wakabi-Kiguwa

East Africa Institute of Social Research, Makerere College, PO Box 16O22, Kampala,
Uganda.

Sex: Male.   *Age:* 3O-39.
Educational qualification: Bachelor's degree.
Formal training: Social/behavioural sciences.
Informal training: Humanities.
Primarily engaged in: Both futures studies and long-range planning.

Areas in which work done (%): IOO In organization primarily concerned with futures studies and/or long-range flanning.
Direction of work in forecasting: Environmental.
Methods used: I Expert panels, 2 Historical analogy, 3 Contextual mapping.
Time range of work: 5 - IO years.
Source of support for work (%): 2O National government.
Work done for (%): I5 National government.
Occupational function: I Administrator, 2 Research worker, 3 Educator.
Worked in education: In research, In administration.   *(188)*

3O1. Alexander King
168 Rue de Grenelle, Paris, 75OO7, France.
Sex: Male.   *Age:* 6O or over.
Educational qualification: Other graduate/professional degree.
Formal training: I Physical sciences, 2 Humanities, 3 Education.
Informal training: Social/behavioural sciences, Humanities, Education.
Areas in which work done (%): 2O In planning unit of an international agency, 2O As individual consultant.
Direction of work in forecasting: I Scientific, 2 Technological, 3 Resources, 4 Manpower.
Direction of work in research: Social impacts of technology, Policy research.
Direction of work in planning: Scientific, Educational.
Methods used: Delphi techniques, Extrapolation techniques, Brainstorming, Statistical models, Expert panels, Relevance trees, Individual expert forecasting, Simulation.
Time range of work: IO - beyond year 2OOO.
Source of support for work (%): 4O Voluntary associations, 6O International agencies.
Work done for (%): 5 Local or regional government, 35 International agencies, 6O Voluntary associations.
Occupational function: I Other, 2 Consultant.
Worked in government as: I Researcher, 2 Administrator.
Worked in industry/business in: Consultancy.
Worked in education: I In research, 2 Teaching.
Additional information: Concerned with science policy, technology assessment, encouragement of research on world and regional models, and advocacy of futures studies.
                                                                                          (335)

3O2. Junnosuke Kishida
15-11 6-Chome, Yutakamachi, Shinagawaku, Tokyo, Japan.
Sex: Male.   *Age:* 5O-59.
Educational qualification: Bachelor's degree.
Formal training: I Journalism, 2 Engineering.
Direction of work in forecasting: Technological.
Direction of work in research: I Social priorities, 2 Policy research, 3 Futures methodology, 4 Social impacts of technology.
Direction of work in planning: I Technological, 2 Environmental.
Methods used: I Expert panels, 2 Brainstorming, 3 Individual expert forecasting.
Time range of work: IO - 25 years.
Source of support for work (%): 2 National government, IO Foundations.
Work done for (%): 5 National government, IO Foundations.
Occupational function: Journalist.

Worked in service sector: Communications media.
Additional information: Concerned with long-range national policy, and technology assessment. *(590)*

303. G.B.E. Kitaka

East African Marine Fisheries Research Organization, PO Box 668, Zanzibar, Tanzania, Africa.
Sex: Male.   *Age:* 30-39.
Educational qualification: Master's degree.
Formal training: Life sciences, Physical sciences.
Informal training: Mathematics.
Primarily engaged in: Both futures studies and long-range planning.
Areas in which work done (%): 70 In organization primarily concerned with futures studies and/or long range planning, 20 In planning unit of a governmental agency, 10 In planning unit of an international organization.
Direction of work in forecasting: Resources.
Direction of work in research: 1 Policy research, 2 Resource utilization.
Direction of work in planning: Resources.
Methods used: Statistical models.
Time range of work: 10 - 25 years.
Source of support for work (%): 85 National government, 15 International agencies.
Work done for (%): 70 Regional governments, 20 National government, 10 International agencies.
Occupational function: 1 Administrator, 2 Research worker.
Worked in government as: 1 Researcher, 2 Administrator. *(555)*

304. Helmut Klages

Höchschule für Verwaltungswissenschaften, 6720 Speyer, Postfach 830, West Germany.
Sex: Male.   *Age:* 40-49.
Educational qualification: Doctoral degree.
Formal training: Social/behavioural sciences.
Informal training: Education.
Areas in which work done (%): 10 In organization primarily concerned with futures studies and/or long-range planning, 5 In planning unit of a governmental agency, 20 As academic, in teaching futures studies or long-range planning.
Direction of work in forecasting: Social.
Direction of work in research: 1 Alternative futures, 2 Social priorities, 3 Value systems, 4 Policy research, 5 The individual in the future, 6 Futures methodology.
Direction of work in planning: 1 Political, 2 Social.
Methods used: Delphi techniques, Scenario building, Contextual mapping, Simulation, Causal modelling.
Time range of work: 10 - 25 years.
Work done for (%): 10 Local or regional government, 20 National government, 5 Voluntary associations.
Occupational function: 1 Educator, 2 Research worker.
Worked in education: 3 Teaching, 4 In research, In administration. *(535)*

305. Gary A. Klee

Assistant Professor, Dept of Geography, San Diego State University, San Diego, Ca 92115, USA.
Sex: Male.   *Age:* 30-39.

Educational qualification: Doctoral degree.
Formal training: Social/behavioural sciences.
Informal training: Peace corps.
Direction of work in forecasting: I Environmental, 2 Resources, 3 Cultural.
Direction of work in research: I Environmental, 2 Resource utilization.
Direction of work in planning: I Environmental, 2 Resources.
Methods used: Individual expert forecasting.
Time range of work: 5 - beyond year 2000.
Occupational function: Educator.
Worked in education: I Teaching, 2 In research.
Additional information: Concerned with long-range resource analysis, and future of cultural systems. *(167)*

306. D. Klein

International Society for Research on Civilization Diseases and Environment, B-1060 Brussels, 29 Square Larousse, Belgium.
Sex: Male.   *Age:* 60 or over.
Educational qualification: Doctoral degree.
Formal training: Life sciences, Humanities.
Informal training: Life sciences.
Areas in which work done (%): 5 In organization primarily concerned with futures studies and/or long-range planning, 20 In planning unit of an international organization.
Direction of work in forecasting: Social, Scientific, Environmental.
Direction of work in research: Social impacts of technology, Alternative futures, Environmental, Social priorities, The family in the future.
Methods used: Expert panels, Individual expert forecasting.
Time range of work: 5 - beyond year 2000.
Source of support for work (%): 20 Foundations.
Worked in education: Teaching.
Worked in service sector: Medicine. *(521)*

307. Francesco Kneschaurek

Ecole de Hautes Etudes Economiques et Sociales, 9000 St Gall, Dufourstr 50, Switzerland.
Sex: Male.   *Age:* 50-59.
Educational qualification: Doctoral degree.
Formal training: Social/behavioural sciences.
Informal training: Journalism, Education.
Primarily engaged in: Both futures studies and long-range planning.
Areas in which work done (%): 10 As academic, in teaching futures studies or long-range planning, 30 In organization primarily concerned with futures studies and/or long-range planning, 30 in planning unit of a governmental agency, 30 In organization concerned with other studies including long-range planning.
Direction of work in forecasting: I Economic, 2 Population, 3 Manpower, 4 Educational, 5 Social, 6 Resources.
Direction of work in research: I Alternative futures, 2 Futures methodology, 3 Policy research, 4 Population, 5 Manpower.
Direction of work in planning: I Economic, 2 Political, 3 Labour, 4 Regional, 5 Educational.
Methods used: I Cross impact analysis, 2 Expert panels, 4 Relevance trees, 5 Historical analogy, 6 Extrapolation techniques.

Time range of work: IO - beyond year 2OOO.
Source of support for work (%): IO Foundations, IO Private business, 8O National government.
Work done for (%): IO Private business, 2O Local or regional government, 7O National government,
Occupational function: I Consultant, 2 Research worker, 3 Educator.
Worked in government as: Administrator.
Worked in education: In research, Teaching.
Worked in industry/business in: Consultancy.   *(79)*

3O8. Heinz H. Koelle
D-1 Berlin 45, Willdenowstr 1O, West Germany.
Sex: Male.   *Age:* 4O-49.
Educational qualification: Doctoral degree.
Formal training: Engineering.
Informal training: Social/behavioural sciences.
Primarily engaged in: Both futures studies and long-range planning.
Areas in which work done (%): 4O In organization primarily concerned with futures studies and/or long-range planning, 4O Teaching in space technology, administration, 2O As academic, in teaching futures studies or long-range planning.
Direction of work in research: I Value systems, 2 Social priorities, 3 Futures methodology.
Direction of work in planning: I Technological, 2 Resources.
Methods used: I Simulation, 2 Causal modelling, 3 Delphi techniques, 4 Scenario building, 5 Extrapolation techniques, 6 Brainstorming.
Time range of work: IO - beyond year 2OOO.
Source of support for work (%): 5O University, 5O National government.
Work done for (%): 2O National government, 4O University.
Occupational function: I Educator, 2 Research worker.
Worked in government as: Researcher.
Worked in education: Teaching.   *(397)*

3O9. Assen Kojaroy
Institute for Contemporary Social Theories, Sofia 35, 'Pionezski Pat' 21, Bulgaria.
Sex: Male.   *Age:* Over 6O.
Educational qualification: Doctoral degree.
Formal training: Philosophy.
Informal training: Social/behavioural sciences.
Areas in which work done (%): IO In organization primarily concerned with futures studies and/or long-range planning, IO As academic, in teaching futures studies or long-range planning.
Direction of work in forecasting: Social.
Direction of work in research: Social impacts of technology, Alternative futures, Futures methodology.
Methods used: I Probabilistic forecasting, 2 Extrapolation techniques, 3 Scenario building, 4 Brainstorming, 5 Historical analogy.
Time range of work: Beyond year 2OOO.
Source of support for work (%): IOO National government.
Work done for (%): 2O National government.
Occupational function: I Research worker, 2 Administrator.
Worked in government as: Administrator.
Worked in education: I In research, 2 In administration, 3 Teaching.   *(593)*

310. Jiri Kolaja
University of Morgantown, 108 Oglebay Hall, W Virginia 26506, USA.
Sex: Male.   *Age:* 50-59.
Educational qualification: Doctoral degree.
Formal training: Social/behavioural sciences.
Informal training: Cinema/television.
Direction of work in forecasting: Social.
Methods used: I Probabilistic forecasting, 2 Expert panels, 3 Causal modelling.
Time range of work: IO - 25 years.
Occupational function: Educator.
Worked in education: Teaching, In research.
Additional information: Concerned with sociology of planning.   *(123)*

311. Gert V. Kortzfleisch
Industry Seminar, University of Mannheim, 68 Mannheim 1, Schloss, West Germany.
Sex: Male.   *Age:* 50-59.
Educational qualification: Doctoral degree.
Formal training: Humanities, Engineering.
Informal training: Social/behavioural sciences.
Primarily engaged in: Long-range planning.
Areas in which work done (%): 30 Consultant, 70 As academic, in teaching futures studies or long-range planning.
Direction of work in forecasting: I Economic, 2 Social, 3 Cultural, 4 Environmental.
Direction of work in research: I Value systems, 2 Social priorities, 3 The individual in the future.
Direction of work in planning: I Economic, 2 Corporate, 3 Environmental.
Methods used: I Simulation, 2 Operational models, 3 Extrapolation techniques.
Time range of work: IO - beyond year 2000.
Source of support for work (%): IOO Foundations.
Work done for (%): 50 Foundations.
Occupational function: I Research worker, 2 Educator, 3 Consultant.
Worked in industry/business in: 2 Management, 3 Consultancy.
Worked in education: In research.
Additional information: Concerned with industrial corporations, religious, environmental, research and development policies.   *(236)*

312. Rajni Kohari
1 Court Rd, Delhi 110054, India.
Sex: Male.   *Age:* 40-49.
Educational qualification: Bachelor's degree.
Formal training: Social/behavioural sciences.
Informal training: Social/behavioural sciences.
Primarily engaged in: Futures studies.
Areas in which work done (%): 20 As individual consultant, 20 Conferences colloquia, 30 In organization primarily concerned with futures studies and/or long-range planning, 30 As academic, in teaching futures studies or long-range planning.
Direction of work in research: I Alternative futures, 2 Value systems, 3 Social Philosophy, 4 The individual in the future, 5 Social priorities, 6 Policy research, 7 Futures methodology.
Direction of work in planning: I Political, 2 Technological, 3 Urban, 4 Evolving intellectual and cultural environment for future outlook, alternative futures, 5 Resources.
Methods used: I Brainstorming, 2 Designing new paradigms for the future, 3 Causal

modelling, 4 Historical analogy, 5 Scenario building.
Time range of work: 5 - 25 years.
Source of support for work (%): 20 International agencies, 30 National government, 50 Own centre.
Work done for (%): 10 Voluntary associations, 20 National government, 20 International agencies, 50 Own centre.
Occupational function: 1 Research worker, 2 Author, 3 Editor.
Worked in government as: Researcher.
Worked in industry/business in: Consultancy.
Worked in education: 1 In research, 2 Teaching, 3 In administration, 4 As editor.
Worked in service sector: 1 Communication media, 2 Social welfare.   *(235)*

313. D. Kuchemann

Aerodynamics Department Royal Aircraft Establishment, Farnborough, Hampshire, UK.
Sex: Male.   *Age:* 60 or over.
Educational qualification: Doctoral degree.
Formal training: Physical sciences.
Informal training: Engineering.
Primarily engaged in: Futures studies.
Areas in which work done (%): 20 As academic, in teaching futures studies or long-range planning, 80 As individual consultant.
Direction of work in forecasting: Scientific.
Direction of work in research: Social impacts of technology.
Direction of work in planning: Scientific.
Time range of work: 5 - 25 years.
Source of support for work (%): 100 National government.
Work done for (%): 100 National government.
Occupational function: 1 Research worker, 2 Consultant, 3 Educator.
Worked in government as: Researcher.   *(99)*

314. Ranjit Kumar

10 Deerbrook Trail, Agincourt, Ontario, Canada.
Sex: Male.   *Age:* 40-49.
Educational qualification: Other graduate/professional degree.
Formal training: Social/behavioural sciences.
Informal training: Humanities.
Areas in which work done (%): 30 In planning unit of an international organization, 15 As academic, in teaching futures studies or long-range planning, 40 Unspecified, 15 In organization concerned with other studies including long-range planning.
Direction of work in planning: Technological, Educational.
Methods used: Scenario building.
Time range of work: 10 - 25 years.
Occupational function: 1 Administrator, 2 Educator, 3 Consultant.
Worked in industry/business in: Management.
Worked in education: 1 In administration, 2 Teaching.
Additional information: Concerned with technology assessment.   *(403)*

315. Kazuo Kuwae

Director, General Manager, Corporate Planning Office, Hitachi Limited, No 5 - 1, 1 Chome, Marunouchi, Chiyoda-ku, Tokyo 100, Japan.
Sex: Male.   *Age:* 50-59.

Educational qualification: Doctoral degree.
Formal training: Engineering.
Informal training: Social/behavioural sciences.
Primarily engaged in: Both futures studies and long-range planning.
Areas in which work done (%): 5 As academic, in teaching futures studies or long-range planning, 30 In planning unit of a business enterprise, 65 In organization primarily concerned with futures studies and/or long-range planning.
Direction of work in forecasting: I Market, 2 Economic.
Direction of work in research: I Alternative futures, 2 Manpower, 3 Resource utilization, 4 Environmental.
Direction of work in planning: Corporate.
Methods used: I Statistical models, 2 Extrapolation techniques, 3 Scenario building.
Time range of work: 5 - IO years.
Source of support for work (%): IOO Private business.
Work done for (%): IOO Private business.
Occupational function: Manager.
Worked in industry/business in: I Research and development, 2 Management, 3 Planning.

(266)

L 316. Igor V. Bestuzhev-Lada

Institute for Social Research, 46 Novo-Cheremnshki, 117418 Moscow, USSR.
Sex: Male.   *Age:* 40-49.
Educational qualification: Doctoral degree.
Formal training: Humanities.
Informal training: Social/behavioural sciences.
Primarily engaged in: Futures studies.
Areas in which work done for (%): IO As individual consultant, 90 In organization primarily concerned with futures studies and/or long-range planning.
Direction of work in forecasting: I Social, 2 Scientific, 3 Educational, 4 Cultural, 5 Environmental.
Direction of work in research: I Futures methodology, 2 Alternative futures, 3 Value systems, 4 Consumer affairs, 5 Social priorities, 6 The family in the future, 7 The individual in the future, 8 Social impacts of technology.
Methods used: I Probabilistic forecasting, 2 Individual expert forecasting, 3 Historical analogy, 4 Scenario building, 5 Delphi techniques.
Time range of work: IO - 25 years.
Source of support for work (%): IOO National government.
Work done for (%): IOO National government.
Occupational function: I Research worker, 2 Administrator, 3 Consultant.
Worked in government as: Researcher.
Worked in industry/business in: Research and development.
Worked in education: In research.
Worked in service sector: Social welfare.
Additional information: Concerned with the future of human way of life. Forecasting in sociology -- the history of modern futures studies.

(243)

317. Eugene C. Lafond

Naval Undersea Centre, San Diego, Ca 92132, USA.
Sex: Male.   *Age:* 6O or over.
Educational qualification: Doctoral degree.
Formal training: Physical sciences.
Informal training: I Physical sciences, 2 Education.

Primarily engaged in: Futures studies.
Areas in which work done (%): 25 As individual consultant, 75 In planning unit of
an international organization.
Direction of work in forecasting: I Scientific, 2 Environmental.
Direction of work in research: Environmental.
Direction of work in planning: I Scientific, 2 Environmental.
Methods used: I Individual expert forecasting, 2 Probabilistic forecasting, 3 Expert
panels, 4 Extrapolation techniques, 5 Statistical models.
Time range of work: 5 - IO years.
Source of support for work (%): IO International agencies, 9O National government.
Work done for (%): IO National government, 9O International agencies.
Occupational function: I Administrator, 2 Research worker, 3 Consultant, 4 Educator.
Worked in government as: I Researcher, 2 Administrator, 3 Elected official.
Worked in industry/business in: Research and development.
Worked in education: In research.   (284)

318. Edward F. Landau

Director Planning and Administration, Allied Chemical Corp, PO Box 1O21R,
Columbia Rd, Morristown, NJ O796O, USA.
Sex: Male.   *Age:* 5O-59.
Educational qualification: Doctoral degree.
Formal training: Physical sciences.
Areas in which work done (%): 8O As individual consultant, 2O In organization
concerned with other studies including long-range planning.
Direction of work in forecasting: I Market, 2 Technological.
Direction of work in research: Resource utilization.
Direction of work in planning: I Corporate, 2 Technological.
Methods used: All methods (see Directory guide)..
Time range of work: 5 - IO years.
Source of support for work (%): IOO Private business.
Work done for (%): IOO Private business.
Occupational function: Administrator.
Worked in industry/business in: I Research and development, 2 Management,
2 Planning.
Additional information: Concerned with technology assessment, long-range resource
analysis, research trends, research administration planning, and marketing research.   (233)

319. Erika Landau

Young Persons' Institute for Promotion of Art and Science, 8 Hess St, Tel Aviv, Israel.
Sex: Female.   *Age:* 4O-49.
Educational qualification: Doctoral degree.
Formal training: I Humanities, 2 Social/behavioural sciences, 3 Education.
Informal training: I Design, 2 Arts.
Areas in which work done (%): IO In organization primarily concerned with futures
studies and/or long-range planning, I5 As individual consultant, I5 In planning
unit of an international organization, 6O Future oriented-education and psychotherapy.
Direction of work in forecasting: Cultural, Educational.
Direction of work in research: I The individual in the future, 2 Value systems.
Direction of work in planning: Educational, Resources.
Methods used: I Brainstorming, 2 Gaming, 3 Scenario building, 4 Historical analogy.
Time range of work: 5 - 25 years.

Occupational function: I Animator, Stimulator, 2 Educator, 3 Administrator.
Worked in education: I Teaching, 2 In administration.
Worked in service sector: Medicine.

(464)

320. Frank Landler

Institut für Sozio-Ökonomische, Entwicklungsforchung, A-1010 Vienna, Austria.
Sex: Male.   *Age:* 30-39.
Educational qualification: Master's degree.
Formal training: Physical sciences, Engineering.
Informal training: Education, Social/behavioural sciences.
Primarily engaged in: Futures studies.
Areas in which work done (%): 80 In organization primarily concerned with futures studies and/or long-range planning.
Direction of work in forecasting: I Educational, 2 Manpower.
Direction of work in research: I Policy research, 2 Population, 3 Manpower.
Direction of work in planning: I Educational, 2 Economic, 3 Political.
Methods used: I Simulation, 2 Causal modelling, 3 Statistical models, 4 Extrapolation techniques, 5 Scenario building.
Time range of work: 10 - 25 years.
Source of support for work (%): 100 National government.
Work done for (%): 100 National government.
Occupational function: Research worker.
Worked in government as: Researcher.
Worked in education: In research.

(548)

321. James A. Lane

c/o International Atomic Energy Agency, PO Box 590, A1010 Vienna, Austria.
Sex: Male.   *Age:* 60 or over.
Educational qualification: Master's degree.
Formal training: Engineering.
Primarily engaged in: Futures studies.
Areas in which work done (%): 100 In planning unit of an international organization.
Direction of work in forecasting: Energy demand.
Methods used: I Extrapolation techniques, 2 Individual expert forecasting, 3 Expert panels.
Time range of work: 10 - 25 years.
Source of support for work (%): 100 International agencies.
Work done for (%): 50 National government, 50 International agencies.
Occupational function: Consultant.
Worked in government as: Administrator.
Worked in industry/business in: Management.
Worked in education: Teaching.

(110)

322. C. Theodore Larson

3575 E Huron River Drive, Ann Arbor, Mi 48104, USA.
Sex: Male.   *Age:* 60 or over.
Educational qualification: Other graduate/professional degree.
Formal training: I Design, 2 Humanities.
Informal training: I Education, 2 Journalism, 3 Mathematics, 4 Social/behavioural sciences.
Primarily engaged in: Both futures studies and long-range planning.
Areas in which work done (%): 100 As individual consultant.

Direction of work in forecasting: I Educational, 2 Technological, 3 Economic, 4 Social, 5 Cultural.
Direction of work in research: I Futures methodology, 2 Social impacts of technology.
Direction of work in planning: I Environmental, 2 Urban, 3 Regional.
Methods used: I Probabilistic forecasting, 2 Statistical models.
Time range of work: IO - 25 years.
Source of support for work (%): IO International agencies, 2O Foundations.
Work done for (%): IO International agencies, 2O Foundations.
Occupational function: I Research worker, 2 Educator.
Worked in government as: I Administrator.
Worked in industry/business in: I Research and development, 2 Management.
Worked in education: I Teaching, 2 In research.
Worked in service sector: Design.
Additional information: Concerned with measurement of comparative rates of change in various fields of activity affecting building and urban development.   *(36O)*

323. André F. Lebeau

Directeur General Adjoint, Centre National d'Etudes Spatiales, 129 Rue de L'Université, Paris - 7C, France.
Sex: Male.   *Age:* 4O-49.
Educational qualification: Doctoral degree.
Formal training: Physical sciences.
Informal training: Engineering.
Primarily engaged in: Both futures studies and long-range planning.
Areas in which work done (%): IOO In planning unit of a governmental agency.
Direction of work in forecasting: Technological, Scientific.
Direction of work in planning: Scientific, Technological.
Methods used: I Extrapolation techniques, 2 Individual expert forecasting, 3 Relevance trees, 4 Simulation.
Time range of work: 5 - 25 years.
Source of support for work (%): IOO National government.
Work done for (%): IOO National government.
Occupational function: Manager.
Worked in government as: I Administrator, 2 Researcher.   *(246)*

324. Leonard A. Lecht

Director, Economic Research, Conference Board, 845 Third Ave, New York, NY 1OO22, USA.
Sex: Male.   *Age:* 5O-59.
Educational qualification: Doctoral degree.
Formal training: Social/behavioural sciences.
Primarily engaged in: Long-range planning.
Areas in which work done (%): IOO In organization concerned with other studies including long-range planning.
Direction of work in forecasting: 3 Manpower, 4 Social.
Direction of work in research: I Manpower, 2 Social priorities.
Methods used: I Social and economic projections, 2 Extrapolation techniques, 3 Statistical models, 4 Individual expert forecasting.
Time range of work: IO - 25 years.
Source of support for work (%): 5O National government, 5O Voluntary associations.
Work done for (%): 5O National government, 5O Voluntary associations.

Occupational function: I Research worker, 2 Administrator.
Worked in education: I Teaching, 2 In administration.   *(78)*

325. Paul Leitzinger

Director, Corporate Planning, Federated Department Stores Inc, 222 West Seventh St,
Cincinnati, Oh 45202, USA.
Sex: Male.   *Age:* 30-39.
Educational qualification: Master's degree.
Formal training: Business.
Primarily engaged in: Long-range planning.
Areas in which work done (%): IOO In planning unit of a business enterprise.
Direction of work in forecasting: Market.
Direction of work in research: Resource utilization.
Direction of work in planning: Corporate.
Methods used: I Causal modelling, 2 Operational models, 3 Individual expert forecasting.
Time range of work: 5 - IO years.
Source of support for work (%): IOO Private business.
Work done for (%): IOO Private business.
Occupational function: I Administrator, 2 Manager, 3 Research worker.
Worked in industry/business in: I Planning, 2 Research and development, 3 Management.
Additional information: Concerned with implications of future trends on profits of a
company.   *(185)*

326. Stuart P. Leland

Executive Director, International Co-operation Council, World Headquarters, 1781 Roscof
Blvd, Northridge, Ca 91324, USA.
Sex: Male.   *Age:* 40-49.
Educational qualification: Master's degree.
Formal training: Social behavioural sciences, Humanities, Mathematics, Education,
Journalism, Religious studies.
Informal training: Social/behavioural sciences, Humanities, Education, Arts, Religion.
Primarily engaged in: Both futures studies and long-range planning.
Areas in which work done (%): 75 International organization primarily concerned with
futures studies and/or long-range planning, 5 As individual consultant, IO Universal
ministry, IO As academic, in teaching futures studies or long-range planning.
Direction of work in forecasting: Educational, Religious.
Direction of work in research: Social impacts of technology, Alternative futures,
Value systems, The individual in the future, The family in the future.
Direction of work in planning: Educational, Religious.
Methods used: Brainstorming, Individual expert forecasting (Prophetic Insight),
Group exploration.
Time range of work: Beyond year 2OOO.
Source of support for work (%): 25 Voluntary associations, 5O Programs, 25 Member-
ships and contributions.
Work done for (%): 75 Voluntary associations, 25 Individuals.
Occupational function: Administrator, Educator, Religious leader.
Worked in education: Teaching.
Worked in service sector: Religion.
Additional information: Concerned with new age emergence in all fields, with
particular reference to consciousness change (universal way of life).   *(549)*

327. Fred B. Lempers

Investigator, Netherlands Central Planning Bureau, S-Gravenhage, Van Stolkweg 14, The Netherlands.

Sex: Female.   *Age:* 30-39.

Educational qualification: Doctoral degree.

Formal training: Social/behavioural sciences.

Informal training: I Mathematics, 2 Education.

Primarily engaged in: Both futures studies and long-range planning.

Areas in which work done (%): 5 As individual consultant, 5 As academic, in teaching futures studies or long-range planning, 90 In planning unit of a governmental agency.

Direction of work in forecasting: Social, Education, Resources.

Direction of work in research: Manpower, Social priorities.

Direction of work in planning: Social, Economic, Labour.

Methods used: Probabilistic forecasting, Delphi techniques, Scenario building, Extrapolation techniques, Statistical models, Expert panels, Operational models, Simulation, Causal modelling.

Additional information: Concerned with future health services, education, labour markets, and social indicators.

(290)

328. Martin Lendi

Institute for National, Regional and Local Planning, Weinbergstr 35, Zurich, Switzerland.

Sex: Male.   *Age:* 40-49.

Educational qualification: Doctoral degree.

Formal training: Law.

Informal training: Social/behavioural sciences, Humanities, Journalism, Administration.

Primarily engaged in: Both futures studies and long-range planning.

Direction of work in research: Policy research.

Direction of work in planning: Urban, Regional, Political.

Time range of work: 5 - 25 years.

Source of support for work (%): IOO National government.

Work done for (%): I8 Local or regional government, 82 National government.

Occupational function: I Manager, 2 Research worker, 3 Educator, 4 Consultant.

Worked in government as: Administrator.

(408)

329. Hans Lenke

Universitat Karlsruhe, Technische für Philosophie, Kollegium am Schloss, Bau II, West Germany.

Sex: Male.   *Age:* 30-39.

Educational qualification: Doctoral degree.

Formal training: Social/behavioural sciences, Humanities, Mathematics, Education.

Informal training: Athletics, Coaching.

Areas in which work done (%): IO As academic, in teaching futures studies or long-range planning.

Direction of work in forecasting: I Cultural, 2 Scientific, 3 Technological.

Direction of work in research: I Value systems, 2 Social impacts of technology, 3 Futures methodology, 4 The individual in the future.

Direction of work in planning: I Scientific, 2 Social, 3 Technological, 4 Education.

Methods used: I Individual expert forecasting, 2 Scenario building.

Time range of work: IO years-beyond year 2OOO.

Occupational function: I Research worker, 2 Educator, 3 Administrator.

Worked in education: I Teaching, 2 In research, 3 In administration.

(54)

330. Ralph C. Lenz, Jr

University of Dayton, Research Institute, Dayton, Ohio 45467, USA.
Sex: Male.　　*Age:* 50-59.
Educational qualification: Master's degree.
Formal training: Engineering, Management.
Informal training: Education, Social/behavioural sciences.
Primarily engaged in: Futures studies.
Areas in which work done (%): 80 Organization primarily concerned with futures studies and/or long-range planning, 10 Individual consultant, 10 academic, in teaching futures studies or long-range planning.
Direction of work in forecasting: 1 Technological, 2 Resources, 3 Military, 4 Economic, 5 Social, 6 Market.
Direction of work in research: 1 Futures methodology, 2 Resource utilization, 3 Social impacts of technology, 4 Social priorities, 5 Alternative futures.
Direction of work in planning: 1 Technological, 2 Military, 3 Urban, 4 Corporate, 5 Regional.
Methods used: 1 Extrapolation techniques, 2 Cross impact analysis, 3 Delphi techniques, 4 Scenario building, 5 Causal modelling, 6 Historical analogy, 7 Relevance trees, 8 Simulation.
Time range of work: 10 - 25 years.
Source of support for work (%): 20 Local government, 40 National government, 25 Private business, 15 University.
Work done for (%): 25 Local or regional government, 45 National government, 25 Private business, 5 University.
Occupational function: 1 Consultant, 2 Research worker.
Worked in government as: In research and development.
Worked in industry/business in: Consultancy.
Worked in education: Research and consulting.　　　　　　　　　　　　　*(565)*

331. Wassily Leontief

309 Li Hauer Centre, Harvard University, Cambridge, Ma 02138, USA.
Sex: Male.　　*Age:* 60 or over.
Educational qualification: Doctoral degree.
Formal training: Social/behavioural sciences.
Informal training: Mathematics.
Direction of work in forecasting: Technological, Economic, Environmental, Resources, Population.
Methods used: Statistical models.
Time range of work: 10 - beyond year 2000.
Source of support for work (%): 50 Foundations, 50 International agencies.
Work done for (%): 30 International agencies.
Occupational function: Research worker, Educator, Consultant.
Worked in education: Teaching, In research.
Worked in industry/business in: Consultancy.
Additional information: Concerned with future of economy and society (and the World).　　　　　　　　　　　　　　　　　　　　　　　　　　　　*(74)*

332. Stanley Lesse

Editor-in-Chief, American Journal of Psychotherapy, 15 West 81st St, New York, NY 10024, USA.
Sex: Male.　　*Age:* 50-59.

Educational qualification: Doctor of medical science, Doctor of medicine.
Formal training: I Life sciences, 2 Social/behavioural sciences, 3 Education, Neurology, Psychiatry.
Informal training: I Journalism, 2 Humanities, 3 Physical sciences.
Areas in which work done (%): 25 Organization concerned with other studies including long-range planning.
Direction of work in forecasting: I Medicine, 2 Social, 3 Educational.
Direction of work in research: I Medicine, 2 The individual in the future, 3 Social impacts of technology.
Direction of work in planning: I Medicine, 2 Social, 3 Educational.
Methods used: I Cross impact analysis, 2 Probabilistic forecasting, 3 Individual expert forecasting.
Time range of work: IO - 25 years.
Source of support for work (%): IOO Self funded.
Work done for (%): 20 Voluntary associations.
Occupational function: Practising Neurologist - psychiatrist.
Worked in education: I In research, 2 Teaching.
Worked in service sector: Medicine.
Additional information: Concerned with the future of medicine, sources of individual and group decompensation and the future of education.   *(573)*

333. Ed Levin

Asst Vice President and Director of Marketing Planning, Gulf and Western Industries Inc, 1 Gulf and Western Plaza, New York, NY 1OO23, USA.
Sex: Male.   *Age:* 4O-49.
Educational qualification: Master's degree.
Formal training: Marketing.
Informal training: Finance and economics.
Primarily engaged in: Both futures studies and long-range planning.
Areas in which work done (%): 5 As academic, in teaching futures studies or long-range planning, 95 In organization primarily concerned with futures studies and/or long-range planning.
Direction of work in forecasting: Market.
Direction of work in research: Alternative futures.
Direction of work in planning: Corporate.
Methods used: Data collecting and analysing.
Time range of work: 5 - IO years.
Source of support for work (%): IOO Private business.
Work done for (%): IOO Private business.
Occupational function: I Manager.
Worked in industry/business in: I Management, 2 Research and development, 3 Planning.
Worked in education: Teaching.   *(375)*

334. Fritz Lienemann

Project Director of Plan Europe 2OOO, c/o Systemplan EV, D-69 Heidelberg 1, Tiergartenstr 15, West Germany.
Sex: Male.   *Age:* 3O-39.
Educational qualification: Master's degree.
Formal training: Social/behavioural sciences.
Informal training: I Design, 2 Journalism.
Primarily engaged in: Both futures studies and long-range planning.

Areas in which work done (%): IOO In organization primarily concerned with futures studies and/or long-range planning.
Direction of work in forecasting: I Social, 2 Economic, 3 Cultural, 4 Technological, 5 Environmental.
Direction of work in research: I Alternative futures, 2 Value systems, 3 Social priorities, 4 The individual in the future, 5 Social impacts of technology, 6 Environmental.
Direction of work in planning: I Urban, 2 Regional, 3 Political, 4 Social.
Methods used: I Scenario building, 2 Contextual mapping, 3 Delphi techniques, 4 Individual expert forecasting.
Time range of work: IO - 25 years.
Source of support for work (%): 5O Foundations, 5O National government.
Work done for (%): 5O National government, 5O Foundations.
Occupational function: Research worker.
Additional information: Concerned with international comparison of urban development trends; international comparison of social indicators concerning quality of urban life. *(108)*

335. S.W. Lim

Design Partnership, 5881 Woh Hup Complex, Beach Rd, Singapore 7, Republic of Singapore.
Sex: Male.   *Age:* 4O-49
Educational qualification: Other graduate/professional degree.
Formal training: Design.
Informal training: Social/behavioural sciences.
Direction of work in forecasting: I Environmental, 2 Cultural, 3 Economic.
Direction of work in research: I Environmental, 2 Value systems.
Direction of work in planning: I Urban, 2 Environmental, 3 Economic.
Time range of work: IO - 25 years.
Occupational function: Consultant.   *(171)*

336. Martti Lindquist

Senior Research Associate, Research Institute of the Lutheran Church, Satakunnankatu 11 B 21, SF-331OO Tampere 1O, Finland.
Sex: Male.   *Age:* 25-29.
Educational qualification: Other graduate/professional degree.
Formal training: 1 Theology, 2 Social/behavioural sciences.
Informal training: Life sciences.
Primarily engaged in: Futures studies.
Areas in which work done (%): IOO Church research institute.
Direction of work in research: Value systems.
Methods used: Content analysis.
Time range of work: Beyond 2OOO AD.
Source of support for work (%): IOO Church research institute.
Occupational function: Research worker.
Worked in education: In research.
Additional information: Concerned with analysis of church related statements concerning economic growth and the image of man in future perspective.   *(67)*

337. Harold A. Linstone

Portland State University, PO Box 751, Portland, Or 972O7, USA.
Sex: Male.   *Age:* 5O-59.
Educational qualification: Doctoral degree.

Formal training: Mathematics.
Informal training: Systems analysis.
Primarily engaged in: Both futures studies and long-range planning.
Areas in which work done (%): 20 Individual consulting, 20 In organization concerned with other studies including long-range planning, 20 Editor of a future oriented journal, 40 As academic, in teaching futures studies or long-range planning.
Direction of work in forecasting: I Technological, 2 Social, 3 Environmental, 4 Economic.
Direction of work in research: I Futures methodology, 2 Alternative futures.
Direction of work in planning: I Governmental, 2 Technological, 3 Corporate.
Methods used: I Delphi techniques, 2 Extrapolation techniques, 3 Historical analogy, 4 Gaming, 5 Cross impact analysis, 6 Scenario building, 7 Relevance trees, 8 Operational models, 9 Simulation.
Time range of work: 5 - 25 years.
Source of support for work (%): IO Foundations, IO International agencies, 20 Private business, 60 National and state government.
Work done for (%): IO International agencies, IO Foundations, 20 Private business, 60 Government.
Occupational function: I Educator, 2 Research worker, 3 Administrator.
Worked in industry/business in: Planning.
Worked in education: I Teaching, 2 In administration, 3 In research.   *(274)*

338. Joseph Lipson
1721 Colonial Lane, Northfield, II 60093, USA.
Sex: Male.   *Age:* 40-49.
Educational qualification: Doctoral degree.
Formal training: Physical sciences.
Informal training: I Social/behavioural sciences, 2 Education, 3 Humanities.
Areas in which work done (%): 40 In organization primarily concerned with futures studies and/or long-range planning, 60 Administration.
Direction of work in forecasting: Social.
Direction of work in research: I Social impacts of technology, 2 Manpower.
Direction of work in planning: I Educational, 2 Technological.
Methods used: I Operational models, 2 Individual expert forecasting, 3 Extrapolation techniques, 4 Causal modelling, 5 Social indicators.
Time range of work: 5 - beyond year 2000.
Source of support for work (%): IOO State government.
Work done for (%): IOO University.
Occupational function: Administrator.
Worked in education: I In research, 2 In administration, 3 Teaching.
Additional information: Concerned with prediction and modification of future society; interaction of education and society.   *(325)*

339. Edmond Lisle
CREDOC, The London School of Economics and Political Science, Houghton St, Aldwych, London WC2A 2AE, UK.
Sex: Male.   *Age:* 50-59.
Educational qualification: Doctoral degree.
Formal training: I Social/behavioural sciences, 2 Humanities.
Informal training: I Engineering, 2 Mathematics.
Areas in which work done (%): IO As individual consultant, IO As academic, in teaching futures studies or long-range planning.

Direction of work in forecasting: I Social, 2 Cultural, 3 Market.
Methods used: I Historical analogy, 2 Simulation, 3 Probabilistic forecasting, 4 Delphi techniques.
Occupational function: I Educator, 2 Research worker, 3 Consultant.
Worked in education: I Teaching, 2 In research, 3 In administration.   *(287)*

340. Dennis Little

Specialist in Future Research, Congressional Research Service, Library of Congress, Washington DC 20540, USA.
Sex: Male.   *Age:* 30-39.
Educational qualification: Master's degree.
Formal training: Social/behavioural sciences.
Informal training: Education, Design.
Primarily engaged in: Futures studies.
Areas in which work done (%): IOO In planning unit of a governmental agency.
Direction of work in forecasting: Social.
Direction of work in research: I Futures methodology, 2 Policy research, 3 Social priorities, 4 Alternative futures.
Direction of work in planning: Social.
Methods used: Library research.
Time range of work: 5 - I5 years.
Source of support for work (%): IOO National government.
Work done for (%): IOO National government.
Occupational function: Research worker.
Worked in government as: I Administrator, 2 Researcher.
Worked in industry/business in: I Management, 2 Planning.
Worked in service sector: Social welfare.   *(563)*

341. Dennis Livingston

History/Pol Sci Dept, Rensselaer Polytechnic Institute, Troy, NY 12181, USA.
Sex: Male.   *Age:* 30-39.
Educational qualification: Doctoral degree.
Formal training: Social/behavioural sciences.
Informal training: I Social/behavioural sciences, 2 Futures studies, International law, science policy.
Primarily engaged in: Futures studies.
Areas in which work done (%): IO As individual consultant, 9O As academic, in teaching futures studies or long-range planning.
Direction of work in forecasting: I Social, 2 Environmental, 3 Educational.
Direction of work in research: I Alternative futures, 2 Environmental, 3 Social impacts of technology, 4 Social priorities.
Direction of work in planning: I Social, 2 Environmental.
Methods used: I Scenario building/science fiction, 2 Extrapolation techniques, 3 Brainstorming.
Time range of work: IO - beyond year 2OOO.
Source of support for work (%): IOO Academic.
Occupational function: Educator.
Worked in education: I Teaching, 2 In research.   *(51)*

342. Robert Logan

Local Gov Rel Div, 240 Cottage SE, Salem, Or 97310, USA.
Sex: Male.   *Age:* 30-39.
Educational qualification: Bachelor's degree.
Formal training: Public administration.
Areas in which work done (%): 100 In planning unit of a governmental agency.
Direction of work in planning: Government.
Methods used: Scenario building, Futures conferences.
Time range of work: 10 - 25 years.
Source of support for work (%): 33 State government, 67 National government.
Work done for (%): 50 Local or regional government.
Occupational function: Administrator.
Worked in government as: Administrator.
Additional information: Concerned with the future of the state of Oregon.   *(244)*

343. Jim Lotz

Jim Lotz Associates, Box 3393, Halifax South PO, Halifax, NS B3J 3J1, Canada.
Sex: Male.   *Age:* 40-49.
Educational qualification: Master's degree.
Formal training: 1 Social/behavioural sciences, 2 Physical sciences.
Informal training: 1 Social/behavioural sciences, 2 Humanities, 3 Journalism, 4 Education.
Primarily engaged in: Long-range planning.
Areas in which work done (%): 20 Personal writing and thinking, 30 In planning unit of a business enterprise, 50 As individual consultant.
Direction of work in forecasting: 1 Social, 2 Educational.
Direction of work in research: 1 Social impacts of technology, 2 Social priorities, 3 Value systems.
Direction of work in planning: 1 Community development and citizen participation, 2 Social, 3 Regional.
Methods used: 1 Historical analogy, 2 Individual expert forecasting, 3 Scenario building.
Time range of work: 10 - 25 years.
Source of support for work (%): 100 Self funded.
Work done for (%): 30 Personal.
Occupational function: 1 Consultant, 2 Research worker.
Worked in government as: Researcher.
Worked in education: 1 In research, 2 Teaching, 3 In administration.   *(64)*

344. Ebba Lund

The Royal Veterinary and Agricultural University of Copenhagen, Dept of Veterinary, Virology, and Immunology, 13, Bulowsvel, 1870 Copenhagen V, Denmark.
Sex: Female.   *Age:* 50-59.
Educational qualification: Doctoral degree.
Formal training: 1 Life sciences, 2 Engineering.
Informal training: 1 Life sciences, 2 Journalism.
Direction of work in forecasting: 1 Environmental.
Direction of work in research: 1 Environmental.
Direction of work in planning: 1 Environmental, 2 Technological.
Methods used: 1 Extrapolation techniques, 2 Expert panels.
Time range of work: 10 - 25 years.
Source of support for work (%): 50 Local government, 50 National government.

Work done for (%): 5 Local or regional government, 5 Voluntary associations, IO National government.
Occupational function: I Research worker, 2 Educator, 3 Administrator, 4 Consultant.
Worked in education: I In research, 2 Teaching, 3 In administration.
Worked in service sector: 2 Medicine.
Additional information: Concerned with water pollution control. *(201)*

345. David D. Lundin
5256 Breeze Hill Place, Troy, Mi 48084, USA.
Sex: Male. *Age:* 30-39.
Educational qualification: Other graduate/professional degree.
Formal training: I Humanities, 2 Journalism, 3 Social/behavioural sciences, 4 Education, 5 Business.
Informal training: I Social/behavioural sciences, 2 Education, 3 Mathematics, 3 Journalism, 4 Humanities, 5 Business, Economics.
Primarily engaged in: Long-range planning.
Areas in which work done (%): IOO In planning unit of a business enterprise,
Direction of work in forecasting: I Economic, Cultural, Market, 2 Social, 3 Auto market.
Direction of work in research: I Value systems, Social priorities, The individual in the future, The family in the future, 3 Auto consumer market.
Direction of work in planning: Market penetration (automobiles).
Methods used: I Statistical models, 2 Simulation, 3 Historical analogy, 4 The individual in the future, 5 Scenario building, 6 Expert panels.
Time range of work: 5 - IO years.
Source of support for work (%): IOO Private business.
Work done for (%): IOO Private business.
Occupational function: I Manager, 2 Research worker, 3 Administrator.
Worked in industry/business in: I Planning, 2 Management.
Worked in education: I Teaching. *(136)*

346. H. Tambs-Lyche
General Secretary, International Council for the Exploration of the Sea, Charlottenlund Slot, DK 2920 Charlottenlund, Denmark.
Sex: Male. *Age:* 60 or over.
Educational qualification: Master's degree.
Formal training: Life sciences.
Informal training: Physical sciences.
Areas in which work done (%): IOO In planning unit of an international organization.
Occupational function: Administrator.
Worked in government as: Researcher. *(269)*

347. John McHale
Centre for Integrative Studies, School of Advanced Technology, State University of New York at Binghamton, Binghamton, NY 13901, USA.
Sex: Male. *Age:* 50-59.
Educational qualification: Doctoral degree.
Formal training: Sociology, Technology, Social/behavioural sciences, Art.
Informal training: Resource analysis.
Primarily engaged in: Futures studies.
Areas in which work done (%): IOO In organization primarily concerned with futures studies and/or long-range planning.

Direction of work in forecasting: Social, Cultural, Technological, Resources, Population.
Direction of work in research: Social impacts of technology, Alternative futures, Value systems, World resources, Human requirements.
Direction of work in planning: World priorities, Human requirements, Resources, Environmental.
Methods used: Contextual mapping, Expert panels, Scenario building, Historical analogy, Individual expert forecasting.
Time range of work: Beyond year 2000.
Source of support for work (%): 100 University.
Work done for (%): 50 University, 25 International agencies, 25 Foundations.
Occupational function: Director of centre.
Worked in industry/business in: Consultant.
Worked in education: Teaching.
Worked in service sector: Communications.   *(586)*

348. Magda Cordell McHale

Centre for Integrative Studies, School of Advanced Technology, State University of New York at Binghamston, Binghamton, NY 13901, USA.
Sex: Female.   *Age:* 50-59.
Educational qualification: Master's degree.
Formal training: Arts, Humanities, Languages.
Informal training: Resource analysis, Population study, Futures studies.
Primarily engaged in: Futures studies.
Areas in which work done (%): 100 In organization primarily concerned with futures studies and/or long-range planning.
Direction of work in forecasting: Social, Cultural, Resource, Population.
Direction of work in research: Social impacts of technology, Human requirements, Women studies.
Direction of work in planning: Human requirements, Social priorities.
Methods used: Contextual mapping, Expert panels, Historical analogy.
Time range of work: Beyond year 2000.
Source of support for work (%): External funding.
Work done for (%): 50 Foundations, 50 International agencies.
Occupational function: Senior Research Associate.
Worked in industry/business in: Consultant.
Worked in education: Educational advisor, In research.
Worked in service sector: Communications.   *(587)*

349. O.W. Mackley

Centre for the Study of Social Policy, Stanford Research Institute, Menlo Park, Ca 94025, USA.
Sex: Male.   *Age:* 30-39.
Educational qualification: Doctoral degree.
Formal training: 1 Social/behavioural sciences, 2 Engineering, 3 Design.
Informal training: 1 Mathematics, 2 Education, 3 Humanities, 4 Law.
Primarily engaged in: Both futures studies and long-range planning.
Areas in which work done (%): 85 In organization primarily concerned with futures studies and/or long-range planning, 5 As academic, in teaching futures studies or long-range planning, 5 Giving seminars, 2 As individual consultant, 2 In planning unit of a government agency, 1 In organization concerned with other studies including long-range planning.

Direction of work in forecasting: I Cultural, 2 Educational, 3 Social, 4 Technological.
Direction of work in research: I Policy research, 2 Social priorities, 3 Social impacts of technology, 4 Alternative futures, 5 Futures methodology.
Direction of work in planning: I Educational, 2 Social, 3 Political, 4 Scientific, 5 Technological.
Methods used: I Policy analysis, 2 Contextual mapping, 3 Historical analogy, 4 Wisdom building.
Time range of work: 5 - beyond year 2000.
Source of support for work (%): 60 National government, 20 Regional government, IO Foundations, IO Consulting.
Work done for (%): 5 Local or regional government, I5 General public, 30 Foundations, 50 National government.
Occupational function: I Research worker, 2 Manager, 3 Consultant, 4 Educator.
Worked in industry/business in: I Research and development, 2 Training.   *(292)*

350. Ted McIlvenne
330 Ellis Street, San Francisco, Ca, USA.
Sex: Male.   *Age:* 40-49.
Educational qualification: Other graduate/professional degree.
Formal training: Social/behavioural sciences, Humanities, Education, Arts.
Informal training: Social/behavioural sciences, Humanities, Education, Arts, Cinema/ television, Theology.
Direction of work in forecasting: Economic, Social, Cultural, Educational, Scientific, Population.
Direction of work in research: Alternative futures, Value systems, Population, The family in the future.
Direction of work in planning: Social, Economic, Corporate, Resources.
Methods used: Network analysis, Operational models.
Time range of work: 5 - 25 years.
Source of support for work (%): 20 Voluntary associations, 80 Foundations.
Occupational function: Administration.
Worked in industry/business in: Research and development.
Worked in education: Teaching, In research, In administration.
Worked in service sector: Medicine, Social welfare, Religion, Communication media, Design.
Additional information: Concerned with future of education.   *(207)*

351. J. Michael McLean
Science Policy Research Unit, University of Sussex, Falmer, Brighton BN1 9RF, UK.
Sex: Male.   *Age:* 25-29.
Educational qualification: Bachelor's degree.
Formal training: I Humanities, 2 Physical sciences.
Informal training: I Mathematics, 2 Journalism.
Primarily engaged in: Futures studies.
Areas in which work done (%): 5 As academic in teaching futures studies or long-range planning, 20 As individual consultant, 75 In organization concerned with other studies including long-range planning.
Direction of work in forecasting: I Social, 2 Economic, 3 Technological.
Direction of work in research: I Alternative futures, 2 Policy research, 3 Social impacts of technology.
Methods used: Various.

Time range of work: 5 - 25 years.
Source of support for work (%): 25 International agencies, 75 National government.
Work done for (%): 25 International agencies, 75 National government.
Occupational function: Research worker.
Worked in industry/business in: I Management, 2 Consultancy.
Worked in education: In research.
Additional information: Concerned with forecasts of food and agriculture.   *(499)*

352. Gerald J. McLindon

Dean, School of Environmental Design, Room 304 Field House, Louisiana State
University, Baton Rouge, La 70803, USA.
Sex: Male.   *Age:* 50-59.
Educational qualification: Other graduate/professional degree.
Formal training: I Design, 2 Engineering, 3 Education.
Informal training: Life sciences, Social/behavioural sciences.
Primarily engaged in: Both futures studies and long-range planning.
Areas in which work done (%): 10 In planning unit of a governmental agency, 10 In
organization concerned with other studies including long-range planning, 20 As individual
consultant, 10 In organization primarily concerned with futures studies and/or long-range
planning, 50 As academic, in teaching futurus studies or long-range planning.
Direction of work in forecasting: Social, Educational, Environmental, Manpower, Resources,
Urban design.
Direction of work in research: Manpower, Value systems, Policy research, The individual
in the future, The family in the future.
Direction of work in planning: Urban, Regional, Educational, Environmental.
Methods used: Extrapolation techniques, Contextual mapping, Brainstorming, Statistical
models, Relevance trees, Network analysis, Historical analogy, Operational models,
Individual expert forecasting, Simulation.
Time range of work: Beyond 2000 AD.
Work done for (%): 10 National government, 15 Private business, 50 Education.
Occupational function: Administrator, Educator, Consultant.
Worked in industry/business in: Management, Planning, Consultancy.
Worked in education: Teaching, In research, In administration.
Worked in service sector: Design.   *(218)*

353. John Maddox

Director, Nuffield Foundation, Regents Park, London NW1 4RS, UK.
Sex: Male.   *Age:* 50-59.
Educational qualification: Master's degree.
Formal training: Physical sciences.
Informal training: Mathematics, Journalism, Education.
Direction of work in research: Resource utilization, Environmental, Popula-
tion.
Methods used: Writing.
Time range of work: 10 - 25 years.
Occupational function: Journalist.
Worked in industry/business in: Management.
Worked in education: In research, In administration.   *(96)*

354. Pentti Malaska
Turun Kauppakorkeakoulu, Rentorinpellontie 5, 20500 Turku 50, Finland.
Sex: Male.   *Age:* 40-49.
Educational qualification: Doctoral degree.
Formal training: I Engineering, 2 Mathematics.
Informal training: I Education, 2 Mathematics, 3 Energy economy.
Areas in which work done (%): 5 In planning unit of a governmental agency, 10 In planning unit of a business enterprise, 25 As individual consultant, 50 As academic, in teaching math modelling.
Direction of work in forecasting: Economic.
Direction of work in research: Alternative futures, Futures methodology.
Direction of work in planning: Scientific, Economic, Corporate, Environmental.
Methods used: Probabilistic forecasting, Delphi techniques, Scenario building, Extrapolation techniques, Statistical models, Simulation, Causal modelling.
Time range of work: 10 - 25 years.
Source of support for work (%): 20 Private business, 30 National government, 50 Personal.
Work done for (%): 20 Private business, 30 National government, 50 Personal.
Occupational function: Research worker, Educator.
Worked in government as: Researcher.
Worked in industry/business in: Planning, Consultancy.
Worked in education: Teaching, In research, In administration.
Additional information: Concerned with future of Finland, new direction for science and technology, technology assessment. 'World Energy Game' is another interest.   *(480)*

355. Ivan Ma'Lex
Hadolinach 18, 14700 Prague 4, Czechoslovakia.
Sex: Male.   *Age:* 60 or over.
Educational qualification: Other graduate/professional degree.
Formal training: Life sciences.
Informal training: Social/behavioural sciences, Education, Arts.
Areas in which work done (%): 10 As individual consultant, 90 Private studies.
Direction of work in forecasting: Scientific, Environmental.
Direction of work in research: Social impacts of technology, Environmental, Value systems, The individual in the future.
Direction of work in planning: Scientific.
Methods used: Network analysis, Historical analogy.
Time range of work: 10 - beyond year 2000.
Source of support for work (%): 100 National government.
Occupational function: Consultant.
Worked in government as: Researcher.
Worked in education: In research.
Additional information: Concerned with future of medicine, biology for the future, science of science.   *(514)*

356. Carlos A. Mallmann
President, Bariloche Foundation, Latin American World Model, CC 138 Baroloche - Rio Negro, Argentina.
Sex: Male.   *Age:* 40-49.
Educational qualification: Doctoral degree.
Formal training: Physical sciences.
Informal training: Social/behavioural sciences.

Primarily engaged in: Both futures studies and long-range planning.
Areas in which work done (%): 100 Organization concerned with other studies including long-range planning.
Direction of work in research: Alternative futures, Value systems, Futures methodology.
Methods used: Normative simulation models.
Time range of work: Beyond year 2000.
Source of support for work (%): 50 International agencies, 50 Bariloche Foundation.
Work done for (%): 100 Bariloche Foundation.
Occupational function: Research worker.
Worked in government as: 1 Researcher, 2 Administrator.
Worked in education: In research, In administration, Teaching.
Additional information: Concerned with science policy, quality of life and world and regional models.   *(570)*

357. Thomas F. Mandel

Policy Analyst, Centre for the Study of Social Policy, Stanford Research Institute, Menlo Park, Ca 94025, USA.
Sex: Male.   *Age:* 30-39.
Educational qualification: Bachelor's degree.
Formal training: 1 Futuristics, 2 Cybernetics systems.
Informal training: 1 Mathematics, 2 Cinema/television.
Primarily engaged in: Both futures studies and long-range planning.
Areas in which work done (%): 5 As individual consultant, 5 As academic, in teaching futures studies or long-range planning, 90 In organization primarily concerned with futures studies and/or long-range planning.
Direction of work in forecasting: 1 Resources, 2 Transportation.
Direction of work in research: 1 Policy research, 2 Futures methodology.
Direction of work in planning: 1 Social, 2 Resources, 3 Educational.
Methods used: 1 Simulation, 2 Delphi techniques, 3 Probabilistic forecasting, 4 Statistical models, 5 Expert panels, 6 Brainstorming.
Time range of work: 10 - 25 years.
Source of support for work (%): 10 Self employment, 90 Private business.
Work done for (%): 10 Consultation, 90 National government.
Occupational function: 1 Research worker, 2 Consultant.
Worked in government as: Researcher.
Worked in industry/business in: Consultancy.   *(15)*

358. Edwin Mansfield

Wharton School of Finance and Commerce, Dietrich Hall, University of Pennsylvania, 37th and Locust St, Philadelphia, Pa USA.
Sex: Male.   *Age:* 40-49.
Educational qualification: Doctoral degree.
Formal training: Social/behavioural sciences.
Direction of work in research: Social impacts of technology.
Methods used: Statistical models.
Time range of work: 5 - 10 years.
Source of support for work (%): 25 Foundations, 75 National government.
Occupational function: Research worker, Educator.
Worked in education: Teaching, In research.   *(39)*

359. Michael Marien
Director, Information for Policy Design, Webster Rd, La Fayette, NY 13084, USA.
Sex: Male.   *Age:* 30-39.
Educational qualification: Doctoral degree.
Formal training: Social/behavioural sciences.
Informal training: Life sciences, Education, Futures.
Primarily engaged in: Futures studies.
Additional information: Concerned with futures documentation.   *(14)*

360. P. Marstrand
Science Policy Research Unit, University of Sussex, Falmer, Brighton BN1 9RF, UK.
Sex: Female.   *Age:* 40-49.
Educational qualification: Master's degree.
Formal training: Life sciences, Applied Hydrobiology.
Informal training: Life sciences, Social/behavioural sciences, Humanities, Education.
Primarily engaged in: Futures studies.
Areas in which work done (%): 10 As individual consultant, 20 As academic, in teaching futures studies or long-range planning, 70 Research.
Direction of work in forecasting: 1 Resources, 2 Environmental, 3 Technological, 3 Economic, 3 Social, 3 Scientific.
Direction of work in research: 1 Social impacts of technology, 1 Alternative futures, 1 Resource utilization, 1 Policy research, 2 Environmental, 2 Population.
Methods used: All methods (see Directory guide).
Time range of work: 10 - beyond year 2000.
Occupational function: 1 Research worker.
Worked in education: 1 Teaching, 2 In research.   *(484)*

361. Antonio de Martini
Via Mercalli 13, Rome 00198, Italy.
Sex: Male.   *Age:* 30-39.
Educational qualification: Master's degree.
Formal training: Social/behavioural sciences.
Informal training: Social/behavioural sciences, Engineering, Journalism, Military.
Direction of work in forecasting: 1 Market, 2 Resources, 3 Military.
Direction of work in research: 1 Futures methodology, 2 Consumer affairs, 3 Policy research, 4 Alternative futures.
Direction of work in planning: 1 Political.
Methods used: Probabilistic forecasting, Cross impact analysis, Scenario building, Brainstorming, Statistical models, Expert panels, Network analysis, Historical analogy, Individual expert forecasting, Simulation.
Time range of work: 5 - 10 years.
Work done for (%): 30 Foundation, 30 Voluntary associations.
Occupational function: Administrator.
Worked in government as: Military.
Worked in industry/business in: 1 Consultancy, 2 Management, 3 Planning.   *(358)*

362. Joseph P. Martino
819 Maple Ave, Fairborn Oh 45324, USA.
Sex: Male.   *Age:* 40-49.
Educational qualification: Doctoral degree.
Formal training: 1 Mathematics, 2 Engineering, 3 Physical sciences.

Informal training: I Education, 2 Humanities.
Primarily engaged in: Both futures studies and long-range planning.
Areas in which work done (%): IO As academic, in teaching futures studies or long-range planning, 90 As staff member of research institute.
Direction of work in forecasting: I Technological, 2 Scientific, 3 Military.
Direction of work in research: I Social impacts of technology, 2 The individual in the future.
Direction of work in planning: I Technological, 2 Military.
Methods used: I Operational models, 2 Relevance trees, 3 Cross impact analysis.
Time range of work: 5 - IO years.
Source of support for work (%): IOO National government.
Work done for (%): IOO National government.
Occupational function: Researcher.
Worked in government as: I Researcher, 2 Administrator.
Worked in industry/business in: Research and development.
Worked in education: Teaching.   *(530)*

363. Eleonora Masini

World Future Studies Federation, Secretary General, Caselle Postale 6203, Rome Prati, Italy.
Sex: Female.   *Age:* 40-49.
Educational qualification: Doctoral degree.
Formal training: Social/behavioural sciences, Law.
Informal training: Education.
Primarily engaged in: Futures studies.
Areas in which work done (%): 20 As academic, in teaching futures studies or long-range planning, 20 As individual consultant, IO In planning unit of an international agency, 50 In organization primarily concerned with futures studies and/or long-range planning.
Direction of work in forecasting: Social.
Direction of work in research: I The individual in the future, 2 Alternative futures, 3 Futures methodology, 4 Value systems, 5 The family in the future.
Direction of work in planning: Education.
Methods used: I Brainstorming, 2 Scenario building, 3 Delphi techniques.
Time range of work: Beyond 2000 AD.
Source of support for work (%): IO Foundations, 20 International agencies, 70 Private association.
Work done for (%): IO Foundations, 20 International agencies, 70 Private associations.
Occupational function: I Educator, 2 Research worker, 3 Consultant.
Worked in education: I In research, 2 Teaching.
Worked in service sector: I Law, 2 Social welfare, 3 Religion.
Additional information: Concerned with education toward the future; changing human needs and values; religion and the future; future methodologies.   *(411)*

364. Roy Mason

3701 Connecticut Ave NW 404, Washington DC 20008, USA.
Sex: Male.   *Age:* 30-39.
Formal training: I Design, 2 Engineering, 3 Mathematics.
Informal training: I Arts, 2 Humanities, 3 Social/behavioural sciences, 4 Journalism.
Primarily engaged in: Both futures studies and long-range planning.
Areas in which work done (%): 80 In organization primarily concerned with futures studies and/or long-range planning, I9 As individual consultant, I As academic, in teaching futures studies or long-range planning.

Direction of work in forecasting: I Architectural, 2 Technological, 3 Environmental, 4 Social, 5 Cultural.
Direction of work in research: I Alternative futures, 2 Value systems, 3 The family in the future, 4 The individual in the future, 5 Futures methodology.
Direction of work in planning: I Urban, 2 Technological, 3 Regional, 4 Environmental.
Methods used: I Brainstorming, 2 Expert panels, 3 Network analysis, 4 Probabilistic forecasting.
Time range of work: Beyond year 2000.
Source of support for work (%): IO Local government, 50 National government, 20 Private business, 20 Foundations.
Work done for (%): IO Local or regional government, 50 National government, 20 Private business, 20 Foundations.
Occupational function: I Consultant, 2 Research worker, 3 Educator.
Worked in government as: Researcher.
Worked in industry/business in: Consultancy.
Worked in education: In research.
Worked in service sector: Design. *(581)*

365. Yoneji Masuda

Executive Director, Japan Computer Usage Development Institute, 4-14-11, Jingumae, Shibuyaku, Tokyo, Japan.
Sex: Male. *Age:* 60 or over.
Educational qualification: Bachelor's degree.
Formal training: Mathematics.
Informal training: Design.
Primarily engaged in: Both futures studies and long-range planning.
Areas in which work done (%): 5 As individual consultant, 15 In planning unit of a governmental agency, 80 In organization primarily concerned with futures studies and/or long-range planning.
Direction of work in forecasting: I Technological, 2 Social, 3 Economic.
Direction of work in research: I Social impacts of technology, 2 Futures methodology, 3 Value systems.
Direction of work in planning: Social.
Methods used: Scenario building.
Time range of work: IO - 25 years.
Source of support for work (%): 40 National government, 60 Foundation.
Work done for (%): 35 Foundations, 65 National government.
Occupational function: Manager.
Worked in government as: Researcher.
Worked in education: Teaching. *(508)*

366. Sydney T. Mathews

Bldg M-22, National Research Council, Ottawa KIA OR6, Ontario, Canada.
Sex: Male. *Age:* 50-59.
Educational qualification: Other graduate/professional degree.
Formal training: Engineering.
Areas in which work done (%): 5 In planning unit of an international organization, 15 In planning unit of a governmental agency, 30 As individual consultant, 50 In organization concerned with other studies including long-range planning.
Direction of work in forecasting: Technological.
Direction of work in research: Environmental.

Direction of work in planning: Scientific, Technological.
Methods used: Probabilistic forecasting, Individual expert forecasting.
Time range of work: 5 - IO years.
Source of support for work (%): IOO National government.
Work done for (%): IOO National government.
Occupational function: I Administrator, 2 Research worker, 3 Consultant, 4 Manager.
Worked in government as: Researcher.
Additional information: Concerned with technology assessment.   *(470)*

367. J. Maurer

Institute for National-Regional Planning, Weinbergstr 35, 88O6 Zurich, Switzerland.
Sex: Male.   *Age:* 4O-49.
Educational qualification: Doctoral degree.
Formal training: Design.
Informal training: I Humanities, 2 Mathematics, 3 Law, 4 Engineering, 5 Social/behavioural
sciences, 6 Education.
Primarily engaged in: Both futures studies and long-range planning.
Areas in which work done (%): 2O As individual consultant, 4O In organization primarily
concerned with futures studies and/or long-range planning, 4O As academic, in teaching
futures studies or long-range planning.
Direction of work in forecasting: Environmental, Resources.
Direction of work in research: Alternative futures, Environmental, Resource utilization,
Futures methodology.
Direction of work in planning: Urban, Regional, Environmental, Resources.
Methods used: Probabilistic forecasting, Gaming, Cross impact analysis, Scenario building,
Extrapolation techniques, Contextual mapping, Brainstorming, Statistical models, Expert
panels, Network analysis, Historical analogy, Operational models, Individual expert
forecasting, Simulation, Causal modelling.
Time range of work: 5 - beyond year 2OOO.
Source of support for work (%): 2O Local government, 8O National government.
Work done for (%): 5 International agencies, IO Local or Regional government, IO National
government.
Occupational function: I Educator, 2 Research worker, 3 Manager.
Worked in government as: Elected official, Administrator.
Worked in education: Teaching, In research, In administration.
Additional information: Concerned with physical environment.   *(409)*

368. T.W. Maver

Abacus, Dept of Architecture and Building Science, University of Strathclyde, Glasgow
G4 ONG, UK.
Sex: Male.   *Age:* 3O-39.
Educational qualification: Doctoral degree.
Formal training: Engineering.
Informal training: Mathematics, Design.
Primarily engaged in: Long-range planning.
Areas in which work done (%): 5O In organization concerned with other studies
including long-range planning, 5O As academic, in teaching futures studies or long-range
planning.
Direction of work in research: I Environmental, 2 Value systems, 3 Alternative futures.
Direction of work in planning: I Environmental, 2 Regional, 3 Urban.
Methods used: I Operational models, 3 Gaming, 4 Statistical models.

Time range of work: 5 - beyond year 2000.
Source of support for work (%): 100 National government.
Work done for (%): 10 Private business, 40 National government, 50 Local or regional government.
Occupational function: Educator, Research director.
Worked in education: In research.
Additional information: Concerned with design and planning of the built environment.

(202)

369. Premysl Maydl

European Centre for Leisure and Education, Jilska 1, Prague 1, Czechoslovakia.
Sex: Male.   *Age:* 50-59.
Educational qualification: Doctoral degree.
Formal training: Social/behavioural sciences.
Informal training: I Humanities, 2 Education.
Direction of work in forecasting: Social.
Direction of work in research: Social impacts of technology.
Direction of work in planning: Social.
Methods used: I Expert panels, 2 Statistical models.
Time range of work: 10 - 25 years.
Source of support for work (%): 50 National government, 50 International agencies.
Work done for (%): 50 National government, 50 International agencies.
Occupational function: Research worker.
Worked in education: In research.

(533)

370. Dennis L. Meadows

Research Program on Technology and Public Policy, Thayer School, Dartmouth College, Hanover, NH 03755, USA.
Sex: Male.   *Age:* 30-39.
Educational qualification: Doctoral degree.
Formal training: I Management, 2 Physical sciences.
Informal training: I Journalism, 2 Social/behavioural sciences.
Primarily engaged in: Both futures studies and long-range planning.
Areas in which work done (%): 40 In organization concerned with other studies including long-range planning, 40 As academic, in teaching futures studies or long-range planning, 20 As individual consultant.
Direction of work in forecasting: I Resources, 2 Social.
Direction of work in research: I Resource utilization, 2 Social impacts of technology, 3 Futures methodology.
Direction of work in planning: I Resources, 2 Urban.
Methods used: I Causal modelling, 2 Simulation, 3 Delphi techniques.
Time range of work: Beyond 2000 AD.
Source of support for work (%): 5 Local government, 35 Foundations, 60 National government.
Work done for (%): 30 Local or regional government, 70 National government.
Occupational function: I Manager.
Worked in government as: 2 Researcher.
Worked in education: I In administration, 2 In research, 3 Teaching.
Additional information: Concerned with resource availability, land use.

(128)

371. Richard L. Meier

Dept City and Regional Planning, University of California, Berkeley, Ca 94720, USA.
Sex: Male.   *Age:* 50-59.
Educational qualification: Doctoral degree.
Formal training: I Physical sciences.
Informal training: I Social/behavioural sciences, 2 Life sciences, 3 Education, 4 Engineering, 5 Humanities.
Primarily engaged in: Both futures studies and long-range planning.
Areas in which work done (%): 20 In organization concerned with other studies including long-range planning, IO As individual consultant, 70 As academic, in teaching futures studies or long-range planning.
Direction of work in forecasting: Technological, Economic, Social, Cultural, Educational, Scientific, Environmental, Manpower, Resources, Population.
Direction of work in research: Social impacts of technology, Alternative futures, Manpower, Consumer affairs, Environmental, Resource utilization, Value systems, Social priorities, Policy research, Population, The individual in the future, The family in the future, Futures methodology.
Direction of work in planning: Scientific, Technological, Social, Urban, Regional, Educational, Economic, Political, Corporate, Environmental, Resources.
Methods used: All methods (see Directory guide).
Time range of work: 5 - beyond year 2000.
Source of support for work (%): IO Private business, IO Misc, IO National government, 20 International agencies, 20 Foundations, 30 Local government.
Occupational function: Research worker, Educator.
Worked in industry/business in: Research and development, Consultancy.   *(515)*

372. Rosa Menasanch

Club de Amigos de la Futurologia, Pvertaferrisa 23, 30, 3A, Barcelona 2, Spain.
Sex: Female.   *Age:* 50-59.
Educational qualification: Master's degree.
Formal training: I Educator, 2 Law, 3 Humanities, 4 Journalism.
Informal training: I Education, 2 Law, 3 Humanities, 4 Journalism.
Primarily engaged in: Futures studies.
Areas in which work done (%): 20 In planning unit of an international organization, 50 In organization primarily concerned with futures studies and/or long-range planning, IO In organization concerned with other studies including long-range planning, 20 Politics, philosophy.
Direction of work in forecasting: I Educational, 2 Cultural, 3 Politics, Philosophy.
Direction of work in research: I The individual in the future, 2 The family in the future, 3 Futures methodology.
Direction of work in planning: I Educational, 2 Political, 3 Philosophy.
Methods used: I Cross impact analysis, 2 Brainstorming.
Time range of work: 5 - beyond year 2000.
Source of support for work (%): 5 Foundations, 5 Private business, 90 Voluntary associations.
Work done for (%): IOO Voluntary associations.
Occupational function: I Research worker, 2 Educator.
Worked in education: In research.   *(445)*

373. Jay S. Mendell
Visiting Professor of Management, Florida Atlantic University, Bola Raton, Fl 33432, USA.
Sex: Male.   *Age:* 30-39.
Educational qualification: Doctoral degree.
Formal training: Physical sciences.
Methods used: Monitoring.
Time range of work: lO - 25 years.
Source of support for work (%): lOO University.
Occupational function: Educator.
Worked in industry/business in: Management.
Worked in education: Teaching.   *(312)*

374. M. Eugene Merchant
Director of Research Planning, Cincinnati Milacron Inc, Cincinnati Oh, USA.
Sex: Male.   *Age:* 6O or over.
Educational qualification: Doctoral degree.
Formal training: Engineering.
Informal training: Physical sciences.
Primarily engaged in: Long-range planning.
Areas in which work done (%): lOO In planning unit of a business enterprise.
Direction of work in forecasting: Technological.
Direction of work in research: Alternative futures.
Direction of work in planning: Scientific, Technological.
Methods used: l Individual expert forecasting, 2 Expert panels, 3 Brainstorming, 4 Delphi techniques, 5 Extrapolation techniques.
Time range of work: lO - 25 years.
Source of support for work (%): 5 National government, 95 Private business.
Work done for (%): 5 National government, 95 Private business.
Occupational function: Manager.
Worked in industry/business in: l Research and development, 2 Planning, 3 Management.
                                                                   (516)

375. Charles Mercieca
Secretary General of the International Assoc of Educators for World Peace, Executive Office of the Secretary General, PO Box 3282, Blue Springs Station, Huntsville, Al 3581O, USA.
Sex: Male.   *Age:* 4O-49.
Educational qualification: Doctoral degree.
Formal training: l Education, 2 Humanities, 3 Social/behavioural sciences.
Informal training: l Journalism, 2 Cinema/television, 3 Arts.
Primarily engaged in: Both futures studies and long-range planning.
Areas in which work done (%): 5 In organization concerned with other studies including long-range planning, 5 As individual consultant, l5 As individual consultant, 2O In planning unit of an international organization, l5 As academic, in teaching futures studies or long-range planning, 4O History and philosophy of education.
Direction of work in forecasting: l Educational, 2 Cultural.
Direction of work in research: l The individual in the future, 2 Social impacts of technology, 2 Futures methodology, 3 Social priorities.
Direction of work in planning: l Educational, 2 Social.
Methods used: l Historical analogy, 2 Technology advance, 3 Expert panels.
Time range of work: 5 - beyond year 2OOO.
Source of support for work (%): 25 Voluntary associations, 75 Personal.

Work done for (%): IO Local or regional government, IO Private business, IO Foundations, IO Voluntary associations, 2O International agencies, 4O National government.
Occupational function: I Educator, 2 Research worker, 3 Administrator, 4 Consultant.
Worked in education: I Teaching, 2 In research, 3 In administration.
Worked in service sector: I Communication media, 2 Religion.
Additional information: Concerned with social relations and international communications.

(457)

376. Cesare Merlini

Director, Istituto Affairi Internationali, Viale Mazzini 88, OO195 Rome, Italy.
Sex: Male.   *Age:* 4O-49.
Educational qualification: Doctoral degree.
Formal training: Engineering.
Informal training: Engineering, International politics.
Direction of work in research: Policy research.
Occupational function: Manager.
Worked in education: Teaching, In research.   *(25)*

.377. Wolfgang Michalski

Director, Institute for Technology and Economics (ITE), Neuer Junfernstieg 21, 2 Hamburg 36,West Germany.
Sex: Male.   *Age:* 3O-39.
Educational qualification: Doctoral degree.
Formal training: Economic.
Informal training: I Law, 2 Design.
Areas in which work done (%): 35 In organization primarily concerned with futures studies and/or long-range planning.
Direction of work in forecasting: I Economic, 2 Resources.
Direction of work in research: I Futures methodology, 2 Resource utilization, 3 Social priorities.
Direction of work in planning: I Economic, 2 Resources.
Methods used: I Simulation, 2 Probabilistic forecasting, 3 Extrapolation techniques.
Time range of work: 5 - IO years.
Source of support for work (%): 5O Private business, 5O National government.
Work done for (%): 5O National government, 5O Private business.
Occupational function: I Manager, 2 Consultant, 3 Research worker.
Worked in education: I In research, 2 Teaching.   *(327)*

378. Clement S. Mihanovich

Prof of Sociology, 221 North Grand Blvd, St Louis, Mo 631O3, USA.
Sex: Male.   *Age:* 6O or over.
Educational qualification: Doctoral degree.
Formal training: Social/behavioural sciences.
Informal training: Social/behavioural sciences.
Areas in which work done (%): 4O In organization primarily concerned with futures studies and/or long-range planning.
Direction of work in forecasting: Population.
Direction of work in research: Value systems.
Direction of work in planning: Social.
Methods used: I Delphi techniques, 2 Scenario building, 3 Expert panels, 4 Simulation.
Time range of work: IO - 25 years.
Occupational function: Educator, Consultant.

Worked in education: I Teaching, 2 In research.
Additional information: Concerned with future of the family. *(300)*

379. Balint Szent-Miklosy
150 Haven Ave, New York, NY 10032, USA.
Sex: Male. *Age:* 30-39.
Educational qualification: Master's degree.
Formal training: Humanities, Design.
Informal training: Physical sciences, Life sciences, Design, Arts, Television/photography, Inventing.
Primarily engaged in: Both futures studies and long-range planning.
Areas in which work done (%): 25 In organization concerned with other studies including long-range planning, 25 As individual consultant, 25 In organization primarily concerned with futures studies and/or long-range planning, 25 Representation.
Direction of work in forecasting: Technological, Societal, Legal, Governmental evaluation.
Direction of work in research: Transportation, Solid waste resource recovery.
Direction of work in planning: I Urban, 2 Technological, 3 Scientific, 4 Regional, 5 Social, 6 Political, 7 Environmental.
Methods used: I Extrapolation techniques, 2 Brainstorming, 3 Individual expert forecasting, 4 Inventive futurism.
Time range of work: 1 - beyond year 2000.
Occupational function: Self employed, Inventor, Consultant, Investor.
Worked in government as: I Administrator, Educator, Consultant.
Worked in industry/business in: I Planning, 2 Management, 3 Marketing, 4 Import.
Worked in education: Instructing in planning, Administration and government.
Additional information: Concerned with solving urban or management problems; cost cutting systems development. *(168)*

380. Thomas W. Milburn
Mershon Centre, Programs of Research and Education in Leadership and Public Policy, Ohio State University, 199 West 10th Avenue, Columbus, Oh 43201, USA.
Sex: Male. *Age:* 50-59.
Educational qualification: Doctoral degree.
Formal training: I Social/behavioural sciences.
Informal training: I Social/behavioural sciences.
Areas in which work done (%): 10 Thinking and research about planning and forecasting.
Direction of work in research: I Futures methodology, 2 Social invention.
Methods used: I Expert panels, 2 Extrapolation techniques, 3 Contextual mapping, 4 Delphi techniques.
Time range of work: 5 - 10 years.
Source of support for work (%): 50 Foundations, 50 University.
Occupational function: I Research worker, 2 Educator.
Worked in government as: I Research and development.
Worked in industry/business in: I Research and development.
Worked in education: I In research, 2 Teaching.
Additional information: Concerned with elements in the validity of forecasts, modes of future orientation, social invention. *(505)*

381. Ian Miles
Science Policy Research Unit, University of Sussex, Falmer, Brighton BN1 9RF, UK.
Sex: Male.   *Age:* 25-29.
Educational qualification: Bachelor's degree.
Formal training: Social/behavioural sciences.
Informal training: Engineering, Journalism, Law.
Primarily engaged in: Futures studies.
Areas in which work done (%): IO As individual consultant, 5 As academic, in teaching futures studies or long-range planning, 2O Teaching social science and group dynamics, 65 In organization concerned with other studies including long-range planning.
Direction of work in forecasting: I Social, 2 Cultural.
Direction of work in research: I Futures methodology, 2 Alternative futures, 3 Social indicators, 4 Social impacts of technology, 5 Value systems, 5 The individual in the future, 7 The family in the future, 8 Social priorities, 9 Policy research, IO Consumer affairs.
Direction of work in planning: I Social, 2 Urban, 3 Regional, 4 Political.
Methods used: I Probabilistic forecasting, I Cross impact analysis, I Scenario building, I Extrapolation techniques, I Contextual mapping, I Statistical models, I Historical analogy, I Simulation, I Causal modelling, 2 Delphi techniques, 2 Expert panels, 2 Individual expert forecasting.
Time range of work: IO - beyond year 2OOO.
Source of support for work (%): 5 Educational institutions, 25 International agencies, 7O Foundations.
Occupational function: I Research worker, 2 Educator, 3 Consultant.
Worked in education: I In research, 2 Teaching.   *(399)*

382. Lynn H. Miller
Office of the Dean, The Graduate School, Temple University, Philadelphia, Pa 19122, USA.
Sex: Male.   *Age:* 30-39.
Educational qualification: Doctoral degree.
Formal training: Social/behavioural sciences.
Areas in which work done (%): IO As academic, in teaching futures studies or long-range planning, 9O Academic administration.
Direction of work in research: I Alternative futures, 2 Value systems, 3 Social priorities, 4 Social impacts of technology.
Methods used: I Extrapolation techniques, 2 Probabilistic forecasting, 3 Historical analogy, 4 Contextual mapping.
Time range of work: IO - 25 years.
Source of support for work (%): IOO University.
Occupational function: I Educator, 2 Administrator.
Worked in education: I Teaching, 2 In administration, 3 In research.
Additional information: Concerned with futures studies in international relations.   *(95)*

383. George H. Moeller
Program Co-ordinator, Pinchot Institute, USDA - Forest Service, 6816 Market St, Upper Darby, Pa 19O82, USA.
Sex: Male.   *Age:* 30-39.
Educational qualification: Doctoral degree.
Formal training: I Social/behavioural sciences, 2 Forestry.
Informal training: I Mathematics, 2 Physical sciences.
Areas in which work done (%): IO As academic, in teaching futures studies or long-

range planning, 20 In planning unit of a governmental agency,40 In organization
primarily concerned with futures studies and/or long-range planning, 20 In organization
concerned with other studies including long-range planning.
Direction of work in forecasting: I Social, 2 Cultural, 3 Environmental.
Direction of work in research: I Resource utilization, 2 Social impacts of technology,
3 Futures methodology.
Direction of work in planning: I Resources, 2 Environmental, 3 Scientific.
Methods used: I Delphi techniques, 2 Scenario building, 3 Extrapolation techniques,
4 Statistical models, 5 Individual expert forecasting, 6 Relevance trees.
Time range of work: IO - 25 years.
Source of support for work (%): IOO National government.
Work done for (%): 5O Local or regional government, 5O National government.
Occupational function: Research worker.
Worked in government as: Researcher.
Additional information: Concerned with social-institutional change as it influences
recreation use.   *(88)*

384. Alberto Fuentes-Mohr

E 9O8O Palais des Nations, Geneva, Switzerland.
Sex: Male.   *Age:* 4O-49.
Educational qualification: Doctoral degree.
Formal training: Economics and political science.
Informal training: Humanities.
Primarily engaged in: Long-range planning.
Areas in which work done (%): IO As individual consultant, IO In organization
primarily concerned with futures studies and/or long-range planning, 8O In planning
unit of an international organization.
Direction of work in forecasting: I Economic, 2 Social.
Direction of work in research: Policy research.
Direction of work in planning: I Economic, 2 Political, 3 Social.
Methods used: I Historical analogy, 2 Operational models, 3 Individual expert fore-
casting, 4 Expert panels.
Time range of work: 5 - 25 years.
Source of support for work (%): IO Voluntary associations, 9O International agencies.
Work done for (%): IO Voluntary associations, 9O International agencies.
Occupational function: I Administrator, 2 Research worker.
Worked in government as: I Administrator, 2 Researcher.   *(245)*

385. Robert T. Moline

Vice President Riverbend Association, 1395 N Washington, St Peter, Mn 56O82, USA.
Sex: Male.   *Age:* 4O-49.
Educational qualification: Doctoral degree.
Formal training: Social/behavioural sciences.
Informal training: Physical sciences.
Areas in which work done (%): 2 In planning unit of a governmental agency, 5 In
organization primarily concerned with futures studies and/or long-range planning,
2O As academic, in teaching futures studies or long-range planning.
Direction of work in research: Environmental.
Direction of work in planning: I Environmental, 2 Regional.
Methods used: I Scenario building, 2 Delphi techniques, 3 Gaming.
Time range of work: 5 - IO years.

Source of support for work (%): 5 Voluntary associations, 5 National government.
Work done for (%): IO Voluntary associations.
Occupational function: Educator.
Worked in education: Teaching.   (57)

386. A. Monnett Jr

Vice President Corporate Planning, United States Steel Corp, 6OO Grant St, Pittsburgh,
Pa 1523O, USA.
Sex: Male.   Age: 5O-59.
Educational qualification: Master's degree.
Formal training: Economics.
Primarily engaged in: Both futures studies and long-range planning.
Areas in which work done (%): IOO In planning unit of a business enterprise.
Direction of work in forecasting: I Market, 2 Economic,.
Direction of work in research: I Resource utilization, 2 Alternative futures.
Direction of work in planning: I Corporate, 2 Economic.
Methods used: All methods (see Directory guide).
Time range of work: IO - 25 years.
Source of support for work (%): IOO Private business.
Work done for (%): IOO Private business.
Occupational function: Consultant.
Worked in industry/business in: Management, Planning.
Additional information: Concerned with resources and markets.   (371)

387. A.M. Mood

Public Policy Research Organization, University of California, Irvine, Ca 92664, USA.
Sex: Male.   Age: 6O or over.
Educational qualification: Doctoral degree.
Formal training: Mathematics.
Informal training: Social/behavioural sciences.
Direction of work in research: Social priorities, Policy research.
Methods used: Statistical models, Historical analogy, Simulation, Causal modelling.
Time range of work: IO - 25 years.
Source of support for work (%): IOO University.
Occupational function: Research worker.
Worked in education: Teaching, In research.
Additional information: Concerned with organizations, communications, and education.
                                                                            (68)

388. Karl Schmitz-Moormann

463 Bochum-Stiepel, Varenholtstr 56, West Germany.
Sex: Male.   Age: 4O-49.
Educational qualification: Doctoral degree.
Formal training: Humanities.
Informal training: I Life sciences, 2 Physical sciences, 3 Social/behavioural sciences,
4 Education.
Direction of work in forecasting: Cultural.
Direction of work in research: Futures methodology, Motivation.
Methods used: I Historical analogy, 2 Brainstorming, 3 Extrapolation techniques.
Occupational function: I Educator, 2 Research worker.
Worked in education: I In research, 2 Teaching.
Additional information: Concerned with motivation of future engagement.   (177)

389. A.T. Morkel
School of Business Leadership, University of South Africa, PO Box 392 Pretoria, South Africa.
Sex: Male.   *Age:* 40-49.
Educational qualification: Doctoral degree.
Formal training: I Physical sciences, 2 Business administration.
Informal training: Physical sciences, Business administration.
Direction of work in forecasting: I Overall view, 2 Technological.
Direction of work in research: I Futures methodology, 2 Alternative futures.
Direction of work in planning: Corporate.
Methods used: I Individual expert forecasting, 2 Nominal group technique, 3 Scenario building, 4 Cross impact analysis.
Time range of work: IO - 25 years.
Source of support for work (%): 5O University, 5O Private business.
Occupational function: I Educator, 2 Consultant.
Worked in government as: Researcher.
Worked in industry/business in: Planning.
Worked in education: I Teaching, 2 In research, 3 In administration.
Additional information: Concerned with methods of technological forecasting to be used as general forecasting for strategy formulation for business.   *(458)*

390. Henry N. Moss
Northern Medical Bldg, Park Ave, and Tabor Rd, Philadelphia, Pa 19141, USA.
Sex: Male.   *Age:* 40-49.
Educational qualification: Doctoral degree.
Formal training: Life sciences.
Informal training: Life sciences.
Areas in which work done (%): 5 In organization primarily concerned with futures studies and/or long-range planning, IO As individual consultant.
Direction of work in research: Resource utilization.
Direction of work in planning: Scientific, Technological, Regional.
Methods used: Brainstorming, Expert panels, Operational models.
Time range of work: 5 - IO years.
Source of support for work (%): IO Foundations, IO Voluntary associations, 2O National government.
Work done for (%): IO National government.
Occupational function: Practising surgeon.
Worked in service sector: Medicine.
Additional information: Concerned with medical care delivery system, cancer, regionalization, knowledge utilization.   *(35)*

391. Pierre P. Mottoros
Vice President, Director of Research, Heinz, Fishbein and Co Inc, One State St Plaza, New York, NY 10004, USA.
Sex: Male.   *Age:* 40-49.
Educational qualification: Other graduate/professional degree.
Formal training: Social/behavioural sciences, Economics, Investments.
Informal training: I Physical sciences, 2 Design.
Primarily engaged in: Both futures studies and long-range planning.
Areas in which work done (%): 5O As individual consultant, 5O In organization concerned with other studies including long-range planning.

Direction of work in forecasting: I Economic, I Resources, I Population, 2 Technological, 2 Social, 2 Environmental.
Direction of work in research: Social impacts of technology, Alternative futures, Manpower, Consumer affairs, Environmental, Resource utilization, Value systems, Social priorities, Policy research, Population, The individual in the future, The family in the future, Futures methodology.
Direction of work in planning: Scientific, Technological, Social, Economic, Political, Corporate, Resources.
Methods used: I Probabilistic forecasting, I Expert panels, I Historical analogy, 2 Cross impact analysis, 2 Scenario building, 3 Brainstorming, 3 Gaming, 3 Relevance trees, 4 Simulation.
Time range of work: 5 - 25 years.
Source of support for work (%): IOO Private business.
Work done for (%): IOO Private business.
Occupational function: Director of research.
Worked in industry/business in: I Research and development.
Worked in education: I Teaching.
Additional information: Concerned with resource shortages, social description, allocation of resources, alternative investment postures.   *(89)*

392. Mario'n Mushkat
Tel Aviv 6117, PO Box 17O27, Israel.
Sex: Male.   *Age:* 5O-59.
Educational qualification: Doctoral degree.
Formal training: Law.
Areas in which work done (%): I5 As academic, in teaching futures studies or long-range planning, 2O International law and organization, and how it will shape the future.
Direction of work in forecasting: International framework.
Direction of work in research: Environmental, International community.
Direction of work in planning: Political, Environmental.
Methods used: Gaming, Scenario building, Historical analogy, Simulation.
Time range of work: 5 - IO years.
Source of support for work (%): IO Foundations, 2O Voluntary associations, 2O University.
Work done for (%): 5 Voluntary associations, IO Foundations, I5 University.
Occupational function: Research worker, Educator, University professor.
Worked in government as: Researcher.
Worked in education: Teaching, In research, In administration.
Worked in service sector: Law.
Additional information: Concerned with future development of the law and the organization of the international community.   *(271)*

N 393. Burt Nanus
Director, Centre for Futures Research, University of S California, Graduate School of Business Admin, University Park, Los Angeles, Ca 9OOO7, USA.
Sex: Male.   *Age:* 3O-39.
Educational qualification: Doctoral degree.
Formal training: I Business administration, 2 Engineering.
Informal training: I Business, 2 Mathematics, 3 Education, 4 Social/behavioural sciences.
Primarily engaged in: Both futures studies and long-range planning.
Areas in which work done (%): IO As individual consultant, 2O As academic, in teaching

futures studies or long-range planning, 70 In organization primarily concerned with
futures studies and/or long-range planning.
Direction of work in forecasting: I Technological, 2 Economic, 3 Social, 4 Educational,
5 Manpower.
Direction of work in research: I Social impacts of technology, 2 Alternative futures,
3 Policy research, 4 Social priorities, 5 Futures methodology, 6 Manpower, 7 The
individual in the future, 8 Resource utilization.
Direction of work in planning: I Social, 2 Technological, 3 Urban, 4 Regional,
5 Educational, 6 Economic, 7 Corporate, 8 Political.
Methods used: I Delphi techniques, 2 Probabilistic forecasting, 3 Simulation, 4 Expert
panels, 5 Gaming, 5 Cross impacts analysis, 5 Scenario building, 5 Extrapolation
techniques, 5 Contextual mapping, 5 Brainstorming, 5 Statistical models, 5 Historical
analogy, 5 Operational models, 5 Causal modelling.
Time range of work: IO - 25 years.
Source of support for work (%): IO Foundations, I5 Local government, 25 Private
business, 50 National government.
Work done for (%): IO Foundations, I5 Local or regional government, 25 Private
business, 50 National government.
Occupational function: I Manager, 2 Educator, 3 Research worker, 4 Consultant.
Worked in government as: Researcher.
Worked in industry/business in: Management, Research and development, Planning,
Consultancy.
Worked in education: Teaching, In research, In administration.   *(398)*

394. Morteza Nassefat

Institute of Psychology, Tehran University, 19, 24th of Esfand Square, Tehran 14, Iran.
Sex: Male.   *Age:* 40-49.
Educational qualification: Doctoral degree.
Formal training: I Psychology, 2 Education.
Informal training: I Social/behavioural sciences, 2 Life sciences, 3 Mathematics.
Occupational function: I Research worker, 2 Educator, 3 Administrator, 4 Consultant.
Worked in government as: Researcher.
Worked in industry/business in: Consultancy.
Worked in education: I In research, 2 Teaching, 3 In administration.
Worked in service sector: Social welfare.
Additional information: Concerned with studies on human resources.   *(282)*

395. Jessie Tellis-Nayak

Programme Director, Indian Social Institute-Dept of Women's Development, John's Hill,
Nandigudda Rd, Athavar, Mangalore 575001, Karnataka State, India.
Sex: Female.   *Age:* 50-59.
Educational qualification: Doctoral degree.
Formal training: I Social/behavioural sciences, 2 Education, 3 Physical sciences.
Informal training: Journalism.
Primarily engaged in: Long-range planning.
Areas in which work done (%): 25 As individual consultant, 25 In planning unit of an
international organization, 50 In organization primarily concerned with futures studies
and/or long-range planning.
Direction of work in planning: Social, Regional.
Methods used: Operational models.
Time range of work: 5 - IO years.

Source of support for work (%): IOO Indian social institute - a voluntary organization.
Work done for (%): 5O International agencies, 5O Voluntary associations.
Occupational function: I Educator, I Consultant.
Worked in industry/business in: I Research and development, 2 Consultancy.
Worked in education: I Teaching.
Additional information: Concerned with analysis of social situations, feasibility studies of planned projects in the field of development.   *(106)*

396. Giorgio Nebbia

Prof of Resources, Universita Internationale, Degli Studi Sociali, Viale Pola 12, 1-OO198, Rome, Italy.
Sex: Male.   *Age:* 4O-49.
Educational qualification: Doctoral degree.
Formal training: Physical sciences.
Informal training: Environmental problems, technology and society.
Primarily engaged in: Both futures studies and long-range planning.
Areas in which work done (%): IOO As academic, in teaching futures studies or long-range planning.
Direction of work in forecasting: I Resources, 2 Environmental, 3 Technological.
Direction of work in research: I Resource utilization, 2 Environmental, 3 Social impacts of technology, 4 Consumer affairs.
Direction of work in planning: I Resources, 2 Environmental, 3 Technological.
Methods used: Historical analogy.
Time range of work: 5 - 25 years.
Source of support for work (%): IOO University.
Work done for (%): IOO University.
Occupational function: I Educator, 2 Research worker.
Worked in education: I Teaching, 2 In research.
Additional information: Concerned with technology assessment of production and consumption pattern.   *(511)*

397. I.A. Newstead

National Telecommunications Planning, Australian Post Office, 7th Floor, 14O Queen St, Melbourne, Victoria 3OOO, Australia.
Sex: Male.   *Age:* 5O-59.
Educational qualification: Master's degree.
Formal training: I Engineering, 2 Economics.
Informal training: Social/behavioural sciences.
Primarily engaged in: Both futures studies and long-range planning.
Areas in which work done (%): IO In planning unit of a governmental agency, 9O In planning unit of an international agency.
Direction of work in forecasting: I Social, 2 Technological, 3 Economic.
Direction of work in research: I Alternative futures, 2 Social impacts of technology, 3 Futures methodology.
Direction of work in planning: Participative.
Methods used: I Scenario building, 2 Delphi techniques, 3 Extrapolation techniques, Brainstorming, Expert panels, Relevance trees, Network analysis, Simulation.
Time range of work: IO - 25 years.
Source of support for work (%): IOO National government.
Work done for (%): IO International agencies, 9O National government.
Occupatiolal function: I Administrator, 2 Manager, 3 Educator.

Worked in government as: 2 Administrator.
Worked in industry/business in: I Planning.   *(503)*

398. Simon Nicholson

180 Woodstock Rd, Oxford, UK.
Sex: Male.   *Age:* 30-39.
Educational qualification: Other graduate/professional degree.
Formal training: Arts, Prehistoric archeology.
Informal training: I Design, 2 Education, 3 Social/behavioural sciences.
Primarily engaged in: Both futures studies and long-range planning.
Areas in which work done (%): 50 Research, 50 As academic, in teaching futures
studies or long-range planning.
Direction of work in forecasting: Social, Cultural, Educational, Environmental.
Direction of work in research: Alternative futures, Environmental, Social priorities,
The individual in the future, The family in the future, Futures methodology.
Direction of work in planning: Social, Urban, Regional, Educational, Environmental.
Methods used: Community participation.
Time range of work: 5 - beyond year 2000.
Source of support for work (%): IO Foundations, 90 National government.
Work done for (%): 50 National government, 50 Curiosity.
Occupational function: I Artist, 2 Consultant, 3 Research worker, 4 Educator.
Worked in government as: Researcher.
Worked in industry/business in: Consultancy.
Worked in education: I In research, 2 Teaching, 3 In administration.
Worked in service sector: I Design, 2 Communication media.   *(248)*

399. Consuelo Nievo

IRADES, Istituto per la Ricerca e la Formazione al Futuro, Via Paisiello 6, Rome 00198, Italy.
Sex: Female.   *Age:* 40-49.
Educational qualification: Bachelor's degree.
Formal training: Humanities.
Informal training: Cinema/television.
Primarily engaged in: Futures studies.
Areas in which work done (%): IOO In organization primarily concerned with futures
studies and/or long-range planning.
Direction of work in forecasting: Social.
Direction of work in research: I The individual in the future, 2 Alternative futures,
3 Futures methodology, 4 Value systems, 5 Social impacts of technology, 5 The family
in the future.
Time range of work: Beyond 2000 AD.
Source of support for work (%): IOO Private association.
Work done for (%): IOO Private association.
Occupational function: Research worker.
Additional information: Concerned with documentation and information in futures studies.
(414)

400. Czeslaw Nosal

Forecasting Research Centre of the Technical University of Wroclaw, Wybrzeze
Wyspianskiego 27, 50-370 Wroclaw, Poland.
Sex: Male.   *Age:* 30-39.
Educational qualification: Doctoral degree.
Formal training: I Social/behavioural sciences, 2 Education, 3 Mathematics.

Informal training: I Life sciences, 2 Humanities, 3 Engineering.

Primarily engaged in: Futures studies.

Areas in which work done (%): IO In organization concerned with other studies including long-range planning, 2O In organization primarily concerned with futures studies and/or long-range planning, 2O As individual consultant, 5O Industrial psychology, psychology of scientific creativity.

Direction of work in forecasting: I Scientific, 2 Educational, 3 Social, 4 Cultural, 5 Technological.

Direction of work in research: I Value systems, 2 Futures methodology, 3 Policy research, 4 Social priorities, 5 Social impacts of technology, 6 The individual in the future.

Direction of work in planning: I Scientific, 2 Educational, 3 Social, 4 Technological.

Methods used: I Brainstorming, 2 Expert panels, 3 Individual expert forecasting, 4 Contextual mapping.

Time range of work: Beyond 2OOO AD.

Source of support for work (%): 5O Local government, 5O National government.

Work done for (%): 5O Local or regional government, 5O National government.

Occupational function: I Research worker, 2 Educator, 3 Consultant.

Worked in government as: I Researcher.

Worked in education: I In research, 2 Teaching.

Additional information: Concerned with the future problem in general (structural analysis of field of problem). The future of education, social indicators (human needs). *(456)*

401. David Novick

David Novick Associates, 1O32 2nd St, Santa Monica, Ca 9O4O3, USA.

Sex: Male.   *Age:* 6O or over.

Educational qualification: Doctoral degree.

Formal training: Social/behavioural sciences.

Informal training: Social/behavioural sciences.

Primarily engaged in: Long-range planning.

Areas in which work done (%): 25 In organization primarily concerned with futures studies and/or long-range planning, 75 As individual consultant.

Direction of work in forecasting: Economic.

Direction of work in research: Resource utilization.

Direction of work in planning: I Economic, 2 Social.

Methods used: I Historical analogy, 2 Individual expert forecasting, 3 Statistical models.

Time range of work: 5 - IO and beyond year 2OOO.

Source of support for work (%): 25 National government, 75 Private business.

Work done for (%): 5 Local or regional government, 2O National government, 75 Private business.

Occupational function: Consultant.

Worked in government as: Administrator, Researcher.

Worked in industry/business in: Management, Consultancy.

Worked in education: Teaching.

Additional information: Concerned with long-range resource analysis at the US Federal Government and large corporations' levels. *(442)*

402. Eiichi Ochiai

Keyakidai 38 - 3O2, Nishimachi - 4, Kokumbumji-Shi, Tokyo 185, Japan.

Sex: Male.   *Age:* 5O-59.

Educational qualification: Bachelor's degree.

Formal training: I Engineering, 2 Social/behavioural sciences.

Informal training: I Trade union officer, 2 Social/behavioural sciences, 3 Education.
Direction of work in forecasting: I Economic, 2 Social, 3 Environmental, 4 Manpower.
Direction of work in research: I Social priorities, 2 Manpower, 3 Social impacts of technology, 4 Consumer affairs.
Direction of work in planning: I Labour, 2 Educational.
Methods used: I Network analysis, 2 Statistical models.
Time range of work: 5 - IO years.
Source of support for work (%): 5 Voluntary associations, 5 Private business, 2O National government, 6O International agencies.
Worked done for (%): 5 National government, 5 Private business, 5 Voluntary associations, 25 International agencies.
Occupational function: Manager.
Worked in industry/business in: I Trade union, 2 Research and development.
Additional information: Concerned with forecasting of social and economic situation. *(448)*

4O3. Saburo Okita
5-13-12 Koishikawa, Bunkyo-ku, Tokyo, Japan,
Sex: Male.   Age: Over 6O.
Educational qualification: Doctoral degree.
Formal training: Humanities, Engineering.
Informal training: Social/behavioural sciences, Education.
Areas in which work done (%): IO In organization concerned with other studies including long-range planning.
Direction of work in forecasting: Technological, Economic, Social, Scientific, Manpower, Resources, Population, Overall.
Methods used: Scenario building, Expert panels.
Time range of work: 5 - 25 years.
Source of support for work (%): National government, International agencies, Private business, Foundations, Voluntary associations.
Work done for (%): Voluntary associations.
Occupational function: Administrator, Research worker.
Worked in government as: Administrator, Researcher.   *(591)*

4O4. Robert L. Olson
Unit One, 7O Allen Hall, University of Illinois, II 618O3, USA.
Sex: Male.   *Age:* 3O-39.
Educational qualification: Doctoral degree.
Formal training: Social/behavioural sciences.
Informal training: I Education, 2 Social/behavioural sciences.
Primarily engaged in: Futures studies.
Areas in which work done (%): 5O In organization primarily concerned with futures studies and/or long-range planning, 5O As academic, in teaching futures studies or long-range planning.
Direction of work in research: I Social priorities, 2 Value systems, 3 Policy research, 4 Futures methodology.
Direction of work in planning: I Political, 2 Educational.
Methods used: Future imagery.
Time range of work: IO - 25 years.
Source of support for work (%): IOO Institution.
Work done for (%): 25 Institution.
Occupational function: I Research worker, 2 Educator.
Worked in education: I Teaching, 2 In research.   *(406)*

405. Akira Onishi

Soka University, 1 - Chome Tangi-cho, Nachioji-shi, Tokyo, Japan.
Sex: Male.   *Age:* 40-49.
Educational qualification: Doctoral degree.
Formal training: Economics.
Informal training: I Social/behavioural sciences, 2 Mathematics, 3 Design.
Primarily engaged in: Both futures studies and long-range planning.
Areas in which work done (%): IO As individual consultant, I5 As academic, in
teaching futures studies or long-range planning, 25 In organization concerned with
other studies including long-range planning, 50 In organization primarily concerned
with futures studies and/or long-range planning.
Direction of work in forecasting: I Economic, 2 Social, 3 Cultural, 3 Educational,
3 Environmental, 3 Manpower, 3 Resources, 3 Population.
Direction of work in research: Social impacts of technology, Alternative futures,
Manpower, Consumer affairs, Environmental, Resource utilization, Value systems,
Social priorities, Policy research, Population, Futures methodology.
Direction of work in planning: Economic.
Time range of work: IO - 25 years.
Source of support for work (%): 2 International agencies, 3 Voluntary associations,
5 Private business, 5 Foundations, 35 Local or regional government, 50 National
government.
Work done for (%): IO Private business, 30 National government, 60 International
agencies.
Occupational function: Manager, Research worker, Educator, Consultant.
Worked in education: Teaching, In research.   *(31)*

406. John Osman

Brookings Institution, 1755 Massachusetts Ave, NW, Washington, DC 20036, USA.
Sex: Male.   *Age:* 50-59.
Educational qualification: Doctoral degree.
Formal training: Social/behavioural sciences, Design.
Informal training: Urbanism.
Primarily engaged in: Futures studies and long-range planning.
Areas in which work done (%): IOO In organization primarily concerned with
futures studies and/or long-range planning.
Direction of work in forecasting: Technological, Economic, Social, Cultural, Resources,
Population.
Direction of work in research: Social impacts of technology, Alternative futures, Value
systems, Policy research, The individual in the future, The family in the future, Futures
methodology.
Direction of work in planning: Urban, Regional.
Methods used: Probabilistic forecasting, Delphi techniques, Cross impact analysis,
Scenario building, Extrapolation.techniques, Expert panels, Network analysis, Historical
analogy.
Time range of work: IO - 25 years.
Source of support for work (%): IOO Local government.
Work done for (%): IOO Local or regional government.
Occupational function: Administrator, Educator.
Worked in industry/business in: Management.
Worked in education: I In administration, 2 Teaching.   *(151)*

407. Hasan Ozbekhan

The Wharton School, Vance Hall, 3733 Spruce St, University of Pennsylvania, Philadelphia, Pa 19174, USA.
Sex: Male.   *Age:* 50-59.
Educational qualification: Bachelor's degree.
Formal training: Social/behavioural sciences.
Informal training: Humanities, Arts.
Primarily engaged in: Both futures studies and long-range planning.
Areas in which work done (%): IO As individual consultant, 60 Academic, in teaching futures studies or long-range planning, 30 Research in futures studies and long-range planning.
Direction of work in forecasting: I Resources, 2 Environmental, 3 Population, 4 Social, 5 Economic, 6 Cultural, 7 Technological.
Direction of work in research: I Futures methodology, 2 Value systems, 3 Resource utilization, 4 Environmental, 5 Alternative futures, 6 Social impacts of technology, 7 Policy research.
Direction of work in planning: I Generalised, 2 Resources, 3 Environmental, 4 Political, 5 Technological, 6 Economic, 7 Corporate.
Methods used: I Scenario building, 2 Delphi techniques, 3 Cross impact analysis, 4 Relevance trees, 5 Simulation, 6 Causal modelling.
Time range of work: IO - 25 years.
Source of support for work (%): 25 National government, 25 International agencies, 50 Private business.
Work done for (%): 60 National government, 30 International agencies, IO Private business.
Occupational function: I Educator, 2 Consultant.
Worked in industry/business in: I Management, 2 Planning, 3 Consultancy.
Worked in education: I Teaching, 2 In research.   *(566)*

408. Pietro Pace

IRADES, Istituto per la Ricerca e la Formazione al Futuro, Via Paisiello 6, Rome 00198, Italy.
Sex: Male.   *Age:* 50-59.
Educational qualification: Doctoral degree.
Formal training: Social/behavioural sciences, Humanities.
Informal training: Education.
Primarily engaged in: Futures studies.
Areas in which work done (%): 25 As academic, in teaching futures studies or long-range planning, 25 As individual consultant, 50 In organization primarily concerned with futures studies and/or long-range planning.
Direction of work in forecasting: Social, Religion.
Direction of work in research: I The individual in the future, 2 Alternative futures, 3 Social priorities, 4 The family in the future, 5 Value systems.
Direction of work in planning: Educational.
Methods used: I Brainstorming, 2 Delphi techniques, 3 Scenario building.
Time range of work: Beyond 2000 AD.
Source of support for work (%): IO Foundations, IO National government, IO Private business, 70 Voluntary associations.
Work done for (%): IO National government, IO International agencies, IO Private business, IO Foundations, 60 Voluntary associations.
Occupational function: I Manager, 2 Research worker, 3 Educator.

Worked in education: I Teaching, 2 In research.
Worked in service sector: I Social welfare, 2 Religion.
Additional information: Concerned with changing human needs and values; education toward the future; religion and the future. *(412)*

409. Leo S. Packer

Director, Technology Policy and Space Affairs, Dept of State, Washington, DC 20520, USA.
Sex: Male.   *Age:* 50-59.
Educational qualification: Doctoral degree.
Formal training: I Engineering, 2 Physical sciences.
Informal training: I Executive management, 2 Engineering, 3 Humanities, 4 Physical, sciences, 5 Mathematics, 6 Education.
Areas in which work done (%): 5 In planning unit of a governmental agency, 92 Management of technology policy in international relations, 3 In organization concerned with other studies including long-range planning.
Direction of work in forecasting: I Technological, 2 Market, 3 Scientific, 4 Resources.
Direction of work in research: I Policy research, 2 Social impacts of technology, 3 Futures methodology.
Direction of work in planning: I Technological, 2 Scientific.
Methods used: I Expert panels, 2 Individual expert forecasting, 3 Historical analogy.
Time range of work: 5 - 10 years.
Source of support for work (%): 10 International agencies, 90 National government.
Work done for (%): 10 International agencies, 90 National government.
Occupational function: Administrator, Manager, Federal government policy director.
Worked in government as: I Administrator, 2 Researcher.
Worked in industry/business in: I Research and development, 2 Management.
Additional information: Concerned with development of US policies on technology transfer, space, co-operation. *(45)*

410. R.W. Page

Science Policy Research Unit, University of Sussex, Falmer, Brighton, BN1 9RF, UK.
Sex: Male.   *Age:* 25-29.
Educational qualification: Bachelor's degree.
Formal training: Social/behavioural sciences.
Informal training: I Arts, 2 Physical sciences.
Primarily engaged in: Futures studies.
Areas in which work done (%): 5 As academic, in teaching futures studies or long-range planning, 95 In organization primarily concerned with futures studies and/or long-range planning.
Direction of work in forecasting: Resources.
Direction of work in research: I Alternative futures, 2 Resource utilization, 3 Futures studies.
Methods used: Scenario building, Historical analogy.
Time range of work: Beyond 2000 AD.
Occupational function: Research worker.
Worked in industry/business in: Research and development.
Worked in education: In research. *(490)*

411. George Paine
Office of Population Censuses and Surveys, St Catherines House, IO Kingsway, London WC2B 6JP, UK.
Sex: Male. *Age:* 50-59.
Educational qualification: Bachelor's degree.
Formal training: Mathematics.
Primarily engaged in: Futures studies.
Direction of work in forecasting: Population.
Direction of work in research: Population.
Methods used: Statistical models, Expert panels.
Time range of work: 5 - beyond year 2OOO.
Work done for (%): IOO National government.
Occupational function: Administrator.
Worked in government as: Administrator. *(326)*

412. A.D. Painter
Project Analyst, Qantas Airways Ltd, PO Box 489, Sydney, NSW 2OO1, Australia.
Sex: Male. *Age:* 50-59.
Formal training: Some college or less.
Informal training: Social/behavioural sciences, Engineering.
Primarily engaged in: Both futures studies and long-range planning.
Areas in which work done (%): IOO In planning unit of a business enterprise.
Direction of work in forecasting: Technological, Economic, Social, Resources, Population, Political.
Direction of work in research: Resource utilization.
Direction of work in planning: Corporate.
Methods used: I Expert panels, 2 Individual expert forecasting, 3 Scenario building.
Time range of work: 5 - 25 years.
Source of support for work (%): IOO Private business.
Work done for (%): IOO Private business.
Occupational function: Research worker.
Worked in industry/business in: I Planning, 2 Management.
Additional information: Concerned with the future business environment and its probable impacts upon the operations of a civil airline. *(501)*

413. Jean-Jacques Paltenghi
Prospective EPFL, Ave Fraisse 12, 1OO6 Lausanne, Switzerland.
Sex: Male. *Age:* 30-39.
Educational qualification: Doctoral degree.
Formal training: Physical sciences.
Informal training: Social/behavioural sciences, Engineering, Education.
Primarily engaged in: Both futures studies and long-range planning.
Areas in which work done (%): IOO Research policy in a university.
Direction of work in forecasting: Technological, Economic, Educational Scientific.
Direction of work in research: Futures methodology.
Direction of work in planning: Scientific, Technological.
Methods used: Expert panels, Individual expert forecasting.
Time range of work: IO - 25 years.
Source of support for work (%): 4O Foundations, 6O National government.
Work done for (%): 4O Foundations, 6O National government.
Occupational function: Educator, Consultant.
Worked in education: Teaching, In research, In administration. *(50)*

414. Gustav E. Papanek

Chairperson, Economics Dept, Boston University, 270 Bay State Rd, Boston, Ma, USA.
Sex: Male.   *Age:* 40-49.
Educational qualification: Doctoral degree.
Formal training: Social/behavioural sciences.
Direction of work in forecasting: Economic.
Direction of work in research: Resource utilization, Policy research.
Direction of work in planning: Economic;
Methods used: Statistical models.
Time range of work: 5 - 10 years.
Source of support for work (%): 20 National government, 20 International agencies, 60 Private business.
Work done for (%): 100 Foreign governments and university.
Occupational function: 1 Educator, 2 Research worker, 3 Unspecified.
Worked in governmentas: 1 Researcher, 2 Administrator.
Worked in education: 1 In research, 2 Teaching, 3 In administration.
Additional information: Concerned with the long-term economic future of less developed countries and the preparation of five year and longer-term plans.   *(469)*

415. Max A. Pape

Illinois Wesleyan, Bloomington, Il 61774, USA.
Sex: Male.   *Age:* 60 or over.
Educational qualification: Doctoral degree.
Formal training: Social/behavioural sciences, Engineering, Journalism.
Informal training: Life sciences, Mathematics, Education, Design.
Areas in which work done (%): 30 As academic, in teaching futures studies or long-range planning.
Direction of work in forecasting: Technological, Scientific.
Direction of work in research: Social impacts of technology, Alternative futures, Environmental, Social priorities, The individual in the future.
Direction of work in planning: Scientific, Technological, Social.
Methods used: Probabilistic forecasting, Delphi techniques, Gaming, Cross impact analysis, Scenario building, Extrapolation techniques, Contextual mapping, Brainstorming, Statistical models, Network analysis, Operational models, Individual expert forecasting, Simulation, Causal modelling.
Time range of work: 10 - 25 years.
Occupational function: Educator.
Worked in government as: Researcher.
Worked in industry/business in: 1 Research and development, 2 Planning, 3 Management.
Worked in education: 1 Teaching, 2 In research.   *(381)*

416. Ralph Parkman

School of Engineering, Dept of Materials Science, San Jose State University, 125 South Seventh St, San Jose, Ca 95192, USA.
Sex: Male.   *Age:* 50-59.
Educational qualification: Doctoral degree.
Formal training: Engineering.
Informal training: Education.
Areas in which work done (%): 50 As academic, in teaching futures studies or long-range planning.

Direction of work in research: I Social impacts of technology, 2 The individual in the future.
Direction of work in planning: Technological.
Methods used: I Historical analogy, 2 Scenario building, 3 Delphi techniques.
Time range of work: IO - 25 years.
Occupational function: Educator.
Worked in industry/business in: 3 Research and development.
Worked in education: I Teaching, 2 In research.
Additional information: Concerned with technological assessment and long-range resource analysis.

(47)

417. C.W. Parry

Manager, Corporate Planning, 1501 Alcoa Bldg, Pittsburgh, Pa 15219, USA.
Sex: Male.   *Age:* 40-49.
Educational qualification: Bachelor's degree.
Formal training: Engineering.
Informal training: I Social/behavioural sciences, 2 Mathematics.
Primarily engaged in: Long-range planning.
Areas in which work done (%): IOO In planning unit of a business enterprise.
Direction of work in forecasting: I Economic, 2 Market, 3 Resources, 4 Environmental, 5 Technological.
Direction of work in research: I Alternative futures, I Resource utilization.
Direction of work in planning: I Corporate, 2 Economic, 3 Resources, 4 Environmental, 5 Political.
Methods used: I Extrapolation techniques, 2 Individual expert forecasting, 3 Statistical models, 4 Simulation.
Time range of work: 5 - IO years.
Source of support for work (%): IOO Private business.
Work done for (%): IOO Private business.
Occupational function: Manager.
Worked in industry/business in: Management, Planning.

(366)

418. J.A. Parsons

Human Resources Laboratory, Chamber of Mines of South Africa, PO Box 61809, Marshalltown, Johannesburg, South Africa.
Sex: Male.   *Age:* 30-39.
Educational qualification: Other graduate/professional degree.
Formal training: Social/behavioural sciences.
Informal training: I Social/behavioural sciences, 2 Personnel management.
Primarily engaged in: Futures studies.
Areas in which work done (%): IOO In organization not primarily engaged in, but concerned with long-term futures.
Direction of work in forecasting: Manpower.
Direction of work in research: Manpower.
Methods used: I Simulation, 2 Extrapolation techniques, 3 Historical analogy, 4 Individual expert forecasting, 5 Scenario building.
Time range of work: IO - 25 years.
Source of support for work (%): IOO Private foundations.
Work done for (%): IOO Private business.
Occupational function: Research worker.
Worked in industry/business in: I Management, 2 Research and development.

(475)

419. Manavasi Narasimnan Parthasarathi

General Manager, Indian Lead Zinc Information Centre, 85 - 27 Safdarjung Enclave, New Delhi 110 016, India.
Sex: Male.   *Age:* 50-59.
Educational qualification: Doctoral degree.
Formal training: I Engineering, 2 Education.
Informal training: I Engineering, 2 Education.
Direction of work in forecasting: I Market, 2 Technological, 3 Economic.
Direction of work in research: Resource utilization.
Direction of work in planning: Technological.
Time range of work: 5 - 10 years.
Source of support for work (%): 10 National government, 10 International agencies, 80 Local or regional government.
Occupational function: I Manager, 2 Administrator, 3 Consultant.
Worked in government as: I Administrator.
Worked in industry/business in: I Management, 2 Research and development, 3 Consultancy.
Worked in education: I In research, 2 Teaching, 3 In administration.   *(230)*

420. V. Patruschev

Institute of Sociological Research, Academy of Sciences of the USSR, Novocheramyshkinskaya 46, 117418 Moscow, USSR.
Sex: Male.   *Age:* 40-49.
Educational qualification: Doctoral degree.
Formal training: Humanities.
Informal training: I Social/behavioural sciences, I Economics.
Areas in which work done (%): 100 In organization concerned with other studies including long-range planning.
Direction of work in research: Time budget.
Direction of work in planning: Social.
Methods used: I Expert panels, 2 Historical analogy, 3 Individual expert forecasting, 4 Extrapolation techniques.
Time range of work: 5 - 25 years.
Source of support for work (%): 100 National government.
Work done for (%): 100 National government.
Occupational function: Research worker.
Worked in government as: Researcher.
Additional information: Concerned with development of time budgets of population.
(502)

421. Raymond Saint-Paul

Conservatoire National des Arts et Métiers, 292 Rue Saint Martin, Paris 2, France.
Sex: Male.   *Age:* 40-49.
Educational qualification: Doctoral degree.
Formal training: Economics.
Informal training: Education.
Primarily engaged in: Both futures studies and long-range planning.
Areas in which work done (%): 25 In planning unit of a government agency, 25 In planning unit of a business enterprise, 25 As individual consultant, 25 As academic, in teaching futures studies or long-range planning.
Direction of work in forecasting: Economic.
Direction of work in research: Policy research.

Direction of work in planning: Technological.
Methods used: Network analysis.
Time range of work: 5 - lO years.
Source of support for work (%): 5 Voluntary associations, 25 Private business, 7O National government.
Work done for (%): lO International agencies, 3O Private business, 6O National government.
Occupational function: l Educator, 2 Consultant.
Worked in government as: l Administrator.
Worked in education: l Teaching.
Additional information: Concerned with R & D policy making.   *(512)*

422. K.L. Pavitt
Science Policy Research Unit, University of Sussex, Falmer, Brighton BN1 9RF, UK.
Sex: Male.   *Age:* 30-39.
Educational qualification: Bachelor's degree.
Formal training: Social/behavioural sciences, Engineering.
Informal training: Working in large organizations.
Primarily engaged in: Futures studies.
Areas in which work done (%): lO As academic, in teaching futures studies or long-range planning, lO As individual consultant, 2O In organization concerned with other studies including long-range planning, 6O In organization primarily concerned with futures studies and/or long-range planning.
Direction of work in forecasting: Technological, Economic, Social, Cultural, Scientific, Environmental, Resources, Population.
Direction of work in research: Social impacts of technology, Policy research.
Time range of work: lO - beyond year 2OOO.
Occupational function: Administrator, Research worker, Educator, Consultant.
Worked in government as: Administrator, Researcher.   *(485)*

423. John D. Pears
37 Baker St, London W1A 1AN, UK.
Sex: Male.   *Age:* 40-49.
Educational qualification: Doctoral degree.
Formal training: l Business, 2 Physical sciences, 3 Mathematics.
Primarily engaged in: Long-range planning.
Areas in which work done (%): lOO In planning unit of a business enterprise.
Direction of work in planning: Corporate.
Methods used: l Extrapolation techniques, 2 Statistical models, 3 Probabilistic forecasting, 4 Individual expert forecasting.
Time range of work: 5 - lO years.
Source of support for work (%): lOO Private business.
Work done for (%): lOO Private business.
Occupational function: Business planner.
Worked in industry/business in: l Consultancy, 2 Management.   *(263)*

424. Karol Pelc
Director, Forecasting Research Centre, Technical University of Wroclaw, Wybrzeze Wyspianskiego 27, 5O - 37O Wroclaw, Poland.
Sex: Male.   *Age:* 40-49.
Educational qualification: Doctoral degree.

Formal training: I Engineering, 2 Physical sciences, 3 Social/behavioural sciences.
Informal training: Social/behavioural sciences, Management.
Primarily engaged in: Both futures studies and long-range planning.
Areas in which work done (%): 20 As academic, in teaching futures studies or long-range planning, 30 In organization concerned with other studies including long-range planning, 50 In organization primarily concerned with futures studies and/or long-range planning.
Direction of work in forecasting: I Technological, 2 Scientific.
Direction of work in research: I Social impacts of technology.
Direction of work in planning: I Scientific, 2 Technological.
Methods used: I Delphi techniques, 2 Cross impact analysis, 3 Relevance trees, 4 Simulation, 5 Probabilistic forecasting.
Time range of work: 5 - 25 years.
Source of support for work (%): 100 National government.
Work done for (%): 100 National government.
Occupational function: I Manager, 2 Research worker, 3 Educator.
Worked in industry/business in: I Research and development, 2 Management.
Worked in education: I In research, 2 In administration, 3 Teaching.
Additional information: Concerned with technological forecasting, research and development and planning.   *(145)*

425. Joseph J. Penbera

5444 Nevada Ave, NW, Washington DC 20015, USA.
Sex: Male.   *Age:* 25-29.
Educational qualification: Doctoral degree.
Formal training: I Social/behavioural sciences.
Informal training: I Social/behavioural sciences, 2 Education, 3 International affairs.
Areas in which work done (%): 10 Futures training.
Direction of work in forecasting: I Technological, 2 Educational, 3 Economic, 4 Cultural, 5 Social.
Direction of work in research: I Alternative futures, 2 Value systems, 3 Futures methodology, 4 Policy research.
Direction of work in planning: I Political, 2 Economic, 3 Educational.
Methods used: I Expert panels, I Individual expert forecasting, 2 Delphi techniques, 3 Scenario building, 4 Extrapolation techniques, 5 Contextual mapping, 6 Statistical models, 7 Simulation, 8 Causal modelling, 9 Gaming, 10 Probabilistic forecasting, 11 Cross impact analysis, 12 Brainstorming, 13 Network analysis, 14 Relevance trees, 15 Historical analogy.
Time range of work: 10 - 25 years.
Source of support for work (%): 100 National government.
Work done for (%): 10 International agencies, 90 National government.
Occupational function: I Administrator, 2 Educator, 3 Consultant.
Worked in government as: Administrator.
Worked in industry/business in: Consultancy.
Worked in education: Teaching, In research, In administration.
Worked in service sector: Social welfare.
Additional information: Concerned with future of agro-industry, development of developing countries.   *(363)*

426. D.W. Pendery
Vice President, Planning, Xerox Corp, Stamford,Ct O69O4, USA.
Sex: Male.   *Age:* 5O-59.
Educational qualification: Master's degree.
Formal training: Engineering, Business administration.
Informal training: Physical sciences, Humanities.
Primarily engaged in: Both futures studies and long-range planning.
Areas in which work done (%): 2O In organization concerned with other studies including long-range planning, 8O In organization primarily concerned with futures studies and/or long-range planning.
Direction of work in forecasting: I Economic, 2 Technological, 3 Market.
Direction of work in planning: Corporate.
Methods used: I Expert panels, 2 Scenario building, 3 Network analysis, 5 Probabilistic forecasting, 6 Delphi techniques.
Time range of work: 5 - IO years.
Source of support for work (%): IOO Private business.
Work done for (%): IOO Private business.
Occupational function: Manager.
Worked in industry/business in: Management, Research and development, Planning. *(139)*

427. Eduard Pestel
Lehrstuhl A für Mechanik Technische, Universität Hannover, Appelstr 24B, 3 Hannover, West Germany.
Sex: Male.   *Age:* Over 6O.
Educational qualification: Doctoral degree.
Formal training: I Engineering, 2 Mathematics, 3 Physical sciences.
Informal training: I Humanities, 2 Social/behavioural sciences, 3 Life sciences.
Primarily engaged in: Both futures studies and long-range planning.
Areas in which work done (%): 2O In organization primarily concerned with futures studies and/or long-range planning, 5 In organization concerned with other studies including long-range planning, I5 As individual consultant, IO In planning unit of a governmental agency, 5 In planning unit of an international organization, 2O As academic, in teaching futures studies or long-range planning.
Direction of work in forecasting: Technological, Economic, Market, Environmental, Manpower, Resources, Population.
Direction of work in research: Alternative futures, Environmental, Resource utilization, Population, Futures methodology.
Direction of work in planning: Technological, Economic, Political, Environmental, Labour, Resources.
Methods used: Scenario building, Expert panels, Hierarchical systems approach, 'Open models'.
Time range of work: IO - beyond year 2OOO.
Source of support for work (%): 9O National government, IO Foundations.
Work done for (%): 35 National government, 25 Club of Rome, IO International agencies.
Occupational function: I Manager, 2 Research worker, 3 Consultant, 4 Educator.
Worked in government as: Elected official.
Worked in industry/business in: I Management, 2 Research and development.
Worked in education: I In research, 2 Teaching, 3 In administration. *(594)*

428. Howard V. Philipp

W.R. Grace and Company, 1114 Ave of the Americas, New York, NY, USA.
Sex: Male.   *Age:* 60 or over.
Educational qualification: Doctoral degree.
Formal training: Physical sciences.
Informal training: Mathematics, Engineering.
Primarily engaged in: Long-range planning.
Areas in which work done (%): 100 In organization primarily concerned with futures studies and/or long-range planning.
Direction of work in planning: Corporate.
Methods used: Probabilistic forecasting, Statistical models.
Time range of work: 5 - 10 years.
Source of support for work (%): 100 Private business.
Work done for (%): 100 Private business.
Occupational function: Administrator.
Worked in industry/business in: 1 Research and development, 2 Planning.   *(141)*

429. Robert Pickus

World Without War Council, 1730 Grove St, Berkeley, Ca 94709, USA.
Sex: Male.   *Age:* 50-59.
Educational qualification: Master's degree.
Formal training: 1 Social/behavioural sciences, 2 Humanities, 3 International affairs.
Informal training: 1 Education, 2 Humanities, 3 Journalism, 4 Cinema/television,
5 Political organization, ethics.
Direction of work in research: 1 Value systems, 2 Policy research, 3 Alternative futures.
Direction of work in planning: 1 Political, 2 Educational, 3 Resources.
Methods used: Expert panels, Network analysis, Historical analogy, Individual expert forecasting.
Time range of work: 5 - 25 years.
Source of support for work (%): 50 Foundations, 50 Voluntary associations.
Work done for (%): 3 Private business, 3 Foundations, 10 National government,
30 Voluntary associations.
Occupational function: 1 Educator, 1 Organizer, Catalyst, 2 Administrator, 3 Consultant,
4 Research worker.
Worked in industry/business in: Trade union.
Worked in education: Teaching.
Worked in service sector: Religion.
Additional information: Concerned with world organization, transnational leadership development, formation of social and ethical perspectives on war, community, legitimate authority forms of conflict resolution.   *(522)*

430. Ithiel De Sola Pool

Centre for International Studies, MIT, Cambridge, Ma 02139, USA.
Sex: Male.   *Age:* 50-59.
Educational qualification: Doctoral degree.
Formal training: Social/behavioural sciences.
Direction of work in research: 1 Social impacts of technology, 2 Policy research.
Direction of work in planning: 3 Technological, 4 Social.
Methods used: 1 Operational models, 2 Individual expert forecasting, 3 Scenario building, 4 Historical analogy, 5 Simulation, 6 Expert panels, 7 Extrapolation techniques, 8 Brainstorming.

Time range of work: IO - 25 years.
Source of support for work (%): 25 Foundations, 75 National government.
Work done for (%): 33 National government, 67 Scientific publications.
Occupational function: I Research worker.
Worked in education: I In research, 2 Teaching.
Additional information: Concerned with assessment of new communication technologies.

(206)

431. Vladimir Poremsky
125 - Bis Rue Blomet, Paris 15, France.
Sex: Male.   *Age:* 60 or over.
Educational qualification: Doctoral degree.
Formal training: Physical sciences, Engineering.
Informal training: Social/behavioural sciences.
Direction of work in forecasting: I Social, 2 Scientific, 3 Cultural, 4 Economic,
5 Technological.
Direction of work in research: I Alternative futures, 2 Social impacts of technology,
3 Value systems, 4 Social priorities.
Methods used: I Scenario building, 2 Extrapolation techniques, 3 Expert panels.
Time range of work: IO - 25 years.
Source of support for work (%): IOO Voluntary associations.
Work done for (%): IOO Voluntary associations.
Occupational function: Research worker.
Worked in education: In research.
Additional information: Concerned with the future of co-operation between western,
central and eastern Europe.   *(435)*

432. Arthur Porter
Royal Commission on Electric Power Planning, 14 Carleton St, 7th Floor, Toronto,
Canada.
Sex: Male.   *Age:* Over 60.
Educational qualification: Doctoral degree.
Formal training: Physical sciences.
Informal training: Engineering, Mathematics.
Primarily engaged in: Both futures studies and long-range planning.
Areas in which work done (%): IOO In organization primarily concerned with futures
studies and/or long-range planning.
Direction of work in forecasting: I Social, 2 Environmental, 3 Technological,
4 Resources, 5 Population, 6 Economic.
Direction of work in research: I Social impacts of technology, 2 Resource utilization,
3 Environmental, 4 Social priorities, 5 Population.
Direction of work in planning: I Regional, 2 Environmental, 3 Technological.
Methods used: I Educating public attitudes, 2 Expert panels, 3 Brainstorming.
Time range of work: IO - 25 years.
Source of support for work (%): IOO Provincial government.
Work done for (%): IOO Provincial government.
Occupational function: Chairman of Commission of Inquiry.
Worked in government as: Researcher.
Worked in industry/business in: I Management, 2 Research and development,
3 Consultancy.
Worked in education: I Teaching, 2 Research, 3 Administration.
Additional information: Concerned with electric power planning for Ontario '1983-1993
and Beyond'.   *(564)*

11

433. B.V. Postell
Vice President, Planning and Projects, Island Creek Coal Company, 2355 Harrodsburg Rd, PO Box 11430, Lexington KY 40511, USA.
Sex: Male.   *Age:* 40-49.
Educational qualification: Master's degree.
Formal training: 1 Engineering, 2 Business administration, 3 Physical sciences.
Informal training: 1 Law, 2 Journalism.
Primarily engaged in: Both futures studies and long-range planning.
Areas in which work done (%): 100 In planning unit of a business enterprise.
Direction of work in forecasting: 1 Market, 2 Resources, 3 Technological, 4 Economic.
Direction of work in research: 1 Resource utilization.
Direction of work in planning: 1 Corporate, 2 Resources, 3 Economic.
Methods used: 1 Scenario building, 2 Expert panels, 3 Extrapolation techniques.
Time range of work: 5 - 10 years.
Source of support for work (%): 100 Private business.
Work done for (%): 100 Private business.
Occupational function: 1 Manager, 2 Administrator.
Worked in industry/business in: 1 Planning, 2 Management.   *(374)*

434. John W. Powles
Science Policy Research Unit, University of Sussex, Falmer, Brighton, BN1 9RF, UK.
Sex: Male.   *Age:* 30-39.
Educational qualification: Bachelor's degree.
Formal training: 1 Life sciences, 2 Social/behavioural sciences.
Informal training: 1 Life sciences, 2 Social/behavioural sciences.
Primarily engaged in: Futures studies.
Areas in which work done (%): 5 As academic, in teaching futures studies or long-range planning, 15 Self-education, 90 In organization primarily concerned with futures studies and/or long-range planning.
Direction of work in forecasting: 1 Health trends, 2 Environmental, 3 Population.
Direction of work in research: 1 Health determinants, 2 Environmental, 3 Population, 4 Social priorities.
Methods used: 1 Individual expert forecasting, 2 Historical analogy, 3 Extrapolation techniques, 4 Causal modelling.
Time range of work: 10 - 25 years.
Source of support for work (%): 100 Social Sciences Research Council.
Work done for (%): 100 Research unit.
Occupational function: Research worker.
Worked in education: In research.
Worked in service sector: Medicine.   *(492)*

435. Robert W. Prehoda
Technological Forecaster, PO Box 2402, Tolula Lake Station, North Hollywood, Ca 91602, USA.
Sex: Male.   *Age:* 40-49.
Educational qualification: Master's and other graduate/professional degree.
Formal training: Physical sciences, Life sciences, Humanities.
Informal training: Engineering, Journalism, Education, Cinema/television.
Primarily engaged in: Both futures studies and long-range planning.
Direction of work in forecasting: Technological, Scientific, Environmental, Population, Astronautics, Economic, Resources.

Direction of work in research: Alternative futures, Environmental, Futures methodology, Astronautics, Resource utilization, Value systems, Social priorities, Policy research, Population.
Direction of work in planning: Scientific, Technological, Environmental, Economic, Corporate, Resources.
Methods used: Synthesis forecasting, Expert panels, Individual expert forecasting, Probabilistic forecasting, Delphi techniques, Cross impact analysis, Brainstorming, Statistical models, Relevance trees, Network analysis, Historical analysis.
Time range of work: 5 - beyond year 2000.
Source of support for work (%): Varies.
Work done for (%): Varies.
Occupational function: Administrator, Manager, Research worker, Educator, Consultant.
Worked in industry/business in: Management, Research and development, Planning, Consultancy.
Worked in education: Teaching.

(568)

436. Ian Priban
90 Portland Rd, London W11 4 QL, UK.
Sex: Male.   *Age:* 40-49.
Educational qualification: Doctoral degree.
Formal training: 1 Life sciences, 2 Mathematics, 3 Engineering.
Informal training: 1 Social/behavioural sciences, 2 Design, 3 Economics, 4 Education.
Primarily engaged in: Both futures studies and long-range planning.
Areas in which work done (%): 40 In organization primarily concerned with futures studies and/or long-range planning, 40 As individual consultant, 20 As academic, in teaching futurus studies or long-range planning.
Direction of work in forecasting: Technological, Economic, Social, Strategic multi-disciplinary forecasting.
Direction of work in research: 1 Policy research, 2 Futures methodology, 3 Multi-disciplinary.
Direction of work in planning: 1 Strategic, 2 Corporate.
Methods used: 1 Probabilistic forecasting, 1 Delphi techniques, 1 Contextual mapping, 1 Statistical models, 1 Network analysis, 1 Historical analogy, 1 A systems methodology, 2 Cross impact analysis, 2 Simulation, 2 Causal modelling.
Time range of work: 5 - 25 years.
Source of support for work (%): 10 National government, 10 International agencies, 20 Foundations, 60 Private business.
Work done for (%): 20 National government, 20 International agencies, 60 Private business.
Occupational function: 1 Consultant, 2 Research and development co-ordinator.
Worked in government as: Researcher.
Worked in industry/business in: 3 Consultancy.
Worked in education: 2 In research, 4 Teaching.
Worked in service sector: Medicine.

(163)

437. Rudiger Proske
Studio Hamburg, 2000 Hamburg, 70-Wandsbek, Tonndorfer Hauptstr 90, West Germany.
Sex: Male.   *Age:* 50-59.
Educational qualification: Master's degree.
Formal training: 1 Journalism, 2 Cinema/television, 3 Physical sciences, 4 Social/behavioural sciences, 5 Mathematics.

Informal training: Life sciences.
Primarily engaged in: Futures studies.
Areas in which work done (%): 70 As chief of the scientific program of North German television.
Direction of work in forecasting: I Population, 2 Military, 3 Scientific, 4 Technological, 5 Resources.
Direction of work in research: I Population, 2 Social impacts of technology, 3 Environmental, 4 Resource utilization, 5 Value systems.
Methods used: I Individual expert forecasting, 2 Expert panels, 3 Scenario building, 4 Brainstorming, 5 Statistical models.
Time range of work: IO - 25 years.
Occupational function: Scientific editor and author.
Worked in service sector: Communication media.
Additional information: Concerned with cybernetics, medicine (immunology, virology, cancer research), military technologies resources, energy, economic, and social trends and indicators.

(104)

438. Donald L. Pyke

Planning Co-ordinator of Academic Planning, University of S California, Los Angeles, Ca 90007, USA.
Sex: Male.   *Age:* 50-59.
Educational qualification: Master's degree.
Formal training: Engineering.
Informal training: Social/behavioural sciences, Education, Design.
Primarily engaged in: Both futures studies and long-range planning.
Areas in which work done (%): IO As individual consultant, 65 In organization primarily concerned with futures studies and/or long-range planning, 25 In organization, concerned with other studies including long-range planning.
Direction of work in forecasting: I Environmental, 2 Educational.
Direction of work in research: I Futures methodology, 2 Alternative futures, 3 Value systems, 4 Resource utilization.
Direction of work in planning: I Educational, 2 Corporate, 3 Urban.
Methods used: Probabilistic forecasting, Delphi techniques, Cross impact analysis, Scenario building, Extrapolation techniques, Contextual mapping, Brainstorming, Expert panels, Relevance trees, Network analysis, Historical analogy, Individual expert forecasting, Causal modelling.
Time range of work: IO - 25 years.
Source of support for work (%): 5 National government, 45 University of S Calif., 50 Private business.
Work done for (%):   5 National government, 20 Private business, 75 University of S California. ,
Occupational function: I Co-ordinator, 2 Administrator, 3 Consultant, 4 Research worker.
Worked in government as: Researcher.
Worked in industry/business in: I Management, 2 Research and development, 3 Planning.
Worked in education: I Teaching, 2 In administration, 3 In research.   *(153)*

Q 439. Brian Quickstad

President, Microfutures Group, Inc, 200 Park Ave, Suite 300 East, New York, NY 10017, USA.
Sex: Male.   *Age:* 30-39.
Educational qualification: Other graduate/professional degree.

Formal training: Law.
Informal training: I Design, 2 Education, 3 Cinema/television.
Primarily engaged in: Both futures studies and long-range planning.
Areas in which work done (%): IO Various organizations, 9O As individual consultant.
Direction of work in forecasting: I Educational, 2 Market, 3 Resources.
Direction of work in research: I Policy research, 2 Alternative futures, 3 Value systems, 4 Resources utilization, 5 Social impacts of technology, 6 The individual in the future.
Direction of work in planning: I Urban, 2 Educational, 3 Organizational/institutional, 4 Corporate.
Methods used: I Contextual mapping, 2 Individual expert forecasting, 3 Probabilistic forecasting.
Time range of work: IO - 25 years.
Source of support for work (%): 45 Private business, 55 National government.
Work done for (%): IO Private business, 3O National government, 6O Own projects.
Occupational function: Consultant.
Worked in government as: Researcher.
Worked in industry/business in: I Management, 2 Consultancy.
Worked in education: I In research, 2 Teaching.
Worked in service sector: I Communication media, 2 Design, 3 Law.   *(459)*

44O. J.B. Quinn
Amos Tucker School of Business Administration, Hanover, NH O3755, USA.
Sex: Male.   *Age:* 4O-49.
Educational qualification: Doctoral degree.
Formal training: Engineering.
Informal training: Business-economics.
Areas in which work done (%): IO As individual consultant, 3O As academic, in teaching future studies sor long-range planning.
Direction of work in forecasting: I Technological, 2 Environmental, 3 Resources.
Direction of work in research: I Policy research, 2 Social priorities.
Direction of work in planning: I Technological, 2 Economic, 2 Corporate.
Methods used: Scenario building, Extrapolation techniques.
Time range of work: IO - 25 years.
Source of support for work (%): 2O Private business.
Work done for (%): IO Education, 2O Private business.
Occupational function: Educator.
Worked in industry/business in: Research and development.
Worked in education: Teaching.
Additional information: Concerned with technological forecasting and evaluation.   *(428)*

441. James A. Raferty
3812 Blue Canyon Rd, Studio City, Ca 916O4, USA.
Sex: Male.   *Age:* 5O-59.
Educational qualification: Doctoral degree.
Formal training: Life sciences.
Informal training: Social/behavioural sciences.
Primarily engaged in: Long-range planning.
Areas in which work done (%): IOO As academic, in teaching futures studies or long-range planning.
Direction of work in forecasting: I Social, 2 Cultural, 3 Environmental.
Direction of work in planning: I Social, 2 Urban, 3 Regional.

Methods used: I Simulation, 2 Network analysis, 3 Cross impacts analysis, 4 Probabilistic forecasting, 6 Contextual mapping.
Time range of work: 5 - IO years.
Source of support for work (%): IOO Voluntary associations.
Work done for (%): 5O Local or regional government, 5O Voluntary associations.
Occupational function: Educator, I Consultant.
Worked in government as: Researcher.
Worked in industry/business in: Planning.
Worked in education: Teaching.
Worked in service sector: Medicine.
Additional information: Concerned with humanistic design of future institutions.   *(19)*

442. Zdenko Rajakovic

Chief, Population Studies and Programmes Sect, Economic Commission for Western Asia, PO Box 4656, Beirut, Lebanon.
Sex: Male.   *Age:* 50-59.
Educational qualification: Doctoral degree.
Formal training: Social/behavioural sciences, Law.
Informal training: Education.
Primarily engaged in: Futures studies.
Areas in which work done (%): 5O In organization concerned with other studies including long-range planning, 5O In organization primarily concerned with futures studies and/or long-range planning.
Direction of work in forecasting: Population.
Direction of work in research: Population.
Direction of work in planning: Population.
Methods used: Administrative works on work programme planning.
Source of support for work (%): 25 National government, 75 International agencies.
Work done for (%): 25 National government, 75 International agencies.
Occupational function: I Administrator, 2 Research worker.
Worked in government as: I Administrator, 2 Researcher.
Worked in education: Teaching.   *(122)*

443. D.B. Reddy

Regional Plant Protection Officer and Secretary, Plant Protection Comm. for South East Asia and Pacific Region, FAO Regional Office, Bankok 2, Thailand.
Sex: Male.   *Age:* 5O-59.
Educational qualification: Doctoral degree.
Formal training: Life sciences.
Informal training: I Education, 2 Social/behavioural sciences, 3 Physical sciences, 4 Journalism.
Primarily engaged in: Both futures studies and long-range planning.
Areas in which work done (%): IOO In planning unit of an international agency.
Direction of work in forecasting: I Technological, 2 Scientific, 3 Educational, 4 Environmental, 5 Resources.
Direction of work in research: I Policy research, 2 Futures methodology, 3 Resource utilization, 4 Environmental.
Direction of work in planning: I Technological, 2 Scientific, 3 Regional, 4 Educational, 5 Environmental, 6 Resources.
Methods used: Expert panels, Network analysis, Historical analogy, Individual expert forecasting, Causal modelling.

Time range of work: 5 - beyond year 2OOO.
Source of support for work (%): IOO International agencies.
Work done for (%): 5 Foundations, 5 Voluntary associations, IO International agencies,
8O National government.
Occupational function: I Adviser, 2 Consultant, 3 Administrator.
Worked in government as: Administrator, Researcher.
Worked in education: Teaching, In research, In administration.   *(232)*

444. J. Van Rees

N V Philips' Gloeilampenfabrieken, Eindhoven, The Netherlands.
Sex: Male.   *Age:* 5O-59.
Educational qualification: Doctoral degree.
Formal training: Social/behavioural sciences.
Areas in which work done (%): IO As academic, 9O In planning unit of a business
enterprise.
Direction of work in forecasting: I Market, 2 Economic, 3 Social, 4 Population.
Direction of work in research: Policy research.
Direction of work in planning: Corporate.
Methods used: I Extrapolation techniques, 2 Statistical models, 3 Operational models,
4 Simulation, 5 Causal modelling, 6 Probabilistic forecasting, 7 Historical analogy,
8 Delphi techniques, 9 Relevance trees.
Time range of work: 5 - IO years.
Occupational function: I Manager, 2 Educator.
Worked in government as: I Administrator.
Worked in industry/business in: I Research and development, 2 Planning.
Worked in education: I Teaching.   *(370)*

445. Carl F. Reuss

Director, Office of Research and Analysis, The American Lutheran Church, 422 South
Fifth St, Minneapolis, Mn 55415, USA.
Sex: Male.   *Age:* 5O-59.
Educational qualification: Doctoral degree.
Formal training: Social/behavioural sciences.
Direction of work in research: I Value systems, 2 The individual in the future, 3 The
family in the future. 4 Social impacts of technology.
Direction of work in planning: I Religion, 2 Corporate, 3 Regional.
Methods used: I Expert panels, 2 Historical analogy.
Time range of work: 5 - IO years.
Source of support for work (%): IOO National denomination.
Work done for (%): IOO National denomination.
Occupational function: Research worker.
Worked in education: I In research, 2 Teaching, 3 In administration.
Worked in service sector: Religion.
Additional information: Concerned with religion and its impact on society; and the
societal impact on religion.   *(308)*

446. Billy Rojas

c/o Alvin Toffler, 4O East 78th St, New York NY 1OO21, USA.
Sex: Male.   *Age:* 3O-39.
Educational qualification: Other graduate/professional degree.
Formal training: I Futures studies, 2 Social/behavioural sciences, 3 Education.

Informal training: I Journalism, 2 Arts, 3 Radio.
Primarily engaged in: Futures studies.
Areas in which work done (%): IO As individual consultant, 65 In organization primarily concerned with futures studies and/or long-range planning, 25 As academic, in teaching futures studies or long-range planning.
Direction of work in forecasting: I Cultural, 2 Social, 3 Educational, 4 Regional, 5 Economic.
Direction of work in research: I Futures methodology, 2 Value systems, 3 Alternative futures.
Methods used: I Historical analogy, 2 Gaming, 3 Scenario building, 4 Brainstorming, 5 Delphi techniques, 6 Causal modelling, 7 Extrapolation techniques, 8 Simulation, 9 Cross impacts analysis.
Time range of work: 5 - IO years.
Source of support for work (%): IOO Self and consulting.
Occupational fu ction: I Research worker, 2 Educator, 3 Consultant.
Worked in education: I Teaching, 2 In research.   *(518)*

447. Neal N. Rosenthal

US Dept of Labour, Bureau of Labour Statistics, Washington, DC 2O212, USA.
Sex: Male.   *Age:* 3O-39.
Educational qualification: Bachelor's degree.
Formal training: Social/behavioural sciences.
Primarily engaged in: Futures studies.
Areas in which work done (%): IOO In organization primarily concerned with futures studies and/or long-range planning.
Direction of work in forecasting: I Manpower, 2 Economic, 3 Educational.
Direction of work in research: I Manpower, 2 Futures methodology.
Direction of work in planning: I Educational, 2 Economic.
Methods used: Statistical models.
Time range of work: 5 - IO years.
Source of support for work (%): IOO National government.
Work done for (%): IOO National government.
Occupational function: I Manager, 2 Research worker.
Worked in government as: I Researcher, 2 Administrator.   *(48)*

448. J. Rotblat

Physics Dept, The Medical College of St. Bartholomew's Hospital, Charterhouse Square, London EC1, UK.
Sex: Male.   *Age:* 6O or over.
Educational qualification: Doctoral degree.
Formal training: Physical sciences.
Informal training: I Life sciences, 2 Education, 3 Social/behavioural sciences.
Direction of work in research: I Social impacts of technology, 2 Environmental, 3 Resource utilization.
Direction of work in planning: I Scientific, 2 Technological, 3 Environmental, 4 Resources, 5 Political, 6 Military.
Methods used: Extrapolation techniques, Statistical models, Expert panels.
Time range of work: 5 - IO years.
Source of support for work (%): 25 Voluntary associations, 5O Foundations.
Occupational function: I Educator, 2 Consultant.

Worked in education: I Teaching, 2 In administration, 3 In research.
Worked in service sector: I Medicine, 2 Social welfare.   *(114)*

449. Brian Rothery
Institute for Industrial Research and Standards, Glasnevin, Dublin, Ireland.
Sex: Male.   *Age:* 40-49.
Educational qualification: Other graduate/professional degree.
Formal training: I Design, 2 Author, 3 Humanities, 4 Social/behavioural sciences.
5 Journalism, 6 Physical sciences, 7 Mathematics, 8 Education.
Informal training: I Design, 2 Author, 3 Humanities, 4 Social/behavioural sciences,
5 Journalism, 6 Physical sciences.
Primarily engaged in: Both futures studies and long-range planning.
Areas in which work done (%): IOO Unit of a research institute.
Direction of work in forecasting: I Industry, 2 Environmental, 3 Resources, 4 Market,
5 Social.
Direction of work in research: I Social priorities, 2 Population, 3 Alternative futures,
4 Environmental, 5 Resource utilization.
Direction of work in planning: I Industry, 2 Resources, 3 Environmental, 4 Urban,
5 Regional.
Methods used: I Brainstorming, 2 Extrapolation techniques, 3 Scenario building,
4 Individual expert forecasting.
Time range of work: 5 - IO years.
Source of support for work (%): IOO National government.
Work done for (%): IOO National government.
Occupational function: I Manager, 2 Research worker, 3 Author.
Worked in industry/business in: I Planning, 2 Research and development.   *(125)*

450. Harry Rothman
Dept of Liberal Studies in Science, The University of Manchester, Manchester, UK.
Sex: Male.   *Age:* 30-39.
Educational qualification: Bachelor's degree.
Formal training: Life sciences.
Informal training: Social/behavioural sciences.
Primarily engaged in: Both futures studies and long-range planning.
Areas in which work done (%): 4O In organization concerned with other studies including
long-range planning, IO In planning unit of a business enterprise, 5O Academic, and
technology assessment.
Direction of work in forecasting: I Environmental, 2 Technological.
Direction of work in research: I Environmental, 2 Social impacts of technology, 3 Futures
methodology, 4 Consumer affairs.
Methods used: I Extrapolation techniques, 2 Individual expert forecasting, 3 Historical
analogy.
Occupational function: I Educator, 2 Research worker, 3 Consultant.
Worked in industry/business in: I Research and development, 2 Consultancy.
Worked in education: I Teaching, 2 In research.
Additional information: Concerned with technology assessment.   *(553)*

451. Hugh Rowlinson
Canadian Industries Ltd, PO Box 1O, Montreal, H3C 2R3, Canada.
Sex: Male.   *Age:* 40-49.
Educational qualification: Doctoral degree.

Formal training: Physical sciences.
Informal training: Law.
Primarily engaged in: Long-range planning.
Areas in which work done (%): IOO In planning unit of a business enterprise.
Direction of work in forecasting: I Market, 2 Economic, 3 Technological, 4 Environmental.
Direction of work in research: Alternative futures.
Direction of work in planning: I Corporate, 2 Technological.
Methods used: I Extrapolation techniques, 2 Operational models, 3 Scenario building,
4 Relevance trees, 5 Probabilistic forecasting.
Time range of work: 5 - IO years.
Source of support for work (%): IOO Private business.
Work done for (%): I Voluntary associations, 99 Private business.
Occupational function: I Manager, 2 Administrator.
Worked in industry/business in: I Research and development, 2 Management, 3 Planning.

(453)

452. Sir Norman Rowntree

Rowntree Boddington Associates, 1 Great Scotland Yard, London, SW1, UK.
Sex: Male.   *Age:* 60 or over.
Educational qualification: Other graduate/professional degree.
Formal training: Engineering.
Informal training: I Engineering, 2 Life sciences.
Areas in which work done (%): IOO As individual consultant.
Direction of work in forecasting: I Resources, 2 Environmental, 3 Technological.
Direction of work in research: I Resource utilization, 2 Environmental.
Direction of work in planning: I Resources, 2 Environmental, 3 Technological.
Methods used: I Expert panels, 2 Operational models, 3 Statistical models,
4 Probabilistic forecasting.
Time range of work: IO - 25 years.
Work done for (%): IOO Local or regional government.
Occupational function: I Consultant, 2 Educator.
Worked in government as: Administrator.
Worked in industry/business in: I Management, 2 Planning, 3 Consultancy.
Worked in education: Teaching.
Additional information: Concerned with water resources.

(16)

453. Milton D. Rubin

19 Dorr Rd, Newton, Ma 02158, USA.
Sex: Male.   *Age:* 60 or over.
Educational qualification: Bachelor's degree.
Formal training: Engineering.
Informal training: Social/behavioural sciences.
Direction of work in forecasting: I Technological, 2 Social, 3 Cultural.
Direction of work in research: Alternative futures.
Direction of work in planning: Corporate.
Methods used: I General systems research, 2 Scenario building, 3 Brainstorming.
Time range of work: 5 - IO years.
Source of support for work (%): 2O Personal, 8O Private business.
Work done for (%): 2O The public, 8O Private business.
Occupational function: Consultant.
Worked in government as: Researcher.

Worked in industry/business in: Research and development.
Worked in education: In research.
Additional information: Concerned with energy.

(52)

454. Rudy L. Ruggles Jr

President, Hudson Institute, Quaker Ridge Road, Croton-on-Hudson, NY 10502, USA.
Sex: Male.　　*Age:* 30-39.
Educational qualification: Master's degree.
Formal training: 1 Physical sciences, 2 Social/behavioural sciences, 3 Mathematics.
Informal training: 1 Humanities, 2 Life sciences.
Primarily engaged in: Both futures studies and long-range planning.
Areas in which work done (%): 100 Organization concerned with other studies including long-range planning.
Direction of work in forecasting: 1 Military, 2 Resources, 3 Economic, 4 Social.
Direction of work in research: 1 Policy research, 2 Social impacts of technology.
Direction of work in planning: 1 Military, 2 Economic, 3 Resources.
Methods used: 1 Scenario building, 2 Extrapolation techniques, 3 Individual expert forecasting, 4 Historical analogy, 5 Expert panels.
Time range of work: 5 - beyond year 2000.
Source of support for work (%): 60 National government, 30 Private business, 10 Foundations.
Work done for (%): 60 National government, 30 Private business, 10 Foundations.
Occupational function: 1 President of institute, 2 Research worker.
Worked in industry/business in: 1 Planning, 2 Research and development.

(574)

455. Jean-Jacques Salomon

Head, Science Policy Division, Organization for Economic Co-operation and Development, 2 Rue André-Pascal, Paris 16E, France.
Sex: Male.　　*Age:* 40-49.
Educational qualification: Doctoral degree.
Formal training: 1 Social/behavioural sciences, 1 Humanities, 2 Life sciences, 3 Journalism.
Informal training: 1 Science policy, 2 Physical sciences, 2 Life sciences, 2 Social/behavioural sciences, 3 Education.
Primarily engaged in: Both futures studies and long-range planning.
Areas in which work done (%): 20 As academic, in teaching futures studies or long-range planning, 40 In organization concerned with other studies including long-range planning.
Direction of work in forecasting: Technological, Economic, Social, Educational, Scientific.
Direction of work in research: Social impacts of technology, Value systems, Policy research.
Direction of work in planning: Scientific, Technological.
Methods used: Statistical models, Expert panels, Historical analogy, Individual expert forecasting.
Time range of work: 5 - 25 years.
Source of support for work (%): 100 International agencies.
Work done for (%): 20 International agencies, 80 Local or regional government.
Occupational function: 1 Administrator, 2 Research worker.
Worked in government as: Administrator.
Worked in education: Teaching.

(158)

456. Paul D. Saltman

Vice Chancellor for Academic Affairs, University of California, San Diego, Ca, USA.
Sex: Male.   *Age:* 40-49.
Educational qualification: Doctoral degree.
Formal training: Life sciences.
Informal training: I Life sciences, 2 Education, 3 Cinema/television.
Areas in which work done (%): IO In organization primarily concerned with futures studies and/or long-range planning, IO As academic, in teaching futures studies or long-range planning.
Direction of work in research: Health.
Direction of work in planning: Educational.
Methods used: I Scenario building, 2 Operational models, 3 Delphi techniques.
Time range of work: 5 - IO years.
Work done for (%): 8O University.
Occupational function: I Educator, 2 Administrator, 3 Research worker.
Worked in education: I In administration, 2 Teaching, 3 In research.
Additional information: Concerned with long-range planning for higher education in the steady state.   *(58)*

457. Sipho David Scamini

PO Box 526, Mbabane, Swaziland.
Sex: Male.   *Age:* 25 -29.
Educational qualification: Bachelor's degree.
Formal training: I Humanities, 2 Journalism, 2 Education.
Informal training: Arts.
Primarily engaged in: Futures studies.
Areas in which work done (%): IO In organization primarily concerned with futures studies and/or long-range planning, 25 As individual consultant, 3O In planning unit of a business enterprise, 2O As academic, in teaching futures studies or long-range planning.
Direction of work in forecasting: I Market, 2 Social, 3 Manpower.
Direction of work in research: I Consumer affairs, 2 Manpower, 3 Social priorities.
Methods used: I Gaming, 2 Extrapolation techniques, 3 Contextual mapping, 4 Statistical models, 5 Brainstorming.
Time range of work: IO - 25 years.
Source of support for work (%): 2O Private business, 5O National government.
Work done for (%): 2O Private business, 5O National government.
Occupational function: I Educator, 2 Administrator, 3 Consultant.
Worked in government as: Administrator.
Worked in industry/business in: I Planning, 2 Trade union.
Worked in education: I Teaching, 2 In administration.
Worked in service sector: I Religion, 2 Social welfare, 3 Design.
Additional information: Concerned with technology and business.   *(431)*

458. Victor Scardigli

9 Allée Berlioz, 948OO Villejuif, Paris, France.
Sex: Male.   *Age:* 30-39.
Educational qualification: Doctoral degree.
Formal training: I Social/behavioural sciences, 2 Life sciences.
Informal training: Social/behavioural sciences.
Primarily engaged in: Futures studies.

Areas in which work done: 8O In organization primarily concerned with futures studies and/or long-range planning, 2O As individual consultant.
Direction of work in forecasting: I Economic, 2 Social.
Direction of work in research: I Ways of life, 2 The individual in the future, 3 Value systems, 4 Alternative futures.
Methods used: I Scenario building, 2 Contextual mapping, 3 Extrapolation techniques, 4 Expert panels, 5 Individual expert forecasting.
Time range of work: IO - 25 years.
Source of support for work (%): 4O National government, 2O International agencies, 4O Private business.
Work done for (%): 4O National government, 2O International agencies, 4O Private business.
Occupational function: I Research worker, 2 Manager.
Worked in government as: Researcher.   *(585)*

459. Dali Schindler
International Creative Centre (ICC), 2O CH, Colladon, 12O9 Geneva, Switzerland.
Sex: Female.   *Age:* 40-49.
Educational qualification: Doctoral degree.
Formal training: Life sciences, Humanities, Journalism, Education, Arts.
Primarily engaged in: Both futures studies and long-range planning.
Areas in which work done : In organization primarily concerned with futures studies and/or long-range planning, In organization concerned with other studies including long-range planning, In planning unit of an international organization.
Direction of work in forecasting: Cultural, Educational, Scientific, Environmental.
Direction of work in research: Value systems, The individual in the future, The family in the future.
Direction of work in planning: Scientific, Educational.
Methods used: I Expert panels, 2 Network analysis, 3 Individual expert forecasting.
Time range of work: 5 - IO years.
Source of support for work (%): IO National government, 9O Private business.
Work done for (%): IOO Expert panels.
Occupational function: I Manager, 2 Administrator, 3 Research worker, 4 Educator.
Worked in service sector: Medicine, Social welfare, Religion, Communications media.
Additional information: Concerned with the future of medicine, environment, education, philosophy, urbanization, arts (synthesis of sciences).   *(552)*

460. Kenneth Schmidt
Manager, Market Analysis, Rexnord, PO Box 2O22, Milwaukee, Wi 532O1, USA.
Sex: Male.   *Age:* 40-49.
Educational qualification: Bachelor's degree.
Formal training: Engineering.
Informal training: Business.
Areas in which work done (%): IOO In organization concerned with other studies including long-range planning.
Direction of work in forecasting: I Technological, 2 Economic, 3 Market.
Direction of work in planning: I Corporate, 2 Technological.
Methods used: I Individual expert forecasting, 2 Expert panels.
Time range of work: 5 - IO years.
Source of support for work (%): IOO Private business.
Occupational function: Manager.

Worked in industry/business in: Planning.
Additional information: Concerned with product planning.

(83)

461. Jerry Schneider

Dept of Urban Planning (JO-4O), University of Washington, Seattle, Wa USA.
Sex: Male.   *Age:* 4O-49.
Educational qualification: Doctoral degree.
Formal training: Design.
Informal training: Social/behavioural sciences.
Areas in which work done (%): 5 Individual consultant, l5 As academic, in teaching futures studies or long-range planning.
Direction of work in forecasting: Economic, Social, Environmental, Population.
Direction of work in research: Social impacts of technology, Alternative futures, Environmental, Resource utilization, Value systems, Social priorities, Policy research, Population, Futures methodology.
Direction of work in planning: Urban, Regional, Environmental.
Methods used: All methods (see Directory guide).
Time range of work: 5 - beyond year 2OOO.
Source of support for work (%): lOO Academic.
Work done for (%): 5O Local or regional government, 5O National government.
Occupational function: l Research worker, 2 Educator, 3 Consultant.
Worked in government as: l Researcher.
Worked in education: l In research, 2 Teaching, 3 In administration.
Additional information: Concerned with urban and regional planning and forecasting.

(200)

462. D. Schumacher

Systemplan E.V. Institut für Umweltforschung und Entwicklungsplanung, D 69 Heidelberg, Tiergartenstr 15, West Germany.
Sex: Male.   *Age:* 3O-39.
Educational qualification: Doctoral degree.
Formal training: Natural sciences.
Informal training: l Political sciences, 2 Social, 3 Engineering.
Primarily engaged in: Both futures studies and long-range planning.
Areas in which work done (%): lO As individual consultant, lO As academic, in teaching futures studies or long-range planning, 8O In organization primarily concerned with futures studies and/or long-range planning.
Direction of work in forecasting: l Technological, 2 Scientific, 3 Integrative.
Direction of work in research: l Policy research, 2 Social impacts of technology, 3 Integrative, 4 Social priorities, 5 Futures methodology.
Direction of work in planning: l Technological, 2 Political, 3 Scientific, 4 Integrative.
Methods used: l Brainstorming, 2 Expert panels, 3 Scenario building, 4 Systems analysis.
Time range of work: 5 - 25 years.
Source of support for work (%): 2O Foundations, 2O International agencies, 6O National government.
Work done for (%): 2O International agencies, 2O Foundations, 6O National government.
Occupational function: l Consultant, 2 Manager, 3 Researcher, 4 Lecturer.
Worked in government as: Researcher.
Worked in industry/business in: l Research and development, 2 Management.
Worked in education: Teaching.
Additional information: Concerned with long-range planning, long-range research and technology planning, including assessment.

(294)

463. Egbert Schuurman

Research Officer, Centrale Interfaculteit der Vrije Universiteit de Boelelaan, 1105 Amsterdam, The Netherlands.

Sex: Male. *Age:* 30-39.

Educational qualification: Doctoral degree.

Formal training: 1 Engineering, 2 Philosophy.

Informal training: Mathematics.

Areas in which work done (%): 30 As academic, in teaching futures studies or long-range planning.

Direction of work in research: 1 Value systems, 2 Alternative futures, 3 Environmental, 4 Social impacts of technology.

Methods used: The immanent-transcendental methods of philosophy.

Source of support for work (%): 100 University.

Occupational function: 1 Lecturer, professor, 2 Educator.

Worked in education: 1 Teaching, In research. *(443)*

464. Nicole Schwartz

22 Rue Saint Ferdinand, 75017 Paris, France.

Sex: Female. *Age:* 25-29.

Educational qualification: Doctoral degree.

Formal training: Social/behavioural sciences, Humanities.

Informal training: Journalism.

Primarily engaged in: Both futures studies and long-range planning.

Areas in which work done (%): 100 As individual consultant.

Direction of work in forecasting: Economic.

Direction of work in research: Alternative futures.

Direction of work in planning: Social.

Methods used: 1 Scenario building, 2 Brainstorming, 3 Statistical models, 4 Historical analogy.

Time range of work: 10 - beyond year 2000.

Source of support for work (%): 100 Private business.

Work done for (%): 100 Private business.

Occupational function: 1 Consultant, 2 Research worker.

Worked in government as: Researcher.

Worked in industry/business in: Planning.

Worked in education: Teaching. *(500)*

465. Peter Schwartz

558 Lincoln Ave, Palo Alto, Ca 94301, USA.

Sex: Male. *Age:* 25-29.

Educational qualification: Bachelor's degree.

Formal training: Engineering.

Informal training: 1 Social/behavioural sciences, 2 Planning, 3 Education.

Primarily engaged in: Futures studies.

Areas in which work done (%): 10 As individual consultant, 80 In organization primarily concerned with futures studies and/or long-range planning, 10 As academic, in teaching futures studies or long-range planning.

Direction of work in forecasting: 1 Governmental, 2 Social, 3 Technological, 4 Environmental, 5 Economic, 6 Educational.

Direction of work in research: 1 Futures methodology, 2 Alternative futures, 3 Value systems, 4 Environmental.

Direction of work in planning: I Environmental, 2 Social, 3 State planning, 4 Corporate.
Methods used: I Divergence mapping, 2 Scenario building, 3 Gaming, 4 Contextual mapping.
Time range of work: IO - 25 years.
Source of support for work (%): IO Local government, 2O Private business, 7O National government.
Work done for (%): IO Local or regional government, 2O Private business, 7O National government.
Occupational function: I Research worker, 2 Consultant, 3 Educator.
Worked in industry/business in: 2 Research and development.
Worked in education: I In administration, 3 Teaching.
Additional information: Concerned with general futures work as applied to specific problems. **(49)**

466. H.W. Schwarz

Vice President, Coca-Cola Company, PO Box 1734, Atlanta, Ga 30342, USA.
Sex: Male.   *Age:* 50-59.
Educational qualification: Master's degree.
Formal training: I Engineering, 2 Physical sciences, 3 Mathematics.
Informal training: I Social/behavioural sciences, 2 Design.
Primarily engaged in: Long-range planning.
Areas in which work done (%): IOO In planning unit of a business enterprise.
Direction of work in forecasting: I Economic, 2 Environmental, 3 Market.
Direction of work in research: I Environmental, 2 Consumer affairs, 3 Alternative futures.
Direction of work in planning: I Corporate, 2 Economic, 3 Technological.
Methods used: I Extrapolation techniques, 2 Individual expert forecasting, 3 Expert panels, 4 Scenario building, 5 Simulation, 6 Operational models, 7 Causal modelling.
Time range of work: IO - 25 years.
Source of support for work (%): IOO Private business.
Work done for (%): 5 Local or regional government, I5 Voluntary associations, 8O Private business.
Occupational function: I Administrator, 2 Manager, 3 Consultant.
Worked in industry/business in: I Management, 2 Planning, 3 Research and development.
(368)

467. Aloys Schwietert

Prognos AG, Basle, Switzerland.
Eex: Male.   *Age:* 4O-49.
Educational qualification: Doctoral degree.
Formal training: Social/behavioural sciences.
Informal training: I Physical sciences, 2 Journalism.
Primarily engaged in: Both futures studies and long-range planning.
Areas in which work done (%): 2O As individual consultant, 2O As academic, in teaching futures studies or long-range planning, 6O In organization primarily concerned with futures studies and/or long-range planning.
Direction of work in forecasting: I Economic, 2 Manpower, 2 Resources, 2 Population, 3 Technological, 4 Environmental, 5 Market.
Direction of work in research: Social impacts of technology, Alternative futures, Manpower, Value systems, Population.
Direction of work in planning: I Economic, 2 Corporate, 3 Regional.
Methods used: I Statistical models, 2 Cross impact analysis, 3 Individual expert forecasting, 4 Simulation, 5 Delphi techniques, 5 Scenario building, 5 Extrapolation

techniques, 5 Contextual mapping, 5 Brainstorming, 5 Expert panels, 5 Relevance trees, 5 Network analysis.
Time range of work: 5 - I0 years.
Source of support for work (%): 25 Local government, 25 National government, 50 Private business.
Work done for (%): 25 Local or regional government, 25 National government, 50 Private business.
Occupational function: I Manager, 2 Consultant.
Worked in industry/business in: Management.
Worked in education: Teaching, In research.
Additional information: Concerned with future economic growth and structural change.
(276)

468. Norman Scott

Director, Trade and Technology Division, Economic Commission for Europe, Palais des Nations, Geneva, Switzerland.
Sex: Male.   *Age:* 40-49.
Educational qualification: Master's degree.
Formal training: Social/behavioural sciences.
Informal training: Physical sciences, Social/behavioural sciences, Education.
Areas in which work done for (%): 20 In planning unit of an international organization, 20 In organization concerned with other studies including long-range planning, I0 As academic, in teaching futures studies for long-range planning.
Direction of work in forecasting: I Technological, 2 Economic, 3 Scientific, 4 Market, 5 Resources.
Direction of work in research: I Resource utilization, 2 Social impacts of technology, 3 Social priorities.
Direction of work in planning: I Scientific, 2 Technological, 3 Economic.
Methods used: I Extrapolation techniques, 2 Contextual mapping, 3 Expert panels, 4 Individual expert forecasting.
Time range of work: I0 - 25 years.
Source of support for work (%): I00 International agencies.
Work done for (%): I00 International agencies.
Occupational function: Administrator, Manager, Research worker.
Worked in government as: Administrator, Researcher.
Worked in education: Teaching.
(369)

469. Graham William Searle

Earth Resources Research Ltd, 40 James St, London, W1, UK.
Sex: Male.   *Age:* 25-29.
Educational qualification: Bachelor's degree.
Formal training: Physical sciences.
Informal training: Social/behavioural sciences, Journalism, Education, Cinema/television.
Primarily engaged in: Both futures studies and long-range planning.
Areas in which work done (%): 65 Organization primarily concerned with futures studies and/or long-range planning, 30 Organization concerned with other studies including long-range planning, 5 Academic, in teaching futures studies or long-range planning.
Direction of work in forecasting: I Resources, 2 Technological, 3 Economic, 4 Environmental, 5 Social, 6 Cultural.
Direction of work in research: I Resource utilization, 2 Policy research, 3 Social impacts of technology, 4 Environmental.
Direction of work in planning: I Political, 2 Resources, 3 Environmental, 4 Economic, 5 Social.

Methods used: I Scenario building, 2 Brainstorming, 3 Expert panels, 4 Extrapolation techniques, 5 Historical analogy.
Time range of work: IO - 25 years.
Source of support for work (%): 5 National government, IO International agencies, IO Private business, 6O Foundations, I5 Voluntary associations.
Work done for (%): IO National government, 5 International agencies, 85 Voluntary associations.
Occupational function: I Manager, 2 Educator, 3 Consultant, 4 Research worker.
Worked in industry/business in: Management.
Worked in education: In research, Teaching.   *(558)*

47O. Jean-Jacques Sengiet
Director, Swiss Federal Bureau of Statistics, 3OO3 Berne, Hallwystr 15, Switzerland.
Sex: Male.   *Age:* 5O-59.
Educational qualification: Doctoral degree.
Formal training: Social/behavioural sciences.
Informal training: I Social/behavioural sciences, 2 Education, 3 Humanities.
Direction of work in forecasting: I Economic, 2 Market, 3 Manpower, 4 Population.
Methods used: I Statistical models, 2 Extrapolation techniques, 3 Probabilistic forecasting.
Time range of work: 5 - IO years.
Source of support for work (%): IOO National government.
Work done for (%): IOO National government.
Occupational function: Administrator.
Worked in government as: Administrator.
Worked in education: Teaching.
Additional information: Concerned with economics.   *(295)*

471. Peter J. Senker
Science Policy Research Unit, University of Sussex, Falmer, Brighton, BN1 9RF, UK.
Sex: Male.   *Age:* 4O-49.
Educational qualification: Bachelor's degree.
Formal training: Social/behavioural sciences.
Primarily engaged in: Futures studies.
Areas in which work done (%): IOO In organization primarily concerned with futures studies and/or long-range planning.
Direction of work in forecasting: I Technological, 2 Manpower, 3 Economic, 4 Social.
Direction of work in research: I Social impacts of technology, 2 Manpower.
Methods used: Historical analogy, Technological manpower, Economic studies.
Time range of work: 5 - IO years.
Source of support for work (%): IOO Engineering industry training board.
Work done for (%): IOO Engineering industry training board.
Occupational function: Research worker.
Worked in industry/business in: I Planning, 2 Management, 3 Consultancy.
Worked in education: I In research, 2 Teaching.   *(486)*

472. Emilio Servadio
4 Via di Villa Emiliani, OO197,Rome, Italy.
Sex: Male.   *Age:* 6O or over.
Educational qualification: Doctoral degree.
Formal training: I Law, 2 Life sciences, 3 Psychoanalysis.

Informal training: Parapsychology.
Areas in which work done (%): 40 Teaching, writing, 60 Individual consultant.
Occupational function: I Consultant, 2 Educator.
Worked in education: I In research, 2 Teaching.
Worked in service sector: Medicine.
(41)

473. Harold C. Shane

Prof of Education, School of Education 328 Indiana University, Education Bldg,
Bloomington, In 47401, USA.
Sex: Male.   *Age:* 60 or over.
Educational qualification: Doctoral degree.
Formal training: I Education, 2 Humanities, 3 Social/behavioural sciences.
Informal training: Life sciences, Journalism.
Primarily engaged in: Futures studies.
Areas in which work done (%): 20 As individual consultant, 10 In planning unit of
a governmental agency, 40 As academic, in teaching future studies or long-range planning.
Direction of work in forecasting: Social, Educational.
Direction of work in research: Value systems, Social priorities, The individual in the
future.
Direction of work in planning: Educational.
Methods used: Probabilistic forecasting, Scenario building, Extrapolation techniques,
Brainstorming, Expert panels, Historical analogy, Individual expert forecasting.
Time range of work: 5 - 10 years.
Source of support for work (%): 35 Foundations.
Work done for (%): 35 Local or regional government, 35 Foundations.
Occupational function: I Educator, 2 Consultant, 3 Research worker.
Worked in education: I In administration, 2 Teaching.
(18)

474. Charles S. Sheldon II

Chief, Science Policy Div, Congressional Research Service, Library of Congress,
Washington DC 20540, USA.
Sex: Male.   *Age:* 50-59.
Educational qualification: Doctoral degree.
Formal training: Social/behavioural sciences.
Informal training: I Social/behavioural sciences, 2 Engineering, 3 Physical sciences,
4 Life sciences, 5 Law.
Areas in which work done (%): 100 In organization concerned with other studies
including long-range planning.
Direction of work in forecasting: I Technological, 2 Economic, 3 Social, 4 Scientific,
5 Military.
Direction of work in research: I Social impacts of technology, 2 Population, 3 Alternative
futures, 4 Social priorities.
Direction of work in planning: I Technological, 2 Scientific, 3 Economic, 4 Social,
5 Political, 6 Urban, 7 Military.
Methods used: Probabilistic forecasting, Scenario building, Extrapolation techniques,
Expert panels, Historical analogy, Individual expert forecasting.
Time range of work: 5 - beyond year 2000.
Source of support for work (%): 100 National government.
Work done for (%): 100 National government.
Occupational function: I Manager, 2 Research worker, 3 Administrator, 4 Consultant.

Worked in government as: Researcher.
Worked in education: Teaching, In research.
Additional information: Concerned with future of medicine; long-range resources analysis; technology assessment; and social indicators.   *(256)*

475. L. Shindler
Director, Research Div, Puget Sound Governmental Conference, 216 First Ave South, Seattle, Wa 98104, USA.
Sex: Male.   *Age:* 40-49.
Educational qualification: Master's degree.
Formal training: Social/behavioural sciences.
Informal training: Engineering, Design.
Primarily engaged in: Long-range planning.
Areas in which work done (%): 40 In organization primarily concerned with futures studies and/or long-range planning, 60 In planning unit of a governmental agency.
Direction of work in forecasting: 1 Economic, 2 Population, 3 Environmental, 4 Technological, 5 Resources, 6 Social.
Direction of work in research: 1 Alternative futures, 2 Social impacts of technology, 3 Environmental, 4 Population, 5 Futures methodology.
Direction of work in planning: 1 Urban, 2 Regional.
Methods used: 1 Statistical models, 2 Extrapolation techniques, 3 Probabilistic forecasting, 4 Individual expert forecasting.
Time range of work: 10 - 25 years.
Source of support for work (%): 25 Local government, 75 National government.
Work done for (%): 100 Local or regional government.
Occupational function: 1 Manager, 2 Consultant.
Worked in government as: 1 Researcher, 2 Administrator.
Worked in industry/business in: Consultancy.
Additional information: Concerned with urban growth, land use, changes in life styles, demand for public services, technology assessment, impact of resources, and constraints.
            (423)
476. Andrzej Sicinski
Head, Div of Social Prognoses, Institute of Philosophy and Sociology, Polish Academy of Sciences, Nowy Swiat 72, 00 - 330 Warsaw, Poland.
Sex: Male.   *Age:* 50-59.
Educational qualification: Other graduate/professional degree.
Formal training: 1 Social/behavioural sciences, 2 Engineering.
Informal training: Design.
Areas in which work done (%): 5 As academic, in teaching futures studies or long-range planning, 35 In organization primarily concerned with futures studies and/or long-range planning, 50 In organization concerned with other studies including long-range planning, 10 As individual consultant.
Direction of work in forecasting: 1 Cultural, 2 Social.
Direction of work in research: 1 Life styles in the future, 2 Futures methodology, 3 Value systems, 4 Social impacts of technology.
Direction of work in planning: 1 Social, 2 Educational;
Methods used: 1 Individual expert forecasting, 2 Extrapolation techniques, 3 Scenario building, 4 Simulation.
Time range of work: 10 - 25 years.
Source of support for work (%): 100 National government.
Work done for (%): 100 National government.

Occupational function: I Research worker, 2 Manager, 3 Consultant, 4 Educator.
Worked in government as: I Researcher. *(529)*

477. Manfred H. Siebker

Board du Souverain 209, 1160 Brussels, Belgium.
Sex: Male. *Age:* 40-49.
Educational qualification: Other graduate/professional degree.
Formal training: I Physical sciences, 2 Engineering, 3 Social/behavioural sciences.
Informal training: Humanities, Arts.
Primarily engaged in: Both futures studies and long-range planning.
Areas in which work done (%): 20 Club of Rome, 80 In organization concerned with other studies including long-range planning.
Direction of work in forecasting: I Technological, 2 Economic, 3 Social, 4 Environmental, 5 Resources.
Direction of work in research: I Alternative futures, 2 Value systems, 3 Social priorities, 4 Policy research, 5 Social impacts of technology, 6 Resource utilization, 7 Futures methodology.
Direction of work in planning: I Technological, I Economic, I Political.
Methods used: I Brainstorming, 2 Contextual mapping, 3 Relevance trees, 4 Operational models, 5 Historical analogy, 6 Delphi techniques.
Time range of work: 10 - beyond year 2000.
Source of support for work (%): 20 Private business, 40 Unspecified, 40 International agencies.
Work done for (%): 20 Private business, 40 International agencies, 40 Unspecified.
Occupational function: Manager.
Worked in government as: Administrator.
Worked in industry/business in: I Research and development, 2 Management.
Additional information: Concerned with technological assessment and forecasting basic motivational analysis. *(449)*

478. Ellsworth E. Sietz

Dept of the Army, 3205 Plantation Parkway, Fairfax, Va 22030, USA.
Sex: Male. *Age:* 60 or over.
Educational qualification: Bachelor's degree.
Formal training: I Mathematics, 2 Education, 3 Engineering.
Informal training: I Mathematics, 2 Education, 3 Engineering, 4 Physical sciences, 5 Journalism.
Primarily engaged in: Long-range planning.
Areas in which work done (%): 50 In planning unit of a governmental agency, 50 In organization concerned with other studies including long-range planning.
Direction of work in forecasting: Technological.
Direction of work in research: Resource utilization.
Direction of work in planning: Technological, Military.
Methods used: Probabilistic forecasting, Extrapolation techniques, Brainstorming, Expert panels, Operational models, Individual expert forecasting, Simulation, Causal modelling.
Time range of work: 5 - 25 years.
Source of support for work (%): 100 National government.
Work done for (%): 100 National government.
Occupational function: Manager, Consultant.
Worked in government as: Administrator, Researcher. *(307)*

479. Clive W.H. Simmonds
Industrial Programs Office, National Research Council of Canada, Montreal Rd, Ottawa
K1A OR6, Canada.
Sex: Male.   *Age:* 50-59.
Educational qualification: Other graduate/professional degree.
Formal training: I Physical sciences, 2 Engineering, 3 Social/behavioural sciences.
Informal training: I Planning-forecasting-futures, 2 Education.
Primarily engaged in: Both futures studies and long-range planning.
Areas in which work done (%): IOO In planning unit of a governmental agency.
Direction of work in forecasting: Interaction of technological economic, human and social.
Direction of work in research: Behaviour pattern analysis and synthesis, Extension of
goals.
Direction of work in planning: Value and function of technology and science in industry.
Methods used: I Behaviour patterns, 2 Analysis-synthesis, 3 Forces for change.
Time range of work: 5 - 25 years.
Source of support for work (%): IOO National government.
Work done for (%): IOO Industry, government, university.
Occupational function: I Research worker, 2 Consultant, 3 Educator, 4 Manager.
Worked in government as: Researcher.
Worked in industry/business in: Research and development, Planning.
Worked in education: Teaching, Research.   *(531)*

480. W.W. Simmons
Planning Consultant, 22 Greenwich Plaza, Greenwich, Ct O683O, USA.
Sex: Male.   *Age:* 6O or over.
Educational qualification: Bachelor's degree.
Formal training: Engineering.
Informal training: Planning.
Primarily engaged in: Both futures studies and long-range planning.
Areas in which work done (%): 5O As individual consultant, 5O Applied futures company.
Direction of work in research: 2 Environmental, 3 Alternative futures, 4 Futures
methodology.
Direction of work in planning: I Corporate.
Methods used: I Brainstorming, 2 Expert panels, 3 Individual expert forecasting.
Time range of work: 5 - IO years.
Source of support for work (%): IOO Private business.
Work done for (%): IOO Private business.
Occupational function: I Consultant, 2 Manager, 3 Educator.
Worked in industry/business in: I Management, 2 Planning, 3 Consultancy.
Additional information: Concerned with business planning, environmental studies.   *(77)*

481. William Simon
Institute for Urban Studies, University of Houston, 5O1 Cullen Blvd, Houston, Texas
77OO4, USA.
Sex: Male.   *Age:* 40-49.
Educational qualification: Doctoral degree.
Formal training: Social/behavioural sciences.
Informal training: I Humanities, 2 Education, 3 Arts.
Primarily engaged in: Future studies.
Areas in which work done (%): IOO In organization concerned with other studies
including long-range planning.

Direction of work in forecasting: I Social, 2 Cultural, 3 Educational.
Direction of work in research: I The individual in the future, 2 The family in the future, 3 Value systems, 4 Social impacts of technology, 5 Policy research.
Direction of work in planning: I Social, 2 Urban, 3 Educational.
Methods used: I Probabilistic forecasting, 2 Scenario building.
Time range of work: IO - 25 years.
Source of support for work (%): 5O Local government, 5O National government.
Occupational function: I Research worker, 2 Administrator, 3 Consultant.
Worked in government as: 2 Researcher.
Worked in education: I In research, 3 Teaching.   *(520)*

482. Max Singer
4 Ben Thbbai, Jerusalem, Israel.
Sex: Male.   *Age:* 4O-49.
Educational qualification: Other graduate/professional degree.
Formal training: Law.
Informal training: Policy analysis.
Areas in which work done (%): IOO In organization concerned with other studies including long-range planning.
Direction of work in forecasting: Technological, Economic, Social, Military, Resources, Population.
Direction of work in research: Alternative futures, Policy research, Population.
Methods used: Probabilistic forecasting, Scenario building, Extrapolation techniuqes, Historical analogy, Individual expert forecasting.
Time range of work: 5 - beyond year 2OOO.
Source of support for work (%): 5O Foundations, 5O National government.
Occupational function: Manager.
Worked in government as: Administrator.
Additional information: Concerned with resource, strategic issues, general.   *(472)*

483. Peter Sint
Institut für Sozio Ökonomische, Entwicklungsforschung, A-1O1O Vienna, Austria.
Sex: Male.   *Age:* 3O-39.
Educational qualification: Doctoral degree.
Formal training: Physical sciences, Mathematics, Social/behavioural sciences.
Informal training: Mathematics, Social/behavioural sciences, Education, Design, Humanities.
Primarily engaged in: Futures studies.
Areas in which work done (%): 95 In organization primarily concerned with futures studies and/or long-range planning, 5 As academic, in teaching futures studies or long-range planning.
Direction of work in forecasting: I Economic, 2 Technological, 3 Educational.
Direction of work in research: I Social impacts of technology, 2 Resource utilization, 3 Environmental, 4 Value systems, 5 Social priorities, 6 Policy research.
Methods used: I Simulation, 2 Statistical models, 3 Scenario building, 4 Extrapolation techniques, 5 Operational models.
Time range of work: Beyond year 2OOO.
Source of support for work (%): 9O National government, IO International agencies.
Work done for (%): 8O National government, 2O International agencies.
Occupational function: Research worker.
Worked in government as: Researcher.

Worked in education: Teaching, In research.
Worked in service sector: Design.
Additional information: Concerned with energy modelling.   *(547)*

484, A.S. Skoe

BC Telephone Company, 768 Seymour St, Vancouver, BC V6B 3K9, Canada.
Sex: Male.   *Age:* 30-39.
Educational qualification: Bachelor's degree.
Formal training: Social/behavioural sciences.
Informal training: Social/behavioural sciences.
Primarily engaged in: Futures studies.
Areas in which work done (%): IOO In organization primarily concerned with futures
studies and/or long-range planning.
Direction of work in forecasting: Technological, Economic, Social, Cultural, Environmental,
Population.
Direction of work in research: Social impacts of technology, Alternative futures,
Environmental, Value systems, Population, Futures methodology.
Direction of work in planning: Corporate.
Methods used: Probabilistic forecasting, Delphi techniques, Gaming, Cross impact analysis,
Scenario building, Extrapolation techniques, Brainstorming, Expert panels, Relevance
trees.
Time range of work: IO - beyond year 2OOO.
Source of support for work (%): IOO Private business.
Work done for (%): IOO Private business.
Occupational function: Research worker.
Worked in government as: Researcher.
Worked in industry/business in: Management, Research and development.
Worked in education: Teaching.   *(444)*

485. Perry E. Smart

52 Forest Road, Wallingford, Ct O6492, USA.
Sex: Male.   *Age:* 30-39.
Educational qualification: Master's degree.
Formal training: I Marketing, 2 Engineering.
Informal training: Mathematics.
Areas in which work done (%): 2O In planning unit of a business enterprise.
Direction of work in forecasting: Market.
Direction of work in research: Resource utilization.
Direction of work in planning: Corporate.
Methods used: I Scenario building, 2 Brainstorming, 3 Individual expert forecasting.
Time range of work: 5 - IO years.
Source of support for work (%): IOO Private business.
Work done for (%): IOO Private business.
Occupational function: Manager.
Worked in government as: Administrator.
WWorked in industry/business in: Management, Planning.
Additional information: Concerned with medicine, and socialized salary structures. *(313)*

486. Lev Pavlovich Smirnov

Kiev 127, Bul 40 - Let Oktyabya 142/144, Institute of Cybernetics of the Academy
of Sciences, USSR.
Sex: Male.   *Age:* 30-39.
Educational qualification: Doctoral degree.
Formal training: Engineering.
Informal training: Humanities, Mathematics.
Primarily engaged in: Futures studies.
Areas in which work done (%): 100 In organization primarily concerned with futures
studies and/or long-range planning.
Direction of work in forecasting: 1 Technological, 2 Economic, 3 Scientific.
Direction of work in research: 1 Social impacts of technology, 2 Futures methodology,
3 Policy research.
Direction of work in planning: 1 Technological, 2 Scientific.
Methods used: 1 Expert panels, 2 Relevance trees, 3 Delphi techniques, 4 Extra-
polation techniques, 5 Simulation, 6 Statistical models.
Time range of work: 5 - 25 years.
Source of support for work: 70 National government, 30 Foundations.
Work done for (%): 80 National government, 20 Foundations.
Occupational function: 1 Research worker, 2 Consultant, 3 Educator, 4 Administrator.
Worked in government as: Researcher.
Worked in industry/business in: 1 Research and development, 2 Planning.   **(542)**

487. B. Smith

Laboratorium Voor Algemene Natuurkunde, Westersingel 34, Groningen, The Netherlands.
Sex: Male.   *Age:* 50-59.
Educational qualification: Doctoral degree.
Formal training: Physical sciences.
Direction of work in forecasting: World modelling.
Direction of work in planning: Technological.
Methods used: 1 Simulation, 2 Causal modelling.
Time range of work: 10 - 25 years.
Occupational function: Research worker.
Worked in education: In research.   **(111)**

488. Tenho Sneck

Technical Research Centre of Finland, Building Laboratory, SF - 02150 Espoo 15,
Finland.
Sex: Male.   *Age:* 50-59.
Educational qualification: Doctoral degree.
Formal training: 1 Physical sciences, 2 Engineering.
Informal training: 1 Design, 2 Education, 3 Journalism, 4 Social/behavioural sciences.
Direction of work in forecasting: 1 Technological, 2 Environmental, 3 Scientific.
Direction of work in research: 1 Resource utilization, 2 Social impacts of technology,
3 Alternative futures, 4 Environmental, 5 Consumer affairs, 6 Futures methodology.
Direction of work in planning: 1 Technological, 2 Resources, 3 Scientific, 4 Methods.
Methods used: 1 Morphology, 2 Delphi techniques, 3 Scenario building, 4 Expert panels,
5 Individual expert forecasting.
Time range of work: 10 - 25 years.
Source of support for work (%): 10 International agencies, 20 Private business,
20 Foundations, 50 Own institute.

Work done for (%):   5 International agencies, IO Private business, IO Foundations, 2O Own institute.
Occupational function: I Project leader, 2 Research worker.
Worked in government as: I Researcher.
Worked in education: I Teaching.
Additional information: Concerned with future of building materials; technology; development of systems for product development.   *(421)*

489. John N. Snell
92O Woodson Rd, Baltimore, Md 21212, USA.
Sex: Male.   *Age:* 4O-49.
Educational qualification: Master's degree.
Formal training: I Social/behavioural sciences, 2 Physical sciences.
Informal training: Religion.
Areas in which work done (%):   IO General systems theory, 9O Planning unit of a governmental agency.
Methods used: Contextual mapping.
Time range of work: Beyond 2OOO AD.
Source of support for work (%):   IOO Own funding.
Work done for (%):   IO General public, 9O Local or regional government.
Occupational function: Economist.
Worked in government as: Economist.
Additional information: Concerned with future of education.   *(220)*

49O. David P. Snyder
Management Analysis Officer, Planning and Research Organization, US Internal Revenue Service, 1111 Constitutional Ave, NW, Washington, DC 2O224, USA.
Sex: Male.   *Age:* 3O-39.
Educational qualification: Other graduate/professional degree.
Formal training: I Social/behavioural sciences, 2 Humanities, 3 Mathematics, 4 Arts.
Informal training: I Social/behavioural sciences, 2 Mathematics, 3 Arts, 4 Journalism.
Primarily engaged in: Both futures studies and long-range planning.
Areas in which work done (%):   5 As individual consultant, 4O In organization concerned with other studies including long-range planning, 5 Writer of futures fictions, IO As academic, in teaching futures studies or long-range planning, 4O In planning unit of a governmental agency.
Direction of work in forecasting: I Technological, 2 Social, 3 Economic, 4 Manpower. 5 Cultural.
Direction of work in research: I Resource utilization, 2 Policy research, 3 Organization and management, 5 Futures methodology, 6 Social impacts of technology, 6 Alternative futures, 6 Social priorities.
Direction of work in planning: I Corporate, 2 Economic, 3 Technological.
Methods used: I Individual expert forecasting, 2 Historical analogy, 3 Scenario building, 4 Extrapolation techniques, 5 Simulation, 6 Network analysis, 7 Delphi techniques, 9 Expert panels.
Time range of work: 5 - IO years.
Source of support for work (%):   2O Self, 8O National government.
Work done for (%):   2O Public sector, 8O National government.
Occupational function: I Consultant, 2 Manager, 3 Educator, 4 Research worker.
Worked in government as: I Administrator, 2 Researcher.
Worked in education: I In research, 2 Teaching.   *(146)*

491. K. Erik Solem
Directorate of Strategic Analysis, Operational Research Analysis Establishment, National Defence Headquarters, Ottawa, Ontario K1A OK2, Canada.
Sex: Male. *Age:* 30-39.
Educational qualification: Doctoral degree.
Formal training: Social/behavioural sciences.
Informal training: I Humanities, 2 Education, 3 Physical sciences.
Primarily engaged in: Both futures studies and long-range planning.
Areas in which work done (%): IOO In organization concerned with other studies including long-range planning.
Direction of work in forecasting: I Technological, 2 Military, 3 Resources, 4 Social.
Direction of work in research: I Policy research, 2 Alternative futures, 3 Futures methodology.
Direction of work in planning: I Political, 2 Military, 3 Scientific, 4 Social.
Methods used: I Statistical models, 2 Causal modelling, 3 Operational models, 4 Probabilistic forecasting, 5 Scenario building, 6 Extrapolation techniques.
Time range of work: IO - 25 years.
Source of support for work (%): IOO National government.
Work done for (%): IOO National government.
Occupational function: I Research worker.
Worked in government as: I Researcher, 2 Administrator.
Worked in education: I In research, 2 Teaching, 3 In administration.   *(427)*

492. Zahari Staikov
Buckston Bl 21, Sofia 18, Bulgaria.
Sex: Male. *Age:* 40-49.
Educational qualification: Doctoral degree.
Formal training: Social/behavioural sciences.
Informal training: I Social/behavioural sciences, 2 Humanities.
Areas in which work done (%): IO As academic, in teaching futures studies or long-range planning, 2O In organization primarily concerned with futures studies and/or long-range planning.
Direction of work in forecasting: I Social, 2 Manpower, 3 Economic, 4 Cultural, 5 Resources.
Direction of work in research: I Manpower, 2 Social impacts of technology, 3 Social priorities, 4 Value systems, 5 Population, 6 The individual in the future.
Direction of work in planning: I Social, 2 Labour, 3 Urban, 4 Educational, 5 Economic.
Methods used: I Time budget, 2 Statistical models, 3 Causal modelling, 4 Simulation.
Time range of work: IO - 25 years.
Source of support for work (%): 5O National government.
Work done for (%): 2O National government.
Occupational function: I Research worker, 2 Administrator, 3 Educator, 4 Consultant.
Worked in education: I In research, 2 In administration, 3 Teaching.   *(434)*

493. Grover Starling
University of Houston at Clear Lake City, 27OO Bay Area Blvd, Houston, Tx 77O58, USA.
Sex: Male. *Age:* 30-39.
Educational qualification: Doctoral degree.
Formal training: I Social/behavioural sciences, 2 Engineering.
Informal training: Physical sciences, Humanities, Engineering, Education, Music.
Areas in which work done (%): 5 In planning unit of a governmental agency, IO As

individual consultant, IO In organization concerned with other studies including long-range planning, 3O As academic, in teaching futures studies or long-range planning.
Direction of work in forecasting: I Technological, 2 Economic, 3 Social.
Direction of work in research: I Policy research, 2 Social impacts of technology.
Methods used: I Delphi techniques, 2 Extrapolation techniques, 3 Relevance trees.
Time range of work: 5 - IO years.
Source of support for work (%): 2O Local government, 2O Private business, 6O University.
Work done for (%): 2O Local or regional government, 2O Private business, 6O University.
Occupational function: Administrator.
Worked in government as: Administrator.
Worked in industry/business in: Consultancy.
Worked in education: Teaching.

(451)

494. Dale W. Steffes
President, Planning and Forecasting Consultants, 863 Frostwood, Houston, Texas, USA.
Sex: Male.   *Age:* 4O-49.
Educational qualification: Bachelor's degree.
Formal training: Engineering, Theology, Business administration, Accounting.
Informal training: Business economics.
Primarily engaged in: Both futures studies and long-range planning.
Areas in which work done (%): 25 As individual consultant, 25 In planning unit of a business enterprise, 5O In organization primarily concerned with futures studies and/or long-range planning.
Direction of work in forecasting: Technological, Economic, Social, Environmental, Resources, Political.
Direction of work in planning: Corporate.
Methods used: I Scenario building, 2 Cross impact analysis, 2 Historical analogy, 2 Individual expert forecasting, 2 Monitoring.
Time range of work: IO - 25 years.
Source of support for work (%): IOO Private business.
Work done for (%): IOO Private business.
Occupational function: I Consultant.
Worked in industry/business in: I Planning, 2 Consultancy.
Additional information: Concerned with natural resources.

(517)

495. Hugh Stevenson
The University of Western Ontario, London 72, Canada.
Sex: Male.   *Age:* 3O-39.
Educational qualification: Other graduate/professional degree.
Formal training: I Education, 2 Humanities, 3 Social/behavioural sciences.
Primarily engaged in: Futures studies.
Areas in which work done (%): IO As individual consultant, 2O In organizational and programme planning, 6O As academic, in teaching futures studies or long-range planning.
Direction of work in research: I Policy research, 2 Alternative futures, 2 Social priorities.
Direction of work in planning: I Educational, 2 Social, 2 Economic, 2 Political.
Methods used: I Probabilistic forecasting, 2 Scenario building, 3 Extrapolation techniques, 4 Historical analogy, 5 Delphi techniques, 6 Cross impact analysis, 7 Simulation.
Time range of work: 5 - IO years.
Source of support for work (%): IO Local government, IO Internal-institutional, 8O Foundations.

Work done for (%): lO Local or regional government, lO Internal-institutional, 4O Foundations.
Occupational function: l Educator, 2 Research worker, 3 Administrator, 4 Consultant.
Worked in education: l Teaching, 2 In research, 3 In administration.　　*(118)*

496. Frank A. Stone
Director, World Education Project, U-32, School of Education, University of Connecticut, Storrs, Ct O6268, USA.
Sex: Male.　　*Age:* 4O-49.
Educational qualification: Doctoral degree.
Formal training: l Humanities, 2 Education.
Informal training: l Journalism, 2 Social/behavioural sciences.
Areas in which work done (%): lO Education for development, international education.
Direction of work in forecasting: l Cultural, 2 Social, 3 Educational, 4 Technological.
Direction of work in research: l Value systems, 2 Alternative futures, 3 The individual in the future.
Direction of work in planning: l Educational, 2 Social.
Methods used: l Network analysis, 2 Extrapolation techniques, 3 Historical analogy, 4 Operational models, 5 Cross impacts analysis, 6 Scenario building, 7 Delphi techniques.
Time range of work: lO - 25 years.
Source of support for work (%): lOO University.
Occupational function: l Educator.
Worked in education: l Teaching, 2 In research.
Additional information: Concerned with educational futuristics.　　*(40)*

497. Helmut Strasser
Institut für Sozio - Ökonomische, Entwicklungsforschung, A - 1O1O Vienna, Austria.
Sex: Male.　　*Age:* 25-29.
Educational qualification: Doctoral degree.
Formal training: Mathematics.
Informal training: Social/behavioural sciences.
Primarily engaged in: Both futures studies and long-range planning.
Direction of work in research: Futures methodology.
Methods used: l Statistical models, 2 Probabilistic forecasting.
Occupational function: Research worker.
Worked in government as: Researcher.　　*(545)*

498. Harlan J. Strauss
Institute of Policy Studies, Dept of Political Science, University of Oregon, Eugene, Or 974O3, USA.
Sex: Male.　　*Age:* 25-29.
Educational qualification: Doctoral degree.
Formal training: Social/behavioural sciences.
Informal training: Social/behavioural sciences.
Primarily engaged in: Futures studies.
Areas in which work done (%): 5O In organization concerned with other studies including long-range planning, 5O As academic, in teaching futures studies or long-range planning.
Direction of work in forecasting: l Social, 2 Cultural.
Direction of work in research: l Policy research, 2 Social priorities, 3 Futures methodology, 4 The individual in the future.

Direction of work in planning: I Political.
Methods used: I Delphi techniques, 2 Expert panels, 3 Historical analogy.
Time range of work: Beyond 2000 AD.
Source of support for work (%): 5 Foundations, 95 Local government.
Work done for (%): I00 Private business.
Occupational function: I Administrator, 2 Research worker, 3 Educator.
Worked in education: I In research, 2 In administration, 3 Teaching.   *(383)*

499. G.F. Streatfeild

Centre for Integrative Studies, School of Advanced Technology, State University of New York at Binghamton, Binghamton, NY 13901, USA.
Sex: Male.   *Age:* 30-39.
Educational qualification: Bachelor's degree.
Formal training: Social/behavioural sciences.
Informal training: Journalism.
Primarily engaged in: Futures studies.
Areas in which work done (%): I00 In organization primarily concerned with futures ·studies and/or long-range planning.
Direction of work in forecasting: I Resources, 2 Social, 3 Cultural.
Direction of work in research: I Alternative futures, 2 Social impacts of technology, 3 The individual in the future.
Methods used: Scenario building, Extrapolation techniques, Brainstorming, Historical analogy, Individual expert forecasting.
Time range of work: I0 - 25 years.
Source of support for work (%): I00 University.
Work done for (%): 50 Foundations, 25 International agencies, 25 University.
Occupational function: Assistant to Director of Centre.
Worked in service sector: Communications media.   *(588)*

500. Ota Sulč

Head of Dept of Prognostics, Czechoslovakian Academy of Sciences, Institute of Philosophy and Sociology, Prague 1, Jilska 1, Czechoslovakia.
Sex: Male.   *Age:* 40-49.
Educational qualification: Doctoral degree.
Formal training: Economics.
Informal training: Humanities.
Primarily engaged in: Futures studies
Areas in which work done (%): 20 As individual consultant, 80 As academic, in teaching futures studies or long-range planning.
Direction of work in forecasting: Technological, Social.
Direction of work in research: Social impacts of technology, Futures methodology.
Methods used: I Delphi techniques, 2 Individual expert forecasting, 3 Scenario building, 4 Cross impact analysis.
Time range of work: I0 - beyond year 2000.
Source of support for work (%): I00 National government.
Work done for (%): I00 National government.
Occupational function: Research worker, Consultant.
Worked in government as: Researcher.
Worked in industry as: Research and development.
Worked in education: In research.
Additional information: Concerned with theory and methodology of forecasting.   *(149)*

501. Gerald A. Sumida

Hawaii Commission on the Year 2000, c/o Carlsmith, Carlsmith, Wichman and Case, PO Box 656 Honolulu, Hawaii 96809, USA.
Sex: Male.　*Age:* 30-39.
Educational qualification: Other graduate/professional degree.
Formal training: I Law, 2 Public and international affairs, 3 Social/behavioural sciences.
Informal training: Journalism, Design.
Areas in which work done (%): 5 In organization concerned with other studies including long-range planning.
Direction of work in forecasting: Holistic.
Direction of work in research: I Alternative futures, 2 Value systems, 3 Policy research, 4 Futures methodology.
Direction of work in planning: I Social, 2 Economic, 3 Urban.
Methods used: I Brainstorming, 3 Expert panels, 3 Scenario building.
Time range of work: Beyond year 2000.
Source of support for work (%): 90 Local government, 10 Private business.
Work done for (%): 10 Voluntary associations, 90 Commission on the year 2000.
Occupational function: Attorney.
Worked in service area as: Law.
Additional information: Concerned with the future of law and social policy in the context of a rapidly-changing society.　　　　　　　　　　　　　　　*(579)*

502. A.J. Surrey

Science Policy Research Unit, University of Sussex, Falmer, Brighton BN1 9RF, UK.
Sex: Male.　*Age:* 40-49.
Educational qualification: Bachelor's degree.
Formal training: Social/behavioural sciences.
Primarily engaged in: Both futures studies and long-range planning.
Areas in which work done (%): 33 In planning unit of a business enterprise, 33 As academic in teaching, 34 in planning unit of a governmental agency,
Direction of work in forecasting: I Economic, 2 Resources.
Direction of work in research: I Policy research, 2 Resource utilization, 3 Alternative futures.
Direction of work in planning: I Economic, 2 Resources.
Methods used: I Scenario building, 2 Individual expert forecasting, 3 Probabilistic forecasting.
Methods used: I Scenario building, 2 Individual expert forecasting, 3 Probabilistic forecasting.
Time range of work: 10 - 25 years.
Work done for (%): 25 National government, 75 British fuel industries.
Occupational function: Research worker.
Worked in government as: Administrator.
Worked in industry as: Planning.
Worked in education as: In research.
Work done for (%): 25 National government, 25 Private industry, 50 Nationalised industries.
Additional information: Working on economic and technological assessment of UK energy policy choices.　　　　　　　　　　　　　　　*(487)*

503. Masayoushi Suzuki

Socio-Economics Studies and Business Planning, Nomura Research Institute, Kamakura, Japan.

Sex: Male.   *Age:* 30-39.
Educational qualification: Master's degree.
Formal training: I Social/behavioural sciences, 2 Engineering.
Informal training: I Corporate Management, 2 Mathematics, 3 Education.
Primarily engaged in: Both futures studies and long-range planning.
Areas in which work done (%): 30 In organization concerned with other studies including long-range planning, IO In organization primarily concerned with futures studies and/or long-range planning, IO As individual consultant, 50 In planning unit of a business enterprise.
Direction of work in forecasting: I Social, 2 Economic, 3 Market.
Direction of work in research: I Value systems, 2 Alternative futures.
Direction of work in planning: I Social, 2 Corporate, 3 Economic.
Methods used: I Delphi techniques, 2 Scenario building, 3 Extrapolation techniques.
Time range of work: IO - 25 years.
Source of support for work (%): 40 Foundations, 60 Private business.
Work done for (%): IO The public, consumers, 30 Foundations, 60 Private business.
Occupational function: I Research worker, 2 Consultant.
Worked in industry/business in: I Planning, 2 Consultancy.   *(29)*

504. William L. Swager

Assistant Manager, Battelle Memorial Institute, Dept of Metallurgy, 505 King Ave, Columbus, Oh 43201, USA.

Sex: Male.   *Age:* 50-59.
Educational qualification: Bachelor's degree.
Formal training: Engineering.
Informal training: I Social/behavioural sciences, 2 Design.
Primarily engaged in: Both futures studies and long-range planning.
Areas in which work done (%): IOO Futures studies and long-range planning in non-profit research institute.
Direction of work in forecasting: Technological, Economic, Market, Scientific, Environmental, Resources, Population.
Direction of work in research: Social impacts of technology, Alternative futures, Environmental, Resource utilization.
Direction of work in planning: Technological, Corporate, Resources.
Methods used: Scenario building, Extrapolation techniques, Brainstorming, Statistical models, Expert panels, Relevance trees, Individual expert forecasting.
Time range of work: 5 - 25 years.
Source of support for work (%): 25 Private business, 25 National government, 50 Own planning.
Work done for (%): 25 National government, 25 Private business, 50 Battelle.
Occupational function: Manager.   *(73)*

505. Alexander Szalai

Study Group for Science Organization, Hungarian Academy of Sciences, Münnich Ferenc-Utca 18, H-1051 Budapest, Hungary.

Sex: Male.   *Age:* 60 or over.
Educational qualification: Doctoral degree.
Formal training: Social/behavioural sciences.

Informal training: Life sciences, Mathematics, Journalism.
Primarily engaged in: Both futures studies and long-range planning.
Areas in which work done (%): IO Organization primarily concerned with futures studies and/or long range planning, I5 In organization concerned with other studies including long-range planning, 1O As individual consultant, 3O As academic in teaching futures studies or long-range planning, I5 In Planning unit of an international organization, 3O Sociological and international organization research and teaching.
Direction of work in forecasting: I Social, 2 Technological, 3 Scientific.
Direction of work in research: I Social impacts of technology, 2 Value systems, 3 Futures methodology, 4 The family in the future.
Direction of work in planning: I Scientific, 2 Social, 3 Technological, 4 Regional, 5 Urban.
Methods used: I Probabilistic forecasting, 2 Cross impact analysis, 3 Expert panels, 4 Statistical models, 5 Individual expert forecasting.
Time range of work: IO - 25 years.
Source of support for work (%): IO Foundations, 2O International agencies, 3O Academy of sciences, 4O National government.
Work done for (%): 5 International agencies, 5 Foundations, IO National government, IO Academy of sciences.
Occupational function: I Research worker, 2 Educator, 3 Consultant.
Worked in industry/business in: Consultancy.
Worked in education: Teaching, In research.
Worked in service sector: Communication media.
Additional information: Concerned with future of international organizations, future and planning of communications, technology assessment.   *(208)*

5O6. Leon Tabah

Director, Population Div, United Nations, New York, NY, 1OO17, USA.
Sex: Male.   *Age:* 5O-59.
Educational qualification: Doctoral degree.
Formal training: Social/behavioural sciences.
Informal training: Mathematics.
Primarily engaged in: Both futures studies and long-range planning.
Areas in which work done (%): IO In organization primarily concerned with futures studies and/or long-range planning, IO As individual consultant, 5O In planning unit of an international organization.
Direction of work in forecasting: I Population, 2 Economic.
Direction of work in research: I Population, 2 Alternative futures, 3 Environmental, 4 The family in the future.
Direction of work in planning: I Urban, 2 Economic, 3 Political, 4 Social.
Methods used: I Probabilistic forecasting, 2 Statistical models, 3 Simulation.
Time range of work: IO - beyond year 2OOO.
Source of support for work (%): IOO International agencies.
Work done for (%): IO Foundations, 2O National government, 5O International agencies.
Occupational function: I Research worker, 2 Administrator, 3 Consultant.
Worked in government as: Researcher.
Worked in education: Teaching.
Worked in service sector: Social welfare.
Additional information: Concerned with long-range resource analysis, regulation, and development.   *(377)*

12

507. Serafin Talisayon

Deputy Dean, Institute of Strategic Studies, Philippine Centre for Advanced Studies, University of the Philippine System, Diliman, Quezon City, Philippines.
Sex: Male.   *Age:* 30-39.
Educational qualification: Doctoral degree.
Formal training: Biophysics.
Informal training: Physical sciences, Life sciences, Social/behavioural sciences, Mathematics, Environmental management.
Primarily engaged in: Both futures studies and long-range planning.
Areas in which work done (%): 5 As a consultant, 5 In planning unit of a business enterprise, IO In planning unit of a governmental agency, 80 In organization primarily concerned with futures studies and/or long-range planning.
Direction of work in forecasting: Technological, Social, Market, Environmental, Military, Resources, Population, International relations.
Direction of work in research: Alternative futures, Resource utilization, Policy research, Futures methodology.
Direction of work in planning: Social, Regional, Political, Environmental.
Methods used: I Causal modelling, 2 Expert panels, 3 Simulation, 4 Delphi techniques, 5 Statistical models, 6 Individual expert forecasting, 7 Historical analogy.
Source of support for work (%): IOO National government.
Work done for (%): IOO National government.
Occupational function: I Research worker.
Worked in government as: I Researcher, 2 Administrator.
Worked in industry/business in: I Consultancy.
Worked in education: I In research, 2 In administration, 3 Teaching.   *(465)*

508. Jan Tauber

Prague 9, Prosck 1187, Czechoslovakia.
Sex: Male.   *Age:* 6O or over.
Educational qualification: Doctoral degree.
Formal training: Life sciences, Social/behavioural sciences.
Informal training: Life sciences, Social/behavioural sciences.
Primarily engaged in: Both futures studies and long-range planning.
Areas in which work done (%): I In planning unit of a government agency, 5 In organization primarily concerned with futures studies and/or long-range planning, 5 In organization concerned with other studies including long-range planning, I As individual consultant, 5 As academic, in teaching futures studies or long-range planning.
Direction of work in forecasting: Economic, Social, Cultural.
Direction of work in planning: Scientific, Social.
Methods used: Probabilistic forecasting.
Time range of work: 5 - beyond year 2OOO.
Source of support for work (%): IOO National government.
Work done for (%): 2O Local or regional government, 3O National government.
Occupational function: Research worker.
Worked in industry/business in: Research and development.
Worked in education: Teaching, In research.
Worked in service sector: Social welfare.
Additional information: Concerned with rural communities, agriculture, social organization.   *(12)*

509. Maria Teresa Tavassi
IRADES, Istituto per la Ricerca e la Formazione al Futuro, Via Paisiello 6, Rome OO198, Italy.
Sex: Female.　*Age:* 30-39.
Educational qualification: Master's degree.
Formal training: Social/behavioural sciences, Law.
Informal training: Documentation.
Primarily engaged in: Futures studies.
Areas in which work done (%): 50 In organization primarily concerned with futures studies and/or long-range planning.
Direction of work in forecasting: Social.
Direction of work in research: 1 The individual in the future, 2 Alternative futures, 3 Futures methodology, 4 Value systems, 5 Social impacts of technology.
Source of support for work (%): 50 Private association.
Work done for (%): 50 Private association.
Occupational function: 1 Research worker.
Worked in education: 1 In research.
Worked in service sector: 1 Religion, 2 Social welfare, 3 Law.　　*(418)*

510. Victor Taylor
Mineral Economics Research Div, Energy Mines and Resources, 588 Booth St, Ottawa K1A OE4, Canada.
Sex: Male.　*Age:* 30-39.
Educational qualification: Master's degree.
Formal training: Social/behavioural sciences.
Informal training: 1 Education, 2 Engineering.
Primarily engaged in: Both futures studies and long-range planning.
Areas in which work done (%): IOO In planning unit of a governmental agency.
Direction of work in forecasting: 1 Resources, 2 Population, 3 Market.
Direction of work in research: 1 Alternative futures, 2 Futures methodology.
Direction of work in planning: 1 Resources.
Methods used: 1 Extrapolation techniques, 2 Historical analogy, 3 Simulation, 4 Individual expert forecasting.
Time range of work: IO - 25 years.
Source of support for work (%): IOO National government.
Work done for (%): IOO National government.
Occupational function: Research worker.
Worked in government as: Researcher.
Worked in industry/business in: Planning.
Worked in education: Teaching.　　*(460)*

511. Gordon Rattray Taylor
The Hall, Freshford, Bath BA3 6EJ, UK.
Sex: Male.　*Age:* 6O or over.
Educational qualification: Some college or less.
Formal training: Life sciences.
Informal training: 1 Social/behavioural sciences, 2 Life sciences, 3 Cinema/television, 4 Journalism.
Primarily engaged in: Futures studies.
Areas in which work done (%): IOO Research and writing.
Direction of work in forecasting: Economic, Political, Social.

Direction of work in research: Social impacts of technology, Alternative futures, The family in the future, Value systems.
Methods used: Historical analogy, Individual expert forecasting.
Time range of work: IO - 25 years.
Source of support for work (%): IOO Self-supported.
Work done for (%): IOO General public.
Occupational function: I Thinker.
Worked in industry/business in: 2 Management.
Worked in service sector: I Communication media.
Additional information: Concerned with elaboration of theory of social process and socio-cultural change.   *(113)*

512. F. Tecoz

Le Clos d'en Coulet, 1162 Saint Prey, Vaud, Switzerland.
Sex: Male.   *Age:* 5O-59.
Educational qualification: Doctoral degree.
Formal training: Humanities.
Informal training: Social/behavioural sciences, Management.
Direction of work in forecasting: Economic, Market.
Direction of work in planning: Corporate.
Methods used: Delphi techniques, Expert panels, Individual expert forecasting.
Time range of work: 5 - IO years.
Source of support for work (%): IOO Private business.
Work done for (%): IO Private business.
Occupational function: Consultant, Non-executive director of corporations.
Worked in industry/business in: Management.   *(567)*

513. S. Temple

Administrative Secretary, The Society for Long-Range Planning, Terminal House, Grosvenor Gardens, London, SW1, UK.
Sex: Female.   *Age:* 30-39.
Primarily engaged in: Corporate Planning.
Occupational function: Administrator.   *(346)*

514. Eduardo Terrazas

Cordoba 23A, Mexico 7, DF.
Sex: Male.   *Age:* 30-39.
Educational qualification: Master's degree.
Formal training: Architecture.
Informal training: Social/behavioural sciences, Humanities, Design, Education.
Areas in which work done (%): 4O In organization concerned with other studies including long-range planning.
Direction of work in research: Social impacts of technology, Alternative futures, Environmental.
Direction of work in planning: Social, Regional, Environmental, Urban, Educational.
Methods used: Contextual mapping, Expert panels, Individual expert forecasting, Brainstorming, Historical analogy.
Time range of work: 5 - IO years.
Source of support for work (%): IO National government, 2O Foundations, 2O Private business, 5O International agencies.

Work done for (%): IO National government, 2O Foundations, 2O Private business,
5O International agencies.
Occupational function: I Administrator, 2 Consultant, 3 Research worker, 4 Educator.
Worked in government as: I Administrator.
Worked in industry/business in: I Management, 2 Research and development.
Worked in education: I Teaching.
Worked in service sector: I Religion. *(534)*

515. Romesh Thapar

Journalist, Seminar - The Monthly Symposium, PO Box 338, New Delhi 1, India.
Sex: Male. *Age:* 5O-59.
Educational qualification: Bachelor's degree.
Formal training: I Social/behavioural sciences, 2 Journalism, 3 Arts, 3 Cinema/
television, 4 Design.
Informal training: I Journalism, 2 Cinema/television, 3 Arts.
Primarily engaged in: Long-range planning.
Areas in which work done (%): I In organization primarily concerned with futures
studies and/or long-range planning, 2 In planning unit of an international organization,
IO As individual consultant, 5O In organization concerned with other studies including
long-range planning.
Direction of work in forecasting: I Social, 2 Cultural, 3 Environmental.
Direction of work in research: I Value systems, 2 Environmental, 3 Alternative
futures.
Direction of work in planning: I Economic, 2 Political, 3 Social, 4 Urban, 5 Corporate,
6 Environmental.
Methods used: I Probabilistic forecasting, 2 Brainstorming, 3 Expert panels.
Time range of work: IO - 25 years.
Source of support for work (%): IO National government, IO International agencies.
Work done for (%): 2O International agencies, 4O National government, 3O Local or
Regional government.
Occupational function: I Journalist.
Worked in government as: 2 Administrator.
Worked in service sector: I Communication media.
Additional information: Concerned with the structuring of society. *(119)*

516. Robert Theobald

Remuda Ranch, PO Box 1531, Wickenburg, Az 85358, USA.
Sex: Male. *Age:* 4O-49.
Educational qualification: Master's degree.
Formal training: Social/behavioural sciences.
Informal training: I Education, 2 Journalism, 3 Cinema/television.
Primarily engaged in: Futures studies.
Areas in which work done (%): 4O Publishing, 6O As individual consultant.
Methods used: I Brainstorming, 2 Scenario building, 3 Individual expert forecasting.
Time range of work: 5 - 25 years.
Occupational function: I Consultant, 2 Educator, 3 Administrator.
Worked in industry/business in: I Consultancy. *(343)*

517. Hugo Thiemann
Counsellor, Nestlé Alimentana SA, Ave Nestlé, 1800 Vevey, Switzerland.
Sex: Male.   *Age:* 50-59.
Educational qualification: Doctoral degree.
Formal training: Physical sciences, Engineering.
Informal training: Life sciences, Social/behavioural sciences.
Primarily engaged in: Both futures studies and long-range planning.
Areas in which work done (%): 90 In organization primarily concerned with futures studies and/or long-range planning.
Direction of work in forecasting: 1 Economic, 2 Technological, 3 Population, 4 Scientific, 5 Social, 6 Environmental.
Direction of work in research: 1 Policy research, 2 Population, 3 Social impacts of technology, 4 Consumer affairs.
Direction of work in planning: 1 Corporate, 2 Economic, 3 Scientific.
Methods used: 1 Cross impact analysis, 2 Scenario building, 3 Brainstorming, 4 Probabilistic forecasting.
Time range of work: 10 - 25 years.
Source of support for work (%): 100 Private business.
Work done for (%): 100 Private business.
Occupational function: 1 Consultant, 2 Administrator.
Worked in industry/business in: 1 Research and development.
Additional information: Concerned with future of large, multi-national food company.
(157)

518. Wes Thomas
606 Fifth Ave, East Northport, NY 11731, USA.
Sex: Male.   *Age:* 40-49.
Educational qualification: Bachelor's degree.
Formal training: Social/behavioural sciences.
Informal training: 1 Cinema/television, 2 Education, 3 Engineering.
Primarily engaged in: Futures studies.
Areas in which work done (%): 100 In organization primarily concerned with futures studies and/or long-range planning.
Direction of work in forecasting: Technological.
Methods used: Brainstorming, Individual expert forecasting.
Time range of work: 5 - 10 years.
Occupational function: Publisher.
Worked in service sector: Communication media.
Additional information: Concerned with communications.
(527)

519. Gordon B. Thompson
Bell Northern Research, PO Box 3511, Station C, Ottawa K1Y 4H7, Canada.
Sex: Male.   *Age:* 40-49.
Educational qualification: Bachelor's degree.
Formal training: 1 Physical sciences, 2 Mathematics, 3 Engineering.
Informal training: Social/behavioural sciences, Humanities, Education, Arts, Mathematics, Design, Cinema/television.
Primarily engaged in: Both futures studies and long-range planning.
Areas in which work done (%): 100 In planning unit of a business enterprise.
Direction of work in forecasting: 1 Economic, 2 Technological, 2 Social.
Direction of work in research: 1 Futures methodology, 2 Social impacts of technology.
Methods used: 2 Cross impact analysis, 2 Historical analogy, 3 Simulation.

Time range of work: IO - beyond year 2OOO.
Source of support for work (%): IOO Private business.
Work done for (%): IOO Private business.
Occupational function: I Research worker, 2 Corporate 'Gadfly'.
Worked in industry/business in: I Research development, 2 Management.
Additional information: Concerned with role of communication in society -- to ameliorate present problems and the foreseeable ones ahead. *(436)*

52O. K.M. Thompson

Head, Economics and Planning Section, Pulp and Paper Research Institute of Canada, 57O St John's Blvd, Pointe Claire, PQ, H9R 3J9, Canada.
Sex: Male.　　*Age:* 4O-49.
Educational qualification: Doctoral degree.
Formal training: Engineering.
Informal training: I Education, 2 Social/behavioural sciences.
Primarily engaged in: Both futures studies and long-range planning.
Areas in which work done (%): IOO In organization primarily concerned with futures studies and/or long-range planning.
Direction of work in forecasting: I Technological, 2 Resources.
Direction of work in research: I Technical innovation.
Direction of work in planning: I Technological, 2 Scientific.
Methods used: I Delphi techniques, 2 Extrapolation techniques, 3 Relevance trees.
Time range of work: 5 - 25 years.
Source of support for work (%): 7O Private business, 3O National government.
Work done for (%): IOO Private business.
Occupational function: I Manager, 2 Consultant.
Worked in industry/business in: I Research and development.
Worked in education: I Teaching.
Additional information: PPRIC is specifically concerned with improving the technology of the pulp and paper industry. *(378)*

521. Willis H. Thompson

Assistant Prof, Physical Science Dept, San Diego State College, San Diego, Ca 92115, USA.
Sex: Male.　　*Age:* 4O-49.
Educational qualification: Master's degree.
Formal training: I Engineering, 2 Physical sciences, 3 Arts, 4 Humanities.
Informal training: Education.
Primarily engaged in: Futures studies.
Areas in which work done (%): 25 As academic, in teaching futures studies or long-range planning.
Direction of work in forecasting: Technological.
Direction of work in research: I Social impacts of technology, 2 Population, 3 Value systems, 4 Social priorities.
Methods used: Teaching.
Time range of work: IO - 25 years.
Source of support for work (%): Personal.
Occupational function: Educator.
Worked in education: Teaching. *(20)*

522. Gerald Thorpe
Dept of Political Science, Indiana University of Pennsylvania, Indiana, Pa 15701, USA.
Sex: Male.　　*Age:* 30-39.
Educational qualification: Doctoral degree.
Formal training: I Social/behavioural sciences, 2 Education.
Areas in which work done (%): 25 As individual consultant.
Direction of work in forecasting: Political.
Direction of work in research: Policy research.
Direction of work in planning: Political.
Methods used: I Simulation, 2 Scenario building, 3 Expert panels, 4 Probabilistic forecasting.
Time range of work: 10 - 25 years.
Source of support for work (%): 25 Foundations.
Work done for (%): 25 National government, 25 International agencies, 50 Local or regional government.
Occupational function: I Educator, 2 Consultant.
Worked in government as: I Elected official.
Worked in education: I Teaching, 2 In research.
Additional information: Concerned with technology, politics and the future; long-term government planning.　　　　*(338)*

523. J. Tinbergen
Haviklaa 31, Den Haag 2023, The Netherlands.
Sex: Male.　　*Age:* 60 or over.
Educational qualification: Doctoral degree.
Formal training: I Social/behavioural sciences, 2 Physical sciences.
Primarily engaged in: Long-range planning.
Areas in which work done (%): 30 As individual consultant, 40 Private research. 30 As academic, in teaching futures studies or long-range planning.
Direction of work in planning: Social, Economic.
Methods used: I Causal modelling, 2 Statistical models.
Time range of work: Beyond 2000 AD.
Source of support for work (%): 10 Foundations, 90 Personal means.
Work done for (%): 50 Voluntary associations, 50 Scientific interest.
Occupational function: I Research worker.
Worked in education: I Teaching.　　　　*(38)*

524. Laurence I. Tobias
Centre for Integrative Studies, School of Advanced Technology, State University of New York at Binghamton, Binghamton, NY 13901, USA.
Sex: Male.　　*Age:* 20-29.
Educational qualification: Master's degree.
Formal training: Geography.
Informal training: Physical sciences, Life sciences, Mathematics.
Primarily engaged in: Futures studies.
Areas in which work done (%): 100 In organization primarily concerned with future studies and/or long-range planning.
Direction of work in forecasting: Social, Population, Resources, Technological.
Direction of work in research: Social impacts of technology, Population, Resource utilization, Social priorities, Alternative futures.
Direction of work in planning: Social, Resources.

Methods used: I Expert panels, 2 Contextual mapping.
Time range of work: IO - 25 years.
Source of support for work (%): IOO University.
Work done for (%): 5O Foundations, 25 International agencies, 25 University.
Occupational function: Research worker.
Worked in education: In research. *(589)*

525. Alvin Toffler
Forty East Seventy Eighth St, New York, NY 2OO21, USA.
Sex: Male.   *Age:* 4O-49.
Educational qualification: Bachelor's degree.
Formal training: Humanities.
Informal training: Social/behavioural sciences, Humanities, Journalism, Education, Cinema/television.
Primarily engaged in: Both futures studies and long-range planning.
Areas in which work done (%): IO As individual consultant, 9O Author, lecturer.
Direction of work in forecasting: I Social, 2 Cultural.
Direction of work in research: I Alternative futures, 2 Social impacts of technology, 3 Value systems, 4 Social priorities, 5 The individual in the future, 6 The family in the future.
Sirection of work in planning: I Corporate, 2 Political, 3 Social.
Methods used: I Individual expert forecasting, 2 Brainstorming, 3 Scenario building.
Time range of work: IO - 25 years.
Source of support for work (%): IOO Personal.
Occupational function: Author,
Worked in service sector: Communication media. *(34)*

526. Bernard Towers
Dept of Pediatrics, School of Medicine, Centre for Health Sciences, University of California, Los Angeles, Ca 9OO24, USA.
Sex: Male.   *Age:* 5O-59.
Educational qualification: Other graduate/professional degree.
Formal training: I Life sciences, 2 Humanities.
Informal training: I Education, 2 Arts, 3 Social/behavioural sciences.
Direction of work in research: I Social priorities, 2 Value systems, 3 The individual in the future, 4 Alternative futures.
Methods used: I Historical analogy, 2 Expert panels, 3 Probabilistic forecasting.
Time range of work: Beyond 2OOO AD.
Source of support for work (%): IO State university.
Work done for (%): I Local or regional government, I National government, IO Voluntary associations.
Occupational function: Educator.
Worked in education: Teaching, In research, In administration.
Worked in service sector: Medicine. *(152)*

527. Carl Townsend
Director, Centre for the Study of the Future, 411O NE Alameda, Portland, Or 94212, USA.
Sex: Male.   *Age:* 3O-39.
Educational qualification: Master's degree.
Formal training: I Engineering, 2 Mathematics.
Informal training: I Religion, 2 Mathematics, 3 Engineering.

Primarily engaged in: Futures studies.
Areas in which work done (%):   5O In organization primarily concerned with futures studies and/or long-range planning, 5O Medicine and computers.
Direction of work in forecasting: Religion.
Direction of work in research: Religion.
Direction of work in planning: Religion.
Methods used: Gaming, Scenario building, Individual expert forecasting, Simulation.
Time range of work: 5 - IO years.
Source of support for work (%):   IOO Private membership.
Work done for (%):   IOO Private membership.
Occupational function: Research worker.
Worked in service sector: Medicine, Religion.
Additional information: Concerned with future of medicine, religion, healing.   *(468)*

528. Gisela Trommsdorff

Universität Mannheim, Sonderforschungsbereich 24, 68 Mannheim, West Germany.
Sex: Female.   *Age:*   3O-39.
Educational qualification: Doctoral degree.
Formal training: Social/behavioural sciences.
Informal training: Social/behavioural sciences, Humanities.
Primarily engaged in: Both futures studies and long-range planning.
Areas in which work done (%):   5O In organization primarily concerned with futures studies and/or long-range planning, 3O In organization concerned with other studies including long-range planning, 2O As academic, in teaching futures studies or long-range planning.
Direction of work in research: I The individual in the future, 2 Value systems, 3 Alternative futures.
Direction of work in planning: Social.
Methods used: Statistical models, Individual expert forecasting.
Time range of work: 5 - IO years.
Source of support for work (%):   IOO Local government.
Work done for (%):   IOO Local or regional government.
Occupational function: I Research worker, 2 Administrator.
Worked in education: I In research, 2 Teaching, 3 In administration.
Additional information: Concerned with images of the future in different social strata and their impact on decision making.   *(199)*

529. Hugo Trux

Research Co-ordinator, Behavioural Sciences Lab, 4O4 - BW 17th Ave, Ohio State University, Columbus, Oh 4321O USA.
Sex: Male.   *Age:*   25-29.
Educational qualification: Master's degree.
Formal training: Social/behavioural sciences.
Areas in which work done (%):   3O As individual consultant, 7O Administering social research.
Direction of work in forecasting: Social.
Direction of work in research: Policy research.
Methods used: I Causal modelling, 2 Simulation.
Occupational function: I Administrator, 2 Consultant, 3 Research worker.
Worked in government as: I Administrator.
Worked in education: I In administration, 2 In research, 3 Teaching.
Worked in service sector: I Religion.   *(219)*

530. Graham F. Tubb
Science Policy Research Unit, University of Sussex, Falmer, Brighton BN1 9RF, UK.
Sex: Male.   *Age:* 25-29.
Educational qualification: Master's degree.
Formal training: I Physical sciences, 2 Humanities, 3 Social/behavioural sciences.
Informal training: Social/behavioural sciences.
Areas in which work done (%): IOO In organization primarily concerned with futures studies and/or long-range planning.
Direction of work in forecasting: I Technological, 2 Social, 3 Economic.
Direction of work in research: I Resource utilization, 2 Alternative futures, 3 Environmental.
Direction of work in planning: Resources.
Methods used: Scenario building, Extrapolation techniques, Contextual mapping.
Time range of work: 5 - IO years and beyond year 2OOO.
Occupational function: Research worker.
Worked in education: In research.   *(497)*

531. Brian Tucker
Chief, Technological Forecasts Division Industry, Trade and Commerce, 112 Kent St, Ottawa K1A OH5, Canada.
Sex: Male.   *Age:* 50-59.
Educational qualification: Other graduate/professional degree.
Formal training: Engineering.
Informal training: I Design, 2 Social/behavioural sciences, 3 Education.
Primarily engaged in: Both futures studies and long-range planning.
Areas in which work done (%): IOO In planning unit of a governmental agency.
Direction of work in forecasting: Technological.
Direction of work in research: I Social impacts of technology, 2 Alternative futures, 3 Environmental, 4 Futures methodology, 5 Social priorities, 6 Value systems.
Direction of work in planning: I Technological.
Methods used: I Delphi techniques, 2 Scenario building, 3 Relevance trees, 4 Cross impact analysis, 5 Brainstorming.
Time range of work: IO - 25 years.
Source of support for work (%): IOO National government.
Work done for (%): IOO National government.
Occupational function: I Manager.
Worked in government as: I Administrator.
Worked in industry/business in: I Management, 2 Planning.   *(432)*

532. Franklin Tugwell
Dept of Government, Pomona College, Claremont, Ca 91711, USA.
Sex: Male.   *Age:* 30-39.
Educational qualification: Doctoral degree.
Formal training: Social/behavioural sciences.
Areas in which work done (%): IO Futures related research, 2O As academic, in teaching futures studies or long-range planning.
Direction of work in forecasting: Political.
Direction of work in research: Policy research.
Direction of work in planning: Political.
Methods used: Probabilistic forecasting, Scenario building, Extrapolation techniques, Historical analogy, Individual expert forecasting.
Time range of work: 5 - beyond year 2OOO.

Source of support for work (%): IO Private business, 9O University.
Occupational function: I Educator.
Worked in education: I Teaching, 2 In research, 3 In administration.   *(55)*

533. Murray Turoff

Newark College of Engineering, 323 High St, Newark, NJ O71O2, USA.
Sex: Male.   *Age:* 30-39.
Educational qualification: Doctoral degree.
Formal traning: Physical sciences.
Informal training: Social/behavioural sciences, Computer science.
Areas in which work done (%): 2O As individual consultant, 2O In organization
concerned with other studies including long-range planning.
Direction of work in forecasting: I Technological, 2 Social.
Direction of work in research: I Futures methodology, 2 Policy research, 3 Social
impacts of technology.
Direction of work in planning: I Technological, 2 Corporate, 3 Social.
Methods used: I Delphi techniques, 2 Probabilistic forecasting, 3 Gaming, 4 Scenario
building, 5 Extrapolation techniques.
Time range of work: 5 - IO years.
Source of support for work (%): 2O National government, 2O Private business.
Work done for (%): IO National government, IO Private business.
Occupational function: I Educator, 2 Research worker, 3 Consultant.
Worked in government as: I Researcher, 2 Administrator.
Worked in education: I Teaching, 2 In research.
Additional information: Concerned with new methods of human communication.   *(351)*

534. Brian Twiss

Director, Technology Management Programmes, University of Bradford, Management Centre,
Heaton Mount, Keighley Rd, Bradford, BD9 4JU, UK;
Sex: Male.   *Age:* 4O-49.
Educational qualification: Master's degree.
Formal training: I Engineering, 2 Business.
Informal training: Education.
Areas in which work done (%): 4O As academic, in teaching futures studies or long-
range planning.
Direction of work in forecasting: Technological.
Direction of work in research: Futures methodology.
Direction of work in planning: I Technological, 2 Corporate, 3 Environmental.
Methods used: I Delphi techniques, 2 Extrapolation techniques, 3 Brainstorming,
4 Relevance trees.
Time range of work: IO - 25 years.
Occupational function: Educator.
Worked in industry/business in: Management.
Worked in education: Teaching, In research.
Additional information: Concerned with technological forecasting; corporate planning.
                                                                            (324)

535. M. Tyler

Head of Economic and Environmental Studies, Long-Range Planning Div, Post Office
Telecommunications, 2O7 Old St, London EC1, UK.
Sex: Male.   *Age:* 25-29.
Educational qualification: Master's degree.

Formal training: I Social/behavioural sciences, 2 Physical sciences.
Informal training: I Design, 2 Mathematics, 3 Engineering, 4 Education.
Primarily engaged in: Both futures studies and long-range planning.
Areas in which work done (%): IO As academic, in teaching futures studies or long-range planning, I5 As individual consultant, 75 In planning unit of a business enterprise.
Direction of work in forecasting: I Market, 2 Economic, 3 Technological.
Direction of work in rsearch: I Policy research, 2 Social impacts of technology, 3 Alternative futures, 4 Resource utilization, 5 Environmental.
Direction of work in planning: I Corporate, 2 Economic, 3 Environmental, 4 Urban, 5 Technological.
Methods used: I Causal modelling, 2 Scenario building, 3 Relevance trees, 4 Operational models, 5 Statistical models.
Time range of work: IO - 25 years.
Source of support for work (%): IOO Post Office, telecommunications.
Work done for (%): 1OO Post Office telecommunications.
Occupational function: I Manager, 2 Research worker, 3 Consultant, 4 Educator, 5 Administrator.
Worked in government as: Researcher.
Worked in industry/business in: Management, Planning, Consultancy.
Worked in education: Teaching.
Additional information: Concerned with potential demand for, and social and experimental effects of, advanced telecommunications service.   **(354)**

536. Vinyu Vichit-Vadakan

Director, Asian Institute for Economic Development and Planning, 22 Soi 24 Suknumvit Rd, Bangkok, Thailand.
Sex: Male.   *Age:* 3O-39.
Educational qualification: Doctoral degree.
Formal training: Social/behavioural sciences.
Informal training: Social/behavioural sciences.
Primarily engaged in: Long-range planning.
Areas in which work done (%): 9O In planning unit of an international organization, IO As academic, in teaching futures studies or long-range planning.
Direction of work in forecasting: Economic.
Direction of work in planning: Policy research.
Direction of work in planning: Economic.
Methods used: I Brainstorming, 2 Statistical models, 3 Historical analogy, 4 Individual expert forecasting.
Time range of work: IO - 25 years.
Source of support for work (%): 3O Foundations, 7O International agencies.
Work done for (%): 1OO International agencies.
Occupational function: Administrator.
Worked in government as: Administrator.
Worked in education: Teaching, In research.
Additional information: Concerned with economics and social development planning. *(283)*

537. John Vaizey

Head, Brunel University, School of Social Sciences, Kingston Lane, Uxbridge, Middlesex, UB8 3PH, UK.
Sex: Male.   *Age:* 4O-49.
Educational qualification: Doctoral degree.

Formal training: Social/behavioural sciences.
Informal training: Humanities, Journalism, Education, Arts.
Areas in which work done (%): IO In organization concerned with other studies including long-range planning, IO Research.
Direction of work in forecasting: Economic.
Direction of work in research: Manpower, Policy research.
Methods used: Statistical models, Individual expert forecasting.
Time range of work: IO - 25 years.
Source of support for work (%): IOO Foundation.
Work done for (%): 5O Local or regional government.   *(98)*

538. K. Valaskakis

c/o Bion Dept, University of Montreal, Montreal, Canada.
Sex: Male.   *Age:* 3O-39.
Educational qualification: Doctoral degree.
Formal training: Social/behavioural sciences, Law.
Informal training: Humanities.
Primarily engaged in: Futures studies.
Areas in which work done (%): IO Miscellaneous, 3O In Organization primarily concerned with futures studies and/or long-range planning, 3O As individual consultant, 3O As academic, In teaching futures studies or long-range planning.
Direction of work in forecasting: I Economic, 2 Social, 3 Technological.
Direction of work in research: Social impacts of technology, Alternative futures, Social priorities.
Methods used: Delphi techniques, Gaming, Cross impact analysis, Scenario building.
Time range of work: IO - 25 years.
Occupational function: Educator.
Worked in education: Teaching, In research.   *(21)*

539. Paolo Maria Valenzano

IRADES, Istituto per la Ricerca e la Formazione al Futuro, Via Paisiello 6, Rome OO198, Italy.
Sex: Male.   *Age:* 25-29.
Educational qualification: Master's degree.
Formal training: Mathematics.
Informal training: I Education, 2 Arts.
Primarily engaged in: Futures studies.
Areas in which work done (%): IOO In organization primarily concerned with futures studies and/or long-range planning.
Direction of work in research: I Futures methodology, 2 Population.
Time range of work: Beyond 2OOO AD.
Source of support for work (%): IOO Private associations.
Work done for (%): IOO Private association.
Occupational function: I Research worker.
Worked in education: I Teaching.
Worked in service sector: I Social welfare, 2 Religion.
Additional information: Concerned with futures methodology.   *(417)*

540. Roberto Vanore

c/o ICE, Via Liszt, 21, Rome, Italy.
Sex: Male.   *Age:* 30-39.
Educational qualification: Doctoral degree.
Formal training: Agriculture, Agricultural economics, Foreign trade.
Informal training: Education.
Primarily engaged in: Both futures studies and long-range planning.
Areas in which work done (%): I5 In planning unit of a business enterprise, IO In organization primarily concerned with futures studies and/or long-range planning, IO As individual consultant, IO Promotional activities, 2O In planning unit of an international organization, 5 As academic, in teaching futures studies or long-range planning, 3O In planning unit of a governmental agency.
Direction of work in forecasting: I Market, 2 Economic, 3 Educational.
Direction of work in research: I Consumer affairs, 2 Educational, economics.
Direction of work in planning: I Educational, 2 Economics.
Methods used: I Expert panels, 2 Brainstorming, 3 Extrapolation techniques.
Time range of work: 5 - IO years.
Source of support for work (%): IOO National government.
Work done for (%): 2O Private business, 2O In-house training, 3O National government, 3O International agencies.
Occupational function: Manager.
Worked in government as: Elected official.   *(303)*

541. A.J. Veal

Centre for Urban and Regional Studies, University of Birmingham, Selly Wick House, Selly Wick Rd, Birmingham B29 7 JF, UK.
Sex: Male.   *Age:* 25-29.
Educational qualification: Bachelor's degree.
Formal training: Social/behavioural sciences.
Informal training: I Social/behavioural sciences, 2 Design.
Direction of work in forecasting: I Recreation, 2 Social, 3 Environmental, 4 Cultural.
Direction of work in research: I Recreation, 2 Social priorities, 3 Environmental.
Direction of work in planning: I Recreational, 2 Urban, 3 Regional, 4 Environmental.
Methods used: I Causal modelling, 2 Statistical models, 3 Extrapolation techniques, 4 Probabilistic forecasting.
Time range of work: 5 - beyond year 2OOO.
Source of support for work (%): 5O Foundations, 5O National government.
Work done for (%): 5 Local or regional government, 5 National government.
Occupational function: I Research worker.
Worked in education: I In research, 2 Teaching.
Worked in service sector: I Design.
Additional information: Concerned with recreational forecasting and planning.   *(463)*

542. P.T. Veelenturf

Topaasstr 51, Boekelo, The Netherlands.
Sex: Male.   *Age:* 30-39.
Educational qualification: Master's degree.
Formal training: Engineering.
Informal training: Social/behavioural sciences, Humanities, Mathematics.
Direction of work in forecasting: Social, Scientific.

Direction of work in research: Social impacts of technology, The individual in the future, Futures methodology.
Methods used: Causal modelling.
Occupational function: I Research worker, 2 Administrator, 3 Educator.
Worked in education: I In research, 2 Teaching, 3 In administration.   *(132)*

543. Frederic Vester
Studien Grüppe für Biologie und Umwel, 8 Munchen 2, Nussbaumstr 14, West Germany.
Sex: Male.   *Age:* 40-49.
Educational qualification: Doctoral degree.
Formal training: Life sciences.
Informal training: Physical sciences, Social/behavioural sciences, Humanities, Mathematics, Journalism, Education, Design, Cinema/television.
Primarily engaged in: Both futures studies and long-range planning.
Areas in which work done (%): 5 As academic, in teaching futures studies or long-range planning, IO In planning unit of a governmental agency, I5 In organization primarily concerned with futures studies and/or long-range planning, 60 Writing, IO As individual consultant.
Direction of work in forecasting: Technological, Economic, Social, Educational, Scientific, Environmental, Resources, Population.
Direction of work in research: I Environmental, 2 Medicine, 3 Social impacts of technology.
Direction of work in planning: I Environmental, 2 Educational.
Methods used: Probabilistic forecasting, Extrapolation techniques, Brainstorming, Statistical models, Expert paenls, Operational models, Individual expert forecasting, Simulation.
Time range of work: 5 - beyond year 2000.
Source of support for work (%): 5 Local government, 5 National government, 30 Private foundations, 60 Television and publishing houses.
Work done for (%): 5 Local or regional government, 5 National government, 30 Private business, 60 Television and publishing houses.
Additional information: Concerned with the future of medicine, long-range resource analysis, technology assessment, the future of technical learning, the future of science and society.   *(467)*

544. Marcelo Ortiz Villacis
San Ignacio 951, Quito, Ecuador.
Sex: Male.   *Age:* 30-39.
Educational qualification: Doctoral degree.
Formal training: I Social/behavioural sciences, 2 Law. 3 Journalism, 4 Co-operative and agrarian reform.
Informal training: Education.
Primarily engaged in: Both futures studies and long-range planning.
Areas in which work done (%): 5 Consultant, 25 As academic, in teaching futures studies or long-range planning, 70 In organization primarily concerned with futures studies and/or long-range planning.
Direction of work in forecasting: I Social, 2 Economic.
Direction of work in research: I Social impacts of technology, 2 Futures methodology.
Methods used: I Historical analogy, 2 Statistical-percentage, 3 Expert panels, 4 Gaming.
Time range of work: 5 - IO years.
Source of support for work (%): IO Students, 90 National government.

Work done for (%): 7O University.
Occupational function: Research worker, Educator, Consultant.
Worked in government as: Researcher.
Worked in education: Teaching, In research.
Worked in service sector: Law.
Additional information: Concerned with social indicators, methods news, and computers.

(293)

545. André Vinette
CIDA, Multilateral Prog Branch, 122 Bank St, Ottawa, Canada.
Sex: Male. *Age:* 25 - 29.
Educational qualification: Master's degree.
Formal training: I Law, 2 International, 3 Humanities.
Informal training: I Law, 2 Humanities, 3 Education.
Primarily engaged in: Both futures studies and long-range planning.
Areas in which work done (%): IOO In planning unit of a governmental agency.
Direction of work in forecasting: I Social, 2 Economic, 3 International.
Direction of work in research: Policy research, The individual in the future.
Direction of work in planning: I International, 2 Social.
Methods used: I Expert panels.
Time range of work: 5 - 25 years.
Source of support for work (%): 5O National government.
Occupational function: I Manager, 2 Administrator.
Worked in government as: I Administrator, 2 Researcher.
Worked in industry/business in: I Research and development.
Worked in education: I In research.
Worked in service sector: I Law.
Additional information: Concerned with future policies regarding international
co-operation, and international law. *(285)*

546. Carlo Virgilio
IRADES, Istituto per la Ricerca e la Formazione al Futuro, Via Paisiello 6, Rome OO198,
Italy.
Sex: Male. *Age:* 30-39.
Educational qualification: Doctoral degree.
Formal training: Social/behavioural sciences.
Informal training: Arts.
Primarily engaged in: Futures studies.
Areas in which work done (%): 20 As academic, in teaching futures studies or long-
range planning, 3O In organization primarily concerned with futures studies and/or
long-range planning, 5O Consultant in the social area.
Direction of work in forecasting: Social.
Direction of work in research: Alternative futures, Futures methodology.
Direction of work in planning: Social.
Methods used: I Scenario building, 2 Historical analogy, 3 Simulation, 4 Statistical
models.
Time range of work: Beyond 2OOO AD.
Source of support for work (%): IOO Private business.
Work done for (%): IOO Private business.
Occupational function: I Research worker, 2 Educator, 3 Consultant.
Worked in government as: I Researcher.
Worked in industry/business in: I Research and development, 2 Consultancy.

Worked in education: I In research, 2 Teaching.
Worked in service sector: I Communication media.
Additional information: Concerned with education toward the future; arts and the future; forecasting methodologies.   *(415)*

547. Aldo Visalberghi
11 Via Spalato, OO198 Rome, Italy.
Sex: Male.   *Age:* 5O-59.
Educational qualification: Doctoral degree.
Formal training: Philosophy.
Informal training: I Education, 2 Social/behavioural sciences, 3 Mathematics.
Primarily engaged in: Both futures studies and long-range planning.
Areas in which work done (%): IO In planning unit of a governmental enterprise, 4O As academic, in teaching futures studies or long-range planning, IO In organization concerned with other studies including long-range planning, IO In planning unit of an international organization, 3O In organization primarily concerned with futures studies and/or long-range planning.
Direction of work in forecasting: I Social, 2 Educational, 3 Economic, 4 Technological, 5 Environmental, 6 Manpower, 7 Military.
Direction of work in research: I Alternative futures, 2 Social impacts of technology, 3 Manpower, 4 Value systems, 5 Social priorities.
Direction of work in planning: I Educational.
Methods used: I Scenario building, 2 Expert panels, 3 Historical analogy, 4 Probabilistic forecasting.
Time range of work: IO - 25 years.
Source of support for work (%): IO Voluntary associations, IO Private business, 2O International agencies, 3O Foundations, 4O National government.
Work done for (%): IO Local or regional government, 2O International agencies, 3O Foundations, 4O National government.
Occupational function: I Educator, 2 Research worker, 3 Manager.
Worked in government as: I Researcher.
Worked in industry/business in: Consultancy.
Worked in education: I Teaching.
Worked in service sector: I Communication media.
Additional information: Concerned with future of education as it relates to social and economic development.   *(342)*

548. Evan Vlachos
Dept of Sociology, Colorado State University, Fort Collins, Co 8O521, USA.
Sex: Male.   *Age:* 3O-39.
Educational qualification: Doctoral degree.
Formal training: Social/behavioural sciences.
Informal training: I Social/behavioural sciences, 2 Law, 3 Design.
Primarily engaged in: Both futures studies and long-range planning.
Areas in which work done (%): 2O As academic, in teaching futures studies or long-range planning, 3O As individual consultant, 5O In organization primarily concerned with futures studies and/or long-range planning.
Direction of work in forecasting: I Social, 2 Resources, 3 Population.
Direction of work in research: I Social impacts of technology, 2 Futures methodology, 3 Environmental.
Direction of work in planning: Social.

Methods used: I Scenario building, 2 Delphi techniques, 3 Cross impact analysis.
Time range of work: IO - 25 years.
Source of support for work (%): IO Local government, 2O National government.
Work done for (%): IO Private business, 2O National government.
Occupational function: I Educator, 2 Consultant.
Worked in education: I Teaching, 2 In research.   *(175)*

549. Fritz Voigt
Director, University of Bonn, Institut für Industrie und Verkeurspolitik, 53 Bonn,
Koblenzer Str 24-26, West Germany.
Sex: Male.   *Age:* 60 or over.
Educational qualification: Doctoral degree.
Formal training: Social/behavioural sciences, Law, Economics.
Informal training: Social/behavioural sciences, Law, Economics.
Primarily engaged in: Long-range planning.
Areas in which work done (%): 30 In organization concerned with other studies
including long-range planning, 2O As individual consultant, 50 In organization primarily
concerned with futures studies and/or long-range planning.
Direction of work in forecasting: Economic, Social, Transportation.
Direction of work in research: Transportation.
Direction of work in planning: Urban, Regional, Economic.
Methods used: Extrapolation techniques, Statistical models, Network analysis,
Historical analogy.
Time range of work: 5 - 25 years.
Source of support for work (%): 50 Local government, 50 National government.
Work done for (%): IO International agencies, 30 Local or regional government,
60 National government.
Occupational function: Research worker, University professor.
Worked in government as: Researcher.   *(278)*

550. Vladimir Stepanovich Volokhov
USSR Kiev 127, Bul 40 - Let Oktyabya 142/144, Institute of Cybernetics of the
Academy of Sciences, UKRO SSR, USSR.
Sex: Male.   *Age:* 30-39.
Educational qualification: Doctoral degree.
Formal training: Engineering.
Informal training: Mathematics, Engineering, Social/behavioural sciences, Life sciences,
Design.
Primarily engaged in: Both futures studies and long-range planning.
Areas in which work done (%): 70 In organization primarily concerned with futures
studies and/or long-range planning, 5 In organization concerned with other studies
including long-range planning, 5 As individual consultant, 5 In planning unit of a
governmental agency, IO In planning unit of a business enterprise, 2 In planning unit of an
international organization, 3 In academic, in teaching futures studies or long-range
planning.
Direction of work in forecasting: I Environmental, 2 Scientific, 3 Technological, 4 Social.
Direction of work in research: I Alternative futures, 2 Environmental, 3 Futures
methodology.
Direction of work in planning: I Technological, 2 Scientific, 3 Urban, 4 Social.
Methods used: I Simulation, 2 Statistical models, 3 Probabilistic forecasting, 4 Extrapolation techniques, 5 Gaming, 6 Operational models, 7 Network analysis, 8 Delphi
techniques, 9 Expert panels, IO Relevance trees.

Time range of work: 5 - 25 years.
Source of support for work (%): 100 National government.
Work done for (%): 10 Local or regional government, 80 National government, 10 International agencies.
Occupational function: 1 Research worker, 2 Administrator, 3 Consultant, 4 Educator, 5 Manager.
Worked in government as: Researcher.
Worked in industry/business in: 1 Research and development, 2 Consultancy.
Worked in education: Teaching.
Worked in service sector: Medicine.

551. Jan Vranken

179 Tiensesteenweg B - 3200 Kessel-Lo, Belgium.
Sex: Male.   *Age:* 30-39.
Educational qualification: Master's degree.
Formal training: Social/behavioural sciences.
Informal training: 1 Education, 2 Humanities.
Direction of work in forecasting: 1 Social, 2 Economic, 3 Cultural.
Direction of work in research: 1 Alternative futures, 2 Social priorities, 3 Futures methodology, 4 Social impacts of technology, 5 Value systems.
Direction of work in planning: 1 Social, 2 Economic, 3 Labour.
Methods used: 1 Individual expert forecasting, 2 Causal modelling, Historical analogy.
Time range of work: 10 - 25 years.
Work done for (%): 100 Voluntary associations.
Occupational function: 1 Educator, 2 Research worker, 3 Administrator.
Worked in education: 1 Teaching, 2 In research, 3 In administration.
Worked in service sector: 1 Social welfare.
Additional information: Concerned with evaluation of basic structures of society.   *(239)*

552. Egbert de Vries

39 Deer Lake Park, Chalkhill, Pa 15421, USA.
Sex: Male.   *Age:* 60 or over.
Educational qualification: Doctoral degree.
Formal training: 1 Agricultural, 2 Social/behavioural sciences.
Informal training: 1 Social/behavioural sciences, 2 Humanities, 3 Education.
Areas in which work done (%): 10 In organization primarily concerned with futures studies and/or long-range planning, 50 As academic, in teaching futures studies or long-range planning, 20 In planning unit of an international organization, 10 In organization concerned with other studies including long-range planning.
Direction of work in research: 1 Social impacts of technology, 2 Population, 3 Environmental, 4 Social priorities, 5 Resource utilization.
Direction of work in planning: 2 Economic, 3 Political, 4 Resources.
Methods used: 1 Historical analogy, 2 Individual expert forecasting, 3 Expert panels, 4 Network analysis.
Time range of work: 10 - 25 years.
Source of support for work (%): 10 Voluntary association, 10 Foundations, 20 International agencies.
Work done for (%): 10 Foundations, 10 Voluntary associations, 20 International agencies.
Occupational function: 1 Educator, 2 Consultant.
Worked in government as: 1 Administrator, 2 Researcher.

Worked in education: I In administration, 2 Teaching, 3 In research.
Worked in service sector: I Social welfare, 2 Religion.
Additional information: Concerned with population; environment, social development.

(134)

W 553. Warren Wagar

Prof of History, Library Tower, Room 809, State University of New York, Binghamton, NY 13901, USA.
Sex: Male.   *Age:* 40-49.
Educational qualification: Doctoral degree.
Formal training: I History.
Informal training: I Humanities, 2 Social/behavioural sciences, 3 Education, 4 Arts.
Primarily engaged in: Futures studies.
Areas in which work done (%): 30 As academic, in teaching futures studies or long-range planning, IO In organization primarily concerned with futures studies and/or long-range planning, IO As individual consultant, 50 As writer and scholar.
Direction of work in forecasting: I Cultural, 2 Political, 3 Social, 4 Educational.
Direction of work in research: I Alternative futures, 2 Value systems, 3 Political systems, 4 Social priorities, 5 Futures methodology, 6 Resource utilization, 7 Environmental, 8 The individual in the future, 9 The family in the future, IO Population, 11 Social impacts of technology.
Direction of work in planning: I Cultural, 2 Political, 3 Social, 4 Economic, 5 Educational.
Methods used: I Individual expert forecasting, 2 Historical analogy, 3 Extrapolation techniques, 4 Probabilistic forecasting, 5 Cross impact analysis, 6 Scenario building, 7 Brainstorming, 8 Statistical models,
Time range of work: Beyond 2000 AD.
Source of support for work (%): IO Foundations, IO National government, 80 University salary and grants.
Work done for (%): IO National government, IO Foundations, 80 University.
Occupational function: I Educator.
Worked in education: I In research, 2 Teaching.

(22)

554. Fred Walden

Director, Socio-Economic Strategic Planning, National Defence, 101 Colonel By Drive, Ottawa K1A OK2, Canada.
Sex: Male.   *Age:* 50-59.
Educational qualification: Doctoral degree.
Formal training: I Social/behavioural sciences, 2 Education.
Informal training: I Humanities, 2 Arts.
Primarily engaged in: Both futures studies and long-range planning.
Areas in which work done (%): IOO In planning unit of a governmental agency.
Direction of work in forecasting: I Economic, I Social, 2 Cultural, 2 Educational, 2 Manpower, 2 Resources, 2 Population.
Direction of work in research: I Futures methodology, 2 Value systems, 2 Social priorities, 3 Social impacts of technology, 3 Policy research, 3 The individual in the future, 3 The family in the future.
Direction of work in planning: I Military, 2 Social, 2 Economic.
Methods used: I Extrapolation techniques, 2 Statistical models, 3 Cross impact analysis, 3 Network analysis, 3 Simulation.
Time range of work: IO - 25 years.
Source of support for work (%): IOO National government.

Work done for (%): lOO National government.
Occupational function: Consultant.
Worked in government as: Researcher.
Worked in education: In research.
Worked in service sector: Social welfare.

(404)

555. Willi Wapenhans

Director, Regional Projects Dept, Europe, Middle East, and North Africa, International
Bank for Reconstruction and Development, International Development Assoc,
1818 H St, NW, Washington, DC 20433, USA.
Sex: Male.   *Age:* 40-49.
Educational qualification: Doctoral degree.
Formal training: Life sciences, Social/behavioural sciences.
Informal training: Education, Management.
Primarily engaged in: Long-range planning.
Areas in which work done (%): lOO In an international agency.
Direction of work in planning: l Economic, 2 Social, 3 Resources.
Methods used: l Expert panels, 2 Causal modelling, 3 Operational models, 4 Simulation.
Time range of work: lO - 25 years.
Source of support for work (%): lOO International agencies.
Work done for (%): lOO International agencies.
Occupational function: l Manager.
Worked in industry/business in: l Planning, 2 Management.
Worked in education: l Teaching, 2 In research.
Worked in service sector: l Social welfare.
Additional information: Concerned with identification, formulation, financing and
execution of priority development investments; and sectorial development planning. *(267)*

556. Jonathan Ward

CBS News, 524 West 57th St, New York, NY 1OO19, USA.
Sex: Male.   *Age:* 30-39.
Educational qualification: Some college or less.
Formal training: l Physical sciences, 2 Humanities, 3 Journalism.
Informal training: l Cinema/television, 2 Arts, 3 Mathematics, 4 Social/behavioural
sciences.
Primarily engaged in: Futures studies.
Areas in which work done (%): 6O Reporting futures studies.
Direction of work in forecasting: Social.
Direction of work in research: Alternative futures.
Direction of work in planning: Social.
Methods used: l Individual expert forecasting; 2 Scenario building, 3 Expert panels,
4 Brainstorming.
Time range of work: 5 - beyond year 2OOO.
Source of support for work (%): lOO Private business.
Work done for (%): lOO Public.
Occupational function: l Reporter, 2 Manager, 3 Research worker.
Worked in service sector: l Communication media.
Additional information: Concerned with general future research. *(162)*

557. John Warfield

System Scientist, Battelle Memorial Institute, 505 King Ave, Columbus, Oh 43201, USA.
Sex: Male.   *Age:* 40-49.
Educational qualification: Doctoral degree.
Formal training: I Engineering, 2 Mathematics.
Informal training: Social/behavioural sciences.
Primarily engaged in: Long-range planning.
Areas in which work done (%): IOO In organization concerned with other studies including long-range planning.
Direction of work in research: I Futures methodology, 2 Policy research.
Direction of work in planning: I Urban, 2 Educational, 3 Technological.
Methods used: I Interpretive structural modelling, 2 Brainstorming, 3 Contextual mapping, 4 Scenario building, 5 Cross impacts analysis, 6 Probabilistic forecasting.
Time range of work: 5 - IO years.
Source of support for work (%): IOO Private business.
Work done for (%): 2O Private business, 8O Public.
Occupational function: I Research worker, 2 Educator, 3 Consultant.
Worked in industry/business in: I Research and development, 2 Planning.
Worked in education: I Teaching, 2 In research.   *(223)*

558. W. Montgomery Watt

Dept of Arabic and Islamic Studies, University of Edinburgh, 7 Buccleuch Place, Edinburgh, EH8 9LW, UK.
Sex: Male.   *Age:* 6O or over.
Educational qualification: Doctoral degree.
Formal training: Humanities.
Informal training: Social/behavioural sciences.
Direction of work in research: Value systems.
Methods used: I Historical analogy, 2 Expert panels.
Time range of work: Beyond 2OOO AD.
Source of support for work (%): IOO University of Edinburgh.
Occupational function: I Research worker, 2 Educator.
Worked in education: I In research, 2 Teaching, 3 In administration.
Additional information: Concerned with future of religion.   *(23)*

559. M.M. Webber

193O El Dorado Ave, Berkeley, Ca 947O7, USA.
Sex: Male.   *Age:* 5O-59.
Educational qualification: Master's degree.
Formal training: I Social/behavioural sciences, 2 Design.
Informal training: Life sciences.
Primarily engaged in: Both futures studies and long-range planning.
Areas in which work done (%): IOO As academic, in teaching futures studies or long-range planning.
Direction of work in forecasting: I Social, 2 Technological.
Direction of work in research: I Social impacts of technology, 2 Policy research, 3 Alternative futures.
Direction of work in planning: I Social, 2 Urban, 3 Regional.
Methods used: Scenario building.
Time range of work: 5 - 25 years.
Source of support for work (%): IOO University.

Work done for (%): IOO University.
Occupational function: Educator.
Worked in government as: Researcher.
Worked in industry/business in: Consultancy.
Worked in education: I Teaching, 2 In research, 3 In administration.
Additional information: Concerned with future of urbanism, long-range effects of transportation and communications technologies.   *(582)*

560. Robert Weeda

Plan Europe 2000, European Cultural Foundation, Amsterdam 1007, Jan Van Goyenkade, The Netherlands.
Sex: Male.   *Age:* 30-39.
Educational qualification: Bachelor's degree.
Formal training: Education, Arts.
Informal training: Social/behavioural sciences, Journalism.
Primarily engaged in: Futures studies.
Areas in which work done (%): 20 As individual consultant, 80 In organization primarily concerned with futures studies and/or long-range planning.
Direction of work in forecasting: Social, Cultural, Educational.
Direction of work in research: Value systems, The individual in the future, The family in the future.
Direction of work in planning: Social, Urban, Educational.
Methods used: Brainstorming, Expert panels, Historical analogy, Operational models, Individual expert forecasting.
Time range of work: IO - beyond year 2000.
Source of support for work (%): 5 Local government, National government, International agencies, 5 Voluntary associations, 30 Foundations, 60 Private business.
Work done for (%): 5 Private business, 5 Foundations, 90 European Cultural Foundation.
Occupational function: I Manager, 2 Consultant, 3 Educator.
Worked in education: I Teaching.
Worked in service sector: I Communication media.   *(254)*

561. Jo Ann Weinberger

Assistant to the Executive Director, Research for Better Schools, 1700 Market St, Philadelphia, Pa 19103, USA.
Sex: Female.   *Age:* 30-39.
Educational qualification: Master's degree.
Formal training: Education.
Informal training: Education.
Primarily engaged in: Futures studies.
Areas in which work done (%): 50 In organization primarily concerned with futures studies and/or long-range planning, 50 Administrative unit of a non-profit corporation.
Direction of work in research: I Education/schooling, 2 The individual in the future.
Methods used: I Brainstorming, I Expert panels.
Time range of work: 5 - IO years.
Source of support for work (%): 75 National government.
Occupational function: I Administrator, 2 Educator.
Worked in education: I In research, 2 In administration.
Additional information: Concerned with future of education.   *(471)*

562. Tom Weiss
302 Nassau St, Princeton, NJ 08540, USA.
Sex: Male. *Age:* 25-29.
Educational qualification: Doctoral degree.
Formal training: Social/behavioural sciences.
Informal training: Education.
Areas in which work done (%): 20 In planning unit of an international organization,
10 As individual consultant, 10 As academic, in teaching futures studies or long-range
planning.
Direction of work in research: Alternative futures, Social priorities, Policy research.
Methods used: Probabilistic forecasting, Scenario building, Extrapolation techniques,
Historical analogy.
Time range of work: 10 - 25 years.
Source of support for work (%): 15 Foundations, 85 International agencies.
Work done for (%): 10 Foundations, 90 International agencies.
Occupational function: Research worker.
Worked in government as: Administrator.
Worked in education: Teaching, In research, In administration.   *(75)*

563. Anthony L. Wermuth
Strategic Studies Institute, PO Box 329, US Army Way College, Carlisle Barracks, Pa
17013, USA.
Sex: Male. *Age:* 50-59.
Educational qualification: Doctoral degree.
Formal training: 1 Social/behavioural sciences, 2 Humanities, 3 Military.
Informal training: 1 Social/behavioural sciences, 2 Journalism.
Primarily engaged in: Futures studies.
Areas in which work done (%): 10 As individual consultant, 10 As academic, in
teaching futures studies or long-range planning, 80 In organization primarily concerned
with futures studies and/or long-range planning.
Direction of work in forecasting: 1 Social, 2 Military, 3 Manpower, 4 Cultural,
5 Technological, 6 Economic.
Direction of work in research: 1 Social impacts of technology, 2 The individual in the
future, 3 Alternative futures, 4 Manpower, 5 Value systems, 6 Social priorities.
Direction of work in planning: 1 Military, 2 Social, 3 Political, 4 Economic,
5 Technological.
Methods used: 1 Individual expert forecasting, 2 Historical analogy, 3 Brainstorming,
4 Extrapolation techniques, 5 Scenario building, 6 Delphi techniques, 7 Expert panels.
Time range of work: 5 - 25 years.
Source of support for work (%): 10 Voluntary associations, 90 National government.
Work done for (%): 10 Voluntary associations, 90 National government.
Occupational function: 1 Research worker, 2 Consultant.
Worked in government as: 1 Administrator, 2 Researcher.
Worked in industry/business in: 1 Research and development, 2 Management.
Worked in education: 1 Teaching, 2 In research, 3 In administration.
Additional information: Concerned with technology assessment, assessment of social
and cultural change, interrelations between armed forces and society, strategic equations.
(297)

564. Roger Wescott

Chairman Anthropology Dept, Drew University, Madison, NJ O7940, USA.
Sex: Male.   *Age:* 40-49.
Educational qualification: Doctoral degree.
Formal training: I Social/behavioural sciences.
Informal training: I Humanities, 2 Life sciences, 3 Arts.
Areas in which work done (%): 5 In planning unit of a government agency, 5 Consultant
to a governmental agency, IO As academic, in teaching futures studies or long-range planning.
Direction of work in forecasting: Social, Cultural, Educational, Scientific.
Direction of work in research: Alternative futures, Futures methodology.
Direction of work in planning: Regional.
Methods used: Probabilistic forecasting, Scenario building, Brainstorming, Individual
expert forecasting.
Time range of work: IO years to beyond year 2000.
Source of support for work (%): IO Local government, National government, Inter-
national agencies, 90 Local or regional government.
Work done for (%): 5 Local or regional government, IO University.
Occupational function: I Educator, 2 Research worker, 3 Administrator, 4 Consultant.
Worked in education: I Teaching, 2 In research, 3 In administration.
Worked in service sector: I Communication media.
Additional information: Concerned with future of sciences.   *(65)*

565. James Wellesley-Wesley

Executive Director, Mankind 2000, 1 Rue Aux Laines, 1000 Brussels, Belgium.
Sex: Male.   *Age:* 40-49.
Educational qualification: Some college or less.
Formal training: Humanities, Agriculture.
Informal training: Social/behavioural sciences.
Primarily engaged in: Futures studies.
Areas in which work done (%): IOO In organization primarily concerned with
futures studies and/or long-range planning.
Direction of work in research: I The individual in the future, 2 Value systems,
3 Alternative futures.
Methods used: I Brainstorming, 2 Extrapolation techniques, 3 Contextual mapping.
Time range of work: IO - 25 years.
Source of support for work (%): IOO Voluntary associations.
Work done for (%): IOO Voluntary associations.
Occupational function: I Manager, 2 Administrator.   *(193)*

566. R.E. Wilkins

Director, Corporate Research and Planning, Firestone Tyre and Rubber Company,
1200 Firestone Parkway, Akron, Oh 44317, USA.
Sex: Male.   *Age:* 50-59.
Educational qualification: Bachelor's degree.
Formal training: Mathematics.
Informal training: Marketing research.
Areas in which work done (%): IOO In organization concerned with other studies
including long-range planning.
Direction of work in forecasting: Market.
Direction of work in planning: Corporate.
Time range of work: 5 - IO years.

Source of support for work (%): IOO Private business.
Work done for (%): 3O Private business.
Occupational function: Administrator.
Worked in industry/business in: Management.   *(367)*

567. Gareth Williams
Prof of Educational Planning, University of Lancaster, UK.
Sex: Male.   *Age:* 30-39.
Educational qualification: Master's degree.
Formal training: Social/behavioural sciences.
Informal training: Education.
Areas in which work done (%): 2 In planning unit of a governmental agency, 3 As
individual consultant, 5 In planning unit of an international organization, 4O In
organization concerned with other studies including long-range planning.
Direction of work in forecasting: Educational.
Direction of work in research: Manpower, Resource utilization, Policy research.
Direction of work in planning: Educational, Labour.
Methods used: I Statistical models, 2 Causal modelling, 3 Simulation, 4 Probabilistic
forecasting.
Time range of work: 5 - IO years.
Source of support for work (%): 2O Foundations, 3O National government, 5O University.
Occupational function: I Educator, 2 Research worker.
Worked in government as: I Researcher.
Worked in education: I In research, 2 Teaching.
Additional information: Concerned with educational institutes.   *(306)*

568. Philip D. Wilmot
Ciba-Geigy AG, KA 83 Basle, 4OO2 Swizerland.
Sex: Male.   *Age:* 50-59.
Educational qualification: Master's degree.
Formal training: Physical sciences.
Informal training: Life sciences, Social/behavioural sciences, Humanities, Mathematics,
Education.
Primarily engaged in: Both futures studies and long-range planning.
Areas in which work done (%): 5O In organization primarily concerned with futures
studies and/or long-range planning, 5O Market research.
Direction of work in forecasting: I Technological, 2 Market, 3 Economic, 4 Social.
Direction of work in research: I Resource utilization, 2 Social priorities, 3 Social
impacts of technology, 4 Alternative futures.
Direction of work in planning: I Corporate, 2 Technological, 3 Economic, 4 Social,
5 Resources.
Methods used: I Scenario building, 2 Expert panels, 3 Brainstorming.
Time range of work: IO - 25 years.
Source of support for work (%): IOO Private business.
Work done for (%): 5 International agencies, 95 Private business.
Occupational function: I Manager.
Worked in industry/business in: I Management, 2 Research and development.   *(523)*

569. Ian H. Wilson

Staff Associate, Business Environment Research and Forecasting, General Electric
Company, Fairfield, Ct O6431, USA.
Sex: Male.   *Age:* 5O-59.
Educational qualification: Master's degree.
Formal training: I Humanities, 2 Social/behavioural sciences.
Informal training: I Education, 2 Economics.
Primarily engaged in: Both futures studies and long-range planning.
Areas in which work done (%): IOO In organization primarily concerned with futures
studies and/or long-range planning.
Direction of work in forecasting: I Social, 2 Political, 3 Economic, 4 Manpower.
Direction of work in research: I Value systems, 2 Alternative futures, 3 Social priorities,
4 Social impacts of technology.
Direction of work in planning: I Corporate.
Methods used: I Expert panels, 2 Individual expert forecasting, 3 Scenario building,
4 Cross impact analysis, 5 Delphi techniques, 6 Historical analogy, 7 Brainstorming.
Time range of work: 5 - I5 years.
Source of support for work (%): IOO Private business.
Work done for (%): IOO Private business.
Occupational function: I Research worker.
Worked in industry/business in: I Research and development, 2 Planning.   *(379)*

570. Robert G. Wilson

Director Strategic Planning, Warnaco, Inc, 35O Lafayette St, Bridgeport, Ct O66O2, USA.
Sex: Male.   *Age:* 4O-49.
Educational qualification: Bachelor's degree.
Formal training: Humanities.
Informal training: Education.
Primarily engaged in: Long-range planning.
Areas in which work done (%): 9O In organization concerned with other studies
including long-range planning.
Direction of work in forecasting: I Population, 2 Social, 3 Market.
Direction of work in research: I Market.
Direction of work in planning: I Corporate, 2 Resources, 3 Social.
Methods used: Cross impact analysis, Extrapolation techniques, Historical analogy,
Operational models, Simulation.
Time range of work: 5 - IO years.
Source of support for work (%): IOO Private business.
Work done for (%): 5 Church organization.
Occupational function: I Administrator, 2 Educator, 3 Consultant.
Worked in industry/business in: I Planning, 2 Management.   *(6O)*

571. Beverly Woodward

148 N St, South Boston, Ma O2127, USA.
Sex: Female.   *Age:* 4O-49.
Educational qualification: Doctoral degree.
Formal training: I Humanities, 2 Social/behavioural sciences.
Informal training: I Law, 2 Arts, 3 Journalism.
Primarily engaged in: Futures studies.
Areas in which work done (%): I3 In organization concerned with other studies including
long-range planning, I3 In organization primarily concerned with futures studies and/or

long-range planning, 40 Writing and political activities, 20 As academic, in teaching futures studies or long-range planning, 13 As individual consultant.
Direction of work in research: I Alternative futures, 2 Value systems, 3 Policy research.
Direction of work in planning: I Political, 2 Social, 3 Environmental.
Methods used: I Philosophical analysis, 2 Historical analogy, 3 Brainstorming, 4 Scenario building.
Time range of work: 10 - 25 years.
Source of support for work (%): 100 Foundations.
Occupational function: I Research worker, 2 Consultant.
Worked in education: I In research, 2 Teaching. *(169)*

572. Yuri Victorovich Yershov

USSR, Kiev 127, Bul 40 - Let Oktyabya 142/144, Institute of Cybernetics of the Academy of Sciences, The UKRO SSR, USSR.
Sex: Male.   *Age:* 30-39.
Educational qualification: Doctoral degree.
Formal training: Engineering.
Informal training: Social/behavioural sciences, Mathematics.
Primarily engaged in: Both futures studies and long-range planning.
Areas in which work done (%): 100 In organization primarily concerned with futures studies and/or long-range planning.
Direction of work in forecasting: Technological, Scientific.
Direction of work in research: Futures methodology.
Direction of work in planning: Scientific, Technological.
Methods used: I Expert panels, 2 Relevance trees, 3 Delphi techniques, 4 Network analysis, 5 Simulation, 6 Extrapolation techniques, 7 Contextual mapping, 8 Statistical models.
Time range of work: 10 - 25 years.
Source of support for work (%): 100 National government.
Work done for (%): 70 National government, 30 International agencies.
Occupational function: I Research worker, 2 Consultant, 3 Administrator, 4 Manager, 5 Educator.
Worked in government as: Researcher.
Worked in industry/business in: Research and development.
Worked in education: Teaching.
Additional information: Concerned with methodology of technological forecasting and language planning.. *(543)*

573. S.M. Zawadzki

Director, Long-term Planning Dept, Planning Commission, Plac Trzech Krzyzy 3/5, 00 507 Warszaw, Poland.
Sex: Male.   *Age:* 40-49.
Formal education: Doctoral degree.
Formal training: Social/behavioural sciences.
Primarily engaged in: Both futures studies and long-range planning.
Areas in which work done (%): 25 As academic in teaching futures studies or long-range planning, 75 Organization primarily concerned with futures studies and/or long-range planning.
Direction of work in forecasting: Spatial.
Direction of work in research: Spactial economy.
Direction of work in planning: I Economic, 2 Regional.

Methods used: I Probabilistic forecasting, 2 Individual expert forecasting, 3 Historical analogy, 4 Scenario building, 5 Extrapolation techniques.
Time range of work: IO - beyond year 2000.
Source of support for work (%): IOO National government.
Work done for (%): IOO National government.
Occupational function: I Research worker, 2 Educator, 3 Administrator.
Worked in government as: I Administrator.
Worked in education: I Teaching, 2 In research.   *(392)*

574. Milos Zeman

Centre for Special Science, Technosports, Kyselova, 1188, 18200 Prague 8, Czechoslovakia.
Sex: Male.   *Age:* 30-39.
Educational qualification: Bachelor's degree.
Formal training: Social/behavioural sciences.
Informal training: Mathematics.
Primarily engaged in: Both futures studies and long-range planning.
Areas in which work done (%): 55 Organization primarily concerned with futures studies and/or long-range planning, IO As academic in teaching futures studies or long-range planning, 5 In organization concerned with other studies including long-range planning, I5 Individual consultant, IO Planning unit of a governmental agency, 5 Planning unit of an international organization.
Direction of work in research: Futures methodology.
Methods used: I Simulation, 2 Statistical models, 3 Causal modelling, 4 Brainstorming.
Time range of work: 5 - beyond year 2000.
Additional information: Concerned with simulation of complex social systems.   *(576)*

575. Charles Zraket

Senior Vice President, The Mitre Corporation, 1820 Dolley Madison Blvd, McLean, Va 22101, USA.
Sex: Male.   *Age:* 50-59.
Educational qualification: Master's degree.
Formal training: I Engineering, 2 Mathematics, 3 Physical sciences.
Informal training: I Engineering, 2 Design, 3 Social/behavioural sciences.
Primarily engaged in: Both fuutres studies and long-range planning.
Areas in which work done (%): 50 In organization primarily concerned with futures studies and/or long-range planning.
Direction of work in forecasting: I Technological, 2 Environmental, 3 Resources.
Direction of work in research: I Resource utilization, 2 Environmental.
Direction of work in planning: I Technological, 2 Environmental, 3 Resources.
Methods used: I Cross impact analysis, 2 Brainstorming, 3 Individual expert forecasting.
Time range of work: IO - 25 years.
Source of support for work (%): IOO National government.
Work done for (%): 50 National government.
Occupational function: I Manager, 2 Research worker.
Worked in industry/business in: I Management, 2 Research and development, 3 Planning.
Additional information: Concerned with long-range resource analysis; environmental plannir intrastructure systems planning.   *(250)*

Organizations - Geographical Index

All numbers refer to entry numbers.

Argentina

Bariloche Foundation (22)
Confederacion de Organizaciones Turisticas de la America Latina (82)
Contracultura (87)
International Association for Water Law (204)

Australia

Australian Post Office, National Tele-communications Planning (18)
World Organization of National Colleges, Academies and Academic Associations of General Practitioners and Family Physicians (434)

Austria

Austrian Academy of Sciences Institute for Research in Socio-Economic Development (19)
Austrian Institute for Economic Research (20)
European Co-ordination Centre for Research and Documentation in Social Sciences (121)
IFES (163)
Institut fur Sozio-Okonomische Entwicklungsforschung (173)
Osterreichische Studiengesellschaft fur Zukunftspolitik (293)
Osterreichische Studiengesellschaft fur Atomenergie (294)
Salzburg Assembly: Impact of New Technology (Saint) (324)

Belgium

Bureau du Plan (37)
Centre d'Etudes des Problemes Sociaux et Professionels de la Technique (56)
Centrum Voor Sociaal Beleid (68)
Commissariat General au Tourisme (77)
Commission Interministerielle de L'Eau (78)
Europe Plus Thirty (117)
European Association of National Productivity Centres (118)
International Society for Research on Civilization Diseases and Environment (223)

Mankind 2000 (242)
Mens en Ruimte (248)
SCIENCE Sprl (330)
World Confederation of Teachers (427)
World Federation of Agricultural Workers[(428)
World Problems Project (435)

Canada

Advanced Concepts Centre (3)
B.C. Telephone Company, Corporate Planning (27)
Bell Canada Business Planning Group (28)
Canada Post Office (42)
Canadian Industries Ltd, Corporate Planning (43)
Canadian International Development Agency (44)
Department of Industry, Trade and Commerce, Office of Science and Technology (97)
Department of National Defence (98)
Institute for Research On Public Policy (185)
MacMillan Bloedel Limited, Strategic Planning and Development (240)
Mineral Economics Research Division, Energy, Mines and Resources (253)
Ministry of State for Science and Technology, Technological Forecasting and Technology Assessment Division (145)
Ministry of Treasury, Economics and Intergovernmental Affairs, Office of Economic Policy (262)
National Research Council of Canada, Environmental Secretariat (271)
National Research Council of Canada, Marine Dynamics and Ship Laboratory (272)
The Ontario Educational Communications Authorities (287)
Operational Research and Analysis Establishment (290)
Pulp and Paper Research Institute of Canada Economics and Planning Section (315)
Science Council of Canada (327)
Seneca College, Centre for International

Programs (334)
Southam Press Limited Tele-Information[
(341)

Costa Rica

Consejo Nacional de Investigaciones
Cientificas y Technologicas (85)

Czechoslovakia

European Centre for Leisure and Education
(119)
Federal Statistical Office (124)
Institute for Philosophy and Sociology
(184)

Denmark

Denmark Towards the Year 1990 (91)
Institututtet for Fremtidsporskning (195)
International Council for the Exploration
of the Sea (211)

Ecuador

Universidad Central del Ecuador, Facultad
de Dere Cho, Instituto Superior de
Investigaciones Sociales (384)

Egypt

Cairo University, Institute of African
Research and Studies, Department of
Natural Resources (41)

France

Aéroport de Paris (4)
Association Internationale Futuribles (16)
Bureau d'Etudes et de Réalisations
Urbaines (34)
Bureau d'Informations et de Prévisions
Economiques (36)
Bureau de Recherches Géologiques et
Minières (38)
Centre d'Etudes des Conséquences
Générales des Grandes Techniques
Nouvelles (55)
Centre d'Etudes sur la Recherche et
l'Innovation (57)
Centre International de Recherche sur
L'Environment et de la Développement
(59)
Centre National D'Etudes Spatiales (60)
Commissariat General Du Plan (76)
Conservatoire National des Arts et
Métiers Institut Technique de Prévision
Economique et Sociale (86)
DATAR (90)
Fondation C.N. Ledoux pour les Réflex-
ions sur le Futur (132)
Hazan International (154)
Institut de Recherche D'Informatique et

d'Automatique (171)
Institut du Transport Aérien (175)
Institute of Legal Medicine and
Criminology (183)
Institute of Social Psychology (187)
International Agency for Research on
Cancer (199)
International Council of Monuments and
Sites (212)
International Council of Scientific Unions
(213)
International Institute for Educational
Planning (in UNESCO) (217)
Laboratoire de Prospective Appliquée (233)
OECD Development Centre (283)
Organization of Economic Co-operation
and Development (292)
Plurilog (305)
Société d'Etudes et de Documentation
Economiques Industrielles et Sociales
(338)
Société d'Etudes et de Recherches en
Sciences Sociales (339)
Thomson/CSF (362)
UNESCO, Department of Environmental
Sciences and Natural Resources
Research (373)
UNESCO, Department of Free Flow of
Information (374)
UNESCO, International Institute for
Educational Planning (217)
UNESCO, Science Sector (375)

Finland

Economic Planning Centre (108)
Ministry of Communications (256)

Guatemala

ICAITI (161)

Hungary

Group of Science Organization (148)
Hungarian Academy of Sciences
Institute of Sociology (160)
ICPS (162)
Study Group for Science Organization,
Hungarian Academy of Sciences (352)

Iceland

Economic Development Institute (107)
National Research Council (270)

India

Centre for the Study of Developing
Societies (63)
Indian Lead, Zinc Information Centre
(166)
Kapur Solar Farms (232)

Philippines

Institute of Strategic Studies (188)

Poland

Planning Commission of the Ministers'
Council (302)
Polish Academy of Sciences Institute of
Philosophy and Sociology Division of
Social Prognosis (306)
Polish Academy of Sciences Research and
Prognostics Committee Poland of
2000 (307)

Romania

International Centre of Methodology for
Future and Development Studies (208)

South Africa

Chamber of Mines Research Organization
Human Resources Laboratory (69)
Council for Scientific and Industrial
Research Information and Research
Services Group for Techo-Economic
Studies (149)
Human Sciences Research Council
Institute for Research Development
(159)
University of South Africa School of
Business Leadership (413)
University of Stellenbosch, Bureau for
Economic Research Unit for Futures
Research (416)

Spain

Club de Amigos de la Futorologia (73)
Instituto de la Juventud (193)

Sri Lanka

Marga Institute of Development Studies
(243)

Swaziland

Geological and Mines Department (142)
Ministry of Industry, Mines and Tourism
(259)

Sweden

Ministry of Housing and Physical Planning
(258)
National Defence Research Institute (268)
Royal Swedish Academy of Engineering
Sciences (321)
Scandinavian Institutes for Administrative
Research (326)
Secretariat for Future Studies (333)
Stockholm International Peace Research
Institute (351)
University of Linkoping (406)

Switzerland

Battelle Geneva Research Centre (24)
Bureau Fédéral de Statistique (35)
Central Office for International Railway
Transport (49)
Commission Fédérale pour une Conception
(79)
Gesellschaft für Hochschule (140)
Institut für Regional und Landerplanung
(170)
International Institute for Labour Studies
(218)
International Labour Office (221)
Neue Helvetische Gesellschaft (275)
Prognos AG (311)
St Gallen Zentrum für Zukunftsforschung
(322)
Société d'Etudes Economiques et Sociales
(337)
Swiss Council of Sciences (354)
Swiss Federal Institute of Technology
Institute for National, Regional and
Local Planning (355)
Swiss Society for Futures Research (356)
UNCTAD Trade and Economic Integration
(365)
UN Economic Commission for Europe
(367)
UN Economic Commission for Europe,
FAO Timber Division (106)
UN Economic Commission for Europe
Projections and Programming Division
(368)
UN Economic Commission for Europe
Trade and Technology Division (369)
Universal Postal Union (383)
World Meteorological Organization (433)

Tanzania

East African Marine Fisheries Research
Organization (105)

Thailand

Asian Institute for Economic Development
and Planning (14)
Economic and Social Commission for Asia
and the Pacific Agricultural Division
(106)
Economic and Social Commission for Asia
and the Pacific Division of Social
Development (107)
Economic and Social Commission for Asia
and the Pacific Population Division (108)
UN Food and Agricultural Organization
Regional Office (370)

Centre for Integrative Studies (58)
Centre for Peaceful Change (61)
Centre for the Study of Alternative Futures (62)
Centre for the Study of the Future (64)
Centre for the Study of Social Policy (65)
Centre for Technology Assessment, Newark College of English (66)
Chamber of Commerce Council on Trends and Perspective (379)
Champion International Corporation (70)
Cities Service Company (72)
Coca-Cola Company Long-Range Planning (74)
Colgate University (75)
Committee for the Future, Inc (80)
Conference on Alternative Economic Futures for Hawaii (83)
Congressional Research Service Environmental Policy Division (84)
Department of Agriculture (93)
Department of Agriculture Graduate School International and Special Programs (94)
Department of the Army (379)
Department of Housing and Community Development (96)
Department of Labour Bureau of Labour Statistics (381)
Department of State, Bureau of Politico-Military Affairs (99)
Diebold Group, Inc (100)
Communications-Electronics, Directorate for (81)
Dreyfuss College Division of the Future (101)
Earthrise, Futures Lab (103)
Education Exploration Centre, Inc (112)
Educational Resources Information Centre Clearing House for Social Studies (113)
Exxon Corporation Corporate Planning Department (123)
Federated Department Stores (125)
Firestone Tyre and Rubber Company Corporate Research and Planning (126)
Forecasting International Ltd (129)
Forum for the Advancement of Students in Science and Technology (131)
Furman University Department of Sociology (132)
Future Options Room (133)
Future Research Corporation (134)
The Futures Group (136)
General Electric Company Business Environment Research and Forecasting (137)
General Electric Tempo (138)

Georgetown University, Centre for Strategic and International Studies (140)
Gulf and Western Industries, Inc Market Planning Department (150)
Harris Associates (151)
Hawaii Commission on the Year 2000 (152)
Hawaii State Research Centre for Futures Study (153)
Hudson Institute (158)
IIT Research Institute (164)
Indiana University of Pennsylvania, Department of Political Science, Institute for the Study of the Future (167)
Industrial Management Centre Inc (168)
Institute for Defence Analysis (177)
Institute for Juvenile Research (182)
Institute for Public Policy Alternatives (349)
Institute for Scientific Information (186)
Institute for World Order Inc (192)
Inter-American Committee on the Alliance for Progress (196)
Interfuture (197)
International Association of Educators for World Peace (201)
International Association for the Physical Sciences of the Ocean (202)
International Bank for Reconstruction and Development (206)
International Bank for Reconstruction and Development, Regional Projects Department Europe, Middle East and North Africa (214)
International Bank for Reconstruction and Development Transportation and Urban Projects Department (207)
International Co-operation Council (210)
International Development Associations (214)
Iowa 2000 (224)
Library of Congress Congressional Research Service, Science Policy Research Division (234)
Local Government Relations Division, Executive Department (236)
Louisiana State University School of Environmental Design (238)
Lutheran Resource Commission (239)
Management and Organization Development Inc (241)
Massachusetts Institute of Technology, Centre for Policy Alternatives (244)

University of Oregon, Department of
Political Science, Institute of Policy
Studies (411)
University of South Florida, Leisure
Studies Program (414)
University of Southern California, Graduate
School of Business Administration,
Centre for Futures Research (415)
University of Washington, Program in
Social Management of Technology
(419)
University of Washington, Urban
Systems Research Centre (420)
The University of Wisconsin, Project
Destiny (421)
Videa 1000 (422)
Weyerhaeuser Company (424)
The Whirlpool Corporation, Technology
Forecasting and Technology
Assessment (398)
World Bank (206, 207, 214)
World Future Society (429)
World Future Studies Federation (430)
World Institute Council (432)
World Resources Inventory (436)
World Without War Council Inc (437)
Zero Population Growth (439)

USSR

Institute of Cybernetics (176)
USSR Academy of Sciences Institute
for Social Research Section of Social
Forecasting (376)

West Germany

Battelle Institut ev (25)
Battelle Institut ev Economics and Social
Sciences Department (26)

Bonn University, Institute of Industry
and Traffic Policy (30)
Bundesforschungsanstalt für Landeskunde
und Raumordnung (33)
Forschungs-Institut für Internationale
Technisch-Wirtschaftliche Zusammenar-
beit (130)
Gesellschaft für Marktforschung,
Marktplanung und Marketingfin-
beralung Mbh (142)
Gesellschaft für Zukunftsfragen (143)
Henkel KGaA (155)
Institut für Angewandte Systemanalyse
und Prognose (169)
Institut für Europaische Politik (170)
Institut für Systemtechnik und
Innovationsforschung der Fraunhoferge-
sellschaft (174)
Institute of Employment Research (179)
Institute for Technology and Economics
(190)
Intergovernmental Committee for
European Migration (198)
International Institute of Management
(219)
Systemplan ev (357)
Universität Mannheim (386)
University of Mannheim, Industry Seminar
(408)
Wirtschafts und Sozialwissenschaftliches
Institut des Deutschen Gewerkschaft-
bundes (426)
Zentrum Berlin für Zukunftsforschung
ev (438)

Zaire

Université Nationale du Zaire, Campus
de Lubumbashi (387)

Organizations - Methods Index

Brainstorming

1 2 3 4 5 7 9 10 11 13 14 15
16 23 24 25 26 27 28 30 31 36
37 39 42 44 46 47 50 56 58 60
61 63 64 66 73 80 84 90 94 99
101 102 103 108 112 117 122 126
129 131 134 137 142 148 152 154
155 158 161 163 165 166 170 171
172 174 175 179 180 182 193 194
195 199 201 204 206 207 208
213 217 220 221 224 227 228 230
233 234 238 240 241 242 251 261
263 265 267 268 270 271 273 274
276 277 278 281 283 284 287 291
292 294 298 299 300 301 309 311
312 318 320 325 326 328 330 337
341 344 345 348 352 353 357 358
361 363 372 373 375 376 377 378
379 380 388 391 399 401 403 415
419 420 423 424 429 430 435 436
438

Causal Modelling

13 19 22 26 27 32 37 44 46 54
63 66 68 74 80 95 96 98 101 108
110 121 125 136 138 147 153 171
173 178 179 180 188 191 206 214
220 226 230 235 237 245 247 254
255 261 268 269 276 280 283 290
300 309 310 311 312 321 322 323
336 344 348 358 372 389 391 396
402 404 408 409 415 419 420 424
433

Contextual Mapping

2 3 13 16 26 58 59 63 66 80 89
90 94 101 107 122 147 176 180
181 194 206 233 238 242 248 252
255 258 268 276 283 284 309 321
326 327 344 347 358 372 377 391
415 420 424 435

Cross Impact Analysis

1 4 8 13 18 23 24 26 28 29 57
62 66 72 77 80 86 91 94 98 101
115 121 122 136 137 151 160 164
171 172 180 189 193 206 208 224
226 229 230 234 238 258 263 264
267 276 279 283 299 302 304 309
312 321 322 330 332 337 344 348
352 357 362 372 391 396 401 413
414 415 420 421 424 425 436

Delphi Techniques

4 11 13 18 23 24 25 26 27 28 32
36 37 38 42 50 62 66 50 57 86
94 101 108 126 129 132 136 137
142 143 148 149 151 154 155 160
163 169 171 174 176 180 187 188
189 191 195 206 208 218 227 229
230 231 234 240 250 251 253 254
261 265 267 268 271 276 279 283
287 291 292 299 305 309 310 311
312 315 322 323 328 330 337 344
345 356 357 372 375 376 378 388
394 396 401 411 415 420 421 424
425 432 435 436 438

Expert Panels

1 7 9 10 11 13 14 15 16 18 21
23 26 27 28 29 34 36 37 38 39
42 44 45 49 50 52 53 56 58 59
61 64 66 67 71 74 75 76 80 82
83 84 86 88 89 90 91 94 100 101
102 107 108 109 110 117 118 119
122 129 135 136 137 140 141 147
152 154 160 161 163 167 169 170
171 172 176 177 180 184 188 193
194 195 196 199 200 201 202 203
204 205 206 209 211 212 213 214
215 216 217 218 220 221 224 225
226 228 233 234 238 240 242 243
246 248 251 253 258 260 264 265
267 270 271 273 275 276 278 279
282 283 284 287 291 294 299 300
301 305 307 309 310 312 314 316
318 319 324 325 327 328 330 331
332 337 344 348 350 351 354 356
357 364 365 366 367 368 369 371
372 373 374 375 376 377 378 379
380 383 384 392 398 400 401 402
411 415 416 420 421 422 424 427
429 430 432 436 437 438

Extrapolation Techniques

1 4 5 6 11 13 17 18 19 20 23
24 26 27 28 30 31 32 35 36 37
42 43 44 45 50 51 52 55 56 57
58 60 62 66 69 74 75 76 77 78
79 80 81 86 89 91 94 97 98 99
101 102 106 107 110 114 115 118
121 122 123 124 126 128 129 132
136 138 142 144 154 155 156 158
161 163 168 170 173 174 176 179
180 182 190 195 196 206 207 218
219 221 230 234 237 238 240 241
242 248 250 254 258 261 264 267
268 273 274 276 278 280 282 283
284 286 291 292 300 305 306 307
309 311 312 315 316 320 322 323
328 329 331 337 343 344 350 351
354 355 362 366 367 369 370 372
376 377 380 381 388 389 391 394
396 402 408 413 415 416 420 421
424 425 426 430 431 436 438

Gaming

13 22 23 25 26 61 63 64 66 94
99 101 103 132 136 171 191 195
206 234 238 255 268 276 277 283
288 290 291 309 335 344 372 378
384 390 391 393 401 415 417 418
420 424 435 436

Historical Analogy

1 9 10 11 13 14 15 17 18 19 26
27 28 30 32 39 45 58 61 63 64
66 69 72 75 80 94 99 101 102
104 106 108 109 110 112 117 136
137 140 142 148 154 158 160 161
169 173 175 180 181 188 194 201
205 206 210 212 214 219 222 225
229 233 234 237 238 240 243 245
247 248 253 261 267 268 270 275
276 283 291 300 301 305 309 312
321 326 330 337 339 341 344 347
350 351 366 370 372 376 378 383
384 389 391 401 402 414 415 418
419 420 424 425 431 436 437

Individual Expert Forecasting

1 3 5 6 8 9 11 13 14 18 21 23
26 27 28 29 31 32 34 36 39 41
45 49 52 53 56 58 60 63 66 68
69 70 71 72 73 74 76 79 80 84
89 90 93 94 99 100 101 105 106
107 108 110 120 122 125 128 134
135 137 138 140 142 143 151 154
158 160 164 165 166 169 177 180

184 188 189 200 202 206 209 211
214 217 218 220 221 224 228 233
234 237 238 240 242 246 248 250
251 252 258 259 260 262 263 264
265 267 268 269 272 276 281 283
284 287 291 292 297 300 301 304
306 307 309 311 312 313 319 321
327 329 331 332 338 341 344 345
350 351 352 353 354 355 358 361
363 364 365 366 367 369 372 374
376 379 380 381 383 386 392 394
401 402 406 413 415 418 420 422
424 429 431 432 436 437 438

Network Analysis

2 4 9 13 14 15 18 26 27 33 52
56 57 62 63 66 73 80 86 94 98
101 107 122 136 151 171 174 175
176 177 180 191 195 206 267 276
279 283 302 309 312 330 337 339
344 347 364 370 372 384 390 391
420 424 435 436 437

Operational Models

1 4 7 19 26 27 36 39 42 43 45
46 47 48 52 56 57 61 62 66 67
74 75 80 92 94 101 107 109 116
125 126 136 141 147 168 175 177
180 193 206 207 208 210 212 214
219 221 233 235 240 245 255 257
261 276 276 283 290 291 300 301
302 303 309 312 317 325 330 344
345 358 364 371 372 373 374 377
380 384 402 408 415 417 418 420
424 436

Probabilistic Forecasting

4 8 10 13 23 24 25 26 27 28 29
36 37 39 43 46 47 52 54 58 60
61 62 63 66 76 83 94 98 101 104
106 124 128 136 138 140 142 144
163 167 171 175 182 187 190 195
200 206 208 209 214 217 219 224
234 237 240 252 254 258 262 264
265 267 272 275 276 279 280 283
286 290 291 300 302 303 305
307 309 311 312 327 328 331 332
337 343 344 351 352 364 367 369
372 373 377 380 384 390 391 393
399 404 415 416 420 424 431 432
436

Relevance Trees

2 13 18 23 25 26 28 43 52 60 66
86 94 101 129 136 149 163 168
171 175 176 180 191 195 206 230

Organizations - Focus of Concern Index

These generic headings refer to:

Direction of work in forecasting
Direction of work in research
Direction of work in planning
where given in each entry.
Where no Direction of Work is indicated
the focus of concern has been interpreted
from elsewhere in the listed information.

Business, including commerce and industry

1 5 6 10 13 15 16 17 24 25 26
27 28 29 30 33 34 39 40 43 57
70 71 72 74 76 80 86 92 97 98
100 101 104 109 115 117 118
123 125 126 128 129 133 134 136
137 142 145 150 154 155 156 165
166 168 169 173 195 219 228 230
240 241 249 251 252 259 262 264
267 269 273 279 282 283 293 298
299 300 302 303 304 306 307
310 311 312 316 320 326 332 333
337 340 341 343 344 345 353 358
361 365 369 372 376 379 381 382
388 390 391 394 396 400 401 408
413 415 417 422 424 425 426

Communications

8 13 18 28 42 76 81 113 121 127
197 200 234 246 256 265 287 297
310 338 341 363 374 383 421 435

Cultural

3 13 16 37 58 72 73 76 87 95
98 102 104 110 117 119 122 129
133 141 145 189 193 195 201 210
212 233 237 254 255 260 264 268
275 277 289 293 298 301 302 306
307 332 333 336 338 344 347 348
350 358 372 376 391 401 415 416
423 430 432

Defence

13 29 76 81 98 99 107 111 117
129 138 140 158 177 188 192 268
290 298 343 344 351 378 380 396
412 416

Economic

1 2 4 6 7 13 14 15 16 17 19 20
22 23 24 25 27 28 29 30 32 33
34 35 36 37 39 41 42 44 48 50
52 57 59 60 63 68 70 71 72 74
76 77 78 82 83 86 89 95 97 98
100 101 102 104 106 107 108
109 110 111 115 117 118 123 124
125 126 128 129 133 136 137 139
140 142 144 145 149 150 152 154
156 158 159 164 166 169 173 176
177 178 189 190 195 103 206 207
209 214 215 224 226 228 229 230
233 237 244 245 247 253 254 257
259 261 262 266 267 268 269 270
273 274 275 276 279 280 282 283
284 286 291 292 293 298 299 302
303 304 307 308 309 310 311
312 313 315 316 319 322 324 327
332 333 337 338 342 344 345 346
348 350 355 356 358 361 364 365
366 367 368 369 372 374 377 379
381 382 384 389 390 391 393 394
396 397 401 408 409 412 415 416
420 424 432 438 493

Education

1 2 7 10 12 13 16 19 21 25 28
31 35 36 37 41 46 47 50 51 53
56 59 63 67 71 73 75 76 80 85
87 94 98 101 104 112 113 116
117 120 122 127 128 131 133 141
151 171 173 179 192 193 194 195
201 208 209 210 213 217 227 237
239 242 243 244 251 252 254 255
257 274 275 277 279 281 283 287
289 293 296 298 301 302 303 306
307 311 318 322 325 333 334 338
344 348 350 352 354 359 360 370
372 374 385 387 391 395 395 399
400 401 402 404 406 410 412
413 414 415 418 419 420 427 429
430 431 432 434 437

Energy

13 39 76 108 123 137 232 253 282
294 310 328 345 361 366 377 405

Environment

1 3 4 6 7 12 13 14 16 22 23 25
26 27 28 33 34 37 39 41 47 50
51 52 54 58 63 72 73 74 76 78 80
84 85 87 90 91 92 95 98 101 102
103 117 122 129 130 133 136 138
142 151 156 160 164 166 167 169
172 174 180 181 187 189 190 191
192 194 195 197 199 201 202 203
208 209 211 213 216 223 224 225
227 229 230 231 232 233 235 238
245 247 248 254 257 258 263 264
267 268 271 275 276 279 283 288
289 290 293 298 301 302 309 310
311 312 313 317 319 326 327 329
332 333 341 342 344 348 350 355
356 364 366 370 372 373 376 377
388 389 391 393 394 397 398 399
401 407 408 409 416 417 420 421
423 424 425 433 436 438

Food

13 45 76 93 94 120 128 195 220
232 250 280

Health

8 13 76 183 187 199 223 251 284
331 339 359 392 434

Labour

1 7 13 14 16 17 25 26 29 30 33
34 35 36 37 41 47 50 51 56 69
76 81 98 101 104 107 108 109
110 111 117 120 122 128 130
137 141 148 151 156 169 173 176
179 195 209 218 219 221 230 237
241 243 244 245 254 257 262 267
268 269 274 279 282 283 286 290
293 298 302 307 312 322 331 333
337 338 342 344 372 381 391 401
404 409 415 416 424 426 427 428

Legal

13 49 76 157 183 204 205 215 222
260 264 403

Methodology

2 13 22 24 25 26 27 28 34 52 54
57 65 76 80 86 92 95 98 101 103
114 116 128 129 136 145 148 149
152 153 168 169 173 180 187 190
195 201 208 210 227 229 230 233
237 238 243 247 264 267 268 276
277 279 283 289 298 301 302 306
307 309 311 312 322 329 332 333

335 337 339 344 347 350 352 355
357 362 366 371 372 376 384 388
391 396 407 412 415 417 421 430
432 436

Policy

1 2 3 6 13 14 17 19 23 28 29
30 41 44 45 49 54 57 61 65 68
71 73 76 80 83 84 85 86 95 96
97 98 99 100 101 102 104 109
110 116 129 136 137 138 139 140
141 145 146 151 152 158 167 169
170 171 173 174 176 177 182 185
193 195 196 204 217 219 233 234
235 236 237 244 245 246 251 252
255 256 258 262 267 268 274 279
283 284 290 295 296 298 301 303
304 307 308 310 312 313 314 322
327 328 329 331 332 333 336 337
344 347 348 349 355 356 357 364
365 366 367 370 371 372 375 389
391 392 395 397 399 401 403 404
407 410 411 412 415 419 430 432
437

Population

1 2 7 12 13 14 16 17 19 22 23
24 25 26 27 34 35 37 41 42 48
51 54 58 73 76 98 107 109 111
117 120 128 138 141 144 145 160
169 172 173 185 189 193 195 198
201 209 214 226 235 237 243 245
247 248 251 254 257 262 267 268
269 274 275 276 279 280 283 285
293 298 302 307 311 313 322 331
332 333 338 342 344 348 350 355
356 358 372 391 393 397 399 408
415 416 420 439

Regional

1 2 9 13 14 24 25 26 29 30 34
37 47 54 62 63 76 78 90 96 101
104 107 108 128 129 149 167 172
194 209 219 231 233 235 238 245
248 257 258 262 267 276 279 289
299 301 302 309 310 311 313 333
342 344 348 355 357 364 366 370
389 391 393 396 397 398 399 400
408 415 417 420 436

Religion

9 13 64 76 210 239 255 350 360

Resources, Natural

1 2 6 7 12 13 14 16 17 19 22 23
24 25 26 29 34 36 37 38 39 41
52 58 59 69 70 71 72 73 76 78
80 81 85 94 95 98 100 101 102
104 105 106 107 108 109 115
117 125 126 128 129 136 139 140
141 145 148 153 154 156 158 164
166 169 173 174 177 181 185 190
195 200 201 204 205 207 208 209
211 213 214 220 230 232 235 237
239 243 245 247 250 251 252 253
254 255 257 258 259 262 263 264
267 268 275 276 277 279 280 282
283 284 290 293 298 299 301 302
303 304 307 310 312 315 319 327
329 332 333 338 342 344 345 348
355 356 358 361 364 366 370 372
373 377 380 382 388 391 393 396
397 398 399 401 405 407 408 415
416 420 421 424 425 428 436 493

Science and Technology

1 2 3 4 6 7 11 12 13 19 23 24
25 26 27 28 29 33 36 38 42 51
52 55 57 58 59 60 63 66 71 72
74 76 78 80 81 85 86 88 91 93
94 95 97 98 99 100 102 115 117
126 129 131 132 133 134 135 136
138 141 142 145 148 149 151 154
160 164 166 167 168 169 171 174
176 177 180 181 182 186 190 191
193 195 199 200 201 202 208 209
210 211 213 215 219 220 229 230
234 244 249 251 254 256 261 263
264 265 267 268 270 272 275 277
279 282 283 284 288 290 293 298
299 301 302 303 304 309 310
311 312 314 319 320 321 323 324
325 327 328 320 330 332 333 334
337 338 342 343 344 346 347 350
352 354 356 357 361 363 364 366
368 369 370 371 372 374 375 376
377 380 382 388 391 393 396 399
401 405 406 407 408 409 415
416 419 420 421 424 425 429 430
432 433 434 436 438

Social

1 2 3 7 11 12 13 14 16 19 21 22
23 24 25 26 27 28 29 32 34 35
36 37 41 42 44 50 54 55 56 57
58 59 60 62 63 65 66 67 68 72
76 77 78 80 82 83 85 86 88 92
98 101 102 103 104 107 109 110
111 113 115 116 117 119 129 132
133 134 135 136 137 139 141 145
151 152 153 154 158 159 164 167
168 172 173 178 179 180 182 184
185 187 189 192 193 194 195 201
208 209 210 213 214 218 219 224
226 227 229 230 232 233 235 237
238 239 242 243 245 246 247 248
251 252 254 255 256 257 259 260
261 262 264 267 268 273 275 276
277 279 281 284 289 290 291 293
299 301 302 304 306 307 309
310 311 312 322 323 324 326 327
329 331 332 333 336 337 338 339
342 344 346 347 348 350 351 352
353 355 356 357 358 364 368 370
372 374 376 379 382 384 385 386
389 391 392 393 394 395 396 397
400 401 408 412 414 415 416 419
420 424 425 427 428 429 430 432
434 436 437 438

Transportation

4 13 30 47 49 76 79 175 203 207
216 261

Urban

1 2 13 14 16 24 25 26 28 30 34
41 54 62 63 72 73 76 78 90 91
92 96 101 104 120 122 129 132
147 151 152 172 187 194 207 231
233 235 237 238 245 248 251 252
254 262 267 276 279 283 289 301
302 310 311 313 317 333 338 339
342 344 355 357 364 372 389 391
393 394 396 399 400 401 415 417
420 438

Individuals - Geographical Index

Argentina
Cano, Guillermo (81)
Grinberg, Miguel (216)
Mallman, Carlos A. (356)
Van Dam, André (119)

Australia
Newstead, I.A. (397)
Painter, A.D. (412)

Austria
Bruckmann, Gerhart (71)
Fleissner, Peter (170)
Fried, Maurice (179)
Gehmacher, Ernst (190)
Landler, Frank (320)
Lane, James A. (321)
Sint, Peter (483)
Strasser, Helmut (497)

Belgium
Baeyens, Herman (28)
Feldheim, Pierre (161)
Haulot, Arthur (238)
Hubert, M. (261)
Judge, Anthony (283)
Janne, Henri (273)
Kennet, Lord (298)
Klein, D. (306)
Siebker, Manfred H. (477)
Vranken, Jan (551)
Wellesley-Wesley, James (565)

Bulgaria
Kojarov, Assen (309)
Staikov, Zahari (492)

Canada
Andrews, Peter (15)
Beamish, R.E. (34)
Bodnar, Laszlo (51)
Clark, Colin W. (99)
Clayton, R.H. (101)
Dator, Jim (124)
Day, Lawrence H. (129)
Dernoi, Louis A. (134)
Doyle, Frank J. (142)
Durie, R.W. (148)
Gillen, R.L. (198)
Harrison, Michael A. (235)

Hoffman, Ben (251)
Ide, T. Ranald (265)
Jackson, R.W. (270)
Kettle, John (299)
Kumar, Ranjit (314)
Lotz, Jim (343)
Mathews, Sydney T. (366)
Porter, Arthur (432)
Rowlinson, Hugh (451)
Simmonds, Clive W.H. (479)
Skoe, A.S. (484)
Solem, K. Eric (491)
Stevenson, Hugh (495)
Taylor, Victor (510)
Thompson, Gordon B. (519)
Thompson, K.M. (520)
Tucker, Brian (531)
Valaskakis, K. (538)
Vinette, André (545)
Walden, Fred (554)

Czechoslovakia
Ma-Lek, Ivan (355)
Maydl, Premysl (369)
Sulč, Ota (500)
Tauber, Jan (508)
Zeman, Milos (574)

Denmark
Anderson, Hans Skifter (14)
Lund, Ebba (344)
Tambs-Lyche, H. (346)

Ecuador
Villacis, Marcelo Ortiz (544)

Egypt
Ghabbour, Samir I. (196)

Finland
Karttunen, Timo (289)
Lindquist, Martti (336)
Malaska, Pentti (354)
Sneck, Tenho (488)

France
Antoine, Serge (16)
Baboulene, M. (27)
Baker, F.W.G. (31)
Batisse, Michel (33)

Decouflé, André-Clement (130)
Ellul, Jacques (153)
Friedman, Yona (180)
Gerardin, L. (193)
Gueron, Georges (222)
Guillemin, Claude (223)
Harrison, James (234)
Hetman, François (245)
Higginson, John (247)
de Jouvenel, Bertrand (281)
de Jouvenel, Hugues (282)
King, Alexander (301)
Lebeau, André F. (323)
Poremsky, Vladimir (431)
Saint-Paul, Raymond (421)
Salomon, Jean-Jacques (455)
Scardigli, Victor (458)
Schwartz, Nicole (464)

Guatemala

Aquirre B, Francisco (18)

Hungary

Forgacs, Pal (173)
Szalai, Alexander (505)

Indonesia

Alisjahbana, S. Takdir (10)

Iran

Nassefat, Morteza (394)

India

Bowonder, B. (61)
Ghosh, Samir (197)
Iyengar, Madhur Srinivas (269)
Kapur, J.C. (288)
Kothari, Rajni (312)
Parthasarathi, Manavasi Narasimhan (419)
Tellis-Nayak, Jessie (395)
Thapar, Romesh (515)

Ireland

Blackith, R.E. (48)
Rothery, Brian (449)

Israel

Berger, L. (39)
Dror, Yehezkel (144)
Elboim Dror, Rachel (143)
Jaffe, Eliezer D. (271)
Landau, Erika (319)
Mushkat, Mario'n (392)
Singer, Max (482)

Italy

Aubrac, R. (24)
Baruchello, Barbara (32)
Cazzaniga, Vincenzo (86)

Ceccato, Silvio (87)
Chullikal, Anthony (98)
Colombo, Umberto (105)
Dante, Caponera (120)
Dadaglio, Paola (116)
De Martini, Antonio (361)
Finetti, Bruno de (164)
Gaja, Maria Cristina (186)
Gori, Umberto (207)
Gozzer, Giovanni (210)
Masini, Eleonora (363)
Merlini, Cesare (376)
Nebbia, Giorgio (396)
Nievo, Consuelo (399)
Pace, Pietro (408)
Servadio, Emilio (472)
Tavassi, Maria Teresa (509)
Valenzano, Paolo Maria (539)
Vanore, Roberto (540)
Virgilio, Carlo (546)
Visalberghi, Aldo (547)

Japan

Eto, Shinkichi (159)
Fujii, Takashi (182)
Hayashi, Yujiro (242)
Kato, Hideitoshi (291)
Kaya, Yoichi (294)
Kishida, Junnosuke (302)
Kuwae, Kazuo (315)
Masuda, Yoneji (365)
Ochiai, Eiichi (402)
Onishi, Akira (405)
Okita, Saburo (403)
Suzuki, Masayoushi (503)

Lebanon

Rajakovic, Zdenko (442)

Malta

Busuttil, Salvino (78)

Mexico

Hodara, Joseph (250)
Terrazas, Eduardo (514)

The Netherlands

Beyer, G. (42)
Cohen, Suleiman (104)
Diemer, G. (136)
van Gelder, H. (191)
Georis, Raymond (192)
van der Grinten, P.M.E.M. (217)
van de Kaa, Dirk (285)
Lempers, Fred B. (327)
van Rees, J. (444)
Schuurman, Egbert (463)
Smith, B. (487)

Dunham, Kingsley (147)
Eivind, Gilje (152)
Emmett, Isabel (154)
Feld, B.T. (160)
Freeman, Christopher (178)
Gershuny, J.I. (194)
Gillett, N. (199)
Goldsmith, Maurice (204)
Gregory, S.A. (215)
Hale, L.J. (227)
Hall, Peter (228)
Hallett, V.D. (229)
Hart, R.I. (236)
Ion, D.C. (267)
Jahoda, Marie (272)
Jeffers, N.R. (275)
Johnson, Brian (66)
Jones, M.S. (278)
Kuchemann, D. (313)
Lisle, Edmond (339)
Maddox, John (353)
Marstrand, P. (360)
Maver, T.W. (368)
McLean, J. Michael (351)
Miles, Ian (381)
Nicholson, Simon (398)
Page, R.W. (410)
Paine, George (411)
Pavitt, K. (422)
Pears, John D. (423)
Powles, John W. (434)
Priban, Ian (436)
Rotblat, J. (448)
Rotham, Harry (450)
Rowntree, Norman (452)
Searle, Graham William (469)
Senker, Peter J. (471)
Surrey, A.J. (502)
Rattray-Taylor, Gordon (511)
Temple, S. (513)
Tubb, Graham F. (530)
Twiss, Brian (534)
Tyler, M. (535)
Vaizey, John (537)
Veal, A.J. (541)
Watt, W. Montgomery (558)
Williams, Gareth (567)

USA

Abler, Ronald (1)
Abraham, K.V. (2)
Adams, Benson D. (4)
Adams, John D. (5)
Adelson, Marvin (6)
Adler, John (7)
Aines, R.O. (8)
Almon, Clopper (11)

Amara, Roy (12)
Anderson, C. Eugene (13)
Arnold, Mary F. (20)
Arnold, R.A. (21)
Aroni, Samuel (22)
Averch, Harvey (25)
Bahm, Archie J. (29)
Becker, Harold S. (35)
Bell, Wendell (37)
Bender, A. Douglas (38)
Berner, Jeff (40)
Bigler, Alexander B. (43)
Bigler, Craig (44)
Bilstein, Roger (46)
Blackman, A. Wade (49)
Bosserman, Phillip (54)
Boucher, Wayne I. (56)
Boulding, Elise (57)
Boulding, Kenneth (58)
Bowden, William L. (59)
Bowman, Jim (60)
Brameld, Theodore (62)
Breuning, Siegfried (64)
Brictson, Robert C. (65)
Bright, James R. (66)
Brockhaus, William L. (68)
Brownlee, Corrin (70)
Brudner, H.G. (72)
Bryan, V.V. (74)
Buchen, Irving H. (75)
Button, Robert E. (79)
Callahan, W. Thomas (80)
Cargille, Charles M. (83)
Carleton, Thomas (84)
Case, Fred E. (85)
Cetron, Marvin J. (88)
Chaplin, George (89)
Chatel, Bertrand H. (90)
Chenery, Hollis (91)
Christakis, Alexander N. (94)
Christensen, Cheryl (95)
Christian, Betsey (96)
Christopher, William F. (97)
Coomer, James (107)
Cook, Blanche Wiesen (106)
Cooper, Kenneth J. (108)
Cornish, Edward (109)
Cover, Dan J. (110)
Craver, J. Kenneth (112)
Coates, Joseph (102)
Crumlish, Joseph D. (114)
Dalkey, Norman C. (118)
Darling, Martha (121)
Darracott, H.T. (122)
Darrow, R. Morton (123)
David, Henry (125)
David, Paul T. (126)

Miller, Lynn H. (382)
Moeller, George H. (383)
Moline, Robert T. (385)
Monnett, A. Jr. (386)
Mood, A.M. (387)
Moss, Henry N. (390)
Mottoros, Pierre P. (391)
Nanus, Burt (393)
Novick, David (401)
Olson, Robert L. (404)
Osman, John (406)
Ozbekhan, Hasan (407)
Packer, Leo S. (409)
Papanek, Gustav E. (414)
Pape, Max A. (415)
Parkman, Ralph (416)
Parry, C.W. (417)
Penbera, Joseph J. (425)
Pendery, D.W. (426)
Philipp, Howard V. (428)
Pickus, Robert (429)
Postell, B.V. (433)
Prehoda, Robert W. (435)
Pyke, Donald L. (438)
Quickstad, Brian (439)
Quinn, J.B. (440)
Raferty, James A. (441)
Reuss, Carl F. (445)
Rojas, Billy (446)
Rosenthal, Neal H. (447)
Rubin, Milton D. (453)
Ruggles, Rudy L. Jr. (454)
Saltman, Paul D. (456)
Schmidt, Kenneth (460)
Schneider, Jerry (461)
Schwartz, Peter (465)
Shane, Harold C. (473)
Sheldon, Charles S. II (474)
Shindler, L. (475)
Sietz, Ellsworth E. (478)
Simmons, W.W. (480)
Simon, William (481)
Smart, Perry E. (485)
Snell, John N. (489)
Snyder, David P. (490)
Starling, Grover (493)
Steffes, Dale W. (494)
Stone, Frank A. (496)
Strauss, Harlan J. (498)
Streatfeild, Guy F. (499)
Sumida, Gerald A. (501)

Swager, William L. (504)
Tabah, Leon (506)
Theobald, Robert (516)
Thomas, Wes (518)
Thompson, Willis H. (521)
Thorpe, Gerald (522)
Tobias, Laurence I. (524)
Toffler, Alvin (525)
Towers, Bernard (526)
Townsend, Carl (527)
Trux, Hugo (529)
Tugwell, Franklin (532)
Turoff, Murray (533)
Vlachos, Evan (548)
Wagar, Warren (553)
Wapenhans, Willi (555)
Ward, Jonathan (556)
Warfield, John (557)
Webber, M.M. (559)
Weinberger, JoAnn (561)
Weiss, Tom (562)
Wermuth, Anthony L. (563)
Wescott, Roger (564)
Wilkins, R.E. (566)
Wilson, Ian H. (569)
Wilson, Robert G. (570)
Woodward, Beverly (571)
Zraket, Charles (575)

West Germany

Boehret, Carl (52)
Flechtheim, Ossip K. (169)
Havemann, Hans A. (240)
Huning, Alois (262)
Jungk, Robert (284)
Klajes, Helmst (304)
Koelle, Heinz H. (308)
Kortzfleisch, Gert V. (311)
Lenk, Hans (329)
Lienemann, Fritz (334)
Michalski, Wolfgang (377)
Schmitz-Moormann, Karl (388)
Pestel, Eduard (427)
Proske, Rudiker (437)
Schumacher, D. (462)
Trommsdorff, Gisela (528)
Vester, Frederic (543)
Voigt, Fritz (549)

Zaire

Babole, Munzadi (26)

Individuals - Methods Index

Brainstorming

2 4 6 8 10 13 14 16 18 20 23 30
35 36 40 43 44 45 49 51 55 64
65 70 75 78 80 81 83 84 88 94
97 98 102 105 107 108 115 117
124 127 129 130 131 132 134 139
145 148 149 158 161 165 166 167
168 169 177 181 182 183 188 189
190 192 194 198 199 201 202 204
206 209 214 215 216 223 225 228
230 234 235 236 239 244 246 247
251 264 265 278 279 280 281 284
285 286 287 289 290 291 297 298 301
302 308 309 312 318 319 326 341
352 357 360 361 363 364 367 371
372 374 379 386 388 390 391 393
397 400 408 415 430 432 435 437
438 446 449 453 457 461 462 464
467 469 473 477 478 480 484 499
501 504 514 515 516 517 518 525
531 534 536 540 543 552 553 556 557
560 561 563 564 565 568 569 575

Causal Modelling

9 20 41 47 49 52 53 69 71 74 75
82 90 98 99 100 102 104 108
115 124 133 137 140 150 153 155
157 159 163 167 168 170 172 174
177 191 197 201 206 218 221 225
226 233 251 256 268 273 278 280 291
304 308 310 312 318 320 325 327
330 338 354 360 367 370 371 381
386 387 393 407 415 425 434 436
438 443 444 446 461 466 478 487
491 492 507 523 535 541 542 551
555 567 574

Contextual Mapping

36 49 50 57 63 75 94 102 115
130 138 148 163 182 185 192 201
218 225 254 270 280 292 300
304 318 334 347 348 349 352 360
367 371 380 381 382 386 393 400
415 425 436 438 439 441 457 458
461 465 467 468 489 514 524 530
557 565 572

Cross Impact Analysis

20 21 23 25 35 43 49 51 52 54
60 70 75 77 78 98 101 102 103
104 108 112 115 118 125 128 129
131 138 168 172 180 181 183 192
193 201 202 206 211 214 219 225
231 232 235 238 251 278 280 292
307 318 330 332 337 360 361 362
367 371 372 381 386 389 391 393
406 415 424 425 435 436 438 441
446 461 484 494 495 496 500 505
517 519 529 531 538 548 553 554
557 569 570 575

Delphi techniques

6 12 20 23 35 38 39 44 49 52
60 61 68 70 72 73 74 75 80 85
88 101 102 110 111 114 115 118
119 123 125 127 128 129 131 132
137 138 142 145 149 150 158 162
168 177 183 190 198 201 202 203
204 206 207 215 219 225 226 231
232 234 239 244 251 269 278 280
289 290 297 301 304 308 316 318
327 330 334 337 339 354 357 360
363 370 371 374 378 380 381 383
385 386 393 397 406 407 408 415
416 424 425 426 435 436 438 444 446
456 461 467 477 484 486 488 490
493 495 496 498 500 503 507 512
520 531 533 534 538 548 550 563 569
572

Expert panels

4 9 12 14 18 20 23 24 25 28 31
33 34 35 44 45 49 62 65 69 70
76 78 83 85 88 89 90 93 97 98
102 105 108 112 115 117 119 125
128 129 130 131 132 134 137 138
139 149 155 160 161 162 165 166
173 179 181 183 188 189 190 192
201 202 203 204 205 206 208
209 211 224 225 234 235 236 237
240 241 242 244 247 265 270 273
278 279 280 289 290 292 293 295
297 298 300 301 302 306 307
310 317 318 321 327 344 345 347

348 357 360 361 364 367 369 371 374
375 378 380 381 384 386 390 391
393 397 400 403 406 409 411 412
413 420 425 427 426 429 430 431
432 433 435 437 438 443 445 448
452 454 455 458 459 460 461 462
466 467 468 469 473 474 478 480
484 486 488 490 498 501 504 505
506 507 512 514 515 522 524 526
540 543 544 545 547 550 555 552
556 558 560 561 563 568 569 572

Extrapolation Techniques

1 2 3 4 14 17 28 29 35 36 39 41
44 46 47 49 50 52 55 60 61 63
66 69 70 71 74 75 77 85 88 93
97 100 101 102 103 104 110 112
114 115 117 122 124 128 129 131
138 140 145 146 151 155 161 162
163 166 168 170 178 182 183 184
190 191 192 193 198 199 201 202
204 206 213 214 215 217 219 225
231 236 238 239 240 243 251 252
260 261 267 277 278 279 280 285
287 290 292 296 299 301 307 308
309 311 315 317 318 320 321 323
324 327 330 337 338 341 344 352
354 360 367 371 374 377 379 380
381 382 383 386 388 393 397 406
415 417 418 420 423 425 430 431
433 434 438 440 441 444 446 448 449
450 451 454 457 458 461 466 467
468 469 470 473 474 475 476 478
482 483 484 486 490 491 493 495
496 499 503 504 510 520 530 532
533 534 541 543 549 550 553 554 562
563 565 570 572 573

Gaming

4 35 36 49 55 60 63 64 65 72
75 84 85 102 110 115 127 131
145 150 159 172 183 185 188 215
225 251 256 280 284 318 319 337
360 367 368 371 385 386 391 392
393 425 446 457 461 465 484 527
533 538 544 550

Historical Analogy

1 2 4 6 10 18 21 28 30 35 39
44 45 46 47 48 49 50 52 53 54
57 60 70 75 78 80 86 102 103
106 115 120 123 128 129 130 131
137 139 140 142 150 153 155 159
165 168 169 170 174 181 182 183
197 198 201 202 205 206 207 214

218 224 225 229 233 235 239 242
243 250 252 254 259 264 267 271
276 278 280 281 291 292 293 296 297
298 299 300 307 309 312 316 318
319 330 337 339 343 345 347 348
349 352 355 360 361 367 371 375
379 381 382 384 386 387 388 391
392 393 396 401 406 409 410
416 418 420 425 429 430 434 435
436 438 443 444 445 446 450 454 455
461 464 469 471 473 477 482 490
494 495 496 498 501 504 505 506
514 519 526 532 536 544 546 547
549 551 533 558 560 562 563 569
570 573

Individual Expert Forecasting

4 5 6 9 12 13 28 35 40 42 49
50 70 71 76 78 86 93 97 100
102 103 112 115 120 123 124 129
130 131 132 134 146 151 153 155
161 166 171 176 183 189 192 198
199 201 202 203 207 208 209
214 219 220 221 223 225 226 232
235 236 237 239 241 242 243 244
246 250 252 264 276 269 270 273
276 277 278 279 280 281 284 286
290 292 297 299 301 302 305 306
316 317 318 321 323 324 325 326
329 332 334 338 343 345 347 352
360 361 366 367 371 374 379 381
383 384 386 389 400 401 409 412
413 415 417 418 420 423 425 429
430 434 435 437 438 439 443 449
450 454 455 458 459 460 461 466
467 468 473 474 475 476 478 480
482 488 490 494 499 500 502 504
505 507 510 511 512 514 516 518
525 527 528 532 536 537 543 551
552 553 556 560 563 564 569 573
575

Network Analysis

17 20 36 43 49 57 70 72 78 94
101 102 115 119 120 130 138 161
180 181 182 183 192 201 202 206
211 214 225 231 232 251 259 271
278 280 318 350 352 355 360 361
364 367 371 386 397 402 406 415
421 425 426 429 435 436 438 441
443 459 461 467 490 496 549 550
552 554 572

Individuals -
Focus of Concern Index

These generic headings refer to:
Direction of work in forecasting
Direction of work in research
Direction of work in planning
where given in each entry.
Because the range of concern is usually
very wide for individuals involved in
futures studies, this index will only give
a very rough indication of their specific
focus.

Business

2   3   7   8   9   11   12   13   21   27   35   36
38   43   44   45   56   61   64   65   66   67
68   74   75   77   79   82   86   88   97   98
101   105   112   117   118   119   123   129
130   132   133   146   149   152   170   171
172   182   190   191   198   200   201   202
203   206   213   212   215   217   226   228
235   236   239   241   243   244   252   264
278   279   280   281   282   284   286   288
289   290   292   297   311   315   316   318
325   330   333   337   339   345   350   354
361   371   381   386   389   391   393   396
402   405   407   409   412   417   419   423
426   427   428   433   435   436   438   439
440   444   445   449   450   451   453   457
460   465   466   467   468   470   480   484
490   493   494   503   504   507   510   512
515   517   525   533   534   535   540   566   568
569   570

Cultural

1   3   10   23   39   40   44   50   68   72   75
78   79   87   88   98   101   102   106   108
112   127   130   131   137   142   151   155
157   176   181   182   185   188   190   192
197   211   216   218   228   238   241   242
243   251   258   264   265   268   276   277
279   280   282   286   287   288   290   291   296
298   305   311   316   319   322   329   334   335
339   347   348   349   350   364   371   372
375   381   383   388   398   400   405   406
407   422   425   431   441   446   453   459
469   476   481   484   490   492   496   498
499   508   515   525   541   551   553   554
560   563   564

Defence

4   36   50   74   80   88   106   122   140
144   160   212   250   268   280   298   330
345   361   362   437   448   454   474   478
482   491   507   547   554   563

Economic

2   3   8   9   11   12   13   14   15   21   27   30
35   36   38   39   41   44   47   50   53   59
60   63   68   69   71   73   74   76   77   78
79   80   85   86   88   89   91   93   97   98
101   102   103   104   106   108   112
114   117   119   121   129   131   132   133
135   138   140   142   145   146   157   158
162   167   170   172   173   174   178   181
182   183   187   191   198   202   203   206
209   211   212   213   215   217   219   223
224   226   233   235   236   238   239   240
241   243   245   251   252   261   268   269
277   278   279   280   281   285   286   288
289   290   292   293   298   299   307   311
315   322   327   330   331   334   335   337
345   350   351   354   360   365   371   377
384   386   391   393   397   401   402   403
405   406   407   412   413   414   417   419
421   425   426   427   431   432   433   436
444   446   447

Education

3   5   6   9   10   17   31   33   36   45   55   59
60   62   65   66   68   72   75   78   80   87
94   96   104   113   118   121   127   129
131   139   143   145   151   156   157   161
163   164   167   182   185   187   192   199
200   201   202   210   212   216   219
224   229   232   234   237   238   240   241
243   246   251   254   255   259   263   264
265   266   273   277   279   280   282   291   29
298   301   307   314   316   319   320   322
326   327   329   332   338   341   343   349
350   352   357   363   371   372   375   393
398   400   402   404   405   408   413
425   429   438   439   443   446   447   455
456   459   465   473   476   481   483   492
495   496   514   540   543   547   553   554
557   560   561   564   567

Resources, Natural

2 8 12 13 14 15 18 24 27 30 31
33 35 36 38 42 44 45 48 49 50
51 55 59 61 63 65 67 68 69 74
76 77 80 81 85 88 93 94 95 98
99 100 101 102 103 104 105
106 120 122 128 129 130 133 138
140 142 147 148 149 151 156 158
160 165 166 167 174 177 180 181
182 183 188 191 196 198 201 205
211 212 213 215 217 219 223 224
229 230 233 234 238 239 240 243
244 250 251 254 264 266 267 274
275 277 278 279 280 281 286 288
290 292 293 294 297 298 301 303
305 307 308 312 315 318 319 325
327 330 331 347 348 350 352 353
357 360 361 367 370 371 377 383
386 390 391 393 396 401 403 405
406 407 409 410 412 414 417 419 422
427 429 432 433 435 437 438 439
440 443 448 449 452 454 461 467
468 469 475 477 478 482 483 488
490 491 492 494 499 502 504 507
510 520 524 530 535 543 548 552
553 554 555 567 568 570 575

Science and Technology

1 2 4 6 9 12 13 14 18 21 23 24
30 31 33 34 35 36 38 39 43 46
49 50 55 56 61 64 65 66 67 68
69 72 74 76 77 83 88 90 93 94
97 101 102 103 105 106 108 110
112 113 115 118 122 128 129 131
138 139 141 142 145 147 148 149
157 160 166 168 171 177 179 180
181 182 183 185 189 197 201 202 204
206 212 215 217 219 223 224 226
232 234 235 236 239 240 241 242
244 245 250 251 252 253 254 259
264 268 269 270 275 277 278 279
280 286 288 289 290 292 296 297 298
301 302 306 308 312 313 314 316
317 318 322 323 329 330 331 334
337 338 344 347 349 350 351 354
355 360 362 364 365 366 371 374
379 383 389 390 391 393 396 397
400 403 406 407 409 412 413 415
416 417 419 421 422 424 425 426
427 430 431 432 433 435 436 437
440 443 448 450 451 452 453 455
459 460 462 465 466 467 468 471
474 475 477 478 479 482 483 484
486 487 488 490 491 493 494 496

500 504 505 507 508 517 518 519
520 521 524 530 533 534 535 542 543
547 550 557 559 563 564 568 572
575

Social

1 3 5 6 7 9 10 12 14 17 20 23
26 34 35 36 37 39 40 42 43 44
46 47 49 50 52 53 54 55 56 59
60 62 64 66 68 69 71 72 73 75
77 78 79 80 84 85 88 89 90 92
94 95 96 97 98 101 102 103 104
106 108 110 112 113 114 115 117
119 121 123 124 125 128 129 130
131 132 134 137 138 140 142 145
148 149 151 152 153 154 155 156
157 158 159 161 163 164 166 167
168 169 170 172 173 174 176 178
180 181 182 183 185 186 187 188
189 190 193 197 199 200 201 202
203 206 208 209 211 213 214 219
221 222 224 225 226 228 229 231
232 233 236 237 238 239 241 242
243 244 245 246 250 251 252 254
257 260 261 262 264 265 268 269
270 271 272 273 276 277 278 279
280 281 282 284 285 286 287 288
289 290 291 292 293 295 296 297 298
299 302 304 306 307 309 310 311
312 313 316 322 324 326 327 329
330 332 334 337 338 339 340 341
343 345 347 348 349 350 351 352
358 360 362 363 364 365 369 370
371 372 375 378 379 380 381 382
383 384 387 391 393 395 397 398
399 400 401 402 403 404 405
406 407 408 409 412 415 416 420
422 424 425 427 430 431 432 434
435 436 437 439 440 441 444 445
446 448 449 453 455 457 458 461
463 464 465 467 468 469 471 473
474 475 476 477 479 481 482 484
488 490 491 492 493 494 495 496
498 499 500 501 503 505 506
507 508 509 511 514 515 517 519
521 523 524 525 526 528 529 530
531 533 538 541 542 543 544 545
546 547 548 549 550 551 552 553 554
555 556 559 560 562 563 564 568 569
570 571

Urban

6 23 27 28 36 42 43 45 47 52 59
63 65 75 88 92 94 110 111 118 129
130 134 152 171 174 180 182 188
192 196 213 214 219 231 232 233

About the compilers

John McHale is Director of the Centre for Integrative Studies in the School of Advanced Technology, State University of New York, Binghamton, New York 13901. Born in Scotland, Mr McHale was educated in the United Kingdom and in the United States and holds the Ph.D. degree in Sociology. He has published extensively in Europe and this country on the impact of technology on culture, mass communications, and the future. His latest books are 'The Future of the Future'(Braziller, 1968),'The Ecological Context' (Braziller, 1970) and'World Facts and Trends'(Collier-MacMillan, 1972). As an artist and designer, Mr McHale has exhibited widely in Europe since 1950. His work includes graphics, exhibition design, television, film, and general consultancy to organizations in the U.S. and Europe. He is a Fellow (and Secretary-General) of the World Academy of Art and Science, the Royal Society of Arts (England), the New York Academy of Science, and the American Geographical Society; awarded the Medaille d'Honneur en Vermeil, Société d'Encouragement au Progrès in 1966, the Knight Commander's Cross of the Order of St Dennis in 1974; member of the American Sociological Association, Institute of Ecology, Society for Advancement of General Systems Theory, Colorado Archaeological Society, and the Scientific Commitee of the World Future Studies Federation. He is a member of the Futures Advisory Editorial Board.

Magda Cordell McHale is a Senior Research Associate of the Centre of Integrative Studies.

FUTURES

The Futures Directory is a special publication from FUTURES, the international journal of forecasting and planning.

FUTURES serves all who are concerned about the future in an increasingly complex world; readers and contributors come from over 60 countries, East and West, developed and developing. FUTURES provides an effective link between academic research and the practice of forecasting and planning. Over half of FUTURES' readership works in government or in industry; over two-thirds of FUTURES' contributors are academics.

Other FUTURES special publications include:

TECHNOLOGY ASSESSMENT AND THE OCEANS
Edited by Philip Wilmot and Aart Slingerland
Proceedings of a conference held in Monaco under the auspices of Eurocéan and the International Society for Technology Assessment. Thirty main papers cover topics ranging from artificial islands in the North Sea through fishing, energy and food, and deep-sea nodule mining, to the application of TA to ocean thermal energy conversion systems. Publication November 1976
305 x 215 mm / 216 pages (est)
Cloth / 0 902852 61 2 / £12.00 net

ADOLESCENCE AND YOUTH IN THE YEAR 2000
Edited by John P. Hill and Franz J. Mönks
A treatise on the socio-cultural, biological and psychological environment for youth and adolescence at the end of the century. Based on an international meeting of experts from many nations and disciplines. The meeting was organized by the Jeugdprofiel 2000 Foundation in Amsterdam.
Publication Spring 1977
210 x 150 mm / 208 pages (est)
Cloth / 0 902852 66 3 / £6.80 net

EDUCATION FOR PEACE
Edited by Magnus Haavelsrud
This book contains over thirty contributions from twenty countries dealing with peace education from early childhood to university level. It contains case studies and proposals for action, and analyses the major problems in peace education from different cultural viewpoints. The contributors include Adam Curle, Jaime de J. Diaz, Paulo Freire, Johan Galtung, Robert Kwaku Atta Gardiner, David Ingram, Masako Shoji, Hisako Ukita and Tarzie Vittachi.
210 x 147 mm / viii + 408 pages
Casebound / 0 902852 43 9 / £5.75 net

HUMAN FUTURES

A discussion on human needs in the stage of transition, new societies to which they may lead, and the technologies necessary for their realization. A collection of papers prepared for the Rome Special World Conference on Futures Research held in September 1973. Published in cooperation with IRADES. Authors: Bertrand de Jouvenel, John McHale, Maurice Guernier, Lewis Mumford, Sam Cole, Craig Sinclair, Jim Dator, William Simon, Harold Linstone, Yehezkel Dror.
147 x 210 mm / 183 pages
Paper / 0 902852 34 5 / £5.50 net

EDUCATIONAL PLANNING IN PERSPECTIVE

Edited by Thomas Green
This book offers the fresh perspective of long-range forecasting to those involved with the immediate issues of educational planning and policy at all levels. Authors: Kjell Eide, Rachel Elboim-Dror, Thomas Green, Michael Marien, Maurice Kogan, Beresford Hayward, Gareth Williams, Peter Armitage, Fritz Stern.
264 x 181mm / 132 pages
Paper / 0 902852 07 8 / £2.25 net

THE PREDICAMENT OF MAN

Edited by Maurice Goldsmith
This book deals in a critical and discursive manner with the environmental, technological, social, moral and spiritual aspects of man's future. The five main sections of the book are: the predicament; man's future; geopolitical man; towards global action; design for society.
297 x 210mm / 189 pages
Paper / 0 85637 001 0 / £7.00 net

FUTURES is published alongside a growing number of specialist international journals dealing with specific policy areas:
Energy Policy
Food Policy
Resources Policy
Science and Public Policy
Policy Publications Review
Marine Policy
Telecommunications Policy

For further details write to:
IPC Science and Technology Press Limited, IPC House, 32 High Street, Guildford, Surrey, England GU1 3EW.